P
B

Seize the Day

DIARIES 1969–1999

ANN ALLESTREE

SINCLAIR-STEVENSON

LONDON

First published in Great Britain by
Sinclair-Stevenson in 2006
3 South Terrace, London SW7 2TB

ISBN 9543520–8–4

British Library Cataloguing in Publication Data
A CIP catalogue record for this title is available from the British Library

Typeset by Rowland Phototypesetting Ltd, Bury St Edmunds, Suffolk
Printed by St Edmundsbury Press Ltd, Bury St Edmunds, Suffolk
Design by Michael Brown
Index by Douglas Matthews

For
LYDIA and SEBASTIAN
and to
NANNY, GLADYS SLUCE
whose eye on the home front
made our travels possible

Introduction

'Let's jump in! We might never get another chance . . .' The ten-year-old girl hauled her father up into the fiacre as they clattered off across the cobbled streets of Paris. The year was 1950. The days of those nimble horse-drawn cabs were indeed numbered, to be usurped by trams and buses. Initiated in the seventeenth century in the fetid Impasse Saint-Fiacre, to navigate the sludge and loosened stones of the city's streets, they were revived under Louis-Philippe's Restoration; speeding by in style, as 'Josephines', 'Hirondelles', 'Gazelles', 'Sylphides' or 'Dames Réunies'.

Instances recalled in our childhood's eye can mark our life's trajectory; like shafts of insight crystallised on the conscience. In one fell swoop on that drizzling spring afternoon in Paris, the girl (and it was I) had seized her chance to grab an opportunity. She had sensed a moment to remember.

This diary has evolved principally through travel and its impact on an open mind. Francis Bacon wrote: 'Travel in the younger sort is a part of education; in the elder, a part of experience . . . let diaries, therefore, be brought in use.' Travel is a perennial education, provoking in us more thought and more action than any other pursuit. A reader of these random entries may find some juxtapositions disorientating; cantering on a pouring wet morning through Richmond Park can be annexed to our arrival in a sultry Baghdad the following afternoon. Diaries, like life itself, have their own peculiar agenda. Drawn from a global canvas, these vignettes are observed rather than analysed. Scenes range from the desert life of Bedouins, to evocative British embassies, to the faded vestiges of inherited opulence.

But the sense of pioneer adventure is heightened by any journey made alone. I still savour intensely that hundred-mile car journey through the Caucasus mountains and a subsequent longer one skirting the Lycian coast; a stunning narrative of Graeco-Roman ruins towering above the sea, where the wooded cliffs plunge to secluded bays and sand shores.

In travelling it is the people of the land – their indigenous habitats and customs – that intrigue. Through the surges and retreats of our changing worlds today, it is the 'primitive' that still fascinates. The line of scarved and squatting women in a field; the water buffalo plodding through rice; the North Yemeni bint veiled in black, with her camel at the plough; the Rajputani women swathed in bright saris and bracelets building a wall, each brick lifted high and cemented like a crown. That innate fastidiousness of Eastern peoples, long forfeited in the West, is a revelation; the grace with which too many ease into a rickshaw denotes respect for another's space; the platform of Kuala Lumpur's Victorian railway station, with its arcades and towers to resemble a mosque, teems with orderliness, clean heads and clean shirts. In Saigon, a tunnelled-out garage serves as an eatery, with white walls, tablecloths, scented flannels and pretty serving girls.

According to Sir Roy Strong, doyen of the arts and the literati, no diary can be complete without references to food, clothes, prices and conversations. Dinner parties, country house parties, shooting parties and even garden parties reflect the social trends of any period – or they did . . . whereas the politics of the day are lost in time. Diary entries by an anonymous pen, of war and régime change, are of little account. By the same token I have referred to such instances to mark the passage of time. Today the media's prerogative holds sway in world triumphs and disasters and the more sensational zeitgeist.

My editor's eye has focused on personal encounters with people and places; he has correctly ruled out my awed outpourings over the Americans' landing on the moon; the Falklands War, which I had chronicled each day, and the stirring scandals closer to home. It is the vignettes of British eccentricity that my editor has championed; the conversations over family dining tables, the time-honoured British humour and the concerns for heritage and tradition. (The demise of unjustified privilege, seeded in the early 1990s, has marginalized whole structures of our society.) And I have felt constrained to note this demise on a global scale; the Rajput maharajahs and the forfeit of their purses and palaces; the Malay sultans and their fear of the people's censor; the descendants of Iran's Qajar dynasty, their political acumen crushed under a doomed Shah. Finally, in July 1991, the Queen of England was called upon to pay her taxes.

Any luminaries who breached our modest horizon were singled out for my close attention: writers, politicians, hostesses, great collectors, the heirs to great houses, and the princes and pundits of distant climes.

Walking up a hill in Asolo with Dame Freya Stark, she paused for breath: 'I am a little puffed' – and catching sight of some orange dahlias – 'such modern, ugly colours.'

Strolling around the theatrical gardens of La Pietra with Sir Harold Acton, he stopped to crumble a spray of mint; it smelt wonderfully pungent.

Lunching with the mellifluous Max Reinhardt at Rules, when the waiter cautioned me: 'Mind your head, madam – that print of Mr Greene juts out a bit as you sit.' Such fleeting moments hang like pictures in the mind.

Travel with the chance to observe is necessarily linked to leisure. It was my privilege to share in my husband Tom's unique agenda – to note and cogitate from a few paces behind.

1969

Tom is valuing Lord Gainsborough's furniture in this large, rambling house. Lady Gainsborough in her early forties with shoulder-length, bright fair hair is excessively compos mentis having had seven children. Soon after our arrival we sat down to a family lunch with Nanny, the governess and girl-groom included. An elegant, enormously tall butler, by name Bottomley, waited on us with stalwart concentration. We ate fried fish fingers followed by two 'family-size' blocks of vanilla ice cream; an accompanying hot chocolate sauce exuded from Bottomley's silver sauceboats. A sensible weekday lunch considering the numbers entailed.

Lord Gainsborough sat at the head of the long table and in a bemused manner surveyed the familiar scene. His three daughters Lady Juliana, Lady Maria and Lady Celestria Noel were eulogising Bob Dylan, folk singer extraordinary; they were ardent fans. His second son, the handsome Gerard, kept silent, and his third son, Thomas, a sparkling twelve-year-old, was uninterested in Dylan and talked instead of his new car, a recent acquisition, second-hand; although, he confided, he had been driving for at least seven years this was his first. The thrill of ownership was still very new as we discovered that evening when he took us out for a flamboyant spin. Edward, the fourth son and youngest of the family, had sat on his father's left. He was flushed and proud from his visit to the dentist; he later disclosed, with a lowering of his eyelashes, that he had 'gone off' vanilla ice cream and preferred old coins.

1970

February 8 Dunlossit House Islay Inner Hebrides Scotland

Islay, 'Queen of the Isles', and what a superb view we have from Dunlossit House, which stands secure and proud in its thick, black, granite, Victorian solidarity, 200 feet above the small harbour of Port Askaig. To the west we are flanked by pine forests and to the east lies the sound of Islay with the 'paps of Jura' rising high into the clouds. The sound boasts a virile tidal flow, sparkling blue and crystalline in the sun; a puckered grey, swirling waste with the fall of winter mists. They say you can see the red deer on Jura on a fine, clear day and to the north one can faintly discern the outlines of Mull. But it is Islay with her pervasive soft green hills and furrows, edged with reeds, gorse, peat troughs, and dry slate walls, that holds the eye. The wild bird life, cattle, sheep, and deer, are protectively swathed in her mists and the distilling (and drinking) of her revered 'Islay Mist' whisky adds a beguiling dimension for the island's inhabitants.

We have been staying at the house for three days, valuing the furniture of the Schroder family, notably Victorian or reproduction. A certain Mr Day from Glasgow once took two and a half weeks to value the contents; Tom has taken two days. No doubt Mr Day wrote in free hand, including such details as the waste paper baskets and lampshades. Tom speaks straight into a tape recorder and sweeps through the job with that invaluable phrase: 'remaining contents, including . . .' These can sometimes constitute three-quarters of a room's furniture if it be of little significance. The house has been a joy to stay in under the care of Morag, the charming and ingratiating young housekeeper. Her excellent cooking and cosseting hot water bottles have been a delight. She did us an exceptionally good turn the day we arrived. There was a power cut at Dunlossit and, on learning that haggis was the sole option at the pub in Port Askaig, she made us cheese sandwiches – a happy alternative.

July 10 Carlton Towers Goole Yorkshire

We dropped in briefly to meet Lord and Lady Howard of Glossop to do a reconnoitre of the valuation entailed in their extraordinary house, a monstrosity of turreted and crenellated Victoriana. On entering the dimly-lit hall, flanked on the one side by a chapel and burning candles, one's eye is further arrested by the very vastness of it all.

Lady Howard is a remarkable-looking woman with finely-drawn features and merry blue eyes. Invalided and sitting in a wheel-chair she talks gaily and asks many questions. She has enormous presence. A couple in their eighties, they have thirty-five grandchildren and confidently expect their first great-grandchild very shortly.

Lord Howard wryly admitted that it was rather a business living to be so old; however, we left them in the throes of expecting forty-two members of the family to descend on them for yet another wedding. 'We have loads of staff,' he assured us, pointing to a formidable tower at the end of the house; 'that's stuffed with them!' He then added as an afterthought: 'Do give my regards to that nice young man, Peter Chance.' (Peter Chance being the distinguished, very middle-aged Chairman of Christie's.)

August 20 Hardwicke House Ham Common Richmond Surrey

Last night we took Beverley Nichols[1] and his friend Cyril Butcher[2] to the soi-disant erotic revue *Oh! Calcutta*. The production sports continuous nudity for the first time in stage history. The censors, faced with this new slant of brazen nakedness and the ubiquitous swinging of private parts, deemed it unlikely to deprave or corrupt the avid public. Potential viewers with secret hopes of being sexually stimulated will indeed have to hunt elsewhere. The frivolous, witty skits that gently deprecate the whole performance and the selection of hand-picked attractive bodies that perform acrobatic, impersonal dances and stances are of more sculptural and artistic impact than sexual.

The music and stage effects were at times admirable, but the dialogue was essentially amateur and unimaginative. Sex, like anything else that is abused and consequently hackneyed, loses its cogent effect. As a small boy who indulges in a surfeit of Mars Bars and is physically sick, so must the public eventually decree that sex when openly exploited loses its savour and finally repels. Doubtless the law of change that hovers over all things will soon prompt us to re-wrap the human body and indulge in its ensuing mysteries with more pleasure.

Beverley himself was shocked by the performance and muttered indignantly from the stalls: 'I have been known to stop a show before

---

[1] Born 1898. Known for his books on gardening, village life and travels. See the biography *Beverley Nichols* by Bryan Connon (1991).
[2] A lifelong companion and part-time actor.

now, you know!' He subsequently recovered his equanimity and wrote a sceptical article for *Woman's Own*.

November 13 Abbotsworthy House Winchester Hampshire

We stayed this weekend with Jennie Enfield – an old friend with whom I have kept in gentle touch since schooldays. Seven years ago she married Tom, the eldest son of the Earl of Strafford, and has since produced four children. Tom tends the rare trees and shrubs at Hillier's Garden Centre. Jennie is a formidable young woman; a member of the Bow Group, she is blessed with a brilliant and incisive mind and remarkable good looks. On top of these major attributes she has succeeded in drenching her house in exquisite taste. Each room has a distinct ambience of its own, induced by subtle colouring and carefully grouped furniture – not least the children's splendid playroom; an appendage of vast proportions on the end of the house and a veritable den of toys, excitement and gymnastic challenge.

New faces and old friends encompassed the leisurely rhythm of delicious meals and conversation. Sue Baring sparkled with her perennial glamour and William Douglas-Home came to dine. His wife was introduced as Lady Dacre, having just inherited her own Scottish title. He was a wiry, charming, alert character, smoking restlessly; he disclosed nonchalantly that he was in the throes of writing a play around a fictitious politician called Brown. He also dwelt on the engaging possibility of devising a 'retreat-pod': an oval egg into which he could escape to a world of private reverie and presumably uninterrupted play-writing.

A surging, bubbling and colourful sea of faces and voices – but there was one particular man who disturbed one with flashes of brilliant insight – namely, Christopher Bland[3]. Until recently he was Chairman of the Bow Group and in the future one can imagine him as Prime Minister. He is in his early thirties. He surveyed the changing scenes of a weekend at Abbotsworthy with bright, calm, intelligent eyes and implanted on one's mind the vivid suggestion that he was going places. If he ever did become Prime Minister, I would risk forecasting a prominent place for Jennie in his Cabinet.

[3] Knighted 1993. Chairman, Board of Governors, BBC 1996–2001. Member, Prime Minister's advisory panel on Citizen's Charter 1991–94.

November 16 Killion Penzance South Cornwall

After a long and circuitous drive through November drizzle and sodden country roads, we arrived at the home of Commander[4] and Mrs Beacus Penrose ('Annie' she advised us after we had set eyes on her for a mere three minutes). The stone Georgian house, set in a rambling park, lay still, dark and wet as we pulled on the door bell. Dogs leapt to attention within and rushed to the door, followed by the slow step of our host Beacus Penrose. He ushered us through a dimly-lit outer hall and by the glow of the wood fire which hissed encouragingly on its four-foot mound of soft, silvery ash, one was aware of his mild, appraising eyes and an imperturbable manner. He led us into the library and with solicitous enquiries after our journey and a distributing of drinks he settled us in comfortable, old chairs.

Suddenly, Mrs Penrose swept into the room on a wave of extravagant welcome. She was 'thrilled and bewitched to bits to meet us both – what youth and glamour – it was altogether just too much. The excitement of having us had kept her awake all night and running like a mad thing all day. How clever of us to finally arrive. And oh that hair! Oh, dirty old Beacus – aren't you just loving that long hair? Well, she must go now and butter the bloody birds'. She shortly reappeared and whirled us through a series of rooms; the dining-room, the drawing-room, outer hall, inner hall, and inner back passage where we breached the kitchen. The attractive scrubbed table was flanked on one side by a tall wide Cornish settle and laid for three.

We had heard that she was an accomplished cook and that it was her habit to refuse her concoctions for herself – preferring instead to skirt the settle and to serve up course upon course and perhaps even to stand still in an unseen corner drinking whisky.

'Sit next to Beacus, darling – he's just loving this. No – I won't join you; I prefer to do a poor man's Madame Prunier, but I may sit between you and Beacus at some stage. Watch out, Beacus! Yes, Tom darling, sit opposite your stunning wife . . .' We had a superb dinner, greatly enhanced by her colourful conversation and fresh crab. Her cheerful monologue was occasionally punctuated by her maid's petulant exclamation of 'Oh, Madam! That word again!' and by the odd quiet aside from Beacus. He confessed to being an easy-going tolerant fellow and was left happily unmoved by her verbal extravagances. We loved it and finally left the table, with every possible sensation of good living.

---

[4] Beacus Penrose was Dora Carrington's last lover and portrayed as the handsome yachtsman in the film *Carrington*.

Annie led the dark and winding trail back to the library, absent-mindedly munching on a Ryvita.

We spent two memorable nights at Killion, while Tom valued the whole contents of the house, ending with the Cavendish room; lavish and unused in its irrelevant, golden-tasselled, red velvet splendour.

Beacus Penrose was previously married to Joy Newton; Annie Penrose was previously married to Joy's brother Bobby Newton – that famous and well-loved example of charm and dissipated talent. Beacus, Joy, Bobby and Annie. What a quartet they must have been; the bright young things of Evelyn Waugh's *Vile Bodies* personified, and living on a vivacious strain in the most southern tip of England. We left them preparing lunch for thirty guests, Annie swearing unabatedly over her knives and mixing bowls. She kissed me goodbye and added as an afterthought: 'You are a beauty, remember, but don't get nibbled on the way up.' With this dark advice ringing in the ears one wondered if there would ever be a chance to see this lovely eccentric pair again.

1971

It was a dark, drizzling evening as we reached the home of Captain and Mrs Beauchamp Blackett – a superb stone manse and reputed to be one of Adam's first buildings; in fact the young architect had been so green at his profession that he had overlooked the positioning of the main staircase, which was ultimately squeezed in, rather ignominiously, through the back of the house. The front elevation has since been contaminated by a cumbersome Victorian porch, which effectively wards off the North Sea winds but simultaneously obliterates the handsome pillar motif. The rooms are well-shaped with the authentic cornices and door architraves intact.

Beauchamp Blackett disclosed that his grandmother had installed all the important pieces in her smaller house on the estate, and that it was she who zealously possessed the key to the silver safe. He then continued in tones of halting awe to put us in the picture as regards Grandma – by name Mrs Blackett-Swiny – a formidable-sounding grande dame who had clearly ruled the Blackett family generally and their fine arts particularly for sixty-odd years. She had refused to cast any of these treasures on her son ('Beechie's' father), claiming that he was ignorant and irresponsible and would have sold the lot and bought new motor cars.

We met this remarkable tour de force the following morning. She proved a distinguished good-looker, pert, slim and upright in figure, and altogether intimidating in presence. She graciously showed us all over her house, with Beauchamp and Sarah Blackett in close tow; they had never been afforded such affable treatment themselves. With tact and subtle persuasion Tom managed to eke out one or two details about the silver and, eventually, her assurance that between 11 pm and 12 pm that night she would get out the best pieces – when nobody was around. Yes – she had quite a collection in the back of the cupboard under the back stairs and even had a record of the important pieces in the safe at the big house. However, she would prefer to wait for the silver expert to call before unlocking it all – thus exposing it to risk and daylight. There was also some fine jewellery for Beechie's wife Sarah; however they were both too young to enjoy it for the moment, she added rather deprecatingly. Our strange interview was thus concluded.

Later that day she produced out of her nefarious back cupboard some select strawberry dishes and important tankards, leaving them in full daylight on her dining-room table, clearly at risk with all her doors unlocked, whilst she pottered nonchalantly in her famous garden. Most women are inconsistent and Mrs Blackett-Swiny, for all her shrewd talents, was no exception.

Her house – 'The House on the Shore' – is well known for its cleverly constructed garden, pervaded with its creator's taste and forceful imagination. It is set off to perfection by its juxtaposition with a remote and peaceful sea shore. But Mrs Blackett-Swiny herself was not a conducive candidate for quietude; a busy life was her essential motivation. We finally saw her driving off upright and determined – to dine alone at the local hotel; apparently she liked to go out once a week and be waited on.

March 20 Hardwicke House

How one savours life when all is clear and true. And oh what hell it was last week, when once again I seemed drowned and bludgeoned by inexplicable depression. My mind and every attitude and breath was totally absorbed in endless negative self-analysis. I confided my bleakness to Tom, he had sensed it all along – even, he confessed, by looking at the back of my head. I rallied and immediately felt more positive, and asked John Flood[1] for more pills. How did I feel? Simply that I had run out of all physical, mental and emotional force, like a car out of fuel, like a diabetic out of insulin; I had become mentally incapacitated with no hold on any one natural moving force or sequence.

How many thousands suffer in this way – and go on suffering indefinitely? Some because they have not the means or opportunity to consult a suitable doctor, some because they are too diffident to relate to a doctor and maybe some who feel that they are surely going insane. Others soldier on, outwardly calm and bright, ashamed to admit to any man the sheer mental torture that infests their every living moment.

It is true that depression, like any emotion or situation, will ultimately change, lift and vanish, but sometimes at too serious a cost to its victim. Personally I now regard these attacks as a chemical deficiency rather than a mental challenge, and only need that pill to put back

[1] The leading psychiatrist at the Priory nursing home, Roehampton in the 1960s and '70s. He practised to good effect the treatment of ECT (electric convulsive therapy) as devised by Ugo Cerletti in 1938.

into the bloodstream the grain of sense and happiness that would appear to have been temporarily sucked dry. Mind over matter is a problem, is a challenge, but mind over mind is a maze that makes one die a little. But oh how one savours the 'ups'. As Rupert Brooke once remarked in writing to his girl friend: 'How one packs things!'

March 21 Sudbrook Cottage Ham Common Surrey

Beverley Nichols entertains. Beaming and benevolent, he leads us through his attractive Queen Anne cottage to the drawing-room. It drips with delicate flower arrangements, hues of palest lavender and snuff. A suffusion of warmth and light pervades the room with the brisk log fire and the soft gleam from wall brackets and picture lights. The scene is swathed by well-known faces – hitherto glimpsed only on the screen or in newspapers. Dame Rebecca West, Mervyn Stockwood, Anton Dolin, Peter and Molly Daubeny, Moura Lympany, Bernard Levin and that incorrigible narcissus, John Gilpin. Others, like ourselves, form a quieter backdrop to these rich personalities.

Dame Rebecca holds benign and vivacious court on three-quarters of a small sofa, a striking woman with dark eyes, alive with wit and intellectual energy. Old now, and fat, she still belies her late seventies with her charm and generous sparkle.

Mervyn Stockwood towers above us with his distinguished head; he looks flamboyant enough in his pink shirt and purple kipper tie – or was it the other way around? He is charming and emanates a nervous vigour. He is a leading member of the Psychic Research Committee and informs us how the USSR and the USA are trading, independently, in telepathic communications. The Americans have even gone so far as to conduct an extrasensory perception exercise with their latest man on the moon, a 'mind mission' apparently successful. He now comes down to earth and talks of wine, a favourite indulgence.

Bernard Levin, on short superficial acquaintance, proves a quiet and unassuming soul; obviously eminently intelligent he is loath to entertain a conversation that breathes of the inconsequential; difficult for the girls to break through to, one would surmise, and yet he is always escorted by beautiful women on his sorties to the opera. He is altogether an unknown quantity, leaving the extent of his colossus impossible to assess.

Moura Lympany spends her evening languorously and palely loitering, closely attended by men and lesser men. She has been ill and is very closely aware of conserving her powers for her next concert.

A mournful creature, her pale oval face and limpid eyes suggesting moonlight, thick with rocking flower scents and sad concertos, all the way down the garden path.

John Gilpin becomes drunk. He has spent most of the evening in poses of orgiastic distortion before Beverley's long wall glass. He is impossible to engage in conversation and finally shows his total disenchantment by relieving himself on the floor of Beverley's cloakroom, whether in protest of the evening's entertainment or of the fact that there is no mirror in the room we do not know. Dame Rebecca remarks wryly that, for a ballet dancer, she is surprised he does not have better aim.

This party was subsequently referred to in Beverley's own words in his book *Down the kitchen sink – Cocktail parties – 'Cause and Cure'*.

May 17 The Ritz Hotel Paris

What delight to be once again swept through these high-ceilinged, rose-carpeted passages, on a wave of bowing, smiling service. The garçon unlocks the bedroom door with minute precision. Long silk taffeta curtains, caught in lush folds with heavy, faded cords, and the bed decked so high in soft deep pillows, linen and sumptuous quilted satin, breathes invitation. There is an aroma and atmosphere unique and peculiar to the Ritz, a distillation perhaps of log fires in bedrooms, black coffee, and excellent cigars that lingers in its seasoned walls and that overall pervasion of dedicated service. The hotel is still presided over by the exclusive concern and inspiration of Count Zembruski. Occasionally he fingers the faded taffeta of the curtains and shrugs lugubriously. He knows he can never replace them.

We bathed and made for the bar on the Rue Cambon. There to our faint surprise sat Dolly Burns[2] – easily distinguishable in her colourful largesse. The last time we had set eyes on her had in fact been in the same bar six months earlier, when she had been sitting on . . . but wait; here he was, and again she hatched the same crushed pallid Russian composer. He looked more alive this time, having just savoured the singular achievement of his music being performed at the Festival Hall.

Some say that Dolly's world-weary air of disillusionment started when, at the age of five, she complained that the sea was too cold. Her resourceful and doting father, the famous Duveen, immediately commissioned one or two kettles of boiling water. A timely oasis of

---

[2] Daughter of Lord Duveen, wife of the surgeon Bobby Burns, and a formidable hostess.

temporary warmth thus enabled this wily little girl to enjoy herself a space.

June 4 Hardwicke House

We arrived at No 9 Kensington Place, the residence of the Philippine Ambassador. It had been attractively re-decorated by Mrs Zobel herself. She effected quick introductions and looked radiant in her fine and delicate Spanish looks with her long gleaming hair elegantly coiled.

Almond-faced Philippines plied us with drinks and attention; the diminutive maids were dressed in bottle-green dresses and starched bibbed aprons.

The guests present were Sir David Scott and his wife – a gentle wild rose of a woman; both were self-effacing and keen, knowledgeable gardeners; Denys Sutton, editor of *Apollo*, and his wife; an ex-English Ambassador to the Philippines by name of Gibbs, other people of equal standing, including the uncle of the present Ambassador.

Denys Sutton was something of a romantic to look at, emanating great charm and distinction; his conversation was original and amusing and he listened with a flattering attention to anything one had to say. He had just returned from Nuremberg where he had covered the 500th anniversary exhibition of Albrecht Dürer. He works hard to produce this magazine with only four aides – to include his secretary. The subscription per annum is £12.00; in January this year a print of a colour block cost him £53.00; in June – a mere five months later – it costs him £82.00. We both agreed that Dürer, taking into account his unimpeachable and formidable talent, was a cold fish; perhaps this rendered him even more fascinating? Denys Sutton was certainly an intelligent and diverting man. His hands and fingers were remarkably small and delicate in comparison with his build. His wife was also distinguished-looking; she had a small dark head and was tenacious in her conversation; a little intense, with a hint of strong passions surging through her slight, upright body; a cross between the Duchess of Windsor and Valerie Profumo in mien.

During the course of a quite excellent dinner – chilled vichyssoise; salmon in a *sauce mousseline* garnished (liberally) with truffles; poussins; and a rich apricot ice cream (and quite good wines only) – I asked the Ambassador's uncle, on whose right I sat, whether he was a gourmet. 'No,' he replied, beaming with a certain relieved pleasure. 'No,' he repeated, 'I have not got that problem. My problem,' he continued, 'is that I have an insatiable passion for a good Spanish omelette. In every country, city and restaurant it is prepared differently. It is a fascinating study. Now – how do you prepare it?' We talked of food for the next half an hour.

June 25 Christie's St James's

For the past week the great rooms have vibrated in tremulous anticipation of the greatest sale of furniture and paintings of this century. Mrs Anna Dodge of Cleveland, Ohio, an American collector of exclusive 'Duveen' repute, died last autumn at the inspired age of one hundred and two. Towards the end of her life, she commissioned Duveen to collect for her the finest continental furniture, paintings and porcelain with the occasional rare influx of Russian pieces. He completed his assignment in three years of frenetic energy and persuasive enthusiasm. His bills were thinly disguised in waves of flamboyant deprecation; at one juncture he concluded a suggestive letter with the frivolous words, 'What is money after all?'

Mrs Anna Dodge proved a good patient and collected well. A few months ago a conspicuously uninterested nephew was detailed to guard a BOAC 707 cargo jet load of these quality goods and, amidst the urbane calm of Christie's at the hammer, each item has been finally sold and formidably accredited. The Louis XVI bureau plat, attributed to Martin Carlin, with lavish ormolu mounts and much Sèvres inlay, fell heavily to French & Co. of New York for 165,000 guineas; a price never before realised for one single item of furniture. We ourselves bought a guéridon Louis XVI table. The bowed ormolu legs, headed with intricate satyr masks and finished in lion's-paw feet, supports a circular malachite top. The vivid green is segmental in design – Russian perhaps?

The sale of the furniture augured well for the paintings. The Boucher, the Fragonard, the Greuze were of the most desirable order, depicting those halcyon days of lush extravagance, when all in the flesh was rosy. The colours glowed powder-bright as the bidding reached and over-reached reserve after reserve. Leger Galleries bought the Greuze for 20,000 gns; Mr Leger was sitting beside me. The subject had a sweet mild face, the letter she was half-reading, the loose white chemise she was half-wearing and the pearly right breast she was half-revealing evoked a languid, light-hearted mise-en-scène. Mr Leger completed his successful bidding and sat back fulsomely in his chair, his face wreathed in agreeable smiles.

'There's a lush bit you have bought,' I ventured. He chuckled. 'Do you know who she is?' I asked. 'She was the artist's chief botherer,' he muttered, 'and cost slightly more when she was alive!'

The four Negro heads – a study of the same man – in four smiling poses fetched 400,000 guineas. A controversial painting and one of Van Dyck's most famous and revered, it was sold by the Derby family[3].

Finally, the Titian – the chef d'œuvre of the sale – owned by Lord Harewood. After straight steady bidding it was knocked down to Julius Weitzner for 1,600,000 guineas. However according to the papers this morning the picture has spent an indeterminate weekend having been lured into the grasp of Mr J. Paul Getty. He plans to loan it to the National Gallery for two years and then to house it in his museum in California.

What a painting! It inspired an intuitive article by a young journalist, Richard Cork, in the *Evening News*; a succinct study of the artist's motive for usurping his usual finished style with this surging restless brushwork: *The Death of Actaeon*. Titian had here chosen to 'let up' and died three years later, aged seventy-six, leaving this last great work – a fascinating deviation; a haunting subject, a mystery of achievement and the whole drenched in the rich harmonious shades of autumn – sepia, russet and deepest red. Any onlooker must be filled with elusive emotion on beholding this painting. When it was originally commissioned in 1559 by Philip of Spain, Titian fervently assured the King – 'In these pieces I shall put all the knowledge which God has given me.'

October 16 Hardwicke House

Beverley Nichols called in for a drink this evening. We had not seen him for some time; he always avoids us in July because our lilies are so good. In August we were in France and he had been completing his latest book *Father Figure*. He has always impressed upon us in low underlined tones of conjured horror how his father was an evil, terrifying man. Tonight he further averred that he was a sadist, a drunk and a potential murderer; all of which we will read in January 1972 when this splenetic and climactic vitriol will be serialised in the *Sunday Express*; which exposure will nicely coincide with the book's final publication in March.

He looked well and was in magnetic humour. Had we heard the latest story about Godfrey Winn? Emlyn Williams was biding his turn in the dentist's waiting room one afternoon this summer; he was reading one of Godfrey's articles – Godfrey expounding on how to

---

[3] This work witnessed the sinister scene on October 9, 1952, of the butler shooting at the thirty-one-year-old Countess of Derby. She had been watching television in the smoking-room. The family considered the painting cursed ever since. (See *Gossip, 1920–1970* by Andrew Barrow.)

be kind to pregnant grandmothers – you know the sort of thing – when a friend of Emlyn's walked in. 'Hullo, Emlyn! Have you heard? Godfrey's dead; he was playing tennis at the time.' Replied Emlyn – 'What a splendid way for dear Godfrey to go; holding his racquet aloft, ready to serve and announcing "Love All".'

How was Cyril and how was Alec and how was the man we no longer mention? (He got drunk one night and punched Beverley on the nose – I think the nose – whereupon Cyril flattened the unfortunate miscreant with two masterly blows; Alec, whose friend he was, was promptly ordered to make other arrangements for this wild hooligan – by then unconscious on the landing; Alec did.)

Alec is now restored to great favour; a pleasant, appreciative and ordinary man. Beverley took him to Paris this spring where the 'pardons', 'toilets' and the odd 'perfume' caused less *honte* than they do on home ground. Beverley remarked that he was improving slowly; 'This afternoon I pointed out to him how the wallflowers – the deep reds – would make a magnificent blaze.' Replied Alec – 'Oh yes! And they have a nice perfume, don't they?' 'No, Alec, we do not say perfume, we say they have a nice scent.' Alec: 'Yes, yes, so we do, the wallflowers have a nice scent and we go to the loo.'

The only other more immediate problem in Beverley's domestic life is that he is 'over-catted'; he maintains three old originals and has just acquired two Siamese; these last on a 'demi-pension' basis.

Beverley finally left with a brown paper bag of my Regale Lily seeds.

1972

We are staying the weekend with Michael and Anne Tree. Cecil Beaton came to dinner; not a man to warm the heart on brief encounter. Pale and interesting, serious, unassuming and rather quiet, his bleak eyes look closely at his neighbour as though singling out all facial imperfections – a cold fish. Michael asked him how he would describe that paragon of style, flair and warped wit, Daisy Fellowes.

'How would you describe Daisy, Cecil?'

'Daisy? She was an aristocratic adventuress, a slut on a large scale.'

April 29 Shute

A wet, windy day. Lord Gage, who had taken the precaution of bringing his own cue, spent the morning playing billiards; a shrewd old codger (at breakfast he had described Archbishop Ramsey of Canterbury as an 'unmade bed'). Lady Gage spread her knees with a sea of intricate embroidery and set to work with an unassailable concentration. Michael and I played an expensive game of backgammon and took a walk round the garden. Despite the rain, his pipe didn't go out.

And what horticultural departures will Anne dream up next? Her imagination has no bounds. Waiting to be decked in climbing foliage and suitable flowers was an ironwork frame of a double four-poster bed, a bedside table, an armchair and a dressing table. 'I am putting roses round the dressing table,' she told me. 'And will you actually sleep out as well?' I asked. She seemed doubtful but had schemes for planting a carpet of bright flowers with her initials in the middle. She also breeds moths; she injects them to death, much to her two adopted daughters' delight, when they are finally dried and mounted on a glass-fronted frame.

Michael looked gorgeous tonight in his red velvet and matching monogrammed slippers. And what fun we had when, with that pipe and its accompanying dribble down his left chin, he showed us Cecil Beaton's watercolours of that seasoned snob, the Countess of Rosse. Cecil Beaton's pet *bête-noire*? For how else could he have depicted with such zealous invective the myriad social details and relationships of that woman's life, in a pen so finely tuned? As Anne remarked, 'I don't think Cecil would have got his knighthood if the Royal Family had seen this.'

August 9 Castellina in Chianti Tuscany Italy

A sparse and rugged landscape, smudged with medieval stone farm-houses and a church spire on every distant hill; olive groves and fig vines and cornfields brush this clay soil with a rash of cool relief. We are poised midway between Florence and Siena, with San Gimignano towering over the hills, but it is too hot for serious sightseeing. A cool pool is the languid prime delight in the midsummer heat of Tuscany.

Down the hill, Ronnie Tree[1] and the vital Marietta[2] have rented a villa. We met them in Asolo, where Ronnie, the epitome of archetype English elegance, had disported himself with grace and dignity. His guests had included David Bruce[3] and the beautiful, tall Evangeline. As they sat in the charming dining-room of the Villa Cipriani, Mr Kamina would swim to their table, bowing and swaying like a cuckoo clock's pendulum. Ronnie's studied attention would never swerve from his party; his distinguished profile carefully averted from such obsequious overtures.

Then Evangeline[4] had been taken ill at Asolo; one moment chic and chatting vivaciously in a white silk trouser suit, her immaculate hair piled high, the next, whisked off to the local hospital with a burst appendix and a cyst on the ovaries. A hazardous operation ensued; a few days later requests for Fiuggi water and bottles of Soave augured well for a quick recovery. She is at present writing a book on Napoleon.

Ronnie is seventy-five and enjoys £200,000 a year income. He cannot afford to live in England and winters in Barbados, on which he has written a book. (Second editions still available at Quaritch.) In the late autumn he sojourns at Baden-Baden; New York houses his more valuable works of art. His life has always been conducted on a rhythmical scale of stylish comfort and orderliness. (It was not so long ago that he and his children would take their own monogrammed sheets when travelling British Rail.) He knows everybody.

---

[1] The Anglo-American private secretary in the Ministry of Information 1940–43. His book, *When the Moon Was High* was published in 1975. Whenever Chequers was too visible to German night bombers, Churchill and his entourage would retreat to Tree's early eighteenth-century home, Ditchley Park, North Oxfordshire.
[2] Marietta (née Peabody) married Tree 1947.
[3] David Bruce, American ambassador to England 1961–69.
[4] Evangeline Bruce published *Napoleon and Josephine* in 1995.

'I have had a tiring morning,' he remarked today as we sat drinking aperitifs by the pool. 'I have been thinking. Now what can I call my next book?' (The subject being his memoirs of peace and war.) Over lunch, *all'aperto*, various ideas were put forward; the final favourite *A Backbencher Looks Back*, was suggested by his house guest Kenneth Harris, the *Observer* journalist and television interviewer; charming and with the admirable ability to listen attentively as well as talk, he later asked my opinion of the title. All were agreed that the strong string of B's sounded effective. 'Too laboured.' I ventured and threw out *A Backbencher's Bygones* as an alternative.

Kenneth was staying in the annexe of the villa, along with Lady Hartwell, the daughter of F. E. Smith. A plump, good-looking woman; her flickering, sharp brown eyes and the indomitable outpourings of her likes and dislikes rendered her intimidating on first encounter. She runs the *Daily Telegraph*.

Susan Mary Alsop[5] was also a guest; the estranged wife of the American columnist Jo Alsop and a lifelong friend of Ronnie's and Marietta's, she told us how David Bruce was first married to the sister of Paul Mellon; an unhappy liaison, where she had jealously guarded her rich independence and had thwarted her husband's every ambition by dragging him across the globe in a vacuum of restless inactivity. It was not until his early forties that Bruce had made his mark in the diplomatic field. With Evangeline on his arm (the former Miss Bell: a formidable linguist and his one-time secretary), they had set a large slice of the world alight with their charm, ability and intelligence; great Anglophiles, they now have permanent chambers in Albany.

August 11 Tuscany

As planned we met him at the steps of the Duomo of San Gimignano; a tall lithe figure in the hot light of the morning sun with his dark hair and white teeth gleaming, André Dzierzynski, a Polish-born British subject, an artist and something of a recluse. Revelling in the peace of the stark Tuscany hills, he paints the environs for his bi-annual exhibitions at the Hamet Gallery in London. Three years ago he bought a mediaeval farmhouse – Le Casette, a mere ruin and an arduous challenge to restoration. With the help of a local builder, glorying in the name of Orlando, he is slowly renovating it – largely with his own hands. He is currently laying the roof tiles, genuine rose-red mediaeval tiles that Orlando had taken upon himself to procure from some local

[5] Her book of letters *To Marietta from Paris 1945–1960* was published in 1975.

graveyard. André's property includes an ancient chapel, a cowshed, a long-disused well and an indeterminate garden. The cowshed will be his studio, with the walls whitewashed to offset the rose-warm glow of the original vaulted brick ceiling. Surrounding him on all sides are acres of rough grass and stunted trees. 'I will plant silver birches,' he averred, although he later confessed that Georgina Masson[6] had strongly discouraged his plan to introduce atypical trees to the landscape. It takes a boisterous climb in his jeep (nine gears and bequeathed him by John Piper) to negotiate the steep, rough approach to his 'ruin'; an even dustier series of slithering jerks ensures an eventual return to the narrow road.

We took him to lunch at La Cisterna, an excellent restaurant in San Gimignano. His mother came too. She felt car-sick in our Jaguar; riding beside André in the jeep proved more conducive to her comfort than power-steered smooth suspension.

André's year is neatly severed with his Tuscan summer idyll and his winters harboured in a London flat, where, from copious notes, he will depict the scenes and colours savoured from his Italian interlude.

August 23 Dunecht Skene Aberdeenshire

We are valuing Lord and Lady Cowdray's furniture for insurance purposes and today waded through the 116 rooms of this mid-nineteenth-century stone pile, a plethora of John Fowler decoration and Victorian four-poster beds, festooned in faded damasks and crewel work. At the extreme end of the east wing we came across the Countess's bedroom, rather splendid in its Victorian faded oak panelling; it sported a good piece of furniture, set in the window and draped with a sheet. At first glance it almost suggested her Ladyship's coffin. We peered under the cloth and saw a superb (Italian) serpentine-fronted commode in faded walnut with elegant inlay. We later coveted a painted bracket clock and the four tapestries in the Long Gallery. These used to adorn the walls of a room at Crockford's – the Cowdrays' original London home.

It is a strange, uncomfortable sensation to meander through a house when the owners are absent. Dunecht was markedly tidy and devoid of personal paraphernalia. But the bowl of faded dead roses in the morning-room appeared beautiful in their floppy soft demise. The photograph of Lady Cowdray in her husband's study denoted a serious,

---

[6] Her most famous book is *Italian Gardens* 1961. In his introduction to *Tuscan Villas* 1973, Sir Harold Acton wrote: 'Miss Masson's *Italian Gardens* is the most important of recent books on the subject.'

sensitive face, young and vulnerable, with lovely, shy, slanting eyes; one wondered if she still resembled it. Her bedroom was feminine and comfortable with its white fluffy carpet, the white frilled dressing-table, the touches of pale pink in the four-poster, the chintz curtains and the inviting chaise-longue of pink taffeta and white velvet. A minute stairway of three steps led from her room to his Lordship's.

August 25 Edinglassie Strathdon Aberdeenshire

Here we met Lady Cowdray; dressed in tartan trousers and a head scarf, she sat on a garden seat, eating an apple. She was charming and looked very young. (Lord Cowdray whom we met later was also charming and looked very old) The eighteenth-century stone house was low-storied and rambling. 'We come here to picnic,' explained Lady Cowdray; even so they maintain a full staff.

December 19 Wilton's St James's

It was Quentin Crewe who referred to Wilton's as a venue for good nursery food served by starched nannies. Presided over through the years by Mr Marks and his socially discerning eye ('Oy trates everybody ze syme'), it has still retained its ambience of aristocratic understatement. Here the upper echelons can mull over their grouse and lobster and nurture any idiosyncrasies, knowing which side their brown bread is buttered.

A quiet haven of polished wood, boxed banquette seats, with an air of intimacy further engendered by hints of Victorian lace and unobtrusive wall prints.

We dined there last night. Sitting across the aisle was Lord Ashcombe and his blonde girlfriend, loquacious on one glass of hock. He meanwhile took care of one and a half bottles of Burgundy and the port. (He eats there so regularly that he may even be guilty of sticking corks back into bottles.) He appeared glum and broody, reputed to be a bad shot with appallingly behaved gun dogs, and very, very rich.

As we sat, swathed in every self-indulgence, half-listening to Ashcombe's assurances to his favourite waitress that he would be eating there for every meal up to Christmas, John Profumo and his striking wife, Valerie Hobson, sailed past. He, suave, slim and charming, and she a galaxy of style and good looks. The wine waiter poked an excited face into mine, 'You, Madam,' he avowed 'look the spit image of Mrs Profumo.' 'Come, come,' riposted Tom gallantly, 'Mrs Profumo looks like my wife.' 'Indeed, Sir,' laughed the waiter, 'and your wife is younger.' He laughed again, all a touch too familiar, one felt.

The next day Tom mentioned to Michael Tree our proximity to Harry Ashcombe, his girlfriend and his bottles. 'Let's ring him!' cried Michael, always eager for frivolous diversion. They found Ashcombe at home rather than at his office. 'Hello, you dirty little Lord. There you were – booze and blondes – at it again. Do you know, Harry? I would simply hate to go to bed with you; it would be so nasty waking up in the morning and seeing your teeth in a mug.'

'I won't ask you to shoot again, Michael,' concluded Ashcombe petulantly, and a week later married his blonde.

1973

The Spanish maid crossed herself as she hurried through the marble hall to open the door to us. It was late, dark and wet, but we were still expected. We plunged into the warmth as an English housekeeper with carpet slippers, a fallen stomach and a stale chignon sidled out of a door. 'She is upset not to greet you herself,' she condescended, 'but she has been unwell again and gets over-excited at night; here, there and everywhere and so difficult to settle her; it's not right for a body to be so full of pills; you know how it is.' With a wary conciliatory look she led us to our room. The maid unpacked, produced open sandwiches and coffee – so deliciously French and different. We fell exhausted into bed.

The Villa is eighteenth-century, stylish and intimate, copiously marbled and mirrored with French windows hung with faded silks. It housed nothing of great import, save for its charming taste and ambience and, of course, Mrs Rosie Chisholm.

She appeared the next morning at eleven o'clock; a frail, minuscule figure, locked in black; black sweater and trousers with her gazelle-like delicate, pale face framed in a black and white scarf. Her whole diminutive frame emanated a heavy, expensive scent; her long be-ringed fingers and her soft American drawl waved all before her on a sea of waffled sweet nothings. She was charming in her fragility and the flutterings of her hopping mind. Erstwhile photographs, drawings and portraits denoted her former beauty, with Vanderbilt blood to boot; a transient, tremulous beauty, but those young clear lines had since gathered storms to cloud her loveliness in sad distortions. She was fifty and looked seventy; a succession of operations on a gangrenous arm, with the physical strain and the drugs entailed, and the recent death of her husband, had left her spent and brittle.

She retired to bed for lunch; her tray went up and came down – untouched. She kept to her bed for the rest of the day. The doctor called, the banker, the masseuse and a heavy woman, with a syringe. Tom visited her before dinner; she entreated us to see her after. She lay diminutive in pink, surrounded by the comforting paraphernalia of wireless, books, drinks (ginger ale and water?), television and cigarettes. We sat down a small distance from her capacious, plump bed. The maid looked in nervously with the next day's menus – tick, tick,

tick, and then, petulantly, 'Quelque-chose mieux pour le dîner.' Next the housekeeper, who, with little ceremony, briskly slid a hot-water bottle under those lost little legs.

Rosie Chisholm remained studiously unaware of these attentions and soon bade us goodnight. However, at midnight, swaying in her nightdress at the top of the curved staircase, she was calling imperiously for the Spanish maid, for the housekeeper and for Tom: 'Those Chantilly knife handles! Where are they?' They were in the cellar; she wished them valued immediately.

April 5 London

We dine with Brinsley and Moorea Black in Holland Villas Road. Their late Regency house is assiduously decorated with a striking use of geometrically-patterned carpets; a handsome foil for their collection of Biedermeier furniture. Rich, sombre, high-ceilinged rooms these, of clever, calculated taste; a little cold.

'It will be in October – you must come of course,' Sir Francis Dashwood refers to his dance to mark his wife Victoria's fortieth birthday.

'I am tired of being placed next to queers.' Pauline Vogelpoel[1] in a weary aside to Tom.

'You have pretty ears.' Peter Coats pays me a compliment. He later refers to Noël Coward, whose ears he assured me were the ugliest pair ever.

'We have a few acres in Derbyshire – a lot of work for my wife, Penelope.' Reresby Sitwell of his splendid home, Renishaw Hall. His dark-haired, vivacious and elegant wife has Brinsley to herself at the end of the table.

'How's Selina?' A leading question from Tom to Moorea; Lady Selina Hastings is her half-sister, aged twenty-eight and currently engaged to Larry Adler, mouth-organist extraordinary and aged over sixty. Moorea establishes that they are still heavily engaged, although her step-mother, the writer Margaret Lane, cannot find it within herself to regard Mr Adler as a 'viable proposition'. Apparently he is in complete sympathy with her feelings. He is also reputed to be 'very good with his hands'.

'Confrey Phillips is my man,' concludes Sir Francis, indulgently; he

---

[1] A ravishing redhead. She directed the Contemporary Art Society from the Tate Gallery basement 1956–82. An avant-garde traveller, she led her CAS groups through Russia, Afghanistan, China and Cambodia.

continues his vapid flow of bemused chatter, laced with louche asides; 'and I will arrange that he procures a string of dusky women naked to the waist.' (A hasty glance at Victoria to see if she had heard this last.) 'They will wear turbans and serve champagne. I have already laid down a thousand bottles of Mumm.' I only hope he remembers to invite us.

April 21 Poulton House Marlborough Wiltshire

'Find the rut that you can afford and stick in it,' proclaims my mother as she settles into her habitual foetal position in the deep fireside chair, her rug notched firmly into every curve of her body. She shivers contentedly at the splattering rain on the newly double-glazed Queen Anne windows. 'Has anybody done the dogs? Ugh! What a night! Where's Steve? Perhaps he's doing the dogs.'

Stephen, my younger brother, aged twenty-six, is a budding tycoon. Having just landed a contract to build the new marina at Weymouth harbour with McAlpines as his eager sub-contractors, he has even acquired an aeroplane. Fitting in flying lessons at every moment he can spare, this new and fascinating toy must pursue him everywhere. Unbeknownst to his mother, an air sock has been installed at the top of the farm. Indeed this twin-engined, orange flying machine is poised for imminent take-off for Schipol, Amsterdam. His parents know about the flying lessons, but not of the plane's existence, nor indeed of its immediate positioning. His unsuspecting father commented only the other day on how ill one of the farm workers was looking. (Poor Arthur had just been treated to a 'joy-ride'.)

June 5 London

Lady Hartwell had invited a substantial bunch of politicians for drinks, together with a sprinkling of outsiders to lend dabs of background colour. We peered a little diffidently through this massed main display. (Why is it that the famous in the flesh lose substance rather than gain?) The party was given for Ronnie and Marietta Tree.

Lady Gaitskell, diminutive and intense, cross-examined Lord Longford on the Press attitude to the latest Lord Lambton disclosures. Longford expressed a vehement disgust – especially so as he had just been photographed kissing Mary Whitehouse goodbye. He stumbled into calmer expletives and a halting dissertation on prisons. The broad shoulders of Reggie Maudling were on perpetual manoeuvres through the glass-clutching throng. Tony Royle[2], upright and handsome, was closely flanked by his soignée, blonde wife Shirley. Jeremy Thorpe, pale and purposeful, twisted a determined path towards his hostess, whilst his new bride, Marion, appeared very tanned and lined with small brown eyes glittering in anticipation. Anthony Barber's pink and white soft face contrasted strangely with Lord Goodman's dark, hirsute largesse. Anne Scott-James towered overhead – dipping a sharp nose into any conversation that wafted her way and tossing it further on a wave of wit. Her husband, Osbert Lancaster, retains his own talent for later publication. Small, rotund, serious and shabby, he is a happy foil for his wife's loquacity.

The Hartwells[3] live in the Queen Anne belt of recherché Westminster, in Cowley Street. An elegant staircase to the first-floor verandah leads past doors thrown open to inviting rooms on either side; one's eye and senses were immediately enslaved by their taste. Pictures were lavishly banked on panelled walls and richly-coloured French carpets exuded an ambience lush with every exotic comfort. The European furniture throughout was exquisite.

One wished that it had rained; that the party had been forcibly held inside rather than on that pokey new verandah that seethed with so many unapproachable faces.

June 25 Eydon Hall Eydon Nr Rugby Northamptonshire

'Do you ever hit your husband?' enquired Lady Ford. 'Or throw things at him?' Sir Edward Ford[4], her Ladyship (a niece of Nancy Astor), Tom and myself were having dinner in their exquisite Adam house, Eydon Hall. The cows mooed mildly beyond the ha-ha; the dining-room was cool and darkening in the summer evening. The butler hovered over the table with more wine and more pudding.

'No,' I replied hesitantly, 'I haven't hit him yet. I did actually shout at him in the kitchen once. He merely told my doctor to change my pills.'

'Oh . . .' she murmured, in the flat and heavy silence.

'Do you throw things at Sir Edward?' I asked tentatively.

'Oh yes!' she responded with renewed vigour – 'the whole time! Anything, everything!'

---

[2] Conservative MP for Richmond-on-Thames 1959–83.
[3] Lord Hartwell was Chairman and Editor-in-chief of the *Daily Telegraph* 1954–87 and the *Sunday Telegraph* 1961–87.
[4] Tutor to King Farouk of Egypt 1936–37. Assistant Private Secretary to King George VI 1946–52 and to the Queen 1952–67. Extra equerry to the Queen 1955. Awarded MVO 1949, KCVO 1957, GCVO 1998.

'And does Sir Edward throw things at you?' I felt emboldened to ask.

'No,' she replied, smiling gaily; 'he shakes me instead. Once he shook me so violently that my teeth really did rattle – just like they do in books.'

There was a peaceful interlude while breakfast arrangements were noted with the butler. She turned to me again. 'What would you do if your husband had an affair? Would you sit it out, be patient – have him back?'

'No,' I told her and catching the gist of her caprice, 'I would rush off and have some myself!' She roared with laughter and added she would throw Sir Edward out on his ear if she ever had any trouble of that kind.

We wandered out on to the magnificent colonnaded balcony reached by a stone staircase from the garden. Handsome Ionic pilasters rested on the red stone façade of the house. And what a house. By no means too large to live in and enjoy; pure Adam, a gem, beautiful from every angle and enveloped by unspoilt rolling country. Walled gardens of weathered warm quarry stone and brick abounded, with a profusion of flowers and shrubs and sweeping cedar trees.

We talked, the four of us, idly into the warm night. It grew colder and I played a little Chopin.

Meanwhile, Lady Ford and I, having established a more gentle rapport on matters matrimonial, had happily exchanged addresses of psychiatrists, furniture restorers and cooking recipes. She gave me her eggs and cream and cucumber in exchange for my pears in gorgonzola.

August 25 Villa Cipriani Asolo Italy

Absorbed in his autobiography, he was resting in the hall of the Villa Cipriani. We met up briefly, Ronnie and Marietta Tree were back again; their brief venture into Florence, with its tourist trappings and overpowering heat, had proved a small disaster. He told me, however, that during their brief stay Kenneth Harris had flown out from London and helped him further with his book; they had now made it to 1939. He also reported that Pamela Hartwell had been around; her chronic interest in politics was now usurped by an acute assault on the arts. She has recently become involved with the V & A, under the aegis of John Pope-Hennessy, whom she now apparently regards as omniscient in all things. 'She follows him around, her mouth hung open like a . . . like a . . . 'Ronnie's voice faded with mild despair . . . 'like a dog,' I suggested lamely. 'She positively flew around Florence.' He sighed quietly and one half–imagined the Red Queen pecking at frescoes with her flamingo.

I told him how much we had enjoyed the party she had given for Marietta and himself at Cowley Street. He had obviously enjoyed the evening himself, but confessed that he had not admired the new extended dining-room; one remembered it as long, dark and red. It had looked like a night club, I ventured. 'A rather bad night club' was his wry rejoinder.

September 1 Asolo

We followed her up a steep, terraced slope which led to her mediaeval tower. Below us lay the rose roofs of Asolo with a swathe of soft, round hills beyond; the plain was hazy, the Euganean hills a frail brush on the horizon. She turned to us, and her eyes, in contrast, glinted as fresh and clear as a Dartmoor tarn, small, deep, reflective eyes. Not for her, Dame Freya Stark, the dimming of time; her happy effervescence, unshackled by the limits of the modern age, rides abreast a new idea, tossing any raw contour into the mould of her own experience.

'I am a little puffed,' she murmured. We paused on a narrow, grass terrace, a small allotment of straggling dahlias nodding in the breeze. 'Such modern, ugly colours,' she mused, and we zig-zagged further up the hill, her sturdy little feet picking through loose stones and deep blue plumbago.

We reached the tower. She bent her small head of thick coiled grey hair over the lock of the heavy weathered door. 'This is your hermitage,' I ventured, and we wandered from ceramic to painting to book; each one a vignette of memory; fixed mosaics in her crowded life. And had she enjoyed Dostoyevsky's *The Idiot*? (I confessed I could not finish it.) She had not finished it either, and anyway, she concluded, Dostoyevsky would not have been an amusing guest for dinner.

Another day we went and took a drink with her in her flat in Asolo; an old apartment house, sandwiched between Duse's old house and the Villa Cipriani. The latter establishment supplied her evening meal. ('A sad little ice,' she commented, as she eyed the bald coffee glacé produced yet again.) 'Here I am secluded and I can look through these hills, each one enfolding the next, into the distance. I love my terrace,' she continued, and showed us how she lowered the awning to form a cool tent.

She was working on her letters and opened a small cabinet, each drawer neatly stacked with piles of sorted correspondence, carefully wrapped in old cream paper. We admired her desk, made especially for her in Asolo to her own design; a wide full moon of revolving chestnut, finished in simple ormolu mounts and handles. 'Here I can sit,' she said, 'with the bits and pieces I love.' She fondled the lapis lazuli handle of her magnifying glass. The handle she told us had come from an old sabre. Her simple chair, its front legs sawn off in a permanent tilt to avoid her back aching, was poised possessively by her busy blotter; the blotter had also been especially made, its tooled brass corners fitting the curved outline of her desk.

Her conversation, like her prose, flowed effortlessly in perfect phrasing, her soft voice with its deep timbre, her knowledge, her humour and her wealth of travel stories complemented each in the happiest mélange. She listened too. Once I asked her what she considered the most important quality in life. 'Accuracy,' she almost snapped. A direct reflection perhaps on a life that had scaled mountains, linguistics and a formidable literary output.

We said goodbye; the flowers on the kitchen table were fresh and carefully arranged. One had a fleeting vision of her happy childhood; the breeze and balm and heather of those days on Dartmoor; and the cool tea-times in Italy with milk and figs and grapes. Her life had been nurtured on well-built foundations, with ever-evolving peaks of radiant achievement. 'One of my favourite maxims,' she said, is that 'this life should be a little seed pot for the next'. These same words, written in Arabic, and simply framed, hung on her bathroom wall.

1974

Peking isn't ready for us! Poised for flight in five days' time; jabbed with inoculations and sustaining jumbled impressions from half-read books, we were ready – twenty of us, from the Contemporary Art Society, with Pauline Vogelpoel at our head – when we were refused visas; no explanations; it happens often.

May in England has every compensation, and what a joy to revert to one's own chosen reading:– Virginia Woolf, Strachey, Carrington; the former particularly. Does she always write with a lump in her throat? Her feeling so intense, so vulnerable; her observation so astute; her understatement so revealing. The distilling passion that pervades her work belies that habitual background of domestic peace. She would make bread and jam, a good year if the quince on the south wall yielded three pounds, and she kept her slabs of butter on a slate in the larder.

Her perception always so deep, her brushes with insanity enhanced her essence and hoisted her on that tight-rope of spiritual awareness; the delicate brain was driven hard in brilliant, barely-recovered swerves. And did she love with a lump in her throat also? And is the purest ecstasy tinged with sadness?

May 18 West Wycombe House Buckinghamshire

The lilac, horse-chestnut candles and heavy-hanging cherry blossom were humped into pyramids of thick profusion; harbingers of spring in every room. The eighteenth-century mahogany staircase gleamed dark and rich from years of tread and polish. It was lunch outside today, under the colonnade. Victoria Dashwood was hurriedly changing over the plates; they were ancestral, the yellow went better; a happier match with the low central flower arrangement; it was done; the perfectionist's touch completed in stolen seconds.

'Can I show you round, actually?' Sir Francis led the way in from the colonnade. We had lunched on pheasant's eggs; a hiatus had then ensued while he wielded pork and charcoal on a newly-acquired barbecue. We had talked to Jack and Sue Gardiner – visiting from Boston, descendants indeed of the incorrigible and fascinating

Isabella Stuart Gardiner. The colonnade was warm and gold in the soft floating sunshine; lunch had finally shunted to a gentle halt; it was four o'clock.

Ornately-painted ceilings, original fireplaces, a superb conglomeration of eighteenth-century furniture, porcelain and tapestries, we ambled through the rooms, each basking in its cherished renovation.

'We open to the public actually. No Sundays in June – and never Saturdays; but Tuesdays, Wednesdays and Thursdays between . . .' Francis maintains a nonchalant attitude to the remunerations of the National Trust and the public. His father loathed the house; its Palladian concept was to him a presumptuous folly. He never lived there; for Francis it has proved a mainspring of creative energy throughout his life. It has been jealously restored and even enhanced by Victoria's unerring taste and colour sense. 'The house is set up for fifty years, actually, and I am collecting Art Nouveau, Gillow and Edwardian for the girls. Emily's not doing too badly, actually, with these Canalettos in her bedroom. We've stocked up with champagne; need it for the children – for the servants too, actually; they preferred it to beer at their last party – Australia is the place; I'm off to Canada in two days. I bought 300 acres on a main road, actually; I think I'll try and buy 500 instead. I might even make five million on it; or at least only lose 20% on the whole deal.'

Again the next day, we lunched on the sun-splashed colonnade. David Hicks sat at one end of the table. We all admired his linen jacket; it was the palest eau-de-nil, with chrome buttons on the sleeves. 'Left-over curtain material,' he confided, with a bland smile; his teeth were dreadful. Morys Aberdare at the other end of the table was reminiscing over the first few years of his marriage to Francis's sister, Sarah. They had had a lodger at the top of their London house; each night, by arrangement, he had left his shoes outside his door, and each night Morys had crept upstairs before going to bed and dutifully cleaned them, whilst Sarah had always placed beside them a thermos of coffee and bowl of stewed fruit. The lodger had paid a comparative pittance in cash. When their first child appeared, the lodger was usurped by a young Swedish nanny. Morys and Sarah paid her £3.50 per week. After two years the girl married but continued her office. However, in return for the keep of her husband, her wages were amicably scrapped.

May 31 The Waterside Inn Bray Berkshire

Ari and Plato solemnly rolled dry sherry around the backs of their
tongues. They were guides from Egon Ronay; slim and elegant, they
more resembled Knightsbridge hairdressers. We studied the menu with
them. Our host, Gregory Houston Bowden and his older brother,
Adrian, completed the party.

'Is the pike pâté hot?' The waiter assured us it was; we were later
further surprised to learn that the soufflé Grand Marnier was cold. The
menu was apparently too short; personally I found it a relief to peruse
a small and well-selected choice.

The Thames and the service spun smoothly around us as we sat in
the glass-enclosed dining-room. One felt in France; the setting, the
presentation of each detail and the ambience were totally beguiling.

Ari, on my right, assured me that the bread roll was excellent in
texture and flavour and baked the day before. Adrian Houston Bowden
– a large, solid man – refused the bread; he was on a diet. He also
refused the pudding, but ended his meal with an exuberant attack on
the cheeses. We drank Meursault. Adrian knew his wines and a plethora of ecstatic description, redolent of bulb catalogues, threw the
company into a frenzy of wine appreciation and stories of ever-greater
superlatives.

'Penelope has had her hair rinsed in Pommery and Greno 1928,'
Tom finally proclaimed. As I was the only woman present, this startling
information hung in the air – a line too improbable and too perfect
to risk unravelling.

Gregory was entranced with his choice of pâté; it was indeed hot
and had a pale green river of contrasting matter streaking its middle. I
detected white cabbage exquisitely seasoned, but Gregory insisted that
it was asparagus tips. He changed the conversation to harpsichords, on
which he had written a book; to Morgans, on which he was writing
a book; and then we were again wallowing in favourite food, wines
and restaurants (on which Gregory was also writing a book). On a
wave of fresh, ingenuous enthusiasm, he was imminently poised for
another epic eating bout in France; certain dishes having escaped his
mind and palate on a previous trip. Brother Adrian (whose diet was
assiduously abandoned during the main course) urgently reminded
him of the egg dish in Lyons: 'a concoction of soft eggs glazed with
truffles and snails and an exquisite sauce of perfectly selected herbs – a
dish that leaps ahead.'

Plato had not spoken; instead he had instigated a hive of nervous
activity around his fast-emptying plates. More and more puddings
were called for: lemon pie, sorbets and sledgehammers of cheese. He

looked pale, thin, intense. Ari told me that his friend expended a lot of energy in other fields and that he knew how to dress. Plato looked up from his plates at this overhead juncture and, with large, hang-dog eyes, announced in a mournful undertone that he had lost weight since becoming an Egon Ronay guide.

June 12 Sudbrook Cottage

Beverley Nichols: 'You play the piano like a man!'
    Me: 'How do you mean?'
    Beverley: 'You play with force and resist all sentimentality.'
    Later.
    Beverley: 'That last cadence was like a tiara worn skewiff – you must practise it; straighten your tiara!'

July 17 Hardwicke House

We went to the theatre last night, *Bloomsbury*. Dan Massey sustained a superb performance as Lytton Strachey. In a finely-evoked falsetto, punctuated with hysterical rants, he managed to convey that incongruous libido; his body becoming more elongated, his hands in perpetual lame distortion, and his fingers appearing whiter and more frail as the play progressed.

Yvonne Mitchell, as Virginia Woolf, portrayed admirably that thin, vibrant body with eyes so vacant, then intense, and that tortured mind that would verge on madness and then gasp at the truth revealed when on its knife-edge rim of acute perception.

Moyra Fraser, as Lady Ottoline Morrell, added a rich eccentricity to the galère and Penelope Wilton as Carrington epitomised a perfect mélange of clumsy insight and headstrong naivety.

We saw Dan after the performance; he was struggling with his false nose and beard. (He needed Carrington to help.) His housekeeper and Lydia Bedford were soon at his side; we left him nicely propped by their every attention.

Those scenes at Ham Spray and Garsington must surely have prompted V. Woolf's last novel *Between the Acts*. The drowsy summer afternoons when the peace and gnats would be suddenly disturbed by the Lady Ottoline's flamboyant arrival; accompanied perhaps by the beautifully-appointed Siegfried Sassoon; an air of sexual inadequacies would hang over the remaining day.

Beverley Nichols was amused to hear about the performance and commented: 'Lytton once tried to seduce me, I was nineteen at the time; at a party in Cambridge. I drank too much and was lying on a friend's sofa – out for the count. I had a dream – that I was head-long in an ant-heap. I woke to find myself smothered by Lytton Strachey's beard. I was sick all over him and called him a dirty old man. He was extraordinarily unattractive – never washed; they none of them did. Virginia Woolf's hair was dirty and awry; she had huge feet; never put them down properly; her clothes were drab. They were a smug lot; the Sitwells would have nothing to do with them.'

August 1 Hardwicke House

Perusing Michael Holroyd's excellent biography on Lytton Strachey, I was musing on Carrington's conquests; wondered if they would halt. Turning to the index, I saw the words – 'a short last love affair'. The man was Beacus Penrose; Carrington, ten years his senior, fell violently in love. Her attentions were mildly reciprocated. She was painfully aware of his comparative youth and beauty; every day was important; 'an uncomplicated morning light played about their love.'

Lytton found this last attachment of Carrington's distasteful; by Bloomsbury literary standards Beacus was limited. Carrington's restless searching was finally dispelled; Beacus sailed off to the Mediterranean and left her. Relieved, she declared that, at last, her 'lusts had run dry.'

August 11 Hardwicke House

When a writer completes an arduous book he often compares achievement to giving birth. When the reader finishes a book, in which he has become fascinated and absorbed, he/she dies a little. Michael Holroyd's biography on Lytton Strachey is a fine book; it enthralled me. Lytton Strachey's legs curled round for ever – as did those webs of passion and intimacies that he delicately wove around him. A perpetual carnival of intense relationships – Carrington, Gerald Brenan, Ralph Partridge, Frances Marshall, Roger Senhouse. These close friends formed the nucleus of Lytton's last years. With tact and sensitivity he presided over this perplexing ebb and flow of relationships. He cherished the peace of his home, Ham Spray, near Hungerford, where the rolling downs were a salve to the fraught sadnesses and the exquisite content that made up his life with Carrington. Carrington! What was it about her?

With Lytton at the helm of her disordered life she provoked the strongest desire and torment in the lives of several attractive men. Yet so often dispassionately described as plump and pale-faced – or red-faced – ungainly, with a flat voice. Where lay her magic?

Beverley Nichols claims she was quiet and would pass unnoticed in a room; perhaps she would be knitting khaki socks for the troops, but suddenly she would speak. Her eyes; large, blue, magnetic, would light up that room with their fleet vivacity. She would fall silent again and listen beautifully, creating in the man at her side the formidable sensation that he alone existed. Her charisma remained as elusive as her hold on life.

August 28 Villa Corner Cavasagra Treviso Italy

Three women in blue on bicycles billowed out of the handsome gates. It was noon. We were calling unannounced on Lady Sands.

Some months before – from a suite in the Dorchester Hotel, London – she had handed over to Tom some jewellery. She had wanted it valued by Christie's. She had also wanted the contents of her seventeenth-century Italian villa valued by Christie's. Recently widowed by the Hon. Sir Stafford Sands – the noted Bahamian – she had had 'flu when Tom called at the Dorchester. Propped up in her lavish négligée, she had been difficult to assess. 'She must have been very striking,' was his wry comment. 'Finnish by birth.'

Within three days of his visit, four independent solicitors acting on her doubtful behalf had intervened. They were unanimous in one respect; no valuations were required. The jewels were returned to Lady Sands, whereupon she had returned to New York, Paris, Rome and, as made apparent by the gardener, had finally retrenched at Treviso.

We were led into a large cream room of marble, glass and rugs. Two huge cream dogs, indistinguishable at first from the deep rugs on which they stirred, bared their fangs. They resembled polar bears.

Bare-footed, Lady Sands, long, tanned legs with thighs as slick as gun-stocks, entered the room; friendly, hand extended, wearing a Pucci bathing costume hugging post-perfection and a wide straw hat half-concealing her world-weary eyes, paired with an indomitable bone structure. She was charming, polite and with large drinks and dogs we were swept through every room in the Villa.

'Don't mind the dogs; when they bare their teeth, they are smiling,' she reassured us lightly.

With drinks trays in every bedroom and an impersonal show of comfort throughout it appeared as a smart hotel rather than a home. No quirk of taste or eccentricity relieved that deadening perfection.

The coup de grâce of this extensive tour was a windowless room; mahogany buffets stood at each end; a long table and subdued lighting completed its dim solidity. In this room, she confided, they ate breakfast, it was agreed that the twilight atmosphere was sympathetic to hangovers. She had hung severe, unframed portraits of Roman emperors over her bed and dressing-table. 'I could not bear to sleep under a Madonna,' she asserted.

Would she like the cellar looked at? she had mentioned it in London – the gardener took us around. It was very ordinary stuff she had assured us; everyday drinking wine. Rows of superb vintages disclaimed this last comment; Lafitte, Rothschild, Haut Brion, Cheval Blanc, Latour, Beausite. Tom made a rough mental valuation of £25,000.

October 19 Beaulieu Hampshire

Colour, class and sexual creed mingled free last night; all barriers lifted by our host – Edward Montagu[1]. Remarried last month to Fiona Herbert – a vivacious and piquante sprite of a woman – he wanted to celebrate. Four hundred guests were invited to his Great Gatsby Ball.

In the Abbey everyone complied with sartorial aplomb. It was only in the middle dawn when feathers became flattened, ludicrously long cigarette-holders lay forgotten on crumpled sofas, and young men twirled tired eyes and boaters, that reality re-asserted itself through this parade of 1930 fantasia.

It was a splendid evening; rich in diversion for every taste. One did not have to be a voyeur to savour the incongruity of Lord Mountbatten dancing on the same floor as Diana Dors. All the boys were there (the evening was notable in its lack of beautiful women). Perhaps the final accolade should go to the beautiful young black. Who was he?

October 22 Hardwicke House

Harold Wilson is reinstated. His mediocre majority has little to fear from the Opposition; the Conservatives are a tired, weak and defenceless body, divided by panic and frustration. The ill-timed eruptions of the 1922 Committee have done little to encourage their disillusioned electorate.

---

[1] His seventieth birthday. Lord Montagu opened the National Motor Museum at Beaulieu Palace in 1972. He was Chairman of English Heritage 1983–92.

Last night we dined with Sir John and Lady Tilney[2]; he, the ex-Member for Liverpool; she, Guinevere, the ex-deputy Chairman of the Conservative Party. At dinner, I sat next to Sir Nigel Fisher – the Member for Surbiton; a small man with long fingernails; he wore rings on both little fingers. He re-affirmed that Ted Heath was an electoral liability; that he was stubborn to an unpalatable degree; that he must be ousted within the next four to six months; above all, he must not be running in the next election, four years hence

Why this untimely panic? Was there no suitable successor? We went through the paltry list: Soames? Whitelaw? Mrs Thatcher? What a ludicrous idea! Sir Keith Joseph? – out – absolutely out! Any politician guilty of such blunt and insensitive indictment of the lower classes and the subsequent naivety in apologising was not worth serious consideration. But was not 99% of Sir Keith's speech admirable? And was not that 1% mindful of what most people feel but dare not say? Maybe . . . pondered Sir Nigel. (I found him paper-thin.) But the inferred arrogance, the political damage – the image–the image! (Always the image.) Could I not see this? And Sir Christopher Soames and William Whitelaw, I rejoindered. Had they never made any political gaffe? No – they were politically wise; their image was still intact. (But had either of them spoken out with real effect about anything ever?) And what about Edward du Cann – the acting Chairman of the 1922 Committee? Sir Nigel Fisher lit up; was Edward du Cann, then, the saving grace of the Conservative party? Sir Nigel insinuated that this might be so; meanwhile (he disclosed) he was making 'discreet enquiries in the City to check Edward's record'.

Ted Heath may have no charm or political candour; but he has calibre and integrity; and he does not depend on a prefabricated image.

November 9 Hardwicke House

Murder! Un crime passionel? Une cause célèbre? The court case of the century? An Earl on the run; a battered Countess; a murdered nanny.

On Thursday (November 7) at 10.10 pm Veronica Lucan, pouring blood from head injuries, rushed from her house – No 46 Lower Belgrave Street – into the neighbouring pub – the Plumbers' Arms – screaming 'Murder! Help me! My nanny's murdered. I think my neck

[2] From 1975 to 1983, Guinevere Tilney was adviser to the Rt. Hon. Margaret Thatcher MP. She was awarded a DBE in 1984. In retirement she listed 'making soup' as a recreation, for her entry in *Who's Who*.

is broken. He tried to strangle me. I am dying – my children – my children!'

She was whisked off to St George's Hospital, where she now assures all and sundry that her husband is guilty. Her condition is reported to be comfortable.

John Lucan has not come forward and has been missing forty-eight hours. Is he alive? He telephoned his mother two hours after the incident, telling her that there had been 'trouble' at Veronica's house that night. Three hours after the incident, his brother-in-law and sister-in-law – Bill and Christina Shand Kydd – were disturbed by their door-bell ringing; there was nobody there. Today they received a letter from John, to the effect that 'his house is in order', and that he is not guilty of murder. He also mentioned that he saw Tom Craig at Christie's eight days ago about selling £8,000 worth of family silver. (Apparently he has been trying to raise money lately.)

We are lunching with Bill and Christina tomorrow. Guilty or not guilty? Is John still alive? His wife Veronica provokes everyone in her unhappy orbit, including psychiatrists and church ministers. Did John Lucan hire a killer? Did the killer mistake the nanny – twenty-nine-year-old Mrs Sandra Rivett of Coulsdon, Surrey – for Lady Lucan? (His intended target?) Was the killing premeditated? (The body was stowed in a canvas sack; a rod of bloodstained lead piping lay nearby.)

Bill's wry comment to a policeman yesterday: 'Damn silly, whoever it was, not to have written off Lady Lucan completely.'

November 10 Grove Farm Linslade Bedfordshire

'Press, police; we've had the lot – short of *Exchange and Mart* and *Farmer's Weekly*.' Bill Shand Kydd shaded his eyes; as yet another car squirmed up the drive. 'Who are you?' 'From the Thomson Press, sir. Can I just ask you, sir – have you any fresh evidence or any personal belief of your brother-in-law's suspected crime?' Bill scuffed the gravel, separated a mastiff and a bull terrier amid blood-curdling growls. 'The pity of it is,' he assured the reporter shortly, 'that Lord Lucan didn't make a better job of it. If I'd been around, I would have finished off Lady Lucan myself.' 'I see how it is, sir.' The reporter scuttled back to his car as though he had suddenly remembered a ton of bacon that needed saving up the road.

Christina looked radiant on no sleep. Roaring fires, drinks all round, children tumbling through the house, a family under immense duress and tension, acting as per normal with aplomb. Bill and Christina took it in turn to pick up the telephone. And then, 'Hullo, who? Oh, God . . . that's it? Thank you, Dominic.'

Dominic Elwes, albeit an unreliable source of information, had been round to Gerald Road Police Station. The case was cut and dried. The canvas sack had been traced to John's house and the lead piping was smothered in his fingerprints. He had known that Thursday was the nanny's night off and had, in the dark, apparently mistaken the slight figure of Sandra Rivett for his wife Veronica. (Sandra had stayed in that Thursday night, her boyfriend had stood her up.) The hope drained from Christina's face; she sank into a chair. 'I will not,' she asserted with revived spirit, 'believe that John has done this until it has been conclusively proved. He has been so calm of late, and has come here almost every weekend with the three children; they adore him. They were all going to stay here for Christmas.' If he was guilty, we assured her, his actions would be exonerated by all who knew him. He had been provoked beyond the bounds of endurance.

Dead or alive? Three days since the murder and John's whereabouts are still unaccounted for. And Veronica sits pretty in St George's Hospital feeling better. She is patently thrilled that John Lucan has at last been 'shown up' in the lurid colours in which she has always painted him.

Amongst the instructions in his last letters to Bill and Christina, John asked them to bring up his children; the only happy issue to evolve from the rotten tragedy.

November 11 Hardwicke House

On the eight o'clock news this morning a statement that the French police were on the alert for Lord Lucan, believed to have been seen in Dieppe last night at eleven o'clock. It appears he is still alive. I am trying to remember the exact context of his two letters to Bill Shand Kydd, written on the night of the incident. We saw photographed copies at lunch yesterday. The first was to the effect:

'. . . Terrible trouble at Veronica's tonight – events of which I have described in some detail to my mother. I was passing by the house and saw an intruder attacking Veronica in the basement. I came between them. I took V upstairs and tried to mop her up. Frances [the elder daughter] saw us upstairs together. V "lay doggo" for a bit and then rushed out of the house. She accused me of hiring a killer. I do not want my children to see their father in the dock for attempted murder. I do not want them to see me in the bankruptcy courts. I will be "lying doggo" for a bit. When they are older, please tell the children the truth and explain to them the dream of paranoia.'

His second letter referred to 'financial matters'. His arrangements for the settlement on the three children; his desire for Bill and Christina to bring them up. He mentioned only Frances (ten years) and George (seven years) in his letter. Camilla (four years) was obviously included. 'Please agree with Tom Craig on reserves for the sale of silver. The sale should be coming up on November 27.'

This morning I telephoned Christina. She had hoped to see Veronica at St George's Hospital last night. Veronica would not see her.

'Hello?' – 'Hello, Christina, it's Penelope. Can you talk a moment?'

'Not really – unless it is something important.'

'Christina – if you need any help this week – collecting the children's clothes from Veronica's house or anything – I'll come with you . . .'

One feels so lame in the face of one's friends' troubles.

Nothing on the one o'clock news.

With regard to Bill and Christina taking over the children, Tom urged them to set it in writing; to obtain some infallible deed from the solicitor, to the effect that Veronica would have no hold on their care and control.

The four o'clock news:

'The theory that Lord Lucan arrived from Newhaven to Dieppe late last night has now been discounted by the police. The search goes on amongst hotels and boarding houses in the Sussex area.'

How greatly were the money worries weighing on John Lucan's mind? Huge gambling debts? Blackmail? Was he fearing literal bankruptcy? Had he contemplated suicide? And if so – realising the liability of Veronica bringing up his children – attempted a plan to dispose of her first?

Seven o'clock.

Tom spent three-quarters of an hour with Bill at his office today. The children are already Wards of Court; the solicitor has agreed, nominally, that Bill and Christina have full control.

The headlines of the evening papers:

'The trail of the Hunted Earl.'

'Who is hiding the Hunted Earl?'

Yesterday at lunch Christina told us that John had called on Sue Maxwell-Scott late on the night of the incident. He had stayed two hours; it was from that house, near Uckfield in Sussex, that he wrote the two letters to Bill. Sue Maxwell-Scott was understandably surprised to see him; she noted that he had blood on his hands and trouser legs. She claims she was astonished to read of the murder the following Friday evening, when her husband arrived from London with an evening paper. It was only then that she reported John Lucan's precipitate visit, to her husband.

November 12 Hardwicke House

The police believe Lucan is abroad and have publicly disclosed him as the murderer of the children's nanny, Sandra Rivett. A warrant for his arrest was released this afternoon. They fear him dead or contemplating suicide.

Today Christina visited Veronica at St George's Hospital. She is badly battered but has no fractures; there is a police guard on her ward.

Bill was televised on the six o'clock news. 'I have known Lord Lucan for many years – since before we married. My children adore him; his own children patently adore him. He and his children have stayed many weekends with us; he was with us the weekend before last and appeared relaxed and happy.' The interviewer, Sandy Gall, asked him: 'Is there anything you would like to say in the event that Lord Lucan is watching and listening to you now?' Replied Bill, 'I would urge him to contact me or his solicitor, David Leverton, and we could go to the police together.'

Dickie Craig [my brother-in-law] telephoned tonight; he affirmed Lucan was charming, affable and intelligent; they had competed together in the Bobsleigh, had gambled on many occasions and had played backgammon recently. The papers this evening are full of Lucan's charm, honour and the obsessive adoration for his children.

It is the first time that an Earl has committed murder since 1642.

November 13 Hardwicke House

Rumours are rife. Lucan is still presumed abroad; in the South of France? With a relative in Haiti?

Veronica left hospital this morning in a police car with a coat over her head. She has returned to 46 Lower Belgrave Street where detectives busied themselves in the gloomy basement.

Tom brought back home a photostat of John Lucan's letter to Bill, dealing with 'financial matters'. Herewith the copy ad verbatim:

'There is a sale coming up at Christie's Nov 27th which will ratify bank overdrafts, please agree reserves with Tom Craig.
Proceeds to go to:

Lloyds, 6 Pall Mall
Coutts, 59 Strand
Nat West, Bloomsbury, Broadway
Who also hold an Eq & Law Life Policy.
The other creditors can get lost for the time being.
          Lucky.'

November 14 Hardwicke House

'Lady Lucan faces the world', with a black cummerbund around her head to hide bandages, her glum set face plasters every front page. She is living under police guard at a secret address in London; she is determined on having the complete care and control of her children.

Meanwhile from Haiti to Newhaven John Lucan is hunted. The police suspect he may have taken his life and today concentrated their search in Newhaven harbour, a day of gales and heavy squalls. The deep-sea divers had a hard time gleaning any likely secrets from that murky water.

The emotional burden on Christina must be appalling.

November 14 Hardwicke House

Today the *Daily Telegraph* telephoned the Christie's press office. Johnny Van Haeften took the call: 'Was it true that Lord Lucan's family silver was up for sale this month?' Johnny laughed with surprise; Tom had kept this pending transaction secret and confidential on John Lucan's express instruction. (He had not wanted Veronica to know of the sale.) The lots are catalogued as 'the property of a Nobleman', albeit the family crest '*Christ is my hope*' bears witness to its provenance.

Not satisfied with Johnny Van Haeften's bemused denials the *Telegraph* telephoned through to Tom Milnes-Gaskell – the silver expert at Christie's. He knew of the sale but again denied any knowledge. Meanwhile Tom alerted Jo Floyd (the Chairman) of the situation. Jo was intrigued to hear that Lucan had made arrangements to sell silver to the amount of £25,000 on November 27, some pieces by Paul Storr and others dated 'pre-charge of the Light Brigade'[3]. Tomorrow he and Tom will meet first thing to decide on a party line towards the Press.

[3] The 3rd Lord Lucan (born 1800) was Field Marshal in the Army and the Cavalry Commander at the fatal Charge of the Light Brigade (October 25, 1854). (On November 11, 2005 a pair of duelling pistols, owned by the 3rd Lord Lucan, fetched £18,000 at Bonhams, London.)

Bill and Christina are weathering the traumas well. Their telephone rings each night until 2.30 a.m. Veronica stays on at her secret address with a nurse and a police guard. The search in Newhaven harbour has been called off; the police are now launching an extensive search in the country houses of John Lucan's friends.

The one a.m. news reveals that Lady Lucan has been granted custody of her three children by Mr Justice Rees. Bill and Christina and close relatives attended the hearing. Has the law no compromise in these emotionally delicate cases?

Tom had lunch at White's with Michael Tree yesterday. The conversation spun around Lucan in every corner. One old codger with a moustache was heard to remark, 'I hear the fellow had a bloody wife.' And another, 'The fellow was a member of the Brigade, wasn't he? He will shoot himself as any member would.'

November 15 Hardwicke House

Today Bill Shand Kydd, Jo Floyd and Tom discussed the pending sale of Lucan's silver with solicitors. It was agreed the sale should go ahead on the basis of Christie's regular policy to honour transactions at the owner's express intent. Lucan had re-iterated his intent in his letter to Bill on the night of the incident. Meanwhile they hope to keep the press – and Veronica – at bay.

The search for Lucan continues through its eighth day. The police suspect he is being harboured by a friend. On the other hand, if he has been eaten by fishes, his body might never be recovered. If he is dead, he will never, by law, be proved guilty. Is this the murder mystery of the century? If, however, he is reclaimed, it is legally permissible for an Earl to be tried by his own peers. In the event of the House of Lords finding a peer guilty of murder, it is written that he should be hanged with a silken cord. Lord Huntingdon revealed this information to my mother-in-law, Diana Garrett, whilst lunching with her at Beaulieu last weekend. (He later confessed that he was personally far more interested in the current divorce of Lady Carolyn Townshend.)

Bill confirmed to Tom today the improbable instance of an earlier press report that John Lucan, on realising his appalling blunder in murdering the nanny, Sandra Rivett, instead of his wife, had apologised to Veronica. She has now returned to her home in 46 Lower Belgrave Street, with the children, where she hopes to continue a normal life, spared of further publicity. (She loves it.) She was pictured on the news tonight, talking beside her front door, and under guard. She has

been given custody of the children until Christmas, when the case will
be reviewed.

November 24

John Lucan is now believed alive and, furthermore, in England. The
police are searching and interviewing a hundred names in Sandra
Rivett's address book. Apparently she was often visited by an unknown
man who drove a Mercedes.

Lucan's silver is up for sale on Wednesday; tomorrow night we take
Bill and Christina to the preview at Christie's.

This afternoon, for the second time, we saw Dr Roy Strong's[4]
exhibition at the Victoria and Albert Museum of 'The Destruction of
the Country House.' As John Cornforth[5] is at pains to point out, there
is a radical difference between the term 'the House in the Country'
and 'the Country House'; the latter denotes a whole community
dependant on the country house, for its life, work and welfare.

Since 1875, 1,551 large houses have been demolished completely.
Since 1920, 1,400. Since 1945, 712. (England having lost 478, Scotland
203.'

In 1955 one house was demolished every five days; they now fall,
on average, one every two weeks.

We first saw this admirably-mounted exhibition on its opening night
in October. A month later we read that Powerscourt, in Ireland,
was burnt to the ground, together with its priceless contents. Tom
telephoned Roy Strong's secretary with the suggestion that a black-
board be erected at the exhibition, marking up the causalities since the
start of the sad display six weeks ago. Today we saw two more chalked
up: Barons Hill, Anglesey, now in the process of demolition, and
Stensham Court, burnt down on October 21.

With owners of country houses having to forfeit a substantial
endowment to the National Trust in return for minimal upkeep and
grants there seems little hope of staving off this holocaust.

[4] Dr Roy Strong, knighted in 1982. Director of the Victoria and Albert Museum 1974–87.
[5] *The Country Houses of England 1948–1998* by John Cornforth reflects some forty years of his
writing for *Country Life*.

November 26 Hardwicke House

Police renew their search for Lucan; today they concentrate on the Sussex downs and the River Ouse.

Meanwhile Veronica is wise to the sale of the Lucan silver tomorrow and yesterday dispatched her solicitor, Mr Swallow (perhaps he flew), to Christie's to verify the fact. Christie's told the beleaguered Mr Swallow that it was not possible to disclose the names of the anonymous clients; if they conducted their affairs on such unethical grounds, they would be out of business.

Tom Milnes-Gaskell told me last night at Christie's preview that he was expecting Veronica to appear at his office today. Jo Floyd[6] is doubtful that Lucan's silver will make the sale; Veronica may yet bring an injunction on vague, temporary grounds that the silver is not in Lucan's absolute possession anyway.

November 26 The evening

Today at Christie's proved a turmoil of press, solicitors, legal knots and loopholes; every mind and person involved running in distracted circles. Mercifully Veronica did not appear.

Jo Floyd called in his old friend Anthony Lousada Q.C. for advice, which he finally discounted; Lousada had raised the extreme point that as Mr David Leverton (Lucan's solicitor) of Payne Hicks Beach had been given no firsthand instructions from Lucan – after the murder – he now had no valid claim to be Lucan's solicitor on this issue. Lousada also urged Christie's to obtain a letter of indemnity from Payne Hicks Beach, in the event of the sale of silver falling foul of any future revelations. Mr Leverton refused to undertake such an indemnity. At the end of the day, Jo Floyd, tired and determined, elected that the sale of Lucan's silver should proceed. Whereupon Bill Shand Kydd (whom Jo Floyd described to Lousada as 'a gay young man'; he had seen him only last night, leaping up and down, half-naked, on the bonnet of a car) telephoned Jo. Bill thanked him profusely for his positive decision and congratulated him on having 'a pair of balls'.

[6] John Anthony 'Jo' Floyd, Chairman of Christie's London and Christie's International 1974–85.

November 27 Hardwicke House

Veronica's solicitors go to court today; their sitting is due at 10.30 a.m. The silver sale will start at 11 a.m. John's silver is Lot 50 and should be through before the case. Will Veronica be at the sale? Christina and I will go together; it is now 7.45 a.m. and I am off for a ride in Richmond Park.

November 28 Hardwicke House

We arrived punctually at the silver sale. It was held in the ante-room on the left of the main stairs. A dozen long-haired photographers angled their baleful lenses on Andrina Colquhoun (John Lucan's last known girl-friend), a diminutive, mousy girl who assiduously noted down the prices of every lot. Bill joined us. The photographers squirmed in the crush around the door for a picture of him with Christina. John's twelve lots came up and fetched a sum of around £18,000. As the silver salvers and crested plates and soup tureens were held up to view, the photographers snapped vigorously. At Lot 60 Christina motioned we should leave. We slipped down the stairs and into the street, congratulating ourselves on eluding the press mob, when they promptly tumbled from the main door. We fled up Duke Street.

There has been little publicity for the sale, and Jo Floyd, much relieved, is delighted that he chose to 'publish and be damned'. He also mentioned to Tom that he felt Lucan's letter referring to the sale should be carefully kept, a document of enormous interest in years to come. Meanwhile, Bill, with the approval of John Lucan's trustees, himself bought back a lot of the silver plates; they will be released to the children when they come of age. If Lucan is now languishing in the Sussex downs, he will be content that his final instructions 'to ratify bank overdrafts' have reached a viable conclusion.

December 9 Hardwicke House

Today it is disclosed that Lucan had a 'bugging' device fitted to his telephone some eight months prior to the incident. He also had a minuscule tape machine fitted to the inside of his coat; this recorded intimate conversations with his wife, whenever he visited her. (Presumably not on his person the night of the incident). Detectives are now engaged in analysing seventy hours of recorded conversation between Lucan and his friends and between Veronica and himself. Somehow, somewhere, one feels, he is still alive.

The other night we had a stimulating dinner with Jeremy and Antonia Maas; he is an expert on Victorian pictures and author of the lavishly-documented *Victorian Painters*; she is engagingly exuberant. Their panelled eighteenth-century house – 10 Montpelier Row, Twickenham – is a triumphant haven of crowded antiques, prints and pictures. I sat next to Michael Holroyd; we focused on Carrington for ten minutes and then got on to him. Having now completed his biography of Augustus John, he is heading for America and Dublin to research George Bernard Shaw. At first glance, Holroyd appears mild, even insipid; with a bad hair cut; on further appraisal one appreciates that callous, yet sensitive mouth, and a humorous glint in the eye.

1975

'Move by friends to clear Lord Lucan.'
'Search for clues goes on as the Lord Lucan mystery
enters third month.'
'Murder hunt police believe peer had an accomplice.'

Brief and intermittent references in the press; the police are mystified and frustrated by one of the most bizarre murder hunts in British criminal history. The inquest on the murdered nanny, Sandra Rivett, will be reopened on March 10 before a full jury.

The police maintain an open mind to all aspects of the case; they have failed, conspicuously, to trace Lucan's exact movements during those four crucial hours between his leaving the Maxwell-Scotts' house in Sussex and the discovery of the borrowed Corsair in a Newhaven side-street the following dawn.

Meanwhile, Veronica continues her life with her children at 46 Lower Belgrave Street; yet another nanny has been engaged; they have come and gone like ships in the night.

Bill and Christina are exerting pressure to re-open the legal case of the children's future care and custody. They have asked Tom to talk with the psychiatrist, John Flood; he, having observed Veronica as an in-patient in the Priory Nursing Home, deemed her fit to look after the children.

February 1 Hardwicke House

Tom left for the Middle East yesterday; he is on an extended tour to woo the Arabs and to inveigle them into visiting Christie's and to buy works of art. As their tastes, to date, extend mainly to jewellery, fast cars and Harrods, and studiously eschew anything 'second-hand' (like antiques) he has a daunting assignment. John Slim[1] has given him personal introductions to:

---

[1] John Douglas Slim OBE, 2nd Viscount, son of the Field Marshal, Governor General of Australia. In 1977, he became Vice-chairman of the Arab-British Chamber of Commerce and Industry.

His Majesty Sultan Qaboos bin Said, The Palace, Muscat, Oman
His Highness Sheikh Zaid bin Sultan al Nayan, The Palace, Abu Dhabi
His Excellency Mr D. J. McCarthy, CMG, British Embassy, Abu Dhabi
His Excellency Sir Anthony Parsons KCMG, CMG, MVO, MC, The British Embassy, Teheran, Iran
Desmond Harney OBE, Morgan Grenfell & Co. Ltd., Teheran, Iran
Peter Stirling, Teheran, Iran.

Tom's route will take in Cairo, Beirut, Jeddah, Riyadh, Muscat, Dubai, Abu Dhabi, Doha, Bahrain, Kuwait, Teheran.

We are still having trouble with his visa for Muscat (the State of Oman requires 'a certificate of good conduct'). Princess Jeanne-Marie de Broglie – the head of Christie's Paris branch – will be joining him for the last lap in Teheran. She is formidably influential – especially so in Iran, having enjoyed a personal friendship with the Prime Minister, Mr Hoveyda.

February 1

Last night I dined with Walter and Katie Saloman. Their house in St James's Place (a modern shell, transformed inside with pine panelling wrested from houses all over England) is crammed with their priceless and comprehensive collection. Thirty-odd Impressionist paintings vie with aubussons, savonneries, Weisweiller cabinets, a superb gueridon Sèvres-plat table from the Fribourg Collection, books, porcelain, fine chandeliers.

Twenty guests in all, we sat down to an excellent dinner; Lord Dartmouth to my left and, on my right, our host. Robin Day and Moura Lympany were present. After the pudding (which appeared as a mound of peppermint ice-cream swathed in spun sugar and served from a floodlit glass-fibre dome), Mr Saloman tapped his Royal Derby 'polite' plate with a heavy cigar cutter. He stated that he wanted to make a short speech on the oil crisis and how we in the West should overcome it. An uncomfortable pause ensued. After a brief, disjointed peroration, Mr Saloman's blond-coiffed butler, Joseph, handed him a slip of printed paper on a silver salver. It was a copy of an article written by our host himself on this worldwide problem; it had been recently published in a German newspaper (*The Times* had declined its insertion). Mr Saloman asked Robin Day to read it out aloud. Robin Day refused, adding that if he himself had subjected his own friends to all the articles that he had written, he would not have any left. He further suggested that, if Mr Saloman wished his views known to his friends, he should hand them each a copy, which they might read at leisure. Mr Saloman, visibly rebuffed at Robin Day's refusal to toe the line, dropped the matter abruptly; whereupon Moura Lympany brought the scene to a low key conclusion, stating that she was always being asked to play the piano and she was not going to oblige that night either. Poor Mr Saloman, the merchant banker! A highly intelligent man, but in his pomposity had proved insensitive to his audience.

March 19 Hardwicke House

Calamity at Christie's! Today it was discovered that £250,000 worth of jewellery was released, unwittingly, to a man who had produced a forged document of collection; the said jewellery fetched high prices at last week's sale. Detectives, lawyers and police have been working at King Street all day.

Secondly, the Chester Beattys, who were selling, anonymously, the portrait of 'Monsieur Patience Escalier' by Van Gogh, telephoned Christie's this morning to announce their decision to withdraw the painting from next month's sale. Buyers from abroad have flown over especially – including Livanos; he is tonight dining with David Bathurst, our head of the Modern Pictures department. Meanwhile the Chester Beattys disclose no reason for this surprise renegation and have refused to speak with Jo Floyd or David Bathurst.

It is now 6.30 pm and we dine tonight with John and Guinevere Tilney; on our way, Tom will be calling on Chet and Helen, at 76 Park Street, and endeavour to talk them round, or at least discover the reason for this sudden withdrawal.

March 20 Hardwicke House

Nothing on the news about the jewellery theft, and no press releases. Tom called on the Chester Beattys last night. He suggested to the butler that he might have a drink with them, although he was not expected. Helen was changing for dinner but came and saw Tom and was most friendly. Chet was in the throes of a business meeting and unavailable. Tom told Helen that he had just returned from the Middle East and was most disturbed and sorry to learn about their decision over the Van Gogh. Helen did not choose to enlarge on the matter and Tom felt that he could not press the point further.

March 21 Hardwicke House

A small mention on the news today reference the jewellery theft. Christie's had a good picture sale this morning, with John and Guinevere Tilney's pair of Alkens fetching 4,000 guineas. We spoke a few moments with David Bathurst. He had just delivered Chet's Van Gogh back to 76 Park Street. Rumours abound of death threats and kidnapping if the sale of the picture had gone through. David observed that Helen had appeared nervous on receiving the picture back – peering through the security hole in her elegant front door before opening it. The expected price on Van Gogh's 'Patience Escalier' (the 'Man with a Hoe') was three-quarters to a million pounds. (It was finally bought by the Lefevre Gallery.)

March 25 Hardwicke House

Sir Oliver Millar, Surveyor of the Queen's pictures, was talking at dinner the other night of Augustus John. He proclaimed that he had always found his talent too facile for serious consideration and that, in his opinion, Gwen John was a superior artist. We drifted on to Turner, agreeing that he could not draw figures, but that he was, indisputably, the best English landscapist. Our conversation was abruptly cut short by the man on my left – Sir Victor Seely – who firmly announced that Turner was a lousy painter. No – he had not seen the present exhibition at the Royal Academy; he had been told that he would have to queue. He never queued for anything. However, to take Munnings; now there was a painter! Sir Oliver disputed this last claim hotly and described Munnings as a coarse and even vulgar painter; keen on the bottle to boot, whilst slapping on another gleaming flank; painting merely to please his indiscriminating patrons. If we were extolling horse painters, why not settle for Stubbs? Sir Victor Seely dug into his crème brûlée and, turning to the lady on his left, asked, 'Who is that fellow who thinks he knows about art?'

April 11 Hardwicke House

Duff Hart-Davis called on me last week to talk about Veronica Lucan. He taped our conversation of one and half hours. It was a pity to waste his charm and intelligence on the sad, warped subject of Veronica. But he particularly wanted to know of my meetings with her and what one might deduce from her behaviour.

It was in March 1973 that Christina asked me to lunch at her house in Cambridge Square, to meet her sister, Veronica. The latter was depressed, listless and diminutive. She was well-dressed in sleeveless green wool and her long fair hair had been newly set. She tapped her foot on the table leg throughout lunch, though appeared attentive to any shred of encouragement I had to offer. I felt that I could help her through my own experience of depression.

We met again a month later – at the Priory Nursing Home in Roehampton. She had gone there for a week, ostensibly to be under Dr John Flood's observation; he was to determine whether or not she was fit to care for her children. At a later date, he declared in the Courts that she was perfectly capable; a verdict that summarily contravened John Lucan's wish that his children could be released from their mother's influence.

She lay on her bed, dressed in a polo neck and trousers. She was bored and vindictive, but later showed me a drawing she had done of the flowers I had sent her. I jollied her along and wrote an encouraging letter.

A few weeks later we met again for lunch at her house. I was shocked at her appearance. She had lost even more weight, her hair was unkempt and her house was shrouded in dust with curtains drawn. Her black velvet coat, which she claimed she lived in (perhaps she slept in it also), was a far cry from the smart dress she had worn when we first met with Christina.

Her children had already eaten their sausages and peas and were promptly ordered upstairs to play. Veronica had no nanny at this time. Camilla (then four) and George (seven) appeared pale, subdued and indifferent to their mother's attentions, or lack of them. Veronica merely assured me that she kept them clean, fed and clothed, and got them to school on time.

We sat there in her large, gloomy kitchen, where streaks of damp had meandered down those basement walls, papered in a sad blue bamboo motif – an undusted piano, dark, untidy corners, large, smeared windows – as drab a scene as one could conjure. Veronica showed me drawings she had done – sexual ones. Her theme expressed the continual exploitation of woman by man. She would like to see their fictitious, boorish sexual superiority exterminated. I cannot remember her exact wording but she seemed to be under an even sicker role-reversal than Edvard Munch's own delusion, to avenge the feminine role. She talked nervously, on a manic key. She wanted to make history. She had done that, naturally, by producing an heir. She wanted to read, to draw, to see her name in print, to see her husband publicly disgraced. She was in a state of vindictive euphoria. I told her to have her hair seen to, even to take a lover, to come down to earth. We parted reasonable friends with little viewpoint in common.

My fourth meeting with Veronica took place three weeks later, at the start of May. She had an appointment with John Flood at the Priory. We arranged that she should come on to lunch at Hardwicke House, with myself and my five-year-old aphasic son, Sebastian.

We started with avocado vinaigrette; her favourite food. The sun poured over a peaceful dining-room scene when suddenly she exclaimed vehemently, 'I loathe my sister Christina.'

I replied, 'Oh, come now, Veronica; Christina is a marvellous sister to you. She is so concerned for you and is trying desperately to help in every way. She is a special friend of ours; I can't have you talk of her like that.'

Veronica retorted, 'You think Christina is a friend of yours? She loathes you! She thinks you are eccentric and badly-dressed. And I don't want your help or your friendship. I think you and your child, your house – everything about you is ghastly.'

Much taken aback I tried to humour her. 'Oh, Veronica, eat up your lunch. It's a lovely day; we might go for a walk in the park.'

Whereupon she half-screamed, 'I don't want to spend a moment longer in your dreary, awful house, listening to your abysmal conversation. I would prefer to be at home.'

'In that case, Veronica,' I concluded briskly, 'perhaps I had better ring for a taxi and you could leave at once.'

She seemed well-pleased with this suggestion. I cannot recall our conversation while waiting for the taxi; perhaps Sebastian and I merely continued our lunch.

I was certainly amazed and shaken at her outburst; it had almost evoked the spite of an Angela Brazil schoolgirl. Equally she had meant what she had said, in that clipped, cool outburst. If I had had qualms as to her mental state, I would have driven her back to the Priory. No, she is a comparatively sane and intelligent woman, but her warped, calculating and malignant disposition proves a wearisome trial to all in her vicinity.

June 26 Hardwicke House

Last Monday week, June 16, began a four-day inquest on the death of Mrs Sandra Rivett, the nanny. The jury of six gave their verdict that Lucan was guilty of her murder.

Police are now closely watching the Belgian-French coast following reports that Lucan has been seen in the area. In today's *Times* it is disclosed that Lucan was apparently seen in Cherbourg, the day after the murder. The police are interviewing others who now claim to have seen the fugitive Earl. Why did they not come forward seven months ago? It seems that memories have been jogged by photographs of the wanted man, issued with the murder warrant for his arrest. Personally, I have always suspected he was still alive; a man in that parlous position after the incident would have been too taxed to enact an effective suicide, leaving no trace of body or teeth.

July 17 The Dance Centre Floral Street

'It need not be high, but it must be correct!' Romayne Grigorova is in the throes of her Saturday morning conditioning class at the Dance Centre. She skims across the studio boards to attend a recalcitrant foot here, a stiffly-extended arm there. An awkward bottom is gently, tactfully righted into a more sympathetic curve. Pert in her middle age, her blonde hair caught in a bright scarf, she trips up the stone stairs to the airy studio. In action she is young, slim and vivacious, carrying the unwieldy class through every mirage of aspiration. Married to a Bulgarian, she has not been a Royal Ballet mistress for nothing; her vitality is remarkable. For one and a half hours at the modest charge of 80 pence per pair of legs (children free) she whirls us through a series of stimulating exercises; and however mean our achievement we come away uplifted with a modicum of satisfaction in our own clumsy efforts, heads and bodies reeling with the perplexing exercise of linking harmony to rhythm.

A motley crew are we of indiscriminate age, sex and colour, the scene more colourful on winter mornings with bright wool sweat socks, tights and jerseys. In summer the black girl twists her hair into splayed spirals; the young tarzan, stripped to the waist, flexes his slim, sharp shoulders; sawn-off jeans with bare brown legs abound, and the long-arched Georgian windows are open to the street below.

The pianist, Peter, with hooded eyes and cigarette-holder, coaxes Tchaikowsky, Verdi, Brahms and Joplin from his isolated corner. A languid beat leads through quiet tragedy and mounts to a riot of clamorous chords for the rumbustious steps.

Grigorova, dapper in skin-tight trousers and tee-shirt, urges us to watch the mirror – to pull in our stomachs mightily and finally to get down on the floor. Spinal cords and neck discs scrunch with that impact of bare boards. No matter, 'Stretch out your right arm as though pleading for a glass of water – four times – and then with the left. Peter, darling, have we any hospital music?' A desultory rendition of *La Traviata*'s death-bed scene ensues. The session ends with a stylised romp of skipping, galloping and a bewildering complication of steps in sequence. It is 11.30 a.m. precisely, when Romayne throws up her slim arms to blow us a kiss. We applaud her.

August 1975 El Cuarton Tarifa Southern Spain

If Nicholas Bethell's[2] cavalier silence throughout the lunch party proved the talking point of the week, Bill Shand Kydd's explosive arrival knocked the record flat. Strutting in sawn-off jeans, his bonhomie instantly doubled the voltage at El Cuarton. Within an hour of his boisterous descent we were speeding through the stark, cork-tree-studded country to see the medieval fortress of Arcos. In a quick about-turn, half the party elected to return to El Cuarton, whilst the rest of us hurtled on further to Seville. (John Wauchope devoured Xaviera Hollander's *Happy Hooker* whole, to relieve his mind from the racing scenery.)

Despite the disparities between their personalities, Nicholas and Bill became fast friends, and later embarked on a two-day trip to Tangier together. (Had Bill had a mystery tip-off on John Lucan's movements?)

El Cuarton, enfolded between Algeciras and Tarifa, is a simple haven conceived by Dominic Elwes; a contemporary prototype of the ideal white-washed village holiday commune, where pools and sun-baked terraces are made even more alluring with the cool, gentle fretting of a breeze. The scorched surround of hills, the Atlantic pounding on those long white tracts of sand, the web of Tarifa's cobbled streets, with intimate shaded courtyards strung with bright washing, all combine for peace. Cornfields and cows stretch to the sand dunes here, where tourist exploitation has magically stopped short.

August 1975 Soto Grande

Dining one evening at an exclusive restaurant in Soto Grande, we caught up with Henry[3] and Toots Cotton (the latter immaculately

---

[2] Lord Bethell's incisive interest in human rights, and in the Soviet Union especially, has engendered a life of travel and writing. His *Spies and other secrets* published 1994 and *The Last Secret* 1974 conjure up memories from the second Cold War.

[3] Henry Cotton laid out the renowned Penina Golf Course in the Algarve in 1963. In an article – *Rice and Cotton* – his friend Henry Longhurst described the difficulties of working in a morass of rice fields and how Cotton insisted on seed from Oregon for the greens. A handsome, stocky man, Cotton had a formidable wife in Toots, daughter of an American millionaire. Toots Cotton would hide her enormous dark eyes behind green-tinted sunglasses and have a ferocious cropped wig. She was painted by the Fauvist Kees van Dongen.

be-wigged in thick chestnut and a heavy fringe). They had been given forty-eight hours to leave the Algarve and have now set up house at Soto Grande where Henry continues to give the odd golf lesson for an exorbitant fee. His once-prized Penina Golf Course is currently being ploughed up by Communists for growing vegetables.

September 1975 Hardwicke House

This month's issue of *Connoisseur* carries an article on Carlton Towers, Goole, Yorkshire. It is described as 'one of the finest series of Victorian rooms in the country. The State rooms at Carlton represent the swan-song of Victorian Gothic Revival in England.' (The house is not open to the public to date.)

October 22 Swinton Park Masham North Yorkshire

The crenellated Victorian Gothic towers stood crimson with virginia creeper as the contents of the house were poised for sale. The incumbent, Lord Swinton, wished to offset vast death duties incurred by the death of his mother in 1974.

Anthony Coleridge, the Christie's Director in charge, had spent a week at the house preparing for the sale, together with a posse of porters, sales clerks and secretaries. An impressive collection of marquetry bombé commodes and cabinets, eighteenth-century German, a superb Meissen dinner service and a huge Landseer oil of eagles attacking a swannery were the star attractions.

Viewing day was last Saturday. The County came in droves while bids from the Continent and America flooded the office. A strong contingent of German dealers descended on the scene and subsequently bought the Meissen and the prized marquetry cabinets. Prices far exceeded Christie's most optimistic reserves. The Meissen service fetched 9,000 guineas having been estimated at 3,500. The contents of the total sale realised £255,575; approximately £30,000 more than Christie's had forecast.

Lady Swinton, confined to a wheelchair as a result of a riding accident, sat in the front row of the marquee throughout the bidding. Her thirty-eight-year-old husband preferred, for sentimental reasons, to roam the grounds out of earshot of the hammered prices. Later eating a picnic lunch off a plastic plate, he explained his sadness and frustration to reporters. Government taxes and crippling death duties had forced the family to sell up, and would he really have wanted to be saddled with a large and unwieldy house? It would appear that his existing arrangement of living in a comfortable bungalow with his invalid wife was a far more viable proposition.

On the morning of October 20, Jo Floyd, the Chairman, had opened the bidding at 11 o'clock precisely. An hour earlier he had read the news of Lord Camoys selling up at Stonor Park. Phillips, Son and Neale, rival auctioneers, had been given the job. Jo had telephoned through to Pellow, Lord Camoys's solicitor, immediately, rightly indignant that he had not been informed of Camoys's decision to sell through Phillips. He would have taken the first car down to Stonor to try and change that irascible mind. Pellow's lame apologies and excuses of how impossible Camoys was did nothing to allay Jo's wrath.

'Going for a Song' was the headline in yesterday's *Express*, with photographs of Swinton Park and Stonor; an accompanying article on the declining funds of English estates made sombre reading. Alternatively, business thrives on their demise and the fact that fine pieces are bought, restored and sold to new collections is in itself an admirable preservation of the arts. The Common Market does not confine its deals to consumer goods alone.

A country house sale entails a ten-day intensive process of assembling and marking pieces, with a huge onus on the porters. The highlight of the two-days auctioneering with the provision of marquees and refreshments is swiftly overtaken by the busy aftermath of clearing goods and arranging collections and deliveries. Albert, the head porter, plays a vital role in these enterprises. A dapper forty-year-old with modestly-dyed red hair, he makes beds for his mates and cooks their evening meals. He can also lay claim to sleeping in some of the most imposing four-posters in the country. On this particular trip I made myself useful in the kitchen and lightened his duties by cooking his team a mammoth Irish stew; it lasted two days – although to everybody's surprise the Aga cooker finally exploded; it was on sale too; a case in point of *caveat emptor*?

November 13 Hardwicke House

We were in Prague this November the seventh. Having visited Russia in 1963 I was mentally pre-armed for that deadening impact of Comintern drabness, depression, loss of individual face and enterprise, that ubiquitous resignation in the crushing force of communism. What I was not prepared for was the fear and uncertainty that pervaded conversation, expression and atmosphere. Since the 1968 Soviet invasion the Czechs have felt the insidious grip of communism tighten.

They are a frightened and powerless people with the fatal knowledge that their situation can only deteriorate; it is anybody's guess how much.

We didn't see many police on the streets, they mostly wear plain clothes. We did see a bottle of whisky marked at L70 (£17). Any Czech who bought it would no doubt have been suspected and clearly questioned.

We were shown the famous Clementinum library, a superb building of Italian Baroque influence. Marble pillars supported a huge long room with a high ceiling painted in the style of the Quattrocento. The books were dusty, dry and untouched. A formidable collection of the larger pigskin volumes had been whitewashed 'to protect the leather', we were led to believe. One pondered deeply on the titles of these tomes that they had chosen to so shamefully obliterate.

The rate of exchange was 21 cronins to the pound; in the street we were approached by a pair of reckless young men, offering us 45 cronins for one British pound. The Czechs are desperate for foreign currency and jobs run on the black market syndrome are rife. Compelled to work for eight hours per day for the State, they get up at 6 a.m. to work in their allotted employment until 2 p.m. Private ownership of any shop or trade is prohibited; in the afternoons they follow their own devices. Their health care is free, but they are not allowed to buy so much as an aspirin. Their education is free, but they cannot choose their subject or specialise to personal tastes. Their underground service is clean; paradoxically their hotels and restaurants are filthy. Their opera houses are beautifully maintained, the seats comparatively cheap, but audiences are subsidised and few foreign artists are invited to perform. Visas are occasionally rendered to those with family or even friends in the West, but they are obliged to produce a passport if visiting in another city of their own country. Meanwhile, their former leader, Alexander Dubcek, is employed as a railway porter in Bratislava.

Our guide, a highly intelligent, erudite, well-travelled woman in her seventies, murmured to me in confidence: 'It is always possible for an individual to somehow maintain his integrity in any society.' Brave words. She reserved the State propaganda commentary for the bus trips; and they were always bugged.

Prague, the crossroads of Europe, a city of hills, spires, misted woods and bridges, is one of the most poignant and most beautiful in the world. With architecture drawn from France, Italy, India and Turkey, the variety of these influences has wrought an amazing and consistent harmony of design and order; the result is unique and unified. Long, tree-lined avenues (the Champs-Elysées?), Baroque, Italianate squares and fifteenth-century clock towers (Vicenza?). A small conglomerate of buildings near the Castle, with their 'wet plaster' façades, evokes an impression of Indian decoration. These Renaissance-style façades have been stuccoed in blocks of dark cement, then coated in a wet, white geometric design; the effect is a striking herringbone finish.

We were in Prague four days only and the weight of such intensive sightseeing in part alleviated our growing awareness of the prevalent angst of the man in the street. We met one citizen, namely Mr Jiri Mucha, the son of the celebrated painter Alphonse Mucha. A thin, tense, nervous man in his fifties, he was yet allowed to live in his father's charming eighteenth-century house. The contents were a fascinating mixture of art nouveau, rococo and eccentricity of taste that naturally included original examples of his father's work. Walls were treble-decked with his familiar paintings of Sarah Bernhardt and the famous Champagne Posters, all lovingly framed in softly-silvered wood.

The whole house was positively choked with the gamut of good to gaudy taste. Biedermeier pieces appeared popular, as were Victorian. A stuffed crow, perched haphazardly on a heavy cheval glass, vied with the books and plastic flowers that cluttered the grand piano. Deep, wide sofas were carelessly draped in carpets and old lace. A bust of a young woman sporting a present-day hunting cap rested alongside an art nouveau 'what-not', which, in the shape of a flower, was curiously hung with cheap, strange necklaces. We were shown into his bedroom; the solid seventeenth-century oak four-poster was unadorned by hangings. A copy of Kingsley Amis's *Lucky Jim* lay on his bedside table, which, on closer inspection, proved to be a small refrigerator. A well-worn easy chair by the fireplace was variously flanked by an electric cooker, an electric kettle, a tin of Nescafé, and a packet of dry biscuits. We were told that he was married but there seemed little evidence of a woman in this confused ménage. We were also told that he was a painter, but later discovered that he had recently been imprisoned as a writer.

No visit to Prague would be complete without a trip to the Jewish Ghetto and its attendant cemetery; a horrifying example, this last, of their congested, segregated conditions in death as in life. Twenty thousand stones of roughened pink marble marked the graves of sixty thousand bodies. This mass compound of the dead beneath the soil told its own sorry tale in the precarious tilt of tombstones. The stark black trunks of the acacia trees with their shivering leaves made daunting props for this memorial. But who could deny that this stark Jewish cemetery was not infinitely more moving than the ostentatious black marble halls, choked with bright flowers, that is Prague's burial ground today?

The Jewish Synagogues, now relegated to museums of their personal collections of Church silver, books, pictures and textiles, demonstrated that assiduous intelligence and taste for expertise and quality. There were some superb pieces of Augsburg silver in museums that were scrupulously maintained and well-documented.

Arriving back in London we felt thoroughly subdued and grateful for our Western way of life; at the same time realising the fragility of its structure and practice in the face of any such radical Comintern bludgeon.

Two days after our return, we heard the Leader of the Opposition, Mrs Margaret Thatcher, speak out. Her words were addressed to the Trades Unions concerning their Labour Relations Bill. She outlined the prime importance of freedom of the press, and the freedom of the individual. She stressed emphatically that we would otherwise be 'no better off than countries behind the Iron Curtain'.

'In Czechoslovakia,' she further warned, 'the Press are bound by one single Union, determining their every action and control. Their attitude to the Soviet Invasion is rigorously checked and questioned. They are impelled to condone it.'

December 12 Hardwicke House

The end of another year races headlong in the familiar frenetic pre–Christmas rush. Inflation has not restrained the shop tills as they jangle overtime. Today, in *The Times*, the leading article states categorically that any forcible wealth tax will make dishonest citizens of us all, while in the same vein Sir Arnold Weinstock (Managing Director since 1963 of General Electric) denounced the proposed nationalisation of the aircraft industry; indeed he pronounced any future nationalisation as the death knell of Britain's solvency. He further indicated that poli-ticians were painfully ignorant of industrial endeavour and were incapable of guiding its future machinations to plausible effect. (But does not the present Labour Government appear ineffectual and a palpable danger to every field of good, sound endeavour?)

It has been a nervous autumn of intermittent bomb blasting in London. The IRA have forced upon citizens in England an acute awareness of their own parlous state in Ireland. The over-riding fear of loss of limb, life, or face disfigurement has turned each Londoner into a wary watch-dog these last five months. Restaurants (mostly Egon Ronay favourites) have been the latest targets; many have sand-bagged their windows. Cars have been other prime scares. We have learned to lock our boots, to report foreign bags in gutters, and to look tentatively between tyres and mudguards. The Police are stalwart and, as Bernard Levin observes: 'Having been frisked vigorously on entering the Royal Festival Hall, it is the first familiar chords we anticipate, not an explosion;' a certain indifference to imminent dangers has set in and a playing down of imagined drama effectively minimises that lurk of horror.

This autumn has also witnessed the loss of two well-loved London clubs. The St James's Club, Piccadilly has closed down and the Guards Club has amalgamated with the Cavalry. A superb if poignant farewell dinner marked the demise of the former. One hundred members attended. The menu read as follows:

> *Coquille – Sauce Newburg*
> *Hot consommé with croutons*
> *Roast Pheasant à l'Anglaise*
> *Fresh French beans*
> *New potatoes*
> *Calon Ségur 1967*
> *Orient soufflé*
> *Coffee*
> *4th December 1975*

Lord Salmon proposed toasts and made no speech. Oh, that dear dining-room with its classic French windows surmounted by those elegant circular fanlights. How often we have relished those crystal rondels; on sunny Sunday luncheons they have been faithfully reflected in the fine Knapton portraits of the Dilettante Society. The self-portrait of Reynolds, hung as always above the fireplace; a pensive, sensitive study. He, along with other treasures, will be removed to Brooks's Club with which the St James's now joins (and where, in time, its whole identity will be lost).

Lord Salmon held the evening with his natural grace and modesty. Who had bought the St James's Club, I asked him? He replied, 'The Devonshire Club; they appear to be a lot of dentists; there is no way in which we would have had anything in common.' One felt they must indeed be a Philistine bunch to have prompted such a curt comment from so kindly and polite a man. 'Changing Guards' was the *Evening Standard*'s own peremptory comment on the dwindling of these long-hallowed bastions. Meanwhile Tom's name comes up in White's in February. And will there ever be 'white ladies' for ladies in White's?

1976

The familiar figure of the Italian Ambassador, Signor Roberto Ducci, neat and dapper, astride his Arab thoroughbred, veered towards me in jerking sidesteps. It was nine o'clock on a mean, cold morning in Richmond Park. How were we? Our respective mares snorted restlessly as off with his hat, his gloves and a proffered hand. I was on my way home to breakfast? Yes? But this last week we had been to Rome? Too many Communist demonstrations for comfort, I told him. Ah yes. In the Piazza di Spagna? He shrugged wryly, and I remembered how the head of the fifty police, overseeing those two thousand youths, had been smoking a cigarette. His troop had been shielded with visors and armed with tear gas and truncheons. There had been no casualties.

The previous week a rally of young women had submerged the Piazza Navona with demands for contraception and free abortion; again no casualties save for a huge effigy of a man which was subsequently burnt. Twenty-four hours later, the Piazza had emerged clean, quiet and empty; the Bernini fountains in all their magnificence and virility had again reigned supreme.

We had called on Christie's newly-acquired rooms at the Palazzo Massimo Lancelloti, where an amiable polo player for the Italian team, Count Paolo del Pennino was in charge. We admired the sixteenth-century coffered wood ceilings, the frescoed ballroom and the assembled miscellanea for sale. Early days but they seemed busy enough.

We were delighted with our hotel, secreted in a vicolo off the Piazza Navona, the 'Raphael'. Devoid of a telex or large comfortable bedrooms, it was accordingly discounted by the ubiquitous Japanese tourist groups and businessmen. Clean and adequate with impeccable service in the old style and manner, the bedrooms were small but the sheets were linen, albeit darned fifteen times to the square foot. The charge for bed and breakfast per day per person was £10. This atmosphere of understated refinement and the peaceful venue by one of the most ravishing squares in Rome was well worth such a conservative price.

One evening we crossed the Piazza Navona to have a drink with Virginia Borghese – a niece of Lord Gladwyn[1]. She was married to

---

[1] Gladwyn Jebb, created the first Baron Gladwyn 1960. Married to Cynthia (née Noble). Ambassador to France 1954–60.

some Italian aristocrat named Scaretti and since divorced. In her early forties, she was a beautiful woman with those delicate, cool, Jebb features. She expressed her disenchantment with present-day culture of Rome, and bewailed the increasing onus of the Borghese fifteenth-century Medici castle in the hills above Florence. Like so many privileged families they were continuously kept down by upkeep.

Her admirer, Signor Umberto Nordi, joined us, a brilliant man with apparent total recall of fascinating statistics. Sophisticated, tall and slim with grey, receding hair and a long nose, he was undeniably attractive and obviously in love. He was the Chairman of Alitalia and regaled us with the associated Communist problems. He felt that he had his men in check, but quoted appalling examples from other industries, notably Fiat; the company was entangled in some strange benign blackmail whereby they regularly paid 2,000 men who rarely turned up for one single day's work.

We later dined at Pasetto's, one of Rome's more distinguished restaurants, succinctly reflected in its elegant clientele and the superb deference of its waiters. The deep-fried artichokes, crisped to the colour of mahogany, were delicious, and could be eaten in their entirety. Like most restaurants in Rome today, the décor was austere, but again there was that sense of style in its very understatement . . .

Another evening we dined at Alfredo Alla Scrofola, a long-time favourite for its fabled fettucini, generously buttered, and its patronage of film stars. It has now lost its one Michelin star and has acquired three tiresome musicians; but we liked it enough and ate there again.

A restaurant named Sans Souci off the Via Veneto should be assiduously avoided. Described as in the 'Grand Tradition' it was steeped in ludicrous extravaganza, sycophantic service, mediocre cooking and young waiters coyly attired in frills and velvet. Empty tables and enormous prices proved an abysmal reward. We walked home through the dark and cold, mindful of mugging in the streets at night. I clutched my handbag as five young men walked briskly towards us, abreast. In the event of us being separated there would have been trouble; Tom pressed me against the side wall. On another occasion we were descended on by gipsy girls in the terraced gardens across from the Colosseum. They hovered around us like flies, chattering loudly; we threw them off with shouts of 'I Carabinieri.'

Rome today is no lively centre of contemporary culture. The opera house resembles a Muscovite community hall, a drab post-war building that holds an indifferent performance once a week; it does not attract any potential intelligentsia. The theatre world is equally devoid of talent and patronage. Film stars and their producers cause the only hive of artistic activity; the Via Veneto is their favourite backdrop. Other fashionable streets of Rome attract the richer residents, a plethora of middle-aged women flaunting their streaked blonde hair, their cheap-looking expensive furs, and the inevitable elegant boots, superbly made in soft rich leather with heels made in one with the sole. A pair bought in Sloane Street could not compare in price or quality.

When in Rome, it is to the magnificence of its past that one pays tribute. The senses are stunned by the feats of architecture, where every piazza overflows with its own beauty, a vast conglomerate of evocative caprice. One is astonished by the quantity of marble alone, whilst Bernini's genius excels all anticipation in his *Apollo and Daphne* at the Borghese Gallery.

Finally we gazed on Michelangelo's ceiling of the Sistine Chapel. What a provenance of angst and suffering! One recalled his desperate discomfort, lying on his back, painting through the harsh heat of four summers that alternated with winter's brute cold. The continual harrying of Pope Pius III must have proved mean encouragement. 'But when will it be finished? Be finished?' Today a sublime and luminous achievement, worshipped by the world. Some years later, Pius III commissioned him to paint the Altar. Michelangelo chose as his theme 'The Last Judgement'. The work has always had a contro-versial reception. Against a brilliant blue sky, straddled with clouds and monolithic bodies, Christ raises up the writhing dead with his one arm and banishes the failures to Hell with the other. Pope Pius IV subsequently referred to this huge painting as 'a stew of nudes'. He later prompted another artist to insert some knee-breeches.

April 20 Hardwicke House

> Except for thy Heaven there is no refuge for me in this world,
>   other than there is no place for my head.

These words, written by the fourteenth-century Persian poet Hafiz Ardabil, are woven into the sixteenth-century Ardabil carpet. Con-sidered by experts to be the most beautiful and important carpet in the world, it has been temporarily released from its glass cage in the Victoria and Albert Museum, where it now breathes freely on the floor. It is a remarkable eye-trainer in the Persian paradise garden concept, where birds, fish and animals disport themselves amidst flowering trees, ornamental ponds and fountains, as rare an example of Islamic art as one could ever hope to see. Meanwhile it is the mammoth festival of Islam that has overtaken London these past weeks.

What is Islam? Stemming from complete submission to Mohammed, a seventh-century BC Arabian camel-trader, it swept a rampant course throughout the Middle East, engulfing Africa, Southern Spain, Turkey and finally India. This staggering force was conclusively stalled in 732 at Poitiers by Charles Martel; hence Islam with its alien and evocative trappings was given no platform in Western Europe. Gleaming mosques blistered the skies in its wake and this rich culture of artistic and scientific endeavour has nudged the souls and minds of men ever since.

London, acting as present host to this conglomerate picture of Islamic arts and tradition, is heaving with splendour in museums, galleries and sale rooms. The Shahbanou of Iran has favoured Colnaghi's for her purchases. Its director, Jacob Rothschild, has amassed a highly important selection of Persian art, to include a Polonaise rug, woven with silver thread on a field of clear oranges, yellows and limes, colours smacking of a John Fowler chintz more than the muted hues familiar to sixteenth-century vegetable dyes. It is to be hoped that the Shahbanou ticked this item on her shopping list, despite comments from connoisseurs that the design is weak and shallow.

Tom has been gratified, and not least his Chairman, to see a steady flow of Iranians at Christie's sale rooms and it was with great satisfaction that he auctioned a sixteenth-century Shahnameh[2] Manuscript to the tune of £75,000. The reserve had been placed at £45,000. The richly-coloured illustration depicted lively warfare with extravagantly-attired riders on leaping horses, alongside dogs, deer and a lurking dinosaur. The vivid blues, reds and yellows, laced with gold and black calligraphy, together with such gruesome details as maroon blood spurting from dismembered bodies and flying heads made absorbing viewing.

With Christie's and Sotheby's 10% commission rate, the dealer had to pay £82,000 for this manuscript.

May 4 Bramham Park Yorkshire

It is six years since we visited this house, the re-valuation of its contents has since doubled in price. George Lane Fox is now ensconced with his wife, Victoria. The gardens, as laid out by Le Nôtre, are superb as ever and are effectively kept up by 'two and a half' gardeners. The Bramham three-day horse-riding event, comparable in popularity

---

[2] The *Shahnameh (Book of Kings)* is Iran's national epic. Originally compiled by Abu'l Qasim Mansur Firdowsi, who died 1025.

to Badminton, is held at the beginning of June, when Princess Anne and Captain Mark Phillips will be competing. They will be staying at the house and obviously enjoy this quiet and informal setting. Victoria Lane Fox commented that the only hazard in this arrangement concerns their own dogs; when they are let out at night a free fight invariably ensues with the security guard Alsatians. Having Royalty to stay must breed as many different complications in as many households.

May 5 Sledmere Driffield North Yorkshire

'Father will be back in a moment; his horse has been racing at Chester this afternoon.' Sir Richard Sykes's second son, Jeremy, was showing us round the house. It was seven o'clock and it would seem that no drinks could be dispensed other than by the old man himself.

We wandered through the superb rooms decorated by Joseph Rose (1746–99). Extensively employed by the Adam brothers, Rose's work can also be seen at Nostell Priory and at Harewood. He must also have been continually rubbing up against Capability Brown, who laid out many parks adjoining these Yorkshire country mansions. Indeed our eyes were becoming well-attuned to Adam ceilings and window friezes with vistas beyond of Capability Brown's famous avenues stretching away into bold green horizons.

As we reached the drawing-room, resplendent with new renovated gold leaf moulding, Sir Richard entered from an opposite door. His three golden greyhounds clung to him possessively before taking up statuesque positions among the gilt wood furniture, their elegance comparing favourably. Sir Richard had had a disappointing day at the races. We talked tentatively for a few moments before going to change for dinner.

Cases had been unpacked, baths run, evening clothes laid out on the bed. It is not often in these stringent days that one enjoys the full comforts of a well-run household. We further noted that the staff were happy, and that the superb upkeep throughout the house extended to the whole estate. Sir Richard later confided that he had not yet been brain-washed by the socialists; it was true that they had modified his address to North Humberside, but he himself still referred to his home county as North Yorkshire. Humberside, he observed, conjured up such horrors as grim dockyards and trades union disputes, a picture at sharp variance to his own tastes.

Sir Richard always changes for dinner at Sledmere, and when dining out with neighbours, however illustrious, he has been known to take along his own mixed cocktail. His devoted valet, Robert, attends to this detail and, in turn, is treated to the odd dinner in a Paris restaurant, if Sir Richard ever finds himself alone, travelling through Europe.

We reassembled in the staircase hall at 8.15; Sir Richard, Jeremy, Tom and myself. Over a drink we talked of London clubs; Whites', Brooks's and the former St James's proved safe havens of conversation. We went in to dinner and sat in a corner of the vast dining-room, nursed by a lacquer screen. The meal was simple: sardines, thin soup, lamb chops, and 'Sledmere's special trifle'. The sardines were nestled artfully in a bed of chopped spring onions and hard boiled eggs, the thin soup excelled in its croutons, and the lamb chops were elegantly trimmed and bread-crumbed. After some hesitation, Sir Richard allowed Jeremy to mix the salad dressing. The Sledmere trifle, thickly blanketed with the estate's own cream, was a final triumph. The cook later assured me that she had never met with such a concoction before, but vowed that she could not improve on the Sledmere recipe.

Later I found myself stumbling through Chopin in the music room. Sir Richard listened graciously and confessed that he was also out of practice with his organ playing. I joined him on the sofa where our conversation switched rather abruptly to Solzhenitsyn.

We left the next morning, not before witnessing a gratifying bed-room scene of two women packing my case and the butler wrestling with Tom's. I also happened to notice, in the study, that the 'Sir Richard's own sweeties', kept in a cardboard box decorated by one of his daughters, contained a mere half-eaten bar of nougat. On our way home to London, we bought him a tin of old-fashioned toffees at Farrah's of Harrogate.

Browsing through the history of Sledmere on our return, I came across an illustrated documentary, compiled by Sir Richard himself. An extract from a letter dated September 8, 1784, written by a house guest, read as follows:

Sir Christopher and Lady Sykes are both extremely obliging, indeed I don't know in what family so nearly strangers to me I could have been so agreeably placed for a visit and of near a fortnight and not tired of it I assure you. Lady Elizabeth Hill [another guest] and I were taught to dread these Wolds, but without perverseness, we are highly delighted and well maybe; nothing can be finer than the pure air here, only 18 miles from Bridlington, the beautiful hill and the dale of the country makes charming rides, etc., and Sir Christopher has formed and is forming great designs in the planting way which will beautify it prodigiously. He is building offices and the House is to be transformed some time. It is now a very good one of its age and reminds me of the Highgate House below stairs.

Here's plenty of books, pictures good and antiques, which keep one in constant amusement, besides organ, harpsichord, etc., which strange to tell, I've exercised my small skill upon before all the party every day; the Wolds inspire me with the courage beyond my expectation and my spirit so good to enjoy and join the laugh with comfort.

I was encouraged by the above to write my own adaptation in thanking Sir Richard for our brief stay with him. He sent me a charming card in return, thanking me for the toffees and adding that he 'greatly enjoyed the adaptation of the letter about Sledmere'.

June 24 Hardwicke House

Back in London, the older generation entertain with plausible panache. Dolly Burns envelops the head of her Mayfair dining table, concentrating her predatory bulk upon the newly-honoured Lord Vaizey. He is pale and slight in contrast to her force and colour. On her left she launches an eager young name-dropper from the US Embassy; her eyes glaze over. She tries to lure Sir John Foster QC, two away, to alleviate this unproductive line. Sir John, bowed down over his plate and past reminiscences, studiously avoids her beady entreaty, and hurriedly invites me to lunch at his flat. At the far end of the table, our host, Bobby Burns, peers suspiciously at an Italian Count who claims Italy would be better run by their communist party. (Who has Dolly gone and asked to dinner this time?) Lady Roberts, spry, petite and Lebanese, has been an ambassador's wife in Russia and Yugoslavia. She concentrates her sleek dark head on dissecting her salmon rather than on this full-blown imbecile.

We leave the table and the men. Dolly offers me a place in her lift where she leaves little room. We arrive at her bedroom in seconds. The impact of shocking pink, purple, mauve and lavender taffeta enhanced by explosions of artificial flowers and feathers is stunning to the worst degree. We finally collapse in faint heaps in the drawing-room below. The men join us promptly. Augustus John's portrait of our hostess in her prime dominates a wall. Full face with her full mouth pursed in amusement. Had she just said something provocative? She looks fun, dynamic. John has captured a rich ray of her former self. Perhaps he was being seduced.

October 18 Hardwicke House

Tomorrow I meet up with Tom in Jeddah, Saudi Arabia, a city described in uncouched terms by T E Lawrence, as deadly quiet, where the air has remained still and stagnant for centuries. A different city now, but perhaps no more enticing. The hot blue sky is stabbed with concrete and the desert all around ringed with oil pipes. Today one of the richest cities in the world, in terms of material potential, Jeddah remains a comparatively dead city to the Western traveller: no alcohol, no cinema, no unveiled women in the street after dark. A city caught up in the escalation of enforced progress without the nous to effectively determine its own adjustments to Western civilisation. A city caught between the desert and the deep Red Sea. Like a child showered with expensive toys too intricate for him to comprehend, the Saudi Arabian is heaped with the rich toys of modern mechanics. But where lies his technology?

   Jeddah can further boast a fish market, Eve's tomb, and a European cemetery. Unfortunately my travel hand-out does not enlarge on these local delights. I am also alerted that, being the penultimate port of call before Mecca, Jeddah throngs with itinerant Muslim pilgrims. An alien world, unseen by most European women today. Having had difficulty extracting my visa, this visit must be cherished.

October 19 – November 7 Jeddah Saudi Arabia

When confronted with the explosive and sudden wealth of his country, the late King Feisal remarked to Dr Kissinger: 'We have oil and we have time'. Was he reckoning with the uninitiated manpower of his country, the inherent laziness and the arrogance? The Saudi in the streets has not changed his spots. He drinks his mint tea, idly waggles his knees beneath his dish-dasher and gazes on the imported labour. It is the Sudanese and the Egyptians who get on with the job in hand. The Saudi will drive his taxi, sound his horn hysterically, heckle over distance, churn up traffic and dust roads with expansive U-turns. But will he grout a bathroom tile? Lay a pavement, a pipe, a table? Oh no! He likes to keep his hands and his dish-dasher clean.

   One blazing morning (they are always blazing in Jeddah), from the top of the Queen's Building (a prestigious pile), we gazed over the dirty hot dust of the town to the Red Sea harbour. The crowded bay positively belched with cargo; baleful grey ships awaiting their dues. It will be months before they are unloaded; the harbour itself will take three more years to complete, we are told.

We look more closely and see helicopters hovering over decks, off-loading single bags of cement. Lowering a fifty-foot cable to secure its bag, each helicopter then heads for the shore, spewing a trail of grey dust as the bag leaks its powder.

'Crazy, isn't it?' A bright-eyed young American stands beside us. 'All that packed-up cargo waiting for customs and red tape; they suspect pork and pornography in every load. The result is delay, chaos and rotten tempers.' We later saw rows of Datsun and Toyota cars on shore. They must have been unloaded weeks ago, so thick were they in sand and cement dust. Would their engines still work?

We picked our way back to the ramshackle Airport Hotel, across rutted roads jammed with recalcitrant, hooting cars, past half-built, half-cracked, cement-faced buildings, perilously propped with wooden scaffolding, a scene of total disorder where building raced with demolition. The few remaining old houses, their foundations visibly shaken by reverberations of the new, stood tall and narrow; their frail brick façades a hovering reminder of a past civilisation, forlorn indictments of this present confusion. We waited in the cool, dusty lobby watching spirals of air-conditioned dust eddying up the marble staircase. The ill-fitting carpet, split on every tread, posed a threat to the unwary heel. We sipped the customary 7-Up and waited for our friend.

Two Arabs sat in a corner with two nondescript British businessmen; the former looked inestimably the more distinguished in clean, white dish-dashers, crocheted skullcaps lining their white kafiahs, encircled with black agals. Their British counterparts were sloppy in short-sleeved shirts, creased travel-worn trousers, barely containing their protruding stomachs.

It is difficult to strike up a ready relationship with an Arab. He will take his time to trust you and resents being told which way to walk, having the freedom of the desert in his blood. He is sensitive over his Eastern domestic habits. He will not easily introduce his wife, or invite you home for a meal; he will in time, if you are proved his friend. But the young Arab, proud of his newly-decorated office with its modern accoutrements, will blandly show off his streamlined skimpy-skirted secretary. She will be European, Lebanese or Egyptian – and young. His office boy will serve you Arabic coffee or mint tea; there will be peaceful silences during the interview as he sums you up and feels your presence. When he has met you four times in as many years you will become his dear, true friend. You will do big business and link little fingers as you stroll through the Souk. You will kiss at airports and may even meet his wives. Meanwhile you leave his office mystified and non-plussed. A row of white kafiahs, encircled with black agals, are perched on a plastic hat stand. (They recognise their own headdress by the smell, you are told.) You lurch into the loud and airless street. Sometimes you wonder what it is all about.

Our friend arrives in a range-rover. Leonard Ingrams[3], brother of the *Private Eye* editor, Richard Ingrams, is working in Jeddah for Barings, principally advising SAMA – the Saudi Arabian Monetary Agency – on how to spend their money. 'You can build a house in Jeddah with four bedrooms for £50,000 and then let it for £20,000 a year . . .' We drove along the Red Sea front to lunch at his house on the outskirts of the town. 'That's King Khaled's Summer Palace . . .' he points out. We swivelled our eyes to take in a mammoth low-lying Moorish pile, coated in sunny cream; a few palm trees rose up behind the encircling walls and waved their desultory salute. We looked out to sea again and to the newly-built promenade dotted at generous intervals with marble bench seats and a snake of marble-topped balustrading. 'The half-finished look is due to looting. Marble disappears by the night. There's my house and just beyond is the Dutch Embassy. They haven't been connected to the telephone yet; it will be anybody's guess before my garden is overlooked.' We admired the oleanders and acacia trees in his courtyard; his garden looked remarkably mature. 'We don't have any water restrictions here, but in the town they feed acacia trees with sewage; the cart goes round every Friday.' Leonard's African-Saudi house boy served us an overcooked, hot khaki lunch of lamb and ratatouille. 'I'm perfectly happy. My wife and three children are in London, she is expecting her fourth. I have my grand piano and my swimming pool and I have even generated a little musical activity in Jeddah. We have a cellist on her way – stuck in Kuwait – visa trouble . . .' We were grateful for his hospitality and impressed by his stalwart enthusiasm in the face of such dry-living as proffered by Jeddah.

John Wilton[4] is the present British Ambassador in Jeddah. He and his red-headed wife are well-versed in Arabian diplomacy; they have been at it for four years. Their charm and commonsense are a refreshment to all who meet them. We arrived for lunch at the Embassy in the midday heat and waited patiently at the wrong door while the door man bowed to Mecca. We admired his well-timed oblivion of our arrival. Having completed his reverences under the shade of the only tree, he re-directed us to the private quarters of the Embassy, a low comfortable building, cushioned by a lush garden.

[3] Founder and Chairman Garsington Opera Ltd 1990. Member Mozart 2006 Committee, Salzburg, 2000. Leonard Ingrams OBE died 2005.
[4] Ambassador to Kuwait 1970–4 and to Saudi-Arabia 1976–79. Chairman Arab-British Centre 1981–86. KCMG, KCVO.

'What will you drink?' Mrs Wilton fumbled in her handbag for her bunch of keys. 'I always keep it locked.' John Wilton remarked that everybody, including the Arabs, expected the Ambassador to serve drinks. He has it sent out from the UK in huge cases marked 'refrigerators'. We had a pleasant informal lunch. The servants, confided Mrs Wilton, in good-humoured despair, never cease to demand more and more for less and less. 'They already have all we can afford, with three children to educate.' We spent an informative afternoon in their air-conditioned Cadillac, touring Jeddah. John Wilton, having only been in office for seven months, was delighted to take the opportunity of looking around.

We drove first to the shanty town district where an attempt had been made to eradicate it with bull-dozers. The demolished area was fouled with dead goats and debris. Aged ex-inhabitants tottered in their filthy rags, in a hideous struggle to salvage their neighbours' belongings in order to resurrect something of their own. A complex of clean, wooden Colt houses on the other side of the road appeared spurned and silent; better the dirt they knew. John Wilton pointed out the modern landmarks; the Queen's Building and the Ministry of Information were handsome and well-built; suitable specimens, no doubt, for those 'industrial architects' who are already scanning the Arabian Gulf for contemporary architecture monuments, to commemorate the fleeting oil age of these future ghost cities.

Muscat Oman Arabia

We waited five hours for our plane to take off from Jeddah. Women sat mute and patient on the airport floor, clutching restless babies. Some were totally veiled in black, their profiles strange and predatory under the clinch of their burkahs. Darkness merged swiftly into dawn and sunrise, the desert was rose, amethyst and clear as we flew towards Oman. Vast drifts of sand, windblown to knife-edge swirls, were shelved into precarious ledges and long empty hollows; silent lakes of sand peppered with shrubs like so many cigarette burns on a beige carpet. We neared Oman, encircled by its range of black volcanic mountains and red sedimentary rock. Good tarmac roads and well-designed ribbon-line development spread beneath us as we landed at Muscat.

The contrast between Oman and Saudi Arabia was a tonic. Efficiency, enthusiasm and cleanliness prevailed; method, good design and good management were conspicuously evident. The young Sultan had spent heavily and well during his five years in power. Despite his extensive and elaborately constructed Moorish palace on the shore of Muscat harbour; his horses, with each loose-box individually air-conditioned with GEC fans; his race course, designed on the lines of Ascot; his passion for parades (on a par with our own Queen's Birthday Parade), and his air displays (on a par with Farnborough); his private VC10, with a full-time team of air-hostesses; his Jersey herd, his speedboats, his shirts from Turnbull and Asser, and his suits from Kilgour, French and Stanbury, he has given his peasants a dignity and purpose; a sense of livelihood and industrial challenge. In time it is hoped that he will give them more hospitals and schools.

Meanwhile the oil in Oman has virtually run dry. It was fortunate that the Sultan had built and designed in such haste after his father was ousted from power in 1971. Due to Oman's strategic position on the Gulf, King Khaled of Saudi Arabia is generous with pocket money. He visits the Sultan regularly and urges him to 'keep the Brits'. The Sultan's army, with the victory of Dhofar to its credit, is now relinquishing the British commanding forces to the Omanis, viewed with mixed feelings by the Saudis and by the British directly involved. It could be surmised that this particular neck of the Gulf, part Arabian, part Iranian, will prove a cockpit of trouble in the future. Meanwhile the mountains are being drilled for copper and other minerals as a possible contingency export. The harsh sweep of mountains in Oman are gashed with lush green wadis, rambling mud and stone villages subsist on the running mountain streams, date groves, banana trees, fat donkeys and thick grasses swaying with wild amaryllis flourishing in these wide valleys. Our car got stuck in one such wadi and in minutes we were encompassed by friendly waving natives, hitherto unseen in the dense foliage, who shovelled us out of the loose wet shale and directed us to their village of Sumayl.

The souk was quiet and sleepy in the humid midday sun. Old men, their eyes glazed with trachoma, sat quietly observing us over wooden troughs of curry, cayenne, rice, lentils, cinnamon sticks and nuts. A Bedouin drew a knife out of his thick leather hunting belt and slit open a sack of dates and offered us one; their dark glistening succulence lured the flies immediately and he carefully pressed the split sides together. More mounds of fat golden dates lay ripening and darkening in the sun, while veiled woman sat plaiting sacks from the sun-bleached fronds of palm trees. A group of children clustered around us as we ambled through the dusty souk; the dim warm light was drowned in hot, sweet spices and their wheedling squeals of 'Baksheesh! Baksheesh!'. A little girl with bracelets round her ankles jumped up and down excitedly, leading the hue and cry.

We wandered through the village, a labyrinth of shady, dry mud lanes hedged by high wattle walls. An old man motioned us from his narrow gate to take tea with him. We entered a courtyard cluttered with chickens and were led to a sizeable verandah adjoining his mud house, and strewn with worn carpets. We took off our shoes and sat cross-legged beside the open arches that gave on to his garden of thick long grass and banana trees. We learnt that he was the retired mayor of the village, and that he had two solemn grandsons, Tariq and Ali, who watched us gravely from his side. Having settled us to his satisfaction, he went in search of tea. He returned first with a jug of water which he explained had been cooled in a gourd left hanging in the trees. There then followed a tin salver of pink rose petals which he insisted we should accommodate; seeing my hesitation he motioned that I drop them into my shirt front. A further foray produced a large dish of dates, and a water melon which he sliced into rounds with assiduous concentration; and finally minuscule cups of mint tea which he took an inordinate pleasure in re-filling again and again until we shook them to indicate we had drunk enough. He watched us with a solicitous pride whilst we took all his offerings in the left hand as is the custom. When we could bear the pressure of sitting cross-legged no more and signed that we should go, he disappeared again and returned with a bottle of duty-free scent. We were copiously sprayed and led back to the gate in his mud wall, with fond and enthusiastic farewells. Standing in his worn dish-dasher, a meagre old man, wreathed in smiles and grimy wrinkles, his two small grandsons holding each hand, he appeared the very expression of peace and human dignity.

October 1976 Abu Dhabi United Arab Emirates

From Oman, the most beguiling corner of Arabia, we flew to Abu Dhabi. Five years ago the aeroplanes landed on the sand; the town had since exploded into a flat, all-encompassing complex of tarmac and cement-block buildings. One redeeming feature of Abu Dhabi is the Hilton Hotel. It stands tall in majestic design and is immensely spacious with a Lebanese staff. Clean, efficient, comfortable and geared to the mores of the European and American businessmen, who can be seen lolling in fat heaps beside the swimming pool. Building construction is now being taken into the Arabs' own hands; Wimpey's past efforts are already cracking and insurance companies are wary over what they underwrite. British Land Rovers have also lost their cachet here, with spare parts and servicing not readily available; the Toyota is now in favourable demand.

We arranged lunch with Colonel Sir Hugh Boustead[5], a legendary British veteran who, after years of distinguished service in the Arab countries, has settled in the desert. Principally he oversees Sheikh Zayed's[6] horses. 'Come immediately,' he urged. We set off to Alain, a seventy-mile drive along a new tarmac road slap through the desert. Sheikh Zayed's ambition to have a hundred miles of trees along this new road seemed remarkably effective, acacias and oleanders lined the start of our route, punctuated by massive roundabouts, stiff with flowers and bright shrubs. The combination of continuous watering and hot sun produces a lush surface growth even in the heart of the desert.

However, it is feared that this whole enterprise might topple in a strong wind, with trees spreading such shallow roots. The straight smooth road belied its danger; every three miles lay crumpled wrecks of twisted cars. The driver had gone to sleep. He had run into a camel. He had careered out of control with a burst tyre. On either side of us the desert billowed away in softly-moulded dunes. A string of camels were sharply reflected in a glassy mirage. Groups of white tents, flaps down, stood in lifeless solitude, defying a tourist's curiosity. A long line of men were panned out along the road, fixing up arc lighting and planting the first frail shoots of endless oleanders. They eased their roots into little saucers of sand. Huge and garish advertisement boards for colour televisions, hotels and ice-cream stood in abrupt contrast to the ever-receding sands. After two hours we yanked the car off the tarmac and followed a rutted sand track to reach Sir Hugh.

'You're early! Wasn't expecting you for another hour; it's this new road, everybody arrives early now.' We remarked on the road's newly-planted trees. 'Ah yes, Capability Brown, we call him.' We followed him out to his straw-covered verandah. A hammock hung from the corner, swathed in a mosquito net. 'Just one fly can worry you to death, old boy; playing on your mouth, but I like to sleep out. Yes, the garden's come on in just two years. It's a good life, four months' holiday a year, my two house boys, and a pint of fresh milk a day from the Sheikh's cows; he wants to fatten me up, he says. Want to see the horses?' We edged round his glorified pre-fabs and crossed over a waste area of sand to the stables. The loose boxes, designed by Sir Hugh, were light and airy. Built in cement with fretted open-work panels on the back walls, and a simple drain-pipe construction barring each front allowed a free flow of air. The floors were sand with a hole

---

[5] *The Wind of Morning* by Colonel Sir Hugh Boustead KBE, CMG, DSO, MC – published 1972, Chatto & Windus.
[6] 'Arabic spelling is based on phonetics. Sir Hugh refers to Sheikh Zaid..(Zayed or Zayeed are equally correct.)

in each corner where the manure was shovelled out. 'Zaid began with eleven horses and now has sixty-one, with mares and stallions in mint condition, what can you expect? There's not enough stabling, old boy, and only twelve saddles . . .' Sir Hugh seemed unperturbed by these immediate problems; apparently his notes in the breeding books are a mass of inaccurate pedigree and gender. The Sheikh is also suitably vague about his ever-increasing stock; however, the whole concern appeared thriving. Healthy-looking, well-mannered stable boys came and shook our hands. 'Nice fellows, mostly Pakistani. No complaints, old boy, except for this prayer-business. These fellows have got it all wrong and think they must do it on the dot of six o'clock; no allowing for any latitude either way, never mind the horses. I tell them, look here, boys! I've read your Koran. No such thing as being on time for a prayer. You don't know your stuff . . .'

The ceiling of Sir Hugh's living-room is a feast of whirring fans. 'I have my own ideas about air-conditioning, you know. I like to feel the real air coming through the windows. We'll draw the curtains and keep the windows wide open. How about our lunch? And then you will have a siesta and then a ride in the evening with the boys. Don't worry about shoes; you can wear mine and I'll give you some socks to pad them out.'

We sat down to an excellent meal, home-made brown bread, fresh salad, king-fish and some white wine (warm and sweet). The two house boys served us with possessive pride. As we finished a fat Indian clutching a crying baby edged into the room. 'Hullo, my friend,' roared our host. 'So you've recovered from your malaria? What is this?' Sir Hugh pointed to the bundle in the man's arms. 'Is that a boy you've got there, or a girl? Are you sure? Well, she's far too fat, like her father.' The child had obviously caught the fever. Sir Hugh opened his medicine cupboard behind his desk. Myriad bottles for local diseases – trachoma and malaria – and an economy-size blue bottle of Milk of Magnesia (conspicuously unopened) were neatly lined along two shelves. The child squirmed with the teaspoonful of medicine. Sir Hugh next injected her, while the father beamed comfortably during the whole performance; he took his leave a happier man. Sir Hugh's informal dispensary is an important part of native family life. He even claims that the trachoma hazard has greatly improved in his area.

We rested for an hour. Sir Hugh roused us at four o'clock. He was off to Abu Dhabi to stay with friends for two days. Jaunty in his Panama hat, full of energy and enthusiasm, thin and brown and wiry, he gave no heed to his eighty years. 'I'm off, chaps. Here are my shoes; now don't complain. The boys will take you out over the dunes; good exercise for bunching up their hind-quarters, old boy.'

It was a new experience to swoop up and down the dunes, with the desert and distant mountains fired with evening sun. The horses broke out in frustrated sweating; one longed to canter on the flat for miles, instead of bunching up their hind-quarters on sand dunes.

Dubai The Gulf States

From Abu Dhabi to Dubai. Here there still remains a distinct essence of old-time trading. Seasoned wood dhows bobbed in the creek that divides the old port of the town from the new. We edged up a dusty road on the old side. The sun was sinking, provoking a mystery and bustle in the Arab quarter. Women in burkahs set up little stores on sandy street corners. Others returned from their food shopping, clutching veil and scampering child. A cow sniffed at a heap of rubbish and a goat picked its way disdainfully through a ramshackle array of tin beds and mattresses, open to the skies. The old brick wind towers with their intricate fretwork marked clinging boundaries of this passing Arabic way of life.

We went up 150 feet in a cement hoist from the roof of a commercial construction (by Al Masaood's, for Sheikh Rashid). We saw the hard lights of modern development across the creek, the hotels and other high-rise conglomerations; the necklace of traffic and the gleam and swank of tarmac. We crossed the creek through a new underground tunnel and drove twenty minutes further up the coast to Sharjah, an even more recent cement eruption. Its prized Carlton Hotel has an air of the sophisticated week-end pick-up joint. Saudis sit on the verandah sipping Heineken; they knock their knees together beneath their white cotton dish-dashers; a cooling process, a gentle distraction. A string of nubile air-hostesses pass through the lobby – International, Eastern, Western – eyes swivel from the verandah, fat necks crane, the moment passes. More Heineken and eyes are settled back to sea.

The stories of the Arabs' largesse in London are legion. I was particularly amused to hear of the Sheikh who arrived for his dentist appointment in Harley Street, clutching a handful of emeralds. He asked that they should be used for his teeth stoppings instead of gold.

1977

Last week we drove 120 miles to Gaddesby to see Colonel Norman Johnstone and his vivacious wife Rosh on his birthday.

We arrived at Park House in darkness, slush and drizzle to be greeted by the Colonel himself in a scarlet track suit. 'They are so practical for feeding the macaws, gardening, walking dogs, and very warm in winter and cool in summer; I live in them. Do come in and let me take your cases; it is kind of you to come all this way. You couldn't have chosen a better moment, I have just upset a whole tray of glasses.' Were they full, we asked? One of the reasons we had made such a pilgrimage was to revel in Norman's cellar. The house was full of greenhouse plants, dogs and log fires. Rosh appeared in a yellow trouser suit, topped by a fur jacket, and freshly-curled hair. She looked gay and young and a million dollars; had she been cooking all day?

'Come along in; come in – mind the dogs.' We sat down in the drawing-room where a home-grown huge camellia stood tall and perfect behind a knole sofa. Norman is an authority on camellias as well as cellars. We drank a bottle of Schloss Johannisberger, Rheingau Spätlese 1971, in the space of ten minutes. A bottle of champagne, Deutz, Blanc de Blancs, non-vintage, quickly followed. We had baths and changed for dinner. The comfort of a four-poster bed further secured our enjoyment of the evening. No fun to drive through narrow Leicestershire lanes after having had dinner with Norman and Rosh[1]. Another advantage of the track suit would seem that it promotes quick changing. In no time Norman was sleek in his dinner jacket, opening the front door to his other guests.

Rosh was a vision in an exotic dark hue with borders of multi-coloured beading and braid. Their guests included Lord Crawshaw, confined to a wheelchair since a near fatal fall, when some twenty years ago he was riding in his own point-to-point. His brother, the Hon. David Brooks, and his sister-in-law, Belinda, together with other country talent. We drank another bottle of champagne, Deutz and Gelderman 1966, this time. Rosh soon whisked us through to the dining-room; clearly there was a lot more drinking and eating to be done.

---

[1] Roshnara (née Wingfield-Stratford-Orr) married secondly Lt Colonel Norman Johnstone, Grenadier Guards. He wrote a wine column for the *Tatler*. Towards the end of his life, he had the stair-lift extended down to the cellar.

The table looked superb, regally loaded with silver. The central candelabra towered as high as the camellia in the drawing-room. Dinner proved an epicurean orgy; game galantine attended by a magnum of Meursault Genevrières 1971, was followed by partridge and another magnum, of Volnay 1966. Next, lamb en couronne exquisitely stuffed and served with Norman's home-grown mashed pumpkin, together with a mélange of courgettes and cheese tossed in a crisp batter. The sauce escapes me. The conversation became general and suffused with bodily satisfaction. Norman sat at the middle of the table, so that he could see everybody and be heard. Rosh, ever-sprightly on her feet, whisked in a final superb finish to the meal, a sumptuous whirl of Camembert mixed with cream and other secrets. We drank a magnum, of Corton Bressandes 1964; Taylor's 1960 was then mingled with bin ends of magnums.

At midnight we moved from the table into the drawing-room. During the two hours of ensuing laughter, contented chat, occasionally punctuated by half-remembered literary quotes on Norman's part, we managed a bottle of Bollinger, non-vintage. In a final burst of enthusiasm a bottle of Krug 1959 was opened at around two a.m. One of Norman's guests fell flat on the doorstep having misjudged some black ice. Norman himself, precariously swaying halfway up a flight of stairs on his way to bed, was given a timely tug by Rosh with her walking stick. We slept like logs and drove back to London the following morning, full of admiration for the zestful and generous way of life prevailing at Park House.

February 6 Hardwicke House

With time and money at a tight premium these days, there is little climate for nurturing the eccentric in man. Eccentricity has always been considered a well-deserved luxury of old age. After a lifetime of distinguished service, scholarship, artistic or literary prowess, a man might be allowed to slacken his grip; to chase perhaps some foible, whim, or mild madness. The older heroes of today do not appear to have such licence. Those who have written, composed, played instruments, advocated justice or painted pictures, for the most part continue to do so. Success has become the hard-gained product of self-discipline and consistent output. Idleness has lost its art, bills and taxes have to be paid.

Sir John Foster QC, stooped in age and salutary experience, practises still. Last year he unravelled the protracted Russell Baby case. Artur Rubinstein performs as dexterously as ever, and without the aid of elastoplast. (Both Joseph Cooper and Alfred Brendel, younger men, bind thumbs and finger-tips with plaster before a performance.) 'I wind it round the base of my thumbs,' Joseph Cooper explained to me. 'Perhaps it is just a psychological habit. Nobody notices; if they do I say I caught my hand in the mower. In fact I think I am missing a joint down there and the plaster strengthens my octate grip. Now Alfred Brendel's finger-tips are almost permanently bound in elastoplast. Incredible, isn't it?'

Beverley Nichols is currently absorbed in another final autobiography. We spent the day at the Colindale Newspaper Museum last week. 'I want to look up my articles in the *Sunday Chronicle* from 1932 to 1936.' When we were settled with the pertinent papers, Beverley urged me to read page 2 of every edition: his page. However the pages 6 proved far more interesting; they sported a serial on Lawrence of Arabia.

Teddy Croft-Murray, one-time Keeper of the Drawings of the British Museum, leads a busy life with his collection of eighteenth-century fiddles, watches and his Regency spectacles in silver frames. He has kept a diary since youth, recording his travels, and has illustrated them with jotted sketches – an Italian fireplace, a pillar pediment, or peasant. Teddy delights in dress. Fur and velvet are favourite touches to his wardrobe, and the fiddle a favourite pastime. He plays it at the local eighteenth-century church on Christmas morning. A near-eccentric?

Lord Huntingdon continues painting his murals. 'Of course England is the wrong country for such a hobby as mine; the weather is all wrong. On the other hand we can thank the rain for stirring England to the greatest literary achievement of the world.' (His paintings are pretty eccentric.)

June 12 Hardwicke House

With a plethora of pageantry, street parties and exuberant decoration strewn over London, we have just celebrated 'Jubilee Week'. The Queen has reigned for twenty-five years. With her consistent standards of self-discipline, good humour, and tireless public performance she has served us better than we sometimes deserve. She looked radiant in her role, which constituted a week packed with monarchical events. She was obviously moved and delighted by the spontaneous crowds as were her subjects by her rare stamina, her approachability and, frankly, her glamour.

Dressed in a bright green coat and a headscarf the Queen first lit a huge bonfire at Windsor Castle; this promoted a circuit of fires to blaze across the country. This initiating ceremony took place at 10.30 p.m. on Monday, June 6. She then drove to Buckingham Palace to appear the next morning in her golden coach. At 10.40 she was driven to the Service of Commemoration at St Paul's Cathedral. She wore strawberry pink with a hat of twenty-five pink silk bells to mark each year of her reign. Prince Charles rode on horseback behind his parents. He confessed later that he was so mesmerised by the spokes of the carriage wheels that when it finally stopped he nearly fell off. The service was splendid and solemn; the Queen looked a little pale, understandably tired and momentarily sad. She then walked through the crowded streets to Guildhall for a banquet lunch. Vivacious, gracious and wreathed in smiles, she chatted away to the Mayor and to the crowd. One small boy presented her with a drawing of her carriage which she took happily, handing it over to her aide a few yards further on. No security measures could have saved her from a single madman's attack.

Speeches at lunch; a banquet the following day at Buckingham Palace for the members of the Commonwealth; a river party the day after, with walks ashore at Deptford; tea at Lambeth Palace; a galaxy of fireworks that night on the Thames; endless late-night appearances on the Palace balcony and a morning ride on her horse to rehearse for her most personally exacting performance of all: the Birthday Parade. This took place in grey weather which terminated in a cloudburst. The Queen led her troops up the Mall and later appeared on the balcony to see the aircraft salute. She was again rewarded with a jam-packed audience. The Mall swarmed with waving arms and flags as she watched from above with her family. The planes flew past, spewing tails of red, white and blue smoke. As the memories of this week recede and Britain takes up the reins of everyday living, let us be thankful for a good and caring Queen; one who has a highly competent understanding of the political scene. In her speech at Guildhall, she referred to her 'Salad Days, when I was green in judgement'. Twenty-five years on, with the passing experience of her prime ministers, she should be a wise counsellor to her future ones.

July Quenby Hall Loughborough Leicestershire

'Let us forget the tax man and dance till dawn. Ladies dress up!'

Edith de Lisle, a petite Peruvian, with an abundance of joie de vivre, was determined to give her friends a whale of a time. Women were encouraged to wear tiaras and to dress in blue, red, white or silver. The tiaras became an issue of mild controversy. Not that Leicestershire society did not own their fair share; they felt it non de rigueur to sport them alongside men in dinner jackets and no decorations. However, a splash of tiaras did adorn the event and one young Grenadier even pinned an elegant Royal Insignia on the centre of his eye patch (a wound sustained during his term in Belfast).

Gerard and Edith de Lisle bought Quenby Hall, the venue for this splendid ball, some three years ago from Sir Harold Nutting. Gerard, half-French, had suddenly inherited 7,000 acres in Leicestershire and the handsome wherewithal to settle in Quorn country. Local eyebrows were raised when he referred to himself in the telephone directory as 'Squire de Lisle', along with numerous numbers. In fact, the de Lisles fast became the butt of many wry asides as they set up their conspicuous way of life. However, when it was a question of a ball and a picnic lunch the following day at the Temple of Venus (an eighteenth-century stone folly set high on a windy hill above Loughborough) there were few refusals.

The de Lisles' hospitality knew no bounds. We were piped up the stone steps into the Elizabethan hall. Sombrely kilted, they played hard. The bare-chested, male–only band in the ballroom could hardly match them for spirit and clamour. A huge crowd of guests swarmed through the Elizabethan rooms, where tapestries, new silk curtains (said to be made by Edith herself), paintings, which would no doubt benefit from the smoke of more such evenings (they had been over-cleaned), comfortable knole sofas, and a hefty expanse of oak to lean on whetted our appetites for the night to come.

We sipped champagne for two hours before being ushered in to a swagged royal blue tent where some 800 guests were placed at separate tables, each name meticulously written by hand. Said John Mackinnon, a past master at enjoying the best of everything: 'They have even spelt my wife's name right – Susana with no double "n" or "h", a thoroughly good show.' Somebody introduced me to the Duke of Rutland. 'Do you live round here?' he asked me. I replied not. 'I didn't think so; you wouldn't last long.' He was gone before I could pursue what might have been a promising conversation.

The buffet tables were laden with every delicacy. A thick coat of caviar masked the soft yellow glaze of the lobster mayonnaise. The strawberries were heaped high in blue and white Wedgwood-style meringue-made bowls. The Jubilee motif of red, white and blue festooned every corner, pillar and person.

We danced and drank exuberantly until dawn. There were more beautiful women than men. In my opinion it was Isobel Barnet who particularly shone. Her chiselled bone structure and superb carriage commanded attention. We left at four a.m, funking the band in the dungeon and the breakfast of soup and croissants.

The next morning we stumbled up the hill for more delectable seafood and caviar-laden mayonnaise. Abysmal weather blew and flattened our hair to rats'-tails. But the sense of revelry ensued undaunted. We satiated ourselves on specially-bottled vin rosé, turkey quiches, and a particularly good ruin of raspberry-filled meringue. We threw off our shoes and danced in the rain. Some threw buns. Back at Quenby Hall, 1,500 associates of the Red Cross and attendant invalids were enjoying the splendid marquee. Edith would be giving exactly the same party next year, it was rumoured.

August Dalcross Castle Croy Inverness-shire

Sun-filled, halcyon summer days. The rose granite seventeenth-century walls of the castle encompass a bevy of friends, children and dogs. The kitchen gardens overflow with bulbous raspberries, and lawns fling comfort to bodies stretched out in the heat. The castle is dim and cool; stone stairs spiral to bedrooms big and small, with dressing tables tucked in turrets. A log fire burns continuously in the high-ceilinged drawing-room, a dark room with deep sofas and heavy red-ruched blinds. The pink bedroom is haunted, the yellow room lists, and the green room buzzes with bees from a nearby swarm.

And did we hear the footsteps on the stairs? With the castle full of children it is impossible to discern any haunting steps. A gust of wind, coupled with the deep, uneven tread of the staircase, certainly can give an illusion of a shove, a push. Despite local interest in how we are making out at haunted Dalcross Castle, we feel no qualms.

Dalcross has been owned by the Mackintosh family for 300 years. The first owners, the Frasers, lost it over a game of cards. The story goes of a young man from the victorious Mackintosh family standing one day in the pink room. He was watching a fight at the Castle front between the two families when he rushed from the room, down the three flights of stairs to bolt the main door and portcullis; he was shot dead as he rounded the last steps.

We wake early. The sun streams through our emerald taffeta curtains, turning them bright lime; the air is champagne. We row on lochs, we plunge in, swim ashore, and picnic. We stretch out on rocks and fish from them. One day the water is so still, it reflects every sunbeam, its surface hard and blazing, a brilliant mirror. The surrounding whorls of rock slap back the heat. Provence with Cézanne close by? Was this really Scotland? Children paddle fearlessly over smooth, round stones. Dogs[2] splash in the silver rills of shallow rivers and drink the clear, peaty water, their coats as sleek as toffee. Another day, a 'soft' day of rain. The loch is puckered and shaved by capricious jabs of wind. Grey and unfathomable, it forbids idle play. The river flows swiftly; the water rises by the hour. The rocks are scuffed with mud-churning water; logs and branches are swung haphazardly along as furious water sucks and hurls. Where there are no rocks, it swells in silent, hefty muscles, powerful, sullen and friend of none.

The carefree month slips by. We drink fabulously from Tom's southern-borne cellar. There is bridge and backgammon and talk late into the nights.

October Afghanistan

Midday in Kabul is hung with dust and haze. The Afghans rest in groups by the side of pot-holed, dried mud roads; the crumbling façades of their primitive shops are boarded up until the evening trade. They bow their turbaned heads and embroidered skull caps over worry beads, chess, trays of tea and crawling babies. The Kabul river weaves a desultory course through the centre of the town. Earlier in the day women have parted their sombre veils to wash bright-coloured clothes in its turgid flow; strips of saffron cotton, beetroot-red, slate-blue and vivid purple are left stretched out to dry on the baked grass banks. Some men take drinks in the shaded Barbur Shah gardens, enclaved by the dun-coloured stone of the old city walls. Dishevelled marble steps and terraces descend through terracotta pots of red geraniums, petunias, and rose gardens, thrown together in haphazard abundance. Three simple fountains faintly screen the hushed fever of Kabul below. In the British Embassy compound there are tall old trees and lawns, large wicker chairs and flowered borders; tea and silver spoons, scones and strawberry jam; the rocking scent of white tobacco plants, holly-hock and rose, shades of Sussex and the British Raj.

With the evening cool, old men pull loaded carts again, ramshackle stalls thrust out fruit and nuts, bulbous tassels of grapes and huge pale melons, marrows and pomegranates on groaning trestle tables. The town is seized with children's games and cries, men and women bargain. The night falls fast in its autumn chill and the mountains etch a stark surround. The dawn will see Kabul refreshed and cool, set in

[2] Porridge, our golden retriever, frolicked so long in the loch on one occasion that the children's nanny announced: 'Porridge has been in long enough.' This moment was published in Jilly Cooper's book *Class* 1979.

a scoop of rose and limpid light, caught in a moment of quiet and prayer before the heat and work raise dust again. Kabul has no architectural beauty, but embodies a monument to the daily craft of living.

From Kabul we flew north in a twin-otter over the Hindu-Kush mountains to Bam-i-Yan. It was dawn. We were the only two passengers, together with a cargo of two thousand hens' eggs. The sun rose promptly; the chocolate pudding mountains glowed with that rosy amethyst light, peculiar to the Eastern world. The steward gave us strong mint tea, as we strained to see the green ribbons of hidden valleys that meander through that impenetrable mountain range.

We soon landed at the village of Bam-i-Yan and were shown our yourt where we would spend the night. It was made from stripped, curved poplar trunks, with a domed roof of goat's hair and rugs, topped with pristine white canvas. In the evening an old man beat off the day's accumulated dust with the leafy branch of a poplar.

We wandered through this remote settlement and stood before the Great Buddha, a monolithic carving hewn out of the face of red mountain rock. It was sculptured during the 3rd or early 4th centuries AD and stands 175 feet. The finely-moulded drapes and folds of the tunic fall to the knees where the massive legs stand squarely embedded in feet with insteps ten feet high. To the right of the Great Buddha loom the ruins of the ancient city of Gholghola standing high on a mound above the valley. From the crumbled soldiers' garrison and the ravaged look-out towers, we watched the village activity below. Oxen threshed the wheat, dragging flat round stones back and forth, while veiled women tossed their sieves and winnowed the grain in the evening breeze – like dancers waving tambourines. The fretted grain grew in gleaming piles beside them. Strings of donkeys ferried balanced loads of firewood, stooks of hay, plump-filled water skins, poplar logs, potatoes and dung-compressed discs for the mud-hut evening fire.

And the oxen drew the wooden plough, leaving the dark soil moist and furled in their plodding wake. Darkness fell as we descended this rough deserted hill. A wizened potter, bending low over his swirling wheel in the shadow of the red mountain, raised his eyes from his encampment of pots and water jugs, eyes glazed with concentration and blood-shot from the dust. Children scampered through his wares like mice; he nodded to the small girl who fixed each curved handle to its neck with slim, deft fingers.

An Afghani with a Peugeot car took us through the heat of the next day from Bam-i-Yan to the miraculous cobalt-blue lakes of Band-e-Amir, a seventy-five-mile drive over white stone dusty roads. A harsh and arid landscape of mud-baked plains. Hard to believe that in spring this vast bleached desert would emerge emerald with grass and rain.

We passed a dishevelled train of nomads, 'Savage, desperate peoples,'
muttered our driver as we rattled along. Only a month ago, he told
us, German tourists driving independently had been viciously attacked.
Their car had broken down as the night closed in on this same lonely
road. Nomads had loomed up and shot them in the legs making off
with wallets and watches. Then there was the American family who
had inadvertently run over a nomad child. They stopped to tend him
when the nomads fell on the car and without a murmur dragged out
a child of equivalent age and slit his throat. Our driver's stories took
on an added morbidity as we passed a posse of hillside graves, each
marked with slate and stone on the face of the loveless, lunar landscape.
Babies die of cold, he assured us, and mothers are kidnapped, ransoms
go unfulfilled and other wives are bought. Our attention was further
arrested by more nomads on the nearside road, busily disembowelling
a cow. The fat and muscle gleamed red and white, a livid prey to the
midday sun and knives. It was with some relief that we saw the cobalt–
blue glimmer of the famous lakes ahead.

The heat was intense and the shimmer from the vast red encircling
rocks that plunged sheer into the 700-foot-deep lakes was hung with
a fierce silence. Five lakes in all, flat round plates and mirror-smooth.
They say a girl from Yorkshire once dived in and she was shot. We
later took the same road back to Bam-i-Yan where the night temperature had dropped to 2° centigrade. We arrived at our yourt exhausted
and caked in the white dust of the road – like split, slumped sacks of
flour.

Early next day we were driven through the mountain valleys of the
Salang Pass, bound back to Kabul. The peasants with their mongoloid
features and slim strong bodies were busy with their land and produce;
women and children, oxen and donkeys worked in biblical harmony.
Ploughed potato fields gave way to harvested plains and tall poplar
avenues. Wide, bouldered rivers frothed through gorges and dwindled
to veins of sapphire. The jade-green of the eucalyptus, the amethyst
clouds of the receding mountains and the blond gleam of the grain
soothed the eye with gentle colour, it was a rare and lovely landscape.

As we drove down the valleys, nearing the comparative heat of
Kabul, the crops became thick with fruit and nuts, apricots and mulberries, walnuts and almonds, and the stained carpets of drying grapes.
The villages became more lively. Women crouched in veiled huddles,
their slim, fluttering fingers shelling the almond haul. Swarthy men
rested beneath mulberry trees and cradled their hands in stony steams,
rubbing teeth and toes before they prayed. They ate in shaded shacks,
a simple meal of unleavened bread with a matt and corrugated crust,
they dipped the bread in thin hot soup and wiped the small bowls

clean. They chewed on dried mulberries. And around them lay the fields of hot swept dust, carpeted with lush cool clumps of grapes, where the sun and night would chill and suck and wrest the juice to turn each raisin, brown, amethyst and purple. Children were spewing out of schools. There were bicycles propped by street bazaars and luridly-painted lorries ferried potatoes, tree trunks, wool and peasants to Kabul. Strings of nomads trailed along with camels piled high with chickens, grandmothers and children, and every bare provision, wending their way to the warmer winter of Jalalabad. Herds of motley-coloured sheep and loaded donkeys followed close behind. And so we reached Kabul again, a basin of faded colour, of rhythm and clamour, echoing with its hive of humanity, thrust back from that huge impassive mountain range.

December Hardwicke House

The darkening days bound inexorably towards Christmas. Into the maze of recalcitrant fairy lights, the intricacies of marzipan, chestnut stuffing, shopping and wrapping, we hurl ourselves, loving it and hating it, everybody doing it, there is no way of evading it. Friends and parties flash by in a kaleidoscope of glitter, fun, effort and exhaustion.

At a private dinner party, Margaret Thatcher, swathed in pale blue, talks sense in a normal voice and listens attentively to Tom's observations on the Middle East.

'The Iranians do not consider themselves Arabs,' she volunteered. She had also realised that she could not tactfully visit Iran and Jordan on the same itinerary. She was planning two separate journeys in the coming year, it would be expensive – but what could she do? She clearly needs more briefing on her respective deserts.

1978

Wreathed in fat smiles and with a comfortable bosom, her dark hair scooped in a bun, our landlady swept us into her warm farmhouse. We had driven through the night to the north-east of Poland. Our plane had landed five hours late in Warsaw and we apologised for keeping her awake. No problem, she assured us, she had dozed 'like a chicken'. Her friendly dachshund, named Frog, bundled ahead.

We were a party of eleven men and myself. We were three Poles, three Americans, and five Dutch. I was the only non-shooting guest accompanying this motley crew on a wild boar shoot. The temperature was 10 degrees below zero and the snow was thick and layered solid. We were glad to arrive.

Amid general bonhomie we unpacked and sipped vodka and hot drinks. The men were sleeping three to a room; my own bedroom resembled a private room in an English cottage hospital, green paint and lino, but with the luxury of a warm duvet.

Despite the long journey we were dressed at seven a.m. and break-fasted hugely on Polish sausage, eggs, white cheese, and thick bread, ladled with black cherry jam. Poland had run short of coffee and I had been detailed to bring Nescafé from England. It was a good meal.

We set off for the forests in a range-rover and an assortment of tractor-driven vans. The young beaters were thirty-strong, wearing bright orange tunics; it was a change from chopping wood. Our spirits were high as we flanked the wood in strategic positions, 200 yards apart, intent on silence and waiting.

Leszek scraped the snow from under our feet and we stood on solid, damp earth. The scrunch of snow if one made a sudden turn could head a boar away and one might even topple, gun in hand, on a slippery pad. The early-morning light was bleak and sunless. The pine-trees soared tall above; the fir-trees were thick with snow, the oak vied with the pine in strong, slender trunks. A beater hollered beyond. More cries and the blast of horns. We stood erect and tense. Several footprints of red deer, fox and boar belied the silence of the forests. Suddenly the dry crackle of a snapped twig and a deer leapt through the trees; a shot in the distance, and another. Loud cries from the beaters grew more spasmodic.

We relaxed and gathered in groups. Two boar had been shot, females only. They were being disembowelled, deflated in death, their warm blood was spattered, freezing on the snow. They were yanked on to a horse-drawn sleigh. We climbed aboard and cosseted ourselves with rugs, swigs of vodka and lively exchanges of shots missed and still to come. The wagons and sleighs hissed over the heavy crust of snow. We passed through wide avenues to the next drives and set up our positions. In each man there was the overriding desire to shoot his boar. It was do or die. Wine, women and song, forget it! After four drives and as many dead targets we hoved to for lunch. The beaters built up a huge fire and snow wept at its hearth. Men rubbed hands and noses, stamped their feet and held out gloves and boots on sticks to the flames. Gallons of hot, red soup, hunks of bread and sausage and the ubiquitous vodka put the guts back into chaps. They were off again.

It was dark each day by four o'clock. At six we were huddled in the warm and steamed-up dining-room eating a three-course dinner. Duck soup, roast goose or boar and stewed wild strawberries – a typical meal. The Americans were tucked up in duvets by eight o'clock. We lingered at the table, talking, drinking and playing backgammon. We laughed a lot at simple jokes.

The farmhouse was situated in the village of Borki, near Kranklanki, in the province of Augustow. Originally German territory this part of Poland boasts vast pine forests, interspersed with lakes and rolling steppes. The solid, stuccoed houses incorporate a wealth of granite. Many foundations of farm buildings are built on hewn blocks of rose and green, naturally-tinted stone. The upper stories are completed in the local red clay brick. They are pleasant buildings. Modern houses are constructed with breeze blocks of cement, slapped with cream, rose or pale-green paint. The wooden Noah's ark-type houses, small and more picturesque, are dotted over the flat central steppes. A varied and pleasing landscape, where the villagers look fit and reasonably cheerful. The women and children are gaily clothed in knitted wool hats and anoraks.

One day the sun shone high and clear. The early-morning rose light suffused the snow with colour and turned the shadows blue. My horse was strong but well-tempered and we rode hard. Intoxicated by the wide avenues, thick with soft snow that seared straight through the pines, we galloped alone. We jumped fallen tree trunks, walked slowly through narrow rides and galloped again. Time stood still in that alien snow and silence, where animal footprints lay frozen and unclaimed.

Our party shot seventeen boar in five days. Braced with fresh air and conquest we took leave of our magnanimous châtelaine and headed for Warsaw. Stàs Czartoryski, a Prince from the past régime, and one of our number, invited us to lunch at his home near Warsaw. His petite, attractive wife Kristina plied us with smoked salmon, excellent boeuf Stroganoff, red wines and vodka. We sat in their glorified Nissen hut, where the modest walls were hung with prints of Czartoryski palaces and richly-clad ancestors. We mused on the guts and capabilities of this resourceful couple.

Unlike many Poles of his generation, Stàs had elected to stay in his country. He and Kristina have eked out a viable existence from the jaws of the Communist bureaucrats. Their endeavours have included breeding turkeys, which proved a lucrative trade with embassies and restaurants. After a period of five years they were ordered to close this line of business. Stàs next involved himself in market gardening and carnation-growing. He has since built up an equally impressive and lucrative business, which is causing concern with the Communist régime. Stàs is philosophical and, in accordance with the cunning of the Comintern, has built up his own. It is the same with every Pole. They appear to have preserved their own identity and spirit more than any other Communist satellite. They argue and complain irrepressibly in the fish queue. When the government raised food prices 100% overnight in the autumn of 1976, they revolted wholesale and sent the edict packing. Prices were reverted immediately and the bureaucrats licked their panic; they realised that the Polish worker wielded more power than they had appreciated. The general food shortage is a butt for many a strike. The men came out in protest at the food queues and position themselves to wait instead of their wives, effectively disbanding all tools for that day. It was recently reported in the British press that the Polish government is now encouraging private enterprise from home and cottage industry. They envisage that economic blame will then be partially levelled at the individual. The indomitable spirit of the peasant has also overthrown the hierarchy's bid to oust collective farming and for the extinction of village life. 8% of the land is now privately owned by the farmers; village life (although private gatherings in the church hall are still forbidden) is being gradually reinstated.

But Warsaw must today be regarded as the most staggering monument to the Polish people. Razed to the ground by the Germans in the second world war, the old quarter of the city has been completely restored to its original fifteenth-century structure. The squares look totally unscathed by previous devastation and recent repair.

Well done, that man who successfully stored the original plans and surveys from the ravages of war.

February 10 London

It is interesting that Sussy, a member of a distinguished Qajar family in Iran, chose to be married in London. Indeed many Iranians from the deposed Qajar dynasty are spending more and more time and money in London. They buy flats and houses and one assumes they will also acquire land. The Shah, having stripped them of their former holdings, can offer no incentive for future aggrandizement in his re-shuffled priorities. The Qajar Society for Teheran are free to conduct their own business and remaining money on a worldwide basis. A tax of £1,000 is incurred each time they leave the country, with the insidious inducement of a free eleventh trip; this poses a popular target. They mix freely with the diplomatic world in Teheran and entertain in a comparatively lavish style (although servants are now on a slope of extinction). These rich Iranians have become progressively more anxious and restless with their restricted conditions. The habitual hassle of disorganised services in Teheran's urban life, the sycophantic obligations to the Shah and his régime, and their own total exemption from political power is fast proving the Qajar's nadir. In no place in the world has their former life-style become more irrelevant than in their own country.

And this old, sophisticated seam of Teheran society was conspicuously absent from the Cultural Festival held in their country last September/through October 1977. Under the combined aegis of the British and Iranian governments, with HRH Princess Alexandra, the Shahbanou and the Princess Fatimeh presiding over ceremonies, there transpired three unprecedented weeks of art and music and literary culture. Each performance and exhibition was well-conceived in elegance and efficiency. One particular event is highlighted in my memory.

The Royal Ballet Corps of Covent Garden sent over their leading artists – notably Merle Park and Michael Coleman – to stage a gala performance of Ashton's *La Fille mal gardée*. There are 850 seats in Rudaki Hall, 150 of which were occupied by the Shah's secret police – Savak. Those of us who had managed to obtain tickets had to produce our passports at the door. We were subsequently seated an hour before the arrival of the Shahbanou, Princess Alexandra and Princess Fatimeh. Rudaki Hall is a severe contrast to the lush red and gilt of Covent Garden, the whole being painted in battleship grey with a lino floor. Soft drinks were served in the interval.

The curtain rose to Barry Wordsworth conducting the music by Hérold with a very adequate Iranian orchestra. We were sitting in the front row with a member of Savak on my right; they are an easily recognised breed; stocky, short with crinkly black hair and busy eyes. It was soon apparent that my neighbour had a cough; one of the unpredictable tickles in the throat that became impossible to quell in pianissimo moments. He spluttered uncomfortably beside me, when finally I rummaged in my bag for throat lozenges. I offered him one; he brushed it aside suspiciously. I took one myself and with his next bout of unsuppressed coughing he grudgingly changed his mind; whereupon I gave him a handful. At performance end the stage was bombarded with yellow and red rose heads. Some minion had clearly been detailed to disgorge a huge drum of them from a balcony. He performed this task with a sober face at punctuated intervals. No bunches were allowed for fear of hand grenades concealed within. It was a stiff and reserved evening with the audience inhibited in their applause. However, our British ambassador, Sir Anthony Parsons[1], afterwards assured us that the Royal Box was glowing like 1,000-watt bulbs.

March 1 Floors Castle Kelso Roxburghshire, and Mellerstain

With the furniture valuation at Floors Castle finally completed we drove down the road and eyed Mellerstain, the superb Adam house, a seat of the Haddingtons. It is now lived in by their son, Lord Binning. We didn't know him and the house was closed to the public until May. We would love to return another day. It looked enticing, set back from the road, in lawns and fields. We felt frustrated as we turned the car away.

The next morning we met up with Hugh Roberts[2], from Christie's furniture department. He wanted to see round Floors and to fill in any gaps of our descriptions with his first-hand knowledge of makers' initials. We mentioned the elusive Mellerstain; had he ever seen inside?

'But my sister-in-law is the groom! I will ring her up and we can have dinner with her!'

This chance proximity – by stable door or by any other door – to our prized goal was a splendid revelation. That evening Hugh telephoned Mellerstain. Lady Binning answered and promptly asked us all to dinner. As we drove to Mellerstain, Hugh disclosed that Binning was planning to shoot a roe deer in order that we could eat the liver for dinner.

[1] Served in Iran 1974–79, to the fall of the Shah. He became UK Permanent Representative to the United Nations 1979–82. His book *The Pride and the Fall* was published in 1984.
[2] Director of the Royal Collection and Surveyor of the Queen's Works of Art since 1996. KCVO 2001.

The house was in darkness save for the converted stable block. We crossed the side-lawn to an open door where a gamekeeper stood talking to a dishevelled figure. I introduced myself rather diffidently. Was this his lordship? I presumed right and Binning in a mild and affable manner waved us through his threshold, over a large pool of blood; the aftermath of the extracted liver. Yes, there it lay, seeping on a plate. On closer inspection, Binning's hands were still smeared in blood; it was all very informal. We need not have rushed.

Lady Binning, dressed in jeans, looked up from chopping cabbage. She took us through to their cheerful sitting-room. They had held the meet at the house that morning and she was all behind as they say. Binning poured us drinks and Prue Binning lit the log fire. Their dogs ambled around and selected the most comfortable sofas. Binning sat in a bemused brown study; he was a silent man. We were startled when he suddenly stood to dramatic attention, staring fixedly at his gin and tonic. 'I hate gin!' he muttered morosely and, shuffling in his stockinged feet, he threw the remaining contents on to the roaring fire.

'Oh! Binning,' remonstrated the glorious Prue, 'not again.'

'I dropped my ash in it,' explained our host. 'Who is cooking my liver?'

Annie, the groom, announced that all was under control and that dinner would be ready in an hour.

'We are always in a state of chaos when Annie has had a few days off. The horses take forever.' And Prue stood by the fire gyrating on her heels to the background music, twisting her thick gold hair into a loose plait. 'Would you like to see the house? And then we can all relax and get warm again.'

Binning opened door after door and we revelled and murmured happily at the precise splendour of it all. The Adam ceilings, newly-painted in their original colours of Wedgwood greens and mauves and palest yellows, were perfectly restored. But oh! how flat and opaquely dull compared to those similar painted ceilings in Italy, where the colour is alive and subtle, receding here, more pronounced there, a suggestion of tempera and age.

The Adam Rooms had an admirable air of imminent daily life. Fine furniture of the period with Italian pictures from the Salting Bequest[3] were in generous supply. One painting particularly caught Hugh's attention. 'Who is that one by, would you suppose?' he enquired of

---

[3] George Salting, a member of the last Lady Haddington's family, collected well and widely from London picture dealers in the early 1900s. In February 1902 he commissioned Agnews to bid for the Franz Hals *Portrait of a Gentleman*. It fetched £3,780 and was presented to the National Gallery to enrich the collection of the Salting Bequest.

the amiable Binning. Our noble host gave the impression of mild uninterest in his heritage, but an enduring dedication to assuaging other people's. 'Some fellow, I forget his name, something like Paravicini.' With this final pearl of improbable information we wandered back to the stable block and promising smells of dinner.

We had a jolly meal in the kitchen and Prue Binning with her striking fresh beauty looked completely happy with her lot. We ate excellent game soup and warmed Arabic bread; they hadn't been able to find baps in Kelso that day. Annie rose from the scrubbed pine table and sliced the liver, it cut like butter. Then fried it lightly on the spot. Binning sat silent and smiling at the head of the table. He seemed well-satisfied with the combined handiwork of picking one's dinner from the woods and having it cooked by one's girl groom a mere two hours later.

Conversation flowed in happy non-sequiturs when Binning abruptly switched our attention to clones and chromosomes and witchcraft. His eyes lit up as he talked in halting, breathless bursts, of ghost stories, true, read and half-remembered. 'Ghosts really make Binning tick,' explained Prue. He left the table. Where had he gone? Prue shrugged unconcernedly. A few moments later he returned, grinning mysteriously, clutching a small leather-bound book of seventeenth-century ghost stories. He began to read in level tones of chests dancing across rooms and of children being shaken off their beds. It brought the evening to a natural conclusion and we had a long drive south the next day.

June 2 Hardwicke House

The Queen stood on the red velvet-festooned balcony of Buckingham Palace tonight. She was dazzling in flame chiffon and an explosion of diamonds. Her smile, her skin, and her hair exuded radiance. Sir Cecil Beaton has often commented on the special sheen of the Queen's skin. Prince Philip was at her side, together with Prince Charles and Princess Anne, whose thick, blonde hair was coiled in a gleaming chignon. They waved to the ecstatic crowd from their floodlit eyrie. The lights snapped out and a lavish display of fireworks splintered the night sky to commemorate twenty-five years of the Queen's reign. The crowd were thrilled and would call her back to the balcony again. 'We want the Queen!' She appeared twice only; her magic must not wane. Tomorrow she faces the rigours of her official Birthday Parade.

June 2, 1953, was a wet, mean day. I watched the Coronation procession with my mother. We sat high up in a Regent Street dress shop. I was particularly impressed by the fat and jolly Queen of Tonga and distinctly remember eating a chocolate éclair as she rolled by below. The grey slurry in the street gutters of wet, squashed newspapers amazed me. How could people have spent such an uncomfortable night of it? I was full of admiration – the thrill, the mingled horror, and delight of the outside world. Boarding school in safe, green Gloucestershire seemed a travesty.

June 3 Hardwicke House

After the wettest May we can remember the sun has blazed on us for a whole week. Fields and banks are foaming with Queen Anne's lace and buttercups. Walls and balconies drip with wisteria and clematis; the air is heavy with their swaying scent. It is strange to recall the heat and hassle of the Middle East. We returned a week ago.

Baghdad was a sad, untidy place. Why had I envisaged faded green copper cupolas, palm groves and fountains, and men in bright turbans sipping cardamom coffee as they played chess on quiet street corners?

The best hotel in town sported the following stern indictment over its entrance: 'The workers of Iraq condemn hireling Sadat.' Our bedroom was dirty and forbidding with a noisy and ineffectual air conditioner. A policewoman conducting traffic below our window with a microphone added to the joyless atmosphere. Later in the drab dining-room the waiters seemed cheerful and almost apologetic; many of them were Egyptian. I practised a little Arabic on them. 'But you must never say "mabsut" here,' I was warned. 'Mabsut means happy in every Arab country except Iraq. Here it means 'kill him'. (I later discovered they meant 'kilim', a type of thinly woven rug.)

We visited the Iraq Museum[4], a comprehensive, well-presented collection of bones, jewellery, pots and Roman remains. We were foiled in our attempts to visit Hatra, the first-century AD Roman city. We would have to wait until Friday. The bus only went once a week, no private cars were available. Private cars were forbidden.

Baghdad has a rich history and culture. Its oil reserves are second only to Saudi Arabia's and may well survive the longest. Its present system and consequent social demise is due to Communism. Baghdad today is totally overrun by Russian infiltration. Its Baathist régime had ringed the city with guns, and Russian-designed consumer and industrial goods are given pride of display in the main street. Every Iraqi of

---

[4] The Iraq National Museum in Baghdad was pillaged during the British and USA invasion, March 2003. In November 2005, 11,500 objects were reported still at large. (*Culture at risk* by Alastair Northedge in the *Art Newspaper*.)

former position and private means has fled his country. We did the same.

Our spirits soared in Jordan's sunny Amman, a tidy, modern city built on mounds. Needle pines and dense-leaved acacia gave shade and breeze along the well-surfaced streets. Many villas, newly–built in the local honey stone, spread out from the town; they were large and opulent and set to stay. Our hotel was luxurious, and the atmosphere relaxed.

Every Jordanian has a job. He enjoys the relative peace and pros-perity induced by King Hussein (who himself was trained at Sand-hurst). A small country with a population of two million, King Hussein wants to keep it that way. The inclusion of half a million Bedouins and half a million misplaced Palestinians are the main outstanding problem. The east bank of the Jordan river has been a militarised zone since the six-day Israeli war of 1967. From high above these parched and rolling hills it is impossible to see the tanks and soldiers hidden in their folds.

We were standing on Mount Nebo where Moses struck up a spring of water. An old man in a voluminous brown dish-dasher strolled towards us with a key in his hand. We had come to see the mosaics in the Church? But first he showed us his binoculars, his whistle, and his gun; they hung haphazardly on his shoulder. His King had armed him. He beamed with pride and next showed us his little girls. They giggled shyly in bright shawls and tunics and then ran off to their primitive stone house and brought out a mug of thick white labaneh; a cheese milk processed from their goat. We took a sip. How old were they? The biggest, declared the old man, was born during the six-day war and the others came after. Arabs have little idea of their own age.

We entered the cool church built up by itinerant monks in the sixth century AD. The cream and green, the coral and ochre, of the local hill stones had been magically transformed into a floor of flowing Byzantine animal mosaics. Fruits and detailed scenes of wine-harvesting were also depicted, each stem and curve mocking the precise effort of chiselling each small square. One floor had only been discovered this past year. Since 100 BC it had lain covered by a layer of stone, protected against alien marauders. It was smooth and fresh, each stone intact over the uneven floor It was the strangest sensation to look at such an ancient creation in mint preservation.

We came out into the bright, dry sunshine. The old man gave us his precious binoculars. In turn we scanned the Mount of Olives across the Jordan river and strained to see the towers of Jerusalem; mere pinpricks in the sky above the mountains. We drove on down to the

Dead Sea; it was quiet and empty on the stony beach. Israel simmered beyond that flat, warm plate of water and Jericho was smothered in haze across the Jordan river. The water was crystal-clear with sleeping black mud in places; there were many coloured stones, rounded and comfortable to the feet, pink, yellow, indigo, and blue. I crouched in the warm water where nothing lives. It is said the extreme salt has beneficial properties for skin and eyes. I stung all over and fought with the buoyant water. My legs flailed in the air as I tried the breast-stroke. Instead I sat in the water, helpless as a baby strapped in a chair. The stinging abated and I stepped ashore, much refreshed, with a white beard rimming my chin.

We saw the Arabian stones in the museum on the hill in Amman; agates worn as healing agents for inflammation of desert-scanning eyes; dark-green 'love' stones worn as an aid to conception and safe delivery in childbirth (always available from the local crone); blackish green stones to be worn at the throat, as a cure for tonsillitis; transparent glass beads worn as friendly talismans; dark-brown stones for warding off headaches; creamy 'milk' beads to induce lactation; and pale-grey beads for healing an abscess or any skin infection. One would be immune to all ills with such a string in the medicine cupboard.

We saw Petra, 'the Lost City'. Re-discovered by the intrepid Jean-Louis Burkhardt in the heat of August 1812, and immortalised in many minds by J W Burgon's 'a rose-red city, half as old as time . . .'

We staggered on horseback through the Siq, a narrow ravine, its sheer craggy sides 200 feet high. Oleander, eucalyptus and fig, half-smothered in dust, veiled the rock face. Our guide, Mohammed, walked beside us with a proprietary air. (There was not one part of my body he had not attempted to touch by the end of our guided tour.) We came to the opening of the Siq and the full drama of the Treasury building.

A few Bedouins were setting up rickety tables and awnings from which to ply their trade of expensive soft drinks and hideous trinkets. They were dwarfed by the huge, pillared rock façade. We rode further into the 'city' where pillars and plateaux, steps to altars and shrines, and gaping caves urged us on to see more. We dismounted and took to our feet. The sun was getting strong; everywhere the salmon rock formation seethed and shimmered in its massive hulks. Great seams of amber, ochre and slate-blue grey ran through its strata, the roofs of caves were waved in colour, half-blackened by the oil-lamps and fires of two thousand years. A smattering of Bedouins in dark goat's-hair tents were set on the plateau; others had taken to the caves, their donkeys and goats nearby. In one tent a young girl had slung a goat-skin between forked sticks. The empty carcass was stretched fat and full with the chuckling milk. She tossed it from side to side, curdling it into yoghurt and cheese. Another woman beckoned us to her tent. She had a transistor radio nestling in the wool cushions and a baby at her breast. We sat down beside her. Her seven other children swarmed around us companionably and asked for nothing. They emptied a little sack of coins and broken pottery at our feet, gathered haphazardly from the ruins of their world; it looked genuine museum material to me. But where could an archaeologist begin or complete his search in such a site, still half-submerged by the silted levels from the wind and rain of centuries? We took our leave from the mother and her suckling child; she flashed her gold-capped teeth in a peaceful smile.

Round the next rock we were encouraged by another family to sit by their cave. Two little girls were jumping in and out of an oil drum. Their hair was matted with dust, but their teeth were white and even. They laughed gaily and their limbs were lithe; cleaned up they could rival the most beautiful child model. We were hoisted on to their donkeys and their naked, puking brother was thrust into my arms. He cried so pitifully I put him back to rest across the silky stomach of a baby goat where he had happily spent the morning. The mother heaved a mat from her dark cave into the sun and motioned us to sit, while she made tea. She piled up brittle, desert scrub and lit it with a match. Her blackened kettle was left to boil. She explained that her front room, which she kept tidy for visitors, was a few yards' walk. We followed her, with the daughter carrying the kettle and an assortment of glasses. We sat in the cool gloom of the cave, made cosy with long padded cushions, covered in gaudy cottons. It was conspicuously free from her attendant livestock and babies. Her son joined us and then her husband, the former looking comparatively clean and smart in an old soldier's uniform. He went to school and spoke English and seemed as out of place in his primitive home as we did. The mother, prematurely old from child-bearing and the severe extremes of sun and snow and squatting life, pressed flat, white goat cakes in our hands. We took our leave, nibbling gingerly while our hostess ambled back to her more utilitarian lodgings. We re-mounted our horses and picked our way back through the dust and boulders of the Siq. We waved to a tourist in the middle distance. He looked incongruous in an old school tie and blazer, a Wykehamist no less! How droll . . .

And we saw Jerash, the remains of a complete Roman city, set in a remote valley thirty miles from Amman. We timed our visit for the late afternoon. There is something infinitely poignant about ruins seen in the glow of a dying sun. Jerash was ravaged by enemy fire in 720 to 747 AD. In 1906 it was re-discovered by the German traveller, Seetzen. Today it is a half-restored relic of that grandiose, flourishing

Roman life. Like Petra and Palmyra the city was a strategic trading and refreshment post for caravans en route from the East Mediterranean to Mesopotomia. Here the travelling merchants would ply their haul of silks and spices. We pottered through a miscellany of broken columns and pediments, hurled inconsequentially from the rigours of ancient earthquakes and half-submerged in silt. Mounds of grass and wild flowers – poppies, anemones and hollyhocks – nudged and cradled their toppled grandeur. In defiance of this colourful dishevelment of nature, attempts were being made to resurrect each relic. Rows of sectional columns, plinths, cornices, and Corinthian capitals were neatly lined up for re-assembly; they must have been waiting some time, like props to be placed in a grand opera. The wild flowers and tufts of grass were already straddling each crevice and village children scampered happily over their capsized heritage.

Our guide pointed out the runnels from the iron chariot wheels; they were clearly visible on the wide square flagstones of the main streets, which, in turn, were flanked by massive pillars. And he showed us the round stone sewage covers let into the roads and the stone drain covers with their pierced petal motif. They knew how to conduct water and sewage to fertile and hygienic effect in those days. 'We have no sewage system there,' lamented our guide as he pointed to the ugly encroachments of the modern town.

I noticed a concrete hut framed incongruously in the arch above a sacrificial altar. The main tarmac road to Damascus ran slap between the peripheral Roman columns, their remaining capitals roughly secured by breeze blocks. The necessity of the new strikes crude and unceremonious blows at the beauty of the old. We returned to the forum and to the amphitheatre, where green hills and plains rose beyond. The columns stood proud in their lines and circles. In that honeyed evening light, the golden stones evoked those ancient calls to prayer, the street criers and the rich merchants with their heavily bejewelled wives, strolling in the bustle of the forum.

From Jerash to Palmyra, the most renowned oasis of them all, a four-hour drive to Damascus, through the Syrian desert along a tarmac road. To the left and right the desert dust tracks wound and twisted as they skirted the base of every mountain. (How well Lady Jane Digby must have known those paths.) The empty, arid appearance of a desert in the hard morning light is deceptive. Bedouins with their attendant livestock and modus vivendi are everywhere hidden in hills and rocks. In spring the desert is brushed with grass and bush and the brightest flowers; it vibrates with its own established rhythm.

We broke our journey at Homs, surprised to see cinemas, university students and shops bursting with electrics and digital watches; even an 'obstetrian' and 'gynologist' was advertising his services. It is always unexpected, a flourishing town in the heart of a desert. We drove on and on conditioning ourselves for the impact of Palmyra. Finally, rounding a steep corner, we saw a vast area of familiar columns and temples. They looked fragile in the distance. To our right waved the palm trees of the oasis, a dense sea of shade, lush and vivid green against the hot blue of the midday sky.

An enthusiastic guide plunged us through four hours of intensive Roman appreciation. Once more we pottered up shallow steps to altars, sat on the statesmen's seats in the scorching amphitheatre, entered the refreshing gloom of porticoed temples, and finally prevailed upon our friend to find us bottled water. We collapsed in a cool and recently-excavated mortuary. As we drove back to Damascus that evening, the yellow and white, the pink and black of the stones of Palmyra mingled in the mind. The fast-sinking sun urged us on; night falls swiftly in the East. Groups of sheep and their shepherds meandering towards the dying light recalled the lines, 'Drop thy still dews of quietness, beside the Syrian sea'. What does he think of, that Syrian shepherd, as he slowly walks, eyes lifted high, fixed intently on the next horizon? Who knows, but that the desert makes one think. Little lights glowed in the darkening distance as Bedouins beside their tents were making fires and dinner.

Damascus is a delight, a city that boasts the oldest of civilisations. The Barada river wending through its centre has provided more tra-dition, trade, and elegance than any oil-well could procure. It branches out in seven channels irrigating the fertile valleys and orchards that surround the city. One is conscious of water everywhere; the city courtyards and cafés tinkle with cascading pools and fountains. We spent an hour savouring the colour and scents of the El-Azm Palace courtyard. Bougainvillea tumbled from balconies, entwining the lam-brequins of fretted stonework. Lilies, iris, and alyssum nodded in white confusion in the shade of orange trees and lemon. Tendrils of jasmine curled and tangled around the large marble bedstead, lulling the air with its astonishing scent. Quiet footsteps, veiled heads, old men in corners fingering their worry-beads, stayed the distant din of the souk and strident calls to prayer. But it is in the cool of the evening when the surrounding mountains have swallowed the sun that Damascus lures the traveller to its oldest quarters. The narrow labyrinth of balcon-ied streets seethes with scampering cats and children. Shy women watch from windows and men spill their wares and handcrafts on to pavements, shrill cries and laughter rise with wafts of spiced lamb and steaming rice. The dark tunnels of the souk are splashed with light from the gaudy booths, cars and donkeys, drink-carts and bolts of cheap, bright cotton are zig-zagged furiously through the covered ways. In the Byzantine grandeur of the adjoining Omayad Mosque, the mosaics, the marble, and the gold gleam quietly in the blue half-light of dusk. Men and women stroll barefoot and cloaked over the 200 Persian carpets that pile its vast floor, while others sit silent by the well in the colonnaded courtyard.

On such an evening, we found the Nassan Palace. Lived in still by an established merchant family, they were preparing for their small son's birthday party. Chocolate cake and jelly and a rocking horse were laid out ready in the flowered courtyard, la plus ça change. A painted dais at the far end was padded with low cushioned seats, suggesting timeless comfort and elegance. Cool, dark, richly-painted interiors led off on all sides. There was a predominance of pale walnut furniture, finely-inlaid with an ivory seaweed marquetry. (This style of inlay workmanship has been abused in recent years by substituting camel bone.) Other pieces were inlaid with apricot, rosewood, green pistachio, and frail bands of lemon.

We were next shown the adjoining workshop of silk looms. Sleek plaits of finest silk ochre, royal-blue, rose, and white, were slung on hooks. Shuttles and treadles filled the gloom of this traditional work-room. Lengths of damask and brocade were being worked today in the tradition of our 'damasks' of yesterday. They were completing orders from all over the world. It takes a whole week for one man to complete one metre of woven silk; the business was thriving.

There are many rich families in Damascus today. They keep a low profile. President Assad has maintained peace and prosperity in his country under his own brand of statesmanship for eight years. It is progressing economically; agriculture and tourism are particularly encouraged. Let us hope that Syria will maintain its independence from total Communism, that Damascus will survive intact as the oldest, most distinguished head of the Middle East.

Our last call was Sana'a, the capital of North Yemen. Termed through the ages as Arabia Felix, the North Yemen lies 8,000 feet above sea level and has a population of six million, twice that of Saudi Arabia. Sana'a has the distinction of being the most ancient untouched city in Arabia. We had longed to see it last November, but our plans were thwarted by the sudden assassination of President Hamdi. It is believed that the Saudis instigated the coup. Hamdi was a young man of thirty-five, with independent ideas. He had wanted the North Yemen to become self-sufficient in crops and industry, to stand up against the tide of Communism on its one flank and the soft belly of Saudi economic aid on its other. The country is now ruled by a more malleable young man, content that Russia supplies arms and that Saudi

supplies pocket money and that the Russians encourage potential
Yemeni students to join their educational establishments for minimal
qualifications. ('Not worth the paper they are written on,' according
to one Western opinion.) The Saudis skim the few trained Yemenis
for labour and rich rewards. The 80% illiterates who are left behind
are encouraged to grow 'gat', an easily-cultivated narcotic with a high
market value and a soft option substitute for the more complicated
crops of cotton and mocha coffee. In order to further ease the life of
the Yemeni, the government allots him a quota of 'gat' each day, to
be chewed in the afternoons and evenings only. He can be seen
dragging his thin brown legs in disjointed lethargy, holding hands with
his boyfriend, his cheek stuffed with gat, virtually all day long. His
curved knife is fastened loosely at his waist. Sleepy soldiers man the
airport, smoking, slumped in chairs, their guns lying untended across
their knees. The heat and the altitude of Sana'a is a killer, the average
mortality is aged at forty years. They are a small and skinny race, lithe
with their knives and renowned as furious fighters.

The pain of industrial birth and recalcitrant infrastructure was apparent throughout the upturned streets, drains, and ubiquitous rubble.
Turbaned workers wielded axes and hand machines in dazed confusion
and dusty slow motion. It was always a relief when evening came and
the dust settled, when eyes would lift to the mountains and gaze in
prayer through the city's mosques and minarets.

From the terrace of our Mafraj (a long, low room, cooled by an
adjacent flat roof walk), we could watch the women walk from the
well with pots and buckets superbly balanced on their heads. Our eyes
followed their swaying, cloaked figures as they vanished down streets
of golden stone and smudged white-washed window-frames. We were
happy in our Mafraj with its coloured glass fanlights and panoramic
view. The sun streamed through the white gypsum tracery and danced
with their vivid panes of yellow, green, red and blue. Long ago these
widely-used fanlights were inserted with thinly-sliced alabaster. Men
would sit digesting their meal, sipping spiced tea, and sucking on water
pipes. They would walk through the arched doorway, stride over the
roof terrace, survey the city below, and sniff for trouble. And we were
happy, driving along the road to Taiz through the fertile Moutane
plain, where peasants and black-veiled wives ploughed little fields with
camels, where children minded sheep and carried feathery piles of
green donkey food on their heads, where azure lizards basked on
round hot rocks, and where we sat high above wide valleys with
minutely-terraced crops that stretched and curved in green necklaces
below. But in the streets of Sana'a we were not happy; the red flag of
the rambling Russian embassy fluttered ominously. The insidious ten-

sion between Saudi Arabia and Soviet communism sent out sinister undertones.

June 24 Udny Castle Udny Green Aberdeenshire

'Let no one bear beyond this threshold hence. Words uttered here in friendly confidence.' This inscription in stone rests above the ladies' stairway leading from the Great Hall of Udny. References to Udnys of Udny first appeared in the fifteenth century, but the original date of the Castle Keep is uncertain. In 1875 John Henry Udny took it upon himself to restore it from centuries of disuse. After nine years, in 1884, he had not only plastered the vaulted ceiling of the Great Hall and panelled the walls, but had also added a vast Victorian wing, almost as high as the Keep itself. His descendant, Lord Belhaven, inherited in 1934 and lived comfortably enough with the post arriving each day at 8.30 a.m. and leaving at 12.20 p.m.

Prayers were at 9.15 a.m., breakfast at 9.30 a.m., luncheon at 2.00 p.m., tea at 5.00 p.m., and dinner at 7.30 p.m.

Something of an Arabist, Lord Belhaven travelled extensively in the East. His visitor's book boasts the following entry in 1937: 'Saud, son of HM King of Arabia.'

A photograph of this exotic party, standing in their white robes and corded headdresses, on a dull, grey day in front of the Castle, bears witness to an unusual visit; they had not discovered oil in Arabia forty years ago, and who would have guessed at the secrets of the North Sea?

At the ripe old age of seventy, Belhaven became father to a beautiful dark-haired daughter, Maggie Schellenberg, the present owner. She inherited in 1961 and a year later there was a three-day sale of the contents. Conducted by local auctioneers, the sum totalled a mere £3,500. She retained the best furniture, pictures and silver, and spent the next two years demolishing the entire Victorian additions. The Castle Keep finally soared supreme as it was in the fifteenth century.

Maggie Udny Hamilton, slim and beautiful, married Keith Schellenberg, a renowned entrepreneur and infectious extrovert, in the early sixties. They settled in Yorkshire with his two young daughters from a previous marriage and soon had a son, Nicholas, and two more daughters, Amy and Rosy, of their own. Keith with his natural energy and Maggie with her inspired style set about converting Udny as their holiday home. They created something so sumptuous and comfortable that they moved in permanently.

The Great Hall, stripped of its heavy panelling and covered in mustard linen and superb pictures, has become a stunning drawing-room. The high Wardrop ceiling, with a design of applied plaster roses, thistles, paterae and the cartouche of the family arms above the fireplace, is painted ivory, a splendid foil to the riches gathered below. Furniture with ormolu and marble decoration, window recesses lined with leather tomes and window seats, enormous comfortable sofas, a roaring fire, massive flower arrangements, and Maggie flooding the whole with her accomplished piano playing, makes a ravishing ambience. The winding stone stairs lead off to bedrooms with four-posters luxuriously layered with White House linen, sunken baths in turrets and recessed dressing-rooms. Maggie's food and flowers and clothes are eye-trainers in excellence. (The coffee beans are specially sent from Fortnum and Mason.)

This particular weekend was the ninth year of Keith's unique innovation, 'The Udny Games'. Eight neighbouring villages – Tarves, Pitmeden, Methlick, Foveran, Newburgh, Esslemont, Cultercullen, and Udny Green – crowded the Castle grounds for a tantalising rout of competitive games and skills. Football, netball, and rounders were succeeded by archery, croquet, boules, target golf, egg and spoon races, obstacle races, flat races, throwing the hammer, tossing the caber, a tug o'war, and finally Highland dancing on well-sprung trestle tables. Bagpipe players, dressed in the Gordon tartan, arrived by bus from Ellon and paraded the Castle front, with their red-tasselled drumsticks. They then sat down to a hearty tea, where we had all enjoyed a hearty lunch and where Maggie later sat down twenty of us to dinner. The long oak table was draped in Madeira linen, silver candlesticks, the Aboynes, the Glenarthurs, the Macleods, and the Campbells. The evening progressed to the Udny Arms where the locals had gathered for a midsummer romp. I had a vigorous whirl with a diver from the Aberdeen oil-rigs. He told me that he ate four steaks a day. I think we were all grateful for the Scots' licensing hours, which enabled us to return to the Castle comforts by midnight.

June 26 Hardwicke House

The coldest June day on record for twenty years. The world news does not cheer either; a massacre of British missionaries in Rhodesia, a bomb blast destroying priceless works of art at Versailles, President al Ghashmi of Sana'a, North Yemen, killed by a booby trap (delivered to his office in a briefcase) followed by a serious shooting in Aden, South Yemen, where it is unknown if the President escaped. The explosion that killed Ghashmi in Sana'a was brought by an envoy from Marxist Aden and it can be surmised that the subsequent attack on

Aden's President was a retaliation from revolutionaries in Sana'a. One wonders if the Russians have instigated this murder, only nine months after former President Hamdi's assassination. He, we remember, was attempting to forge closer ties with his Marxist neighbour; this ploy displeased the Saudis and led observers to speculate over their responsibility for his sudden death on the very eve of his visit to Aden. It is stated in *The Times* today: 'Observers now believe that yesterday's attack may well have been an attempt by South Yemen, or elements sympathetic to it, to create renewed instability in North Yemen and wean the country away from the conservative Saudi régime.'

A month ago we were there; we smelt trouble; the British Ambassador smelt it too. 'The Russians would love to get their hands on this place' was his wry comment.

June 27 Hardwicke House

Today it is confirmed that the President of South Yemen, Salim Rubayya Ali, was executed by firing squad along with two of his ministers. The two coups were presumed to have been carried out by pro-Soviet elements, namely in protest at North Yemen's outright friendliness with Saudi Arabia and South Yemen's ready acceptance of Saudi aid.

July 3 Hardwicke House

The Arab League, which was founded in 1945, has agreed, for the first time in these past thirty-eight years, to boycott a member state: the South Yemen. President Sadat of Egypt has already expressed his concern about the Communist expansion in the Arab world; the Vice-President of America meets him to discuss this issue; Israel will no doubt take second place on their agenda.

Communism versus the Muslim faith; which will prove the stronger? Time, rather than these troubled times, will finally tell.

This stringent withdrawal of economic and technical aid from South Yemen should throw that country in a stranglehold of helplessness; it has always depended on Kuwait, and Saudi Arabia for main supplies. However, five unnamed countries have elected not to bow to the boycott. Iraq? Libya? Syria? It is possible that these leftist states, together with the full brunt of Soviet ire, will be instrumental in forcing the South Yemen and the whole southern entrance to the Red Sea, inexorably, into the Soviet camp. Have the conservative Arabs been too quick in their boycott decision? Cannot Russia and East Germany supply the South Yemen as readily as the Saudis?

July 6 Cadogan Place London

'Do please sit! I can't possibly stand any more. I'm eighty!' The dapper man with the incisive eyes waved me abruptly to a sofa. I was introduced to Field Marshal Sir Gerald Templer.[5] 'I am an old solider these days; don't enjoy meeting people any more; fed up with this mediocre modern age. I'm happy to sit quietly with a good book. Do you know? I sometimes fall asleep after breakfast!' Despite his affected gloom and irritations, the Field Marshal carried the evening on a wave of Machiavellian wit and vivacity. His beautiful wife, her elegance and sparkle undimmed by age, assured me that she adored meeting people and loved spending money.

We were dining with Anthony and Shirley Royle; Shirley looking young and radiant despite her father-in-law, Sir Lancelot Royle, dying three weeks ago and her daughter, Susannah, flying through the windscreen of her car, a week later. She had provided a delicious summer dinner, asparagus mousse (Sir Gerald had more), two salmon trout nestling in succulent curves, a green salad, cheese, a peach and raspberry compote.

On my right sat Norman St John Stevas, our Conservative Shadow Minister for education and culture. He assured me that too many books were published; he didn't know who had the time to read them. I asked him if he had read Paul Erdman's *Crash '79*, which I felt was an imaginative and pertinent observation of the Middle East oil boom turned crisis. He replied that he had no interest in the oil states; the Middle East was not his province. His mind and mouth shut like a clam. I suggested that the Shadow Cabinet was not as well-informed over the Middle East as it should be and mentioned to him that Margaret Thatcher had asked naively of my husband (before her recent visit to Teheran) – 'The Persians do not consider themselves Arabs, do they?' (That *Private Eye* had also quoted Jonathan Aitken as commenting that Mrs Thatcher would merely equate Sinai with the plural of sinus, I felt would be an equally unpopular observation.)

On my left, Sir Gerald was receiving general acclaim, led by Sir Anthony; he pointed out that, due to the Field Marshal's sharp words to Mr Heath, the latter was now publicly prepared to fully support

[5] Sir Gerald Templer, director of military intelligence, War Office 1946–48 and ADC general to King George VI, 1951–2 and to Queen Elizabeth II 1952–54.

Mrs Thatcher in an imminent election – 'The change in leadership makes no difference to my determination to install a Conservative government in office,' Heath had that every evening assured a Penistone by-election meeting. At this high point in the evening's conversation, Sir Anthony and Norman St John Stevas abandoned their pudding and hurried off to vote on the Finance Bill. 'Yes – yes,' murmured Sir Gerald, 'I saw Heath a few days ago in Oxford. He was eating peaches in Trinity College common room at eleven o'clock in the morning. I went up to him; told him to stop playing the fool; to get off his stubborn high-horse attitudes. He grunted and walked away. He used to live opposite us in Wilton Street. Do you know? I never once saw him say good morning to the policeman on guard or say a word of greeting to his chauffeur.' Here, Shirley flew to Heath's defence. She assured us there was not a dry eye amongst the staff when he left No. 10; that one and all refused to stay on for Harold Wilson; that each Christmas Heath gave a splendid party at Chequers for his domestic staff. Perhaps his awkward manner was due to social insecurity, I suggested. 'She's plumb right,' said Sir Gerald, and we rose from the dining-table.

August 17 Quiberon South Brittany France
(my thirty-eighth birthday!)

The sun shone all day on Belle Ile, the escapist island where Sarah Bernhardt would rest from her hectic life in Paris and where Claude Monet painted several canvases in 1866. Breeze-blown heather swept up from cadaverous cliffs and burnt-cream coves. White cottages with grey slate roofs straddled the grass hillsides and stony lanes dipped up and down across furls of scrub and stubble. Sheep grazed and cows chewed drowsily to the lazy tinkle of their bells. Children dabbled in rock pools, dug wet holes in moist sand, and splashed in the gentle sea. The noon sun beat down, engulfing each limb, each pore of skin. Through half-closed eyes, the plaited straw of my hat was golden filigree mounted with myriad sapphires and diamonds. The heat and haze of the afternoon turned the sky to palest aquamarine. Dogs panted in caves and bushes. Women knitted and talked incessantly. The ice-cream man touted his bounty of blackcurrant ice, passionfruit, and chocolate; his fresh warm doughnuts oozed with myrtle jam.

With the shiver of the evening breeze we caught the return ferry boat to Quiberon. A full load of family outings crowded on board. Bars of bread stuck up from capacious handbags, Alsatian dogs licked fathers' arms and babies; mothers and grandmothers clasped food and coats and children. They were large simple women with arms like croissants, creased and fat, baked gold in the sun. Good, wholesome wives, who would cook moules delectably, wring the duck's neck, bone and stuff it in a trice; knit heavy jerseys in cable stitch, and crochet babies' boots . . .

Those August nights were warm and dark. One night the weather broke, a slurry of rain clouds sponged the frail slice of the new moon and veiled Quiberon in billowing drizzle. We saw the tent of streaming colours; its flaps were up with invitation. Children, dogs and tired, damp mothers were drawn, like moths, to that seething merry-go-round of screaming cars and whirling aeroplanes, yellow, green, hard, shiny red, like puffed-up insects in distress; their giddy lights swirled in snakes and ribbons of hectic colour; the wheel turned faster, faster. A white-faced young man with a red beard hurled rubber balls and bright tassels of shredded wool into the excited fray of children's arms and heads and fingers. A cacophony of discordant colour, speed and sound; a child's own mecca. Too soon the wheel slows down, the music dies, the lights cut out. Children slump in seats, glowing in their swift-captured delight, their mothers' arms and the promise of another *glace*.

Our own children adored their first *goût* of France. And will they remember the peace and green profusion of those hills and lush, dark valleys? The Normandy cornfields and poplar avenues? The shady village squares of the Dordogne? The shuttered houses with window-boxes of cascading red geranium? The stone trough drenched in hydrangea – the palest blue and rose? The clash of honeysuckle, petunia and rose that showered their mingled scent on the evening air? But they would sit chatting about the beach; sip their grenadine and coke. And will they remember those tartes aux fraises, bulging with crème patissière; those croissants encasing half-melted chocolate; that sea-food platter and that unremarkable and ubiquitous white fish that is transformed to epicurean perfection with its cream mousseline sauce and attendant pastry crescent? It was good to be in France again.

September 15 Chatsworth House

We hurtled through the front door, whipped on all sides by a sudden autumn squall. The wind whined and shuddered through windows and passages and the young butler strained to shut it out again. 'Her Grace is expecting you. Please come this way.' We followed him upstairs and through corridors, hung with damask, pictures, prints and portraits, and all the sumptuous paraphernalia of widely-assembled elegance. Flowers, plants, and Labradors signalled that we had arrived in the Duchess's private wing.

She greeted us with all her natural spontaneity, radiant in her charm and fresh good looks. She introduced us to her two companions, Lord Oaksey and Mr Harold Macmillan. The latter was struggling to rise out of his easy chair. 'Please, sir, don't get up,' I motioned, as I shook the great man's hand. 'How very nice,' he murmured and re-settled himself. Lord Oaksey was preparing to leave. 'Must you go, Baldy? What are you doing for lunch?' 'Oh,' he replied, 'I'll pick up a sandwich, but I'll be back for dinner.' 'I wish you would stay for dinner, Uncle Harold. We have J. J. Astor and Professor Wall.' 'By Jove, how very nice. But I must get back tonight.' The old man looked perfectly content at the prospect of lunching with this charming woman. She explained to him that she was about to take us round her private rooms. 'Oh! for another look at the Vandervaart violin. Perhaps it could be brought to me here?' He chuckled quietly and it was only later when we saw this superb feat of trompe l'oeil – the famous violin painted on a simulated panelled door, that we appreciated his mock wistfulness.

The Duchess showed us her sitting-room with the specially-cut out window opposite her desk. 'I can always see who is coming up the drive.' We all sat in the chair to have a peek. It was a small and cosy room with favourite things, to include a prominent photograph of John F Kennedy. We moved on to her bedroom and its ravishing view. 'I would love to extend the formal garden to the river; but it is further away than one thinks. This is my mother, by Helleu.' And then she pointed out another enchanting drawing that he had done of his wife, nestling back on a heap of white pillows, her hands cradling a huge cup of coffee? Chocolate? Which completely obliterated her face. A small and lovely room with the four-poster hung in white and blue, two dog baskets, one white satin hanger hooked on a cupboard door, a cairn of books by sisters, Nancy Mitford and Jessica. (A recent biography of Unity rested on a chest of drawers.) She finally left us to the grand tour of the main rooms and the remembered pleasure of her company.

December 3

Rahmi Koç's[6] yacht, *Nazenin* (Coquette), built in 1977, was a riot of well-appointed, expensive machinery, fitted carpets, efficient lavatories, showers and bidets, spare socks and shoes and sweaters, cassettes

[6] Rahmi Koç is one of Turkey's leading industrialists. Widely travelled, he has collected antiquities from the Graeco-Roman and Byzantine eras. He has restored the finest remaining yalıs on the Bosphorus.

and televisions, a discreet and unobtrusive crew, a continual flow of drinks, sturgeon and mackerel stew, and an adoring blonde. His tall, elegant son, Ömer, talked infectiously on a wide range of subjects to include his own treasured piece of information that English women could boast of such fine, white skin that black grapes could be seen passing down their throats.

We set off for the sea of Marmara and shortly anchored by Büyükada, the main Princes' Island. There we drank too much tea with the man who sold us too many kilims. Emré Gönensay[7] wedged himself in a corner and dozed. He was nearly suffocated with the mounting pile of carpets, while Rahmi, who has traded in cars, condemned each worn offering as a 'chassis'. We laughed and argued in that hot little steamed-up shop and settled on £50 a purchase. We returned to Istanbul with radar controls at full throttle. It was evening and the Topkapı Palace, the Blue Mosque, the domes of St Sofia, the Sheraton Hotel, the Hilton, the whole of Istanbul with its splendid miscellany of hills and lights, had never so attentive an audience as we cruised up the Bosphorus passing slowly under the famous bridge.

December 5 Kuwait

A wheeler-dealer's mecca to end them all? Kuwait looks better at night. There are shadows, secrets and perspective. Multi-coloured, computerised advertisements – the most sophisticated in the world – flash their rays on the predatory cranes. Kuwait is a vast flat conglomerate of office blocks, tower blocks, hotel blocks and circular blocks. Spheres, minarets and domes erupt from this urban stronghold and add a garish gloss with their coats of gold and mosaic. Pillared villas are tucked around with blankets of jealously-watered grass, and tall eucalyptus, huge bastions of privacy marooned in sandy wastes and rubble where cigarette ends eddy in the warm desert breeze.

By day the town throbs to the ubiquitous road drills and the hooting of badly-driven American cars (the air conditioning in the plush interiors boasts of special 'below the navel air-flow'). The smooth sweeping roads hug the sand-ruffed Gulf coast.

This whole industrial enterprise is dependant on an Egyptian, Indian, Turkish, Yemeni and Palestinian labour force. Potential revolutionaries? The population of Kuwait, this year, stands at 100 million, of which 30 million are Kuwaiti and 70 million are of mixed nation-

---

[7] Professor of Economics. Foreign Minister of Turkey from 1996.

alities. European technologists are imported to assemble this daunting morass of money and uninitiated labour into viable shape.

The famous gold souk is swamped with women swathed in black and bartering hotly through their veils. Gold watches, bracelets, necklaces, and earrings are weighed and re-weighed, while the husband undertakes the more menial matter of buying groceries.

Up the coast at Samieh we ate well in a small restaurant. The men ate below and mixed parties climbed the stairs to above. We ordered the good local fish, hamour, a white, thick-textured variety heaped with large, fleshy gulf shrimps. Later we talked to an Indian. Kuwait is a place to make money, he informed us, but no place to live. A man dangling a fishing line from a jetty claimed he was a Palestinian guerrilla. 'The Kuwaiti considers only God and his stomach,' he warned us direly. He continued his desultory attempt at fishing and assured us that he himself was only there for the money.

One night, we were invited by a tall, charming and handsome Arab, Mr Al-Hassawi, to take tea and cakes with him and his family after dinner. A white Rolls-Royce collected us. His house was a vast glittering fairground of hastily-purchased trophies. Our host referred to it as his 'shop'. It was Harrods gone mad. Such blistering, shining new clutter, and thick florid rugs. A posse of highly-coloured Gallé-style vases were lined up at the end of one room and several large suites of nineteenth-century French gilt furniture were grouped uncertainly throughout: the desire to acquire gone crazy. Bright lights glared overhead.

There was cake in every room, trays of cakes peering from beneath thin embroidered cloths, symbols perhaps of that old desert hospitality when every caller at a Bedouin's tent would be automatically offered refreshment. I sat on a high French settee and nibbled a crumbling concoction of flour and cinnamon. Above, the chandelier dripped with seemingly brown beer-bottle heads, a strange assortment of glass pendants which would have tempted the aspiring marksman at a fairground booth. And everywhere gaudy cushions, crudely embroidered with shining gold thread, segments of mirror, tapestry and velour.

The wife was quiet as though dazed by her lavish spending and the resulting disorder. She picked up the heavy Sèvres tureen by one handle and shyly offered me another cake. She spoke no English; I tried to speak a little Arabic. She smiled happily at my attempts and pointed with pride at the blown-up coloured photograph of herself and her husband. I admired it profusely, indeed they made a handsome pair. The charming daughter, who spoke perfect English and knew London well, explained that we also could have the same portrait done at Harrods.

1979

Work to rule picketing; lorry drivers on strike; train drivers on strike alternate days; ambulance drivers on strike (with the comment from their spokesman 'so be it'). Lives have been lost as the result of their action. We are in the midst of the worst snowfalls and frozen conditions since 1963; the gritting trucks are on strike; as the lorries which deliver the grit and salt are also on strike, the problem becomes ludicrously academic; surprisingly few lives have been lost on the frozen motorways; people are determinedly getting to work. Today the Chairman of United Biscuits, Sir Hector Laing, has succeeded in pushing through an injunction against secondary picketing; it is an unprecedented triumph for the rule of law. The whole country must now be questioning the credibility of this inane and fatuous government.

Ten days ago the Shah of Iran[1] scooped up a small heap of his native soil and left his treasured land in tears. The Military had persuaded him in vain to stay on the throne; their loyalty is still strong; one soldier even stooped to kiss his Shah's feet as he finally boarded his private plane for Egypt.

The acting government chaired by Dr Shapour Bakhtiar immediately released political prisoners, disbanded Savak, and welcomed the return of the Muslim leader, the Ayatollah Khomeini.

The ensuing ten days have resulted in religious demonstrations with Communist undertones and frenetic demands for the return of the Ayatollah. Dr Bakhtiar has assured him via a personal messenger to Paris that Iran is ready for his return; the Military have simultaneously ringed Teheran airport, and, contravening Dr Bakhtiar's statements, have made it impossible for the Ayatollah to land. Air France has conveniently refused to fly him in.

There has been extensive and hysterical demonstration in Teheran today, when thirty-five lives were lost. The situation is unclear; it would appear that Dr Bakhtiar has lost control over the Military. He has no plausible relationship with the Ayatollah and an ambiguous

---

[1] On Tuesday, January 16, the regime of the Shah of Iran ended with a whimper. Unable to face the press, he flew off with the Shahbanou at 11 o'clock in the morning to the clatter of accompanying helicopters. *The Priest and the King – an eyewitness account of the Iranian Revolution* by Desmond Harney, published 1998, British Academic Press.

standing with the deposed Shah. Clearly the Ayatollah has no sympathy with Dr Bakhtiar's middle-line approach; his threatened arrival in Teheran must evolve into extreme clashes and more bloodshed. Finally, the Military, sickened and frustrated by this crippling disruption, could defect; could shoot up both Bakhtiar's régime and the potential Ayatollah's; could place themselves in charge of this appalling holocaust. They might even demand the re-instatement of their Shah? He and the Shahbanou have been resting at the invitation of their dear friend and political ally, President Sadat[2] of Egypt; they have accepted a further invitation to stay with King Hassan of Morocco. President Carter has not proffered any such invitation; the Shah has consequently revoked his plan to visit America.

January 27 Hardwicke House

Nelson Rockefeller died in New York yesterday of a heart attack. We saw him over a year ago in Teheran; he was opening the new copper-roofed Modern Museum, a concept of the Shahbanou and her architect cousin, Kamran Diba. It was a crisp sunny October morning; Rockefeller looked stocky with a blotchy complexion. He made a fulsome speech, professionally delivered, and praised the Shahbanou for her vision and energy. Word of her collection would reverberate and ricochet throughout the world, he confidently predicted. Today, this new museum is burnt and looted.

February 16 Hardwicke House

Dr Shapour Bakhtiar was marched through Teheran a few days ago, a rope around his neck and hustled like a cow. His gallant stopgap government has fallen to the Ayatollah Khomeini; the Marxists are sweeping through the debris of shattered Iran. They will no doubt take over the country, Ayatollah and all. Hundreds of veiled women demonstrating for an Islamic republic are reported to be Soviet militants in the disguise of traditional Iranian wives. As feared, the whole recent holocaust in Iran was not an essentially religious ferment; it was not an outright revolt against the Shah. It was the ubiquitous Soviet infiltration leaking its poison through the cracking fibre of Iranian society. America, Europe, and Britain have sat on the fence through

---

[2] The President was destined to be shot dead in Cairo, October 6, 1981, by a posse of his own soldiers, as he watched a military parade.

the whole débâcle; they now climb down, gingerly placating the new powers in Iran with formal recognition.

In the early '60s the Shah developed a 'folie de grandeur'. He instigated his own Coronation and conferred Imperial rights upon his wife and family. He bought and spent profusely; his land appeared to flow with oil and money. Europe aided and abetted his largesse. It suited the Western world to supply him with arms and technologists. But he became isolated in his power; his closed aides feared to caution him, to the detriment of their own positions. Those who did were promptly ousted. The Shah was hoist by his own petard and finally crashed.

March 8 West Wycombe Buckinghamshire

Marcella Dashwood, Francis's second wife, skilfully effected introductions among her forty-four guests. We drank champagne in the newly-decorated drawing-room – ablaze with colour and a log fire. Reresby Sitwell, with his moon-faced, rosy dial, his stocky body swaying like a well-regulated pendulum, wafted amiably around the room. His beautiful wife, Penelope, was enveloped in a long black dress, elaborately encrusted in swirls of pearls and gold filigree. Betty Kenward[3] with her habitual hump of spun-sugar hair, slashed with that black velvet ribbon, purred away quietly and sniffed for la crème. There were many little black dresses, jokes and trays of drinks. Francis looked young and happy. A rumour that we would be subjected to four hours of sixteenth-century madrigals after dinner caused some uneasy speculation.

We were soon swept into the dining-room where I was placed next to Sir Harry Ashcombe. We talked about food; the price of salmon at Wiltons; (he had only just begun looking at the menu) and had I tried Michel Guérard's new hors d'oeuvre? After a dinner of avocado (topped with caviar), gammon with fresh apricots and some delectable pudding – a coffee mousse, double-decked with slivered roast almonds and whipped cream – we were coaxed towards the ballroom.

We sat dutifully in rows when six beautiful young men (engaged from King's College, Cambridge) sang us nostalgic songs: 'In the Mood' and 'Yesterdays'. Their rounded notes, naked of any accompaniment, suggested they must have had an equally good dinner themselves. Lady Ampthill, chic and French, shook uncontrollably in her

---

[3] Betty Kenward was the doyenne of the social scene for forty years. Her exhaustive 'Jennifer's Diary' in *Harpers and Queen* was avidly read. Celestria Noel was the first to succeed her in the early 2000s.

black lace; she had the giggles. Lord Ampthill told us afterwards that he had urged her to look at the painted ceiling – 'choose a bottom and stick to it.' As there was a plethora of luxuriant bottoms, she must have found it difficult to select just one.

March 9 Hardwicke House

'Appeasement is the father of war. Watch it! It is all beginning again.' Harold Macmillan was televised live last night, making a speech on behalf of the Conservative Party. He began by complimenting Mrs Thatcher on her courageous and competent performance as leader of the Opposition. She had played this difficult and thankless role for four years; his recognition of her good hard work drew applause from the audience. He feels that the whole cycle of industrial discontent which wheeled through the 1930s, culminating in World War II, is in danger of repeating itself. We are again squabbling over higher pay and work to rule attitudes; let us be thankful, instead, for the discovery of North Sea oil, he continued; it could open up new horizons, on the same scale that the discovery of coal precipitated in the nineteenth century. Let us forget our differences and strive for a new and united moral nationality. He looked frail as he spoke and his voice quavered as he ended his speech with the words: 'God bless you in your labours.'

In yesterday's *Daily Telegraph* the Shah of Iran is quoted: 'I think that all of Western Civilisation is in danger.'

May 15 Meridien Hotel Damascus Syria

A persistent knocking drills into the brain. I lurch through our darkened bedroom to the door. It takes two hands, numbed in sleep, to turn the handle. The waiter stands tall and accusing, sharply etched in the bright light of the corridor; his tray, held high, is poised for entry. 'It is only 7.15 am,' murmurs Tom from the bed. The assembled breakfast, set for one, steams with tea rather than coffee. Wrong room! The waiter, unmoved, knocks relentlessly on the adjoining door.

Yesterday our breakfast was an hour late, Tom's trousers were returned from pressing with tram lines. The day before the room was not made up until we protested for service at seven o'clock in the evening. Food, service, general upkeep and attitudes have spiralled down since we stayed a year ago. Could the recent declarations of closer ties with Iraq bear rotten fruit so soon? An air of makeshift mediocrity now pervades the hotel; young men look grim in the city's streets, now more dusty and dishevelled. For what gain is Damascus fast forfeiting its pride, its relative peace and prosperity? The air is thick with the deadening clutch of Communism.

It is impossible to sleep again. The wild winds of last night have stilled to a calm and golden morning. Damascus holds its breath, a last clear moment and now the onslaught of another day. Dust and noise and toil. Loudspeakers wail from a police patrol car jarring the air with staccato urgency. What are they warning, shouting, ordering? A screech of brakes and horns. Soldiers march in the compound below; they incant some uniform call in uniform step. The city heaves with mounting heat and action. The haze and hassle suck all into its vortex.

We take the bus to Aleppo and see the rich plains through Homs and Hamar. Peasants in bright silks bend over cornfields and carry their heads in green haloes of animal fodder; old men tie the lush vines, stoop over sheep, round up lean cows; the young boy urges on the donkey, that urges on the herd of black-haired, straggling goats; sons and fathers rest under olive trees and poplar, their women at a distance, weeding, bent and busy. Fields of vivid green and gold rise swaying from the rich red soil; striations of nature's harvest that stretches for miles untrammelled by fence or hedge. Those plains towards Aleppo are high and catch the rains. The barren inland towards Palmyra is rough and hard with sand and stone. Rounded slopes are surmounted by the occasional village, small, square, clay and wattle holdings, moulded by hands and smoothed by rain, baked pink and brown and hard. The dome of a mosque shines white, a cemetery lays bleak, pale stones in rows. They bury their dead with more ceremony in this peasant world. The Bedouin will merely mark his grief with the nearest stone. Quaint, conical out-houses annex the farms and village homes, an extra habitat or storage for grain. Made in the same pink clay, they are as much a feature of these plains as the oasthouses of England's Kentish Vale. Cool in summer, warm in winter, they bear redoubtable witness to the thermal properties of Syrian clay.

Our bus nears Aleppo; we have been on the road for four hours. The vibrations of the formidable Mercedes engine and the rasping pitch of the horn have silenced the peasant load. Young mothers are trim in sober cottons, with pale-skinned oval faces framed in pink scarves, their eyes so black and full and bright, Arabian eyes like garnets set in crystal. Children loll in the laps of fathers, who nuzzle them with curly beards and shake their worry beads to amuse and soothe. The old man slumped in sleep and wrinkled grime has not stirred since Damascus. All now wait for Aleppo.

The co-driver fills again our paper cups with water from his yellow plastic can; it is smudged with oily hands but the water pours clean and cold and thirst makes men take risks. The pot-holed road curls down the hill. Tall tenement blocks, faceless in cement and glass, escort us to the bowl of the town. The ancient ramparts of the stone citadel gleam gold and massive in the evening sun.

We haul our cases through the fast-darkening main street, Baron Street. Ramshackle cars lurch and hoot their passage through the loitering crowds. Unlike Damascus, there is no 4 p.m. embargo on their horns. We reach the wide steps of the Baron Hotel, an imposing edifice, built in 1910 by an Armenian. His son, the present proprietor, sits languidly on the front terrace, his plump, English wife rises heavily from a wicker chair. She has shared his life for thirty-two years. And does she sit here each evening, amidst this twilit dust? A golden retriever drags its matted tail and sniffs us with forlorn tenderness. The proprietor explains that she is unwell, her puppies lie dead in her womb. The vet has prescribed medicine that will dissolve the foetuses; the bones will in time be absorbed with her own. We offer tired concern. We are expected, the proprietor assures us, and the British Ambassador, James Craig, is also due to arrive.

He leads us through tall doors and towards large rooms of high-ceilinged, stone-floored gloom. Double doors of dark-polished wood open on to a dining-room. Further wide passages lead to more doors and more rooms of indeterminate function. They appear sparsely furnished with brown leather sofas, hard-backed chairs and empty tables caught in corners. Up more wide stairs and, with footprints of the day etched thickly in dust on each red-carpeted tread, we are shown our room. I push open the slatted wooden shutters and face the blare of the street below. A small stone balcony supports an iron rail that whines and trembles in the rising breeze. And this is Aleppo? Warm, putrid gases from the drone of traffic waft through the open window. A man from the house opposite peers at me narrowly from his evening perch. My spirits rise with the comparatively clean bathroom. Tom is amused by the capacious bidet, it is amply designed to accommodate the fuller oriental bottom.

To give dimension to the evening we thread our way through Baron Street to the recommended Strand restaurant. We pass narrowly by the sturdy young girls in the ubiquitous headscarf; bevies of young men in jeans hang around neon-lit shop fronts eyeing Seiko wrist-watches. Old men scuttle by in trousers, close-fitted on their bandy shins and calves and cascading in folds over their receding bottoms; ideal attire for sitting long hours astride a donkey. An old woman, veiled in black, staggers down a side-street; she is bent double with her bulging bags of food, her chador caught fast in gold-capped teeth. Barbers and shoe-shine shops do a brisk trade for men only, their dusty doors thrown open to the soft, dark night. Waves of exhaust, dust and sweat mingle with the acrid fatty fumes from rotating doner kebabs.

We have a wretched dinner. (How could Aleppo give us better?)

The tough, overcooked lamb weeps and splutters with burnt fat as they pile our chipped plates. We buy the best bottle of red wine – French – expensive, rough and a bad colour. We should have stuck to arrack and hot mint tea. We spurn the limp lettuce and finish the abysmal meal with crumbling wedges of goat's cheese. An hour later the restaurant is still filled with the same men, talking over the same glass of arrack, tea or cup of Arabic coffee. The bare floor, the neon lights and the steamed window are no inducement to linger; the airless room thickens with cheap tobacco, cardamom and breath.

Our stomachs take revenge, together with the ceaseless din of traffic and a persistent mosquito. We breakfast well on fat olives, oranges, baps and thick apricot jam. We wander through hot and ugly streets to the Souk, which is reputed to be the oldest in the Arab world. Through the frenzied beating, drilling and welding of the copper-smiths, their braziers red hot and roaring, past the bakers with their cairns of muffins and steaming pizzas, past the carpet dealers with their cloying plea to drink tea and see their wares, past the soap stall with the round cakes as big as stiltons, where huge vats of detergents are ready-mixed to a viscous white paste, and past mounds of rice – yellow, red and brown, and black and wild in sacks. We come finally to the quiet nooks of the string Souk; white string, red and yellow and green string; thin string and fat string, snugly-coiled; whiskered string or thick and fluffy as a cat's tail. Everywhere hangs that salubrious smell of string – salt and clean.

With difficulty and halting Arabic we found our way to a small sun-lit courtyard. Here lived an octogenarian Austrian, Dr Pocher. His collection of miscellaneous antiques is renowned. The door was opened cautiously by a minuscule old woman and we explained that we were not expected; the telephone system had proved impossible. We waited in the cool, dim passage, lined with gaunt, fifteenth-century Venetian chests elaborately carved and gleaming darkly with age and patina. A tall, spare man in a dark suit walked slowly towards us. He looked frail and wasted; should we not have disturbed him? On the contrary, he was delighted to show us round his home; the family had lived there for nearly 200 years. We spoke in French.

The old woman appeared again with a tray of lemon drinks, mutter-ing that we must put the empty glasses back on the tray when finished. She was too old and blind to traipse through too many rooms to recover them. Dr Pocher rested his foot on a commode and struggled with his shoe laces. I had noticed they were undone, but felt inhibited about alerting him; such detailed exigencies of dressing were perhaps beyond him. His bent body swayed alarmingly as he completed his task. Clutching our glasses we felt inadequate to help. Slowly he straightened up and we followed him through the rooms, sitting a space, here and there, and asking gentle questions.

The house had an Italian flavour with shades of the East. The rooms were small and intimate with ribbed wood painted ceilings. They were comfortably cluttered with well-bound books, Roman glass, French porcelain, prints and portraits. Family photographs, brown with age, were lavishly framed in swirls of tarnished silver. Next, Dr Pocher showed us the room where he was born, cool and quiet, festooned in faded green silk with a delicately-painted ribbed ceiling, a Venetian retreat indeed. We sat awhile in his library, admiring his pair of small Ladik rugs which had been hung to effect in two niches on either side of the fireplace. He led us through to his patio, beguiling enough in the evening with its clay pots of haphazard flowers and lemon trees. The distant minaret sharpened its narrow pinnacle high above the rosy roofs. But, from the height of that hot, sunny room, the garden looked a sorry shambles of dust and half-dead flowers. We left the old man to his books and pictures and his quiet reclusive memory and later sent him flowers.

Back at the Baron Hotel, we joined the Ambassador for a drink. The proprietor mixed us his own concoction of fernet-branca to quell our churning stomachs. For our part, we had failed to penetrate the Citadel. We all commiserated on our exacting timetables; we had to catch the bus back to Damascus that very afternoon.

The Ambassador sipped his drink aloofly. He was a tall, spare Scotsman, dour and scholarly with generous eyebrows. I asked him why Aleppo was called Aleppo. From *halib* – milk, he replied; some myth claimed that Abraham had milked his goats on the outskirts of the city. I was left to digest this information with the fernet-branca, since the Ambassador did not seem conducive to further exchanges.

Instead I mused on the economic derivation of Arabic words; a root of a verb leads to the noun. For example; *darras* (to study) to give us *madressa* (school). There is also an engaging simplicity in many Arabic second names. No doubt many have been assumed by the recent escalation in urban life. We have met *Asayeed Kalil* – a Mr Small, *Asayeed Tayyib* – a Mr Nice, *Asayeed Mubarak* – a Mr Lucky, *Asayeed Shammas* – a Mr Sunny, That redoubtable Sheikh Al Mardi-Tajir (now the owner of Mereworth in Kent) can be accurately translated as Mr Yesterday's Trader. As he made his fortune thirty years ago by enabling whisky to pour through the Bahrain Custom Control to the tune of his own 100% bribery, his name is deservedly and accurately construed.

June 29 The Belgian Embassy Belgrave Square

The Ambassador, Robert Vaes, a charming, well-preserved man of
fifty-odd years, has no greater ambition than to extend his term in
London indefinitely. He has served two and a half years, has married
his pretty daughter to an English lord and, together with his attractive
wife, is enjoying the ubiquitous popularity.

A placement board, propped in the hall, reveals that we are twenty-
four guests, I am sitting between Hardy Amies[4] and the boyish David
Sutherland[5]. Martha Windisgraetz, a handsome Hungarian, and her
Austrian husband Vincent are present. They are on a week's break
from Vienna – where they live in a modest flat and Vinci acts as
Christie's representative. Martha paints oilscapes – and reminisces on
the former glory and gaiety of Bucharest; she complains about life in
Vienna which she finds parochial in comparison. The indomitable
Raine Spencer flounces into the reception salon in a whirl of aquamarine frills and a voluminous bow caught at the waist. She supports
the arm of her newly-acquired husband, Earl Spencer. He has just
recovered from a severe stroke.

Her doll-like face with its clear skin is framed in a precise brown
cloud of curls. She surreptitiously peeps at her compact mirror and
hastily smoothes her cheeks with another coat of white powder.

HRH Princess Michael of Kent arrives. Madam Vaes introduces her
round the room; she is a large handsome young woman with a bold
profile and fine blue eyes. We have met her previously as Marie-
Christine, an Austrian separated from her English husband, Tom
Troubridge; but she would not now care to remember all that. Her
heavy hair is caught in blonde veils and a brilliant diamond clasp. (In
Richmond Park I have seen her hair fly loose as she canters by on her
chestnut mare.) HRH Prince Michael does not appear. We soon pass
in to dinner.

The pillared dining-room is made warm and elegant with a hanging
tapestry; the rich colours are effectively repeated in a cascade of fresh
flowers that splay from a superb silver urn. We are served an exquisite
dinner with a different wine to accompany each course: a chilled
cucumber soup; skate gleams delectably in its ribbed white flesh,
girdled with pastry boats each with a cargo of mushrooms; pink slivers

[4] Pioneer in British fashion and designer by appointment to the Queen, since 1955.
[5] Recruited by David Stirling 1942, into the first SAS regiment, along with Fitzroy Maclean
and George Jellicoe. Sutherland and Jellicoe shared hair-raising operations in the Special
Boat Section (merged with the SAS). See *Drums of Memory* – autobiography – Stephen
Hastings MC.

of lamb nestle in aubergines, emerald courgettes and baby carrots. A silky vanilla bombe concludes the meal in a halo of spun sugar.

Hardy Amies tells me he has been 'in fashion' for fifty years and promptly changes the subject. He is enjoying Wimbledon, goes each day but has to walk the last mile; the marathon queue of cars this year is quite unprecedented. He looks remarkably trim and young, the combination of a devoted mother, regular meals, servants and work. I wonder what he must think of Raine Spencer's dress sense. She sits at the adjoining table, ecstatic and gift-wrapped. She resembles a little girl at a children's tea party, waiting to clap the conjuror.

On my right, David Sutherland urges me to resist buying flies in London. 'If you are fishing in Scotland, get the local ghillie to advise you. They always sniff in despair when one proudly opens one's fly box.'

Opposite us, a Russian, by name of Prince George Vassiltchikov[6], talks engagingly with a stutter. From his first-hand knowledge of the Caucasus, he assures me that there are inaccuracies in Lesley Blanch's amazing book *The Sabres of Paradise*. He has felt compelled to write to her and promises to send me a list of her errors. Having just read the book, which I found remarkably evocative and brilliantly written (it took her four years to complete the two volumes), I will be fascinated to read his adverse comments.

The women leave the dining-room. As we pass through the hall, the door bell rings. 'My husband!' exclaims Marie-Christine. She kisses Prince Michael lavishly as he walks towards Madame Vaes.

'Oh! But he must be introduced to all these ladies!' cries Marie-Christine as we stand aside in an uncertain line. Madame Vaes is leading HRH Prince Michael firmly towards the dining-room to join the men. 'What an opportunity we are missing!' Marie-Christine sounds very put out. The Ambassador's wife replies with every ounce of diplomatic politesse: 'His Royal Highness will meet the ladies presently, of course.' 'Oh' is the perfunctory rejoinder and HRH Princess Michael of Kent stomps up the stairs to powder her nose.

[6] The younger son of an old aristocratic family who left Russia in 1919 for Lithuania, Georgie Vassiltchikov became an international conference interpreter, notably with the United Nations. His elder sister, Marie ('Missie') Vassiltchikov, wrote *The Berlin Diaries*, published 1985 Chatto & Windus.

October 23 Ellel Grange Nr Lancaster

A sunny day in Lancashire with an east wind tugging at the marquee, its roofing flapped and billowed monotonously. A remarkable attendance of furniture-dealers and local buyers, huddled in anoraks and worn tweeds, sat through the morning's sale. The contents of Ellel Grange were fetching record prices. The house was built in 1860 by William Preston, a former mayor of Liverpool. The present owner and descendant, Miss Betty Sandeman, looked dejected and smoked continuously as she led an old black Labrador through the upturned rooms. She had already moved into the stable block.

The large and lugubrious ground floor, panelled in heavy oak linenfold, the countless bedrooms, cold and severe with faded, tattered damask curtains, solid Waring and Gillow beds, marble-topped washstands, and vast mahogany wardrobes were hardly conducive to the comfortable retirement of an ageing spinster. No single item had ever been removed from the house since its purchase over a hundred years ago.

Onlookers gasped as £1,000 was fetched for a small and modest walnut table with one central drawer, another Waring and Gillow example, especially made for the house and intact with its original label; a piece not to be sniffed at. What would its Chippendale counterpart fetch today? The afternoon wore on with the lots of nineteenth-century oriental porcelain and simulated Venetian glass, a huge and ugly array. Christie's head porter, the red-headed Albert, bought Lot 581, a blue and white porcelain cat seated on a tasselled porcelain cushion. He paid the sum of £110, and, on learning that it was his twenty-first house sale, Christie's contributed £50 towards the coveted cat as a celebratory gesture. Albert was delighted and said that his landlady in Hendon would also be pleased. She had never 'abided' his real live one which he had been forced to relinquish. A rusted old bicycle brought in from an outhouse fetched £55 and the sale of Ellel's remaining contents came to a quiet and irrevocable end. The marquee emptied rapidly and frozen, clumsy bodies tripped their way along overgrown garden paths to the car park, warmth and dinner.

October 31 Hardwicke House

Our next assignment was at Dunlossit House, in Islay in the Hebrides, the home of Bruno Schroder, which we first visited nine years ago. The valuation of the contents needed updating.

We flew in a Trislander from Glasgow, a narrow three-engined

commuter airline that seated sixteen passengers, as tightly packed as a
cigar tube. It was a remarkable morning – a clear blue sky with the
Irish Sea as flat and delicately ridged as a Canaletto. Bute and Gigha
lay in soft overlapping mounds of wrinkled gold, strewn with little
lochs of transparent, deepest blue.

Piffa Schroder was staying at Dunlossit with their five-year-old
blonde daughter, Leonie, who pranced behind us in thick warm
clothes and pink ballet shoes. She was an enchanting child and acutely
aware of her Hebridean environment; she loved the rolling mists on
the Sound of Jura, the peeking sun, the sudden showers and frequent
rainbows, the many varied species of birds and the deer. Her desire
for knowledge and her observation of the continually-changing scene
was insatiable.

Piffa has the rare and unusual distinction of winning the Edge
Challenge Cup at Bisley, the first woman in history to win the event
since it started nearly ninety years ago. She invited me to join her
deer-stalking in the afternoon and, suitably swamped in green and
khaki, we set off into the hills accompanied by a young keeper. It was
an afternoon of showers and bright sun and in one instance I saw three
rainbows glowing simultaneously. We clambered up the face of a hill
in close consort, through sodden turf and peat. An hour passed and
my nose began to run. I wiped it surreptitiously on a white handkerchief, fearing that my breach of camouflage would be espied by Piffa,
who I had noticed possessed one of perfectly matched green. I wondered when we would ever see a deer, when suddenly the keeper
flattened himself behind a crag. We followed suit immediately and
cautiously raising our heads we saw around twenty beasts in the glen
below. With his binoculars trained, the keeper even detected a humel,
a hornless stag. Were they rare? Were they impotent? He assured me
shortly that a humel could manage right enough!

As the object of the afternoon's exercise was to thin out the old and
mangy hinds before the onset of the winter months, it was decided
that Piffa should include the humel as a target, as scruffy a beast as any.
Piffa cocked her gun; her elegant green wool turban, her long fingers
further embellished with enviable long nails and gold rings, belied the
deadly act she was about to perform. She shot the humel, a hind and
its calf. It was an impressive bag in the space of minutes. The beasts
were then gralloched and the keeper thrust his knife through the
jugular veins. The blood spewed out sickeningly like an emptied hot
water bottle. We left the forlorn and sunken heaps to be picked up in
the morning and walked back down the deserted glen in the cold
damp dusk.

Back at Dunlossit we revived ourselves with Morag's succulent fruit cake, as dark as a brick of peat, and, afterwards, eyeing Piffa's magnificent selection of unctuous bath essences, I opted for a mustard one, which, when mixed with the steaming brown water of Islay, became an amazing brew.

November 6 Hardwick House

It is dubbed the party of the year in this morning's papers. The Prince of Wales danced through the dawn (he didn't; he left at 2 a.m.). Last night, at the Italian Embassy, the Ambassador, Roberto Ducci, and his Polish wife Wanda did indeed give a splendid ball in honour of His Royal Highness. Against the blaze of chandeliers and flaming candelabra, the richly-coloured French tapestries, jewelled combs and pearls and diamonds that glistened through elaborate veils of hair, the sparkling silk dresses and slim bare shoulders reflected in the suffused glimmer of tall Venetian mirrors, the night became alive with glamour, music, and dance. Henrietta Tavistock looked particularly beautiful in a jewelled jacket and her clear pale profile with its hint of the Asiatic was framed in a cloud of dark waves swept up high from her forehead.

Prince Charles held the centre of the floor. A steady flow of blondes would waft towards him at each suitable pause in the music and keep him dancing continuously to his obvious enjoyment. Margot Fonteyn[7] was also present. She electrified the floor, a radiant wisp in swirling white chiffon her small dark head pivoting from side to side to her own ecstatic rhythm. Her partners followed her steps gingerly.

And, meanwhile, Roberto's favourite tapestry (admirably described in his little book *Twenty-Four Hours at No 4 Grosvenor Square*) of the young woman by Pietro Fevere, sleeping peacefully in the Tuscan countryside, slept on. Only she would look as beautiful and as fresh this morning as she did last night.

November 15 Harwicke House

Sensational news this evening! Sir Anthony Blunt, surveyor of the Queen's pictures for over twenty years, has been publicly exposed as a Soviet agent, the wanted 'fourth man' who helped Burgess and Maclean flee Britain in 1951. We are also informed that, as long ago

[7] Prima Ballerina at the Royal Ballet and President of the Royal Academy of Dancing from 1954, Died 1991.

as 1964, Sir Anthony was persuaded to confess his involvements with Russia, the Attorney-General having offered him immunity from prosecution, believing that it was in the interests of the United Kingdom and its security forces to receive his information on Russian intelligence. A dubious barter.

Sir Anthony will be stripped of his knighthood as from midnight. Where is he? The porter from his block of flats off Edgware Road, who described him as 'a courteous man who always hailed his own cabs', has disclosed to reporters that Blunt left early yesterday morning and, taking a lot of luggage with him, said that he was off to Italy on holiday.

It was only on Monday morning this week that Sir Anthony was lecturing to a group of us at the Christie's Fine Art Course. Who would have guessed that this tall, spare, and erudite man (who like all accomplished lecturers had succeeded in stacking his slides upside down), standing before us expounding on the merits of Poussin and commenting wryly on the profligate attentions of Apollo to Daphne, should be the very man most wanted for treason to his country? Or could he be a double agent? The greatest spy on Britain's behalf that we have ever known?

December 8 Hardwicke House

Having last visited Moscow in 1963, I was fascinated to note any marked changes; there were plenty. A recent article, describing Red Square on a snowy winter's night, wrote of 'black, rain-washed cobbles like wrinkled prunes, dusted with icing sugar'. It then went on to describe the splendid impact of this newly-illuminated night city. Red Square in 1963 was dimly-lit and almost deserted by night, save for bedraggled old women sweeping and hosing down the streets. Their middle-aged daughters would be seen by day, wielding pickaxes and working road drills. Sixteen years later, Red Square is indeed a revelation. In preparation for the Olympics next year, the hot red bricks of the Kremlin have been newly scrubbed and repointed, the splendid epidemic of golden cupolas are lavishly gilded, the ministerial houses and public buildings are repainted in superb Schönbrunn yellow with immaculate pale-green coated roof tiles (a colour combination often used in eighteenth- and nineteenth-century Russia). St Basil's Cathedral is a veritable feast. Those absurd onion domes have been decked in brutal primary colours, striped and checked and dotted in such a way as to conjure up an exotic confection – liquorice allsorts came to mind. And over all flew the illuminated red flag, briskly, purposefully, a proud tongue of flame from the highest tower, it never droops. Sir William Hayter, our British Ambassador to Moscow from 1953 to 1965, suggested to me that an artificial air-vent secures its fierce and unabated flutter, but our Intourist guide assured us that the prevailing wind was strong at that height and always blowing in the same direction . . .

Red Square on this November night was alive with light and foot-steps. Gum, the main shopping centre with its labyrinth of bridged stairs and passages and its huge vaulted glass ceilings, was doing a brisk trade at 9 p.m. Men with upturned coat collars and heavy fur hats vied for service with women, who queued in belted mock-leather and high boots, for bread and cake, for shoes, for tinned groceries and cosmetics. Young couples loitered in front of the stalls, holding hands, talking intimately, stealing kisses – a social revelation indeed! The frosted wind cut sharply as a keening knife as we crossed the mammoth square to watch the changing of Lenin's guard. Two tall lean young men, their hair cropped short under their military peaked hats, marched from the Kremlin to that agate red marble mausoleum, every hour on the hour. Their iron-capped boots rang out on the cobbles as they kicked their legs high with each imperious step. They usurped their colleagues' guard in a trice and, in turn, stood motionless, taut with swords and iron concentration.

Back in the Intourist Hotel, the lobby surged with ferocious central heating and tentative commerce. Americans, Germans and Swedes, sporting newly-bought fur hats, checked in, clocked out, sent cables, oversaw luggage and porters. Moscow was on the secular map, it would seem. Indeed the heavy traffic from Sheremetevo Airport to the heart of the city and the wide, well-built underpasses had already proclaimed this spectacular evolution. In 1963 the roads to Moscow had been uneven, dark and empty, the city dead by 11 p.m. with most windows darkened and shops emptied of stock.

But with the evolution of material progress march those impercep-tible retrogressions, intourist pollution for one. In 1963 we were served caviar, sturgeon and vodka at the start of every meal, then chicken Kiev appeared with monotonous regularity, wreaking havoc on shirts and ties with its spewing butter, and we were treated to mounds of excellent silky ice cream. Sixteen years later, the food is indifferent and pared to a thrifty art, borscht and dubious meatballs, eggs and sausage meat and shashliks.

The Intourist Hotel in Moscow was adequate on every count, but how one hankered for those marbled halls and monolithic pillars, those high mirrored walls, and the handsome sweep of that carved wrought-iron staircase of the old National Hotel on Red Square. It is now mostly commandeered for offices and the Soviets are proud to accommodate us instead in their faceless modern comfort.

I gave the concierge a rouble or two for some bottled water, she handed me my room key and resumed her television-viewing. Television! I recalled momentarily that stern old woman in the National, fat, in black, with scraped-back hair, her châtelaine dangling and clanging round her thick, wrinkled trunk, as she waddled down the wide dark passage to unlock my room. Each room key remained clustered round her girth as she kept her gloomy vigil through the night. There were no books or radio or television then to relieve her surly unremitting guard.

December 23 Hardwicke House

It was a month ago that I made that journey to Tsinandali, the summer residence of the Tchavtchavadze family; it was a mean November Sunday morning and a malevolent mist hung across the mountain range. Before leaving Tbilisi I persuaded the driver and my guide Lali to drive up to the old quarter of the city and to show me Lermontov's[8] house. Painted a bright sky-blue with a white wooden balcony and veranda it was perched in a square, reminiscent of so many quiet, lost corners in Istanbul. Acacia trees, with their late autumn leaves turned brown, stood dripping and shivering alongside. We did not enter; the house was lived in and washing swung from the balustrades.

It was a hundred-mile drive to Tsinandali; the low flat valley of the Kura soon gave way to rolling plains that rose to wooded hills and attendant valleys. We stopped and drank from a roadside spring and met a busload from Odessa. Their blond young courier, a Georgian called Vadim, came and talked to Lali. He spoke excellent English and looked forward to seeing us again at lunch in the Intourist Hotel at the fortressed town of Telavi. We continued our journey while Lali fed me with a potted résumé of Georgian history. I tried to dissuade her from dwelling too deeply on Jason and his hopeless quest for the Golden Fleece and to talk instead of those nineteenth-century contretemps between the Russian forces and the Caucasian Murid bandits, and of the celebrated kidnapping of the Tchavtchavadze princesses, but she drew a veil over such comparatively recent activities.

We entered Kakhetia, the wine country of Southern Russia set in the fertile Alazani plain. Mile upon mile of vineyards stretched to

---

[8] *Lermontov, Tragedy in the Caucasus* by Laurence Kelly. Published by Constable 1977. To evoke the poet's struggle for political freedom and his deep love of the Caucasus.

the distant shrouded mountains. Screens of poplar and wide fields of harvested stubble were interspersed with small, straggling villages. Houses were built with large squares of pinkish local stone, with brick quoining to frame the windows; each walled garden was crammed with its own small vineyard and persimmon trees, while the gleaming orange fruit still clustered the stripped winter branches.

The road became narrower and our driver slowed the car as he navigated the rutted surface strewn with puddles, mud and loose stones. We passed ponies and donkeys driven by old women in black, with their cartloads of grain sacks, a dead pig or sheep. Men, young and old, stood in groups on the village corners; it was Sunday, a day of remorseless inactivity on this drizzling, cold November morning. Lali pointed out to me the different variety of fruit trees by the roadside, in the gardens and fields; mulberry, apricot, walnut and olive. The mulberries were still decked in bright yellow leaves and each slim trunk stood in a ring of fallen gold. One imagined this landscape in the spring in the smouldering heat of summer and then in the autumn, when the vendange would be in full spate, when this same road with its lush, green verge, and its screen of sheltering vine canopies, would be harbouring hot donkeys, ponies and peasants in its shade.

We arrived at Tsinandali. Despite the unremitting grey morning it looked superb. The indigenous combination of pink stone and inserted brick markings gave it a warmth that, together with the adjoining delicate tracery of the Moorish veranda, proved an irresistible invitation to enter. The park with its long-established and varied specimens of trees, many of them coniferous and some even sub-tropical, belied the winter starkness; it must be a veritable jungle in the summer, vibrant with birds and fountains and the deep glow of roses.

We entered the modest hall and were immediately confronted by that flight of wooden stairs down which one of Shamyl's 'turbaned monsters' had leapt in one bound with Mme Drancy[9] in his arms. We walked up and were surprised to find a large and voluble gathering of cameramen, cables and flash bulbs. An anxious woman barred our way to the main rooms. It was not possible to see round the house today, she explained; as we could see they were filming. An old peasant woman shambled past us with some logs in her twisted hands. Peering through the arms akimbo that defied our entry I saw a ravishing raven-haired young girl, warming herself by the roaring fire. Were they filming the story of Shamyl's invasion and kidnapping of the

[9] The governess to the princesses; they were held together in Shamyl's mountain eyrie for four months, until spring 1855. Drancy published a memoir, *Souvenirs d'une Française, Captive de Shamyl*, in 1857. Sales were low; the adventure was over and with no redeeming romance.

Princesses,[10] I asked ingenuously? No, a documentary, was the curt reply. I wondered, could that beautiful girl have been cast as the Princess Anna or Nina? Lali explained to them that I had come from London specifically to visit the house and reluctantly we were allowed into the old drawing-room. The rooms were in understandable disorder due to the filming session and we were urged to make haste, while the camera crew looked askance at our unceremonious interruption. We saw many photographs of the family, an oil painting of them dining in full evening dress on the veranda, and another, a charming, poignant portrait of the Princess Nina Griboyedova-Tchavtchavadze, slim-waisted in a black dress, widowed already at eighteen, her gazelle-like eyes and luminous pale face framed in veils of dark hair.

The family piano stood in the corner of the drawing-room and elegant French windows that were locked led on to the veranda. Could they be opened, I ventured? The answer was, No. I stood there, fingering the ivory-inlaid lever handles; this was the veranda where Lermontov must have paced, in between chapters and inspiration for his *Demon*. Finally they opened the windows for me and I wandered slowly up and down this hallowed walk that had harboured so many family scenes and secrets.

Lali was annoyed with me when I slipped through to the back rooms; they were not for public view and she called after me. However, I effected not to hear and saw for myself the children's bedrooms, now dark and deserted with wooden floors left bare.

Outside in the park, I walked up to the attractive brick stable block from where the Murids had begun their dawn attack. I imagined them careering on their excited horses down the cobbled pathways to the house. I asked Lali if she could show me the hollowed-out oak tree in which Princess Sophie had hidden and thus escaped, but Lali was tired and cold and it was time for lunch at Telavi. The oak tree was like any other oak tree with a hollow trunk, she assured me. By the handsome iron gates, she pointed out a dejected-looking stag, the last of the family's herd; the poor beast looked wet and half-dead.

We had a jolly lunch at Telavi, the old fortressed town nearby, the view again sickeningly obscured by the mist. Vadim joined us for a glass of wine. I suggested that I had been more trouble to Lali that morning than his entire busload from Odessa. I asked them if it were possible to buy a bottle of the best white wine and the best red. The young hotel manager, a good-looking sallow-faced Georgian with dark Byronic curls, promptly gave me two bottles as a present. The

[10] *The Sabres of Paradise* by Lesley Blanch, published by John Murray 1960. The stirring chronicles of the Caucasian wars waged between Shamyl (the Imam of Daghestan) and Tsar Nicholas I.

red was Mukhuzani, November '79 vintage, and the white, Gurjaani, November '79, both from local villages. I gave my handsome benefactor cigarettes and some 'pop-up' pens from Harrods in return, whereupon he picked me some French marigolds, which I assured him I would wear in my hair to the opera in Tbilisi that night. We drove back through the damp dusk and heard on the car radio, loud and clear: Tbilisi beating Mukhuzani three goals to one.

1980

Undeterred by the usual sensationalist media reports of heavy blizzards, overturned lorries in snow drifts and cars marooned on impassable roads in the Scottish border, we set off at 6 a.m. for Dumfriesshire. As a precaution we stowed a hefty garden spade, along with brandy, biscuits, candles and rugs. We reached Portrack, the white-painted late-Georgian manse of Sir John and Lady Keswick, for lunch. Our arrival happily coincided with a skene of geese streaming high over the house in spectacular ribbon formation, honking and curling through the low, heavy cloud. 'A magnificent show,' remarked Sir John reverently, 'grey-lag or perhaps even pink-foot! They come from Iceland to feed on my grass fields over there; ruinous to any autumn seeding.'

We were standing beside the front lawn, where a smooth sweep of snow had formed an arresting dais for a life-size boar, modelled in bronze by Elizabeth Frink. Lady Keswick sailed to the door and caught us up in a rush of welcome and warmth. We had never met before. Sir John, a former Chairman of Jardine Matheson of Hong Kong, and his wife Clare must be renowned for their years of formidable hostmanship. He was awarded the KCMG for his quasi-ambassadorial services and is reputed to be one of the richest men in Britain.

Each room and passage was elegantly enhanced with a graceful overflow of Chinese fine arts. Large urns and porcelain cache-pots exuded enviable plants and flowering camellias; lacquer and gilt embellishments abounded; expansive Chinese watercolours in delicate monochrome and spattered with hieroglyphics hung in profusion on high walls; whilst exotic birds and dogs and an unexpected collection of three-legged toads were liberally displayed in cabinets and book-shelves or seated low beside hearthstones – a house so packed with beautiful things that it might have again evoked that comment of mock-horror from Virginia Woolf who, whilst staying with the Freshfields in Sussex, exclaimed, 'There is not an ugly thing in it!'

Lady Keswick led us through to her drawing-room where we were further enveloped in warmth from a roaring wood fire and more eye-catching objets d'art. An early bronze group by Henry Moore nestled on a pie-crust table, while a small Degas and a Rodin vied for attention on another. An evocative evening landscape by Edward

Burra hung above the fireplace (he and Sir John were schoolboy friends) and charming watercolours by Gwen John were propped along a bookcase. Lady Keswick put some heavy unwieldy logs on the fire. 'Don't move, don't move,' she urged us when we offered a hand. She was an extremely good-looking, well-preserved woman. Her exceptionally good teeth, her clear, pretty complexion and her indomitable energy totally defied her seventy-five years.

We lunched on pheasant while a diminutive Chinese darted in the background with neat, quick attention. After the meal Sir John suggested we needed fresh air to combat the long drive from London; he wished to show us his Castle. We obediently clambered into a land-rover, but Lady Keswick, looking handsome in a deerstalker, said that she did not want to see the Castle that afternoon. We left her to tend her charming bird-cote; its miniature pointed roof was swathed in fronds of fresh yew and hung with cylinders of appetising nuts. It was placed close to the dining-room window and during lunch I had noticed a constant swoop of little coloured wings. Lady Keswick was concerned that the rinds of cheese that she had left out for them that morning might not be to their liking.

Swinging down narrow lanes, banked with snow, we shortly turned down a small drive and came suddenly upon Merkland, a miraculous pink finger of stone rising tall and sheer in its original sixteenth-century simplicity. Around, the snow lay white and smooth, marked only by the footprints of geese and deer. The small frozen lake beyond glowed with the deep red tracery of dogwood. 'The pink-foot will settle here with the thaw,' Sir John assured us, 'and the golden orfe will swim to the surface again.' It was a grey and sullen afternoon, but how ethereal this rare, unexpected scene must appear, lit up with sunlight, this intimate vignette, a castle standing free in snow, shielded by hornbeam, birch and flowering cherry, with its lake of ice beyond, an iridescent drama of white and silver, red and gold.

A worn marriage stone, faintly inscribed with the date 1590, lay embedded in the rough granite lintel above the broad oak door. Sir John, whose absorption with his castle was fast becoming infectious, turned the key with impish delight. The narrow stone stair curled away to our left; to the right of the minuscule entrance opened a dark, dank bothy. Sir John indicated the small hole cut through its vaulted ceiling and explained how household animals and even a sheep and goat or two would have been stalled in this cave-like pen; their emanating body heat would have heated the floor above most effectively.

We followed him slowly up the stairs and wandered through intimate rooms where wide stone fireplaces, niches in walls and enchanting turrets invited the imagination to furnish and make habitable.

'I don't count sheep at night any more,' confided Sir John, 'I climb my castle instead and plan each bath, electric plug and table. I fall asleep before the top turrets. I think we need a sitz-bath in that turret and come and take a look at my lavatory in this other.' He urged us to squat in a sitting position and thus enjoy the view. Each room was fundamentally well-restored with new beam ceilings and repointed stone walls. 'One summer evening,' he continued wistfully, 'Clare and I shall hold a picnic party and have pipers along. We will dance all night by the side of the lake. Come, we must go back home. I have more treasures to show you.'

Sir John's proud collection of James Cox trinkets in silver gilt and semi-precious stones proved a small travesty. We first helped him move old leather suitcases, painted Chinese boxes, and cylindrical Chinese hat-boxes into the drawing-room. It seemed as though we were about to embark for a long trip on the Orient Express, I ventured, and helped him set up a pair of card tables on which to rest his florid trophies. He unpacked them lovingly, one by one. First an elephant, carved from amethyst, prancing joyously on a mother-of-pearl drum with a gold filigree umbrella precariously poised in its trunk; next, exotic orbs, snuff-boxes, clocks, watches and musical boxes with fanciful birds a-flutter were lined up in slow succession before our admiring protestations. Gem-stones glittered provocatively and small silver gilt lids opened smugly to reveal their pink and gold satin cavities. Sir John sighed happily to see his toys spread out before him. I fingered an oval casket of cream agate, which encased a vivid green miniature dog. It was very charming and Lady Keswick explained how the tiny dog so often went missing that they had designed for him this special kennel. She also pointed out another oval box of jade, rare and yellow, which when opened sprung forth a delicate butterfly in amethyst. We dutifully helped Sir John pack his treasures away into their enticing containers and the drawing-room was reassembled to its normal contours.

We bathed and changed for dinner, fearfully enjoying the privilege of dusting the body from a pair of priceless Chinese bowls with lids and finials intact. Sir John, looking dapper in tweed trousers and a capacious Chinese padded dinner jacket, poured us champagne from a glass jug decanter. He blundered and broke its slender neck on my glass. Oh, the angst and the mortification. The loss or breakage of a beautiful possession is always debilitating to the soul and nobody indulged more deeply in his grievous misfortune than Sir John. Conversation faltered and dinner guests stood still in awkward sympathy until he had recovered his habitual, urbane calm, when finally Lady Keswick whirled into the room on a sea of floating pink and seed pearls, and kissed him better. Somebody suggested it might be repaired Chinese fashion with gold insertions, thus even embellishing it. Or should it just be thrown away? Lady Keswick concluded most satisfactorily that she would buy another.

February 22 Cairo Egypt

We landed at Cairo at 10 p.m. Young soldiers in tin hats man the airport with a nonchalant guard. Glinting bayonets are hoisted high on each narrow shoulder. Security is extreme and our name and destination are meticulously noted at every check point. Faint breezes stir in the warm night as a Mercedes taxi whisks us along smooth straight roads lined with waving palm trees and eucalyptus. Neon-advertisements and high-rise lego tenements sweep us to the heart of the city and the wrinkled black coil of the Nile.

The Hilton has no rooms; we have arrived one whole day late. We were indeed expected yesterday but not today. We take a taxi to the Méridien and pore over gin and fruit and coffee, clinging to their hesitant assurances of a room at 5 a.m. Tom addresses himself to this familiar Middle Eastern hassle and the *Times* crossword. I lose myself in bouts of Virginia Woolf's diary, 1915–1919, and make tentative enquires as to the possibility of watching the sun rise through the Pyramids. Could I take a taxi at 5 a.m.? But nobody would be there, exclaims the surprised manager; most people visited the Pyramids at 9 or 10 a.m. Too dangerous to go alone, concludes Tom, and I sink once more into the blue butterflies and mushrooms of Virginia Woolf's beloved Sussex downs.

February 23

We wake late to a cloudless sky with the Nile rippling and blue below our room. The shores are lush with palm trees, mango and acacia, and the gnarled thick trunks of the banyan tree shade the wide corniche. A miscellaneous concrete jungle rises high and hard from the brushed green fringes of the water's edge. A cluster of bamboo shacks nestles below us, where an old turbaned man in a dish-dasher waters exotic plants and tubs of banana trees. With the aid of ragged little boys he is harbouring a thriving nursery garden – the Cairo equivalent of Rassells of London, it would appear. A rich stench of camel dung ensures this flourishing establishment and I resist the temptation to buy a potted banana tree. Another turbaned old hand called

Mohammed offers me a trip on his motor boat, *Arabia*. I again resist and spend two absorbing hours in the Egyptian Museum.

Young guards in pairs tickle each other and giggle as they sit, bored and sleepy in the great ill-lit rooms. A dishevelled display, the familiar relics of Tutankhamen[1] jog one's memory of that superbly-mounted exhibition at our own British Museum. A friendly guard interrupts my dazed assimilation of Neolithic pots and jewellery, of huge gesso couches, shrouded mummies, and strange hunting weapons, by suggesting he show me a stuffed desert dog and some fossilised BC loaves of bread. The bread looks remarkably fresh considering its ancient provenance.

I walk back through the crowded dusty streets along the waterfront. Meagre grey donkeys draw carts of fruit and wood and builders' rubble, and ponies stand by for carriage rides. The juxtaposition of the ancient and the modern jostles incongruously. The Mercedes honks at the donkey, the old men, their heads piled high with bread, shuffle barefoot past the Hilton. I meet Shahira Khayat who owns a gift shop and hand her a letter from her aunt in London. Shahira's family home was recently sold to the American Embassy and subsequently demolished. She invites us for a drink at her apartment opposite the famous Gezira Sporting Club. She assures me it is safe to see the Pyramids at dawn if I take a limousine rather than a dilapidated taxi. And did I ride well? She has a friend who rides and warns me that the horses go at a fair gallop in the desert zone.

The evening falls into night. The traffic hoots and growls continuously whilst loudspeakers wail their calls to prayer.

February 24

At 5.15 a.m. I set off in a reliable taxi through the ramshackle sprawl of Cairo's suburbs. It is still dark when we arrive at the Pyramids. The huge sharp piles are etched against a black sea of stars. Ahmed, my driver, suggests we walk around the second number, a clumsy exercise in the half-light with loose sand and hefty rubble strewn around. I regret wearing new Italian shoes and feel a hole in my favourite Dior stockings. In the grey dawning light a solider looms. He speaks briefly to my driver and indicates that I should follow them back to our car. I am alarmed at this sudden interception. Ahmed explains to me that our friend suggests we have been making love and that he must see

---

[1] Following on from the exhibition of the British Museum, 1972, *Tutankhamen* comes again to the Dome in 2007.

our passports. I suggest Ahmed persuade this surly interloper that I am merely in love with the Pyramids. Further desultory argument ensues and with the final admonition that the Pyramids are 'not open' until 9 o'clock, we are left in peace. 'You do well to come here before the crowds and the hotting,' retorts Ahmed as we watch the soldier's retreat and, finally, 'He only wanted money!' It is my first sharp introduction to the corrupt seams of the Egyptian modus vivendi.

The sky becomes streaked with broken bars of rose light and a pale sun reveals the sharp peaks of those golden limestone cones. The timeless beauty of that ravaged Sphinx appears indomitably square-jawed in profile; but, on facing those full soft lips, the high rounded cheekbones, and the wide set of those magnetic sightless eyes, one stands before a monument of unassailable serenity and mystery and power. A wrinkled old Arab with a rough tweed coat thrown over his cotton dish-dasher beckons me to ride his camel. The animal bares its teeth, regurgitates its cud and growls disconcertingly as it sinks to its knees. I clamber aboard, clinging to my handbag and the wooden pommel as it hoists its humps. The Arab leads me through the cool early morning past tombs and round the Sphinx. I think how pleasurable, indeed unique this start to a day as my camel lurches and swaggers on his sandy beat. There is nobody abroad except a few desert dogs; they are well-fed on bread that still costs one half pence a loaf. I am lowered to the sands again and two avid Arabs lure me to the tomb of King Tut. We lever ourselves backwards down a notched stone shaft; with torches they light up a long deep trough of red granite; its heavy stone lid is supported at an angle. The tomb is empty save for sand and long-bleached fragments of bone, not the remains of King Tut, they assure me, just a few bones thrown in by tourists.

Back at the hotel it is too lovely a morning to go inside. The sun is up and it is only 7 a.m. A horse is tethered to a rail below the concrete complexity of the hotel's foundations. It munches on a pile of stringy spinach leaves, unperturbed by the busy corniche below. I walk towards a mosque, which rises at the end of a small back road skirting the Nile. The road is flooded in parts and steeped in silt and litter. The air smells of watered shrubs, dung, orange peel and the ubiquitous stench of warm decay. I reach the mosque where a young man in a white crocheted skull-cap stands before the high open doors and waves me away disparagingly. I resolve to return by the inner main road, but here the flooding proves even worse, a municipal overflow rather than the Nile, it would appear. Women in long skirts and many veiled in black chadors are taking off shoes to wade through the dirty flow. I follow a young woman in a blue knitted turban secured with pearl hatpins, who effectively navigates this morass of mud and water. I hear her tut-tut with indignation, suggesting that these untimely conditions are not a regular hazard on her way to work. Clinging to railings we catch each stepping stone as it is bared from the tidal flow of the wheels of passing cars and buses, but to no avail, even she and I take in water at the end.

In the evening we go to Shahira's drinks party. Her apartment is a pastiche on French lines. The parquet floors, high ceilings and doors lead to spacious rooms of nineteenth-century fauteuils, mirrors and commodes, interspersed with heavy dark Syrian pieces inlaid with pearl and bone. Her elegant turbaned black manservant plies us with spiced canapés and a cream dip of mint and yoghurt. There is much talk of fast-increasing wealth, despite inflation, of the accelerating noise, dirt, rush and ubiquitous corruption that follows in the wake of prosperity. There is dark reference also to the growing undercurrent of student unrest, more particularly to the recent upsurge of young women who walk the streets, flaunting their black chadors and shouting anti-secular propaganda. The Government is acutely aware of this insidious subversion, but concludes warily that Sadat is a good man, a man well able to contain a bad situation.

Later, returning to the Hilton, we see for ourselves, four black shrouded young women stationed in the all-night café. They look as ominous and as predatory as the witches in *Macbeth*.

February 27

I take a taxi to the old quarter of Cairo. Again one is struck by this crazy, harmonious confusion of the progressive marching with the retrograde: the Mercedes alongside the donkeys, inert shapeless bodies sleeping undisturbed in well-tended public gardens. Goats are curled beside chattering grandmothers while grubby children carve the dust with stones and fingers. Old men smoke and drink and spit.

The mosque of Ibn Tulun is empty, dark and cool, with high-arched windows of variously-carved latticed stone. Sunlight and the faint clamour of the city filters through each fretted arch; their tracery seems frail as lace. Birds chirp and fly in from the sun-baked courtyard to the cool colonnades of the mosque. They settle, chattering on the minutely-carved wood pulpit, a masterpiece of Islamic art. Sunlight plays on the ancient gold and glass mosaic of the prayer-niche.

Alongside the mosque I wander through the old house of Gayer Anderson, an English doctor who lived there from 1938 to 1945, filling it with choice chattels gleaned from his Eastern travels. There are balconies with secretive little wooden shutters, cool summer verandas, lined with ivory-inlaid caskets from Damascus, and silk rugs from Isfahan and Istanbul; dim bedrooms with dark, richly-painted wood ceilings and couches for the master and one for his boy. The dining-room strikes a surprising note with its complete suite of Queen Anne furniture. A self-portrait reveals Dr Anderson in Arab headdress and beside him hangs his Arab servant, a beautiful young boy, again painted by his master and obviously adored.

In the evening I ride at Giza with Angus Hay, a friend from Perth-shire, whom we last saw reeling in his kilt at the Buchan Barn Dance in August. The old stables in the shadow of the Pyramids hand us nimble horses and lend me boots. We gallop over dunes dipped in arrows of light and violet shadow. The Pyramids turn gold, then grey, their precision softened by the minute. Cairo is spread low before us, a wide basin of green and stone and fading minarets. We hear the faint calls to prayer. Turbaned Arabs take our horses and lead us through the dishevelled stableyard of sand, amok with puppies, dogs and peck-ing hens. Through the evening rush-hour traffic Angus talks of his ambitions to set up a trading establishment on the lines of Jardine Matheson.

Cairo has fast become a ripe centre for business deals, but is hindered by uninitiated business sense – save for its own suffocating corruption. Government officials are paid a mere £200 a month, but 'clear a lot on the side'. The Government itself has recently elected to spend four million pounds in Mercedes taxis to boost the comforts of tourism, but with the population of Cairo rising to twelve million, the added accommodation needs for tourists must pose insoluble problems.

We spend a late evening at the Méridien where a lavish floor show complete with vigorous belly-dancing and fire-eating lasts one and a half hours. A comparable outing in London could cost £150 for three people; in Cairo it cost less than £50.

February 29

A scholarly woman, Layla al Hakim, drives us to see the tombs of Saqqara. We take the canal road through Memphis and the flat, fertile plains of Mitrahina. We pass tall stooks of clipped sugar-cane, heaped palm fronds and the familiar assortment of turbaned children, peasants, dogs and donkeys. Bevies of gay young women in bright long skirts, their heads piled with bundles of dirty linen, wend towards the canal. Here a frenzied activity of slapping clothes on round flat stones and a fierce jabbing with bare feet proclaims it is Friday – a day of cleanliness and prayer. Bedouin mud and wattle huts are lined beside summer houses; constructed on Ottoman lines in local red brick or white and gold sandstone. Layla is critical of both extremes of habitat.

At Saqqara we admire the 'graffiti' on the walls of tombs; friezes of fish and animals and toga-ed and fezzed hunters, with slim bare legs and torsoes, are exquisitely etched into the stone and coloured in the natural stone-ground pastas of red and ochre. The patina is enhanced by the inclusion of egg white in this colouring process, an art form that seems to epitomise the primitive and the sophisticated simultaneously. There is no glass protection on these relics open to the wind and dust and we again discuss the lamentable state of the Cairo Museum. Layla claims there would be an uproar if anything were sold and that any proceeds would be misappropriated anyway.

In the evening we have drinks at the British Embassy, a white pilastered mansion built on a generous scale by Lord Cromer in 1894. (He was mildly reproved for exceeding his budget of £30,000.) Soldiers with bayonets stand at the wrought-iron gates and railings, protected in turn by a barrage of sandbags. The present incumbent, Sir Michael Weir[2], was educated at Aberdeen Grammar. He and his second wife prove a modest, young couple with undertones of social insecurity. The days of a sophisticated embassy run on the old Etonian network are clearly past.

Armed with drinks, Sir Michael and his wife give us a conducted tour of the main rooms. Sir Michael's own penchant for modern art is clearly misplaced in these imposing Regency-style proportions. His David Hockneys and Ivon Hitchens are unfavourably shown against a backdrop of high white panelled walls and delicately painted ceilings in the Wedgwood style. Lady Weir is particularly anxious to paint out the ceilings, preferring a monastic effect. However, with their grant of only £25,000 to redecorate, it will be difficult for them to misman-age the funds too dramatically since it would cost them at least £5,000 to curtain one room alone. We discover a handsome bombé black lacquer cabinet in the cluttered billiard room, together with a pair of elegant carved wood fauteuils and some Chinese lamps. We persuade them to move this loot into the main rooms and thus eliminate some indifferent pieces already ensconced.

With their further encouragement a friendly process ensues where we suggest and effect more moves with furniture, rugs and lamps. Their two-year-old son, clutching a mug of cocoa, is delighted with this sudden game of general post and we leave our hosts with assurances to come again.

---

[2] Ambassador, Cairo 1979–85. Narrowly missed death when Sadat was assassinated eighteen months later. Sitting fifteen yards from the President, Weir flung himself to the ground and was unhurt.

March 1

A windy day with fractious eddies of dust blown in from the Sahara. A young girl, Mia El Monasterly, drives us to her grandmother's house on the Nile, an imposing edifice of Spanish/Ottoman proportions with the stone façade washed a dull hot red. Built in the 1950s during the Revolution, it took seven years to complete, and appears as though it has stood for a hundred. Mia's grandmother is Turkish by birth, formerly married to an Egyptian diplomat. Now widowed and in her eighties she is grappling with deafness, a failing hip and the escalating theft of her priceless collection by dishonest servants. Her jade pieces have diminished alarmingly; rugs disappear by the week and Mia tells us how prints and objets are regularly found, artfully secreted in drawers, a popular one-remove to their final abduction. On her death the house and contents will be sealed off by the Government who, having already taken their own surreptitious pick, will condescend the remainder to her next of kin at a tax rate of 70%. Mia has meanwhile persuaded her bewildered grandmother, who is now beset with an overriding distrust that even extends to her family, to sell the priceless Isfahan rug and the 300-piece Meissen dinner service.

A desultory black servant draws upon tall, creaking shutters in the drawing-room. Dusty sunlight spills on a sea of glorious colour, mellowed reds and peacock-blues; saffrons and olive-greens, rich with age and the faded passing of time. The carpet is a little worn, but in overall excellent repair. Mme El Monasterly paid £8,000 in 1940, a huge sum in those days. Tom suggests it is now worth between £50,000 and £60,000.

We wander through vast rooms of marbled grandeur, supported by pillared arches and concave niches, some dark and shuttered, all layered in the dust of neglect and crammed each one with exquisite rugs, Chinese ceramics, huge porcelain lamps and jardinières. Chandeliers of Venetian glass and richly-coloured Bohemian hang dejected in their dust-dimmed long-forfeited elegance.

The Meissen service is stored in a back-room cupboard. Assiettes are still wrapped in their original brown tissue paper, untouched, some since their day of purchase. Is it eighteenth- or nineteenth-century? The pristine condition obscures its age. Dust lies thick in this little room and cobwebs obscure the only light afforded by a narrow window. We remove ornately trellised fruit baskets, tureens and oval fish dishes to the sunlit drawing-room. I hold them to the light as Tom photographs and measures. A servant brings us coffee and gives the table-top a cursory dusting. As I stand before the wide tall window with the Meissen in my hands I hear the Nile lap at the walls of the house. Across this stretch of blue I see peasants stooping over green tomato clumps. A fishing boat drifts past, the sail is furled and three men nod their turbaned heads in greeting. Sparrows chirp in the eucalyptus tree that trails limp, pale branches across the balustrades of the narrow garden terrace. Another fisherman in a more modest craft glides by; his weathered wicker basket is secured by strands of sisal and two heavy stones. I lean out of the window, its ledge thick with the red dust from a nearby brick factory. I see the barges weighed down with their cargo of bricks. Young men in tunics dart back and forth from the barges, bare-legged in sandalled feet; others, in waves of red dust, quickly fill their brick hods. As the load is dissipated the barges slowly rise in the water.

I hear a shuffling step and Madame la Grandmère edges across the large room with the aid of an invalid walking rail. 'Qu'est-ce qu'ils font?' she asks me in alarm, pointing to the Meissen pieces. 'On compte les pièces, Grandmamère,' calls Mia from the nether regions of the store-room. We are introduced and the servant brings a tray of more sweet black coffee. 'Grandmamère' looks remarkably intact, with a lilac crocheted scarf wound round her little head, from which escapes wisps of white curls. Her skin is soft and smooth. She had obviously been a renowned Ottoman beauty and from the few watercolours of her hanging in her bedroom one could easily recognise the woman of forty years ago who, stepping out in furs, reclining in pearls, or elegantly erect in a hat, could boast an aristocratic hook to the nose, the highest cheek-bones and the most alluring slant to the hazel eyes. She talks exquisite French in a deep, low voice and bewails the lack of servants. We humour her, with assurances that the demise of servants is a world-wide problem.

What did she do all day, we ask Mia as we drive away through the ubiquitous noise and upheaval of the Cairene streets. 'Oh,' says Mia airily, 'the same as she's always done. She rests, looks after herself, takes her rejuvenating monkey gland pills. Friends still call in the afternoon, and three years ago she took herself off to Russia, felt she ought to see it, a backlash of that old tribal Caucasian blood, you know.'

At 4 o'clock we fly Finnair to Istanbul.

March 2 Istanbul Turkey

I spend the day in bed, sneezing pleasurably from a desert cold. The terraced plot of vegetables is still meticulously-tended beneath our same bedroom window and the two slender minarets of the Dolmabahçe Mosque are faintly discernible through swathes of mist. All seems quiet with little traffic. It is 37°F and there is no coffee. Turkey out of coffee! 'We have no money to import,' explains an apologetic waiter. (Meanwhile in the North Yemen, a main source of supply, coffee cultivation has been largely substituted for the more remunerative narcotic 'Gat'.) Having read some weeks ago that not even Lord Carrington was offered a cup in Ankara during his talks with the new President Demirel, I have brought with me six pounds of Kenya, Mocha and French Continental beans from the Richmond Coffee Centre, to give to our friends. Aylın and Emré Gönensay dine with us tonight and Rahmi has sent us white freesias. He is in Izmir today.

Emré and Aylın, she is as beautiful and as voluble as ever in her grey tweed trouser suit and single string of pearls. They talk of their repressions augmented by the worst winter they have suffered for thirty years, of fuel scarcities with no import of logs, of whole families moving in together to keep warm, and of meat prices rocketing to 400 per cent. Their whole economy is grabbed by the throat; devaluation choked by an absurd 100 per cent-inflation. Meanwhile they are heartened by the Western world's strong reaction to the Soviet invasion of Afghanistan; it might so easily have been them. Now with the bolstering of Western loans and the promise of American arms they feel encouraged.

There is an average of three street killings a day in Istanbul alone; young soldiers guarding banks and public buildings are popular targets, with their guns an enviable prize. Despite these grim reports Emré is confident that under Demirel's strong lead, with the loyal support of his police and militia, the situation will improve. Turkey will rise again from its present nadir.

We eat and drink well at a small underground restaurant. A piano is being played and the bill is a modest £5 a head. At the end of the meal a waiter ceremoniously ladles a small warm scented towel on each plate with sugar tongs and hands us Turkish delight.

March 4

Thick fog over the Bosphorus this morning. A shaft of rose light breaks through and sweeps a momentary trail, a ball of white sun and then all is blanked grey again. We breakfast on white cheese, olives, bread and tangerines and drink strong tea. Tom visits a Mrs Dokunter, she has an ikon and a watch to sell. Ships and boats pass through the leaden, misted Straits. How often must Atatürk have sat and watched these waters from his palace on the shore. Often lugubrious and depressed, his spirits must have soared to see this arresting landscape in all its changing mood and light. The bars of strident colour swivelling on the sunset waves, the dim faded blue of the Anatolian hills beyond and domes and minarets inked black against the moon. Turkish naval authorities detained a Yugoslav destroyer last week. It sailed through the Straits, on its passage from the Black Sea to the Mediterranean without permission – and Tito lingers on.

March 5

A radiance of sun and mist and snow. We walk gingerly down the hillside to the Dolmabahçe Palace, slowly picking our way through ice and thaw. The guard at the baroque Regale Gate denies us entry. We peer fretfully through the imposing vista beyond: fountains, a frozen central pond, stone statuary brushed with snow, still, dark cedar trees and pine, and the final soaring whit-marble pillar parapets, and lavish Rococo crenellations of the Sultanate's Palace.

It has always proved difficult to see round the Dolmabahçe Palace.[3] Last year it was closed due to bouts of vandalism and for years before it was in the throes of extensive restoration. Now it is only possible to be taken round in small groups of eight or ten. We wait an hour. Soldiers change guard with much saluting and long lithe steps. They are young and strong and flex their thigh muscles as they stand at ease. Tom remarks on their dirty boots. I wander along the marble landing stage, beside the Dolmabahçe Mosque, an arresting site. The old bronze cannons and the two worn bollards talk still of launchings and home-comings long since past. Seagulls wheel and scream above the lapping waves and Leander's little tower stands poignant and forlorn in mist. I rejoin Tom at the Regale Gate, still half-opened to its tantalising treats, when a guard, observing our own determined stand, inexplicably waves us through.

To our right an ornate white-gated quay stretches the length of the Palace, almost a thousand feet along the Bosphorus shore. We approach the Palace doors up an imposing flight of narrow marble steps, whereupon an eager nimble Turk sweeps us through the salons, chambers, reception rooms and up the famous crystal staircase, where a line-up of fire buckets catching discordant drips from the leaking glass dome above somewhat reduces this sumptuous grandeur to a more domestic level.

We are led through countless rooms, long dim passages, up more

---

[3] *Cabbages and Kings* by Ann Allestree; an article, with photography by Fritz von der Schulenburg, of the Dolmabahçe Palace. Published February 1983 in *The World of Interiors*.

stairs and down. Some two hundred rooms we see and four miles we seem to walk. A palace of such overpowering magnitude and opulence, one feels cowed. Each massive mahogany door is richly-carved and ornamented in gold leaf. Every ceiling, wall, and alcove is exquisitely-frescoed, painted, or festooned with silks and lace and velvets. Skins of brown Siberian bears, teeth bared in hefty heads, hug the inlaid parquet floors. Everywhere there is an explosion of mammoth chandeliers, brilliant faceted wall glasses, and crystal fireplaces studded with Sèvres. Not even the solid radiators are left unadorned; each fluted pipe is washed with gold. Countless Chinese urns, French clocks, commodes, and gilded pieces have their pair. Elaborate gifts from every world-wide potentate swell this prolific collection, and Queen Victoria, not to be outdone, commissioned yet another ugly legacy of conspicuous largesse – a four-ton chandelier.

Next we are shown the Sultan's bathroom, a feast of alabaster with silver knobs at every turn, and next the secluded harem baths, light with iznik tiles of lavender and lime. We pass through the Harem corridor where fanlights of deep blue glass look to the sea. They are tinted blue to conceal any perambulations from the eyes of lusty sailors. Many panes are broken, shattered from an explosion between two tankers on a fog-bound night some months ago.

Finally to Atatürk's modest suite, a simple study with a worn, brown leather chair and commanding views of the Bosphorus. I sit at his desk and our guide hurriedly opens the small left-hand drawer and shows me the master's favourite glass hand-blotter. The bedroom too is simple, sparsely-furnished in heavy walnut. Beside the silk-covered bed stands a glass-fronted cabinet, lined with half-full bottles; Atatürk's medicine chest, explains our guide. The stale dark sticky medicaments are more suggestive of liqueurs. Also stacked are many long-sealed packets. Tobacco? No. His Excellency's favourite chocolate, declares the guide. Atatürk died in this room on the morning of November 10, 1938. The clock still stands at 5 past 9. Next his simple white-tiled bathroom with a secret door that opens ingeniously through the mirrored plate of a bombé display cabinet to the reception room beyond. We walk into sun again and as a special concession are ushered through the heavy windows to the porticoed balcony. We scan the Bosphorus through the master's telescope and finally descend that illustrious crystal stairway down to earth.

March 6

A freezing day with a white and wintry sun. The leaden domes and gold finials of mosques gleam palely. We reach the Blue Mosque, which is closed, but nevertheless are given permission to enter with the small proffer of a bribe. It is damp inside but wonderfully blue and dim. A blackbird flits high in the painted domes; two men perched on wooden scaffolding re-set priceless tiles with much raucous clearing of throats and irreverent spitting. A brisk walk to the Bazaar where we admire more kilims, drink tea, and compare prices with a view to buying on another day. One is particularly attractive – a 'Yoruk' – in limes and corals with knotted tufts at random on its field.

March 7

The boom of cannon fire at 8.30 a.m. from a visiting German training ship; sixty-one blasts of greeting reverberate alarmingly through the morning mists. Later we see young sailors devouring chocolate cake in the Hilton lobby and bargaining for Turkish delight, cigarettes and cheap lace petticoats in the bazaar.

We buy three kilims for a total of £300, quite cheap, a Denizli Panutale in faded pinks and mauve, a Konya-Obrak in saffron, browns and blue, and an Aydin-Helvace with a strange rambling motif of coral rings and medallions.

We visit the Museum of Turkish and Islamic Arts and are surprised to see it celebrate its opening day after months of restoration. We are swept in on a wave of police and ministers of art and culture. The outer courtyard is en fête with a flurry of carnations, tulips and trailing ribbons. The Minister talks too long in unintelligible Turkish to the accompaniment of flashing bulbs, heavy coughing and much excited chatter from women with a tossing and fondling of animal skins slung round their shoulders. We finally enter the white-washed stone vaults and see splendid kilims and cimcims, ugly incense sprays, large unfamiliar pedestals of mother of pearl, Koranic manuscripts and a few rare broken tiles.

The German boat is ringed with fairy lights at twilight. A glittering thread of gold and silver beads it is a pendant jewel that sways on soft, black velvet air. We dine with boisterous friends of Rahmi, burly, bearded men who ply us with Veuve Clicquot, a flow of loud jokes in Turkish, and much thigh-slapping. Wives scuttle around quietly with laden dishes and a respectful waiter in a white jacket notes down how sweet each guest takes his Turkish coffee. I am wedged next to a

thick grey beard upon a bulky torso who tells me he exports fish to
Scotland; Scotland, he reminds me darkly, would like to be independent
of England.

The steep cobbled lanes of Tarabya suggest the opening scene of
Cavalleria Rusticana; the morning is warm and bright with sun. Women
in scarves and shawls peer out of old windows. One shakes dust from
her hand switch, another empties a pail from her upper storey, and
washing hangs by every blistered wall. A young man with a pony and
cart trundles by, wailing sonorously for scrap metal, Aylın gives us
coffee on her sun-baked terrace with the Bosphorus blue below. We
lunch on mullet and blue fish on the Marmara shore. Cloud descends
with drizzle as we drive through the toll gate of the Bosphorus bridge
and arrive on the Asian shore. We take tea with the ex-Turkish
Ambassador to London, Nuri Birgi[4]. His old Ottoman wooden house
is largely shuttered and he apologises for cold rooms. We sit over an
elegant brass brazier and prod the glowing charcoal with a fork.

His spectacular view is marred with mist and rain; the grey blurred
shapes of boats and ships and huddled fishermen drift past his wide
windows. We meet Lord John Montagu Douglas Scott[5], a younger
son of the Duke of Buccleuch; he looks thin and cold and tall. He
talks quietly and pleasantly of his endeavours to learn Turkish and to
study eighteenth-century Ottoman painting. We ask him to lunch
on Monday, after his Turkish lesson in Bebek that morning. Tea is
announced and we enjoy a seated ceremony of silver pots, gadrooned
wide salvers filled with scones, and a succulent apple flan made by the
Austrian pastry cook. A charming lady unexpectedly produces a Mogul
dagger from her handbag; it is sheathed in shagreen and generously
studded with rubies and curves of jade. Tom thinks it worth £10,000;
she elects to sell it and buy her son a flat in Ankara.

Later we dine on the Asian shore at Rahmi's old white-painted
house. We are ferried across the Bosphorus in his motor launch,
together with an exotic bombe surprise specially ordered from the
Divan Oteli. We step from his landing stage to softly-lit rooms, strewn
with old carpets and elegantly-dressed guests and waiters serving caviar.
Rahmi's blonde German housekeeper, a Mrs Fratesi, with the formid-

[4] His Excellency was the popular ambassador in the 1950s. After diplomatic postings round
the world, he restored his early nineteenth-century yali (a wood waterfront house) on the
Bosphorus. Filled with his collection of opaque glass – Beykoz ware – and furnished in
European/Oriental style, the house has spectacular views across the water to Topkapí Saray.
Visitors welcome.
[5] In 1982 John Scott founded and edited the magazine *Cornucopia* to span the culture and
economies, the shores, the landscapes and architectural history of Turkey. Articles by writers
from the art world, the diplomatic, travellers and historians. The magazine is sold at Daunt
Books, 83 Marylebone High Street, London.

able qualification of being a former employee at Claridges, ensures an evening of stylish proportions. We drink champagne and Beaujolais '79 from silver goblets and later take coffee in an upstairs room, which is given over to ships' instruments and low seats, draped in more carpets. Waiters with silver salvers weave their way through highly-polished helms and binnacles, telescopes, and compasses.

March 9

A wet grey day with pavements smeared with mud, shop fronts heavily grilled, the Bazaar closed, and little life in the streets save for shoe-shine men on corners, bread vendors, and steaming braziers of roasting chestnuts. Young men in groups stand idly round, smoking, watching nothing, and talking less.

Aylin takes tea in our bedroom with her twelve-year-old daughter Nazlı. We order cake and coca-cola and ice-cream. Nazlı eats slowly with relish and delights in washing her hands again and again in warm water, which at home is saved for baths alone. It rains remorselessly. On an impulse we drive in Aylın's car to Beşiktas and find the Şamil apartment block. Here live the descendants of the Imam Shamyl (Habibe Erkan, the elderly surviving daughter of Emiré-Nafisette and grand-daughter of Khazi Mahommed and great-grand-daughter of Shamyl, Inal her nephew, and Şamil his son). We are not expected, although all week I have been making tentative enquiries as to their whereabouts. There are many pretenders to the hero's throne.

Habibe, a waif-like creature with a proud ferocious head, scans us closely with her deep-set eyes. She is dressed in a long brown velvet dressing-gown, but, despite our audacity in appearing unannounced, she beckons us into her dim and modest rooms. From a large black glass-fronted armoire she produces faded brown family photographs. I tell her of my recent visit to the Caucasus and the drive to Tsinandali. She has never seen this rugged country of her ancestors and is fascinated to glean details of the Tchavatchavdze home. Her lugubrious nephew, Inal, a man of sixty, appears with a faltering step. He is very tall, with the unmistakable high-boned features of his fore-fathers. Unshaven and remote, he has been meditating and apologises for his delay in greeting us. He is surprised that an English lady should be interested in the family legend; he thought it forgotten. I assure him that Lesley Blanch, in her matchless record in the *Sabres of Paradise*, will captivate readers for many generations.

Inal lives with his son Şamil on the floor above Habibe. He invites us up the stone stairway to see further relics. Do we like cats? The

Imam Shamyl liked cats and this great-great-grandson shares his penchant. The ill-lit rooms exude a pungent stink. Well-worn books on
metaphysics and witchcraft line the shelves and strange Nazi symbols
are scattered on his desk. 'We study the supernatural,' explains his son
Samil and shows us a sinister photograph of his mother dressed in
white and holding high a candle. Inal looks disapprovingly at his tall
son, dressed in jeans. 'My son is always fighting in the streets, that old
tribal blood, you know. In the summer months he works at the
discothèques in Antalya.' With these summary introductions we are
shown a finely-turned silver hexagonal pocket casket. It contains
Shamyl's Koranic scrolls. The Iman would lead each battle with this
travelling Koran hoisted to his banner. We finger it with reverence.
More faded photographs, sheathed kindjals and promises to meet again
conclude this eerie interview.

March 10

Princess Neslishah[6] and Lord John Montagu Douglas Scott lunch with
us at the Hilton, an unlikely quartet, but the young and old seem
pleased to meet. John enjoys a square meal and ventures a rather
inarticulate view on Turkey's political future. Princess Neslishah,
beautiful and a little tragic, delicately reminds us of her husband's
recent death. 'He couldn't die; it took so long.'

At 6 p.m. I have a rendezvous with Habibe to meet her niece Bedia,
a great-great-grand-daughter of Shamyl. Bedia offers us Nescafé and
sponge cake. She is a tall, slim charming woman in her thirties, with
grave wide hazel eyes set in the familiar high cheek-bones. She is
flattered at my interest and amazed at my meagre account of their
long-lost Caucasus. Did I photograph Tsinandali? I promise to send
her my written impressions of that day. Her eight-year-old daughter
stares inquisitively at the lace on my cream silk shirt. She is called
Ganja, named after a village in South-East Caucasus. I compare her to
the photograph of her great-grandmother Emiré-Nafisette, pictured
in the arms of Khazi Mahommed's second wife, Habibette. They look
alike with their soft brown curls, their delicate pointed noses, chins,
and large reflective eyes.

Bedia carries in a black velvet dress, richly-embroidered in gold –
great-grandmother Habibette's – and then a child's velvet dress. It is a
deep sea-green and stitched with gold stars and borders of filigree;

[6] Her Imperial Highness, granddaughter of the last Sultan, Abdul Hamid (died 1915), and
the widow of Prince Abdul Muneyim, son of the last Kediv of Egypt.

both Emiré-Nafisette's dresses are of great value, in excellent repair. We hold the green against Ganja for size and, caught with our enthusiasm, the child dances Caucasian reels and softly hums the age-old chants. Her lilting and hopping recall a Scottish reel and so she dances round the room, in her white-stockinged feet and grey school skirt, the great-great-great-grand-daughter of the Imam Shamyl, the Lion of Daghestan.

I give Habibe and Bedia my two remaining pounds of well-travelled coffee beans; they are charmed and delighted, whereupon Habibe gives me a paper knife, beautifully chased in brass and copper and blue and rose enamel. 'You read so much,' she murmurs.

March 23 Wrotham Park Nr Barnet Hertfordshire

Today we lunched at Wrotham, a large handsome house of grey Georgian proportions with the further embellishment of a domed conservatory, set in a landscape of sheep, a lake, and uninterrupted rolling fields. It has the staggering distinction of lying a mere fifteen miles from Hyde Park Corner. We approached the estate through the anonymous suburbs of Ealing and Hendon, where the almond and hawthorn blossomed. In Ealing, women with kerchiefs gripped to their heads were streaming out of churches, Polish Catholic, no doubt. With the Katyn Memorial finally established in nearby Gunnersbury Park, Ealing has become a favoured zone for their community.

Julian and Eve Byng greeted us in their newly-decorated front wing with its walls and ceilings of palatial dimensions, marbelised and stippled in the height of elegance with windows luxuriantly hung in swagged silks and tasselled cords. Having inherited the house two years ago, or rather having tactfully ousted Julian's ageing mother, they are now set upon a course of daunting renovations. The house has been neglected for two generations.

We sat down to a table gleaming with Gerald Benny silver; their original services had been stolen; Eve only discovered the theft a few days later when she espied a stray fork dropped on the lawn. Gerald Benny's silver is ugly in my opinion. Those heavily-proportioned knives and forks with their flat, squat handles and wide steel blades are more a service for trenchermen and hardly commensurate with our first course, which comprised stuffed eggs.

Julian later walked us round the house, describing with gusto and illuminating anecdotes, the Francis Grant family portraits. Staffords and Byngs stared down at us dispassionately. One great-aunt, lavishly depicted by Sir John Sargent in cream taffeta with her slender hands demurely folded, was said to have hired the services of a Parisian courtesan to instruct her in the ways of love-making. However, her startled bridegroom reassured her – or perhaps even warned her – on their wedding night in this instance ladies are not expected to 'move'.

One by one we stole back to the main body of the house to retrieve coats and furs as we were led into more and more cold, undecorated wings.

The rooms were banked deeply with French furniture: ormulu and Sèvres plaques; boulle and counter-boulle abounded, with many pieces the veneer and brass inlay springing haphazardly from their natural confines. Julian is characteristically optimistic that, in time, he will be able to re-establish his inheritance to its original immaculate order. To be born with a silver spoon is a mixed blessing in these days of retrenchment.

April 2 Hardwicke House

Emré Gönensay has been staying a few days. He arrived exhausted from a lecture tour of the USA. 'And what was the burden of your song?' enquired Nicholas Bethell, who dined with us last night. 'To urge America and the NATO countries to supply us more arms, more military stations on the Mediterranean and Black Sea – and more money' was Emre's exacting reply. Turkey is now the last viable territorial link between Europe and the Middle East oil supply. With the devastation of Iran, the unabated Soviet offensive in Afghanistan and the disturbing pocket eruptions of anti-secular Islamic revival, the West is urgently boosting this last strategic platform.

After dinner we watched Nicholas recorded on the television, proposing the debate: 'Détente has failed.' He was ineffectually opposed by a Labour MP. The very word 'détente' has its own special ambiguity; the dictionary reveals it as: 'cessation of strained relations between States.' When 'détente' was evolved in 1975 one imagined it to mean tentative communication between countries to the mutual well-being and benefit of all. Of course it has failed; the Comintern has run consistently rough-shod over human rights as well as dead bodies; it has called its own tune loudly and we in the West have merely lent it a defensive ear.

Emré dutifully admired Nicholas's performance; however, the vision of streaming, celebratory lavatory rolls on that Match of the Day programme might have stirred him more; he remarked at the time that lavatory paper had now become a luxury in Turkey. And as for that £100 worth of daffodils showered at Joan Sutherland's feet after her live performance of Lucrezia Borgia at Covent Garden! He must have inwardly despaired at our extravagant profligacies. Or perhaps he admired them also?

June 4 Reddish House Broad Chalke Nr Salisbury Wiltshire

We parked the car in a lush meadow adjoining Reddish House, the rose-red Charles II gem, which the late Sir Cecil Beaton had cherished for over thirty years. It was up for sale, together with the prolific accumulations of his stylish life. In the timeless peace of Broad Chalke, a Wiltshire village nestling in a green hollow, where the banks of the meandering river Ebble are thick with willow trees, it stands diminutive and eloquent. It is a mild revelation that so small a façade can project so much graceful details and still retain its supreme understatement.

Two grey stone pilasters with Corinthian capitals nicely divide the eight front windows, which, in turn, are framed in stone and the whole further contained in angle stone quoining. The white-painted panelled door with its elegantly-arched frieze and the brick pediment with its central oeil-de-boeuf window complete this combination of mellowed colour and traditional proportion.

Old-fashioned roses drooled in pink and milky profusion on the warm south wall. The little terrace and stone balustrade overflowed with creeping tendrils and pastel colour and cool green hostas, alchemilla and ferns sprung their flat leaves from the more shady corners. A small party of us, privileged to have been afforded a preview of the house and contents, sat sipping champagne in the garden. It was a languid, hot, drowsy afternoon, but Margaret Argyll[7] remained cool in brown and cream linen and chattered vivaciously. Her thick glossy chestnut head was as immaculately coiffed as ever and her legs as slim as wineglass stems tapered into an enviable pair of brown and cream narrowly-pointed shoes. I later saw her nicely framed as she sat beside the garden gate gazing across the water garden to the grey church spire beyond. She had known the house and had been a favoured subject of Sir Cecil's brush. A removal man pinned 'Toilets' on the wall beside her; another heaved a defective lavatory from the mobile Ladies' cloakroom, and one felt a fleeting stab of regret that the house was to be so swiftly and irrevocably stripped of every vestige of its late illustrious owner.

Sir Cecil's secretary and long-time friend, Eileen Hose, seemed

[7] Margaret, Duchess of Argyll, daughter of George Hay Whigham and first married to Charles Sweeny. A legendary beauty, identifiable at a distance by her sculptured head of hair. She led her second husband, the eleventh Duke, such a dance that the publicity made him forgo his membership at White's.

cheerful enough. She would keep her cottage nearby but could not bear to be present on the day of the sale. Sir Cecil had spent the final years limping between his converted cottage studio and his winter garden, she told us, working to the end with his left hand, the right side of his body having been largely paralysed by a stroke.

We wandered in and out of the house at will, the flagged stone floors in the hall and the small simple dining-room exuded a cool and sober backcloth to the ubiquitous elegance. Large ceramic pots and vases were filled with flowers from the garden – lilies predominated. An enticing assortment of parasols stood in the doorway beside a handsome Regency steel garden seat. Oval medallions of white marble portraits and gilt wall brackets hung on the walls and many modern pictures ranged through Rex Whistler, Augustus John (his Dorelia in the garden at Alderney, looking ravishing in a voluminous red apron), Graham Sutherland and David Hockney. An eclectic choice of sculpture and bronzes was liberally interspersed.

Sir Cecil's penchant for Louis XVI furniture was given full vent in his drawing-room, which he had extended on to the house, a veritable pastiche of exclusively French taste, with the added pretension of Ionic support pillars and niched walls. The faded chintz curtains were edged with bobble fringe and frilled taffeta borders and the deep scalloped pelmets were similarly trimmed. Ruched taffeta pull-up blinds hung from behind the curtains and peacock-blue linen lambrequins, dripping with cream lace, further peeped from behind this whole adornment.

The drawing-room led through to the winter garden, a sun-filled arbour of trailing jasmine and every type of variegated frond; plumbago drooped in thick blue clusters and the pendulous trumpets of a white datura loomed high from its terracotta tub. A nettle had sprouted in the shade of a geranium, as delicate and beautiful a soft silky pale-green nettle as one could ever wish to see. Charming blue and white Chinese porcelain garden seats were grouped as further inviting backdrops, as were the maestro's wicker chair and the cushioned window seat where he must have sat so often. A spout of water trailed into the goldfish pool where three fat fish swam peaceably in wide, distracted circles.

To Sir Cecil's bedroom: the solid Georgian four-post bed had been placed in the middle of the room where it claimed a glorious view of the garden. A handsome capacious rug of beige wolf fur was thrown over it, and who wouldn't covet that? It was a peaceful room in muted tones of cream and brown with a black and gold Chinese lacquer screen lending a striking, rich accent. A selection of his typically wide-brimmed hats were heaped in a corner, all for sale. (One wondered where he wore the red one.) And how many different Continental suns must have beaten down on those seasoned sombreros?

June 7 Shute House Donhead St Mary Wiltshire

'Her Ladyship is playing billiards, sir.' And there was Anne Tree, tightly packed in a red anorak, together with Adrian Daintrey, a man of artistic talent who, Anne later confided, found billiards sexually arousing. We all walked back through the house to the library; the passage was lavishly pampered with Anne's treasured flowers, and deep, green nests of trailing scented plants embroidered every corner. Michael joined us in pillarbox-red slacks and Princesse Jeanne-Marie de Broglie flew in from Paris. Nobody quite knew why she had asked to come.

Over drinks before lunch the conversation turned to Isabella, the spirited, raven-haired schoolgirl daughter.

'How often has Isabella been sacked now?' asked Adrian Daintrey.

'Twice,' answered Anne. 'Her friends planted a tree to her memory at the second school.'

'You never know, she will probably turn out to be an authoritative schoolmistress herself one day,' ventured Adrian.

'An authoritative mistress, more like,' concluded Anne wryly. However, as the child appeared popular and beautiful and highly intelligent, with O-levels already to her credit and serious aspirations to University, nobody seemed too concerned with her more immediate shortcomings.

The weekend progressed on gentle waves of comfort and laughter, with the food and drink comparatively unremarkable. Two close friends of the late Sir Cecil Beaton came to dine: Bill and Frank, the former most elegant in one of the maestro's bequeathed shirts; it had been especially designed by Sir Cecil, a busy flecking design of what appeared to be black tadpoles on a white ground. Anne's uncle, Lord David Cecil, was expected for Sunday tea but then postponed his visit to drinks before dinner; he finally cancelled the whole venture. Meanwhile, Michael, Jeanne-Marie and I took an invigorating walk across the top of the chalk downs. The world looked totally green and global as Michael pointed out the blur of the Isle of Wight to the south-west, the unspoilt undulations of Dorset, the Mendip Hills behind us and the Blackmoor Valley beyond. Jeanne-Marie dwelt briefly on the frenetic social whirl of Paris society; hostesses were hiring lavish venues for huge parties as though there were no tomorrow, she told us; one naturally presumed that she would be a prominent guest at these elaborate functions. The conversation switched to Russia whereupon Michael proclaimed that the only way to make them feel on the defensive instead of us was to offer them candid advice in the face of their inept misconceptions of modern technology and of ultimate authority; an attitude of cajolement once advocated indeed by President Roosevelt.

But it was Anne's miraculous garden that surpassed the weekend's whole enjoyment; her outdoor bedroom had come on a treat with the four-poster bed and bolster neatly clipped in box, the four support poles were festooned in vines which even promised their fair share of grapes, and the winged chair was wreathed in a shapely tangle of briar rose which gave a flowered chintz effect. She had not planted the carpet in thyme as originally planned, but was considering instead the effect of a gravel parterre.

Through the old brick garden wall was spread a profusion of exquisitely-orchestrated colour and design. Old-fashioned roses, potentillas and every conceivable shrub and leaf and ornamental thistle grew in the most subtle order. Water from the River Nadder cascaded in wide silver rims between these scented borders, and the effect of the water tumbling over specially-made copper mouldings gave each graded rill a contrasting musical note. Arched supports dripped with wisteria. Suggestions of Italy prevailed amidst handsome statuary and ornamental terracotta tubs placed strategically through vistas of light and shade; a further platform of water with wide grass walks thick with arum lilies and lissom blue iris recalled a cool, quiet veranda, and the parterres of roses enclaved in clipped low hedges called to mind an intimate grouping of salons and ante-rooms. It proved impossible to select any one place to sit; one was too eager to round each corner and then repeat the preamble.

June 9 Reddish House Broad Chalke Wiltshire

'I offer you Reddish House, ladies and gentlemen. What am I bid for Reddish House? . . . £200,000? I'll take it in tens. £220,000? I'll take it in fives. £220,000. Are you finished? £225,000 on my right. Can I say 30? £225,000 for the last time – it's yours, sir.' And so the house was sold with little ceremony to an anonymous bidder. Sir Cecil Beaton had paid £10,000 for it in 1947. An anxious voice rose above the ensuing babble.

'Who is the new owner? The people of Broad Chalke would like to know!'

The auctioneer assured the harassed inquisitor that he did not know himself, as yet, but would certainly find out.

The marquee was packed with an essentially English crowd. Dealers were far outnumbered by private collectors who, determined to secure a coveted memento, shot the bidding up to the most desperate heights.

An elegant brass bath rack, complete with soap tray, a cigarette container, a mirror, and detachable reading stand fetched £520 as opposed to its estimated price of £80–£120. A modest two-seat sofa basking in a rose-patterned chintz especially printed for Sir Cecil from an old fragment tumbled heavily for £1,600. 'That's set them all talking,' muttered a dealer, as he hoisted himself up on a chest of drawers. The finer items, such as the Louis XVI tulipwood commode and the charming parquetry bureau, fetched £10,000 and £7,000 respectively, prices more commensurate with their value.

The marquee emptied visibly after the first fifty lots and a rise and fall of jubilant conversation wafted from the refreshment tent. An air of a garden party or even Derby Day hovered over the garden as people opted for a good lunch and drinks all round. Pinneys of Carlisle, looking decorative in straw boaters, did a popular trade in smoked salmon. The sunlit lawn and borders exuded spice and sweetness after the night's heavy rain, though the greenfly were having a menacing field day.

Walking through the upturned house, one was prepared for the inevitable debilitation of dust and dejection, but the line of Sir Cecil's Louis Vuitton luggage, and the wicker hampers, the famous hats, the Malacca walking sticks, and enchanting linen parasols evoked instead a theatrical memory of Madam Ranyevskaya's retreat from her beloved cherry orchard, and under far more poignant circumstances, after all.

A silver soup spoon, askew on the floor of the blue bathroom, caused a moment's mild surprise from Christie's head porter when told of its inappropriate whereabouts. Meanwhile back to the bidding where the seventeenth-century fruitwood statue of a half-clothed female still raised her left hand to the rostrum, and where the white marble bust of another still proffered her imperturbable pretty profile as she gazed through the open flaps of the marquee to the garden beyond. Sir Cecil's grey morning suit was knocked down smartly for £400, and the day's sale totalled a gratifying £219,914, with a promise of further rich surprises in the morrow's pictures and sculpture. Finally, a rumour that the house had been sold to a Dutch woman named Lady Chichester leaked its balm on the apprehensive locals, who had been speculating uncomfortably on Mick Jagger or even Kevin Keegan as being their new neighbours.

August 20 Florence

The rungs of shade lay unevenly spaced on Sir Harold Acton's[8] drive, The recent plague on cypresses, similar to our own English elm disease, is taking its toll throughout Italy. Where there are still unbroken ranks of tall sleek spiralling green, a closer look reveals brown brittle patching, a prelude to demise. Sir Harold's prized old avenue with his seventeenth-century villa, a beckon of enchantment at the end, sustained its own irredeemable gaps.

Sir Harold was lunching out. A stooped and wrinkled gardener swung open the handsome gates. He propped us up solicitously enough on the low entrance wall and shuffled off into the gate lodge returning with a copy of the Old Testament in Italian. We were offered it as suitable diversion while waiting for the master. He himself promptly took over our large glossy copy of *Tuscan Villas* (written by Sir Harold). A few chickens strutted unceremoniously across the drive and two more gardeners ambled by with unwieldy garden trugs suspended on poles from their shoulders. (Sir Harold later informed us that he maintains the garden with five and a half; the box parterres and extensive topiary are still clipped by hand.) We finally abandoned our friend. Sir Harold's lunch had extended to tea-time and we resolved to telephone him instead.

He invited us for drinks the following evening, along with George and Jean Galitzine, Joan Haslip[9], and Margaret Drabble accompanied by a sturdy girlfriend. Sir Harold was immaculate in dress and manner and, notwithstanding his bald, monk-like pate and thin high voice, radiated immense charm and enthusiasm. 'Have we met before? and I am expecting Margaret Drabble. Do you know her, dear?' This last addressed to Joan Haslip, who commented that she wrote good books on suburban love affairs amongst the meritocracy. 'Not quite your scene, Harold,' she concluded.

Margaret Drabble finally joined us on the terrace; stocky and blue-eyed with short sensible hair, she was with her girlfriend who had even shorter, more sensible hair and a furry upper lip. Sir Harold once again rolled out his customary red carpet of welcome and we all descended through ravishing platforms of terraced parterres, ornamen-

[8] Remembered as a tall, kind boy at Eton with exotic tastes and Chinese-looking eyes. At Christchurch, Oxford, Acton sashayed through a literary galère of sophisticates – notably Evelyn Waugh, Peter Quennell and Cyril Connolly. Acton's *Humdrum* in the late '20s was spurned as much as the *Memoirs of an Aesthete*, 1948, was acclaimed.
[9] Author of several evocative biographies, including *Lady Hester Stanhope*, 1934. *Elisabeth of Austria*, 1965, and *The Sultan, Abdul Hamid*, 1958. She listed 'conversation' as a favourite recreation and relished a touch of gossip.

tal pools, and pleached walks. Seventeenth-century stone statuary, collected by his father, Arthur, sprang strategically from shaded green corners. Tall backdrops of ilex and yew screened the open-air salons and were intermingled with elaborate balls and crenellations of clipped box. We came to the ultimate drama of the intimate little theatre; from a row of footlights (again clipped in box) the stage sloped upwards with delicately-carved figures peeping invitingly from several wings of clipped yew. Sir Harold pointed out the piper, the lady with a dulcimer, another with fruit and flowers; even cups of chocolate appeared to be on offer by a further half-screened figure. The domes and campanile of Florence lay below us and beyond, through the ilex trees.

'The new owners of Villa Palmieri have painted it white, you know,' remarked Sir Harold witheringly. 'Italian too; they should know better.' He crumbled a sprig of wild mint in his fingers; it smelt wonderfully pungent, together with the pine and yew and the rocking scent of gardenias lined up in great terracotta tubs. He pointed with pride at the lemon garden alongside the villa; the stone walls were inlaid with intricate seventeenth-century rocaille work and surmounted by the original busts. Each terracotta tub has to be carried into the shelter of the limonaia at the start of winter, a daunting exercise that demands eight men for almost two weeks.

In the cool gloom and elegance of the high-vaulted drawing-room we were handed drinks and trays of delectable canapés. Sir Harold signed our book, together with his young German friend, Alexander Zielcke, who had taken all the photographs with a Leika. The conversation became a little hushed and halting in this rarefied quattrocento ambiance and Margaret Drabble sat diffidently on the edge of a deep shiny leather chair, wondering, no doubt, how she could evoke such a scene in her own more utilitarian backgrounds.

August 22 Tuscany

Today we lunched at Cetinale near Siena, a captivating seventeenth-century villa newly restored from a state of dereliction by Tony Lambton. Sir Harold Acton wrote of it: 'Cetinale in its decay evokes the legend of the Sleeping Beauty.' Set against a steep hillside of dense ilex woods, secreted among chapels and statues, the Baroque façades are dramatically approached by long, straight rides on either side. The lemon garden, the parterres, and the cypress avenue are now perfectly recovered, and the imposing first-floor rooms, approached by a horse-shoe of stone steps from the garden, are bright and elegant with the paraphernalia of exclusive taste and fine furniture; much of the contents were brought over from England. Four-posters hung with old silk make for inviting bedrooms and, throughout, the original floors of glazed terracotta tiles add a cool austerity.

It was an informal lunch party. The children were given a picnic on a marble table beside the swimming pool. Tony Lambton, rather stooped with thinning hair, greeted us in his habitual dark glasses. His long slim brown legs were shown off to advantage in an old pair of shorts. He is establishing residency in Italy to offset tax duties; an exercise that will surely save him millions. They say he is bored in his self-imposed exile.

Claire Ward, his devoted paramour through many years of vicissitude and not a little scandal, arrived late and a degree dishevelled from marketing. There was a hiatus over the number laid for lunch, which provoked a little petulance from his lordship. However, he readily redeemed this flash of irritation by serving everybody at the table with the most attentive detail. He also took off his glasses and we talked at length about travels in the Middle East. He particularly recalled his time in Aden and how before the evening curfew bodies would gush out of buildings like bathwater as they raced to their own habitats.

On my left sat Lord Wilton, a man in his fifties, with a quiet, ponderous charm and his blonde wife, who looked enviably cool and soignée in a shift of white, embroidered lawn. We talked of Ramsbury Manor, Rahmi Koç (an unlikely friendship considering their totally disparate backgrounds) and the pleached avenue at Hillbarn House, Great Bedwyn, Wiltshire. Having embellished these two properties, which he had previously owned, John Wilton has now opted for a house in Egerton Terrace and no upkeep; he confessed he would never invest in an estate abroad.

Large friendly dogs, including an Alsatian, roamed freely through the rooms and set off a wild round of barking in the middle of the pudding. Nobody seemed in the least perturbed and the noisy mêlée soon raced off into the gardens to thrash out their differences.

Claire later told us that Tony knew no Italian and was not even considering learning any. She had found him, only the other day, commanding the gardener with mounting frustration to dig a hole! 'Dig a hole, a hole in the ground! A hole!' The gardener had merely looked on in mild astonishment.

Would I like to see round the bedrooms? He puffed peaceably on a cigar as I dutifully padded along behind, then down the marble stairway to the entrance hall with its fanlights, and on down to the cellars and old deserted kitchens, complete with bread ovens. We wandered back through the kitchen gardens and into the cypress avenue. The trees showed the tell-tale brown, dead patches. He had

had them all cleaned out last year, but the disease was obviously rampant. We stood back and gazed on the exquisite and classical understatement of the north façade. The double flank of cypresses half-hid it from view. Perhaps it would even enhance the impact of the villa if the trees were removed anyway, he surmised.

We drove back through the nearby village of Sovicille where the old walls dripped with wisteria and trailing lines of washing. Acacia trees shivered with shade in cool corners and a posse of labourers, stripped to the waist, were comfortably slouched on the church steps. An air of cornucopian languor hung over the surrounding patch-work of vines and olive groves, rustling maze and neatly stooked hayfields, halcyon days of hot, white August sun, with the vines so lush and pendulous, and ripening further, in this lull before the autumn 'viaggiatura'.

Such vignettes of peace seemed whole worlds away from any agita-tional propaganda; yet only the other evening we had seen ominous red flags swinging from the ramparts of San Gimignano to indicate a Communist rally. But why dwell on the disturbing vagaries of hot political wrangling when the glorious landscape evokes instead the cinquecento tranquillity of a Giovanni Bellini and the evening skies are suffused with rose and amethyst?

August 23 Florence

'And do you think he is bored? What did you have for lunch? A friend was given pears and custard . . .' We were taking tea with Joan Haslip, or rather iced tea, while the children scooped up delectable home-made strawberry ice-cream and the tiniest tomatoes gleaned from the garden. Here, in her enchanting small house set in the silvery light fuzz of olive groves on the hillside of Settignano, Joan Haslip oversees Florence, her biographies and every conceivable antic and provocative comment that blows her way. Her vigorous red curls and freckles gave her a more youthful glow than she could honestly claim. She walked cautiously with much self-reassuring clucking over the uneven levels of her sloping garden, a veritable mignon bower of trailing green fronds and interlacing branches, colour, scent and two somnolent cats. We stretched out on deck-chairs and addressed ourselves to the pleasurable exercise of listening to more.

They say he is bored; no knowledge of Italian and not even writing a book; and then that spiteful article on poor Pam Hartwell. His only excitement is the prospect of a lunch invitation from Harold Acton. The racy commentary accompanied us further in jerky spurts as we descended the little hill and wandered through the exquisite gardens of Villa Gamberaia below. Seated amidst the rhapsodic splendours of stone mosaic pathways and ornamental pools, intricate topiary and clipped box parterres, we heard fatuous claims that Lesley Blanch was a dishonest writer (a reference here to *The Wilder Shores of Love* with the criticism that too much copy had been taken from biographies) and that George Weidenfeld, in her opinion, was not to be trusted. (W reminded her that he published all her books.) We were finally gratified to learn that Jean Galitzine (who, together with George and their daughter Katya, had just been staying with her) looked wonderful at breakfast and that a new biography by our entertaining albeit rather dangerous hostess, on the Austrian Emperor Franz Joseph and his long relationship with Katarina Schratt, had just been completed. She writes extremely well.

September 29 Hardwicke House

We dined with Patrick and Amabel Lindsay; their son Ludovic (tall and dashing in black tie and narrow tartans) and daughter Laura, who must have lost a stone through travelling the world. Ayesha Jaipur was present, with her youthful beauty become a mite fatigued. But that soft, lilting voice and infectious charm made for compelling appraisal. It was a warm night. We stood talking to Patrick on the pavement of Lansdowne Road. It was midnight; we were to give the Maharani a lift back to Cadogan Square. A blithe figure on roller skates swerved up the road; Zsa Zsa Horne (Alistair's daughter) twirled to our feet, glorious in hot pants and padded knees. 'May I introduce the Maharani of Jaipur[10]?' Patrick relished the moment; and a memorable one for Zsa Zsa, to be suddenly confronted by this distinguished elegance in flowing aquamarine.

November 5 Hardwicke House

I returned from China a week ago. It was an interesting experience on all counts, but sometimes experiences of the most intense interest are subtly divorced from enjoyment. The demands on mental and physical energy were heavy as we were buffeted along a collision

[10] In 1976, a stunning autobiography *A Princess Remembers* was published by Her Highness. Born Gayatri Devi, daughter of the Maharajah of Cooch Behar (an old Etonian) and third wife of the Maharajah of Jaipur (died June 24, 1970, playing polo at Cirencester). Ayesha Jaipur describes a life of grace and bravery.

course of rare, bright treasures and habitual poverty. Treasure? With Chiang Kai-shek's final retreat to Taiwan on the wave of Mao's 1949 revolution, the country was left virtually bankrupt; the few remaining gold reserves were accommodated, along with as much Imperial loot as could be safely evacuated. The world had also appropriated a large slice of China's rich heritage. One was therefore surprised and disappointed by the comparative dearth of beautiful things to be seen in China today. However, with the formidable wealth still stacked beneath its soil in the form of still-sealed tombs and burial vaults, who knows what fascinating and incredible rarities will be recovered in the next twenty years? Their Ming inheritance may be dispersed throughout the museums of the world, but their BC relics must constitute a horde of untold rich potential.

Touching down at Peking airport after an eighteen-hour flight, the first glimpse of China was impressive. It was evening and the sky was a furnace of rose lights with a ring of distant mountains clouded in a mauve haze. The long straight road to the hotel was screened with poplar trees and willow. The meticulously-tilled red soil was striped green with winter wheat, cabbages and cotton bushes. Small adobe houses were clustered in a labyrinth of arid lanes, with white goats and black pigs tethered among milling chickens. Washing and bedding were strung to air between sycamore trees, and, with dusk falling, it appeared that these modest establishments had electricity. We passed little on the road, a few donkey carts with women in coolie hats and children nestled in their laps – returning from marketing their vegetables no doubt.

In Peking we were swept up in a tinkling sea of black bicycles and unisex trouser suits pedalling incessantly through the wide grey faceless avenues. Democracy Wall was perfunctorily dismissed; now boarded up with consumer advertising, our guide explained its demise as a public platform. 'People served too many complaints. Our country was not in good order with old men at the top. Our new leader Zhao-Ziyang is fifty-five. He is an economist. He looks for better science and technology. Education is the best thing and then we think better. Our children learn English from the age of ten.'

Arriving at the Friendship Hotel, we were formally acknowledged with the words 'Dear friends, we welcome you as guests to our country'. In the face of this tacit desire to please and to communicate, we determined to be good ones. (Unpunctuality was taken as a personal affront – lesson No. 1.)

Ensconced in the hotel, for the most part Russian-built and barrack-like, we forgave the dirt (a long accumulation of cursory cleaning with cane whisks and mops), the elusive hot water, the scanty bath towels,

and the rogue lavatory, in the happy realisation that we left our belongings scattered in unlocked rooms with impunity. Petty corruption is
eradicated by peer influence wielded in localised street committees
and land communes, a remarkable do-it-yourself legal system, which
reflected on the enviable discipline of that vast, close-knit society.

A room boy hovered with smiles. We asked him for extra blankets
and coat hangers. He also carried up our suitcases when so prompted,
but his prime desire was to practise English. He was robbed of his
studies by the Cultural Revolution, and two and a half years of crucial
education were spent in rice fields. A worn, prized copy of English
Book II was produced. Could I help with this translation and would
I speak into that Japanese cassette recorder?

He was engaged to Chung, a technician. When would they marry?
It depended on what? On time. He explained that efforts to induce a
low birth rate dictated marriage for a girl at twenty-five. One child
was encouraged with the attendant perks of better job and housing, a
third was currently aborted; and pre-marital sex incurred six months'
imprisonment. We later learned that directed labour, with some married couples parted for months at a time, precluded much subsequent
contact. Indeed this all-pervasive platonic harmony was a revelation.
Throughout China we would see girls in the ubiquitous trouser suit,
their hair bobbed or caught in pigtails, talking and laughing freely to
young men with no overt physical contact. The less you have the less
you want? And a bicycle was usually propped between. I found this
total lack of romance and any concession to feminine allure very
unnerving, depressing too. What did the room boy think? He
remarked that the Chinese were a quieter people than those of the
Western world and that any stepping out of line as regards women's
fashion would be laughed at and condemned as bourgeois. Did Chung
ever wear lipstick? Oh no! He laughed incredulously at such an idea.
And Madame Mao? He looked uncomfortable. I had gone too far?
'We hate her,' he volunteered and twisted his hands in a mock stranglehold. 'What would become of her now?' I felt emboldened by his
sudden candour. 'No chop,' he assured me, 'she would merely be
imprisoned and re-educated.'

The foreigners' dinner at 6.30 was a standard array of courses. We
gathered in a large, high-ceilinged room, made harsh with shiny cream
paint and bright lighting. Clusters of white bulbous globes were caught
in nets perhaps they were prone to explode. Cheerful young girls plied
us with course upon course and replaced our chopsticks as they fell to
the floor through our clumsy, unaccustomed manipulations. With
constant use we soon mastered this art and the longest noodles and
the most slippery water chestnut jelly were magically despatched. We

ate from attractive late Ch'ing-design dishes and were surprised that the meal concluded with soup, said to combine the juices of every previous ingredient. The food was always nutritious, with every farinaceous combination. A variety of shredded root and green vegetables would be served with fish, pork, chicken, goose, or duck.

The first night we were treated to Peking duck. The skin was glazed as a T'ang horse and we fastened small portions into pancakes together with chives and soy sauce. We drank Mao Tai, the heady rice wine, but soon gravitated to the light Tsingtao lager or jasmine tea for everyday drinking. Steamed carp, shad, or perch were staple offerings, spiced with ginger, chilli beans or caramelised in sweet and sour. The sweet potato scones, fried and filled with chestnut paste, were a delicious novelty, as were the crisp batter rolls which encased every variant of highly-spiced meats or herbs. A banquet would run to twelve courses of elaborate presentation with complementary colour and texture.

We enjoyed such a meal at Canton, held in a private room that resembled a colourful glass cabinet with its expansive screen of windows stained with fruit and bird motifs. The menu included steamed fresh prawns, roast crab, goose skin on toast with plum jam, chicken with cabbage hearts, fried rice, rich pastries, and a sweet snow fungus soup swimming with lotus seeds. The scented flannels and the finger bowls filled with warm jasmine tea added a final touch to this culinary marathon. We felt surprisingly underfed after such meals; small samples from each dish and slow eating with chopsticks worked wonders with the digestive system and most of us lost weight.

Peking woke early. From six o'clock a ceaseless throng of trams, buses, police jeeps and three million bicycles vied with vegetable-laden hand carts and donkey-loads. Joggers weaved through solemn figures gyrating to Tai Chi exercises. Vegetables and fruit were laid out on pavements. The odd pig and goat strayed nonchalantly through the clamour, while seasoned shoppers handled each cabbage, each fish, and each egg, with due consideration before their modest purchase.

We drove north of the city through the fertile plains that led to the thirteen Ming Tombs. Private plots were encouraged, said the guide, with the produce sold to townspeople. 'The peasants like to save for their children's marriages.' Peasants, perched in persimmon trees, were toppling the orange fruit with long poles. Others stood below and caught the fall in linen canopies stretched with sticks. Thirty-six pairs of hands worked this half-acre. Further on a row of women thrashed soya branches with whisks and separated the cotton balls. Oxen ploughed and peasants, with tin drums of water hooked on shoulder poles, watered the crops from the narrow dikes. One sensed the profound relationship between these workers and their motherland. Despite efforts to mechanise labour, the feudal rhythm stoically persisted. With a ratio of 100 handlers working 500 acres and 50 million waiting for a job, how could such displaced labour be re-incorporated anyway? The walking tractors and the larger 80-horsepower models were used instead for transport and power generation.

The tombs were finally approached through the four-mile 'spirit way'' an imposing avenue of monolithic fifteenth-century stone mandarins and animals with willows bowing in between. Red pagodas dotted among the foothills like snug weekend chalets guarded each tomb. The mountains, rising up on three sides, were proclaimed to be an effective barrier against wind-blow evil spirits. The Ding-ling tomb, the only one to have been fully excavated, lay beyond terraced flower gardens, peach trees (the fruit of longevity) and pine. Orioles and sparrows chattered in the upturned eaves of the Red Pagoda. A series of dank, white stone vaults and passages led to the Burial Chamber of Emperor Wan-li (died 1619) flanked by his two Empresses. These three large, plastered chests, recently painted a dull red, presided over the comparatively empty vaults. A few excavated relics were housed in a small museum alongside this complex. There seemed to be some discrepancy over whether certain items were a hundred or a thousand years old and the handsome Phoenix Crown topped with a show of kingfisher feathers was falsely claimed to be original; it was a copy. Meanwhile rumour had it that the scenic position of the tombs has prompted speculation for a golf-course. The mind boggled.

Driving west we reached the Great Wall at the Badaling Pass, a snake of stone that swoops and zigzags its amazing course almost 3,000 miles over the hills to far Mongolia. We had been warned to wear rubber-soled shoes and warm clothes to combat the slippery stone surface and the proverbial howling wind; however, it was a warm autumn day and we were hot and puffed as we scaled the steep slope to the nearest crenellated watchtower. The view was superb, with deserted soft-peaked hills smothered red with fonye trees (a type of Chinese maple) rolling into the distant blue beyond.

Back in Peking it proved impossible to see the entire profusion of palaces, temples and lakes. Our brief stay of even three days was suddenly caught short by the vagaries of the haphazard Chinese tourist system; overseas missions and delegations loomed unforeseen with priority over transport and hotel rooms. (Our visit to Shanghai was also blocked from our itinerary due to similar mismanagement; advance planning was an anachronism to the Chinese, it seemed.)

But the Forbidden City with its 9,000 rooms under those golden waves of curved ceramic roofs did not escape us. Cobbled yards and stone terraces led to tree-shaded courtyards, each more intimate than the last. The interiors with their painted angled beams and pillar supports varied from the garish to the sombre. Some housed a wide variety of Imperial treasures and a rich parade of rare bronzes jostled with jewellery, porcelain, and paintings. Others had been so brightly restored in livid primary colours – yellow, red, and green with a plethora of painted golden dragons and phoenixes rampant throughout – that one gasped at such crudeness and Harrods at Christmas sprang to mind. Crowds of Chinese and gaily-dressed schoolchildren wearing the red neck-tie of the Young Pioneers and clasping packed lunches thronged the vast precinct with a proprietary air. (Our guide later confessed that he preferred the Boston Symphony Orchestra and Western ballet to Asian architecture.)

We left Peking for Xian, another principal city in North-West China, an ancient departure point for the silk route through to Syria which retained a distinctive Middle-Eastern flavour. Domestic life spilled on to pavements as chickens were plucked, balls of stuffed dough, deep-fried in woks, and steaming noodles were ladled from huge wooden vats, and tables set up for the evening meal. And every-where patches of corn and millet were laid to dry on the roadsides where no birds pecked (they had been caught in nets and eaten).

In the neighbouring village of Lin Tong we saw the exquisite newly-excavated terracotta warriors complete with their horses and bronze weapons. Housed in the sacred vaults that guarded the still-sealed tomb of China's first Emperor, Qin Shi Huang Di (229–201 BC), they are a major archaeological find of this century. The whole burial complex engaged 700,000 men over a period of thirty-six years. On completion the outer door was lowered into place, entombing the remaining craftsmen. Total secrecy was thus preserved.

The finely-executed sculpture was a revelation in its detail and sophistication. The individual physiognomy of each head was said to bear a direct resemblance to the Emperor's own guards; young, old, humorous, sober, and stern, with long hair elaborately knotted and knopped to equal any *Vogue* hairstyle. Discovered in 1974 by peasants digging a well, the excavation was in full swing with the delicate scraping and unearthing of relics continuing before our eyes. This whole intriguing enterprise was the highlight of our trip.

Eight-five kilometres from Xian on the Liangshan Hill lay the Chienling Tomb with another remarkable 'spirit way' of stone T'ang animals and armoured Chihke Generals. Stepping aside from this ancient avenue, we were amazed to be peering down into a present-day subterranean village. Mud dwellings had been dug twenty feet deep, complete with courtyards and apple-trees. Fruit and grain were drying on mud-baked sills. A dog stretched; a baby crawled, and a curious mother stepped out from her mud door with its astonishing Gothic-style moulded arch.

Further south in Sichuan Province the terrain was rich and hilly. The neat, terraced slopes were clumped with banana-trees and orange groves. Rice fields abounded with water buffaloes ploughing, being slowly coaxed by peasants. Bare-legged in the deep mud with capes of plaited palm fronds thrown over their shoulders they hissed encouragingly at the plodding beasts.

In Chungking, the main mountain town that straddles the Yangste and the Jialing rivers, we saw the famous Sichuan opera. A hypnotic performance of shrill singing (not unlike a cat's chorus or Arabic calls to prayer), an exotic parade of elaborate headdresses of tasselled seed-pearls and encrusted glitter, hot red eye make-up on whitened faces, and an intriguing manipulation of fans and fingers to the accompaniment of guitar, dulcimer, strange wooden hammers, and cymbals. (The steady hum of voices in the audience and deep-throated spitting made for startling noises off-stage.) It was an old audience inured to the cherished traditions of Chinese opera; their enrapt faces, hollow-cheeked in the flash of the stage lights and shadow, recalled Van Gogh's *The Potato Eaters*.

The young people flocked to Western music. Hearing strains of *Madame Butterfly* one night floating from the mammoth People's Hall in Chungking, which adjoined our hotel, I hurriedly went to investigate. Soloists from the Shanghai opera, sporting Western dress, were singing excerpts from *Figaro, Carmen* and *Madame Butterfly* to a packed audience. A certain Li Fuseng was hailed with ecstatic applause. A rotund avuncular figure in a white dinner jacket, he commanded numerous encores. A woman pianist in a long evening dress with a hint of glitter in its folds was the single accompaniment. At the performance-end a stampede of bodies and excited babble rushed out through the foyer into the dark wet night. Brightly-coloured umbrellas bobbed away on a sea of noisy hilarity.

From Chungking we cruised up the Yangste River through the three famous gorges. Ming scroll landscapes came alive as we gazed on those sheer misted crags, plumed with wind-worn pines, like so many perched cranes. We passed a miscellany of fishing-boats and one vast log raft complete with a rough wooden shack strung with washing and a quaint window box of chrysanthemums.

Peasants trotted along hillside paths under their shoulder poles and one was seen striding through the rain with his black pig on a lead. Junks slid by with muddy sails, and seven oarsmen standing in a sampan chanted a rhythm as they rowed. The boat was warm and comfortable enough, but cockroaches in the cabins were a hazard; it was prudent to sleep with the lights on.

Arriving after this three-day trip at Wuhan, we were escorted round a hospital, a school, and invited to tea with a retired grandmother. Flanked by her strong upright children and grandchildren, her hand-crocheted antimacassars, her radio, her simple bamboo bed hung with mosquito nets, her rudimentary kitchen with its calor gas stove, its old stone sink and its one cold tap, she appeared as content as any Western housewife.

The children's school was a tidy, cheerful institution with three to seven-year olds enjoying the odd march and sing-song to the teacher's tambourine. 'They are singing slogans,' explained the guide. And what slogans were they? 'Study well, make progress, build up strong bodies.' They were then whisked away to eat an apple and take a rest.

The typical provincial hospital was a thirty-year-old birch-built model with draughty stone passages and unheated rooms. We sat in one which was markedly colder than all the rest and smelling faintly of fly-killer. We were handed tea in lidded mugs and three doctors in spruce white housecoats informed us that Chinese traditional medicine was still largely practised with Western methods playing an accompanying role. Indeed Western medicine was being widely researched. Meanwhile their traditional cures were more in evidence as we were conducted to a patient, who held a pair of acrid jumbo joss-sticks as he singed his shins to ease his vertigo condition. Another lay in complacent mood under a fleet of pins that tended his facial paralysis. A third was undergoing massage for arthritis, a vigorous rub down with knuckles rather than the palm of the hand; it looked most painful.

China had half a million tourists this year; they hope for three to five million next. Is it on the brink of a tourist invasion? I am glad to have seen it now before a more streamlined tourist system blurs that sense of ready communication. It was an instructive and interesting departure, but I found the lack of romance and individual colour a dampener to the spirit.

November 25 25 Kensington Court Gardens London

Cella Roberts, sleek and diminutive in an Egyptian silk brocade dressing-gown ('from my honeymoon trousseau. I have just begun to wear it again, so fashionable to look ethnic these days'). She raised her pert, dark head to Dolly Burns; they made an incongruous coupling: Cella, the supreme hostess for all her slightness, and Dolly, a voluminous travesty in taffeta, blue-rinsed bouffant hair, with eyes now garaged behind diamanté-rimmed spectacles. 'I had a cataract in both eyes,' she explained mournfully.

Sir Robert and Lady Bellinger arrived. The former's modest start in 1910, son of David Morgan Bellinger 'of Cardiganshire', education Church of England school, catapulted to high platforms in the City of London. At the ripe age of fifty-two he married his vivacious Belgian brunette, Christiane Marie Louise. He became Lord Mayor and a knight in 1966. Tall, slim and thin-lipped, he attributed a deal of his incisive success to exercise and diet. Never eat too much citrus fruit, he warned; it brings on rheumatism.

We passed through a narrow corridor, glowing with Russian ikons, kelim rugs, and saddlebags. In the dining-room Cella's bright collection of Bohemian glass glinted from corner cabinets. She has left them to the Victoria and Albert Museum, which accepted with alacrity. Used to a former life of Embassy trappings she talked nostalgically of chefs and chauffeurs. But her excellent chicken and rice and home-made coffee ice, spiked with ginger, belied such former dependence on kitchen staff.

Frank asked me about China; as our ambassador in Moscow (1960–62) he would have liked to compare the two systems; he had never managed a visit. He was heartened that I did not enthuse; the West was too precipitate in acclaiming the Chinese as new-found friends, he felt. He would always feel more attuned to Eastern Europeans; better the devil you know. And who could ever trust the inscrutable Asians?

December 12 Hardwicke House

Warm, wet December days; grey and windy; yet the berries are astonishingly thick and bright, forerunners of a cold winter, they say.

The world erupts and wails with its usual quota of disasters. The appalling earthquake in and around Naples two weeks ago claimed about 3,000 lives instead of the few hundred originally feared. Relief was slow and haphazardly discharged, and Black Market deals heaped poison on the agglomerate of death and decay.

John Lennon, the ex-Beatle, was shot dead this week in New York, some deluded assassin from Honolulu. A re-surge of Beatlemania now romps home with an unprecedented demand for old records. The EMI factory at Hayes, Middlesex are keeping up with overtime. His widow, Japanese Yoko Ono, implores fans not to commit suicide over her husband's death, there have been two cases in America already. She advises: 'When something like this happens, each one of us must go on.' A daunting exercise, it seems, when we read in today's *Sunday Times* that any man aged twenty-five to forty-four in New York city is now more likely to be murdered than to die from any other cause.

In Peking, Madame Mao's trial lurches dully on its course. Monosyllabic, she has kept a low, apathetic profile until yesterday when she hurled abuse at her judges and called them criminals. She was hustled out of court. Verdict by year-end, we are told. Open prison? Hard labour? 'No chop' was predicted by our guide in China. 'She will be re-educated.'

Christie's had three painful blows this week. Paolo del Pennino, our man in Rome, was arrested for harbouring drugs and guns and a rocket launcher. (What did he want with a rocket launcher?) A personable, charming man in his mid-thirties, we were all very surprised. And he was a good polo-player. The second ignominy was the sale of a (questionable) Bernini bust at Sotheby's for £110,000; it was sold at Christie's South Kensington last year for a mere £110. Thirdly, the Leonardo Codex (a handsome red leather-bound tome crammed with manuscripts of the master's study of hydrodynamics) was finally bought by an American oil millionaire for £2.2 million. Sold by Lord Coke of Holkham, excited speculation had reckoned on a bid of £5 million or more from the Italian Government.

1981

Saturday, January 17 dawned wet and windy. Undeterred, Spencer Le Marchant, Conservative MP for High Peak, Derbyshire, celebrated his fiftieth birthday in exuberant style. A morning shoot on Mike Crawshaw's Leicestershire estate, Whatton Hall, culminated in champagne, roaring fires, and much stamping of mud through the large, galleried stone entrance hall. An ox roasted furiously in the misted garden (it had hung for seventeen days). Lunch for 150 in the dining-hall proved a long, jolly combination of good wine, warmth, and badinage. At dusk an elaborate firework display on the west stone terrace must have further astonished the surrounding villages.

Three days later Tom and I flew to the sun and heat of India. His second trip, my first. Last October he had sown seeds of communication with redundant Maharajahs, rich middle-class industrialists and sharp traders in jewellery, Indian miniatures, carpets, swords, daggers and European miscellanea. In the face of India's unrealistic export laws (nothing over a hundred years to leave the country), Maharajahs and the once privileged private sector are being steadily milked of their heritage. The attractive asset of ready cash from unscrupulous dealers balances such undesirable exchanges, it would seem, and black money, the name of the game, flutters freely on a brisk breeze of corruption. Would an above-board two-way trade be preferable? Works of Indian art scattered throughout Europe and America could be re-instated with a reciprocal transfer of European collections from India. Hoards of Indian mementoes from the century-old Raj connections still lie forgotten in British attics, while European pictures languish in the dust and humidity of enfeebled Indian palaces.

On arrival at the luxury Taj Hotel in New Delhi at 2 a.m., there was the usual hassle of the room not yet ready. We sat in the spacious white marble lobby and watched the busy spray and trickle of a central fountain. Finally a houseboy, resplendent in scarlet turban, tunic and white jodhpurs, ushered us up to our quarters.

The morning revealed a lush landscape of Lutyens's garden city spread far and wide below, but New Delhi, with its wide boulevards, its majestic Government compounds and well-kept parks, gave no hint of India's real essence, its ubiquitous teeming life, its dirt and colour and decaying grandeur. In Old Delhi the sensations were dramatically redressed. Chandni Chouk Avenue was jammed with scooter taxis, bicycle rickshaws, horse-drawn carts, stray oxen, and a motley over-flow of humanity. A car was being festooned with marigolds (the flower for sacred festivities) in preparation for a wedding. 'Speed thrills but kills,' exhorted a hoarding alongside, an irrelevant-enough warn-ing, as our car sat stationary in the milling crowd, while beggars (a lucrative profession, we had been warned) leaned on the windows with arch pleas.

At the Red Fort we were waylaid by a man and his pair of dancing monkeys. They wore green tunics and were caught on a lead. A snake-charmer, with his sitar, competed nearby, while a plausible act of levitation beyond was well under way beneath a huge counterpane. But such intriguing distractions could not compete with the impact of that seventeenth-century Moghul magnificence. Created by Shah Jahan, the red sandstone crenellations and domed kiosks, hot and sharp against the deep blue sky, bounded a host of peacock-arched halls and pavilions, where intricately-fretted marble screens and thrones inlaid with pietra dura opened on cool lawns and flower parterres.

Taking the Mahatma Gandhi marg, we came to Humayun's tomb. Considered to be the forerunner of Shah Jahan's Taj Mahal, its hand-some domes and arched colonnades of red and ochre sandstone were again offset by a Moghul-style garden. Water and shade were effec-tively contained in the symmetry of rectangular pools, flanked with trees; subsidiary water channels enclosed the formal surround of the rose parterres, a little unkempt. An ox grazed on the lawns and the pools and rills were empty. Water shortage and diminished labour had taken their toll. Green parakeets darted shrilly in and out of caves and arches, while pale chipmunks with dark-striped backs scuttered up the Ashoka Avenue. (The ashoka is a long-revered Indian tree, a symbol of peace and harmony, often referred to in BC Vedic Literature.)

We later dined with Patwant Singh[1], a genial Sikh in a navy turban and Gucci shoes. He was reading Graham Greene's *The Bomb Party*, beside a wood fire and a fierce-looking doberman pincher. He had a stylish house, built in 1937 with a twin-fronted curved façade and an adjacent spiral staircase leading to his first floor. A broad balcony, clustered with white bougainvillaea, overlooked his garden below and the sixteenth-century Lodi Park beyond. He liked to walk in the park in the evenings among the fortressed monuments, lakes, and rose gardens. His studio living-room was a colourful mélange of contem-porary art, sculpture, string effigies, pottery and hand-woven durries.

[1] *The Sikhs* – an inspired and definitive history – by Patwant Singh was published in 1999 by John Murray.

(We promptly bought one for £8.00.) An articulate man, with a full deep voice, he rounded on every topic of conversation with relish. An architect by profession and editor of *Design* magazine, he was a leading protagonist for the conservation of New Delhi's inherent town planning and deplored the recent rash of high-rise luxury hotels. He had written on international affairs. His books *India and the Future of Asia* and *The Struggle for Power in Asia* are widely acclaimed.

A wizened housekeeper tended the fire and led out the dog for its nightly airing. We ate rice, curries, kebabs, and pistachio ice-cream. A cook and a bearer served us solicitously. We drank lager. (We never acquired a taste for the harsh Indian wines.) With a final invitation to join him at his farmhouse thirty miles west of Delhi over the weekend, we were driven back to the Taj by his turbaned chauffeur.

Lunching in his country garden, under a bright red parasol appliquéd with blue elephants and parrots, he explained the concept of the Sikh religion. The youngest religion and a distillation of them all, a philosophy of behaviour rather than a religious practice. There are five cardinal rules. The five *Ks* comprised: the wearing of long, uncut hair (Kesh) for virility; a comb (Kanga) to keep it tidy; a steel bracelet (Kara) on the right sword arm to parry blows; a sword (Kirpan) for protection; and, lastly, long underpants (Kaccha) as a symbolic restraint from lust. He later complained that his turban (seven yards of muslin) gave him trouble when travelling; he could never get it starched properly. After lunch his bearer laid out a large carpet on the lawn, and our host, rolling himself up under the rug, took a long nap.

We later walked through the surrounding mustard fields and arid marshlands fringed with palm-trees. The Aravalli mountain range rose clouded and purple in the evening distance. Hedgerows were clustered with pink and yellow wild flowers. Myna birds, sparrows and partridge flew about, chattering loudly. Field, tree, soil, and mountain were rolled in the fading rose light. On our return to the farmhouse we sat drinking before a log fire and admired the old chairs of stripped Burma teak and Singapore cane. There was a sudden violent thunderclap. Hail, the size of walnuts, beat the slate roof like gunshot. The lawn flashed white in the lightning. Terrified birds swooped back and forth in the veranda as the amazed servants rushed out with torches, scooping up the icy balls for us to marvel at; nobody had ever seen the like. The lights failed, a regular hazard in rural areas, and we bathed from buckets of boiled water.

At breakfast the following day, our host appeared sans turban. Sitting on the veranda with his greying hair wound in a thick top-knot, his nightshirt swathed in a blanket, he resembled a kindly ayah. I assured him he looked younger without his customary head-gear.

The following Monday morning of that redoubtable Republic Day Parade was cold and grey, with low cloud. Would they cancel the fly-past? We took our seats on the Raj Path, where a well-disciplined crowd of two million had been converging since dawn. Lutyens's Presidential Palace (Rashtrapati Bhavan), remote in its classical restraint, dominated that broad, majestic route. A helicopter, wittily disguised as an elephant, weaved up the avenue, trailing red rose petals, while our programmes urged us to refrain from eating picnics; food attracted birds and could endanger the planes.

Anticipation was first rewarded by Mrs Gandhi's appearance, in a long grey coat and white headscarf, waving from her open land-rover. She was followed by the Mexican President Portillo. (Their talks on oil loans had been reported as 'warm and friendly'.) He was given a 21-gun salute. A sophisticated stream of gleaming nuclear warfare glided past to subdued applause: rockets, submarines, tanks (air-conditioned), and a MIG fighter – Indian-built to Russian design. Then came the whole gamut of the Indian armed forces (one of the world's largest and best-trained). Their brisk march off-set a wide range of sartorial extravaganza topped with plumed and studded turbans. Elephants swayed magnificently under scarlet-swagged, gold-tasselled howdahs with their silver-fringed red, green and white umbrellas perched high. Drums, trumpets, and cymbals heralded an exotic spate of flower-garlanded floats from every state. Goa was especially festive with bronzed dancing girls, gyrating sinuously to a disco band. Their show of exuberant joie de vivre seemed incongruous on that dull grey morning. The fly-past was limited to three planes spewing out the tri-colour national colours, and the crowds, as vividly clothed as the Parade itself, dispersed to their own business of the day.

The next morning we caught an early flight to Agra and the Taj Mahal. It glistened supremely white and translucent against an electric-blue midday sky. Shah Jahan's seventeenth-century monument to con-jugal love. His adored second wife, Mumtaz Mahal, had died in childbirth aged thirty-nine, after having already borne him fourteen children. The delicately-arched façades and soft rounded domes ema-nate an undeniable tenderness. The river terraces and shaded lawns, alive with peacocks and parakeets, suggest as near a paradise garden has one could wish to see. We walked across the wide marble foundation to the far balustrade. The Jumna river below, with its silted banks and empty tracts of marsh, was a peaceful scene reflecting a train of camel carts, an idling boat of fishermen and a young girl paddling with two frolicking dogs. It was surprisingly dark inside; the white marble walls and the lace screen now dimmed to ochre. A scent of stale frangipani pervaded the tomb below. A wrinkled proprietor lit candles, mumbled prayers, and gathered up rupee notes, left casually on the sacred slabs. All was exquisitely inlaid with rich Italianate colours, flower motifs, and arabesques of agate, jasper and lapis lazuli. Out in the bright sun we watched young men half-heartedly scrubbing the marble walls whiter with chemicals and ammonia.

We drove on to Fatehpur Sikri, the red sandstone long-deserted city. For fourteen years (1570–1584) it had served as a brief and glorious capital for Moghul emperors, but was soon abandoned through lack of water. The terraced courtyards, colonnaded pavilions, pools, and narrow steep stairways to miniature wind temples are evocative pointers to an enchanted court life. From the kiosk of the Manch Mahal we saw the seven-mile span of the crenellated fortress, with the artificial lake now sown with wheat.

Driving back to Agra through country roads and villages the evening streamed with life and colour. Goats and pigs rootled through rubbish, mud and dust. Oxen with brightly-painted red and blue horns strayed through the milling streets and camels with bells round their knees pulled sackloads of grain. Food stores and fruits were propped between the 'Kwality' ice-cream booth, the barber, the tailor, and the general store. A vulture plunged like some huge black flapping umbrella on a dead dog while women swayed by imperturbably in sarees of vivid orange, pink, red, and green, their heads lost in heaped mustard flowers, hay, grass fodder, firewood, and wicker baskets, piled high with dung disks. The men were more soberly clothed in rough wool shawls thrown over their cotton dhotis with every head swathed in some soiled haphazard turban. Poultry farms and fields of sugar-cane, wheat and mustard stretched out from whitewashed, humble courtyards and rickety, cane-roofed holdings. Tethered black cows, colourful washing lines, and stooked pyramids of hay gathered shadows while blackened woks steamed with stews and frying fat.

Then to Jaipur, the pink sandstone capital city of the north-western desert state of Rajasthan. We arrived after midnight at the Rambagh Palace Hotel, once the home of the late Maharajah. Our room had gone. Would we take the Maharani's suite for the night, for £100? After much deliberation between the management we secured it for £30. It comprised four high-ceilinged rooms where large ugly fans alternated with chandeliers. The bathroom was a luxurious complex of mirrored walls, the colour of curry. Water spurted from a silvered lion's mask in the recessed bath and an adjacent shower cabinet with twelve powerful jets proved highly invigorating. A basket of fruit, of chikus, mandarins, and seedless grapes lay on a low table, and a finger bowl with floating marigold petals. Mrs Gandhi, photographed on the front cover of *Imprint* magazine, gazed up with a proprietary air, an ironic touch as she had recently imprisoned the former châtelaine of these very rooms. (The present Raj Mata, Ayesha Jaipur, had refused to relinquish her gold.)

Built a hundred years ago, the peacock-arched marble colonnades support a baroque confection of balconies and domes. The terraced lawns were bright with vast flowerbeds and peacocks strutted between the weeping bougainvilleas. An over-attentive musician played a repetitive ditty on his sitar as we lunched on the marble terrace. On a far lawn, two men in flame-orange turbans were peacefully employed charming a nine-foot python, while a tethered mongoose close by was driven to distraction.

Jaipur, built in 1727 by Maharajah Jai Singh (an astronomer of fabled repute), is a well-planned city of long broad streets, skirted by hills and pinnacled forts. The uniformly old pink buildings are bunched with overhanging balconies and balustraded façades, topped with frail wind palaces, and miniature temples. Wild monkeys group themselves at will among these assorted crenellations. Arched doors and windows elaborate with perforated screens are hung with green wooden shutters. At sunset, the rose suffused glow of the stone is magical and lighted windows glisten like honeycombs.

We strolled through the familiar Indian evening scene. Wafts of musk, aniseed, dung and curry hung in the still warm air. An old man sat cross-legged on a rattan bed, sharpening knives, a woman spread freshly-dyed yarn in her courtyard; two boys mended bicycle tires and soled shoes with the discarded rubber scraps. We watched a wedding parade pass by. The resplendently-dressed groom, astride a horse garishly decked in bright cloth and tinsel, was heading for the bride's home. The women followed in gold-threaded sarees, silver anklets, and rings in their noses. There was a blast of trumpets from the accompanying men, an everyday occurrence. The pavements spilled out baskets of sweet limes, mangoes and mandarins (mostly imported from Bombay). Jaipur is a sheep-farming, carpet-weaving community, and cotton, brought up from the southern state of Gujarat, provides a big trade in hand-block and screen printing.

Sanganer, a village close to Jaipur, has become an internationally-acclaimed centre of cotton hand-printing; a serious young man called Satyendra Singh (Sunny for short) offered to drive me there. It remains essentially a family business with the feudal machinations of output unchanged through success and world demand. We strolled through a labyrinth of narrow streets and mud-baked shacks where stray cows, half-clothed babies, and the rhythmical slap of washing on stones induced a sense of that unhurried preoccupation with age-old daily life. Hand-scooped gutters ran with dye – blue, red, and purple. Young men whipped broad lengths of raw cream cotton on any handy block of stone, which softens the fabric and reduces the chemical content. Crumbling roofs and parapets were strewn with bright printed cotton lengths; four days under the hot, clear Rajasthan sun would ensure permanent colour. Meanwhile, in bare-boarded attics under ramshackle tarpaulin covers, and in roughly assorted premises below, men and women wielded their screens wet with paint and small wood hand-blocks were precisely dabbed on to the cotton lengths stretched taut on trestle tables. From such a rudimentary provenance are those prized fabrics seized upon by the world's most exclusive fashion houses. No machine could compare with that unique and dextrous craft.

Back in Jaipur Sunny showed me round his carpet and rug factory. Women and young children manned the hand looms or sat cross-legged untangling the yarn looped round their bare feet. In another makeshift attic an entire family – especially imported from a local village – were variously employed on a 22 by 40 foot carpet, a private commission for a room in Kansas City. A bedraggled grandchild toddled happily over the smooth pile of pink and palest lavender. Again, this primitive enterprise supplied world orders. (David Hicks is a regular customer.) There lay a world apart between these finished creations in situ and their primal starting point.

At Amber Palace, seven miles from Jaipur and once the capital of the state, we trundled up the steep winding approach on an elephant. A turbaned monster accompanied us with his sitar until we threw him a rupee, whereupon he conveniently waylaid another party on its descent. The elephants had elaborately-painted trunks and we noted how their knees were absurdly close to the ground. A placard nearby warned that 'the trading of elephant goad is prohibited'. From our elevated howdah we saw the old Lake Palace garden below. Once a prized Moghul conception of intricately-carved stone-work enclosing bright flowers like gems in a crown, it was now furred with weed and neglect. Having reached the fortressed summit, we disembarked and wandered through the deserted palace, a series of intimate salons, with coloured marble inlay and Persian mosaic, open-air pavilions, and court-yards. In the Chamber of Mirrors (the world's best, they said) an old man lit a match to indicate the reflections as myriad as the night sky.

The Moghul garden at nearby Sosodia is kept up to heartening standards. An eighteenth-century Summer Palace set in a dell of surrounding hills, it sports a sparkling river terrace lined with cypress and conical clipped ashoka. The garden walls are luxurious with orange and red bougainvillaea; flower beds cascade from the top lawn (where a large and lively lunch party was in full spate).

Our new friends, Bonny Singh, his wife Ganga and Sunny, took us one evening on a picnic. In his capacity as Ayesha Jaipur's financial adviser and general factotum, Bonny had arranged for the Jaipurs' Ramgarh shooting lodge as a venue. Built in 1920 on sixteenth-century Italian Renaissance lines, it stood deserted beside a lake, enclosed by hills, which had once been thickly wooded and full of wild beasts. Tiger and panther hunts had been a regular sport under the late Maharajah. Bonny had brought his gun, despite the recent ban on shooting. (The Jains, a religious sect who adhere to non-violence or killing of animals and even cover their mouths to avoid swallowing insects, had filed a successful petition on this front.) Undeterred, Bonny had already attempted an abortive shot from the car window at a partridge, and on arrival at the lodge set about getting a boat round to the jetty; he had seen greylag geese across the water. We chugged out, but due to the noise of the engine and the swift falling dusk he again misfired on the startled birds. Meanwhile a bevy of old retainers had placed wicker chairs on the rough grass terrace where we ate our picnic under the stars.

The house and garden seemed poised on the brink of resuscitation or decay. Bonny said it was still used for occasional parties. A stuffed tiger, a lion, and a leopard were strategically positioned in the marble hall. A pair of prized elephant tusks had apparently been stolen from their customary home on a writing desk. Bonny later questioned the servants on the matter. An illuminated photograph of Ayesha at the zenith of her youthful beauty conjured up those stylish carefree days of long nights of dancing on the lake-bound terraces and mid-night swims in that long-emptied pool. Prince Philip had been a favourite guest.

The warm dark night encircled us and, as so often happens in congenial company one hardly knows, we all talked freely. Only Sunny seemed subdued. His wife, currently away in Delhi, having just given birth to a son, was of the Brahmin caste. Sunny was a Rajput. It had been a 'love marriage', a rare occurrence; most marriages are still procured with parental dexterity. His father had been gravely upset and had effectively banned him from the family home in Udaipur. It then transpired in conversation that the Brahmin caste was intellectu-ally superior to the Rajputs. One would have supposed Sunny had bettered himself by the liaison? Apparently not, caste was caste. (Any attempt at our understanding the contradictions and strange dichotomy of that complex society is like skinning a tightly-packed onion.) What were their views on Mrs Gandhi? They insisted she was corrupt, that she was stashing billions in Italy (it appeared her son Rajiv had married an astute Italian), that she surrounded herself with parasitic ministers, opportunists like herself and mostly Punjabs (further derision here as they were basically a Pakistani race). She also pandered to the Muslim community, with oil in mind. Fair enough, one felt. The rouble-rupee was another favourite working exchange, but she had at least upbraided Brezhnev over Afghanistan? Her police force was undeniably corrupt. Why? She paid them £5 a week; they had become hostage to bribes from the rich middle class. Young men caught raping village women would buy their way out of trouble. Finally she traded on the country's 80% illiteracy, setting herself up as a benign fairy godmother and paying for busloads to bring in their unwitting votes. Harsh indictments, but they seemed tolerably inured to her power. After all, who else could sort out that whole hapless confusion? It is a free country at least. An interesting fact is the richness of the middle classes. Only that day we had been invited by a Jaipur jewellery dealer (the tenth most important in the town, he had modestly insisted) to a wedding. He had hired the Rambagh Palace services for an al-fresco dinner, dancing and a firework display; the guests numbering over two thousand.

From Jaipur we flew over desert terrain darned with wheat fields and villages to Udaipur, the lake city sometimes termed the Venice of the East. It is greener due to the artificial dams and lakes. The country-side is rich in sugar-cane, wheat, mustard, mango and banana-trees. The setting of the Lake Palace Hotel (again playing a reverted role of mild debilitation from privately-owned bygone days) in the centre of the Pichola Lake was breathtaking. Across the water the high façades and temple spires of the white stone city are reflected in spectacular rose and gold at each rising and setting of the sun. At such moments a muffled rhythmic splutter echoed from the far shores as women slapped their washing on stones.

The hotel was casually run and a degree less comfortable and sophis-ticated than the Rambagh. Not surprisingly the bathwater was rancid. After ordering a picnic, we set off in a hired car on a three-hour drive to Ranakpur to see the renowned fifteenth-century Temple. A fascinating journey, despite our tiresome driver, who exercised his appalling English in a high-pitched whine, and studiedly lit patchouli joss-sticks when I occasionally chose to smoke a cigarette. Through rugged hill country with the Aravalli mountains ever-receding we passed several archaic wooden water-mills turned by oxen. We ate our lunch under a mango tree and soon attracted an audience; two old men squatting behind a cactus watched us with grave fascination. Camel carts, women with anklets and arms jingling in silver and ivory bracelets as they supported brass waterpots, herds of cows and goats, and clutches of children chewing on chapattis, passed before us with unhurried purpose. Bequeathing the half-finished beer to our mute admirers we soon arrived at Ranakpur, a must on any Rajasthan itinerary.

Marble Buddhas strewn with scarlet hibiscus and faded rose petals in dark niches stared fixedly with glass eyes glinting above folded arms. The marble maze of thick, white encrusted pillars, each differently carved and open to the skies, was set in a remote valley where no harsh winds blew, a valley temple magically protected by its position and untouched by time. We pottered about the roof with its eruption of domes and spires, each pinnacle was topped with a tall iron rod, hung with tiny bells and fluttering pennants, signals of welcome we were told though to us they resembled so many ugly television aerials. The place was deserted save for two old men sitting at the entrance clutching a worn visitor's book and a pretty barefoot little girl, who pleaded for pens. Drawing a blank she admired my amethyst ring, persuading me to let her try it on. For one fearful moment I imagined her scampering off with it through that marble labyrinth; however she graciously accepted that the ring belonged to its owner and was given a rupee for prompt exchange

On our return to the hotel we were told that the Maharana was pleased with his copy of *The Christie Year Book*[2]. He would like to entertain us the following day. (Tom had already explained in writing that we were booked on an early flight to Jodhpur in the morning.)

The Jodhpur Palace Hotel is a monstrosity supporting a dome the size of St Paul's. The red stone foundations were laid in 1929, it took twenty years to complete. (The brochure candidly pointed out that employment was thus given to thousands during several years of drought and famine. It also referred to 'beautifully manicured lawns and gardens'. We laughed at such fatuous licence, the parched lawns were as ragged as the desert beyond.)

We had arrived on a 'dry day', with the added annoyance of daily electric cuts from 10 a.m. to 5 p.m., hot water was a moveable feast. We signed our names in the candle-lit foyer while pigeons and sparrows flew blithely in and out, roosting in the vast complex of the central dome. We lunched, again in candle-light, in a large and lugubrious dining-room hung with the Jodhpur Maharajahs; their dark oval eyes stared balefully beneath plumed turbans studded with aigrettes. We spurned the continental menu of shepherd's pie and fried cabbage, for the inimitable Indian curry; diarrhoea was to set in with venom for the next week.

---

[2] A handsome volume, edited 1969–83 by John Herbert, Director of Christie's and Head of the press department. An annual publication it focussed on lots of special interest that had passed through the sale rooms. *Inside Christie's* by John Herbert, published by Hodder & Stoughton 1990. An intriguing up-date of the years 1958–88.

The medieval fort at Jodhpur, towering 400 feet above the plain, had been described by Kipling as 'a work of the angels, fairies and giants'. We walked up the steep approach, sharply-angled to impede any untoward rush of elephants or foe, and were guided through halls, pavilions, and high-walled courtyards of finely-perforated stone work. It housed an extensive and fascinating collection of well-exhibited howdahs, palanquins, royal cradles, and impressive armoury. Swords with vicious blades three feet long were being polished vigorously; word was going round that the young Maharajah was to visit the fort that very afternoon. Indeed the sound of a hooting car and frantic strumming on sitars at the entrance gates proclaimed his arrival.

That evening we were invited to a drink with him and his wife. Aged thirty-two with thick black hair and large eyes that evoked an erotic Indian miniature, he greeted us in a midnight-blue velvet dressing-gown, that half-concealed a loose linen suit and an ample build; his hands were surprisingly slender in contrast. His wife, slim with fine features, acknowledged us more coolly, her head covered with the drape of her scarlet saree. She struck an aloof pose throughout, motioning to the bearers in undertones and kissing her son and daughter a peremptory goodnight.

His Highness, glorying in the name of Bubje, had just returned from a two-year posting as the High Commissioner in Trinidad and was now busily engaged in setting his museums in order. (A pity he had not at the same time accepted the Taj Group offer to set his Palace Hotel in order.) His own apartments were spacious enough. Lalique was a favourite embellishment.

A sudden stir and his mother, the Raj Mata, entered the room; the daughter-in-law stooped to kiss her feet. The lady seemed charming, with that habitual grey pallor of the older Indian woman.

From Jodhpur we drove five hours through arid desert to Jaisalmer, another medieval fort, pitched like a ring of giant sand-castles in the extreme west of Rajasthan. Again we had been intrigued by the ceaseless activity of the desert. Animal husbandry was the chief means of livelihood, with goat-herds, camels, and sheep subsisting largely on cacti, thorn trees, and some shrub with a bitter milky sap that was neither cactus nor eucalyptus, but resembled both; and again that exotic parade of sarees and elegantly-balanced pots. Neat farm encampments with rondavels of pitched oblong stone slabs were topped with thatched roofs and made one convinced that rural poverty was a deal more palatable than any urban alternative.

Jaisalmer is an enchantment. The yellow sandstone glowed apricot in the evening sun as we meandered through its web of cobbled mud streets. Unlike other desert fortresses it was still inhabited as it had been since millennium. Balconies, galleries, façades and tiny stone latticed windows opened on intimate courtyards and homes dug out from the hard yellow stone. Each floor gleamed like polished marble. Here sat a woman sifting rice on a wide brass plate; another spun lamb's wool on a wooden wheel. Children danced round us impulsively, shouting, 'Good morning, what is your name. From where is your country? OK. Thank you. Goodbye.' But there was no begging and they were soon lost again to their games of hopscotch and marbles. Oxen, goats, and dogs were tethered haphazardly along the alleyways, where life had been made easier with electricity and a newly-constructed water tower, though neither amenity had enhanced the aesthetics of their ancient structural treasure trove. Power lines were criss-crossed at random against the old walls, and the handy water supply had encouraged rough plumbing, with sewage dispersal steadily eroding the foundations.

We entered the Jain Temple courtyard where a bent crone swept up dust with her cane, scooping it into a brass bowl. She motioned us to take off shoes and leather belts. The Temple was empty save for one ardent follower who wailed an interminable offering before the central Buddha. He was accompanied by two drummers beating hard on their stretched lambskin. In a candle-lit cell below we were shown a rare twelfth-century manuscript written on two long palm fronds, sandwiched between the original painted wood covers.

Down the street, an old man half-naked sang joyously as he rubbed his hair dry, a small boy alongside cried petulantly as his mother sluiced him soundly under the cold communal tap. An ox nearby munched on hay from a bowl of camel hide, while another seemed content with a cardboard box. In the town below our guide pointed out a lake, the original water supply, where mallard and pintail bobbed between the marooned summer pavilions. We walked through streets of five-storied havelis, the intricately-carved twelfth-century stone houses of former rich merchants and intriguing legacies of more prosperous days, when the ancient Middle Eastern trade routes passed through Jaisalmer to Delhi and Agra. Dusk fell swiftly. A young man untied the blindfold from his ox; all day it had been turning the wooden wheel that crushed the oil seeds, which had yielded a full vat of foaming white cream lather to be processed into soaps and frying fat.

The long drive north to Bikaner was enlivened by the occasional black buck leaping skittishly across the road, and a flat tire, rapidly changed by our driver, who attacked the job with the first show of urgency we had seen throughout India. (The Maharajah of Bikaner later told us that he always travelled with two cars as punctures were an everyday hazard on those hot, rough desert roads.)

We finally arrived at the red stone city and headed for the Lallgarh Palace Hotel. An air of somnolent dilapidation hung about the place and another huge confection of pepperpot kiosks hovered above the solid bastioned front built at the start of the century. We were allotted a large ground-floor room overlooking a courtyard of acacia trees, comfortable enough with its wide brass bed, but any released bathwater had a habit of regurgitating up a drain vent in the opposite corner. Peacocks whooped their raucous mating call as the evening darkened, while bats and pigeons swooped between the silhouette of turrets.

Dinner was a frugal meal, the incumbent Maharajah being a tee-totaller and a vegetarian. We met him the following morning, his large girth caught loosely in a sweater and wide trouser-legs belying his régime. A crack shot at clay pigeons, he had been a member of the Indian team for twenty years and was writing a book on his shooting travels through Russia, Iran, and Europe. His father, on the other hand, had been a full-blooded sportsman. He led us to a sombre room hung with seventy-two species of beasts that had been shot. The walls were smothered with stuffed heads of zebra, giraffe, bear, rhinoceros, buffalo, hyena, deer, and black buck. Good Indian rugs were strewn through his large apartments, and he owned a large collection of Daniell lithographs. Signed photographs of the British royal family were propped on tables between reproduction teak furniture made in Calcutta. (His forefather had received King George V and Queen Mary at Bombay in 1911.) A large cut-glass central vase, filled with plastic gladioli, added a crude splash of colour in the main drawing-room, together with his Highness's own attempt at modern art. An amiable man with no pretensions, he welcomed a new system of social democracy, but he sighed heavily at mention of Mrs Gandhi. He swore she was the epitome of corruption.

The sixteenth-century Bikaner fort was built of red and yellow sand-stone. The painted wood ceilings were exquisitely worked with arab-esques and colourful fruits and flowers. Richly-lacquered doors opened on salons of mirrored walls appliquéd with delicate gold leaf trellis work. In 1900 a 'cloud' room had been created to explain to children the mysteries of rain and storms. Great whorls of bright blue tempera romped across the walls and ceiling, and tongues of flame zig-zagged in and out to resemble lightning. At dado level there was a naïve attempt at rain, altogether a dramatic portrayal of the vagaries of nature.

We finally packed our bags on Rajasthan and flew south to Bombay and the luxury of the old Taj Hotel. Our room overlooked the harbour and its Gothic-style surround of high brick buildings with palm-trees waving in between. The air was warm and balmy after the colder nights of the desert. We dined in an expensive apartment where our diminutive hostess complained of the unseasonal chill. She had donned a warm trouser suit in lieu of a saree. Her turfed roof garden whispered with ferns and bamboo and the muffled surge of the Arabian sea below. Late that night I flew to London, together with a gaggle of old women wearing thick wool jerseys under their sarees and sensible walking shoes over long wool socks.

February 18 Hardwicke House

Today I lunched with Max Reinhardt[3]. He fixed the date weeks ago and I half-wondered if he would remember, but on arrival at The Bodley Head, No. 9 Bow Street, I was promptly told fourth floor.

Mellifluous and urbane, he settled me in a deep chair with that disarming level gaze and a tumbler of Beaujolais. He exuded an air of languor. He was off to Spain in the morning; he hated going away, that last-minute exercise of bedding shelved problems. His eyes lit on photographs of the Queen and Prince Philip scattered on his desk. 'Here you see me in illustrious company.' He plumped up with remembered pleasure.

'She's enjoying herself, isn't she?' The Queen was indeed laughing delightedly. Was she watching a horse race? No, in his capacity as executive chairman of the Royal Academy of Dramatic Art, he and Sir John Gielgud had been entertaining her with a pair of actors, a wrestling act. 'She asked me if we had many students from established acting families. I replied, "Yes, Ma'am, but they seem inhibited following on in famous footsteps." Do you know? She looked me straight in the eye and said ingeniously, "But doesn't that happen to so many of us?" I fell in love with her from that moment.'

His office was padded with books; old periodicals, piled in haphazard cairns, aided the comfortable disarray. 'You see those old Penguins? We started them. They are prized possessions now.' He took one down and fondled it tenderly. 'You see that?' The modest sum of 2/6 was scrawled in pencil on the cover.

He attributed his success in publishing to good friends and never harming them, a modest simplification. Printing costs were appalling; unions were a lurking threat, so far abated. He had a good staff, some of them had worked with him for twenty-five years. 'We thrive on a patriarchal attitude. Muriel Spark has come over to us from Macmillan and we are doing well with Georgette Heyer. I am persuading

---

[3] Max Reinhardt Ltd was founded in 1948 and in 1956 he bought The Bodley Head. Reinhardt was Chairman 1981–87 and joint Chairman Jonathan Cape 1973–87.

Margaret Lane to write her biography. Here, take a copy of Graham
Greene's latest *Ways of Escape*, autobiographical.' He pressed his desk
bell. 'Antonia? Is Stanley downstairs?' We passed through the downstairs lobby heaped with newly-delivered jiffy bags. 'Not for me, I
hope,' he observed in mock alarm.

Stanley deposited us at Rules in a swift Jaguar. 'Good morning, Mr
Reinhardt, sir. Two champagne cocktails? Certainly, sir. Mind your
head, madam, that print of Mr Greene juts out a bit as you sit.' Smoked
salmon was neatly overtaken with succulent grilled sole heaped with
tartare sauce. We drank more Beaujolais and subsided into gentle
observations on life, relationships, plans, regrets. He left me over the
coffee, complimenting me on my own remarkable bladder. And why
had he treated me to such a lunch? 'Your diary,' he ventured, 'perhaps
you need some directive?' How could I ever submit my loosely-woven
ramblings to such an incisive professional?

March 29 Hardwicke House

Described by her father, Lord Spencer, as 'a beautiful physical specimen', at time of birth, and as 'preppy' by an enthusiastic media on the
occasion of her engagement last month to Prince Charles, Lady Diana's
passage through the maze of royal decorum and avid publicity seems
smoothed with approval. We are even endeared to those bitten nails
so carefully secreted from the cameras as she proudly displayed the
ring and her appearance in jeans for that first breakfast at Clarence
House, where she had been so hurriedly deported from her Kensington
flat, and the adventurous décolletage of that black taffeta dress for her
first public engagement at the Goldsmiths' Hall. Her shy lovely eyes
peep elusively from her bang of blonde hair (that will have to go, they
say, in deference to the tiaras), and her open smile seems untrammelled
with regrets for past freedom or fears for her monitored future.

The Queen recently described her as a 'shy, malleable girl', perfect
material indeed for cutting and polishing to the rigours ahead. The
luck of the Royals to secure such a gem with that flawless past! Has
Prince Charles had his cake and eaten it? But why not? He must surely
realise his good fortune and have eaten a slice of humble pie in a
private corner. (A pity though that he conveyed his wish for Lady
Diana's hand by merely telephoning her bemused father, in lieu of a
timely letter or an invitation to lunch.)

Her mother, Frances Shand Kydd, catapulted from a lulled life on
her second husband's farms in Scotland and Australia, has also inspired
a warm press. 'But why do you walk so fast?' panted photographers at

Heathrow on her speedy return from Sydney, at the time of the announcement. 'I have long strong legs like my daughter', was the airy retort. In a matter of hours we saw her on the evening news, immaculate in platinum hair, pink silk and pearls, voicing her pleasure at the engagement.

Last week we met her at Christie's attending an evening view. I remarked on her poignant observation that the pre-engagement holiday with her daughter in Australia would be their last alone. 'I felt forlorn,' she said wistfully, 'as I saw Diana off at Sydney airport.' Her husband, Peter, later remarked blandly, 'If I had been around in the Spanish Civil War, I would have been a Republican – and I still am! We will be lucky to squeeze in three close friends round the font at the wedding.' He must have been exaggerating?

And what are the chances of Bill Shand Kydd (Peter's half-brother) and his wife Christina getting an invitation? They seemed doubtful of one last week. Had any amusing anecdotes transpired from their peripheral role? Christina admitted it had been easier booking tables at restaurants. She had also been tapped for a royal warrant by a man who had covered her sofa. And she mentioned besides that her sister, Veronica Lucan (currently suffering from semantic delusions), had volunteered: 'It's a myth that men are put off by bitten fingernails; Prince Charles is marrying Lady Diana and Lord Lucan married me.'

Meanwhile the tourist trade has bucked up with every conceivable memento of the happy couple, spewing out its future of the past. And the Queen Mother? The perennial darling of the monarchist stage? She must be tickled pink with this whole outcome, her lady-in-waiting is, after all, the grandmother of the future bride.

May 28 Hardwicke House

The traumas and titillations of interviewing are one thing to contend with, but the wrath of an editor is most unnerving.

It was some months ago that I pressed a front-door bell in Cadogan Square and embarked with trepidation on my first assignment – to interview Stanley Falconer, an interior designer with the fabled house of Colefax and Fowler. He was charming, articulate, warm, and enthusiastic. 'I like tricking the eye,' he averred with relish. Indeed the solemn confines of his Edwardian flat appeared to have leapt into the ambience of a French country house. Trompe l'oeil abounded with trick panelling, marbleised eighteenth-century cornices and a fake painted extension to his bookcase, which flaunted fanciful tomes: *Never Complain, Never Explain* by Stanley Falconer and *Good Taste*.

James Mortimer photographed him, and we conducted a companionable interview between takes. I scribbled notes at random while asking him some twenty questions, Many were summarily dismissed while others led to a spate of views and colourful copy. The following day, I was heartened by the material I had gleaned and recalled. I enjoyed chronicling it into an article and quoted him accurately. I presented my piece to my editor – triumphantly.

Robert Harling, the editor of *House and Garden*, a journalist, novelist and typographer to the *Sunday Times*, and self-styled king of Fleet Street, seemed reasonably pleased with my first effort. though he warned me off 'purple prose' and put a line through some coveted observations. It was duly published this month and I was paid £65.

My second interview, with John Siddeley, third Baron Kenilworth of Kenilworth in the County of Warwick, was swallowed whole with no adverse comment. But my third attempt, with George Ciancimino, a half-Sicilian, half-French designer of modern furniture, has incurred a paroxysm of hiccoughs from Mr Harling. 'Too many views, not enough narration. What about his early years? And his training? More flesh and blood needed for a personality piece,' and then the most unexpected kick below the belt: 'If you wish to opt out of these hardships of apprenticeship, you must tell me, and I will go back to the earlier arrangement and do them all myself. So much quicker, if less beguiling.' The editor is clearly disenchanted. After months of open adulation and expensive lunches at the Westbury Hotel, where lustful references to below the belt seemed more the order of the day, I feel soundly toppled.

Robert Harling is a well-preserved specimen of seventy. His trousers are cut so tight that he must surely lie down to ease them on. (I am told that his wife then irons them in place.) He wears a high, hard hat, as we saunter from Hanover Square to the Westbury in Conduit Street. Over lunch and a customary half-bottle of warm, sweet German wine, his conversation becomes flushed with flattery and sexual allusion, warmly embracing his own virility. He suggests that my determination to become a journalist is sheer masochism and that his own commitment to my cause is prompted by my pretty nose and legs, rather than any suspicion of talent. I emerge from these sparring sessions with a hectic sensation of having been alternatively rolled in the mud and doused in the sweetest scents of Araby. I like the man though; he is a professional.

Beverley Nichols came to tea today. Frail and tottering and complaining of failing sight, he carefully laid his hat and walking stick on the hall table. We slowly edged up the stairs to the sitting-room where I had a coal fire burning and where I knew that the profusion of wisteria on the balcony would please him. He was clutching a book, *Are They The Same At Home?*, a series of interviews conducted by him as a young man, 'fifty years before you were even born,' he commented gaily. In fact it had been first published in 1927. What a gallery it contained. Here he breakfasted with Lloyd George, there he sauntered through Trafalgar Square with Sir Edwin Lutyens. Arnold Bennett, Diaghilev, Aldous Huxley, Osbert Sitwell, H G Wells, Duff Cooper, Somerset Maugham (whom he modestly termed 'dark and difficult'), a veritable galaxy of men from every walk of life romped through the pages, interleaved with a sprinkling of stars such as Melba, Rose Macaulay, Rebecca West, Lilian Baylis, Edna Best; and even the decorative tennis player, Señorita de Alvarez, whom he claimed has especially charming, having miraculously escaped the pitfalls of too much muscle or too much temperament. He paints their views and personalities with an enchanted, deft insouciance and is shamelessly subjective throughout. A touch of purple prose here and there as from his interview with Lloyd George.

'And he glowered ahead of him, the sunlight from the window making his eyes glisten like a cat's. There was so much concentrated righteous indignation in that glance that, had he wished, I believe he could have withered the blossoms from the almond tree.'

Dear Beverley. At the fag end of his life, he is still working with money necessarily in mind. His latest venture into poetry has fallen foul of publishers, but their world is in a perilous state these days. However he is doing well with his children's books. 'You know, the world seems such a sad muddle that it gives me a sense of real pleasure and relief to take on the metamorphosis of a wicked witch,' he concluded with a hint of his old humour.

June 27 Abbotsworthy House Kingsworthy Nr Winchester

Only the gnats disturbed that brief enchantment of a still June evening, whilst a number of us – perhaps 200 – drank champagne on the terrace of Abbotsworthy House. The high eighteenth-century bow-fronted walls were knotted thick with roses – pale pink, red and yellow – and recaptured the bright flutter of taffeta dresses below. We were celebrating Jennie Enfield's marriage to Christopher Bland; the final seal on their ten-year love affair. Her husband Tom, heir to the Earl of Strafford, had mercifully fallen for a widow in Winchester some months previously.

'It's wonderful to be Christopher's wife at last, rather than his titled mistress,' volunteered Jennie, radiant in a froth of cream lace.

We later dined in a flower-filled marquee on smoked salmon, rare beef and raspberries.

Lady Antonia Pinter was there; dressed in white, her perennial youth and beauty was favourably enhanced beside the unremarkable dark looks of her newly-acquired playwright husband.

Leon Brittan, MP for Cleveland and Whitby and recently elected as the youngest member of the Cabinet, had trouble manoeuvring his well-worn white mini over the soft grass of the improvised car park. 'I must invest in a new model,' he reflected ruefully. Could it be that one day he would be whisked everywhere in security-guarded limousines as our future Prime Minister?

July 11 Hardwicke House

Is the art boom over? 'Market in Old Masters Collapses' is the sober indictment in *The Times* today. Sixty-five percent of Christie's major summer sale failed to reach reserves yesterday, with the Goya portrait of *Doña Francesca Vicenta Cholet y Caballero* bought in at £900,000. Sotheby's fared little better on Wednesday when fifty-six per cent of their major picture sale was unsold. There are two other potential nails poised to drive the London sale rooms into the ground. A consortium of influential London dealers is due in October, to take legal action over the buyers' premium of 10%; if they win their case, the ensuing financial redress to buyers over the past few years would virtually bankrupt the salerooms. Furthermore, the EEC are trying to introduce a new fifteen percent tax on all antiques entering Britain. This would effectively diminish London as the world centre of art dealing.

Gloomy forecasts are ubiquitous on many fronts these days. With the possibility of a Labour government in two years' time, private education will be a priority abolishment, together with many other established cores and privileges of our society. And will the Monarchy be at stake? Meanwhile a rash of street violence in our northern cities and in and around London has caused untold damage and fear. The Government is soundly shaken by such an unprecedented show of riot. Are these disturbances due to unemployment? Racial unrest? Anti-Royalism? Or due simply to the ravings of a disillusioned country, tired of the recession, tired of hope and hell-bent on flouting every vestige of moral and civil order? Can they be controlled by our stalwart police force? Or will the Army move in with attendant street curfews? Too many unnerving imponderables pervade our country today. Nearer home, the King's Road is now rumoured to be the next prize target for violence and looting. Many shops and restaurants have been boarded up in wary readiness, while 'we are open', 'business as usual', is chalked up on their baleful frontages.

July 24 Hardwicke House

There is nothing remarkable about the Swiss Ambassador and his wife, Monsieur and Madame Claude Caillat; he is an economist with a long nose and a lean figure, whilst she is no beauty; but with their modest charm and quiet aplomb they have a capacity to attract the most sophisticated and influential to their table. Their dinner party last night at the Embassy in Bryanston Square was given in honour of Sir Ian Gilmour, Lord Privy Seal, and his wife Lady Caroline. A relaxed, informal atmosphere overrode the evening dress, and the formal introductions; Swiss bankers and French industrialists mingled with Lord Home and his wife, quiet and gentle in duck-egg chiffon; Roy Jenkins who, in the customary social absence of his wife, seemed happily paired with the raven-haired Patricia Rawlings; Lord and Lady Chalfont, Lord and Lady Gibson, and the Belgian Ambassador and his wife, Madame Robert Vaes. A plumper, rosier edition of Lady Diana Spencer, in the form of her elder sister Lady Jane Fellowes, was the youngest guest. At dinner I was seated next to her husband Robert, a correct young man as sleek as a beagle, and obviously well placed in next week's proceedings for the Royal Wedding; in his position as assistant private secretary to the Queen and brother-in-law to Lady Diana, his main duty of the day will be to escort 'my mother-in-law and step-mother-in-law up the aisle'. He later confessed to being 'a baked beans man myself'; was he being facetious? On my left a Monsieur André Bernard, Managing Director of the Royal Dutch Group, spoke warily of President Mitterrand; 'He wants to make his name in history; to introduce a new socialist order.' To what degree had Mitterrand manipulated the Communist sector and in turn been manipulated? '*Moitié-moitié*' was the sanguine reply. It appeared that a strong Communist element had been willingly planted in his Cabinet, in the top levels of industry and in the press and television.

The dinner was immaculately presented and served, though unimaginative; a consommé was pursued by salmon, veal and a fruit salad, the last concealed in scooped-out halves of pineapple and blanketed with baked Alaska. Monsieur Caillat finally rose to his feet and made a brief speech of welcome to Sir Ian and Lady Caroline Gilmour. He alluded to Sir Ian's 'wit and delicacy' and the esteemed presence of Lord Home and Roy Jenkins. Sir Ian was then persuaded to reply, 'My wife,' he claimed, 'always complains when I don't make a speech and is then embarrassed when I do.' As he was due to speak for thirty-five minutes first thing in the morning at the House of Commons on the Brandt Report (reference Western aid to Third World countries) he voiced his thanks and appreciation with economy. The women then withdrew. Over the coffee, Anny Vaes complimented our hostess on her transformation of the ugly, modernised rooms. The Caillats' personal collection of seventeenth-century Flemish portraits and handsome Oriental rugs had indeed done much to mellow the impersonal austerity. The conversation then veered to the Royal Wedding and to the Vaeses' 'fireworks' party at the Belgian Embassy the preceding night. From Belgrave Square one should have a good vantage of the display in Hyde Park.

The evening, like all diplomatic evenings, ended promptly. I should mention that our own had started in the hallowed precinct of White's Club, where a cocktail party was held to 'honour the occasion of the Royal Wedding'. A ticket charge of £25 to include one member and one 'lady guest' did not deter a throng of 680 people. We all, at some stage, eased our way up the crowded stairway to see the dining-room with its arched and coffered painted ceiling and crimson damask walls, whilst the management warned guests not to congregate there in large numbers, in view of an unfavourable report by the building surveyors.

July 30 Hardwicke House

Wars and weddings have always inspired the British, especially when on the grand scale. Yesterday's momentous event, the marriage between the Prince of Wales and Lady Diana Spencer, with its attendant pomp and pageantry, invoked an unprecedented show of joy and spontaneity from the British public and, indeed, the world. In a pandemic of television-viewing, close on one thousand million people could share the entire gamut of visual and musical thrills.

The sun – as rare this summer as good news – shone lovingly with temperatures in the seventies, as the Royal Carriage Procession rolled its way from Buckingham Palace to St Paul's Cathedral. In the words of Dr Runcie, the Archbishop of Canterbury – it was a 'fairy tale wedding'. It was also, at Prince Charles's request, an especially musical one. The Maori soprano Kiri Te Kanawa soared sublimely into Handel's 'Let the bright Seraphim' during the signing of the register. (She had put on weight, looked more jolly than beautiful, in a dress as bright as a bunch of sweet peas.) Elgar's incomparable 'Pomp and Circumstance no 4' rounded off the service. The swell of music flowed up and around the vast dome, as a good wine curls over the palate.

The bride was breathtaking in her 'nonpareil luminance' and her pure silk ivory dress; a magic confection with a twenty-five-foot train, a low flounced neck, lined with pearl-encrusted lace and a voluminous tulle veil, hand-embossed with mother of pearl sequins. But not even the Spencer diamond tiara, perched strategically above her famous blonde fringe, could match her sparkling radiance and her captivating sidelong smile; a smile already fabled for its hint of mystery and private amusement. She is exceptionally beautiful; tall and slim, her flawless complexion and perfectly-formed limbs and teeth epitomise the delicate English rose. Her inherited Stuart blood and height will certainly refresh the physical stature and looks of the future Royal line. Prince Charles, relaxed and dapper in his full-dress naval uniform, appeared enthralled.

Side by side, at the start of the Service, the couple fluffed their responses: Lady Diana, bestowing upon Prince Charles the first name of Philip; an understandable error which caused a ripple of surprised amusement in the Spencer pew; (it must often prove a hazard to remember the correct order of Charles, Philip, Arthur, George). The groom, in turn, bestowed upon his bride 'all thy worldly goods', and was heard to whisper 'well done' when these customary hurdles were finally breached.

The train was skilfully manipulated by the two senior bridesmaids, Lady Sarah Armstrong Jones and India Hicks; around corners, up and down red-carpeted steps, bundled in and out of carriages, it rippled and shimmered like mercury. The three younger bridesmaids, Sarah Jane Gaselee (the daughter of Prince Charles's horse-trainer), Catherine Cameron (a former school pupil of Lady Diana's), and Clementine Hambro, a diminutive blonde grand-daughter of Sir Winston Churchill, entranced all.

Security along the processional route had been stepped up to the hilt. With the disturbing shooting attempt at the Queen at last month's Birthday Parade, nothing had been left to chance. Armed police, disguised as footmen, were planted in each Royal carriage. The entire route was flanked by police facing the crowd with their backs to the procession; sniffer dogs were never far away. The mock shot at the Queen in June had emphasised Royal vulnerability to good effect.

Throughout the day, ecstatic crowds clamoured for more. Balcony appearances at Buckingham Palace were enlivened by thumb-sucking Clemmie Hambro, the Prince and Princess of Wales kissing full on the lips (just once) and the Queen Mother, her head a froth of crème de menthe feathers, dabbing her eyes. 'The Queen Mother is not well,' warned more than one commentator. (Her eighty-one years already suggest the next occasion for Royal circumstance.) A wedding breakfast for 120 guests, of lobster and a sumptuous-sounding dish, 'Suprême de volaille, Princesse des Galles', was especially presented by the Queen's chef, Mr Peter Page (a mélange of chicken breasts, stuffed with lamb mousse, covered in brioche crumbs and sautéed in butter). Strawberries and Cornish cream followed and vintage wines, Krug 1969, Latour 1959 and Taylor's 1955.

Meanwhile Prince Andrew and Prince Edward (now both taller and more handsome than their elder brother) had arranged for twenty blue and silver heart-shaped gas balloons and the message 'Just Married' scrawled in red crayon on brown paper, to be fastened to the going-away landau. The waiting crowds along the route to Waterloo station roared with delight at this unexpected touch of fun. The Princess of Wales looked more delectable than ever in her tricorn hat, fluttering with white and coral ostrich feathers. Her pale pretty arms were set off by the trim of white lace on her short-sleeved coral silk suit and her neck was caught in a deep pearl choker. What a day she had given us. A week ago she had enquired of some unwitting onlooker in a crowd, 'Will you be watching the wedding?' Yes, was the reply. Would she? 'I'm in it,' she answered disarmingly. We were also amused to read of a former pupil who, when asked 'What was she like?', replied diplomatically, 'I don't know. She never told me.' And so it all happened. In today's *Evening Standard*, we read the headline 'Gone Fishing'. The couple have at last found peace and quiet on the banks of the Test at Broadlands, Romsey, the former home of Prince Charles's adored late great-uncle, Lord Mountbatten.

We have undoubtedly witnessed the happiest marriage of a Prince of Wales in years. The former George IV was described as 'looking like death and full of confusion' on the day of his wedding to the flamboyant Princess Caroline of Brunswick in 1795. In March 1863, Edward, Prince of Wales, son of Queen Victoria, married Alexandra of Denmark, described by the Poet Laureate of the day, Tennyson, as a 'Sea King's daughter from over the sea'. It was a wedding fraught with unfortunate incident. Queen Victoria, still in mourning for Prince Albert, even suggested that St George's Chapel, Windsor should be entirely draped in black. She wept throughout the service, while the future Kaiser, Wilhelm II, then aged five, disgraced himself by flinging his Highland dirk across the floor. He next fell to biting his uncle's knees. Worse was to come, when, finally, after the wedding breakfast, the Prince and Princess travelled by Great Western Railway to their honeymoon on the Isle of Wight. On their departure, the Duke of Cambridge, in a traditional gesture, flung Princess Louise's shoe after them; it caught the groom full in the face. There were no such untoward gaffes this time, except, perhaps, the unfortunate display of

Understanding Cystitis, a book on public view, along with other gifts, at St James's Palace. Tom was in France over the wedding, together with Sebastian, staying in the Champagne country, near Rheims; they watched the whole televised show against a lush backdrop of vines. Lydia, on holiday with friends in San Francisco, must have watched it early in the morning. I stayed at home for the event.

A party at the Belgian Embassy on the previous night had proved another marked occasion, in which Raine Spencer, step-mother of the bride, had asked to be included. She arrived in a Rolls-Royce through crowds thronging Hyde Park for the evening's mammoth firework display. She looked bright and happy, in pink, white and blue voile, silver kid sandals, and heavy make-up. Her husband Earl Spencer, father of the bride, had sensibly opted for an early night. With his health in a parlous state after two recent strokes there was natural concern for his performance the next day. 'What will you say to your daughter as you lead her up the aisle?' invited one reporter. 'England's Kings are old friends of ours, I expect I'll say,' he replied wistfully. (As a younger man, he had been equerry to both George VI and to the present Queen.)

I had friends to lunch on the day of the wedding. With smoked salmon, smoked turkey and pâtés, together with Tom's superb wine, we celebrated in some style. From the moment the couple were pronounced man and wife, we opened a bottle of Laurent Perrier and continued through lunch with Mouton-Rothschild 1961. Nick Bethell came armed with an enchanting enamel box, no 217 from a limited edition of 250, commemorating the Royal Wedding. Hand-painted with the Prince of Wales's feathers in blue, gold, and white, it prompted Georgie Vassiltchikov to explain the origins of the feathers and the motto 'Ich dien'.

July 30 Hotel Royal Champagne Champillon Epernay France

Rheims, Epernay, Champillon, where every southern slope is ruffled green in a sea of vines. The evening sun is suffused with a thin wash of cloud; the air soft and damp at the promise of more rain. too much rain, complain the locals, as each grape clings to its clump, tightly-packed, and as pale as raw peas. Only the sun can stoke the skins to swell the flesh to loosen the full flow for the autumn vendange. It will prove a disappointing year for the purists; better to stock up with more 1976, '78 and '79.

August 1 La Petite Auberge Vaux-sur-Yonne Auxerre

We overlook the river from La Petite Auberge, a converted farmstead where the old beamed dining-room winks with glass wall-lights, copper pans, and fresh bright flowers. The towpath is jubilant with cottage gardens, where old women knit and cats curl in baskets of stiff, dried washing. The cherry orchard by the lock gate, where hens peck around the tethered goat, the willow, the poplar, the long lush grass and the river, flat, deep and green, give a sense that Sisley was here. Up the rue des Lauriers and down the rue de l'Eglise to a quiet dinner, we are lulled with the scent of petunias, good local wines and the final creamy delight of 'gratin de fruits rouges'.

August 2 Chablis

Market day at Chablis, the main street with its restrained eighteenth-century elegance of tall houses in pale, gold stone; now choked with bustle and produce. Hand-plaited straw baskets; as squat and firm as their robust saleswomen, the rich splash of vegetables and fruit, and the fish, translucent, slate-grey and pink, the spread of cheese on straw trays; camembert, brie and pont l'évêque, their ribbed crusts as gold and powdered as crumbling stone façades, welling soft cream at the point of a knife; the goat cheese beside, grey and cold as though rubbed in mildew.

August 3 Chagny

Chagny, ten miles south of Beaune. We lunch at the 3-star restaurant Lameloise, excellent at £22 per head to include the full-bodied burgundy, Morey-St Denis. We drive through the 'routes des grands crus': Meursault, Puligny Montrachet, Chassagne Montrachet, to the red burgundies of Gevrey Chambertin and Chambolle Musigny, vineyards, each intimate and cherished, each stylishly marked by its attendant château. Villages of golden stone where every trough, tub, urn and barrel brims with geranium, petunia and marguerite and where the clustered red-tiled roofs are shielded by the stocky bell-tower of a modest church. In the fifteenth century, the Ducs de Bourgogne declared themselves '*Les Seigneurs des meilleurs vins de la Chrétienté*' and presented their wines to the King. It is said that Louis XIV preferred *les vins de nuits*; Mme de Pompadour, la Romanée Conti, Napoleon *le*

Champ de Bertin, and that Dumas declared Puligny Montrachet to be drunk *à genoux et tête découverte*.

August 4 Auxerre

Through undulating cornfields, oakwood, and the green glint of maize, brushed lightly with its ginger ear to Auxerre, the substantial market town where every three months Colette's mother would journey six hours in her Victoria to buy groceries. The sugar loaf in its oblique wrapping of indigo paper, the ten pounds of chocolate, the vanilla, the cinnamon, the nutmeg, the rum for grog, the black pepper and the white soap.

We drove to Avallon and Vézelay where city walls and ramparts still soar above medieval streets, haphazard cobbled pavements and the Roman-built Basilica of Sainte Madeleine, with its white stone interior, cool and intricately carved.

August 6 Saint-Sauveur-en-Puisage

To Saint-Sauveur-en-Puisage, le pays de Colette and the home where she was born. Described in her own words: 'The house was large . . . the upper garden overlooked the lower garden . . . where the smell of tomato leaves mingled in July with that of the apricots ripening on the walls . . . In the rue de l'Hospice, a two-way flight of steps led up to the front door in the gloomy façade . . . but its dignity was upset a little by the steep gradient of the street, the stone steps being lopsided, ten to one side and six on the other . . . a large solemn house, rather forbidding with its shrill bell and its carriage entrance . . .'

The uneven stone steps are still there and the austere façade unchanged, save for the mundane intrusions of an auto'école alongside and the baleful glare of a dentist's neon light in the front window. The narrow road with its high old walls, voluptuously swagged with wisteria, is quiet. Could one scent ripe peaches from the garden beyond? The high-arched carriage door is there and through the worn keyhole I saw a white rabbit; compact and hunched it sat on the sun-warmed cobbles of the inner courtyard, a small, contented memorial to those late-nineteenth-century days, when this home vibrated to the cries of children and the cherished cats and fruits and flowers of that busy mother.

August 8

Chenonceau, Azay-le-Rideau; châteaux of the Loire; strategically sited
on the river's bank, where the ornamental gardens of topiary and
blazing parterres give more hint of past grandeur than their sparse
interiors. The furnishing of these castles was always reduced to essen-
tials; with incumbents travelling from one seat to another, packing up
tapestries and chests of silver and plate as they went.

The Loire Valley is flat and wide; though endowed with its full rich
quota of woods and farmland, it lacks that enchanted intimacy of
Burgundy. Houses of grey stone and pale weathered stucco stand
sombre under slate roofs. But flowers are everywhere, jostling for space
and clashing colour in window boxes and spilling over each stone
cottage doorstep. Neat avenues of clipped lime, beech and acacia lead
to the open road, where grass banks are crocheted with the tangled
white heads of cow parsley and dance with blue scabious and poppies.
And here a field of sunflowers with each negroid pate flared yellow
to the sky.

Villandry, an elegant Renaissance château, fifteen kilometres to the
west of Tours, where terraced, ornamental gardens are manicured with
box hedges and baluster yew trees. 'Gardens of Love' are symbolised
by minutely-designed parterres; shaped in fans, masks, hearts, horns
and swords; each like a jewel case, brilliant with flowers. The 'Jardin
de potager', where Brunswick cabbages, the yellow marrow peering
shyly from its floppy mantle, rhubarb with stalks as slim and as luminous
as the stem of a red Bristol wine glass; leeks and crimson beetroot
leaves – and all alternately planted with design in mind; an impression
of a multi-coloured draughts board with standard roses and bowers of
jasmine for scent and decoration in between. A vision of exquisite
order and artifice best seen from the shaded walks above of vaulted
lime trees and vine arbours. A dream conception evoked from the
Middle Ages and scrupulously maintained.

September 9 10 Milner Street London

It was a relief to sit down to lunch and to know that the quiddity of
further talk could pass unrecorded. I had been interviewing Michael
Inchbald[4], the interior designer. Descended on his mother's side
from the first Earl of Chatham (William Pitt the Elder), Michael

---

[4] The eclectic interior designer whose career spanned forty years. In 1960, he founded the
distinguished *Inchbald School of Design and Decoration*.

Inchbald certainly inherited a fair degree of his ancestor's rhetoric. His favourite quote 'Only the rich can afford to rectify their mistakes' has been referred to by his peers for years. For the past hour and a half, his childhood, his career, and his commissions had bounded unchecked through my brain and scribbled notes. A career spanning three decades, to include work on ocean liners, several American banks, the Plessey Telephone Exchanges, Claridge's Penthouse, the River Room, the American Bar at the Savoy, the Banqueting Suites and Perroquet Restaurant at the Berkeley, Dunhill tobacco shops throughout the world, and the complete redesigning and furnishing of the Crown Estate Commissioners' Headquarters in Carlton House Terrace.

He recalled his work on the Cunard *QE2* where jobs had been allocated in a straight competition as a formidable challenge. The main saloon, the Queen's Room, had been his own prestigious assignment. Faced with a low ceiling height of 9'6", he had dared to suggest he be allowed to lower it still further with textural interest to give the illusion of height. 'Absolutely not,' he was told. People would feel claustrophobic and it was too low anyway. With professional artifice he had finally created his illusion of height by exposing the criss-cross of steel girders from the deck above; he had then wrapped them in white fire-proof 'marinite' and had covered the whole with a lit-up glass screen. 'It had the effect of a sun-lit lattice. I next divided the room into a nave with two aisles supported on fibre-glass columns. The head of each column was splayed in a drawn trumpet shape which automatically took the eye longer to travel. It was an exercise in aerodynamics really, with a lot of white and silver chrome to aid the effect of height and light.' And so he had continued and I had scribbled, although his final exposition on the merits and failures of the right and wrong diagonals had left my brain high and dry and unheeded.

Tall and slim with fine incisive looks of an aesthete, and the barely-curbed nervous energy of an artistic temperament, he had at last come to rest. That whirlwind recall of past accounts and achievements could once more be stored away in the cool, tidy larder of his mind. It was time for lunch. we talked of Turkey, of India and Samarkand.

The wide high rooms loomed obsessively with the Classical and the Baroque, the Greek sculpture and the Egyptian. We sat in an alcove suffused in their richness, while the warm sun-gold light played on a tall Victorian window. A stooped old woman served the meal, of meat and mushrooms, followed by a crisp bread and butter pudding deliciously coagulated with every kind of sweet spice. Good nursery food must be a rarity in such a decorative ambience.

Was he busy today? 'Trade is very up and down would be my

cynical answer. Basically I am happy to design anything from a tart's bedroom to a gymnasium, but everything is so expensive, one gets fewer chances these days.'

We sipped black coffee companionably, then I finally left him to compile his career in my own tenuous hand.

October 22 Udaipur Rajasthan India

The billowing scent of pink jasmine pervades each corner of this sun-drenched courtyard. An old man in a scarlet turban pours my breakfast cup of coffee. A fountain plays in a pool of lotus flowers; the pigeons coo and everywhere is lush and brilliant after the summer rains. Bougainvillea swings from the fretted balconies in a collision of red, pink and orange. Glossy-leaved pagoda-trees shade their sweet-smelling flower; each wax-like creamy flute is plashed rose and prim-rose. There are orange-trees, too, and hibiscus. A woman in a yellow saree meticulously weeds a flower bed of bold marigolds while a lithe young boy, barefoot and black, balances a clay bowl of earth on his turbaned head, backwards and forwards he walks and fills a small parterre. At sunset he will wash the bowl and from it eat his frugal meal, a portion of mutton broth perhaps and rice.

What indolence to sit and smell and watch when all around pulsates with the heat and rhythm of a morning's work. Across the lake the narrow galleried streets of this white stone city teem with the confusing chaos that is India. The sweeping, squatting, sharpening, the bicycles, the tongas, the rickshaws; the restless monkeys poised narrowly beneath fragile eaves and the cows that stumble and sleep; the din of transistors and horns, shrill bells and crying children; the hammering of brass, of nails in shoes, and the frenzied whir of old sewing machines; the dung and the dust and the dignity and everywhere that remarkable tolerance between each man and child and beast. No angry voice is raised, no cry of fear, no hasty push or shove, rather a timed manoeuvr-ing of adroit lean bodies. The Indian is a master of that balance and deportment long steeled to necessity. His air is free but his space must be assiduously gained.

Last week we were in Turkey. We cruised three days on the Sea of Marmara with our friend Rahmi Koç. Warm and sleepy, idle days and then a force-six Russian wind that set the boat racing on a boisterous sea. We bathed and fished, slept, drank, and talked. We listened finally to General Evren. In a tentative bid for future democracy, he had appointed a consortium of 160 prominent men to assist him in the first faltering steps to civil rule. They appeared an old team. 'Sleeping minds,' commented Aylın Gönensay, whose economist husband, Emré, had narrowly missed being called. 'Too many military men,' observed Rahmi, 'and no leading industrialists.' Notwithstanding their disdain, they all conceded that Turkey had been tranquil and orderly under Evren's two-year military hold.

From Istanbul via Athens to Delhi and on to Jodhpur, a rigorous stint of thirty-six hours' travel. The final lap from Delhi to Jodhpur took nine hours on the road. A sturdy Sikh in a mauve turban had driven his Australian Ford hard. The long flat roads banked by pampas grass and mimosa were jarred with sprawling villages, choked with haphazard congestion, their noise and colour relieving the monotony of our relentless trail. Through the fast-falling night and the rutted desert road we finally reached the Jodhpur Maharaja saloon with an hour to spare. Silver-plated fittings gleamed on the finely-inlaid Burma teak. The table was set for dinner with stiff white linen napkins shaped as peacocks. Soup, fish, curries and an elaborate iced cake were served by two bearers. The train steamed and stopped and spewed its smoke with each successive village. Feet pattered on the roof above where heaped bodies slept in spurts. We hugged our bunks, exhausted, and next morning woke in Jaisalmer.

We approached the pitched medieval fortress in camel carts. Jaisalmer revisited with friends, still gold and glorious and unheeded by time. The same parade of children admired and gingerly fingered our bracelets and rings, but, soon distracted, they tossed their proud heads in waves of broken English, and scampered off. There was much scrubbing of walls and refacing with fresh dung and sand. Diwali, the annual festival of lights, would soon be upon them.

In the evening we drove to a far burial ground where the faint breeze murmured through desolate temples. The distant citadel was clasped in the rose and amethyst of the sinking sun. We later dined and slept on the train, reaching Jodhpur early next morning. The towering fort and the wide streets below scowled red. We bathed and breakfasted at the lugubrious Palace Hotel where five turbaned waiters produced limp toast and pale small eggs. Packed lunches followed as we set off again through hours of arid scrub, scarcely interrupted with the splash of bright sarees and the tended herds of goats and camels, a thinly scattered life.

We reached the fifteenth-century Jain temple of Ranakpur at sunset. The terrain had changed dramatically with the Avavalli wooded mountains. Wild monkeys grouped in shade, clung together and chattered inanely. The Jain temple with its intricate labyrinth of marble pillars stood cool and empty, save for a boy who mixed saffron paste in a marble bowl and daubed each glass-eyed Buddha.

And so to Udaipur, which lies white and shimmering beside its lake. The frowning red of Jodhpur and Jaisalmer's gold stand hours away. Tomorrow we leave for Jaipur, the capital city of Rajasthan, a city of pink stone, wind palaces and wide balconied streets where every arched window is shielded by its delicately-fretted screen.

October 27 The Rambagh Palace Hotel Jaipur Rajasthan

Diwali in Jaipur is a rare, visual feast. The wide streets, always throbbing with colour and activity have today reached a crescendo of exuberance. Branches of ashoka trees and fat necklaces of marigolds festoon each house and meagre shop-front. Stooks of sugar-cane are propped on every street and swept away on heads and bicycles. A plethora of sweet-shops display bright chunks of pounded coconut and sticky rice balls, steeped in honey. Sweets and fireworks and a burning oil light are the essential household props for celebration. Diwali, the festival of lights, denotes the start of the Indian winter and the New Year. It also invokes the Goddess of wealth, Lakshmi. Businesses are blessed with the worship of office safes and ledgers, a prime task. For days the shops have been open until midnight, spilling out extra produce under their gaudy awnings, while villagers from far afield have converged on the city to sell and buy.

Dusk falls and each clay pot of oil is lit. Fairy lights snake over roof-tops and across streets canopied in tinsel. Children in turbans and family jewels dance to itinerant musicians and the blare of relayed songs. Night at last and firecrackers are lit recklessly. Gambling follows praying, with every winner ensured rich takings in the year to come; losers shrug off hopes.

We approach the City Palace; it is 7.30 p.m. The Maharaja Bhawani Singh of Jaipur ('Bubbles' for short; champagne flowed in torrents at his birth some fifty years back) has invited us to his fireworks party, an annual event when family and friends step back 200 years. Our car is jostled and jammed as crackers explode without heed in all directions; frightening really. There will be casualties, they say, and houses burned.

We enter the courtyards of the City Palace; it is strangely silent and empty. An old servant stoops arduously over each clay pot and wick. He refills them with oil from the long-curved spout of his brass water-pot. The towering pink stone domes and marble-pillared prayer halls are suffused in a soft rose glow of dancing light and shadow. Through wide marble archways and spacious rooms of painted walls, hung with armour, we reach a long colonnade; it opens on the Moghul garden, where water terraces and subsidiary rills sparkle with ornamental fountains. Carpets border the water bed that passes from the gardens through the colonnade to the inner hall.

Some two hundred guests have been invited. We hear voices from the roof terrace far above. A servant indicates a steep, carpeted ramp, the main ascent. Bubbles' grandfather, rumoured to have weighed twenty-one stone, instigated the approach and was carried up and down in a sedan-type chair. The roof terrace seethes with colour and proud tradition. The men wear Rajput dress with every red turban adding stature to their swarthy features. Their white jodhpurs are offset with long high-necked black coats. The women are heavily jewelled with diamond pendants secured above their lotus eyes and hair entwined with pearls and rubies. Sarees of dark silks and satins glint with appliquéd gold and silver thread.

The whole carpeted area is encompassed by a low stone balustrade and grouped with divans and low sofas. Drinks are replenished liberally, as we gaze on the fountains and parterres below, where feathery-leaved Golmohur trees are flood-lit, red as cinnabar, and oil lights cluster on the lawn in the shape of elephants. The fireworks boom and soar rapturously, spluttering silver rain on the glinting waterways.

It is essentially a family party. The Raj Mata, Ayesha Jaipur, sits radiant, her dark hair and eyes gleaming, beside her three-year-old granddaughter, the child of her only son Jagat (a pale young man with a mop of tousled curls) and his Thai princess. The women pass before the Raj Mata, making obeisance as they swoop to touch her feet. Bubbles' wife, too, is a beauty. Her heavy-lidded oval eyes and curved full lips evoke visions from the *Kama Sutra*. Estranged for some years, she always returns for Diwali; it is rumoured tonight that the marriage may even be redressed. Bubbles' younger brother, the Maharaj Joey Jai Singh, always enjoys a party; he drinks incessantly. His redoubtable wit is laced with jovial badinage. 'What the hell are you doing, kissing my feet when all I want is more bloody booze?' His unfortunate subject laughs nervously and scurries off for whisky.

Fireworks are followed by gambling. We move downstairs to marble assembly rooms, bright with chandeliers and mirrors. Card tables have been set up around the central roulette table. Bubbles turns the wheel. Red turbans form a bobbing arch above the baize. Jewelled fingers throw and grab, whilst Bubbles, his handsome face beaded with sweat and wreathed with smiles, slips off his shoes.

The party at the City Palace ends at 11 p.m., when the family and few friends drive away to Ayesha Jaipur's home for dinner. More drinks are served, more fireworks on the lawn. Small tables are set for dinner on a terrace flanked with swaying banana leaves. The air is cooler; Diwali is the start of winter, we are warned again, when the moon is new and the sun rises south of the Equator. Mosquitoes too will be banished by the festive smoke.

We are served curries and chapattis, fish and meats and salads. Sweet rice balls follow and some pale pink mousse. We are finally handed glistening vine leaves stuffed with betel nuts and cardamom, a good digestive. I am seated next to an Indian general. He claims that Rajasthan is the seat of Indian culture and tradition, the quintessence of its intrinsic art and structure; where villagers walk tall and lean and proud. 'In southern states,' continues my companion, 'the people are darker, short and fat; they lack elegance and looks and even their cows appear demoted.'

October 28 Bombay

'He is my brother, he come too.'

A little youth squirms into the front seat beside the suitcase. Our two larger cases prop up the boot.

'Which country you from?'

'From India. We live in India,' Tom replies.

The taxi driver is poised for a swindle. He ponders our reply.

'You from India? Not America? Germany? Not England?'

It is 9 p.m. He drives too fast; his right index finger presses the horn incessantly; his left hand barely touches the wheel. He shoots red lights with jubilant abandon and follows hard behind each vehicle passing on the left and right. 'Slowly, slowly,' I squeal, to no avail.

It is a long drive from Bombay airport to the Taj Hotel. Firecrackers explode and flare; it is New Year's Day and sounds like civil war. We turn off into a dark side-street. The taxi falters; it shudders and stops. Our two friends alight languidly. The bonnet is raised. We watch the boot, the cases.

'My fan-belt breaks,' whines the driver. 'You go with my friend in the taxi behind.' A new accomplice waits conveniently. I watch the boot whilst Tom checks the recalcitrant fan-belt. It is in perfect order.

'No, sir, it is broken, sir, you must pay me now. I cannot drive you.' He mentions a ludicrous sum. We fluff his game.

'Your fan-belt is not broken,' we urge. 'Drive on.'

He moans dejectedly and rolls his eyes.

'No, sir, you must understand me, sir, please. My friend takes you now, you pay me.'

It is dark and silent in the street, yet another taxi draws up and blocks us in. We move into the taxi behind; lynx-eyed, we watch the clumsy transfer of our luggage.

'Sorry for the trouble, sir,' reiterates our friend. 'Now you pay me.'
We tell him to accompany us to the hotel where he will be paid.
'No, sir. I must not leave my taxi.'
'If you want to be paid, you come with us to the hotel.'
His accomplice looks bored; our friend looks worried.
'Your fan-belt is not broken,' we assure him. He changes his tack.
'I take you, sir. You come with me to the hotel. You come in my car.'

We agreed to this new departure. Once more our luggage is transferred. The taxi jerks to a start. Three hundred yards from the hotel he tries his game again. We urge him on. We finally arrive and within minutes we have a security officer at hand. Our driver is questioned briefly, his licence confiscated. We make a statement. He will appear in Court.

'There are many robbers in the airport road,' records our prompt redeemer. His quick action and help has meanwhile wiped away our fear and momentary anger.

1982

January 3 Hardwicke House

After two weeks of heavy snow-falls, the most belligerent assault of the stuff since 1941, Christmas Day did in fact dawn white and gleaming. Sunshine streamed through the house. For years now the sun has shone on Christmas Day, forcing us to close a dining-room shutter as the brightness catches somebody in the eye. The lights on the Christmas tree play second fiddle yet again.

We went to early Holy Communion at St Peter's Church, along the road in Petersham, a gem of an eighteenth-century church, dating in part from Domesday. It nestles in the corner of Petersham meadows where milking cows still graze. A member of the congregation ambled in ahead of us with his young red setter. Lunch was a full house of family ranging from five to eighty-five. We were fifteen in all with the youngest children overflowing into the panelled hall, where we had lit a coal fire. For the first time in ten years we sat down without Beverley Nichols, too ill to come. He has momentarily lost the will to live. I had sent him a bowl full of African violets a few days previously. He wrote to me in a wavering hand, 'Your flowers are out of this world, lucky things!' His companion of some fifty years (Cyril Butcher) came as usual, giving us all a moment's panic as he choked fulsomely over his plum pudding. 'It is only an air-lock,' he gasped, crimson in the face. He survived the attack with admirable equanimity while our attention was next caught by Hugo, our blond three-year-old nephew. Seemingly disenchanted with his newly-acquired space invader gun he had ransacked the toy cupboard upstairs for older and noisier distractions.

The polo ponies and their riders pranced in for their customary glass of champagne on Boxing Day. There was some consternation when Billy Walsh's mount tore a liberal hunk out of the yew tree. Billy, downing his second glass of whisky, called frantically to a stable girl. She deftly (and very courageously, I thought) snatched the poisonous fronds from the nether regions of the pony's jaw.

On New Year's Day we were seventy-five for lunch. Oxtail and a whole ham were substantial items on the menu. Polish friends came in force. We heeded the popular slogan, 'In the window of every home, hang a candle for Poland,' and lit a tall one to burn in the eighteeth-century Dutch oil lamp that hangs from the drawing-room ceiling. Friends donated cheques to the 'Polish Knights of Malta Association' for hospital aid and equipment.

There is little news of Poland that we can depend upon as true. Polish radio is selective, propagandist and defensive. We read an account of how the two-week sit-in strike of some one thousand miners at the Katowice colliery ended on December 28, with the men coming to the surface 'to be reunited with their families'. We hear unofficial accounts of how the said miners were forced to capitulate by the army first flooding the colliery and then shooting the hapless victims as they rose involuntarily to the surface. NATO meanwhile flounders in customary dissension. Will it ever agree as one body over a crisis? The Soviet invasion of Afghanistan and the seizing of the American hostages in Iran provoked similar indecisions of policy. President Reagan holds implicitly that the hand of Russia is responsible for the whole Polish mayhem, and has exerted trade sanctions. In Europe we sit on the proverbial fence, weighing up the economics and effect of our own potential action. Russia must be revelling in this familiar parlous state of the Western Alliance.

January 27 Hardwicke House

Veronica Lucan telephoned me tonight in a pitiable state of despair. Sobbing and hiccupping, she squealed down the line as though utterly broken down. Of course I would go and see her. How long had she been so depressed? I made her write down 11.30 a.m. on Friday when I would certainly be along. 'Thank you, Penelope,' she gasped in a small voice drowned in misery. I assured her it was always flattering for a friend to be approached for help. 'I have no friends,' she wailed alarmingly. I can believe her. I have seen her twice in the last few months, the first time for seven years.

We had met for lunch in October last, in one of those quiet sombre little eating holes off Ebury Street. She was fatter and even more disillusioned, critical of her children, her few relatives, her solicitors, and her financial depletion. She was living at 5 Eaton Row, a poky mews house, made even less wholesome by her total lack of interest in keeping it clean, hardly a conducive ambience for her teenage children to heave to for their school holidays. However, they all managed well enough, she assured me stoically, and it must be admitted that Veronica is a stoic at heart.

She was then on a mild dose of anti-depressant pills, namely one or two 'Parstelin' a day. She claimed she kept going happily although I could not imagine how she filled her time; some drab musician, an

impecunious one, apparently called most days to play her piano. Not
surprisingly it was in better condition than his own. I took her out for
lunch a month or two later on our return from India. Her physical
and mental state was unchanged. I suggested she might like to help
feed lunch to the spastic children at the day centre in Cheyne Walk;
she complained of being unable to find any part-time work. She liked
the idea but never followed it up, although I had subsequently paved
her way in this direction. I liked her, but forgot about her. An invitation to lunch here in January with her children was rather rudely
declined. 'Her children had so many friends in London they were not
tempted to spend a day on Ham Common with a family they had
never met.'

I telephoned her sister, Christina, immediately after this sudden
impassioned plea for help. 'Yes, it is very bad with Veronica, very bad,'
commented Christina. She herself had been seeing her daily for some
weeks. It transpired that, on New Year's Eve, Veronica had downed
more cheap red wine than was good for her. The combination, with
her regular dose of pills, had been explosive. She had attempted to
throw her television set out of her bedroom window, cutting her
forehead badly in the event. Returning to bed for the remaining
holidays with a nurse hovering, she was dismayed that her children
had reacted with understandable disdain, and to a certain degree
renounced her. It cannot have been easy for them to witness their
mother propped up in bed, continually crying, complaining and retching. Veronica had been removed to a nursing-home when the children
returned to school. She had completely broken down. She had dismissed herself after a week on account of feeling no better and loath
to pay for this doubtful privilege. A few days back in her throttling,
stale little bedroom with the curtains permanently drawn had finally
brought on this ultimate cri de coeur.

January 29 5 Eaton Row

I stood waiting on the doorstep, clutching an old mushroom basket
of grapes, apricots and an ogen melon, a neatly-wrapped offering in
polythene from my Turkish greengrocer in Putney, and adorned with
a hideous red rosette. Veronica's window box was a forlorn sight
where a few tender shoots of grass shivered in the cold wind. The
door opened furtively and Veronica in a cheap cotton nightdress, her
face as long as a poker, her hair straggling in greying strands down
her back, peered narrowly out. 'Come in, Penelope.' I followed her
upstairs to the curtained bedroom, a mustard-coloured hole with long

crumpled cotton bedsheets of sad brown roses. She made some coffee and we propped ourselves on her bed for an uncomfortable hour, Veronica no doubt feeling hopeless, helpless and utterly dejected, and myself feeling totally inadequate to amuse her or alleviate or even analyse such a parlous condition. I elicited from her the history of the television débâcle. 'There must have been meths in that red wine,' she observed and talked of the nursing-home, the fearful behaviour of her unfeeling offspring, who indeed were doing remarkably well at school (the eldest child, Frances, even planning to go to university), and finally mentioning that a new set of doctors were being brought in to review her case early next week. The situation, thus objectively reported, seemed hopeful. On leaving her after an hour, I promised to see her again, perhaps next week.

January 30 *Hardwicke House*

I slept badly. Getting up at 2 a.m., I wrote what I hoped was a constructive letter to Veronica. It was delivered by hand this morning as we were passing by on our way to Christie's. The letter urged her to like herself more;
> to wash her hair;
> to eat sensible food;
> to clean the house.

February 7 *47 Galveston Road Putney*

Bearing in mind his privileged and indeed glamorous provenance, it is surprising to see Brian Sweeny squeezed into a modest Victorian terraced house off Putney High Street. It must seem even more surprising to his mother, Margaret, Duchess of Argyll. She received us gamely, to the tune of a ding-dong bell, in the small front hall where the Victorian tiled floor nicely offset the stained glass motifs of the front door. She has recently broken her hip and leaned lightly on a stick; superbly elegant, as always, in a tweed coat and skirt, a green silk shirt, a handsome pearl choker; the whole surmounted by her habitual crown of up-swept hair.

Brian looked radiant; the epitome of marital content. His pretty, plump, dark-haired Dutch wife Judith entered the drawing-room, proudly bearing their five-month-old son, Charles. I remarked on the child's likeness to his father.

'I cannot see that he looks like anybody,' commented Margaret

Argyll airily. She chucked her youngest grandson under the cheek whereupon the child screamed vehemently.

'Oh, I am going to get to know you in time,' she assured him cheerfully and added: 'Babies always like shining things, you know'. She flashed her gold rings before the little screwed-up eyes. Charles was not to be won over so easily and was promptly borne away in stubborn tears.

We all admired the pristine unimaginative decoration of the rooms. The small garden in front and behind had been generously manured and mulched and planted up by Brian's sister, Frances, Duchess of Rutland.

'Frances brought down a whole heap of stuff from Belvoir and got down to the job in jeans and gumboots,' Brian beamed happily. 'And Judith has made all the curtains.' She also produced an excellent lunch of pâté and poussins, shamefully uncomplimented by Brian's offering of cheap wines.

February 16 5 Eaton Row

This morning I again stood on Veronica Lucan's bleak doorstep. Had she heard the bell? I tried the knocker. To my dismay the dwarf tulips I had planted ten days ago had been dashed to the ground, the old wooden window box shattered.

Veronica appeared at the door; 'the window cleaner,' she explained as I pointed to the sad ruin of her window box – 'and he also broke my front curtain rail.' She signed wearily, half-dressed with bare legs and feet, her hair uncombed. She looked pitiful and plain. 'The house is being cleaned.'

She waved a hand at two workmen who hovered in a dishevelled corner of the drawing-room. 'Let's go up to my bedroom.' She made mugs of black coffee and we settled once again in her darkened bolt-hole; the sheets had been changed to faded blue roses as opposed to the brown variant two weeks ago. The room smelt stale as before. Veronica swivelled her legs and thick grey skirt under the duvet; back where she belonged, a bed, an airless room where the world passed by unseen, unfelt and uncalled for.

She had spent the last ten days at the Charter Clinic in Radnor Walk. Scooped up by Dr Christian Carritt on that same afternoon that I had surreptitiously planted her bulbs, she had been whisked briefly into a busy, ordered world of appointments, massage, hair-washing, baths and exercise classes. She had been visited three times by a new psychiatrist, Dr Lipsage. New pills, new faces, and now thrust back to the old lonely régime of 5 Eaton Row. She had loathed the clinic and was pleased to be home.

'I am not depressed,' she told me, 'merely desperate. My problems are insoluble. My children are parasites; they loathe me. They give me no happiness, no love; I loathe them in return. I am so lonely. How will I ever find another husband? Life has been so cruel to me and left me nothing. If only I could induce sleep all day long, I could forget.'

How to counter such wretched apathy? Should she have a dog, I suggested tentatively. 'I thought of that,' she murmured, 'but I would be so tied.' As she was permanently tied to her bed anyway, I could not appreciate her argument. A dog would get her out of the house and give her life a new dimension; it would love her, need her, follow her like a Chinese servant, jealous of her every mood. I talked away enthusiastically. I had visions of a King Charles spaniel, embedded in the folds of her blue duvet; a pastiche of Veronica as Elizabeth Barrett Browning with her faithful dog, Flush. 'I'll think about it,' concluded Veronica listlessly.

Later I telephoned her sister with the idea. 'She couldn't cope with a dog,' warned Christina. 'She wouldn't begin to feed it, walk it, or even love it. It would spend its life in that stuffy little bedroom. But I must find her something to get her out of that house; a job of sorts for two days a week.' What a strain this whole saga is for Christina; an appalling strain with no foreseeable turning point. How is it possible for a human being, with so many tangible blessings to moan her life away in a supine heap, subsisting on cold tinned spaghetti and tangerines, spasmodic visits from perplexed doctors and no books or newspapers. Withdrawal is a form of slow suicide. But what can any of us do to relieve Veronica's despair and bitterness?

February 17 Sledmere Driffield East Yorkshire

'How are you, Michael?'

'A little older and fatter, sir. Would you care to wait in the boudoir? Sir Tatton will be down right away to see you, sir, madam.'

A log fire burns in the boudoir and in the adjoining staircase hall. The ageing staff of Sledmere, unchanged since Sir Richard Sykes's death in July 1978, are still obviously bent on keeping to their well-established standards.

A light step in the hall and Tatton appears. He welcomes us warmly. His hair is considerably shorter than when we last saw him, some years previously at the house sale of Rudding Park. With his dark flowing curls and soft faint voice he had, on that occasion, been mistaken by the bidding office for a woman. He has grown a moustache in the intervening years, whilst his whole mien now denotes that he is clearly the master of his domain. Highly intelligent, he talks with an easy poise, choosing his words fastidiously. He is acutely aware of the responsibilities of inheriting one of the finest estates in England, and waves slender hands to emphasise a point.

'My father was always too proud to ask for advice,' he noted. 'He regarded it as a sign of weakness. Whereas I ask for it constantly, and usually take it.'

I suggest that Sir Richard's diffidence on this point was more due to an inborn shyness and insecurity.

'Yes, I think you are right, Father was always insecure, despite his forbidding front.'

There have been innovations to the house under the guidance of the historian John Cornforth and the architect Francis Johnson. Tatton has instigated the elaborate vaulted ceiling of the long gallery library to be picked out in gold. It was in 1790 that Sir Christopher Sykes had engaged Joseph Rose, the favourite plasterer of both Adam and Wyatt, to decorate the ceiling. There had been talk, then, of gilding it, but the work was never executed. Tatton today, with his enthusiasm for Renaissance grandeur, has taken this plunge. It looks magnificent and must be a feast of dancing lights on a sunny day.

Next, using a watercolour of the Music Room, painted in 1847 by a daughter of Sir Tatton, 4th Bart, as a reference, he has reinstalled the fine eighteenth-century organ case and has redecorated the room to its former style and colouring; namely dove-grey walls, with the cornice of winged lions picked out in white and coral; elaborate grey silk curtains with deep swagged pelmets are trimmed with a heavy coral fringe.

Finally, in deference to his father, Tatton commissioned his aunt Lady Antrim (Sir Richard's sister) to design three stained-glass windows in the Roman Catholic chapel. They were erected in 1979; the central window depicts St Mark the Evangelist; the window on the left is dedicated to St Hubert, Patron of the Chase, and the window on the right portrays St Cecilia, Patroness of Music; apt reflections of Sir Richard's two main loves, horses and music.

Jeremy, Tatton's younger brother, arrives in a flurry as we sit and talk over drinks in the Staircase Hall. He is currently selling Japanese cars for a firm in Bridlington. He has also distinguished himself by getting engaged to a plump, blonde, thirty-year-old twice-divorced North Country woman called Pamela. We are told that Pamela is changing for dinner and to find our way to the Green Room and do the same.

A house run by a bachelor and old servants inevitably dictates that Tom's suitcase is unpacked rather than mine (Imperial Leather soap and Boot's 'honeysuckle flower garden' talcum powder).

We meet again in the Staircase Hall at 8.15. Tatton is resplendent in a bottle-green velvet dinner jacket and white loafers, whilst Jeremy favours a black satin ensemble. Pamela is duly introduced. Her long blonde hair is caught hard behind her ears which swing with an enormous pair of gilt discs. She is snugly poured into a diaphanous black dress and beams happily as she pronounces herself pleased to meet us. Farming neighbours, Sir Ian and Lady Macdonald, and a Mrs Richard Marriot make up the party.

Glasses are filled with the magnum of non-vintage champagne, produced by Tom, to celebrate Jeremy's engagement. We move into dinner whilst I ascertain that Lady Macdonald breeds dogs. A good meal of clear soup, creamed ris de veau and zabaglione with a magnum of plausible claret is served by Michael. A bust of Sir Horace Walpole in a far corner, sporting sunglasses on the end of his long nose, gazes coldly on the scene.

Pamela appears totally at ease with her new situation. She and Jeremy marry on March 27 in the local registry office. A small reception at the house will follow. They plan to convert the eighteenth-century stables into a home where her horse has already been comfortably ensconced. She rides for an hour through the park each morning and twice a week visits a psychiatric ward of old men.

I like her; she is essentially individual and appears to exude a natural joie-de-vivre and a quiet self-assurance. (Sir Ian remarked to Tom in the boudoir, after dinner, that the atmosphere at Sledmere had noticeably improved since her arrival. He hinted that she was tending to Tatton's needs as well as Jeremy's. 'She moves through the household,' was his candid observation.) It appears that Pamela, despite her parlous provenance, is set fair for a happy run at Sledmere. I wonder what Sir Richard would have made of her?

She produces chocolates. Tatton congratulates her on her choice. 'That is an exceptionally good box of chocolates, Pamela, and I will tell you why; there are no revolting marzipans. I know, because yesterday I tried to find some for the dogs.' His two gross bull terriers – Lamb Chop and Bluebell – are promptly given almond whirls.

Tatton follows us to the Green Room as we finally go to bed. He is upset we cannot stay longer. Why do we have to leave so early in the morning? He will still be breakfasting in bed.

February 26 Hardwicke House

This afternoon I brought a smart white plastic window box for
Veronica, and a fresh assortment of tulips and daffodils. It was drizzling
as I heaped the broken wooden shafts of her old box into the boot of
my car and scooped up the scattered earth into the new trough. The
plants looked very well with the original dwarf tulip bulbs pressed
down between. I felt pleased with my brief handiwork and glad for
the rain that watered it.

Veronica has been staying a week in Herefordshire with an elder
sister. In her absence Christina has moved fast, the whole house has
been professionally cleaned and a telephone extension fitted beside her
bed. She is due back on Monday. Christina has also arranged for a
nurse from the Social Services to call on Veronica each day. It is a case
of the doctors reaching an impasse and handing back the burden of
their perplexing patient to the family.

February 27 Hardwicke House

A cold grey afternoon. I lit a fire in the sitting-room as Tom and I
watched the 5 o'clock news. A hijacked plane – one hundred hostages
from Dar es Salaam – three heavily-armed Tanzanians claiming
membership of some Revolutionary Youth Movement. After a circuitous flight via Nairobi, Jeddah and Athens, the plane has finally been
given permission to land at Stansted. And then: 'Lady Lucan is tonight
ill in hospital. Neighbours raised the alarm last night. She was taken
away in an ambulance. Attempted suicide is suspected.' Dear, tragic
Veronica. What have you done?

February 28 Hardwicke House

This afternoon we went to the Landseer exhibition at the Tate Gallery;
some flattering oils of Queen Victoria in the bloom of youth, on
horseback; charming pen and wash studies; sentimental dogs but too
many garrotted deer and dead birds for my taste. I bought some cards
and wrote a line to Veronica on the back of Meredith Frampton's
'Portrait of a Young Woman' 1935 – simply saying, 'Darling Veronica
– we all love you – when can I come and see you? – perhaps Tuesday
morning? And I thought you were still away in Herefordshire!' I
delivered it at the hospital desk, together with a bunch of spring
flowers bought from the conveniently sited stall. My offering was

received suspiciously. 'Lady Lucan is not here,' and then 'she is seeing nobody'. I persuaded the porter that I was one of the few friends she had and would he kindly see that my note and flowers were delivered to her room? He would enquire through the 'nursing office', he assured me, in a surly tone and continued to read his newspaper.

Christina telephoned me at 8 o'clock. Veronica had received her flowers, but was in no state to see anybody for the time being. It transpired that, after a row with her sister, she had hired a car and been deposited back at 5 Eaton Row on Thursday evening. She had taken an enormous dose of some pills and drunk a bottle of neat whisky. She was subsequently appalled to find herself alive at Friday lunchtime. She had then attempted to hang herself – to no avail; her knot was not good enough. Slashing at various parts of her body with a razor proved another failure. In desperation she drank a whole bottle of bleach. This put her into such a paroxysm of agony that she telephoned the ambulance of her own accord. 'Drink plenty of water,' they advised her and quickly persuaded her to open the door. They had not bargained for the blood and rope. Veronica is tonight reasonably comfortable. Dr Peter Dally, a leading psychiatrist, is now in charge of her case.

March 6 Hardwicke House

It was a morning ceremony that took place this cold, sunny day. Sir Bernard Braine (MP for Essex South East division) spoke from a modest dais, commanding the wrapt attention of some hundred people. We were grouped on the small triangle of grass at Thurloe Place opposite the V and A Museum. Behind him towered the half-constructed Ismaili Centre where the whine of a woodsaw vied with his strong voice despite his microphone. We waved and shouted at the offending builders and they were momentarily stilled; leaning nonchalantly against the scaffolding supports, they too watched the unusual happening below. We stood around a newly-erected stone sculpture; it had been conceived as an atonement for the allies' hasty repatriation of some 30,000 Russian refugees to Yalta at the end of World War II.

Sir Bernard spoke with compelling passion of our shameful act. Sitting on his left was an attractive pale-faced woman – Zoe Palmer. Dressed in black and a smart hat, she repeatedly dabbed her eyes with a white handkerchief. Sir Bernard introduced her as a Scottish housewife; he next recounted the horrifying story of her miraculous and circuitous wartime escape from her native Russia to Scotland.

Aged thirteen she had been hurled into first Auschwitz, then Dachau, from where she subsequently fled to Austria. Believing herself to be safe at last she had in fact landed in the perilous grip of a Yalta round-up. Tipped off by a soldier, she again escaped, continuing her staggering bid for safety, crossing the Alps, finally to gain a permanent refuge in Scotland.

On Sir Bernard's right sat the sculptress of the monument, Angela Connell. She looked jaunty in tan knickerbockers and a peaked cap. Standing on either side of Sir Bernard were Count Nikolai Tolstoy and Lord Bethell. Historians both, they had each written a book on this sorry saga. It was largely through Nicholas Bethell's initial instigation that the ceremony took place today.

A Russian choir, massed between us, sang a prayer. At its conclusion, Zoe Palmer stepped down from the dais; solemn and dignified, she pressed a button; water spouted from the slim curved arm of stone that arched above the structure. The needle of water swayed the saucer of stone below from side to side, splashing softly into the circular trough; a symbolic creation, indicative of those victims' helplessness, as they were tossed to and fro by the vagaries of their appalling fate.

Princess George Galitzine[1] looked elegant and sombre in a black turban and matching coat. Vane Ivanovic – the Consul General for Monaco – looked equally elegant, though frozen, in morning dress with no coat; whereas Prince George Vassiltchikov was warmly attired as if for a rugger match. We later all converged on the nearby Rembrandt Hotel for 'refreshments'. On seeing the proffered tea and sandwiches, George Vassiltchikov opted for the bar and promptly bought me a welcome glass of Dubonnet.

March 15 6 Gerald Road

A strange, though not unenjoyable evening. Having been invited to dine by Lady Abdy, the whimsical owner of the Bury Street art gallery, we were subsequently surprised to learn that her guests were to be photographed.

'Harpers and Queen want to photograph us having pre-prandial drinks for an article on dinner parties.' She chose to inform us on the day. We were most disconcerted and felt decidedly put-upon. However, rather than make an embarrassing fuss we turned up as bid.

[1] Recalled by many as the ethereal beauty, Jean Dawnay, who became a front-page model girl in the 1950s.

'You are very naughty, Jane – such a vulgar idea!' I remonstrated half-laughingly, as we arrived. Our hostess, dressed in clinging dusty pink, her hair caught up in its habitual loose swoop of curls, appeared a little unnerved as she coaxed us up the stairs to the drawing-room. A keen scholar of Sara Bernhardt, Elinor Glyn, Helleu and Boldini, Jane Abdy affects a figure from that same nineteenth-century milieu. Her excessively slim figure could certainly be compared to that of Sarah Bernhardt, once described as so thin that she could skip between raindrops.

Jane had described her house as 'romantic – Winterhalter, Napoleon III' and suggested that nostalgic dress would blend. A posse of cringing photographers in her drawing-room and bright wattage did little to convey a romantic ambience.

The Countess of Rosse sat bolt upright in a far corner while John Cornforth, the architectural authority and contributor to *Country Life*, mused on why Jane's drawing-room looked so different. I enlightened him on our parlous situation; he was horrified; he had not been alerted. We drank our champagne stiffly and waited awkwardly for the final guests to relieve us of this initiation. They arrived at last and Jane cajoled us into groups. We were urged by the photographers to look convivial. John Cornforth muttered darkly and Lady Rosse sat stubbornly on her high chair in the corner; she took a lot of persuading to move into the orbit of the merciless lens.

'Come, come, Anne,' admonished Jane. 'After all, when I lunched with you recently, your son snapped away all through the meal!' It was all over in minutes and the drawing-room promptly resumed its soft-lit – romanticism? Hardly. A large Winterhalter portrait took up the whole of one wall, while a big, uncomfortable grey silk love-seat usurped the middle of the room; grey ruched taffeta blinds formed a steely back-drop. No fire and no flowers; a cold room. The dining-room was a minute box with a round table. A good dinner ensued with excellent conversation. Upstairs, Jane's bedroom proved a concoction of dusky pink and Biedermeier. The evening ended at 11.30 p.m. when Lady Rosse's chauffeur called to drive her back to Nymans. John Cornforth stolidly put on his gumboots and, thrusting aside all offers to drive him home, strode into the night.

April 9 (Good Friday) Hardwicke House

Apprehension and the insidious fear of the unknown hang over the International world today. It was on April 2, a week ago, that Argentina caught the British Government unawares with a sudden act of unprovoked aggression; they invaded the Falkland Islands. For over a hundred years the Argentines have laid claim to these minority outposts and for over a hundred years these islands have been under British Sovereignty; the largely British inhabitants have wanted to keep it that way. Eight thousand miles separate the Falkland Islands from Britain; a mere 1,800 inhabitants live on them.

Lord Carrington, our Foreign Secretary, resigned on Tuesday, appalled at the very great national humiliation he had inadvertently bestowed upon his Government and country. Margaret Thatcher sadly accepted his surprising? altruistic? resignation and appointed Francis Pym – the former Leader of the Commons – to fill his place. John Nott, our Minister of Defence, was also quick to tender his resignation; Mrs Thatcher chose to refuse it, quite rightly; blunders are never rectified by running away. Mr Nott, meanwhile, has miraculously improved on his image during the week. He has become less a frightened rabbit and more a guerrilla, as, each day, he outlines determined tactics of confrontation.

The rightful ownership of the Falkland Islands has always been a hard bone of contention but British Intelligence underestimated the latest threatening rumbles that preceded this surprise invasion. It's even hinted that President Galtieri of Argentina knew nothing of the proposed assault. Russia again? Up to her old tricks of fishing in troubled waters? The offensive was certainly carried out in that rapid and incisive kick-off, indicative of the Russian heel.

Mrs Thatcher, holding fast to her reputation as 'The Iron Lady', rapidly deployed a fleet of the Royal Navy Task Force to steam into the teeth of trouble. HMS *Invincible* (19,500 tons) set off from Portsmouth on April 5, stocked and armed for war, with a crew of 1,000 and 3 vertical take-off Harrier jets on deck, 180,000 hen's eggs and Prince Andrew. HMS *Hermes* (18,700 tons) with 1,800 crew and marines followed twenty miles behind. The nuclear submarine HMS *Superb* has already reached her destination; three others follow. The luxury liner, the *Canberra*, finally left Southampton at 8 o'clock tonight. She docked two and half days ago after a world cruise. She was stripped of deck–chairs, chandeliers and other leisure niceties while a landing deck of steel plates was hastily fitted.

All week we have witnessed the tearful farewells of wives and children as they wave off their men from the docks. And the Queen? What can she be feeling tonight? Are her fears for her son's safety compensated by her pride? As a Sub-Lieutenant pilot, Prince Andrew will help seek out and destroy Argentine submarines if the islands are to be forcefully re-captured.

International opinion appears to back Mrs Thatcher; trade sanctions and import bans are being considered at her urgent request. America, a strong ally of both Britain and Argentine, finds herself awkwardly placed. President Reagan voices a repeated hope that 'unnecessary disagreement' will be settled peacefully without bloodshed. His Secretary of State, Alexander Haig, dined with Mrs Thatcher last night. Their meeting took five hours. Mr Haig declared today that he could see 'no ready solution' but that he had been impressed by Mrs Thatcher's 'determination'. This morning he flew off to Buenos Aires to the second stage of his peace mission.

Mrs Thatcher's 'determination' to regain the Falkland Islands at virtually any cost has unnerved us all. Sane left-wingers even suggest she is laying on a spectacular show to boost her political position and her dwindling popularity. Denis Healey – the Shadow Foreign Secretary – claims she should have already resigned. Undeterred in her resolve, Mrs Thatcher refuses to negotiate on a single point until the islands have been re-claimed by Britain. Yesterday she announced a 200-mile war zone around the territory. If any Argentine warships are seen within this zone, as from this coming Easter Monday at 5 a.m. GMT, they will be liable to attack. 'We will shoot first . . . we will sink ships . . . we will storm the islands,' proclaimed Guerrilla Nott with untypical Churchillian gusto. And Argentina's reply? 'If they blockade us – we will bomb them.' The Argentines, equally unnerved by Mrs Thatcher's strong bellicose reaction to their false move, are swiftly preparing for a war they had never envisaged.

What will be the cost of Mrs Thatcher's enterprise? She and her Ministers have assiduously evaded this issue. 'Our hard-line decision is to maintain British sovereignty of the Falkland Islands and to save the islanders. Costs are not being considered,' is her airy reply. Leon Brittan, Chief Secretary to the Treasury, has vaguely alluded to a future rise in prices and taxes – but argues that the basic economic strategy of the Conservative Party will not be seriously affected. His comments smack of euphemism. It is obviously impossible to hazard even an estimate of the cost of this vast venture. Figures of such magnitude as £20 millions' worth of fuel for ships (they use up to £2,000 worth a day), of danger money for sailors rising from the normal stipend of £150 a week to £400, a replacement value at £10 million for a Harrier jet, and £170 million for *Invincible* if she is destroyed – it is all too bewildering even to contemplate.

What of the islanders? Any news? They were originally under house arrest and liable to fifteen days' imprisonment if they said anything derogatory to their captors. An ex-islander in London heard two days ago from a relative left behind. They are reported to be 'calm, with their tails rampant', though naturally apprehensive. 'The Argentines are trumped-up terrorists,' concluded our informer. Francis Pym in a special Easter message to the islanders assures them: 'We will do anything to come to your aid as peacefully as possible.'

Thus we wait for Monday's uncertain dawn. Would a sanguine evacuation of the islanders have been more prudent? Followed by a financial compromise over the islands? We would have forsaken the principles of British Sovereignty. And is it commendable to risk human life in the name of human rights? Will the islanders be massacred in the final hour of their release. Will our ships be bombed 200 miles away from their goal? Will Prince Andrew be killed? Has Russia initiated this whole débâcle? If so, we are right to show every bit of determination and force, thus deterring any future assault on us. But the one disturbing element of this potentially lethal confrontation is that both the British and Argentines are prepared for loss of blood in preference to loss of face.

April 15 Hardwicke House

Today I took Veronica Lucan out to lunch. Over a bottle of Soave, and pasta and prosciutto, in a cheerful Italian restaurant, we talked openly about her suicide attempt, her subsequent hospital treatment and, more importantly, her future. She is now back at her home in Eaton Row for the first time since that desperate afternoon when she tried to end it all. 'It is very hard to commit suicide,' she observed, half-laughingly, half-rueful. (She later insisted on a mild demonstration of how she had jumped in vain from the kitchen draining-board, the rope of the skylight above wound haphazardly around her neck. The workman re-papering her staircase wall looked on fearfully.)

With the children back at school next week she will again be alone. Christina has suggested a refresher typing course. 'I badly need to make money and feel useful,' commented Veronica. Her positive approach was encouraging. On our return to Eaton Row I telephoned the St James's Secretarial School in Kensington. The Principal, a cheerful woman, to whom I briefly explained the position, arranged an appointment; it could prove an important first step towards a more fulfilling life for Veronica.

April 20 Hardwicke House

This morning I telephone Veronica. Had she kept her appointment
with the St James's College? Sounding smug she told me she had spent
almost an hour with the Principal, Mrs Hewetson. She would be
starting her course next week. Non-committal, comparatively pleased,
she thanked me briefly. How would she get to Kensington from Eaton
Square? Was there a bus? 'I intend to walk.' I suggested that would do
her figure a world of good. She graciously agreed. The two weeks of
heavily-sedated sleep in hospital have made her swell alarmingly.

April 23 Poulton House Marlborough Wiltshire

I am alone with Sebastian – my son who is dumb – dumb since birth
and yet full of mirth. He loves the moment – never heeding the next;
the last gone for ever – for ever? No. He recalls places, faces, traces of
smells, smiles, silhouettes, each sense acute. He hears too loud, he sees
too sharply, he smells and remembers, he tastes with delight and feels
spontaneously; tears and laughter; quick to come, to change, to go, to
return. Sometimes he is cross and stamps and slams. What else can he
do? He is dumb. That moment vanishes too – no sulks. Boredom?
Self-awareness?

He is now thirteen. Tall and strong with solid limbs; slim now from
sawing wood and growing, growing. His hair glints with health, his
skin is clear, his eyes are bright and blue and grey; they challenge
direct for they know little guile as yet. And yet? What does he think
all day? Does he exist in being and seeing and feeling and giving? He
thinks of others and passes marmalade and salt; he opens doors, fetches
and finds, puts table-mats away; knives and spoons are laid where forks
should be. Who minds? He is trying to help, to please, to be loved
and petted, to be good and clever. He is now thirteen and tall and
handsome. What lies ahead? Love for a girl? Who knows what puberty
will wreak in him? His skin is smooth, his cry is high, and his testicles
lie unconscious, limp, unformed. But he will love and relate as he
always has, deeply, wholeheartedly and fearless of where he lays his
admiration. His charm secures the world. He is changing, maturing.
He is neat and proud of dress and appearance. He rides a 14-hand
pony and screams when she canters, then laughs; then canters on. He
can barely swim, the dog-paddle in a pool perhaps. The sea is not his
friend; a vast imponderable; a cold, capricious foe; an alien to his
self-imposed bounds of security. He likes to cook; the cheese sauce is
lovingly stirred, seasoned and tasted, the pastry is rolled and cut; the

bread is kneaded (with a spoon); he does not understand a dirty hand. He is maturing and changing; saws wood; soon he will be taught to carve a leg, a table top, a chest, a drawer – a dovetail, or will he farm or garden or weave rugs and baskets? He will do all he can to be a whole man.

He turns the pages of *Country Life* carefully from the right tip of each page. He is always careful; fearful of his feet, his balance and the laws of gravity and accident. Soon he will come to a pretty girl; more houses still; Savill, Hampton, John D Wood; gardens, stables and houses still; mock–Tudor, Victorian, Georgian, Queen Anne; another page, and then – the pretty girl! What a smile she has! Miss Sheila Allison of Hampton, Middlesex. Was she waiting for his touch? To be revealed in radiance on her page? The pretty girl! Sebastian shrieks with glee to see. He is changing, maturing, to balance, to rhythm, to a sense of things; his own. One slow step in front of the other with prints unheeded; forward he travels. God speed his gallant passage.

May 30 Woolbeding House Nr Midhurst

Acquired some ten years ago by the National Trust from the Lascelles family, Woolbeding has bloomed again. It was in a state of advanced decay when handed over in lieu of exorbitant tax payments. Entirely due to Simon Sainsbury, who persuaded the Trust to allow him the daunting privilege of undertaking its total restoration, it again stands glorious and complete. He has the loan of the house for his lifetime.

We lunched with Simon at Woolbeding today; a wonderful summer's day when even the A3 appeared delightful with its lush verges and high banks sprinkled with buttercups, clover, wild sorrel and daisies. The house stood back from a quiet country lane; an immaculate 1720 façade of honey-gold ironstone. Standing before it, one's eye was swept up through a wide grass avenue – as smooth as a bowling green – lined with huge oak trees and lime.

Simon guided us to the terrace and introduced us to his guests; they included two Australians from Sydney; the younger, Miles, was slim, blond and beautiful and later flexed his rippling body to admirable advantage in the pool; his older companion, Bill, was clearly an inveterate traveller and something of an aesthete. He wore a shooting cap and a tailored, thick tweed jacket and still appeared enviably cool. He was poised for the Dordogne the following week.

Across the lawn stood a small stone church of Saxon origin, with rolling fields and grazing sheep beyond. There has always been a church in a meadow at Woolbeding; the house itself pertains to Domesday foundations. The river Arun still flows through the estate.

Moving in from the terrace to the dinning-room, we were served an excellent lunch by Simon's Spanish couple; salmon, a dry Graves and a succulent apple tart. After dawdling pleasurably over our coffee, Simon showed us the garden. Again, it had been exquisitely restored and re-planted with his unerring touch. Perhaps the pièce de résistance was the cast bronze model of the sixteenth-century Rustici fountain, sited in an intimate flower-filled patio. The original work used to stand before the house; it was acquired by the V and A at the time of the Trust take-over, when Simon insisted the replica should be made. (Rustici, Giovanni Francesco, a Florentine sculptor, was a renowned pupil of Leonardo da Vinci.)

Borders, parterres and stone-flagged paths were thronged with flowers and shrubs; graded in pastel colour with an air of orderly profusion. The swimming pool was discreetly screened by a clipped hornbeam hedge; as we sat at its far end, Simon spied a potential niche for a further statue. Through the narrow gap of hornbeam there was a vista of clipped yew beyond; a perfect siting for something, he felt; something in bronze. 'Why not marble?' I suggested. It would be so effective against that dark backcloth. 'In stone perhaps,' he compromised. Wandering back through the cobbled courtyard of the stable block we saw the burgundy-painted loose-boxes with their polished brass rings intact. 'Racehorses,' he explained; they were out to grass for the afternoon.

We entered the house and admired again the Indian and Persian carpets, the furniture, the paintings and the decoration (the foremost British designer, David Mlinaric). His style and feeling for understatement, coupled with his essential knowledge of beautiful and old things, have created an exquisite house in Woolbeding. The 'Victorian' room was another masterpiece; a mélange of solid maplewood furniture, set against William Morris wallpaper which was hung in turn with touches of Bloomsbury. A portrait of E M Forster by Roger Fry competed with another of Lytton Strachey. Dora Carrington's vigorous oil 'The Mill at Pangbourne' added further élan.

June 21 Hardwicke House

'Fair and beautiful'; 'blue eyes like his parents'; 'cries lustily'. The country has waited all day for the news; tonight at 9.03 p.m. the Princess of Wales gave birth to a 7lb son in the Lindo Wing at St Mary's Paddington. She had been taken there by Prince Charles this morning at 5 a.m.

There was a carnival atmosphere in the crowds around the hospital and later around Buckingham Palace (details of a Royal birth are always hung on the front railings). The press has waited anxiously all day for tomorrow's front page. Would it happen in time?

At one stage a bunch of blue flowers was accepted and a pink confection turned away. Rumours of a boy! Now, finally, the announcement of this very special and historic birth, a new heir to the throne, second in line. His name? He will be addressed as HRH Prince . . . of Wales. Names tipped for choice are: Albert, George, Edward, Frederick, Charles, and from the Spencer family 'favourites' John, Edmund, Edward, Charles. Even Louis might have a look in? Or Philip? Or indeed Andrew. After his performance in the Falklands, speculation is cast widely on the new Prince's name.

June 22 Hardwicke House

Jubilation rules the day and messages of joy and congratulations have streamed in from the world. Prince Charles, photographed on the front page of *The Times*, appears suitably exhausted. After spending sixteen hours beside his wife yesterday, he was finally present at the birth. 'It is rather a grown-up thing, I found,' he commented ambiguously. 'Rather a shock to my system.'

June 22 25 St James's Place

A fork-truck millionaire might suggest a raw and stocky, raunchy man, but Sir Emmanuel Kaye, on first encounter, surprises one with his slight build, his quiet voice and his shy smile.

From a modest education at Richmond Hill School and Twickenham Tech., he took over Lansing Bagnall Ltd in 1943 (with his late colleague, Mr J R Sharp). After fifteen years they became the largest manufacturers of electric lift trucks in Europe, with Royal warrants and awards to further boost their prestige.

Sir Emmanuel has invited us to lunch in his magnificently-furnished duplex apartment in St James's Place. Commodes of superb English gesso (I thought they were Italian), delicately carved armchairs in Indian ivory (not to be sat upon), a priceless burr-walnut bureau, another in English gesso, Gainsborough drawings, paintings by Tiepolo and Stubbs, eighteenth-century carpets, handsome marble busts, and colourful Chelsea porcelain fill rooms to groaning with a surfeit of superlative quality, that is strangely overlooked on immediate appraisal.

One's attention is perhaps initially usurped by those ponderous swagged pelmets in coffee silk; the coffee walls with an appliquéd wood cornice with its gilded finish; the huge sofas and the vast, plump cushions with their deep frilled and tasselled trim; the thick fitted carpet of mottled mustard and the bilious lime pile that swept us up the front stairs. The impact of these ugly soft furnishings detracts alarmingly from the gracious colour and lines of the antiques and beautiful 'objects' all around.

Sir Emmanuel's wife is visiting relations in Canada; her place is filled by a sombre blonde, a German lady named Princess Hohenlohe. The party is greatly enhanced by Denis Healey and his literary wife, Edna. At the moment she is writing the biography of Mrs Darwin. She talks fondly of 'Charles', remarking on his constant and debilitating attacks of nausea at sea; indeed she cannot understand how he ever achieved so much with that appalling handicap.

Mr Healey enjoys his second helpings and talks articulately on any point that is even half-raised. His eyebrows burgeon and his stomach bulges. His voice is rich and furry and he would like to see all the Falklanders repatriated to New Zealand or to Scotland. The alternative of guarding them with a permanent garrison of 5,000 is not feasible, of course. He recalls in 1977 the Labour Government avoided the whole débâcle; they had heeded the threats and rumbles from Argentina and had despatched a brigade, a submarine, and a frigate or two and the trouble had died down in the space of a couple of weeks.

Sir Emmanuel is a quiet, solicitous host who listens more than he speaks. We ate far too well and drank white and red wine. A cheese soufflé filled with fresh asparagus tips was followed by roast veal with an array of bright vegetables and highly-seasoned sauces; a strawberry meringue, oozing cream.

'I really must get back to the House,' concluded Mr Healey as he downs his second cup of coffee. Snatching up a final sugar almond he takes his leave. The room is a lesser place without his zest and highly-tuned mind.

August 1 Tuscany Italy

Sesto Calende, 6.30 a.m. The Alps are flushed with early sun; oleander, hydrangea, and roses hug the platform palings. The train lurches away and gathers speed for Milan.

A farmhouse in Tuscany, strategically poised between Florence and Siena, was our final destination. Friends stayed and played and ate and drank and swam. We explored ruins in ilex woods, medieval churches, hilltop fortresses, small shops in smaller streets, village grocers, and village butchers, cafés in wide piazzas, and in quiet corners. Our days were crowded with sun and wine and talk, encircled by the glorious view from our house, the dense woods, lilting fields of stubble, red plough, and vines. Olive-trees fringed the terraced hills in silver and everywhere cypress pressed their ink-green palms in prayer while high church towers called faintly from villages beyond.

Lunch with the Ricasoli/Lovatelli family at their enormous house – Cacchiano – made an indelible impression. Their vineyards and woodland swept for miles far below with a few decaying farmhouses for sale on the estate. I was tempted to buy one and to convert it, but the thrill of possession was finally discounted by the problems of making such an enterprise viable.

We lunched in the butler's pantry, a dark room with a sink at one end and hearth the other. A thick plastic cloth was thrown over the table, and the plates were paper. The house red and white wine was excellent, although the meal was frugal. The stacking of paper plates later proved a challenging exercise with the family silver cascading to the floor. The party consisted of widowed Contessas and children; it seemed indelicate to enquire of their husbands' respective fates. However, with their good looks and charm, one felt they would find more consorts; life on one of the largest Chianti estates was obviously a struggle to make vineyards meet.

September 28 Hardwicke House

A bright sunny day with scurrying clouds; in Richmond Park the oak-trees toss their seasoned old branches in a brave jig to the sharp gusts of wind. The willows ripple and flatten their silver leaves. A stag – magnificent with some 15 points to his antlers – stalks arrogantly across the road and then quickens his pace as he chases off some young pretender; a youngster with 10 points whose modest aim to lure away just one hind from the governor's herd is again thwarted. The rutting season is full of disappointments.

I am taking Veronica Lucan out to lunch. She sounded composed on the telephone yesterday, though monosyllabic. She was having a terrible time with the press, she assured me. I suggested we talk about it when we met. She was referring to a rumour at the start of this month, that John Lucan had been seen in South America; wearing a droopy moustache and beard – red, this time – and flanked by a pair of tall heavies in dark glasses; he was said to have accepted a bag of money – lots of money.

Parking the car carefully in the congested mews at 5 Eaton Row, I knocked on the door; a bad start. Veronica shortly appears.

'Why not use the bell? It works now. I only heard you knock because I was expecting you.' Would she like to lunch in an Italian Restaurant at Sloane Square? And shall we walk? It is such a lovely day.

'Must we walk? My hair will blow,' she moans.

'Oh, come on! It will give us an appetite. Take my scarf.' I wind it round her loosely.

We walk up Eaton Square. I compliment her on her figure and her looks generally. She has lost weight and looks trim in a smart black coat.

'Oh! My hair,' she moans pitifully; 'I have an appointment this afternoon. It will look terrible.'

'Is it an interesting appointment?' I ask cautiously.

'Who knows? And why haven't you shown me any sympathy over this dreadful press harassment? I need protection. My story will go down in history. Do you realise? What sort of friend are you? I may as well tell you – directly to your face – that I have always found you a pain in the neck. I think you are a totally uninteresting person. I certainly don't want to lunch in your company. Your husband is a saint to put up with you; all those silences he puts up with when you are in a depression. I hope what I am saying now will send you into a bad depression . . .'

And so it goes on; a spirited diatribe which I do little to combat. We have turned back and on finally recovering my car at 5 Eaton Row I assure her that, despite her present brutality, I have always considered any time spent with her worthwhile.

'I am sure you find my company worthwhile; after all I am a very interesting person.'

What to make of her? She is mad, of course. It is to be hoped that she will go on believing in herself.

5 o'clock

The telephone rings; it is Christina.

'Hello? Penelope? I hear you met Veronica today!'

I explain to Christina that our meeting was cut short very abruptly.

'But Veronica said you had lunch together! In an Italian restaurant . . .'

I compare my notes with Christina's. Veronica is telling her little lies again; on purpose? Or is she unaware of right and wrong, correct and incorrect, good and evil?

How is she? Complaining about being alone; longs for love and affection; yet does she ever give it to her children? Bored now with the idea of a job. Why should she work anyway? Christina has finally suggested that she visits the Heather Jenner Marriage Bureau.

Perhaps that was the appointment for which Veronica was so anxious to protect her wind-blown hair?

1983

January 1 Hardwicke House

A mean grey day with persistent drizzle and stormy winds that rattle the bare bones of beech-wood and oak. We press forward, Sebastian and I, wrestling with mud and rain and one shared umbrella. We bump shoulders as we shuffle through sodden leaves and mud. Porridge bounds ahead through Richmond Park, under siege of gale and damp misery.

Three months since I wrote a line. A long bout of depression has wiped away all zest. It had held me in its merciless thrall, a blackness, with a detachment that freezes all feeling, save fear and suppressed panic. Sense and joy is for other people, the people who belong to life and cheerfully accept their due and debt. How I envy them. Will I ever be involved again?

January 4

Sunshine, a rare commodity these dark, muddy days. Sebastian and I ride in Richmond Park. Our stolid ponies circumvent the deeper puddles and squelch laboriously through others. The air is clear and tinged with northern snows. An atom stirs my brain; spirits rise a little, a precious and rare elusive moment. I touch on sense and freedom, truth and peace of mind. It will come, it will come.

February 20 Steep Farm Nr Petersfield

'Hello! How do you do?' Sir Bernard Burrows, swaddled in layered jerkins and baggy, oil-smeared jeans, helped me ease my Mercedes between a line-up of farm machinery. 'I won't shake hands.' He spread out black, oily palms in explanation. 'Working on a greenhouse.' He guided us through a small porch hugged with logs.

Our Ambassador in Turkey twenty years ago, he and his wife have retained their love and interest of the country with regular return visits. Our mutual friend, Mrs Aylın Gönensay, from Istanbul, had effected this visit; an informal Sunday lunch in their rambling, beamed farmhouse.

Lady Burrows (a staunch aide to the Anglo-Turkish Society) greeted us warmly. She apologised blandly for the 'mess' which, to the casual eye, appeared perfectly settled, bundles of magazines on one chair, knitting on another, piles of mending, clothes for jumble, papers and huge rolls of some white insulating stuff which she was tucking in between the ceiling beams; 'to make the rooms warmer,' she assured us.

Lunch was promptly announced by the cook who was clearly anxious to get back to Petersfield. As Aylin and I had just spent four revitalising days of slimming, saunas, steam and massage at the nearby health hydro, Forest Mere, we had urged our hostess not to serve us anything exotic. Sir Bernard carved the roast chicken and offered us a straight choice of beer or water. There was a gallant display of cottage cheese and celery. By some unfortunate sleight of hand I acquired Sir Bernard's white paper napkin; apologising, I handed it back to him, and fumbled in my lap for my own; to no avail; no matter; it must have slipped under the table. Sir Bernard went to a drawer in the pine dresser; after a brief rummage. 'Eh, darling, have we a napkin crisis?' 'Yes,' answered Lady Burrows.

Sir Bernard, a tall slim man with craggy, boyish features, smiled benignly throughout the meal, which he concluded with an enviable slice of home-made cheese cake. With my trip to Cappadocia in mind I quizzed him on lesser-known wonders. He laid a map across the table and pointed out a canyon with frescoed churches. 'Go to Ihlara,' he urged. 'Pronounced Uhluru; sound the "H". And see the Sultan Han – second-century – where travellers and horses would spend the night . . .' Our brief excursions across the Anatolian steppes were cut short by the cook, standing conspicuously in the doorway. Sir Bernard abandoned Cappadocia and cheese cake and drove her home to Petersfield.

Lady Burrows poured out the coffee. Pre-Raphaelite? Arts and Crafts? Bloomsbury? Certainly an unusual creature nearing seventy, she had the figure of a girl; her tight-fitting cord trousers and her bangs of hair suggested the stage, literary circles? Art schools? Her diplomatic life had left little stamp on her original mould.

March 21 Folkestone to Florence

Tall, terraced houses with cramped façades, sad and damp and surrounded with the grime of the train window. Drizzle. The train jolts though a final point of muddy waste ground spattered with litter. Ditched machinery lies dripping in dismembered piles.

A French boat; a choppy channel; snowflakes in Calais, spiteful whips of wind on the platform. We bound into our overnight train.

On a wet spring afternoon Northern France is comfortably uninspiring, flat plough land, flat wheat, willow and poplar as frail as fish bones. A stone trough, a dung heap in a stableyard, three white geese, a manor house with pink bricks, and stone-coined windows – St Armand.

A fitful night's sleep; much shouting and shunting at Basle.

March 22 Florence

We are swirled in a bus to the Pensione Medici, a few hundred yards from the Piazza della Repubblica. It is cheap, clean, and central, and a free flow of self-service ristorante adjoins. The lift, an old-style contraption, whines it way, laboriously up and down the dark stone stairwell, creaking pitifully in its iron grille cage.

Our party consists of twenty-four sixteen-year-old aspiring school-girl art historians, their headmistress, Margaret Blyth, her daughter Sally, and myself. My own tenuous link to the party is through our daughter, Lydia. *Habeo ut dem* – 'I have (in order) to give', a doubtful school motto for young girls to brandish in Italy perhaps and admirably fielded by the typed memo: 'Female students may have to cope with persistent distracters of attention in Florence. Do not be distracted.'

Attention is promptly tested this afternoon. Lusty Latin youths in tight jeans and padded anoraks are persistent indeed. Finally they feign prayer in Santa Croce. The girls sitting in pews opposite listen dutifully to their tutor, a graduate from the Courtauld Institute.

A break for cappuccino and cioccolata con panna heralds a fresh swarm of ardent suitors; but now it is the hour for Giotto and Donatello, the mysteries of fresco and bas-relief and of International Gothic and Gothic Renaissance. Pens fly and minds boggle. Art on sight leaves the schoolroom standing.

Lucinda, Annabel, Suzannah, Harriet, Nicola, three Sarahs, Lydia, and more. Now Lydia is 'Fresco' and Sarah is 'Doric'. Annabel is 'Pasta' and Nicola 'Jacopo'. What a feat of new forms, new arts and structures; what food for thought and palate. A Doric column? A man all-powerful as constructed by Sansovino for his Mint edifice on the Canale di San Marco. Corinthian? A woman, decorative, most favoured of all. Ionic? A neuter, studious, prevalent with libraries, seats of learning and law. The girls gaze and scribble, walk and steal a giggle. Too much to see and remember and feel?

March 23 Florence

A jubilant profusion of bunched violets, hyacinth, daffodils and pink tulips smother a cart in via Medici. There is the habitual growl and stench of traffic and then the reverberating hum of voices in the Cathedral, the hushed dark corners, candle-lit shrines and the Deutsch in droves. We wander and wonder. The cupola interior is swathed in green waterproofs. *Ristorazioni!* From the stifling whiff of glue it is clearly a case for sticking back mosaics. The Cathedral façade gleams with more scaffolding. Ladders zigzag up through wooden platforms. One man scurries up on a length of cord; next a folded cane screen – to render each wooden platform even more snug and less conducive to hard work?

Brunelleschi, Ghiberti, Della Robbia . . . enough. It is time for lunch.

A ristorante with slabs of Brescia rose marble on wooden peg-leg tables. Yellow wet-strength cloths. Marble-tiled floor. Ceramic-tiled walls. One realizes how rich are the Italians in indigenous materials. Chianti, macaroni, cheesecake.

Piazza della Signoria. A man hoses down the steps of the Palazzo Vecchio with a foam gun. A huge tub container loaded on to the back of a van provides his ammunition. His labours might be as effectively employed on monolithic Hercules and David, stained and soaring alongside.

Bright sun this afternoon. The senses are heightened to the wonderfully-defined contrast of sun and shade and narrow streets with open bright squares beyond. Campaniles and bell towers, pediments and ornamental finials dart up behind the rose roofs of piazzas. Operatic vistas everywhere.

Outside the Chiesa Santa Maria Novella children prance and tear around the grass parterres of the piazza. A fat crumpled man on a bicycle empties litter bins into his black bag. He stamps hard on coke tins and squashes them flat. Inside the dim church the sun filters through stained-glass windows. The tall stone columns glow red, blue and gold; translucent in such rich reflections. A richer larger church than Santa Croce, the intricate vault supports are decoratively painted – a church of the Dominican order. The roof of Santa Croce was of plain bare beams, widely used in the poorer Franciscan churches.

I see a dress of tempting yellow silk chiffon – £220 – too much; Lydia fares better in the market with a cotton shirt for £7.

La Contessa Capponi invites us to family supper on Friday. 'You can't miss the Palazzo; it is well-lit. Nicolo is anxious to show you the family paintings.' Our anticipation is spiced with conjecture.

March 24 Florence

Drizzle and cold. The streets reverberate to grinding dust carts, the wail of police cars, shouts, slamming car-doors, horns. Our guide, David, sports a Panama hat, his customary jeans, and a black wool coat, dressed for any weather contingency. He leads us to his favourite Piazza Santissima Annunziata, a fine example of understatement. Brunelleschi's Foundling Hospital, with its elegant arched colonnades, dominates the whole structure of the square. The church interior is swamped with glitter and gold making it a travesty of its original fifteenth-century restraint.

'Galerio David', written on brown card in red and black ink, summons us to feast upon and admire that hunk of perfect manhood. Michelangelo's David. The girls advance excitedly on their hero, pencils poised. They sketch the familiar torso rapidly, thrilled to replace old postcards with some rendition of the real McCoy.

'It's much paler than I expected.'

'I thought it would be bigger.'

'But it's tiny!'

Nor do they heed our David's comment that the hands and feet are disproportionately big. Next their attention is caught by the *Incompiuta* blocks of *The Slaves*. Figures originally commissioned for the tomb of Pope Giulio II, they were never completed, trapped fast in their marble blocks, a fascinating study in Michelangelo's system of carving statues. He hacked the solid blocks at every level and depth to release his works from within.

Cries of surprise as the girls discover a familiar Benozzo Gozzoli, a Filippo Lippi, a Fra Angelico, the illustrated text is swept aside by the reality. We are in the Chiesa San Lorenzo, a richly-adorned Medici church, where vast circular stone columns with important Corinthian and Ionic capitals were each constructed in one piece of locally-quarried stone.

It is time for tea and coffee and shopping in the market. The rain tumbles and pavements run with muddy water. I am forced to buy an umbrella; the tough Italian cotton stands up well.

March 24 Florence

Armed with a cheerful red and white cineraria, I stand outside the high brown-painted gate. I light a cigarette, revelling in the comparative quiet, away from Florence below. The rain has stopped at last, releasing a watery sun. Birds sing in the ilex trees. A man saunters by. I dally no longer and press the bell.

Joan Haslip welcomes me in her bright dripping garden. Plump and a little puffed, she glows in her copper head of hair and a vivid blue dress. 'Look at my camellias! They are just beginning to flower.' Her pansies nod in profusion from their little terracotta troughs. We move in from her paved and gravelled courtyard to a choice of two sitting-rooms. 'Let us sit in this one; it has all the light and sun. What will you drink? This?' She waves a bottle of Punt e Mes. As there is no alternative readily available on the tray I accept immediately. 'Ice?' 'No, thank you.' Mild relief sweeps her face. I am determined to be a convenient guest. It is her maid's day off. We talk about people and prices.

'My maid tells me coffins cost 900,000 lira here, that is £450 sterling. Prices in Florence have become exorbitant. I happen to know for instance that coffins in Verona cost 350,000 lira. Servants it seems are getting richer and richer and more scarce. They even drink whisky, bad whisky of course. No wonder they can afford it. A butler alone can charge £50 for his sole service at a small dinner party. Harold Acton has terrible problems keeping up his domestic standards. I am lunching there tomorrow. His good-looking young butler has just left; starting a restaurant.'

We eat a simple lunch, white wine, kedgeree, salad, and melted ice cream. Joan insists that we do not wash up, she has trouble making me coffee. Where is the coffee kept? The cups she finds but where are the matching saucers? The sliding cupboard door is solidly wedged by a stuck spoon. Milk is arduously procured from the fridge behind the larger door which is also stuck. It succumbs to a hefty kick from my exasperated hostess. The frustrations of the maid's day off! I sip my coffee. The two cats leap nimbly on to the dining-room table, sniff disdainfully at a plate of sugary biscuits and retreat with as much dignity as the wrath of their mistress will allow.

How is she making out with Marie Antoinette?

'Oh poor girl, she had such an appalling time with Louis XVI. Nobody appreciates how much she suffered. He sweated horribly in bed. I will finish it next year. I am usually late with my books. *The Emperor and the Actress* doing wonderfully in America, better than in Britain, the English have always found Franz Josef boring.'

March 24, 1983 (Evening) Capponi

Lydia and I dine with the Capponi family at their fifteenth-century Palazzo, which overlooks the Arno.

The heavy outer door gives on to a deserted hall and an antique lift. We squeeze inside and are hoisted to the second floor. The elder son, Nicolo, a tall hefty young man, greets us unctuously through his pipe and luxuriant beard. After preliminary sips of Capponi sweet white wine, Lydia is ushered to the kitchen where the eldest daughter, Tessa, is assembling a salmon mousse and an avocado mousse. 'A pink mess and a green mess; I hope it looks all right.' Tessa's talents are gauged to higher duties than making mousse on the maid's night out. She is a fully-fledged interpreter. Lydia watches and admires and listens. Disparity of age and circumstances breeds no barriers; Tessa is a real friend and Tessa is wonderful.

In the small sitting-room, cosy with terracotta-tiled floor, oriental rugs, and deep sofas, Nicolo expounds with relish on the family history. His beautiful mother, Flavia, sits a little nervously beside him. Are we bored, or amazed by her exuberant son? Sebastiano, aged twelve and as startlingly beautiful as any fined-down Tiepolo cherub, shakes my hand briefly. Apparently he is unwell and returns to his bed and to his television with rapid relief. It is Pierrot who inevitably makes the most dramatic entrance. He is eighteen; severely mentally handicapped, slim, strong, and seemingly physically double-jointed. He leaps nimbly on to the sofa, throwing his long legs askew on to his mother's lap. She points reproachfully at his one foot with a missing shoe. Pierrot curls up his legs beneath him and sings ecstatically to a long shred of newspaper, which he winds round and round his index finger. His tutor therapist sidles up and sits firmly between Pierrot and his mother. His charge, who clearly thrives on a new distraction a minute, kisses his tutor on the ear, resting his dark curly head (and beard) on his tutor's narrow, angular shoulder. Pierrot croons his strange lullaby and dandles the strip of paper before the poor man's nose.

It is time for the Grand Tour. Nicolo leads Lydia and me to the lower main floor of the Palazzo complete with the Capponi family chapel. To Lydia's alarm he insists that we enter the little chamber. 'Now I shall turn out the light; can you see the brilliance of the stained-glass window?' He holds a candle high behind the window. Yes, we see perfectly and can we come out now? High painted walls and ceilings – coffered or vaulted, Gothic or Renaissance: shrouded grandeur, dustsheets, dust, marble tops, gesso, gold and gilt, heavy richness put to sleep to be woken, revived, and polished for rare occasions alone.

Meanwhile the Queen's salon is let to a photographer; not even his startling equipment can dent the space and height of such a room. Huge black tripods to vie with any Tanguely machine; a red bicycle on a white sheet? 'Our friend works on commercial art lines,' explains Nicolo.

We return to dinner, the family, the upper floor, and Count Capponi himself. Tired from his professional day lecturing on art history, his eyes light up as he puts his arm round his son; he fondles the back of his neck, mumbles endearments. Pierrot receives this attention restlessly. Count Capponi turns his mind to Lydia.

'And what period of art do you particularly prefer?' Lydia hesitates before answering firmly.

'I think I like the Post-Impressionists best and . . . er . . . Pop Art.'

'Which are your Post-Impressionists, I don't think I know them.'

'Van Gogh, Cézanne, Seurat.'

'I see. And your Pop Artists?'

'Well, David Hockney? Peter Blake? And Andy Warhol?'

'I don't know them either.' Poor Count Capponi. It can't be a comfortable ride through such unfamiliar avenues of art and expression.

And his own favourite artist?

'Fra Angelico,' he states decisively.

Does he like Filippo Lippi?

'He's amusing.' Count Capponi is very precise. During dinner we stumble in the ambiguous foothills of Byzantium and Pierrot leaves the table before the pudding. This is a pity because it is a brilliant red round of redcurrant jelly lavishly decorated with frothy whipped cream, or as Tessa may have described it; 'a red mess and a white mess'.

March 26 Venice

We are driven by coach through the Appenines to Urbino. Rivers swollen and silted by the heavy rains charge through boulders. Waterfalls spew down from rocky ravines and vines are bare, their outstretched twigs form contorted stands, like so many Chinese working at their Tai Chi positions.

Justine Hardy feels sick. After a breath of fresh air and a seat in front, she feels immediately recovered and sits beside me. We talk of her famous father, actor Robert Hardy. He is at present hot and uncomfortable in India's Rajasthan, dressed up tight as some British Army General. M M Kaye's *Far Pavilions* is being filmed from that exceptionally long book.

Susannah Starkey feels faint at the Ducal apartments of Urbino's Ducal Palace. The long-departed incumbent's small study with its teasing trompe l'oeil of marquetry walls proves too overbearing. I lead her to the small outside balcony, worse, much worse, and helpless tears. We walk down stairs, ramps, and terraced paths to the comforts of the car park and a cappuccino. After lunch in a hut behind some garage at Pesaro, it is Ravenna at tea-time.

The church interiors are unusually dark in the heavy afternoon rain. We throw our heads back and gaze on the finest mosaics in Europe, a point lost on the girls, but this first introduction clearly fascinates them. Figures, still and exotic, stare into mysterious space, their wide eyes lined with black. The irregular placing of each cube catches the light; doves drink from the fountains of life, peacocks invite mortality and stags represent souls. Decorative architectural backgrounds, swagged curtains and columns, flowering trees and gardens evoke the East with the glorious power of imagery. We are looking at Byzantium in all its initial brilliance. Ravenna captured by Byzantine Emperors in 540 AD can confidently claim the origin of its unique mosaics from that ancient age. And are they cubes of glass or stone? The coloured cubes are of stone we are assured; the brilliant green and blue and red are indigenous, cut and highly-polished. And the gold? Gold leaf is sandwiched between glass. So many questions come to mind.

It is dark when we arrive in Venice. We clutch our cases and wedge ourselves on a vaporetto. The girls are quiet and absorbed with the strange magic of the Grand Canal. Their city of so many imaginings. They are not disappointed. Venice at night with lit windows in palaces is a handsome alternative to the tear-stained façades by day perhaps. The water is high with Piazza San Marco gently awash. We pad through puddles across the square and turn down a narrow *calle* to our Hotel Atlantico. It rejoices in small bedrooms with adventurous wallpaper; my own huge mongrel orange poppies flop, clumsily, over ceiling and walls. A canal and a bridge below and a tip of the Campanile through the window are rich compensations.

March 27 Venice

'*Per tutti gli studenti. Non gettare niente dalle finestra, specialmente acqua, sulle gondole de passaggio nel canale*[1] . . .' indulgence in medieval water games has clearly caused trouble in the Hotel Atlantico.

We set off this morning (the sky and water as pellucid and blue as the guide books describe) to the Accademia. We attempt to forget the Florentine School in order to assimilate the Venetians. Our new team is rapidly formed and Tintoretto (the son of the dyer), Titian,

[1] 'To all students. Do not throw anything from the window, especially water, on the gondolas passing in the canal.'

Tiepolo, Giorgione, Veronese, Bellini, and Carpaccio become our new classmates.

Ca' Rezzonico (once rented by the poet Robert Browning) is our next port of call. Here a breathless blonde from Dublin University spills it all out at such a pace, with such expressive gesticulation and emphatic tossing of her Titian locks that the girls are mesmerised by her performance; Tiepolo floats way above them on the painted ceilings and Sir Stephen Spender[2], white-haired and wind-blown, passes by unnoticed on the stairs.

To the Frari Church, where the girls, refreshed from lunch, take earnest notes on the huge Titian altar piece, but Justine has had enough. Stretching out her jean-clad legs through the open-fronted pew she gently waggles her feet, colourful in yellow socks and red flat shoes. She strokes and dandles her new bone bracelet, lovingly opening and shutting the silvered clasp.

On again to the Scuola San Rocco. Here the grandiose Tintorettos, in their full drama of light and dark, depress them. For today they have seen enough.

March 28 Venice

The trash of Venice is an excellent antidote to the treasure. The gift boutiques, glittering enamels, cheap glass, and alabaster revive the eye that is sore from culture. The girls revel in these cheap colourful trinkets and face Byzantium in San Marco refreshed. I delight Sarah 1 with more statistics: Venice is built on 117 islands, with 400 bridges, with 150 canals, with 190 churches.

A long dissertation on the Gothic entrance to the Doges' Palace; they enjoy its adventurous and flamboyant style and *La Porta della Carta*. Why 'The Paper Gate'? David doesn't know. My Michelin guide explains that it was so-called because of the placards bearing decrees posted upon it. For the release of prisoners in the Palace cells perhaps? Perhaps.

The Campanile fell in 1907, David tells them. A huge crack appeared; photographers stood by and people waited. It fell at last and crushed the Loggetta. The girls want to know more, much more. We are late for lunch and Sarah 2 catches her fingers in the gothic tangle of the hotel banisters. I give her plaster and Germaline ointment.

---

[2] The notable poet and critic. Born 1909 and knighted 1983.

March 29 Venice

The rain has been bucketing down since 4 a.m. It will continue until Ottobre, warns the porter with mock horror. Those without umbrellas mask their heads and feet in polythene shopping bags and those with umbrellas find they leak under such a barrage of rain.

Another morning of churches. From the fifteenth century they seem to take on the appearance of theatres or drawing-rooms, possessed by Imperial patronage in every guise. The rich and sometimes florid decoration of paintings, and sculptures, the riches of bas-relief and mosaic suggest grandeur rather than the spiritual. In the church of San Giovanni Crisostomo columns are hung in red and gold cut-velvet damask. The elaborate torchères and silver lanterns, the oval portrait (bad) of the Madonna, and hideous silver hearts (sacred?) framed in glass are not immediately conducive to prayer.

The impression is happily redressed in the enchanting church of San Giorgio degli Schiavoni with the deep Carpaccio frieze of artfully-depicted fables of rural scenarios. Here is charm and understatement. The floor of red Verona and cream marble is set with deep pews and elegant torchères. The walls are lined with walnut panelling and benches and the painted ceiling beams complete this intimate interior where colour is muted and decoration is tranquil.

March 30 Venice

Piazza San Marco is dry again. There is much wiping down of marble thresholds as the shops start to roll up their shutters at nine o'clock.

I hire a gondola and take Lydia (Fresco) and Annabel (Pasta), myself and luggage to the station. They are thrilled and so are their friends who stand on the bridge to witness our stylish departure. I am appalled at the state of the gutters at water level and the fumes from motorboats that pound past us are another hazard to enjoyment. Fresco and Pasta revel in the experience and talk of honeymoons and grandchildren. The numerous columns on the passing frontages afford an excellent revision on architectural points. Arrival at *la Ferrovia* concludes ten days of immeasurable experience if not tangible knowledge.

April 20 Garden Cottage Udny Castle Udny Green Aberdeenshire

Nobody could be more snugly ensconced than in this granite cottage sheltered by an avenue of ancient beech trees and the high brick wall of the Castle kitchen gardens. Our own garden lawn is trimmed with bright polyanthus and dwarf daffodils. Spring arrives late and dies hard in the north.

In the kitchen, cosy with a brown tiled floor, wood shelves and cupboards, the table is laid with homemade scones and shortbread. We enter the sitting-room, warm and eminently inviting with plump sofas and a wide wood fire. The front hall sports a piano for those who care and an exquisite bedroom leads off. My friend Jane sleeps there in a froth of cream lace that shrouds the four-poster. Up the stairs leads to Sebastian's room, blue and red and boyish; my own, across the landing, is a confection of pink and white spotted muslin.

We are spending a week's holiday here as guests of Maggie Udny-Hamilton. Through keen winds, soft rains, and sea mists that leave the ploughed fields teeming, we have discovered woodland walks, the teeming bird life of Newburgh sea shore, the French-style garden at Pitmedden House, and the pink harled sixteenth-century castles, Fraser and Craigievar.

Aberdeenshire suggests that life begins and ends with its neat fields sown and ploughed and bounded by firm stone walls. An air of content enwraps these villages: Methlick, Tarves, Pitmedden and Udny Green, where the haphazard general store does as big a trade as the Spar self-service company. A spacious rolling landscape swept by a cruel sea wind, it appears clean and brave and clear of any crowding.

Sebastian and I ride each day from a stable near Methlick. Here the county is hilly and more wooded. We trot along narrow lanes edged with grassy banks clumped with wild daffodils. Chortling burns make muddy margins beside the fields. A large long container lorry of cows deposits its sleepy load in a field; ambling back from the dairy with a herdsman and his stick is now an old memory. The sun comes out, shy and pale. In the distance the sun dapples the plough a deep purple and on a green hill far away the sheep are gleaming white specks. The black great dane bounds down the curved drive of the stables. His ears cocked, and his long slim legs set firmly apart, he stands silhouetted against the brightening evening sky to give his handsome welcome.

May 7 Istanbul Turkey

At the airport we hear 'Istanbul! Istanbul! Passengers this bus please!' We descend from the plane and file towards the proffered bus.

'Wrong bus! Wrong bus! That one please!' We hesitate. Is he right? No. A dyed blonde hurls herself between the throng of befuddled passengers.

'Wrong! All wrong! This bus, Istanbul, that bus Ankara.'

We are finally shepherded into the blonde-designated bus and driven off smartly. At the airport building a major hassle awaits us, nicely packaged in lame excuses. No room at the Hilton. No room at the Sheraton. The Divan? No. Greeks have thronged to Istanbul to celebrate their orthodox Easter. A major fire has incapacitated a major hotel. Could we fly to Ankara? No? Then it is decided, we are booked at the Oriental. We arrive. 'We have one room only; we thought you were two newspaper men!' Two rooms are finally found at the Harem Hotel on the Asian shore at Üsküdar. The magnificent view of Topkapı wipes out the dim state of the hotel plumbing.

Under the aegis of the Turkish Tourist Ministry we are on an assignment, Duncan McNeill and I. He to photograph the delights of Turkish cuisine and restaurants and I to write them up.

Our guide, Oktay, asks, 'Which restaurants you wish to visit? Abdullah? We dine there tonight?' On my list of restaurants, compiled from quizzing Turkish friends, Abdullah features indeed. It proves a mild disappointment; food adequate, dining-room de luxe, and featureless. We are looking for a spread of colourful, enticing dishes, a cornucopia of mouth-watering fish, of bright vegetables artfully stuffed, of glistening pastries, with a proud chef in a white toque standing all before.

May 8 Istanbul

Sunshine after yesterday's rain. Duncan is restless to shoot. We see two restaurants, on my list described as 'fashionable, le dernier cri'. They are closed and forlorn by day, alive with candles and mirrors by night. Maybe! Oktay suggests the Konyalı restaurant at Topkapı. Too touristy, we complain. 'There you will see a show,' he insists. A handsome chef, complete with hat and yellow sun umbrella, sharpens his knife as he slices wafers of pressed lamb from his doner kebab. He flares the charcoal grill with a wooden fan. Ethnic, colourful. Duncan shoots.

We go to Tarabya, a pretty bay ten kilometres north of Istanbul. Huge catches of succulent fish are displayed on the approaching sea walls. Turbot sells at £1 per lb. Mackerel, sea bass, tuna, and shrimps are laid out in colourful profusion. Another shot. Fish restaurants with red-checked cloths spill over pavements. The world is eating Sunday lunch.

May 9 Istanbul

More sun; a day devoted to fish photography. Fat smiling chefs stand alongside tasteful heaps of turbot, sea bass, sole, crab, and shrimps superbly fresh from the Marmara, Black Sea and the Bosphorus. A difficult exercise extracting recipes of stuffed peppers, mussels and vine leaves. The Turkish measure of a tea glass is reduced to two table-spoons. We arrange with a chef at the Divan restaurant, chic and central, to have a further display for tomorrow.

May 10 Istanbul

At the Divan: the young chef, Huseyin, proudly hands me a beauti-fully-compiled list of recipes in unintelligible Turkish. He abandons dressing a ponderous-looking red bass, due for some banquet, and shares his views on Turkish cuisine; the Italian restaurant manager interprets in French and English. Huseyin concedes that Turkish cuis-ine does not look so beautiful as French dishes, but declares that it tastes better and is fresher.

The Turks are to be congratulated on their ability to use natural products to the best effect. Aubergines, considered to be their king of vegetables, are served in forty different ways. Yoghurt is cajoled into numerous creamy sauces and olive oil is worked into everything. Spain and Greece, with virtually the same products, have totally failed to produce a palatable cuisine. Duncan shoots the whole gamut of hors d'oeuvres, meat, fish, and vegetable dishes, and the rice pudding. Do we have to have the rice pudding, I inquire ingenuously? Huseyin insists that it is one of the most popular desserts. Reading six yolks of egg in the recipe, I am faintly reassured, perhaps it will taste like crème brûlée.

Pleased with the pictures under Duncan's belt, we saunter out of the Divan. I open my bag and discover the definite loss of 20,000 Turkish lira (£60 sterling). I persuade the Hilton to place my £1,000 traveller's cheques in a safe.

We lunch with Nuri Birgi, the ex-Turkish ambassador to London. His elegant nineteenth-century Ottoman *yalı* is perched on the old defence red wall. The view is exquisite: caiques, jaunty steamers, and huge ugly Russian tankers pass to and fro on the swift, tidal Bosphorus. Topkapı Sarayı framed in the Selamlik window competes with the awe-inspiring Haghia Sophia mosque. 'Every window is a picture hanging there,' observes Nuri bey

In Nuri bey's long, blue and white dining-room adorned with blue and white Chinese porcelain and blue Polish kelims, we sit, a small assembly of English visitors and Turkish friends. The main course of Circassian chicken holds everybody's rapt attention. A famous dish from the Black Sea area where walnut trees have usurped the olives. The breasts are coated in a creamy pink sauce; it is served cold. Nuri bey's Austrian cook later reveals every detail. In the stock of the boiling chicken soak white bread, red pepper and chopped walnuts. Is that all? Make it the night before, she urges; leave in a cold place and the sauce will thicken.

Nuri Bey's garden is full of flowers and thick with shady trees. Huge gloomy old umbrella pines tower over the judas trees, hundred-year-old pomegranates and quinces. The yuccas, agapanthus, and oleander flower profusely on sloping banks of liriope grass. A garden of shade and secret corners. The sun goes in; birds swoop above. 'A sign of rain,' sighs Nuri bey. We see clouds edge up the Bosphorus and over the towers and kiosks of Topkapı beyond.

Our evening flight to Ankara is graced by a slice of currant cake, a paper beaker of thick brown apricot juice, and short, stocky business-men in pale suits. We speculate on our hotel. It is dark on touch-down. A girl guide this time searches the disgorged passengers anxiously. Plump and pleasant with excellent English, she is called Şerife. She loves her Ankara, insisting that it has a livelier core of culture and intelligentsia than does Istanbul. She is probably right, but who could prefer the flat dust bowl of Ankara to that magical sweep of spires and domes beside the Bosphorus? This sprawling city has been built up only since the 1920s when Kemal Atatürk adopted it as his strategic base for founding the Modern Turkish Republic.

We are driven through wide, straight boulevards flanked with acacia trees in full, white bloom. Our eyes are dully tuned to faceless concrete when Şerife nudges us sharply. Set up high, floodlit on the ebony backcloth of the night city, is a striking, pillared block of gold lime-stone. From a distance it looks imposing and in its classical simplicity resembles the Parthenon. Atatürk's Mausoleum was completed in 1953; it is an impressive blend of ancient and modern concepts.

Our Hotel Bulvor Palas is a barrack-like establishment with vast public rooms. Under dimly-lit high ceilings with pillar supports, we dine on blue fish, after the turbot was recommended enthusiastically, but then retracted by the chef who judged it none too fresh. A dessert of fruit is offered – apples and oranges. No more choice? No. On the next table we see cherries and are promptly offered strawberries instead.

May 11 Nevşehir

A four-hour drive from Ankara to Nevşehir, in the Province of Cappadocia. Here we will photograph and describe the extraordinary phenomena of this volcanic belt. The flat Anatolian country outside Ankara is relieved with soft, peaked hills. No fences to interrupt the wide sweeps of ploughed winter wheat, corn and mustard fields. Flocks of black and white sheep orbit round isolated farmsteads of old-style buildings of lime-washed mud-brick. There are gypsies too, moving back north to spend their summers with a full complement of tents and caravans, children and livestock.

After an unmemorable lunch we glimpse the Hasan Daği mountain. The snow streaks its tip and shoulders like glistening sea foam. In 2,000 BC this 10,000-foot mountain erupted, pouring its lava on the plains below, and Cappadocia with its grand canyons, rushing mountain rivers, and fantastic rock formation evolved from this volcanic upheaval.

We arrive at the Ihlara valley. Sir Bernard Burrows had strongly urged me to see it. There are some amazing churches here, gouged from the sheer 300-foot rock face and subsequently frescoed.

Duncan galvanises his equipment for descent; I plead to take his tripod. He allows me five minutes of this dubious pleasure before persuading me my hands are too small. The rush of the Melendiz river is muffled by thick screens of poplar and willow. As we near the final steps Şerife sees pistachio trees and walnut. Over narrow grass troughs and boulders we are led by the village guide to the Beneath the Tree Church, The Church of the Serpent, The Dark Church, The Church of the Hyacinths, these simple descriptive names given by peasants through the ages. First hewn out of the rock in the first century by Christians escaping pagan persecution, these churches through the centuries were artfully shaped with free-standing columns, cupolas, and apses. The barrel-vaulted naves and walls and niches were frescoed in the eleventh and twelfth centuries. The Byzantine mosaic technique is prevalent; the backgrounds and clothes are filled with typical flower and geometric motifs. Duncan's flash lights up the rich, colourful details. I motion to the guide the scratched-out eyes and forms of some figures. He explains to Şerife that peasants in fear of being pestered by the evil eye have caused this damage. Moslems, who condemned portraiture, are also guilty. Notwithstanding this inevitable toll through time, these churches are acclaimed as the rarest legacy of Christian and Byzantine art.

We ramble back to the head of the valley. We cross a glade of waving wild asparagus and we pick enough for a banquet.

May 12 Ankara

After a night of fierce thunder and lightning the sun is up early. We are on the winding road from Nevşehir (a dreary town, smothered in cement and coaches) to Göreme. A stunning drive through a panorama of tufacious wind-sharpened cones, rising from wind-moulded rocks that resemble soft pink heaps of helva. Towering canyons of red rock and yellow ochre are patched purple in the bright sun; a fauvist's landscape where colour is vibrant and vivid but flits restlessly with the constant switch of sun and shade. The valleys, fertile from the volcanic soil, and a softening contract with winding rivers, are fringed with poplar and willow and orchards of plum, apricot and pomegranate; there are vineyards too. Cappadocia combines space and intimacy, the savage and softly sensual, the harsh and the lush, in a miraculous juxtaposition.

A cuckoo is singing in the Göreme valley; a beautiful amphitheatre at the head of a long, low enclosure of rocky hills. Pigeons swoop to the dovecots notched in the cliff-face. We enter the Church of the Apple named after the nearby orchards. It has a barrel-vaulted nave leading to an apse with a horse-shoe arch; the basic Greek cross structure of so many of these rock churches. Elaborate domes in a cluster and seemingly supported by pillars. Often these free-standing pillar supports are eroded, and hang nonchalantly in mid-air; gravity is flouted and mocked in many such examples. The frescoes here are bold and colourful scenes from the Scriptures and the Life of Christ; the strong Byzantine designs are painted in terracotta, blue-greys and ochre.

Serife takes us to lunch at a 400-year-old stone farmhouse. Part of it has been converted to a simple restaurant, advertising 'Western toilet and bar facilities'. We sit outside on a stone wall covered with faded kelims, sipping raki, the national drink of distilled grapes and aniseed. An old crone crouches beneath a mulberry tree that spreads its shade over a large part of the courtyard. She stokes a primitive stove with bundles of firewood and bakes muffins on the flat iron plate. A young boy nearby makes up kebabs; cubes of lamb, pearl onions, pepper, and tomatoes are placed on slender, red tamarisk twigs. Tamarisk adds a distinctive aroma to the meat as it grills above the charcoal flame.

We eat in the cool, dim interior where kelims drape walls and floors and benches. The red-and-white-check cloth is strangely out of step. Home-made feta cheese, pickled peppers, and raw shallots are accompanied by the muffins still warm from the stove under the mulberry tree. The kebabs follow on a mound of tomato-stained bulgar rice; bulgar or buckwheat is the staple diet of peasants. Glasses of tea cool the palate admirably and, waving aside a further offer of a muffin from the resident baker, we take the road to Avanos. The soil turns red as we approach this village perched beside the Kızılırmak (red river), which is famous for its soft polished red pottery and the river that runs red from the local clay. We are lured into a cavernous grotto hewn out of the red rock face of the valley. Our host sits us down in his Aladdin's cave of pots and kelims and throwing wheel. He gives us local wine in red clay bowls and a quick demonstration of turning his simple crude ware.

May 13 Ürgüp

With Mustafa Halıcı, a renowned carpet-dealer in Ürgüp. We spend an absorbing hour in his shop stacked high with wool and silk carpets, ancient and modern, and kelims from the Caucasus, Iran and Anatolia. Prices start from £70 for a kelim and can reach £700. A new wool carpet he sells at £70 a square metre. Mustafa Halıcı comes from three generations of carpet-dealers and is proud to sell his collection throughout the world. As we sip away at a continual flow of tea he bemoans the commission he has to charge some buyers. If they come in a group with a guide, he is bound to charge any buyer an extra 30% on the goods; 20% goes automatically to the guide (an introductory commission) and 10% to the guide's agent, a case for buying on one's own from a reputable dealer. From Ürgüp, we take the road to Avanos again, branching off right to a parched and desolate plain where on the horizon we see the impressive silhouette of the Sarı Han (Yellow Inn). These Hans or caravanserais line all the main Anatolian silk routes; many still survive as proud witnesses to the Seljuks who built them. Seljuk tribes (from northern Persia) invaded the Anatolian plateau in the eleventh century. They proved to be doyens of venerable architecture.

Standing in the silent half-crumbled courtyard one conjures up the clatter and cries as men and horses once went about their business. In these handsome service stations, horses and camels were stabled in monumental elegance. Under a soaring stone-vaulted roof that smacks of a Norman cathedral, pointed arches lead off a central aisle to their spacious bedding. The central dome is pierced with decorative holes to give light and air. I notice the simple stone sculpted loop-handles that held the reins in the stable arcade. Surrounding the court-yard are doors and arches, elegantly incised with plaited and geometric incisions; here was the lodging for travellers and drivers, the wash-rooms, kitchens, living-rooms, and workrooms. Resident doctors and vets and carriage mechanics were also at hand. Now they stand redundant, magnificent still in their solitude. It was Bernard Berenson who once exclaimed: 'What a miracle is this Seljuk architecture! It has an elegance, a distinction of design and a subtle delicacy of orna-mentation surpassing any other known to me since French Gothic at its best.'

May 15 Ankara

We leave Şerife in Ankara and fly back to Istanbul. Duncan returns to London tomorrow, where we hope the editor of *House and Garden* will lap up his cuisine photography. And who will fall for Cappadocia? Working free-lance has its pitfalls.

May 16 Istanbul

I stay a few days with Rahmi Koç in his nineteenth-century white-painted yali slap on the Bosphorus. From his son Mustafa's bedroom I see the medieval ramparts of the Rumeli Castle and the twinkling lights of Bebek Bay. Water laps the jetty below; lazy, languorous days. Rahmi helps me plan my long-imagined trip down the south coast. In a typical generous gesture he presents me with a car and driver. My friends warn me against bathing on deserted beaches or wandering alone through ruins.

May 21 Cennet Motel Side

The open-air dining terrace is drenched in the scent of honeysuckle and roses. I eat alone with a book. Many Germans and Turks, a few French, no British. A lovely arc of sand at the foot of the colourful garden curves to distant ruins where the layered stone seats of a Roman theatre are clearly seen. The sea is lukewarm with strange, cold currents that come and go. I see Perge and walk the marble streets, the mosaic road, and marvel at the dishevelled pile of toppled columns and capitals.

Wild flowers – poppies, cornflowers and stars of Bethlehem – straddle green empty spaces. Sun and colour everywhere. Here, on the lush Pamphylian plain at the foot of the Taurus mountains, the corn is a crust of gold with tall purple thistles bowing majestically between. We drive to the ancient acropolis of Silliyum and leave the car in a farmyard. A young boy with painfully torn trousers leads us up the vast mound of rock. He points to the crumbled ruin of the *Hamam* (bath house). We admire it dutifully, though there is little left. He hands me a mulberry. A herd of cows saunters down the hill with two young girls, heads wrapped tight in scarves, sitting astride donkeys. His sisters? We follow them down to the farm, where peasants with lean handsome faces sit idly watching us. We take to the rough road again and are surprised by two armed soldiers. My driver shows his identity card. We are motioned to the side; there we remain. General Evren is passing on the main route ahead. We wait. In the distance we see a stream of black gleaming cars. They hurtle past, some fifteen in all. As we near the main road I notice hedges thick with camouflaged soldiers. We drive on to Aspendos. Approaching the site over a remarkably preserved Seljuk hump-backed bridge we see the theatre. It is closed with a handsome pair of iron gates. I peer inside; it is probably the most immaculately preserved Roman theatre in Turkey. The setting sun silhouettes the superb stretches of the aqueduct alongside.

May 23 Side

I establish a routine of working on my articles each morning, a stretch on the beach after lunch, a bathe and then sight-seeing in the evening sun. This evening I walk along a country road to Side, some half a mile away. Donkeys, sheep, and ponies stand grazing in juicy green meadows. The hedgerows burn with bright flowers and everywhere the corn gleams gold like rippling silk. The village of Side consists of a central street, crammed with rough carpet shops, kebab houses, pastry shops, and all the paraphernalia of emergent tourism. It is not unattractive. The small harbour makes a colourful vista before and the Roman theatre towers loftily behind.

I call on Selman Taranto, a friend of a friend. An old man guides me through a back street to her house. She is startled to see me; an American man has also just called on her by dint of some introduction. She settles her new acquaintances on her red-tiled veranda. Her house was a ruin, she explains, a genuine Roman ruin, now converted with the old pink stones and enclosed with rustling umbrella pines and mulberry trees. We sip raki. She deplores the building activity in Side but still manages to bathe undisturbed from the Agora. The Agora? The old Roman market place where toppled marble door pediments, columns, and capitals blaze white in the sun, perfect backdrops for a bathe in that brilliant, azure sea. A helicopter drowns our idle conversation. Selman sits up startled. That must be General Evren. Had we seen him? He was said to be passing through Side today. We shake our heads. He is like the Scarlet Pimpernel, this indefatigable potentate! After an hour of Selman's charming company I extricate myself from her verandah, her raki, and her hazelnuts. She urges me to see the theatre now, at once, at sunset.

To stand on the top perimeter of an ancient monument spells instant excitement, couple it with the sea and waves below and the thrill is intense. I look down the sheer rows of stone seats with the area far below heaped with customary marble remains. The setting sun suffuses each stone in a smoulder of gold and rose. A sword of light straight as a Roman road glances across the sea from the shore to the horizon. I walk back to the motel along the beach. Each time I look behind I see the theatre fade as little by little the arc of stone is drained of gold and pales to amethyst and dust in the sinking sun.

May 24 Phaselis Olympus Myra

We leave Side early this morning. My driver is intent on saying his prayers. I cannot imagine what else he can be muttering over as the road is clear and the sun is beaming. He has another habit at the wheel, he burps brazenly. Notwithstanding these small indulgences, he is a friendly, conscientious man with a delightful smile. 'A clear-cut Anatolian,' was Rahmi's own description. His name is Yaşar.

From Antalya the coast road becomes more dramatic. Steep hills of pine unfold to valleys of rushing mountain rivers, rich agriculture, livestock, farmsteads, and peasants. The soaring belt of the Taurus mountains stands back in a haze of dense blue as their foot-hills slope down to hidden shores. So many beguiling coves we pass, glistening white sands licked with that tongue of aquamarine. 'Don't bathe on deserted beaches,' warned my friends in Istanbul.

We turn off down a rough road through a pine forest with steep, bouldered hills. A ruined aqueduct limps into the distance. Here is Phaselis, the Graeco/Roman city set strategically in a little bay. Here Poseidon stood when he watched Odysseus sail 'over the deep' (on Mount Solymnus, as immortalised by Homer). I see the spot, a high mount of red rock thick with waving pines. The marble street with its indomitable columns leads off from the beach to hamams, agoras, and rich merchants' mansions, half-grounded and crumbled by the wind and rain of centuries. I sit on an upturned Corinthian capital beside the old street. What silence. I savour that rare circumstance of total solitude in a place of beauty. The sea, the mountains, and the vestiges of a powerful age combine in a poignant impact upon the senses. I sigh and walk on through a riot of flowers, bees, and vivid blue and orange butterflies.

Down a steep, winding rock road we lurch and rattle. Through thick pine-woods we reach a clearing, a sort of wadi where rivulets wind through heaped boulders and pebbles. A young girl on a donkey laden with wooden boxes of green peppers directs us to the track ahead. We set off through a patch of pink oleanders and finally abandon the car. We walk towards the shore through a narrow pass in the woods, and are rewarded with another miraculous stretch of beach. In a cool cave men are making screens from willow and cane. They direct us back through the woods to the elusive ruins of Olympus. We find a low stone wall which looks promising. Yaşar intimates that it is an old Roman drain and that there are snakes in the grass below. We walk gingerly along the precipitous relic, which mercifully leads us back to the car. Referring to my guide book I read that the ruins of Olympus are in a perilous state.

We lunch in Finike on some simple type of tasteless fish. Our rudimentary inn overlooks a newly-established marina. Tourist amenities are extending to every dimension. Turkish coffee attended by crème de menthe is an unexpected pleasure; in such a rough house one expects at best a glass of tea. Is it on the house? I forget to note the bill save that it is 2,000 Turkish lira (£6), a quite substantial charge for no wine or Western facilities; presumably the crème de menthe was booked.

'They are Philistines in Finike; they grow oranges and tomatoes.' This harsh indictment from friends in Istanbul prompts us to drive straight on to Myra. The valleys are certainly swamped with tomato houses swathed in polythene. From the hills they resemble so many landing strips. At Myra the theatre is roasting hot. A limp heap of hay takes pride of place in the arena together with a generous load of dislocated seats and fine Ionic capitals. It will take centuries to fully excavate and restore the gracious treasures of this magical court. Perhaps they are best left to crumble; an elegant ruin will sometimes convey volumes while a clumsy restoration can blur its truth and beauty. The curved seats of the theatre are furred with moss and softly-waving grasses. Orange groves, banana-trees, and tomato houses stretch for miles below. I stagger down through rocks and clumps of wild pink columbine. Handsome tombs are carved out of the rust cliff face, architectural masterpieces that have defied the elements remarkably well. A group of tanned peasant women sit chatting under an orange-tree. One breaks away and leads me purposefully to her greenhouse. She offers me a basket of cucumbers and indicates I should pay. I throw out my empty hands in mock apology; she shrugs and smiles and promptly withdraws her loot.

We drive through the evening sun and the familiar vignettes of pastoral life; old men and young boys tend sheep and goat-herds. In lush meadows the black cows graze so sleek and plump. Willow, poplar and wild olive fringe fields and rivers. Women stand bent in line as they hack the rich soil with picks; acres of lettuce stripe the red furrows brilliant green. It is dusk when we reach the Dostlar Pansiyon, 'Friends' pensione', at the coastal town of Fethiye.

May 25 Dostlar Pansiyon Fethiye

After a restless night of mosquito attacks, and cats' chorus, emerging with the lively dawn chant of cocks I enjoy the customary Turkish breakfast: black olives, hard white feta cheese, bread, honey and tea. We set off for the local 'Dead Sea': a stale plate of water hugged by rocks and rushes. I indicate to Yaşar that I would prefer to bathe from the adjoining wide cove. On a round smooth rock I scorch blissfully, eyeing with near-incredulity the blazing blue sea. The mountains tower behind, their tips swathed in mist; they look strangely menacing. I walk over the hot white sand to the foaming waves. They are higher than I imagined. In seconds I am bundled over and over and retire breathlessly to my sun-baked rock.

This evening, I bought a pretty kelim in faded corals and limes with a handsome knotted fringe. It cost me 25,000 Turkish lira (approx. £75). A piece made in Kayseri, according to my vendor, Ayşe. She and her husband, Fatin, are good friends of Rahmi; they run the best hotel in Fethiye, where the business is still young (and doubtless disorganised) compared with Marmaris or Bodrum where prices are double. Armed with this information and the kelim I repair to Dostlar Pansiyon for another adventurous night.

May 26 Marti Hotel Fethiye Marmaris

This morning I was plagued by a hysterical starling. Despite my soft entreaties and opening of windows, it swooped backwards and forwards at a hazardous level of five feet. I packed and dressed, bent double. A mesmeric cliff-road drive, where the view of sea and virgin sandy inlets made one marvel at each successive curve. Yasar rolled ahead. As usual the road was free, save for a few thundering lorries. We reached Marmaris in the late afternoon. A well-built modern town, it was re-styled in local white stone after the devastating 1958 earthquake. Avenues of stout seventy-foot palm-trees seemed to have escaped the holocaust. I called at the yacht hire agency. A personable young man who spoke impeccable English assured me that Marmaris has a sophisticated approach to tourism. To my tentative enquiries over hiring a yacht, he marched me off to the harbour nearby We boarded a couple where I noted inadequate washing facilities and narrow berths. The third looked possible; two shower closets and wider berths whetted my interest considerably. My salesman encouraged by my obvious enthusiasm waxed lyrical over the spacious sun deck, the varnished wood padded with blue linen squab cushions, and the brass rail surround that winked temptingly in the sun. We returned to his desk where I collected the pertinent information. In May or October the charge for *Tuna* would be US$150 per day; June through September $200. This included a Captain and two crew, catching of fish and cooking; between six of us it did not sound immediately prohibitive. With fond imaginings of a future trip on *Tuna* (which translates as Danube as opposed to tuna fish) we arrived at the Hotel Marti, an enormous de luxe-style hotel with the advantage of its own beach. Indeed its strategic all-encompassing position left no room for competition.

May 27 Marmaris Kuşadası

Another arresting drive cutting inland through rocky ravines and past the spectacular Gölu Bafa (Lake Bafa), the landscape was less lush and colourful than the earlier Pamphylian Coast road, but no less beguiling. Vast groves of olives brushed the hills under a hard sun. Wide stretches of cornfields with attendant donkeys undulated down to the old Ottoman town of Muğla. The quaint narrow streets were flanked by beamed old houses with brown-painted balconies, verandahs, and the typical deep eaves that lend added shade to the windows below. Shops and houses carried on the quiet rhythm of an old provincial town; metalcraft, woodcraft, weaving, sherbet booths, carpet-sellers, and eating houses merged with modern shoe-shops and pharmacies. Many sellers and buyers seemed content to sip tea, smoke, and talk under canopies of vine leaves attached to the old façades.

We pressed on to Miletos, once the principal and richest port on the Ionian coast. Its former prime position is now clogged by marshland. The occasional cypress trees gave further forlorn touches to its demise. As I wandered through the temples, hamams, and markets, I saw a fat tortoise ambling over a heap of chopped columns.

The temple at Didyma was impressive. Well-restored in the con-genial setting of a tidy village, it was perhaps less evocative than Miletos; but nobody could dispute the drama of those colossal col-umns, some ten feet in diameter. The bases were exquisitely-incised with floral and scroll motifs. The capitals were missing; in fact the whole edifice, conceived in 300 BC, was never completed through five successive centuries. On one particular massive column, which still sported a crumbled Ionic head, two herons had taken a possessive perch and the wisps from their large wings waved unceremoniously in the breeze.

We lunched in a gazino at the seaside village of Altınkum (golden sand). I suggested to Yaşar that he might prefer grilled chicken as a change from the proverbial kebab. He agreed cheerfully and then took the precaution of ordering a huge plateful of kebabs to follow. No wonder his digestion works loudly overtime. As we drove on to Priene, we saw a herd of white, silky cows preening themselves upon the sun-baked shore.

It was in 334 BC that Alexander the Great seized Priene and defrayed the cost of its completion. It commands a superb position high above the rich agricultural Meander Valley. The corn crops and poplar-groves stretch for miles to distant mountains. The Temple of Athena, sited before a towering rock mountain, was one of the most moving sites I have seen. The five fifty-foot fluted columns had retained their Ionic capitals, although their former precision had been eroded to resemble soft dough. Tumbled columns and much evidence of egg and tongue on toppled architraves were indicative of past elegance and grandeur. A forest of pines, latched on to the base of the mountain rock wall, whispered and whined in the hush of a gentle wind. It was eerie. The cry of a bird above me, the hum of a passing bee, and a sleepy cricket were reassuring. The sun blazed as I walked slowly down the steps and ramp towards the village. I saw the local men in the square far below. In the shade of pine-trees they drank tea, talked, listened, looked. I longed to linger too. I spent that night at the

Kizmet Hotel in Kuşadası[3], where in great comfort on a promontory overlooking the pretty bay I ate and slept to the full.

The final days of my journey with Yaşar passed in a familiar kaleidoscope of rich, beautiful country, heightened by the stunning ruins of Ephesus and Bergama. At Izmir with its grand long façade, flanked by harbours and vast squares, we called on his sister and brother-in-law. In their dark little house in the old back-streets they gave us tea with hot sesame bread rings and feta cheese. Their ten-year-old boy proudly showed me his English book. Today English is the first language taught in schools and German the second. At Bursa, where the peaches are the finest in Turkey, I stayed at the Çelik Palas Hotel, a 1930 landmark, where Atatürk once frequented the resident hot mineral bath. Finding my way to the famous marble sanctuary, I gingerly joined a half-dozen hefty Turkish men, lazing in the steaming water. Circular and vast with a high-domed ceiling, it was a soothing resting place after days of travel. A friendly young man sidled up to me in the water; he assured me I had come at the right time. Some ninety people had passed through the same water that morning!

July 10 Folly Farm Hungerford Wiltshire

The powerful revving of an open nine-seater Rolls-Royce (vintage 1926) grated over the cornfields. An old sports car and a handsome Ferrari took up the clangour, the cherished toys of the Hon. Patrick Lindsay, Christie's Old Master specialist. His Spitfire, his Puss Moth, and his single-seater acrobatic stood by to perform above the strawberry luncheon. Ecstatic sun and heat with wine and beer and coca-cola flooded from makeshift bars in the cool barns. Tables, chairs, and rugs nudged for space and shade on the lawns; an intimate garden of 'salons' caught behind yew hedges and hooped rose bowers, an enchanted garden laced with roses that rambled, trailed, clambered and cascaded over bush and branch and hedge. Patrick's wife, Lady Amabel, is as talented a gardener as she is an interior designer. Cool in white, with long brown legs, sipping champagne, the perfect hostess who, having set her stage, enjoys the show as would her most carefree guest. She had plunged each urn, tub, trough, and vase with stunning colour.

The Christie's Summer Sports Day, an event without precedence, or indeed precedent. Cricket, tennis, bowls, and snooker. The heat-wave drove many into the pool while an Italian ice-cream van was parked

[3] Kuşadası means Island of the Birds.

strategically alongside the improvised cricket pitch. A picnic of chicken legs, scotch eggs, strawberries, chocolate cake and ice cream was enlivened by Patrick looping and swooping in his spitfire above. No sooner had he landed than another daring fellow stalled and twisted in paroxysms of fearful magic. This spectacular rush of noise goaded Lord Fermoy from the marching estate to telephone his marked disapproval; he was in despair over his sheep's comfort and peace of mind. Meanwhile swollen bodies briefly caught in bikinis lay strewn in hot heaps; some teetered to the barn bars where they encountered equally bare clerks and porters. More car rides for all. Patrick, his grey wavy hair flying from his vivid yellow t-shirt, led a final trail around the fields. What a party! We walked away bare-foot through long grass. How cool it felt as toes threaded through the strands.

July 29 Renishaw Hall Derbyshire

A bent elbow was silhouetted against a far window of the hall. Was somebody there? Again we pushed the front-door bell. Our host, Reresby Sitwell, bustled out to meet us, all cigar and confusion. Had we been waiting long? His torso was tightly bandaged in a pale blue denim jacket. We entered the cool hall. The elbow now confronted us in the form of one of a pair of eighteenth-century wooden soldiers – a laughing soldier and a frowning soldier, commented Reresby; he had adorned the latter with a pair of rimless spectacles. He felt his soldiers were of Venetian or even Polish origin as no other eighteenth-century Europeans wore moustaches. Could they be Turkish? Reresby thought not, although it was the time that Turks always wore moustaches. We moved through the dark hall of Renishaw cluttered with gleaming black oak and dramatic moonlit paintings of Venice and Renishaw by John Piper. Settles, dressers, elaborate carved screens, benches and tables and cushioned sofas created a haven of quiet crannies in which to read and browse.

The north façade of Renishaw with its Gothic-style roof crenellations could be described as grim and austere. The walls of soot-stained and eroded limestone – legacies of the surrounding coal belt – speak of centuries daunted by dirt and weather. The ghost wing (comprising a concealed dark passage running the length of the ballroom) manifests itself in a row of blank glass windows. Tales of ghosts abound, particular of 'the Boy in Pink', Henry Sacheverell. He died young and apparently compensates for his lost manhood with his habit of 'kissing' the ladies goodnight. Moura Lympany was a recent target and reported his kiss to be a wet one.

Staying at Renishaw over a summer weekend is sheer languorous pleasure. Cool rooms burgeon from the seventeenth-century central plan. The eighteenth-century high-ceilinged ballroom, billiard room and dining-room are crowded with beautiful things and laced with comfort. The eighteenth-century Elizabethan-cum-Italianate-style gardens are lined and quartered with sturdy, clipped yew hedges and imposing pyramids. The water garden, the statuary, the terraced lawns and fountains, the ancient lime avenue, awash with daffodils in spring-time, the rose walks, and the lake beyond invite every conceivable reverie and dalliance. Reresby's fabled vineyard, the most northerly vineyard in Europe, is a further distraction. We strolled round the prized two acres and strained to see the grapes. They were pinheads. Reresby confessed that he had not enjoyed good harvests in recent years. In 1976, the summer of the drought, he had produced 900 bottles, last year nine only. I suggested his fortunes could be compared to a good or bad year at Lloyds.

The weekend passed in the happy diversions of walks and talks, resting and reading, punctuated by meals in the elegant dining-room. We were a party of twelve including the delectable Lady Deirdre Grantley in a pastel kimono nipped with wide taffeta sashes, a denim skirt, or a pink cotton dress with puffed sleeves; she looked uncommonly innocent and beautiful as the virgin dawn. Johnny Grantley looked tired and smoked his Silk Cuts mild. I sat with him in the back of the car as the four of us snatched a quick trip to Chatsworth. Deirdre Grantley had never been before. After a rewarding and eye-boggling hour, we returned to the car. Deirdre was in dire need of tea. Johnny urged her to find a table at the Cavendish Arms at Bakewell, saying, 'If I go in, they don't want to know.' Although Johnny Grantley was no exceptional beauty, I felt that he underestimated himself most painfully.

Back at Renishaw, our striking, dark-haired hostess, Penelope, was manoeuvring her guests, her slim staff, and Reresby in the right directions at the right time. Reresby was not always amenable to punctual meals or interceptions. He might be engrossed in concocting a last-minute cup of vineyard wine or expounding on some ancestral lore or producing the tiniest pair of chamois gloves magically contained in a walnut shell. Hoisting his flag each day (yellow lions on a green field and *Ne cede malis*) was a lengthy process for which he actually allowed time. I don't ever remember him being retrieved from the rooftops. 'I'm coming, old thing.' Just so would he airily call to his beautiful Penelope. And she, supreme and organised, set the pace, informal ('DIY' service, she called it). The kitchen for breakfast, but a black tie for dinner.

Walking the many rooms I conjured up that other ghost, Dame Edith Sitwell, Reresby's aunt. I imagined her an unhappy lonely girl, too tall for comfort with a long nose, unloved by her mother. A childhood touched in coldness with the rough wild winds and rains of this northern country adding to the gloom. Such bleakness may have proved as conducive to her creative instincts as it had proved to the Brontës.

From beside our high capacious bed I picked up an edition of Dame Edith's *Collected Poems*. In the preface she comments: 'My poems are hymns of praise to the glory of life.' I copied a few lines:

> The cold wind creaking in my blood . . .
> In the cold wind, towers grind around
> Through avenues of lime-trees
> Where the wind sounds like a
> Châpeau Chinois, shrill, unkind . . .

(The Gothic-style wooden weather-cock towers perched on the roof of Renishaw: the 200-year-old lime avenue: the wind howling through the nursery wing as the dressing-up box was upturned for a Chinese cap. How well we see Renishaw reflected.) Then, after the wind, the rain:

> Still falls the rain
> Dark as the world of man,
> Black as our loss . . .
> The mauve summer rain
> Is falling again
> It soaks through the eaves
> And the ladies' sleeves
> It soaks through the leaves . . .

Dame Edith also observes in her preface: 'I was always a little outside life . . .'

To her the unknown was more real. With her courage and her highly-tuned imagination she dared to throw herself over that abstract edge.

August 20 Ochr-y-Fforest Llandovery Dyfed

'My poor old table! It will get ants,' whereupon Lady Aberdare rushed to the kitchen cupboard for her Hoover extension and thrust the nozzle at the offending sugar. Inadvertently I had spilled a spoonful between the joints of the two massive oak planks that joined her handsome dining-table. Sarah Aberdare is particular around the home; with no help save a cleaning woman once a week and with relays of visiting friends and grandchildren, her zealous attention to dirty detail is understandable. Guests soon become indoctrinated to house rules: no dirty feet through the front door; no sitting in wet clothes on the pale chintz covers; mats under every drink; a place for everything and everything in its place. After dead-heading the roses with her secateurs, I felt uncomfortable leaving them inside the back-door. Sure enough they belonged inside the front.

Sebastian and I spent two days with Morys and Sarah and their son Charlie. From their charming stone farmhouse embedded half-way up a Pembrokeshire valley, the view is an untrammelled panorama of rounded peaks and moorland sloping to hedge-hemmed cornfields, tree clumps, white-washed cottages and farmsteads. Sheep and black Welsh cows dotted the pockets of green, only the menacing dark patches of fir-trees, commandeered by the Forestry Commission, were at variance with the pastoral harmony.

We brought rain with our arrival; Morys was ecstatic, the first they had seen for a month. What thoughtful guests. We walked up the hill for the sheer pleasure of breathing it and seeing the fields take colour again. Sarah produced delicious, elegantly-prepared meals, and to my embarrassment, on discovering my birthday, she smuggled in a chocolate iced cake from a neighbouring farmer's wife.

Morys soon lost his rain and the Red Admirals again petted the deep mauve buddleia and Sarah's four-year-old garden was drenched in scent, old-fashioned roses, pale pink, deep pink and white, and clumps of purple lavender, a pastel garden, with two central urns festooned in white geraniums, stylishly silhouetted against the green valley below. 'Take care of the plants underfoot, darling. I do believe you have an amaryllis between your legs.' It was impossible to concentrate on a serious job with Sarah around; better to laugh and loiter. Her flair and zest combine in infectious repartee.

Sebastian had his own fill of entertainment. Charlie had resurrected his huge Hornby train set in the old barn, complete with a newly-hand-painted landscape. Sebastian sat watching for hours as Charlie manipulated the intricate controls. This was better than walking those steep hills. Charlie's taste for milk and lemonade also matched Sebastian's and, when his hero's rugger shorts came out pink in the wash, that was magic too.

That Wales was on the way to Cornwall, our next destination, was arguable. A mist hovered over the River Usk as we set off early, for St Ives. An uneventful journey of hot sun and a salad in Launceston, followed by a large slice of Bodmin Moor. It succeeded in looking remarkably bleak on a summer's day, and there, Jamaica Inn, as immortalised by Daphne du Maurier, glowered in grey granite by the roadside. 'Pony Trekking' swung alongside. We stopped to make enquiries and to peer inside these ominous precincts. A plump, red-haired young man with a beard and a rakish hat was doubled up behind the bar; he appeared to be hurling empty bottles upon more empty bottles. No, there had not been pony trekking for these last three years past. 'Them was an old sign them was.' A summary glance at the dining-room, the Smugglers' Bar, and the scruffy garden, and we left rapidly. The dark-latticed windows with their black frames frowned after our hurried departure.

In contrast the Tregenna Castle at St Ives spelt porters, chambermaids, clean light rooms, televisions with the ultimate luxury of bed switches, clean sheets daily, dinner accompanied by a pianist, voluptuous pudding trolleys, advice on numerous coastal walks and picnics to order. The bi-weekly coachloads of Americans and Australians did little to dispel this convivial comfort.

We rode each morning from stables meticulously run by a pair of middle-aged spinsters. Horses and ponies were vigorously rubbed and polished by a team of well-built young girls, while little girls hung eagerly in the wings for any menial task that fell their way. The stableyard was thickly bedded in sand and assiduously raked each morning. Hanging baskets of lobelia, petunias and geraniums hung from the spinsters' adjacent white-washed cottage.

Over National Trust hills fern-clad with disconcerting slabs of granite, it was the rolling views of distant sea and farmland that proved preferable to the going. But with much opening and laborious shutting of gates by our groom, Nicola, we picked our canters through private woods and fields. In between bursts of action Nicola disclosed that her parents owned the Cottage Hotel at Carbis Bay. It was a misnomer by the sound of the packed programme afoot. 'My parents have 200 for a wedding reception today and then a big private dinner for 100.' As the wedding party was not arriving until 3 o'clock, it seemed a hectic schedule. Nicola confessed she was glad to be out of the way with dressage. 'Mind you,' she added cheerfully, 'my father was a farmer before we took on hotel work. He's used to everything happening at once.'

The days sped by with so much to see and do and find. We climbed the steep cliff to the twelfth-century castle of St Michael's Mount, where the vast refectory table gleamed like glass. 'Just bees-wax and elbow grease,' insisted the sturdy woman guide. 'Yes! We walk up and down to the Castle each day, the family also.' She lowered her voice confidentially. 'The family sometimes use a Land Rover tucked away in the side of the hill.' The present Lord St Levan succeeds 300 years of family ownership of the Castle. We didn't brush against him or his wife. Their portraits in a narrow gallery denoted a good-looking, serious couple set against rugged backdrops of sea and cliff.

Our evening at the Minack Theatre by Land's End proved a memorable outing. Built in 1952 on ancient Graeco/Roman lines this stone amphitheatre soars from the cliff face high above the sea. We went to a performance of *The Magic Flute* by the London-based Beaufort Opera Group. The waves kept muted time below to Mozart's masonic beat. The soprano Queen of the Night fluffed her high notes dismally, poor girl, as the heavens and gravity waged war in her pretty throat. The orchestra, complete with black tie, wafted her through her trouble most skilfully. The audience subsisted happily on hot soup, digestive biscuits, and Mars Bars with rugs and cushions as further aids to warmth and comfort. One woman, vast in white, swayed to her seat further laden with wicker baskets. Her husband (diminutive, dark, bearded, a reincarnation of D H Lawrence) clutched more baskets as he followed in her billowing wake. A cluster of daughters were weighted down with rugs and shawls. Pottery bowls were next handed round and were studiously filled from more pottery bowls. Potato salad? Yoghurt? Cucumber? Brown bread was cut. But it was the large chocolate cake in the cardboard box that served the final indictment of home-cooking. Husband and daughters fell on it with undisguised relief.

Back at St Ives it was the bright yellow local train that took Sebastian's fancy. Licking Cornish maple ice creams, we established from the platform board that its run was short and sweet. We leapt aboard as empty carriages escorted us with toots and jolts. Looping round estuaries, cliffs, and beaches, we reached our destination, St Erth, a brief expectant pause, when we about-turned, even more depleted, to St Ives, past the cottage platforms where palm-trees waved possessive fronds over a profusion of scarlet fuchsias, purple buddleias, and dashing flame crocuses. The next day we read in the *Sunday Times*, 'The slow train to yesterday'; Sebastian's train at St Ives was further described as 'the most romantic little branch line in the West', and threatened with closure. Our trip was timely.

Each evening on the cobbled quays the whelks and crabs and cockles did a rollicking trade and the mackerel catch was hauled into crates. The fudge shop, granite-walled and smelling ready to melt, sold peppermint fudge, ginger, chocolate, coffee, and rum and raisin. The ubiquitous congestion of ugly limbs, voices, litter, amusement arcades, fast foods and ice-cream floats cannot endanger the essential magic of St Ives. The artists, Whistler and Sickert, heralded a trail of painters to this sleepy fishing town, its unique, clear light initially attracting them and continuing with such notables as Ben Nicholson and Dame Barbara Hepworth. They nurtured their 1940 modernist movement at St Ives (and also triplets, but their relationship foundered).

One hot afternoon, having lunched in a seafood inn above a cobbled side-street, where white-washed houses daubed with gull's mess had slate roofs daubed gold with lichen, we tramped up the curling lane to Dame Barbara Hepworth's Sculpture Museum. Opening time was at 2 o'clock. We were too early; the sun was too hot. Armed with yet another packet of irresistible Cornish fudge, we rested it in the shade of the Dame's doorstep and took up waiting positions from another. A Tate Gallery representative soon returned from her lunch. 'Yes, we might leave the fudge on the doorstep, but she could not let us in just yet.' Finally we were let in, five minutes early. A charmingly-conceived museum, the original small home and garden of the sculptress, surrounded by tall, rustling trees of palm and pine and clumped bamboo, where spheres and torsoes of bronze loomed, variously polished or unpolished. Outside the gulls cried, the church bell rang, and the softly persistent dove sang, while the sun splashed grass and forms. Sebastian was not inspired with this play of ghoulish effigies and intimated that we move on. A seal sanctuary, a bird's paradise, the 'Land's End Experience', and the intimate disclosure by the headwaiter that Sir Michael Sieff (with the three blondes) liked ice in his rooms each evening for a glass of St Michael's sherry, brought our Cornish dalliance to a close.

September 16 Hardwicke House

Beverley looked as frail as old porcelain this Wednesday afternoon. I took him a small pineapple. He felt like fruit, he assured me, and would dear Cyril bring him tomato juice tomorrow? He was drowsy with drugs, content and comfortable. A recent fall on his eighty-fifth birthday had engendered this final brief stay at Kingston Hospital. I sensed he was dying fast. How could his scant, debilitated frame combat the force of drugs? 'The nurses keep injecting me,' he mused. (The medical profession studiously evade the euthanasia issue, though they practise it already.) I left Beverley dozing. His face was flushed. He gave a small convulsive swallow. I made a silent farewell.

On my way home to Ham Common, I called at Sudbrook Cottage. Cyril was at home. Yes, he knew about the tomato juice. How did I find Beverley today? He could go at any moment, I blurted out. But then, I added hastily, I was a natural pessimist. Cyril looked dashed;

subconsciously I wanted to prepare him. Handsome and carrying his own seventy-five years well he muttered darkly, 'I have a pair of strong shoulders. Who knows? There may be better news when you get back from France.' We smoked a cigarette in the shadowy drawing-room. The faded colours drained grey in the dwindling evening light. Beverley's grand piano loomed shut and silent. I remembered a fleeting time when he sat with me as I played Chopin's Nocturne No 1.

'You must practise those bars again, they are like a toppled tiara!' And through the little door to the garden such vistas of colour with secrets beyond. 'Do look at this myrtle, it buzzes with blossom.'

Beverley was an incorrigible enthusiast. Acclaimed at Oxford in 1923, his meteoric literary career promptly enthroned him as President of the Oxford Union Debating Society. His autobiography *Prelude* had proved a fat trophy under his slim belt. He also wore suede shoes. Beverley sustained a full life of writing while lovingly tending his many interests and talents. If he never became the great literary figure that his youthful peers had predicted, he was essentially a human one. His friends, his gardens, his music, and his cats made demands, which he faithfully cherished. Yesterday he died.

September 18 The Golf Hotel St Cyprien France

St Cyprien Plage, the most southerly Mediterranean stretch of golden sand in France. Here I luxuriated in the tail of the hot September sun. An *hors de saison* peace hung over the beach with its handful of bright umbrellas, a solitary windsurfer with the waves to himself and his red and yellow sail, and a dog or two. The sea was warm and cobalt. Tom preferred the challenge of the golf course. He played with the young black professional, newly hailed from Senegal, whose crinkly hair came in handy for lodging his tees.

At Collioure, a little harbour further south, we dined at La Balette, a charming al fresco terrace, which overlooked the medieval castle that flanked the sea wall below. The sinking sun, the soft lights of the town, with stars and moon in swift pursuit, made an entrancing tableau for our dinner. The restaurant L'Olivier at Béziers, a small inland town, rose up to expectations. 'Here, I have 2 stars in the Michelin, if I become a 3 star restaurant I would not change my style or seating numbers. Forty-two is my limit.' We assured the manager that small is beautiful and bemoaned the late lost star of Le Père Bise (Talloires, Lac d'Annecy). They became bigger? Folie de grandeur? 'Oui, oui, madame. It became too big and Mme Bise added bedrooms.' In his neat and comfortable restaurant where every table boasted a cache-pot of fresh bright flowers, we ate a memorable meal. Tom's salmon en papillote, recumbent in a tent of silver foil, boasted a slice of goose liver alongside, an incongruous combination and apparently delicious. My own sweetbreads and mushrooms glazed in a rich brown sauce were excellent.

We drove on to Carcassonne, a medieval fortressed gem perched on a hill. Vineyards spread for miles at its feet. A beautifully-preserved little town with cobbled streets and beamed houses, shops and a central square for that welcome beer or citron pressé. Tom urged a visit to the Musée des Beaux Arts in the main town below. We were not disappointed. The chef d'oeuvres were an exquisite Chardin still-life of fruits and faïence pottery: badly cleaned in parts, but the faïence had remained astonishingly luminous. The curator informed us that there were no exhibits on the ground floor. As the large stone hallway was blatantly usurped by bicycling young boys, we were not surprised.

From the foothills of these Pyrenees we planned a trip to Andorra, the small principality on the French and Spanish border. A distant cousin, Ian Craig, to whom Tom is a trustee, was the main raison d'être for this ambitious detour. We were also curious to see this city perched 7,000 feet in mountainous anonymity. Ian Craig was delighted to accept our invitation, proffered a few days previously. His wife (French and difficult from various accounts) would not join us, she had to feed the animals. It was also clear that we were not welcome *chez eux*. He suggested we meet at Le Roc Blanc hotel at 12.30 p.m.

September 22

We made an early start. Vineyards gave way to peach- and apple-trees as we circumvented hills and mountains. We had expected colder weather but the height seemed to add intensity to the hot sun. We were waved through the border with no ceremony. The scenery was not remarkable: soaring mountains smothered in fir-trees with herds of cows clinging to grass clearings. Beside the road their hides for sale flapped in the wind. The road dropped 1,000 feet to the city of Andorra; we were surprised, having imagined it perched high on a mountain plateau with spectacular views. We were also disappointed; the hemmed-in sprawl in the valley was devoid of taste or distinction. The majority of houses smacked of post-war monotony and an unhappy alliance of mediocre present-day.

Having established Le Roc Blanc we waited in the sun over a bottle of wine. By 1.15 our elusive guest had still not appeared. Tom telephoned his house. Indeed the wretched Ian had waited at the hotel from 11.30 until 12.15 and then had returned home. Tom feigned surprise that he could consider lunching at 11.30 a.m. How sad. No, we couldn't invite him to dinner; we were on our way to Sauveterre de Comminges in Gascony. It was a strange rebuff. We suspected the French wife had engineered his curious behaviour. A quick lunch at Le Roc Blanc was redeemed by an excellent wine. Our first choice, a Chablis, was maderised. Bottled in 1974 it had turned sour with age. The wine waiter returned hastily with a choice of red. Tom chose a Moulin à Vent 1976, bottled by the renowned Alexis Lichine. It was full and fruity and cost a modest £4. In London it would fetch £25.

September 24 Les Sept Molles Sauveterre de Comminges

Superb country set in a lush green bowl of rich farmland, vineyards and wooded hills. Soft bells tinkled as cows meandered deep in grass and daisies; old women in straw boaters drove them along the lanes to be milked. Sheep were another picturesque hazard to the motorist. Apples and pears and maize were golden and beamed barns had lofts stuffed with hay. Only the piles of neatly-stacked logs in farmyards gave a hint of cold to come. Barbazan, Luchon, Valcabrière, local villages with names that tempt a visit. The old façades of crumbling yellow stone, the curved terracotta roofs, and everywhere flowers, dripping over doors and balconies, breathed peace and time arrested. The medieval stone church at Valcabrière had a distinctly Tuscan flavour with its solitary tall tower and its shelter of cypress trees. At St Bertrand de Comminges we wandered up the quaint old streets and were reminded of Carcassonne in miniature.

One day we drove to Lourdes. Despite the crowds and commercial trinkets lining every route to the shrine, it was a moving and memorable scene. Immaculate nurses and nuns handled the sick as they made their slow pilgrimage to the grotto. Those in wheel-chairs were pushed by young volunteers. Music was everywhere, relayed from the Gothic-style church, as priests and congregations joined in hymns and responses. Old and young filed past the Madonna perched high on a ledge in the rock grotto. The four-foot candles that I had seen so many carry (and at first imagined them white sticks for the blind) blazed below. A few hundred yards away the River Gave flowed swiftly by and vast wooded hills climbed to the Pyrenees. Due to fourteen-year-old Bernadette, a local country girl, and her visions of the Virgin, nations have trooped to her grotto for a hundred years or more.

Back at our comfortable hotel where the decorations were adventurous more than elegant (a propensity to mix purple and orange was popular), we indulged in excellent specialities. The young chef, who was sometimes seen naked to the waist on some hurried visit to the garden – perhaps to collect a vital herb – regaled us with moules au saffron and his own brand of charcuterie and pâté. His wife took the orders in the dining-room with charm and efficiency. She also did the marketing and took care to keep her little daughter quiet and happy, a daunting exercise. As for the chef's mother, who sat at the desk, she liked to be in charge. When the heat became too much she re-arranged her fat little body on a comfortable sofa by the doorway. She occasionally hung out the bath towels in a corner of the garden beside the duck pond and would take her Yorkshire terrier. Whenever he shot after the geese and ducks she yelled at him with gusto.

September 26 Eugénie-les-Bains Landes Sauveterre

We made a leisurely start from Sauveterre and lunched at the restaurant Pierre in Pau, an elegant town with an unbeatable panorama of the Pyrenees, a town once favoured by Queen Victoria and a host of English. The mountains, the air, and the thermal water cures were then a popular draw. We drank our bottle of Pétrus 1975 with the happy conviction we were downing gold. An exclusive vineyard of Pomerol, it is also a very small one. The wine breathed in the glass becoming fruitier through the meal. Tom doubted if any restaurant in London would have a bottle of Petrus.

At Eugénie-Les-Bains that redoubtable restaurant/hotel where the chef, Michel Guérard, famed for his imaginative cuisine minceur, had established a stage par excellence. Together with his equally redoubtable wife, Christine (whose dowry consisted of several spa hotels), the quintessence of the hotel was its cuisine. The luxurious thermal treatments, bedrooms, interior decorations, pool and flowered park served as enchanting props to this main performance. Funnily enough, having made his name with cuisine minceur, Guérard did little to encourage his guests to sample it. It was, for example, necessary to give twelve hours' notice of your intention to order and to eat at twelve noon. Tom elected to play golf at Pau on the day I had chosen for the 'minceur' experience. As he sat over lobster and a view of the Pyrenees, I also settled for a lobster salad, a minuscule plate of six teaspoons of lobster, three lettuce leaves, a few threads of beans, carrots, tomato and celeriac, and a dab of pink mayonnaise. *Veau en habit vert* was swiftly brought to follow. The waiters were anxious to get us slimmers out of the way before the rush of the standard gourmand

lunch, another reason for Guérard's curious back-pedalling on his
minceur menu. Inserted between the veal and its coat of one spinach
leaf lurked a mirepoix of carrots, onion and tomato, an obliging pool
of thin white celery purée masked the plate. All minceur meals ended
with a pudding and we were not spared. A pineapple sorbet, exquisitely
piped, was piled into the handsome halves of fruit. The creamy froth
was pierced by a surprise trough of raspberries. It had been a satisfying,
pretty meal, but only led to a greater appetite for dinner. Ah! Those
dinners. Perhaps *Les trois salades simples impromptus* were the greatest
deception, with its avocado wrapped in smoked salmon, foie gras
nestling with smoked eel and slivers of quail, and where cress and
carrot struggled to be seen. *Les Ravioles de truffe à la crème de mousserons*
could also sound misleading; the paper-thin crêpes were stuffed with
truffles and rested in a sea of deliciously-flavoured cream and mushrooms. Each dish was presented with a flourish as the young waiters
whisked off the silver tureens, and each dish was distinctly seasoned
with fresh herbs. In a corner of the park was a meticulously-labelled
herb garden of *thyme, menthe, estragon, marjolaine, cerfeuil, ciboulette*, and
verveine. An old gardener kept it trim and green and clipped the
box-hedge surrounds.

Madame Guérard passed through the dining-room one night. She
wore a loose white dress and her long dark hair hung straight behind.
She had an inordinate love of things 'white': carpets, walls, curtains,
chairs, flowers, sun umbrellas, wicker chairs (in one she had sat a black
dummy). Huge rush-woven log baskets in the drawing-room were
painted white to great effect and planted with palms and vivid bright
banana leaves. Three weeks before, she had given birth to her first
child, Eléonore. 'Madame worked in her office the day before and
was returned again after a week. Birth is no problem,' concluded the
young girl who massaged me (a gentle procedure under warm spurts
of thermal water). No cream. No soap. The water had a remarkably
soft and silky property. Did she believe in these thermal treatments?
As she pinched and slapped and rubbed, my friend tossed her wet
head. *Enfin, Madame, pour moi ce n'est pas grand' chose! Tout ce vapeur et
cet eau me fait gonfler.'* She pinched her plump young thighs with a
rueful sigh.

The garden boy was sweeping up the crisp yellow chestnut leaves
as we took our leave of the white-shuttered, greige walls, where
nineteenth-century elegance mixed with sumptuous comfort, style,
and gastronomic *aventures*. At the next village, Aire sur l'Adour, we
espied a beckoning slate beside a modest shop. Freshly-made produce
and pâté prompted a timely purchase of the finest local *foie gras d'oie*
at £60. North of Bordeaux we pottered around the *premier cru* vine-

yards. The vendange was in full swing. Students from all over the world vie for the over-subscribed job of picking the grapes. They made a colourful group at Château Margaux. One tall slim girl as black as night with intricately-coiled hair lay luxuriously on a grassy bank smoking a cigarette. A young Englishman, absurd in white cotton sun-hat and hairy legs, caught in Wellingtons, was endeavouring to press his suit. The comptroller strode towards them. '*Venez, Monsieur! Soyez raisonnable un peu.*' The young man merely continued his dalliance with his beguiling heroine. The rest of the young team obligingly cut the clumps with little secateurs. They emptied their full baskets and hods into the steel tips loaded on to vans. At the wine press we watched an ingenious machine separate the stalks from each grape. It was inconceivable how so many lush acres could be hand-picked in the space of two weeks. The elegant gold stone château stood serene in waves of green. Red and yellow roses swayed in colourful rows lining the edge of each plantation.

Coquilles St Jacques at Calais perfectly concluded our idyllic passage through France. Never had we been more *bouleversé* by the sheer beauty and her ubiquitous elegance, her admirable fastidiousness and care, and that detailed presentation of all things to the best possible effect. The streets were spotless, shaded by well-clipped trees; the profusion of flowers in towns and villages was meticulously tended. No hint of vandalism or dilapidated lethargy to mar that ravishing land. Holiday glasses are naturally rose-tinted; however, even with a menacing Monsieur Mitterrand at the helm, I felt France and her innate and exclusive qualities were essentially intact. She has always made a formidable study of the art of living.

October 26 The Sheraton Hotel Dubai

Sultry black air, tinged with the whiff of oil, the temperature at midnight is 82°F. The Sheraton looms in glittering light from the bank of the creek; an explosion of triangulate architecture, the whole is louvred in white fibreglass. A palatial main marbled hall where water terraces appear to plunge down a central stairway. A row of pretty Chinese girls welcome us and waft us to our room.

October 27 Dubai

The Dutch hotel manager, John Roosemond, is gloomy about the Gulf's future. The hotels are only 25% full, a reflection on precarious politics and slackened trade. The Iran/Iraq war hits hard. Trade with India takes longer and Turkey has run out of lorries. The head of the Arabian Gulf is stuffed with mines, effectively trapping oil-carriers. Will the dire predictions of the industrial architects be indicative of whole Arabian cities being racked by financial ruin and becoming ghostly hostages to bygone fortune? Maybe, but the dazzling blue and white carpet that surrounds the pool beams with a luxurious optimism. We sip iced French wine and momentarily put aside fears. John Roosemond picks up his *Oil and Gas Journal* and leaves us to indulge in a Gulf Sea Food Platter.

We visit an art exhibition of nineteenth-century and contemporary English artists sponsored by the Royal Academy. There is a new awareness of things cultural. Noël Coward's *Hay Fever* with a cast to include Moira Lister and Patrick Cargill has arrived for a two-week showing.

The setting sun blazes across the creek as the day fades into amethyst, a space of tenderness before the black pall of night. An Arab saunters beside the water, a faint brush of white against the black hulks of tethered dhows. He raises his arm, a falcon is perched on his leather-bound wrist.

Dubai will always retain its essential charm and trading character. The notorious creek has held sway through the centuries; the pearls of yesterday may have given way to today's miscellany of beds, air-conditioners, and Rolls-Royces, but the wooden dhow is still the prime mode of transport and the old brick wind towers still nudge the urbanised shore and the seagulls still scream. The quay-side pulsates with drilling and chugging and hammering, while the boys from Bombay scrub the hulls and sing their alien shanties. Dubai hums purposefully. In the affluent, soaring edifices it is an exacting exercise to wield the rich new toys of high technology. Dubai may not always flourish but it will survive.

October 31 The Raj Hotel Bombay Indai

A depression in the Arabian Sea spells 93°F with humidity and a heavy sun. Ten lengths in the pool, a blistering sauna, a freezing hip bath, and a luxurious massage with coconut oil nicely completes an otherwise enervating morning.

We lunch with Jamshed Bhabha in the rooftop Rendez-Vous restaurant. He is General Manager of the Tata family world-wide trading emporium, an influential rich Parsee, warm, intelligent, charming and close to Mrs Gandhi's ear. Are we comfortable in the hotel? He looks anxious. There has been union trouble, Communist infiltration; the room-boys played up. 'But our main problem is that we are more and more. Bombay's population has exceeded nine million with around five million squatting on the streets. The resulting filth is appalling and worsening each year.' Our host believes the problem is exacerbated by the police; in exchange for half the beggars' takings they allow them to stay put. The street advertisements – '*Don't give alms to those extended palms*', '*Discourage able beggars*' – would seem at variance with the law. 'We are a crooked city, corrupt through and through. And so crowded. Such noise pollution. Things have deteriorated these two years past.'

Would a fresh-water system help the country? Jamshed Bhabha looks doubtful. After all, the resulting benefits to health would swell the population. There had been a fresh-water scheme conceived by an old retired soldier; a simple theory, it would involve siphoning off the major rivers in India into a linked canal network. The even flow effected would avoid loss of water through spate and drought. However the machinations of such a scheme were not considered cost-effective at the time.

A phenomenal downpour interrupts the afternoon. One and a half inches bucket from the leaden sky in one and a half hours. The squatters scuttle under lorries and sling tarpaulins over their meagre shanty roofs, others squeeze snugly into sections of jumbo drainpipes scattered conveniently beside the road. Roads flood and gutters gurgle furiously, spewing silt and garbage. We sit steaming in a traffic jam and Tom sees a rat. (There are an estimated 900,000 in the city.)

November 3 Bombay

I join a city tour. The bus lurches through the crowded heart of the city. We are driven to the original fishing village of Bombay straggling along the shore, a scene of intense activity – cleaning of boats and mending of nets. An excruciating stench from fish hung to dry in the sun and salt air pervades. The provenance of the notorious Bombay Duck, which arrives on the plate a shrivelled, tough, pungent little carcass, is considered by many a delicacy. Further along the old shore road the banks are draped with sheets and unfurled turbans; shirts and towels billow in the wind: the local laundry department. Dhobis charge one half-rupee for each garment and call once a week. Heavily-soiled items are slapped on stones in the sea; our guide persuades us that the stones wear out faster than the clothes. It sounds a remarkably well-run service.

We veer round to the central city and are let loose in the Prince of Wales Museum. A comprehensive show of Indian miniatures – amber, jade, porcelain, glass and archaeological treasures – is well-displayed on three floors. A stylish late-nineteenth-century building with a hand-some dome has been heavily endowed by the collections of the Tata family, the Parsee philanthropists par excellence.

Our next port of call is Gandhi's tomb sited on a hill. In the rush to get back to the bus for the Jain temple, our next tryst, I fail to find the inner precincts of the tomb.

The heat and dust mount with midday as the bus lumbers up a steep hill to the temple. A large sign by the arched marble door reads: 'Women with monthly periods are forbidden to enter.' Impurities are not tolerated in the Jain religion. Neither is leather. We discard our shoes, but defiantly clutch handbags. Pigeons flutter blithely through the arches and perch on balustrades and galleries. A venomous-looking old man clangs a bell to ward off evil spirits. Strange offerings are scattered on silver tombs, a handful of rice, a sugar lump, two plastic necklaces. Plastic flowers, dead flowers, the sickly wafts of incense, the baleful Buddhas with glass eyes are everywhere. '*C'est trop chargé,*' exclaims a French woman and plaintively goes in search of her shoes. Outside on the pavement, a baby is having a bath in a red plastic pail.

Bounding along streets with alternate whiffs of sea, sewage, and sandalwood, we are unceremoniously disgorged at the Hanging Gardens. Our young guide explains the origin of their existence. 'The Parsee race leave their dead to the vultures. Do you see them circling above that tower, the Tower of Silence?' We dutifully follow her gaze. 'Many years ago this garden where we stand did not exist. Here instead we had the main reservoir of Bombay. Its position posed a problem; the vultures would fly over, dropping portions of flesh from their beaks. The people complained.' The people's reaction to such appal-ling water pollution sounded remarkably long-suffering. Patience was finally rewarded by a rich Parsee who 'hung' the present garden over the municipal reservoir.

November 4 Bombay

The Indian Goverment considers changing the financial year from April 1 to Diwali. This makes sense. Diwali is the Festival of Lights when the Goddess of Wealth (Lakshmi) is worshipped and when office safes, account books and business deals are blessed. These past three days have rocked to ear-splitting fire-crackers and frenzied street activity. Shops and garages groan under garlands of marigolds and fairy lights. Sweet-stalls multiply over-night, sweets and cakes are the traditional gifts at Diwali. It is essentially a time for the family to come together.

'Diwali symbolises the illumination that dispels the darkness of ignorance, and brings in knowledge, wisdom and prosperity.' It is an obvious starting date for new financial ventures.

November 5 Bombay

We lunch with Mrs Silloo Mody at the exclusive Willingdon Golf Club, nicknamed by all discerning members as the 'WC'. An imposing Victorian edifice isolated in wooded green acres, it is appropriately stuffed with Burma teak furniture and faded chintz. Comfortable cane chairs are drawn up and grouped along the wide verandas; here the breeze cools on marble floors and tickles the generous pots of fern. It all looks very agreeable, but according to our hostess there has been trouble – 'bearer' trouble. Communist unions were inciting strikes for wage rises. 'For a month we members manned the whole club ourselves.' She leads us upstairs to the dining-room, a wide, ugly extension. We are to join her friend, 'Parsee like myself, from a very good family. They all had bungalows.' This statement could denote a contradiction of terms unless one appreciates that the Indian bungalow can rival an embassy for size.

Silloo's friend is very charming, anglophile and nondescript. She has no more bungalows. The conversation is lively, led predominantly by Silloo's wrath over Mrs Gandhi's weaknesses, the corruption of the police, Bombay's filth, the tax inspectors, and the scandal of extortionate practices in the building fraternity.

'Such greedy men! They bring in cheap labour from the countryside and pay them five rupees a day. These boys find ten rupees down the road and more are pulled in from the country again. The population in Bombay swells daily with such greedy manoeuvres. It will be another plague that eases our number.'

The meal concludes with prune pancakes, a Diwali delicacy served with 'gravy' (which is the Indian term for cream). Silloo is anxious to drive us through the cemetery area, the site of the 'Tower of Silence'. It is thickly-wooded and secluded, an oasis of peaceful green. As we drive through the leafy lanes leading uphill to the Sacred Tower Silloo enlightens us on the niceties of the Parsee ceremonial.

'We shroud the body in white linen. Yes, the face is uncovered and the palms of the hand are folded on the breast. There is a dog . . .' She navigates a shop corner. 'Yes, a dog . . . it can be your own dog. No, it doesn't tear at the body. It is just there to ascertain the body is dead. It is an old precaution, a ritual.' And then? 'The body is put on the top of the tower. I will choose to be cremated.'

On our return to the hotel Silloo drives us through the 'Caves' (the brothel area). The brightly-painted jolly-looking girls are a refreshing antidote to the sinister goings-on at the Parsee cemetery. But Silloo disillusions us again. The girls, some aged as young as nine, are now so indelibly diseased that even the sailors are forbidden 'access'. It may be a corrupt city but the old bad traditions die hard. We thank our hostess effusively for introducing us to her club, her cemetery and the city 'caves'. Nobody could have improved on such a diverting programme.

November 8 Delhi

I stroll down the Garden City avenues, the majestic concept of their architect, Sir Edwin Lutyens. Lines of flowering trees lead to vast landscaped roundabouts; one such is a miniature park of two acres where a fountain billows like voile and banyan trees, ashoka, and clipped yew give shade to brilliant red, yellow, and pink canna flowers. A stately white ox, tethered to the hood of a moving machine, is cajoled by two little boys to pull the unwieldy contraption. The operation succeeds while cars and scooter taxis circle this oasis of colour.

November 22 Delhi

It is pleasant to lunch at the Gymkhana Club in winter. A faint breeze rustles the ashoka trees. The sun is still hot enough to shield with shade. My host, Kuldip Narang, has selected fried fish, salad, and beer for our degustation. He talks volubly with the mind of a vital intellec-tual. As a younger man he was an economics professor at Edinburgh University. Could he foresee a revolution in India? He looks startled. 'I think India is heading for big trouble,' he admits hesitantly. 'The telephone system does not work. When essential communications break down it is the start of trouble . . .' Was Mrs Gandhi keener on Russia or America? 'Mrs Gandhi has no ideological hang-ups over either power. But she has not advanced this country or improved the lot of the poor.' I suggest she is a good housekeeper and gives his vast country a semblance of order despite no big leap forward. He agrees wanly. It is too complex a problem to lick over lunch.

We wander across the lawn to the club house, a spacious conglomeration of rooms, full of string matting, marble floors, huge rooms, empty, silent, sombre rooms with forgotten wicker chairs and tables. From the billiard-room two young men cry out to Kuldip. They entice him to play a shot. 'And now I take you to the Pundit.' I am startled. 'The Pundit? Who is this?' Kuldip is amused at my alarm. He is a wise man, a Brahmin scholar. He will tell you things, past and future things.' Lulled by beer and sunshine I am persuaded to meet the Maestro.

Kuldip sits me on the edge of an old bed in the recesses of the Pundit's dusty veranda. There is a servant with a sturdy frame and mop of grey curls. He smiles companionably. Kuldip explains to me the delay; the Pundit is taking a bath. His 'toilet' is soon completed and an emaciated figure, with a shaven head, draped in a white sheet beckons us to join him in the sunshine. A Gandhiesque figure smiles at me. He writes busily on a small pad of paper. 'Your question please?' He looks briefly at my right palm. I am unprepared.

'My son,' I call out, 'what future for our son?' He hands me the writing on the paper. 'Mother's body-aches and high fever; son's impediment will never be cured.' I am aghast. It was my Asian flu coupled with tetracycline that certainly caused Sebastian's embryonic brain damage and aphasia.

'What else? More questions.'

'And my daughter?'

Again he is writing rapidly. I read 'Art. She will have a career in art.' He is right again, but before I asked the questions he has written replies. For myself? He predicts more travel. For my husband? An ambitious career and a divorce in three years. I am horrified. Kuldip pats me on the hand. We are going. His own cousin has arrived, a smart businessman in a dark suit with a wife in a brilliant red sari. Kuldip waves to them and we take our leave of the Pundit's small veranda.

'So, you did not want to hear the bad things? Don't worry. You must not have anxiety syndromes. My cousin there, he has a big problem. He has to choose between Hong Kong and Singapore for his family and work.' How clairvoyant was that man?

November 12 Delhi

We leave New Delhi. A fresh coat of tar is rolled over the Raj Path in anticipation of the Queen of England's imminent visit. On our way to the airport we see the garden roundabouts being assiduously watered. Bright new flowers cram every bed. The Indians' sense of colour and ceremony is inseparable.

1984

David Mlinaric, the ultimate British interior designer, cradles a plastic beaker of coffee. For three days he and his team have been transforming Christie's Great Rooms into some fantastic semblance of the Kasbah – that cut-throat venue of the Moors and Arabs – perched above the ramshackle old harbour of Algiers. 'A Night at the Kasbah' as conceived by Christie's and embellished by over 500 guests in Arab or Levantine dress should prove an exotic pursuit.

Tom mentions my idea of sandalwood joss-sticks. We bought them in the East with the party in mind. Mlinaric approves. Could we *stab* them in orange halves? And have we any whining Arab music to waft up the front stairs?

With three days to go, David's team is up ladders or sprawled over Moroccan scenery. Palm-trees with trunks wonderfully gnarled by rolled newspaper are wheeled into likely positions. Carpets and tapestries are hung on walls and suspended in magic curves across ceilings. (A cadaverous Moroccan is propped on one, in a lolling position with a glass in his papier-mâché fingers.) Settings of courtyards, pavilions, and secret gardens are skilfully daubed on boards. Army camouflage netting swathes the ceiling of the ballroom. Foliage and twists of cotton in orange, purple and yellow make mats of effective colour and shade. A tunnel of greenery and camouflage netting arched over the main staircase has been disbanded; the camouflage in the guise of leaves proved dangerously inflammable. Dunking the nets in dustbins of fire-proof solution (the operation was conducted on the roof), and subsequently drying them in the boiler room, apparently proved the nets as inflammable as ever.

January 10 Christie's

The night of *A Night at the Kasbah*. The East went straight to people's heads; a sea of turbans magnified with feathers, jewels, and glitter towered above each owner's head. Many people were unrecognisable in degrees of dark make-up, beards, and moustaches, and dyed hair. The sensational head-dresses swayed and nodded up the staircase, where a green tunnel of laurel and lemons had been masterfully created., The sandalwood-scented rooms were dim-lit – as in a souk. Carpets loomed everywhere, while the painted outline of the Kasbah glowed down upon the ballroom. The floor was packed until 4 a.m. – closing time. A camel made a brief entrance. It was said that half his legs were French. A white bear chained to a shapely, half-naked woman encircled by a fat silver snake put in a longer appearance.

There were no scandals or disasters (except for one towering young man's riposte when introduced to Lord Snowdon: 'I knew what you looked like but had no idea you were so small'). The fire protection body breathed freely again and so did Tom. As Chairman of the Ball his week had been jolted with fears and contingency plans for disaster. Despite paying Mlinaric £5,000 for the decoration, the Ball raised substantial sums for the Irish Georgian Society and the National Trust for Scotland, for Chastleton[1] and for the house of Dun.[2]

February 9 Hardwicke House

Dr Roy Strong, director of the Victoria and Albert Museum, suggests that references to food and dress are sadly omitted by diarists. He has consistently emphasised the importance of daily detail and habits. How much more palatable is Pepys than the involved precepts of a lawyer or politician. Written words, like possessions, can spell excess lumber through the long passage of life. But written words with which we identify, the humorous and the mundane, live sharply through genera-tions, to startle and delight.

Last night we gave a dinner party where the men wore the custom-ary black tie. With Dr Strong in mind, I made mental notes of our female guests' sartorial accomplishments.

Denise, Lady Ebury[3] would look sheer enchantment in any old thing. Nearing seventy, with the provenance of a famously beautiful mother, she is still ravishing. Her douceur and sensibility were shrouded in a long dove-grey chiffon dress with a wide neck bordered with deep sunray pleats. She wore pearls, with her short hair swept in soft grey waves from her face.

The Viscountess Weir, an intelligent Swiss lady, excelled herself in three-quarter-length black crêpe. A wide satin sash in vivid Schiaparelli

---

[1] Chastleton House, Oxfordshire. Built 1612 and conserved in its Jacobean state, aided by one family ownership.

[2] The House of Dun, Perthshire – designed by William Adam.

[3] Denise Ebury's mother (née Jessie Smither) married three times and had ten children. Her first husband, the 3rd Lord Churston, was the father of Denise, together with her sisters, Joan Aly Khan, Lydia Bedford and Primrose Cadogan.

pink was caught in a voluptuous bow at her waist. Sleeves elegantly tapered to the wrist and her exquisite Schiaparelli pink suede shoes poised high on black patent heels. The contrast of black and pink made a smart statement. A four-strand necklace of pearls fastened low on the breast in a clasp of stones set in gold. Intriguing gold combs caught blonde hair, thick and loosely coiled.

Mrs Reresby Sitwell and Mrs Tim Rathbone had also opted for black. Mrs Sitwell sported sequinned tramlines of peacock blue and black down her bodice. She later complained that the black satin skirt of her three-quarter-length dress kept clinging to her. As she has a beautiful figure nobody complained. At her neck another enviable four-strand pearl necklace with a brooch-fastener as elegant as Lady Weir's.

Mrs Rathbone has an exquisite figure. Her long black wool crêpe skirt appeared slit revealing beautiful slim legs at intervals. An amethyst pendant hung low from a black velvet ribbon. She resisted that old temptation of teasing it with the fingers or indeed of putting it in the mouth. A black sequined butterfly masked her neat waist and diaphragm.

So there it was; the proverbial little black dress won the night. Sequins and pearls added their own perennial glamour. The claret, Cheval Blanc 1966, added a final distinction to the evening.

October 31 Istanbul

'A new, very sad link in the chain of atrocity that is staining the world in blood,' states the Pope.

Mrs Indira Gandhi was shot this morning in the garden of her New Delhi home. Two of her trusted body-guards rained bullets on her chest and stomach as she walked across a lawn to her office.

Nuri Birgi told us the news. We were talking to him on the telephone. 'Not such a bad thing,' was his bland comment, 'after all, she has killed so many herself.'

The Pope, President Sadat, Mrs Gandhi; all moderate, balanced leaders and right-wingers. Is that the motivation for these attacks? I am convinced that each single strike, act of terrorism, revolution and assassination, throughout the world, is masterminded by Russia.

At noon we heard the BBC World Service from Countess Ostrorog's eighteenth-century Bosphorus bedroom. Mrs Gandhi had died on the operating table. (And wasn't Princess Anne due to dine with her in two nights' time?)

Her son, Rajiv Gandhi, has been sworn in as Prime Minister. Aged forty and relatively inexperienced in political fields, he is described as a reluctant heir.

The Countess nursed arthritic feet; a handsome woman of seventy, she looked well in a simple white cardigan, resting her head against a bois-clair Biedermeier bed-head. Golden furniture, corn-yellow walls and ceilings, elaborately appliquéd with white-painted carving, and the Bosphorus below, made a ravishing perch for a convalescent. 'But nobody is left in Istanbul,' she moaned. 'This yali was full all day of friends.' Indeed her enchanting waterfront home was a popular retreat in summer.

A pretty maid in white knee-socks entered the room with a silver tray. An old Albanian butler hovered beside her, straightening rugs and re-arranging side-tables. We were offered white wine and kir and the pretty maid, Gül, which means rose, offered us fish canapés. I commented on Gül's poise and looks. 'She's a darling,' agreed the Countess, 'but you should stay clear of my Polish witch in the kitchen . . .' A cosmopolitan ménage, all told.

Tom and I lunched comfortably at the well-known Liman (Harbour) restaurant. The 1930 décor boasted fanciful fish tanks and gleaming metal pillars; the towers of Topkapı Palace loomed across the Golden Horn. Our 'Bosphorus catch – Liman style' and a bottle of Doluca white wine 1976 cost us £9 per head. Good traditional service.

Istanbul appears quiet and orderly. Armed soldiers are liberally planted. This national concession of overhead military surveillance under General Evren, with Turgut Özal running civic security, works well. But what chance of continuing peace under the eventual return to civil rule? But Istanbul is quiet today. And she is prosperous? Gaping holes on main street pavements, mire-spattered cars, empty houses with blackened façades dangerously supported by their decaying neighbours; is this prosperity? A dingy, wet October afternoon begs the question.

November 1 Istanbul

On Reuters' ticker-tape we read of India. Army troops are on alert throughout the country, a show of strength against city riots, with rioting in Calcutta, our next port of call. Everywhere Hindus are venting their fury on Sikhs. I tell Tom that I will not follow him to Calcutta. He feels that business gives him some magic immunity from trouble.

1985

Why has Mr Patel abandoned his delicatessen? Fiercely proud of his eight-year tenure, he had keenly lorded it over his more inconsistent neighbours, the itinerant Ugandans, Indians, and Chinese.

I saw Mrs Patel a week ago. She was smothered in fur as far as her ankles; her newly-coiffed black hair tumbled to her shoulders. She graciously inclined her heavily-laden head and body towards me, and now she is gone. They struck it rich somehow.

The pile of daily fresh croissants alongside the Eastern hodge-podge of halva and harem navels that swam in honey; and, indeed, the Ugandans next door have all disappeared in the illustrious wake of the Patels.

Who have we now? British traders! A young, efficient, clean, well-mannered (white) team of men and women. The greengrocer's shop, the former Ugandan lair, is now bright with colour and clean display, even the clementines sit proud on purple napkins. As for Mr Patel's successor, Philip, and his sumptuous cheeses: 'Yes, madam, I used to be a chef.' In his capacious green apron 'Philip' adds a certain style to the Parade. I was even more surprised when he announced to me that the birth of his third child was expected that very weekend. It is heartening to see the British at good shop-keeping once more, taking over where the East let go.

January 30 Ham Common

A quiet day, a quiet time of year. Moist, grey air, unseasonably warm at 54°F. The mud riding-tracks in Richmond Park were cratered with puddles this morning. My polo pony Princess took exception to such heavy going and trotted in stubborn protest. But again in the afternoon I felt drawn to the park. Porridge and I walked for one and a half hours. At Pen Ponds, the water was high and cleansed from the recent snow and ice. It jostled the reeds invitingly as Porridge plunged for sticks. There were few people about and they were mostly joggers, alarming young men whose powerful physique belied their belly-aching breath.

January 31, Hardwicke House

Today I lunched with Rosemary Fergusson, our doctor's wife. Their comfortable Regency house is set on Richmond Green, where the crouching cupolas of Richmond theatre are seen in the distant corner.

A natural delicacy had deterred me from asking my hostess whether the occasion was 'tête à tête' or to be graced with a wodge of women. I find lunching with undiluted women uncomfortable. ('What do you *do*?' 'Do about what?' I retaliate.)

Rosemary stood expectantly in her polished hall. We kissed briefly through wafts of steaming – osso buco? – and the fresh scent of daffodils. I noticed the dining-room had been cleared of the *National Geographics*; an embroidered froth of blue and white linen and gilded china heralded a party. We were steered to the log fire in the drawing-room and offered sherry; we comprised a genteel and gracious band of eight. A spinster regaled me with her career in historical research. She had written her book on Madame du Barry's inheritance (her jewels were stolen on the death of Louis XV's death – remember?). Another woman talked about her work with a famous Appeal Fund; another expounded on life in the Barnes Advice Bureau. Mercifully, nobody asked me 'what I did'. But when the chicken liver pâté, the spinach flan and the orange and pineapple salad were safely despatched, the lady with the nose from Twickenham fairly upset the applecart. The refusal of the Oxford dons to confer on Mrs Margaret Thatcher her time-honoured degree was the issue under fire.

'They are a lot of Marxists' – 'It was a political protest' – 'A disgrace' – 'Childish arrogance' – 'Hooligans'.

The Lady from Twickenham squealed shrilly above our indignant offerings.

'They need the money! The scientists have suffered crippling cuts! They were right to seize this platform for political ends!'

Her outburst was summarily ignored as we busied ourselves with coats and departure.

February 1 49 Belgrave Square

'The food is legendary,' muttered my friend Georgie Vassiltchikov. He steered me to the dining-table. Glistening mousses – red, saffron, rose, and green – welled out from their garnish of brilliantly-plumed birds. Wafer-thin cuts of smoked meats, fish, and poultry were flanked by tempting sauces and salads. Two pagodas of profiteroles soared over all, amply swathed in spun sugar. ('I always prefer them with chocolate sauce,' pronounced Peregrine Worsthorne.)

Some forty guests were dining at the Argentine Embassy, an imposing bow-fronted house set on the north corner of Belgrave Square. The resident chargé d'affaires, Juan Eduardo Fleming, and his tall, nymph-like wife Mathilde, are a glamorous and popular couple.

'Has Mrs Thatcher called for you yet?' Tom teases Juan Eduardo. Recently he introduced him to Lucius Falkland. And if a photographer had snapped Mathilde Fleming, 'beautiful wife of the Argentinian chargé d'affaires in tête-à-tête with Lord Falkland', at the Royal Festival Hall earlier on in the evening, it would have made provocative copy.

March 9 The Constable's Tower Dover Castle Kent

The twelfth-century Keep stamped high against the bright sky frowned down upon us. We stood below, beside the more comfortable contours of the Constable's Tower and breathed in the keen air. Brigadier Lee was whisked up the approach road and deposited at the Victorian oak door, complete in his camouflage fatigues. The khaki driver handed him papers, files, boxes, and other paraphernalia relating to the morning's business.

'Come on in – ugly, this bit – 150 years old at the most. Put them in the Queen Mother's room, would you?' Our cases were spirited up the red-carpeted stairs and Michael, honouring his finest hour as keeper of the Constable's Tower, Dover Castle, marched off to change for lunch.

A recent guest had had the misfortune to break a vase; a young girl, she had thrown her head back on the sofa, sending the wretched object skimming over the table behind. We picked our way carefully through the Queen Mother's room, spotless in pink (her favourite bedroom colour) with a pristine clutch of snowdrops on the dressing-table; there was nothing obviously breakable. In the large bathroom, I coveted a round pink tin of cucumber and roses talcum powder (Marks and Spencer). Our hostess, Jane, later told me that it replaced a crystal bowl that had been broken. One of those occupational hazards of tower life where gravity works overtime?

We had an excellent lunch in the twelfth-century dining-room. Steam from a fish pilaff rose to the vaulted ceiling; a salad of artichoke hearts and wedges of avocado was soon swept aside by hot chocolate soufflés. The army excels in domestic services. Dishes heaped with food, dirty dishes, empty glasses, and discarded trays are zealously repaired for further disorder.

The afternoon found us swaddled in mists at Walmer Castle, the neighbouring Cinque Ports stronghold at Deal, which leaves an impression of long passages and little rooms, some dark and many curiously rounded or subtracted by the Tudor Rose design of the Castle's perimeter. 'In this room Wellington died.' The guide pointed to a cadaverous wing-chair, the arms of which looked ready enough to grab another victim. 'And there lay the beautiful young Lady Curzon, racked with fever for three whole weeks.' The damp and unhealthy atmosphere of Walmer Castle is perhaps enhanced by the melancholy of its clipped ink-green Elizabethan garden, its skirt of stony shore, and the incessant sea beyond.

Back at Dover Castle, snug in the tower with tea and Victoria sponge, we heard the fog horn, as faint and persistent as a distant snore. Was it Francis Sitwell? But no, Francis was tucked up in his tweed turn-ups eating cake by the log fire. And then it was black ties for dinner, to include an opera singer, a novelist, the county sheriff, a picture-restorer and excellent wine. The bulging armoury glinted in the corners of the dining-room and we inwardly applauded Michael and Jane for entertaining so generously on the ludicrous army entertainment allowance of £5 per day.

March 13 Hardwicke House

Mr Mikhail Gorbachov (the *Daily Telegraph* persists in calling him Gorbachev) has been sworn in to lead the Kremlin. A new, young broom to sweep out the ossified cobwebs of the old guard. President Chernenko's death last week left only a shadow of public regret; he was in power for a mere year. At fifty-four Gorbachov is hailed as a bright herald of better relationships. 'I like Mr Gorbachov,' claimed Mrs Thatcher, in December, on the occasion of his London visit. She committed herself further. 'We can do business together.' He is certainly reputed to prefer butter to guns.

Described as short and stocky, he appears to have a purple dribble – a birthmark- to the right of his forehead. He prefers a trilby to the ubiquitous fur titfer and can boast a smart, fashion-orientated wife. There is already conjecture that Gorbachov – chev? – will initiate a big divide between America and Europe over nuclear policies.

April 19 Euston Hall Thetford Norfolk

We are forty-five in all, unanimously bent on soaking up the Baroque extravagancies of William Kent, that prodigious eighteenth-century builder, furnisher, and landscapist. The Norfolk seats of Euston Hall, Holkham, and Houghton promise a rare weekend of Kentian culture. Members of the Furniture History Society are we, and avid for absorption in another age.

The Duke of Grafton, owner of Euston Hall, stands upon the plinth of his sundial. Sixty-ish, piercing blue eyes, open shirt, and tennis shoes, he gives a genial address of welcome and a summary history of Euston's shrunken provenance. It had twice been burnt, leaving one extant wing of little consequence. We gaze on an ugly red brick rendition of William Kent's original designs.

Her Grace appears at the main door, good-looking and friendly, in a scarlet silk shirt that flares in the warm breeze. She leads us through the house. Shocking pink cinerarias billow from eighteenth-century wine-coolers and blazing red tulips flop wide open on polished tables. The Duke indicates his collection of Royal Stuart portraits.

'According to Sir Oliver Millar, the originals are everywhere but on these walls.' The furniture is good, solid, predominantly brown. Our expert takes care to point out Kentian swags and flourishes. The Duke asks him the date of the Japanese lacquer cabinets on stands. '1665,' volunteers the Victoria and Albert Keeper of Woodwork. 'Much later,' mutters Tom. '1780, more like. These purists don't know their furniture. They never handle it like dealers.' Our visit ends with a pilgrimage to the Kent temple. It is set above a field of cows, overlooking the seventeenth-century elegant little Euston church.

April 19 Blakeney Hotel Holt Norfolk

From our bedroom window a sombre scene of marsh, reeds, grey skies, and inanely bobbing boats. The sun is gone and the wind is risen. We eat a meal of asparagus soup (tinned and bland) and dark overcooked vegetables. One woman orders pineapple, it arrives under a mound of shaving cream when she had hoped for a dash of kirsch. Sailing masts glide past the dining-room windows in conciliatory silence.

After dinner our several experts regale us with slides and talks in a darkened convention room. It shares a gallery passage with the sauna and swimming pool complex. Scantily-draped bodies go about their business as we concentrate on ours. I nod and droop over Holkham and Houghton. Tom nudges me and hands out toothpicks; chewing on their menthol shreds keeps me awake. We spend two nights at the Blakeney. Our large room with its seaweed carpet and private bathroom, our breakfast and dinner costs a basic daily rate of £52 per person.

April 20 Holkham Hall Norfolk

Holkham Hall was built over thirty years (1734–1764). A pale-gold stone façade; impressive, stark almost, and 380 feet long. Inside the famous white marble hall with its vanishing sweep of stairs, our expert eulogises over this fabulous example of Kent's architectural exuberance. We are led through state-room upon state-room. Massively-carved door frames, white and gilded, support white marble busts in their broken pediments. Elaborate Kentian fireplaces swagged with flowers and grapes and the ubiquitous acanthus leaf raise the eye to the gilded coffered ceilings. Gilt and marble and wood combine in a uniform statement of Kentian grandeur. I find this very consistency a trifle tedious.

Lord Coke joins our party in the Brown State Bedroom. Aged forty-nine, decidedly handsome, he is said to have domestic troubles, but from the appetising wafts of chicken coming from the private apartments it is clear he is not without a cook. From the conspicuous void of fresh flowers we can assume he lacks a wife. He holds his head of thick hair erect and talks amiably to his son, a pleasant-looking youth with his father's admirable deportment, further emboldened by nicely-faded jeans.

The surrounding park with lake, barns, the monument and ilex groves, and the stylised parterres and fountain statuary are further expression of Kent's creative powers. We picnic by the Temple. Sir Nicholas Goodison (Chairman of the London Stock Exchange) looks frozen and clicks his bony knees; his sparse weft of hair is tugged awry in the wind. A clever man, he wrote a book on English barometers. Somebody mercifully lends him a coat. Our silk scarves prove useless against the bluster. The pretty Duchess of Somerset alone remains neat with her page boy hair-cut. We drink sherry and shiver companionably.

April 21 Houghton

We are greeted by the news that Lady Cholmondeley (over ninety years old) is confined to bed from a fall. Her housekeeper conveys to us her Ladyship's disappointment. (We also note no ice-cream in the house.) The minuscule housekeeper, elegant in raspberry tweed and matching wool stockings, walks with a stick. She is a mine of information and our experts are momentarily flawed by her spiel of detail and anecdote.

Houghton, built spasmodically between 1722 and 1785, is essentially a grander-styled house than Holkham. Allegorically painted ceilings abound, together with marble pilasters and arched recesses. The brass hinges on the magnificently-carved and -gilded mahogany doors are massive and gleaming, securing with screws of three-quarter-inch diameter. The housekeeper is at pains to point out a snail, two caterpillars, and a bee, minutely moulded in the recesses of an encrusted marble fireplace. (Her observation makes a change from 'tasselled swags, festoons of grapes, acanthus, etc.')

It is perhaps the sumptuous use of mahogany that especially impresses. A timely tax reduction on wood must have been a keen incentive. The door friezes and pediments are carved with the true style of Kent; the foliate scrolls, egg and dart and Greek key, are indelible eye-trainers.

The chirpy housekeeper is finally spent. We walk to our cars through grand green vistas. Two peacocks flounce their fanned tails at a white hen; she is rooted to the grass, stolidly unimpressed by such arrogant advances.

June 2 Paris

Relishing fruits de mer on a sunny corner by the Madeleine and indulging in today's copy of *The Times* (what comfort and companionship is the printed word to one who eats and drinks alone). I scan the leaders, the diary section – what's this?

'Going Batty.' 'Christie's is facing a boycott by leading London art-dealers after introducing numbered ping pong bats known as 'paddles' which bidders must wave in its King Street auction rooms to identify themselves.'

The art-dealer Hugh Leggatt comments: 'It is all so un-British, picked up from our American cousins.'

Comments Colnaghi's: 'These paddles don't exactly fit in with

Christie's refined image. They make you feel like a child with a toy. One day someone's going to get hit by one . . .'

Another of the Hon. David Bathurst's American affectations; the paddles are dispensed in the Great Room from a type of winkle bar.

July 20 Hardwicke House

David Bathurst's head has rolled, in a shameful debâcle disclosed by the New York art world.

It was in 1981 that Bathurst, then Chairman of Christie's New York, falsified the prices of two Impressionist paintings; they were in fact bought in. The untrue announcement that the Van Gogh and the Gauguin together fetched $3,400,000 (£2,554,000) incensed their Swiss owner/dealer, a Mr Jodidio. He promptly sued Christie's on grounds of inflated representation of the paintings' worth, in order to secure business. (Mr Jodidio is clearly not a man to play clever games with.)

David Bathurst subsequently contended in Court that his false figures were a tactical attempt to protect the art market generally and Mr Jodidio in particular. (Jodidio had indeed put up eight Impression-ists for sale, only one of which reached the reserve.)

This month, four years later, the case hearing was conducted in the Manhattan Supreme Court. Outrage and shame has fallen on the shaken house of Christie's New York, where our successive incumbent has had his auctioneer's licence suspended.

In today's *Times* we read: 'Christie's Chairman who lied, resigns.' And the shares are down 15%.

September 8 Le Club Cavalière Le Lavandou Côte d'Azur

Britain has had a lousy summer, the wettest, greyest offering since 1980. Persistent troughs of depression, cold fronts, north-westerly air-streams combined to obliterate sea resorts and sodden herbaceous borders. Despite the added doldrums of unemployment and the habitual disen-chantment with a mid-term government the British beat it abroad. Tourist agencies are as flooded as the flattened cornfields.

August, time for loosening belts and brain, is the 'silly season'. The media slackens its political bite and other more edifying output appears. Was it in the *Times* diary that I read of a pair of knickers belonging to a sixty-year-old woman living in Clifton Road, Twickenham, stolen from the washing line last Saturday morning? Two pegs were also taken.

The Prime Minister takes a break and re-shuffles her press-battered ministers. Tightened with lateral moves, promotions, and the introduction of the incisive Norman Tebbit as her new Chairman, she fastens her resolve and her cabinet on a third win. I admire Mrs Thatcher.

In France, I admire the French. Their cherished attention to domestic detail – *soin*, do they call it? Their stylish placement of goujonettes de sole wreathed in bright slivers of carrot and courgette set in a delicate yellow sauce, and their reverent pouring of a modest local wine. A meal engenders ceremony, whether at a station hotel, auberge, or three-star restaurant. Here in the Côte d'Azur we hug the sun and heat; an excellent vendange is forecast. They have had no rain for three months.

September 12, 1985

We drove through Provence, Cézanne's own landscape ledged with a hundred greens. Coastal palm-trees waving fronds and fans soon parted for wide river-beds and willows. Villages dabbed rose with terracotta set up on their mounds each topped with a spire. Vines tumbled down the slopes. At Châteaueuf du Pape we lunched at a reputable *hostellerie*. A nineteenth-century Gothic-style extravagance set high on its own *vignobles*. An unfortunate mix of chrome tables and reproduction Louis Quatorze chairs did not detract from the excellent rognons d'agneau.

September 13 Vonnas

A Swiss-style immaculate village, *bouleversé* with flowers that hang from canal bridges, streetlamps and every window-ledge clashing pink, orange, purple, red. Flat, peaceful Lyonnais country with cornfields, woods, and plump white cows. The young proprietors Monsieur and Madame Georges Blanc run their renowned three-star restaurant to superlative standards. The service, food, and presentation are equal to none. The ancient stone flagged dining-room floor, scattered with rich-coloured rugs, the hanging wall tapestries, and handsome furniture are nimbly circumvented by bevies of young waiters with their tureens and tempting trolleys. The sommelier of this illustrious establishment is a young Englishman, a triumphant promotion from his training at Britain's Bell Inn at Aston Clinton, Buckinghamshire. Despite his youth, his indifferent French, and the understandable indifference of some French patrons, he does a remarkable job. The 'cave' on the ground floor is elegantly structured on the finest gravel to absorb damp. Peter Lowe, a well-built six-footer, smoothes down his black leather apron. 'I carried in each case by hand,' he recalls lovingly.

We cruise through neighbouring villages; Vandeins, Buellas, and St Rémy are sleepy in September sun and the cooing of doves. Whiffs of wood-smoke hint of autumn. We potter through their sixteenth-century little churches, with simple red clay floors, rough-hewn stone walls; empty save for the sun leaking through their open doors. Sturdy and snug they stand, each with its rounded *auvent* buttressed to the winds.

September 14 Mâcon

Today we lost the car keys. We retraced our steps laboriously; telephone kiosks, a pharmacy, gutters and window-ledges scanned in vain. The sun beat down, the Mercedes depot shut for lunch and the Hôtel de Ville, with its invaluable department of 'objets retrouvés', promptly closed for the weekend. After lunching in the best auberge in town (a town of no particular charm or distinction, commensurate perhaps with its Beaujolais Mâconnais), we inveigled a mechanic from Mercedes into offering his services. Descending on the car with long wires and hooks he probed at locks in optimistic defeat. The quiet square reverberated to his tinkling; shutters opened from disturbed siestas and householders idly speculated on his efforts and our discomfort. This unproductive scenario was mercifully cut short by two bearded young men girded with shorts and plastic bags. Yes – they had our keys! Found in the first telephone kiosk! Lunch and shopping had intervened with their safe return . . .

September 17 Au Beau Rivage Condrieu

Along the flat, fertile banks of the northern Rhône the terrain changes imperceptibly as you follow it south. Wide valleys bristling with fruit orchards – pears, apricots – and scattered cabbages narrow dramatically to produce the Rhône's first major vineyards of Côte Rôtie. Steep, rocky hillsides are precariously terraced with narrow vineyards twisting tier upon tier (a Herculean task to harvest). Facing south and east across the river an intense summer heat generates, and the battle of root and rock is won in the finest bottles.

Three miles south of Côte Rôtie lies the village of Condrieu. The narrow stone streets cling to the shade from the baking sun. A quiet place with painted window shutters of faded sang de boeuf, pale chocolate, and grey. Quaint dark shops and alleyways evoke passages from Emile Zola's *Thérèse Raquin*: 'The pale and serious profile of a young woman . . . stood out dimly from the darkness filling the shop.' And more romantically: 'Thérèse in her petticoat . . . there was about her a scent of white linen and newly washed flesh . . . her penetrating scent of violets.' In the close streets of Condrieu, caught between the Rhône and jagged hillsides, one senses that same tide of lives and loves still swelling behind the shutters.

Madame Castaing has presided at the Beau Rivage for fifty years. Bandaged in white starched linen she greets us at room temperature. Her large, pale head, illuminated with a keen pair of eyes and a severe grey chignon, inclines us to our room. She next turns her attention to a stout American heaving in his open shirt and shorts. '*Vous voulez vous réguler, Monsieur?*' Matron dispensing an aperient comes to mind.

We eat well and reasonably in Madam Castaing's long-noted establishment and reflect on what a million pounds could do to redress its gentle decline. Sited on the Rhône with a terrace and shaded garden it can boast – apart from the Père Bise at Talloires – one of the finest positions in France. In deference to Madam Castaing, time has stood still for the Beau Rivage, and they are booked solid all year.

December 13 Hardwicke House

In the drizzle of today, the glitter and gold of last night's musical assembly at Lancaster House seems a mirage. The Friends of the Victorian Society had organised a prodigious turn-out of some 700 guests in the presence of their Patron, the Duke of Gloucester. Women were encouraged to wear Victorian dress. A vocal concert was followed by a buffet; a band, rejoicing in the name of the 'the Prince Albert Ensemble', played Victorian waltzes, quadrilles, and gallops throughout the reception.

The former Stafford House was built by Benjamin Wyatt in 1825 as a suitable residence for the Duke of York, young brother of George IV. On his death in 1827, the Government took over the project and eventually sold the lease to the Marquess of Stafford (later the Duke of Sutherland).

What a feat of gilded extravaganza! Vast domed and intricately-coffered ceilings supported with solid marble pillars, a plethora of elongated wall glasses and elaborate panelling, the whole seething

with gold leaf, rich colour, and reflection. 'I have come from my
house to your palace,' once remarked Queen Victoria – a regular
visitor – to the 2nd Duchess. And, as we strolled through these sumptuous Sun King-style halls and galleries, the redoubtable days of the
Marlborough House set and the 'Souls' were easily evoked by such
weekly events as:

1) 11th May 1859. 'Matinée Musicale in aid of Neapolitan Exiles';
2) 4th May 1899. 'Mrs Charles L. Carson and Miss Maude Danks'
   Grand Morning Concert in aid of Lady Henry Somerset's Industrial
   Farm colony';
3) 13th June 1899. 'Grand Afternoon Concert in aid of the Metropolitan Association for Befriending Young Servants'.

Now they make quaint reading.

We finally sank into fauteuils in the south-west Green Drawing-
Room and chatted with Cath Cawdor[1], the chosen consort of this
year's bachelor Lord Mayor of Westminster Roger Bramble. Beautiful
and petite in a froth of rose champagne taffeta, Cath talked vivaciously
of her role. Somebody complimented her on the cobweb of rare seed
pearls that veiled her pretty neck. 'This necklace used to sit better
before the dog tampered with it,' she replied laughing. We walked
back down the red-carpeted stairs, the shallow steps adding to their
grandeur. Charles Barry redecorated the Great Staircase Hall in 1843,
another explosion of mammoth architectural extravagance, which only
to see is to believe.

---

[1] Cathryn, Countess Cawdor. First wife of the 6th Earl. Daughter of Major-General Sir
Robert Hinde.

1986

Patrick Lindsay was once described as part Biggles, part Casanova and part Lord Clark (of *Civilisation*). He would turn his head slowly, chin held high; not the arrogant gesture it might first appear but the legacy of a broken neck, the first of many body blows sustained in a life of spectacular daring; 'His own long series of games played, often, eye to eye with death,' wrote Lord Oaksey in a remarkable obituary.

A comparatively young man – fifty-seven years of life, severed short by cancer. A packed life of sporting feats and artistic endeavour; a veteran car racer, ace flyer, revered connoisseur of Old Master pictures. He would break auction records and in turn save a wealth of pictures from banishment abroad. He wanted no memorial service; a hero of his time, such a farewell would have unleashed a flood of friends. Instead we converged today on St Mary's, Chilton Foliat, a little old church in a Wiltshire village.

The bell tolled remorselessly while the candles guttered in the grey afternoon. Tall, tapering columns of yew, pierced with orchids and lilies, stood sentinel beside the rood screen and the coffin beyond. The organ fiddled in waiting. The family arrived in a rush; Patrick's three sons in cheerful kilts escorted his wife, Amabel, and daughter Laura to the altar enclave. (Laura in red under her black and Amabel with a black ribbon circling her red cloche hat.) A simple service, no address; the lessons were read eloquently by his children, to include the stirring *Airman's Ecstasy* by John Gillespie Magee[1]:

> 'Sunward I've climbed and joined the tumbling mirth of sun-split clouds – and done a hundred things you have not dreamed of; wheeled and soared and swung high in the sun-lit silence . . .'

A German dirge – 'Bist du bei mir' (J S Bach) – fell in comforting waves from the gallery.

We were invited to walk to the open grave; an overflow of guests had stood outside the church. A well-trodden grassy path was smeared with mud and bordered with bunches of forced spring flowers. The tall, distinguished man with silver hair pushed the wheel-chair where

---

[1] John Gillespie Magee, a nineteen-year-old American pilot, killed in December 1941, while serving with the Royal Canadian Air Force.

the dark man sat palely and strained to see. The field beyond the graveyard sloped steep in emerald. A dull afternoon, no wind. A small child, vivid in red wool, walked beside its mother across the horizon. What is this? An air-splitting scream; a Spitfire darts from the heavy cloud. It rolls above us with mischievous aplomb. Just once it comes. 'Who was that?' asks one. 'Patrick, of course,' replied another. And then a small miracle; a flash of sunlight. The bare trees fork the field in shadows; then, just as suddenly, the bright light dies.

May 15 Monkton House Chichester Sussex

'Our man in charge of Monkton is off-duty today. It is five miles through the woods on a single-track road.'

We stood in the hallway of West Dean Park in the high Gothic, oaken gloom of it all. And was it not possible to see Monkton today?

The little Lutyens[2] house in the woods, the famous folly created by Edward James, a veritable jewel-box of surrealist art and eccentric 1930 decoration, it had to be seen. Our informant finally agreed to escort us. It was a sunny morning and this unscheduled drive through the beech-woods and bluebells had obviously appealed.

Edward James (1908–1984) was the fifth child and only son of William James and the beautiful Evelyn. It has been suggested that King Edward VII was little Edward's father; he certainly agreed to be the child's godfather. Edward James's fertile imagination and vast wealth culminated in his scholarly patronage of the Surrealists. Monkton became a favourite refuge and rich depository of his whims and commissions.

We arrived at the house and parked in the small forecourt enclosed with yew. 'Edward always wanted to plant a maze in front of the house; he couldn't stand his elder sisters (Milicent, Alexandra, Silvia and Audrey) and felt it would bar their entry.'

The plastered, purple façade with its pink front door would have surely appalled Lutyens; perhaps in deference to the old master, Edward James had hacked a hole in the rendering to reveal the original orange brickwork. We stepped inside on to the famous green carpet designed with Edward James's Irish wolfhound's paw-marks. 'He dipped the dog's feet in ink and made him walk on paper for the effect.' The incongruous result of paw-marks straddling the stair treads does not detract from the original conception. And there was the pair of sofas

[2] Sir Edwin Lutyens, 1869–1944, objected to 'the pointed arch'. He is particularly remembered for his architectural planning of New Delhi, 1912, and hailed for the simplicity of the Cenotaph in Whitehall', his *War Stone*.

especially designed by Salvador Dali in the shape of Mae West's lips. Their scarlet lushness was strangely patched in dabs of green. 'This house is a moth's paradise,' explained our informant. 'They made a hole in one of the lips. Edward had it patched in green and liked the effect so much he patched the rest for fun. All these thickly-padded and quilted walls, buttoned sofas and that study wall covered in men's navy suiting is just asking for trouble.' We admired the pair of Dali lampstands, tall stems of metal champagne glasses in tandem – curiouser and curiouser.

On the stairs we passed a circular fish tank, let into the wall and visible from a bathroom above. The staircase was solid and widely-curved, reminiscent of a 1930 ocean liner's and designed by Edward James. (Again Lutyens must shudder. Where was his?) And what have we here? Simple net curtaining dipped in gold lined the bedroom walls and shimmered like priceless silk. A chest of drawers is made fresh and fanciful covered in printed chintz with a frilled valence. And in Edward James's bathroom the sun and the moon glow through alabaster panels at the touch of a switch.

Should Monkton be saved for the Nation? Could anybody be rich or crazy enough to buy such an inaccessible folly? The mangled bones of Lutyens and the exotic flesh of James are a strange marriage. And the peacocks screech in anguish for their past and for their future.

June 4 Le Club Cavalière

Père Guillemin – dapper in scarlet slacks – lifts his chin to the sea; he sniffs the Mistral.

'Déjà c'est le deuxième jour que ça tient.' With the streaming rain of Dover fresh in our minds we have no complaint. The evening sun skims sand and restless sea. Fronds of palm trees dance to the breeze. Père Guillemin suavely circulates his guests while *fils* compliments us with a glass of champagne on the garden terrace. Yes – those are the Golden Isles; Porquerolles is a fifty-minute trip from Le Lavandou. Yes – the hotel is full – Yes – Yes – Cavalière is a backwater – and guests return. But in Nice and Monte Carlo the coffers are dry. Terrorism versus tourism has taken its toll on the annual American trade – the casinos are dead.

June 5

A sulking grey sea but the wind has dropped. *Nice-Matin* with my breakfast tray proclaims rape in Lyons, a rare sighting of a *tombre* (water spout) off St Tropez, and murder in Marseilles. The first forest fires have swept through Var, a legacy of last week's heatwave.

My mother and I face the lurching rigours of our hired Peugeot to Le Lavandou. We lunched lightly on langoustines and Beaujolais Nouveau. There is comfort in red wine on a mean day. Our bill at this seemingly modest harbour restaurant, Au Vieux Port, soars to 327 francs.

Days follow swiftly, hot days now with a flat and azure sea. A profusion of flowering grasses, poppies, and the sharp yellow discs of wild achillea choke the winding coast road; red rock and terracotta roofs simmer in blue-green distance. Umbrella pines ink in cliff and cape and every cove is an idle lap for waves.

We drink kir with stockbroker John and pretty Rosemary from Chiddingfold. They leave tomorrow and dwell on tips. The old beach hand of fifty years' employ takes precedence; he secures your fiefdom of sand. And the caviste, the femme de chambre, the waiter, the obliging porter – our friends' position, as regular habitués of Le Club for the past twenty years, costs them dear. For us – mere parvenus – the prix-net basis (1,200 francs *par jour* on one-half pension each) comprises all.

A predictably delicious dinner is immaculately presented and served and Porquerolles fades soft grey in an amethyst dusk. Bouillabaisse with cairns of cream and croûtons, a typically nondescript white Mediterranean fish metamorphosised to excellence with juliennes of red pepper, courgettes, and a mantle of sabayon, a nouvelle sorbet of crushed rosemary and vodka (to clear the palate), noisettes d'agneau, tiny, tender and pink, a cheeseboard to end them all, and finally a striped slice of chocolate ice/gateau. 'We haven't had a potato since we arrived,' observes my mother wistfully.

And the clientèle? The Swedish girl with the dolly blonde hair, scooped in baubles, her bronzed body and décolletage as smooth as satinwood and her hairy escort incongruous in clothes (an Adonis on the beach); the two German fraüleins, dyed blondes and caught again in baubles and shiny belts, journalists? The French, compact and smart and self-assured, and the young Belgian couple (la jeunesse dorée personified), who stroke each other sore. No unclaimed man, no single girl, no Americans, the British all to come. And Père Guillemin, in white and primrose, is in his element. It is Saturday night.

June 9

Church bells echo through the narrow, cobbled streets that is the labyrinth of old St Tropez. It is 12 noon and the harbour bulges with its catch of yachts and gin palaces. The water is scribbled with colour from their ensigns – red, yellow, blue and white and green. The British, the Italian and the French flaunt a marked presence in this elegant hardware. A handsome schooner raises her brass-railed gang-plank and eases out of port. Three-masted (a British flag), she motors majestically to the open sea – the *Shenandoa*. The scene before us is exuberantly recorded in La Musée de L'Annonciade, alongside the harbour. Signac, the first Impressionist to fête the little fishing village of St Tropez, is well represented, together with Matisse, Dufy and Seurat. The stark white walls and pale marble floor are an effective foil for so much vibrant colour. Sturdy bronzes by Maillol are strategically placed.

Into the sun and mounting heat where canopied cafés are brightly laid for lunch and stalls exuding fruit and fish and flowers are spread over pavements. Boutiques abound for every purse – 'Le Must' de Cartier vies with the 'Sweat Shirterie', and everywhere from terracotta troughs and ample urns spill out petunias and hydrangeas – red, purple, pastel pink.

We drive to the hillside village of Grimaud where all is cool and green in the shade of the ilex-trees and rowan. At Les Santons we eat well and expensively. The heavy-beamed ceiling, the wall display of copper moulds, the gemütlich interior where all is rose and orange are stock inducements to the appetite. We take the inland road back to Cavalière through a lush extravaganza of fresh green vineyards, sloping to the densely wooded hills. The evening sea is warm and looped with sun. We watch it fade a translucent, pearly grey. Will it be fine in the morning?

June 10 Côte d'Azur

'Let's try that beach we saw in La Musée de L'Annonciade.' My mother refers to the enchanting painting by Henri Cross of *Plage de Saint-Clair*. A short drive towards Le Lavandou and there it is, swamped with ice-cream vendors, kiosks of garish beach paraphernalia, and a jammed car park.

'Rather different from 1906,' remarks my mother, and we try our luck elsewhere. The *Plage de Tamaris* beckons us down a dust track where all is peace and comparative desertion. Tamarisk trees spread shade over the hot mid-day sand. Birds sing, a small yacht is anchored below a villa. Stone balusters are half-glimpsed through pinewoods, descending steeply to a private jetty. We picnic and bury our boiling legs in sand. 'Is that a drain?' My mother spies a tell-tale pipe lurking in the cerulean shallows; a faint whiff. We pick our way to a beach shanty and drink coffee in the shade of an expansive old plane-tree. A tall, handsome man sits at a nearby table. I think he resembles Lord Lucan. My mother does not agree. His young wife chivvies him to put on a pair of dry trousers. Only in France could a man look like Lucan, smoke a cigarette, gulp coffee, curse his wife, squeeze his long wet legs into a second pair of tight trousers, and be sitting in a café, simultaneously.

June 11 Porquerolles

In our quest for a perfect beach we take a pleasure boat to Porquerolles, an island of five miles by one and quarter miles. After a calm crossing with the world and its French wife (infinitely more palatable to the ear than a horde of British trippers), we embark in the heat of 11 o'clock. I am glad of a heavy cardigan that shields my shoulders from the blazing sun.

Porquerolles induces a gentle lassitude more akin to the heat and dust of North Africa than Provence. The modest square, once the province of Napoleonic parades, is marked by a simple church. The windows of coloured sections of glass have an understated charm, but the Michelin instead guides our attention to the wooden wall plaques depicting Christ's crucifixion, 'carved by a soldier with his penknife'. The boulders in the foreground bear witness to a knife at work, but the figures of this whole extreme drama are eloquently chiselled.

We turn down a sand road, thickly bordered with eucalyptus, olean-der, and dense Mediterranean vegetation, variously scattered with unidentifiable pink and yellow flowers. The drowsy scents of tangled honeysuckle, lavender, and myrtle lure us to the sea. La Plage d'Argent is our goal, with an enticing sign alongside – Le Langoustier. Could a seafood restaurant even be awaiting us? We stagger on to a beach, thick with the prickly residue of surrounding pine-woods; the desul-tory waves are clogged with seaweed. We have an adequate lunch, on a raised terrace; raw carrot, doused in dressing, with hunks of grilled chicken and camembert. Le Langoustier in fact refers to a Grand Point, a highly recommended walk, together with the 'Phare', both of which we chose to forgo.

June 12

A rest day. My mother and I exchange reading matter. While she chuckles indulgently over the escapades of my Emile Zola I borrow her *Yalta Victim* written by Zoe Polanska-Palmer and published this year. With her Russian family safely dead and free from any reprisals, this remarkable woman recounts her story, a shattering record of Nazi torture, imprisonments, her protracted escape and ultimate survival. Her tale lends significant irony to this week's landslide victory of Kurt Waldheim as President of Austria. It is rumoured that he was a junior lieutenant in the German army. But the Austrians of today are largely determined to overlook any incriminations of the past. 'Jetzt zurück zur Zukunft' (now back to the future), they exhort their leader, a suave anti-Socialist and fellow countryman. But the world feels differently; a network of international enquiry is already shuffling through this man's questionable past. And remarks an old Viennese:

'I have never forgotten the fact that proportionately to population there were four times as many Austrian war criminals as there were Germans.'

Zoe Palmer's devastating account of the Argyll and Sutherland Highlanders forced by the British Government – some at mutiny point – to sling innocent Soviet refugees into cattle trucks, to their final death, or moral destruction, makes the blood curdle. This scene that she records took place near Linz in Austria.

On the last day, from the cool of my marble room, the sea sounds quiet; no breath of wind, the sun subdued in haze; it will be a scorcher. Last night the sea was a caress, a benediction. One could not have enough of those warm and lulling corridors of water. Now it ends this 'réalité de rêve', and for the last time *gentil* Jean retrieves our car from its steeply-parked perch, as he might catch an errant pony.

September 30 Hardwicke House

An Indian summer we are having of it, the air soft and the clear light as gold as a dessert wine. The trees are distilled in deepening rich colour, their leaves unshed. We have had no wind for days.

July and August brought a procession of friends to stay; feast days and quiet days; strawberries and salmon; holidays in France and stays in cottages – Devon, Norfolk. Norfolk, where the dense green of broad and bank and wood clouds every horizon greener. And Devon bright and patched with pocket fields, red mud, corn and cottage gardens. Sara's home-smoked haddock with a bantam egg and Vanessa's nectarines glazed with burnt cream and amoretto. Walks with Porridge dog through Ham woods; to Pen Ponds for his plunge for sticks, and along the heavy-scented avenue of limes to Ham House. One evening we saw the South Terrace alive with party-goers; elegantly-dressed guests strolled and laughed and chatted against that handsome Jacobean backdrop.

And then that memorable August day at Tintagel Castle. Unremitting strident rain with a capricious Cornish wind. I leant against it; as strong as a wall support it was, when suddenly it veered off, leaving me as defenceless as the ruins. Between the crumbled walls of St Juliot's chapel, I sensed the momentary hush and shelter and a thousand secret years. On misty days you may share the old custodian's sinister sensation: 'I feel this pressure at the back of my neck and know that I am being watched . . . take care with the wind . . .' he warned me, as I set off with my pen and notebook. A useless endeavour; the rain and wind made notes impossible. For two hours I skirted the castle ruins on this clenched fist of land so tenuously linked to the mainland by a narrow strip of rock. The tide was out and Merlin's cave – cut clean through the neck of the island – was open to the winds. I scrambled through this dark vaulted tunnel – a popular tourist site. Slate boulders were tumbled over pink marble stones, that led to the cove on the other side. English Heritage had asked me to write an article on Tintagel's myths and its maze of archaeological and historic claims; a fascinating exercise and finally completed in the comfort of the sitting-room back home.

October 6 Hardwicke House

Susanna Avery is as bright and neat as befits a senior student at the redoubtable St Paul's School, Hammersmith. She is interested in Interior Design. Would she like a cold drink? Fresh orange is very acceptable and we walk up to the first-floor landing to discuss a new pair of curtains for the Regency window. The old white curtains are pitifully frayed and Porridge has long hastened their demise with a generous bite in the hem.

Susanna is delighted with the house and the panelling. 'What colour would you choose for this window, Susanna?' First she thinks red, inspired by the tattered blobs of geranium on the balcony beyond. But no – that would clash with the pink toile de jouy, visible through the open sitting-room door, she quickly observes. 'But blue would be nice

– you've got blue in the rug.' I have to confess to Susanna that I am allergic to blue – too cold. I hasten to add that I like navy blue (and she looks smart in her navy jersey with her white collar peeking out from the neck). She looks reflectively into her orange juice and says: 'Do you know something? I read in a magazine that people in blue rooms switch on the fire sooner than people in yellow rooms.' We laugh at this timely revelation. I show her a photograph of the Regency pressed-brass frieze we plan to fix up as a pelmet. I explain that it is an egg and dart design. 'That's right! It means life and death; the egg is life and the dart is the arrow of death!' What a fund of knowledge and enthusiasm she is.

I show her round the house, her blonde hair swings and her cheeks are pink as she half-prances through the rooms. With her father's provenance as deputy keeper of the V and A Bronze Department and currently the director of Christie's European Sculpture Department, Dr Charles Avery's enchanting daughter should go far.

November 4 Warwick House Stable Yard St James's

Ambrose Congreve's bland good looks exactly compliment the lush décor of his large drawing-room, but the pale pinks and greens of sofas, the indifferent carpets and pictures are fortuitously overwhelmed with his exquisite French furniture. A plethora of ormolu-mounted porcelain and Louis Quinze clocks surmounted by bronze embellishment (to include an elephant) compound the grandeur. We are invited to dinner, a party of twenty-four.

Ambrose Congreve has a wife, marginally senior to his own eighty years. She is present and sits swathed in fur and is said to talk about her health for which she has a compulsive fear and interest. But Ambrose also has Geraldine, unmarried and spry and decorative as a porcelain figurine. Geraldine Critchley orchestrates his social moves and his prodigious collection of all things bright and beautiful. (His eighteenth-century London home is a drop in the ocean compared with the splendours of his Southern Irish seat, Mount Congreve.) The party is complete. We are led down a circular stair to the dining-room, while Ambrose remonstrates mildly with the peruked Baron di Portanova. 'Why did you bring your own cigars? We have everything here.' The unfortunate Baron has stuffed a posse of his own cigars in his breast pocket.

Our host is renowned for his collection of silver. No table could look more magnificent. Each guest has his own set of eighteenth-century salts and peppers and the line-up of finely-turned candelabra and sticks support some fifty burning candles. Three-tined forks and pistol-grip knives are further eye-trainers in excellence. Tom is seated on Geraldine's left. Yes, the servants do loathe cleaning it all, she assures him, and she herself is hopeless at flowers. Does he see the footman in the corner? He came this week from the Brazilian Embassy, a magician with flowers. She has always contracted out for the job – so exorbitant. And the banked table display of white phlox, freesia, and lily bears witness to his deft fingers.

The first course incurs Geraldine's faint displeasure, an assortment of fish fingers nestling in game chips. The stuffed veal promises better, although a khaki ratatouille and duchess potatoes do not enhance. A chocolate roulade with a scattering of tiny raspberries is very accept-able. Coffee follows, when Tom espies an electro-plated nickel-silver teaspoon in the sugar bowl. What is this? He teases Geraldine and makes to put it in his pocket. She feigns mock horror and summons a footman. 'Bring Mr Craig a Queen Anne teaspoon immediately,' she urges him. Yes, they are low on teaspoons. Tom advises her to go to Mr Silverman of the Silver Vaults to recoup their losses. 'He sells them for £30 each. We bought six the other day, to replace the odd ones that have been lost or mangled in the waste disposal.'

The women leave the table and Geraldine takes us upstairs to Ambrose Congreve's bedroom. A pair of newly-laundered white silk pyjamas, piped in navy, repose on his turned-down double bed. In his immaculate white marble bathroom, I take care to leave the roll of lavatory paper exactly poised for its next rotation. Geraldine flings her neat little body into a chair. Her elegant legs sparkle with diamanté ladders. 'And we were twenty-four last night; tomorrow I am opting for a boiled egg in my room at the top.' She is very vivacious and pretty and all of fifty. We return to the drawing-room where the men have promptly reappeared. Mrs Congreve is re-settled in a corner. She is knitting a shawl, which she conveniently drapes over the parts her stole cannot reach.

Ambrose Congreve leads me to a carved gilt sofa. 'Don't look up at the ceiling. That ghastly late nineteenth-century plaster moulding in the middle is quite out of keeping with the original wood carved cornices.' He talks briefly of his fear of a future Labour government. 'And they are certain to abolish fox hunting, and pheasant shoots. I don't shoot but I like breeding pheasants. Did you know the French are running short of frogs? I'm thinking of rearing them at Mount Congreve. Now who haven't you met?' I indicate a handsome man, pale and interesting and framed in dark curls. He is lured to the gilt sofa. A strange and mournful conversationalist, this one, with an obsession for why and for what. 'Extraordinary show downstairs, d'you know? Ambrose has two lavatories and three handbasins. Why three? And why do we all meet and extract words and eat and drink and smile, for what?'

November 21 Florence

Beautiful cities breathe in the winter months. The Piazza Signoria is stripped of tourists and café tables. The evening sun glances on the damp stone façades and the puddles are gold. An old lady pads slowly behind her old dog. The statues stand high and unheeded in their arresting stance. And the fountains play on this empty stage. I sit in the solid comfort of the Rivoyre Café; a gentle trade in espresso, hot chocolate and patisseries lingers beside its carved wood walls and marble tables. It has been an uneventful trip from Pisa airport; back gardens, where little oranges bowed down their leafless trees, sidling past the window, and the umbrella pines a perennial vivid green against the faded fuzz of woods and hills. A man has slumped opposite me, snoring over his open novel and a dead cigar; another idly twiddles his black curls between finger and thumb.

Now we sit, Lydia and I, in the brick-vaulted bowels of a bistro, off the Duomo.

'I have something to confess,' she volunteers. 'I should have told you three months ago!'

Is she pregnant? An abortion? Had she married him? An Italian? Is she an alcoholic? Become a Catholic?

'Let's wait for the wine, darling,' I suggest weakly. The bottle of Corvo arrives.

'I've got a mini-moped! A sort of bicycle with an engine. It's second-hand and eleven years old with the make Sabrina written all over it. It's sweet – a scruffy cream – but it really works; not more than twenty miles an hour. The lights work. The licence costs nothing.'

'How splendid, darling. Do you wear a helmet?'

'All the students in Florence have mini-mopeds and nobody wears helmets.' After dinner she props the back wheel upon the pavement encircling the Duomo and, with feet flailing and blonde hair flying, she is off into the night.

The following evening we have supper in her minuscule rented apartment – tiled floors, beamed ceilings and whitewashed walls. She has become immensely house-proud. Oh, the thrill of independent possession. We celebrate her scrambled eggs (excellent) with duty-free champagne and marvel at her prowess in La Pubblicità. Her first job (unpaid) with an advertising fashion company has temporarily overtaken any absorption in the opposite sex. 'I work from 9 to 6.30. How long will it last, Daddy?'

'Another 39½ years, my love, and then you might qualify for a pension.'

1987

'You want a fast ride, lady, or a slow one?'

I recalled yesterday's alarming speed trip up the Avenue of the Americas, the wet road and the bevy of fire engines confronting us head-on as they wailed their perilous trail against all traffic. 'A slow one, please.' The yellow checker taxi cab took us sedately through Central Park to the Metropolitan Museum of Art. He was a British driver. 'I stopped off here thirty-eight years ago, on my way to Australia, but I decided to stay.' For two days I had stared at the bare trees in Central Park from the elegant confines of the Knickerbocker Club. What were they? I hated my ignorance. 'All sorts, lady, oaks, elms, sycamores – trees donated from any country in the world except America.' I ventured that New York seemed quieter than our visit twenty years ago, certainly quieter than today's London; less screaming police cars, uncrowded roads and pavements and women nonchalantly parading full-length mink coats, whereas in London one creeps around Knightsbridge in fake fur and Loden. 'New York City is as dangerous as ever it was, lady. But this now is the slow season. Crime and crowds pick up in the spring through summer. You find real trouble starts at 96th Street.'

We enjoyed the specially-sponsored Van Gogh exhibition (pronounced Van-Go in America). It comprised his prolific output of pictures painted in Provence and at Auvers during the last two years of his life. Olive orchards, wheatfields, the asylum garden, village scenes, and his wondrous jugs full of iris and white roses. A poignant legacy which he cut short with his revolver behind a haystack aged only thirty-seven.

Relentless rain all day. Where to lunch? We eschewed all invitations on West 55th Street to fine cuisine lunches and 'ice-cream diners'. The ice rink at the Rockefeller Centre was deserted, but flags and fairy lights made a cheerful-enough backdrop to the Sea Grill restaurant – our final choice. We ate broiled chicken with sliced summer fruits. After an indulgent breakfast of eggs sunny-side up and corn muffins we had little appetite. The Napa Valley wine was excellent and the ladies' powder closet boasted a push button lavatory seat that spewed out a fresh plastic-wrapped arc for each proffered posterior.

We spent the afternoon at the Frick Collection in the high opulence of this privately-styled mansion, resurrected in 1913–14 on eighteenth-century European lines. We absorbed ourselves in the Boucher Room, the Fragonard Room, and the superb collection of eighteenth- and nineteenth-century English portraits and landscapes.

Back at the Knickerbocker Club, built in 1915, again on European lines and marked with all the attendant grandeur, we snoozed in our comfortable bedroom. An exclusive venue to stay where rules are observed:

'Gentlemen are to wear coats and ties in the dining-room. No cigars or pipes in the ladies' dining-room. No business papers to be left in the public rooms. Tea is served for lady guests in the Library and in the Master of Fox Hounds room.'

The main rooms, with their fine Georgian-style windows and high ceilings, abounded in portraits of former members, glorious in 1930 hunting dress, and assorted twentieth-century English sporting prints. Gleaming black leather chairs and sofas and well-worn backgammon and chess tables evoked a sense of space and leisure. We later dined at nearby Harry Cipriani's, where the whole of upwardly social Americans seemed to have converged. All the girls wore outsize gold hooped earrings and there was hardly a straight nose to be seen.

March 2

Today Tom and I spent five hours at the Manhattan Eye and Ear Hospital where I underwent tests and photographic sessions on my right eye. Dr Fred Jacobiec, the resident head ophthalmic surgeon, agreed with Mr Tim ffytche of Moorfields, London, that the vascular tumour at the back of my eye was benign. He also agreed that its position, attached to the retina, was remarkable; he had never seen such a rare combination. In all confessed modesty he could prescribe no definite treatment, either for its removal or for the improvement of my sight in that eye. He suggested that it should be checked each month for the foreseeable future and that I buy a pair of big glasses with side protection.

Mr Robert Ellsworth, his colleague at the New York hospital, agreed with this diagnosis with the further suggestion of possible radium therapy. But he was unconvinced that it would help the remaining vision.

Our second opinion venture in New York has proved a worthwhile exercise and cheap at the price. Moorfield's suggestion of laser treatment would certainly put paid to any remaining peripheral vision and should, in my view, be discounted for the present. The tumour, as

Mr ffytche originally observed, is in 'tiger country'. It appears that any such treatment would be fiddling with a fuse box. Why not leave well enough alone and see, in time, what nature might dictate?

March 13 Castel del Drago Bolsena Italy

The dashing Don Giovanni del Drago had expressly invited us to troop through his castle on the hill. We admired the faded frescoes on his walls, his stone carved fireplaces, and his glazed tile floors, and expressed amazement at the newly-restored coffered oak ceiling of his top-floor drawing-room. It had previously been exposed to the winds for fifteen years. Downstairs, he offered us coffee and English tea. A liveried footman was busily engaged in retrieving hot coals from the stove and transporting them on a little brass shovel to a samovar. It was all very quaint and friendly. Don Giovanni's local friend, Francesca Chigi, had been invited in to help with the entertainments, while a large fluffy white Labrador looked in from outside, thrusting its head in and out of the heavy iron window grille. Tom took a photograph of this restless animal (which subsequently came out better than the frescoes).

'He is not the marrying man,' muttered our erudite guide, Marchesa Maddalena Patrizzi. 'What a waste. So attractive and so charming.' The women in our party had unanimously invested our host with the most manly and desirable attributes. Would not his plump little friend Francesca foot the bill? We finally left our engaging hero and presented him a copy of the Furniture History Society's booklet on Italian Collections. Our cultural party repaired to the bus and to the Villa Lante gardens, set above the old village of Bagnaia.

Armed with Sir George Sitwell's famous dissertation *On the Making of Gardens*, it was a delightful exercise to follow the amazing play of waterfalls and fountains in situ. The whole effect was dramatised by thick encrustations of ice that clung to bronze statues and hung in sturdy icicles from colossal river gods and ornamental basins. Notwithstanding these winter conditions, the pools on this sunny morning reflected pure azure. Sir George's description of 'darkest bronze, blue pools and golden light' held true. We later staggered up the hill of the nearby Villa Farnese and wandered through the Renaissance grandeur of its famous Caprarola pleasure gardens. The statuary band of jovial Therms stood guard against their towering hedge of green, and again one recalled Sir George Sitwell's words: 'These old Italian gardens with their air of neglect, desolation and solitude, in spite of the melancholy of the weed-grown alleys . . . have a beauty which is indescribable . . .'

We saw many private palaces and gardens during our tour of Rome and revelled in the architectural extravagances of trompe l'oeil, boiserie, and rich ceiling decoration. Bernini, Borromini, Barberini – the old architects of Rome's splendour fast became a glorious jumble in the less initiated mind. But it was perhaps the Principessa Elvina Pallavacini-Rospigliosi who afforded us the greatest treats. Confined to a wheelchair with multiple sclerosis, she was nevertheless a remarkably beautiful woman. She invited us in to her palace for a sumptuous tea and we all embarked on a unique perambulation through excellence. Her pictures (including three Botticellis) and her entire collection were superbly housed in gloriously-decorated rooms. In such a setting her obvious penchant for coloured glass Venetian chandeliers even looked well. In a parting speech, Tom congratulated her on her rare and beautiful 'assemblage', which had been evidently created with love and affection. She was clearly moved by his words and her fat, black mongrel (originally liberated from the piazza below) barked on approvingly.

The Barberini gardens, at the Pope's summer residence, Castel Gandolfo in the Alban hills, proved another feast. A grand and immaculate concept of wide-terraced walks, cool ilex-groves, tier upon tier of elaborate parterred gardens, and serried lemon jardinières. It was all exquisitely tended by the assiduous attentions of eighteen full-time gardeners. A herd of cows is said to be kept on the slopes below to supply milk to the Vatican. These gardens are closed to the public, but are open to group tours by special request. One wondered how often the Pope himself could appreciate the seasonal displays.

Our visit to the Villa Aldobrandini at Frascati also comes to mind. We arrived at dusk but could still discern the austere seventeenth-century conglomerate positioned theatrically on a mount above the town. We gazed on the gold stone façade with its elaborate breakfront pediments. A peasant maid let us in to a cold, dim interior. Swathed in a heavy wool scarf and a blue overall, stretched over layers of rough clothes, she padded ponderously behind us as we filed through rooms of heavy Roman pieces and gilded seat furniture. She barred up the shutters as we walked on and on through this seemingly abandoned home. She offered us orange juice, wine and salami before we fled gratefully back to the warm bus. The Principe Camillo Aldobrandini and his Principessa Luisa prudently live elsewhere during the chill winter months.

And I remember with affection the Villa Bonaparte; now the residence of the French Ambassador to the Holy See; originally a home of Napoleon's favourite sister, Pauline Borghese. According to Maddalena Patrizzi, our aforementioned guide, the delectable Pauline had frail health and regularly visited her other home in Lucca, where she would 'take the waters'. His Excellency greeted us warmly and invited us to enjoy a glass of pineapple juice as we admired the Empire-styled interiors. The marble floors were zealously polished and Pauline's Napoleonic mahogany bed, sofas and chairs were upholstered in glow-ing satins and taffetas. This luxuriously-appointed villa overlooked a well-tended garden of decorative parterres, sheltered by a thick screen of ilex and umbrella pines, orange trees laden with fruit, flowering camellias and two swarthy gardeners in recketts-blue dungarees, dig-ging a bed beneath the brilliant yellow plumes of a mimosa tree. All evoked the colours of a French Impressionist painting. In a simple grotto, guarded by a handsome pair of terracotta youths, was enshrined Pauline's pale grey marble bath, into which she was wont to be carried by a gigantic negro.

May 2 The Keswick Hotel Keswick Cumbria

A howling gale last night; the solid Victorian granite walls of the hotel braced themselves as windows shuddered. We woke to sun with surrounding hills and peaks glazed with snow. Only last week, Cumbria basked in 70°F, the hottest, driest spring in Britain since 1947.

Over a traditional breakfast of poached eggs and pan-fried black pudding, Uncle Dickie scours the English Lakeland brochure for a suitable walk, a long and challenging walk in the hills. (Yesterday morning Sebastian and I had failed dismally. In durable drizzle we took the local 'Mountain Goat' bus to nearby Lake Buttermere. 'An easy little four-mile stretch,' assured the driver. 'You will be picked up again at 5 o'clock.' We stumbled out, clutching our Barbour jackets in the bitter rain. The lake was invisible in mist. 'No, we will come straight back to Keswick with you now,' I had said, resolute and panic-stricken.

We collect ourselves and our walking books in the oak-encrusted hall of the Keswick Hotel: Uncle Dickie, Aunt Valerie, Sebastian, me, and Greedy, their diminutive Shih Tzu dog. (Would it ever survive the rigours?). Meanwhile a plaque on the wall advises us of the 'Rules of the Tavern':

4 pence a night for bed
6 pence with pot luck
2 pence for horse keeping
No more than 5 to sleep in one bed

No razor grinders or tinkers taken in
No dogs allowed in the kitchen
Organ grinders to sleep in the wash house.

I suggest a walk to the hamlet of Watendlath in the Borrowdale Valley, to my mind the most evocative and romantic landscape of the Northern Lakes, immortalised by Hugh Walpole, in his popular chronicles of the 'Rogue Herries' family. He wrote of Watendlath:

'Watendlath was an exceedingly remote little valley lying among the higher hills above Borrowdale. It could indeed be scarcely named a valley; rather it was a narrow strip of meadow and stream lying between the wooded hills . . . utterly remote with some 20 ducklings, a dark tarn and Watendlath Beck that ran down the Strath until it tumbled over the hill at Lodore.'

In blustering wind we climb some thousand feet up a rock path from the village of Rosthwaite. The sun is chased by a storm cloud and we see the peaks behind rapidly blanketed in a heavy shower. The sleet soon engulfs us. We press on up and, doubled into the wind, are soon rewarded with Watendlath below, on the other side. The tarn is slate-grey. As we drink coffee beside the 'Judith Paris' rambling farm-house, chaffinches descend on us for sugar lumps. The landscape is rugged and entices us on past becks, through woods and fells. Three and a half hours later, we tumble cold and sodden into the pub at regained Rosthwaite.

No boots or dogs in the saloon bar and no more sandwiches. Hot soup? We never serve it! Such dire inhospitality is incredible after our heroic trek! Our southern souls are sorely tried. A more accommodating farmhouse in the next village of Grange offers us cottage pie and carrot cake. (But no smoking or drinking allowed.) However, our boots and trousers drip unheeded on the slate floor.

Back in Keswick, we potter through antique shops crammed with cut glass, sturdy, stray jugs, and plates and brass. We glut ourselves in the sheepskin and wool shop and once again omit to buy Greedy her rightful tin of Top Dog. The complimentary Trust House Forte chocolate wafer can hardly suffice her needs a second night running. Valerie takes courage and ringing Room Service is presented with a hefty portion of last night's mutton, complete with cereal bowl and a bowing waiter.

May 3

A divinely sunny day. We drive through Ambleside and Windermere to Kendal and feast on azure lakes, snow-capped peaks, and all the riotous green and blossom of spring.

An appetising whiff of meat and onions steals through the sixteenth-century oak-panelled rooms of Levens Hall, mingling with an all-pervading fragrance, sweet and cloying. Is it some special furniture wax polish, incorporating all the locally renowned scents? But no; huge white rhododendrons placed in every room – the Princess Alice variety – prove the source. And Mrs Bagot, the young châtelaine herself, has freshly-arranged generous bowls of flowers, narcissus, yellow prunus, and coral chaenomeles, splayed wide against the dark panels. (A motor rally of thirty-six Austin Healys is expected.)

We pad through the cherished rooms of ornately-carved seventeenth-century four-poster beds, decked in demure patchwork and linen coverlets, worked in silk thread. The old leather walls from Cordoba prove less durable than wood. An exquisite William and Mary secretaire of walnut and marquetry inlay catches the eye. The famous and meticulously good view from the panelled bathroom reveals every parterre below as little blue seas of forget-me-nots; most effective this. But the Gothic-style, elaborate plaster ceilings I find lugubrious.

Back at Townend House in the village of Troutbeck, a narrow, winding lane leads to this seventeenth-century farmhouse, owned for 300 years by the Browne family. (The National Trust came to the rescue in 1948.) A veritable 'time-capsule' of the Cumbrian farmers' way of life through the centuries. The original furniture is intact, made largely from carpenters on the estate. Some zealous joiner has even sized up the ornately-carved bedposts to tally with the precariously-sloping oak floors. Two fat ladies from the local National Trust office sit by the log fire in the small granite-floored hall. They rise to their feet and, with majestic bosoms heaving in local knits, expound possessively on the substantial record of the Brownes.

May 4, 1987

Our proposed week of serious walking subsides into leisurely strolls beside Bassenthwaite Lake and Derwentwater. Valerie is good on birds; her binoculars pick off sandpipers, grey lag, wagtail, and a stray oyster catcher. She and I even stumble upon a stray man lying amongst cowslips beside a river. Whereas Wordsworth would have clinched this vista in verse, we women are momentarily startled. Why does one always delude oneself that rape is in the offing? A sign of these crime-wary times?

And we visit Cockermouth, the modest, market town where Wordsworth was born. Valerie buys an old willow basket; I find a hand-made thick glass vase, tall and wide enough to take the longest-stemmed irises and roses. 'A good hunk of glass,' remarks the dealer in 'collectables'. 'Shall I say £15?'

Wordsworth House itself is a charming Georgian townhouse, washed in a pale pink with stone-framed windows. (Sebastian elects to remain outside with Greedy.) Positioned between the river (banked with daffodils) and the church, the well-proportioned, uncluttered rooms exude peace and respectability. They are charmingly furnished in the period by the National Trust. Wordsworth's father was given the house in lieu of his duties as attorney-general to the local estate-owner. But father died young. William and sister Dorothy must have found simple Dove Cottage at Grasmere a humble comparison.

Finally I should mention the restaurant at the Sharrow Bay Hotel, Pooley Bridge on Ullswater. Here Dickie put his head on the block and gave us all lunch. There was a marked contrast in attitudes and cuisine between this august establishment and the pub at Rosthwaite. Again we arrived in boots and Barbours, to be speedily ushered into a haven of luxurious clutter, where every tasselled sofa and silk cushion was at our immediate disposal. An excellent meal ensued to include a delectable amuse-gueule of Ullswater trout bathed in lobster cream sauce. The chef, rejoicing in the good looks of a Noël Coward toyboy, solicitously checked our progress throughout the meal, offering us his home-baked bread from a silver salver.

May 4 Hardwicke House

Porridge, our darling golden retriever, was put down today, at teatime. He spent a happy-enough morning, rolling in the fallen petals of the pink cherry tree. But last night he went blind.

What a wonderful dimension is a dog in family life. Ten happy years he gave us all, of love and protection, the truest friend and comforter. I feel him everywhere and I touch him in my mind. Those fluffy wisps on the underside of his tail (which he hated to be brushed); the coarse whorls of curly hair on his back; the silky ears and that bushy froth around his throat; those tender inlets of his paws; how he loved his paws and pads to be fondled.

The grandson of a champion retriever, he taught us manners, the joy of the moment, and unequivocal loyalty.

May 24 Giverny Vernon France

Nobody can dispute Gerald van der Kemp's ultimate elegance. And, on this sunny May morning, a pair of scarlet socks complement his meticulously-polished handmade shoes. He sits beside a bed of brilliant pink tulips, armed with a walking stick and a small cigar. After a decade of exacting toil and enterprise he can afford a rest and to enjoy the sun that gilds his completed dream. We are in Claude Monet's cherished garden at Giverny, forty miles north-west of Paris.

It was ten years ago that the Académie des Beaux-Arts invited Gerald van der Kemp to restore Monet's garden, his house, and studios. Neglected for over thirty years, the famous water-lily pond with its Japanese bridge was a pool of black polluted oil. Tree shoots and fungus were eating into the fabric of the house and studios. The furniture was rotting in the damp and the famous collection of Japanese engravings was mildewed. Worms were everywhere.

With his redoubtable American wife, Florence, to encourage and support, Gerald agreed to undertake the entire renovation of Giverny. After thirty years previously engaged in his magnificent restoration work on Versailles, and with the accolade of the *Légion d'honneur* given to him after the Second World War, in recognition of his saving half the Louvre, Gerald van der Kemp was a big fish. Today he and Florence are fêted as ever; money from illustrious American friends – the Astors, the Annenbergs, the Heinzes, and the Rothschilds – still flows like honey to beautify and improve the Musée Claude Monet. 'I am good for nothing except painting and gardening,' was Monet's modest refrain. Today he would have been amazed by the world interest and love for his accurately-recreated garden, always his essential studio.

We sit long over a leisurely lunch on the wooden balcony of Monet's second studio, now lived in by Gerald and Florence. Her Mexican maids have served us well and we linger over coffee and the exuberant company of a Canadian billionairess; tossing her red hair and bangles she expounds on the novel delights of her husband's new jet-plane with its brace of deluxe double bedrooms. 'But there's just no place in the world far enough, to enjoy a full night's rest,' she comments ruefully. She next admires Florence's delectable dessert, an apple tatin. Could the chef make her one too? Florence finally whisks her off to the newly-renovated stableyard, a handsome complex of stone and beamed barns, set around a cobbled yard. It is currently used for housing visiting students and a bevy of Florence's especially-imported Negro garden boys. 'This is where your donation went,' Florence tells her guest and the donor is clearly satisfied with the picturesque result.

Florence, chic in Chanel and oversize sun-glasses, continues her
stately passage through another busy Sunday at Giverny. There are
letters to sign, the Museum shop and restaurant to oversee, the greenhouses to check, next month's seasonal bedding to arrange, and her
Mexican maids to round up for their return to Paris, and more entertaining round the clock. We say goodbye to her and Gerald amid the
congenial clutter of their garage. The maids circumvent old wicker
chairs, boxes of plants, boxes of discarded, drying bulbs, bicycles, and
boots, as they pack the car with plants and produce for Paris.

Tom and I stroll again in Monet's garden, empty now from the
throng of weekend visitors. 'See it between six and nine in the
evening,' advised Gerald, 'when the colours and effects of light are at
their best.' A lone black trout sidles between the lily pads. The white
wisteria heavily festoons the Japanese bridge; scent and colour is everywhere and everywhere reflected. Monet's flat-bottomed boats are
tethered to the willow trunk. It is all just as he painted.

Before the house itself, glowing in its crushed pink stone façade and
emerald shutters, the beds and bordered paths are a vibrant testimony
to Monet's favourite flowers; the iris and clematis in full bloom, with
the roses soon to come.

July 5 Poulton House Marlborough Wiltshire

My mother's delphiniums have never looked more beautiful; the tall
spires of deep blue, delicate blue, every tone of blue, as varied as the
hues of ancient porcelain. I sit in her herbaceous border where colours
and scents pulsate riotously under the hot sun. Nature's vibrations are
savoured more keenly in the face of my father's death.

They kept his body for me to see at my request. I had driven from
London through darkening sunset and calm of a summer's night. A
new moon hovered. It was Friday night, he died, July 3 at 9.15 p.m.
I was beside his bed by 11. His forehead felt warm, but how pale the
skin on his diminished head, tightly-stretched and spent with the
exertions of death. The plump Irish nurse touched my elbow. 'Your
mother had a nice little moment with him at the end. Cradling his
head, she was.' They had washed him – the two nurses – but his
mouth gaped horribly.

We sat in the drawing-room below, my mother, my brother and
the nurses. Lights were on all over the house; the atmosphere was
peaceful, happy almost, after the strain of the day. We drank whisky
and beer and smoked and talked and waited for the undertakers. (They
had been recalled by the doctor from the local pub earlier.) They

brought my father down the fine eighteenth-century oak staircase on a long stretcher. He was over six foot tall even in death. He had been covered in a green tarpaulin. My mother could not watch his final leave of her. She wrapped herself, despite the exceptionally warm night, in a plaid rug. Father was driven off into the night. I stood in the light of the front doorway and watched him turn the corner of the drive, out of sight. Late that night I felt pulled awake – inexorably. I sensed rare vibrations of love – ecstasy almost; the moment passed quickly. I believed it was my father. He had longed to die, but he was afraid to die. Had he found joy?

July 27 The Town Quay Southampton

The *Lord Nelson* is a 141-foot, 3-masted barque. Sebastian and I board at 1400 hours and are rapidly initiated in safety drill on the top deck. We are fifty aboard. An assemblage of ten permanent crew, twenty physically disabled, and twenty able companions. Orange life-jackets are awkwardly hoisted and strapped. We are next commanded to muster at our stations. Sebastian and I are posted to Aft Port for the ten-day voyage. Haydon, a sprightly Welshman from Tenby area, assisted by Simon, a Scot from the Isle of Mull, attempt to unravel for us the mysteries of the ropes – sheets? – braces? We practise the pull and let go; pull and let go; make fast handsomely and coil. I notice in the middle of this exercise that Sebastian has wrong-footed his new yachting plimsoles. The general activity switches to starboard. I shield him from view as he settles himself on a bollard to adjust his footwear.

I am next persuaded by the zealous Haydon to clamber forty feet up the rigging of the main sail. I funk the final rungs to the crow's nest. The clouds scud in a fresh breeze and seagulls wheel noisily around. I descend cautiously to deck. And where is Bass? 'He's on galley duty!' An official-looking man wearing a sweat shirt emblazoned with 'For Fox Sake – Stop Hunting!' seems to know everybody's immediate movements. I discover Bass enjoying an early supper of fried fish and icecream with a bevy of fellow helpers in the galley. He later serves us plates of food in the main lower mess, clears them and dunks them in pails of soapy water, prior to stowing them in a food hoist.

A very mechanised boat this, enabling the handicapped to work alongside the able-bodied. There are six wheel-chair cases on board; they manoeuvre themselves adroitly from deck to deck to the bridge, on specially-designed chair-lifts.

July 28

Day 2

'Bracing stations!' 'Bracing stations!' I share a fat, long sheet with a diminutive young man called Abdul. Is he English? We haul in the sheet companionably and converse, through bursts of wind and breath. 'I was born in Zambia and my parents are Indian.' His provenance proves as intricate as the coils and rigging.

'Clean up the spaghetti!' yells Haydon. Again we coil and hook the sheets. A coffee break and 'smoko' ensues. Lunch of cold mackerel, hunks of cheddar, salad, and Kitty the cook's succulent flapjacks, appears at midday. We disembark down Southampton Water at 1400 hours. Bass and I are on night-watch duty. At 3 a.m. Haydon calls a break; we drink hot tea in the warm galley and eat more flapjacks.

July 29 Normandy France

Day 3 At 1400 hours we arrive at Ouistreham on the Normandy coast. In a persistent drizzle we motor eight kilometres up the canal to Caen. Our narrow route is lined with purple buddleia and waving fishermen. The sun emerges as we moor on the outskirts of the town; suddenly it is hot. Bass and I walk a mile into Centre Ville and drink citron pressé in this pleasant country town, famous for its golden stone. We walk beside the handsome marina taking care not to trip over the painters; our newly-acquired sea legs are unsteady on shore.

Back on board, the beautiful young Bella is on galley duty. The bawdy supper table teases her about 'what' and her private education. She plies them with their curried chicken and fields their noisy badinage with aplomb.

Francis, the assistant boatswain (a Tarzanian six-footer with rippling upper arms that only look at home when hauling in the sheets), gives a demonstration of wind and sail on his large model ship, while Lorna, the hefty paraplegic table tennis champion, catches up with two bowls of lemon meringue; she had been too sea-sick to eat her lunch.

Day 4

Bass and I take wheel-chair-bound Sue into Caen. Pushing her proves good exercise. After lunch we leave for Cherbourg – seventy-four miles as the gull flies. I watch from the bridge as Haydon patiently demonstrates to Bass how to coil a rope. He is later given thirty minutes on the helm and is inordinately pleased with his newly-acquired nautical abilities.

Day 5

A force 6 wind and tacking in the Channel is vastly extending our seventy-four-mile voyage to Cherbourg. We sail all day. Bass is commissioned to clean the ship's large brass bell. He later fastens an even better coil. At tea break the Captain calls us all to the lower mess. We are urged to spruce up the ship with even more vigour; Prince Philip plans to board her at Cowes on Monday. In preparation for our night watch from 2000 to 2400 hours I retire to my bunk with its own porthole and its own pair of curtains. A headache induces two hours' welcome sleep.

Bass and I muster in the chart room at the start of our watch. We pick up a distress call on our radio – 'Willow Wind, Willow Wind – can anybody hear me out there?' – 'Lord Nelson for Willow Wind – where are you heading?' The owner of *Willow Wind* explains that he left Chichester at 4 a.m. and now at 2000 hrs, sixteen hours on, he is lost somewhere between Alderney and Cherbourg. 'Poor devil,' mutters our navigator, Paul. 'Probably got his wife and kids on board.' 'Lord Nelson from Willow Wind, I am heading for Cherbourg.' Paul puts him on course. 'Thank you, Lord Nelson. Willow Wind, Willow Wind, now on course for Cherbourg.' But at 2130 hours he is back on the air. He has in fact been heading for Ouistreham, and has grounded his yacht on a mudbank.

We sail through the night, tacking at 2400 hours off the Cherbourg promontory. Round the head proves a rough, fast sail.

August 1 Cherbourg

Day 6

At 1200 hours we reach Cherbourg in bright sun and calm. The Captain informs us that, due to the persistent west wind, our seventy-four-mile journey from Caen to Cherbourg, when finally completed, covered 234 nautical miles! A pleasant afternoon; we wander through the streets of enticing food shops with our cavalcade of wheelchairs. Haydon buys a crate of Stella Artois beer. I telephone Tom from a street kiosk to report our rough and tumble progress. He reminds me that I can always jump ship on to the *QE2* for a more comfortable channel return.

Day 7

A misty, dull morning. Bass and I take ourselves through the town to the Yacht Club marina. The mast halyards are in full chorus, and in the old stone church the organ and congregation put on a hearty performance. Nearby a bronze statue of Napoleon, on a prancing horse, is embellished by beds of blue ageratum and scarlet begonia at his feet. At 12.30 we embark for the Dorset coast.

Straightforward sailing through the afternoon with the wind a more moderate force 5. Haydon and Francis give a demonstration on sheets and sails. Most of the nautical jargon flies over my head into the winds; but it is pleasant by the bowsprit with the evening sun throwing a wide golden shaft on our portside. It grows cold and Trev in his wheelchair becomes nervous (quite rightly) about my ability to hold him steady. And numb with cold I lurch with him and his chair back to the stair lift and the warm comforts of the lower mess deck.

Bass and I struggle with the confined shower arragements (a space of four feet square to include the lavatory) to wash our hair in prep-aration for HRH's teatime visit tomorrow. We spend the second night running in warm trousers in anticipation of our dawn watch.

August 3 Cowes

Day 8

Having anchored at 1300 hours off Swanage Bay, we set sail for Cowes in the morning sun and a south-west wind. Past Studland Bay, Lymington, and the Needles finely silhouetted to our starboard. A riot of striped and spotted spinnakers – yellow, blue, red and green – race towards us and about. We approach Cowes proudly, all sails ahoy; boats of all sizes eddy in our wake and take a closer look.

Prince Philip comes aboard at 1800 hours with a small entourage of naval officers in hats and uniform. He does a turn round the decks. Bass and I stand by the bowsprit. 'Where are you from? How did you hear of the *Lord Nelson*? And you are off back to Weymouth?' We have quite a little exchange. I whip off my sunglasses, not knowing whether it is rude to gaze through a dark lens at royalty.

August 4 Cowes

Day 9

I am on twenty-four hour galley duty. A sunny day but a cold north wind. Small yachts scurry by on race courses best known to themselves. A huge warship fires a 21-gun salute after breakfast in honour of the Queen Mother's birthday. The smoke and fire balls look furiously alarming, even against the bright sunlight.

Many of our crew go ashore in a rubber dinghy. Bass and I clear lunch and pile dishes into a very small dishwasher. It takes at least five loads to mop up after thirty for lunch. Simon, a nice young man with a beard and confined to a chair, helps us. He takes such a possessive interest in loading and unloading the biggest plates that the whole exercise is delayed a little. Bass spends a happy afternoon with Kitty, the cook. He whips cream and crushes raspberries through a sieve, to concoct a fool. He then encourages the Lord Mayor of Cowes and other visiting dignitaries to dip their fingers in the bowl.

At 1900 hours we leave Cowes for Weymouth, our final port, having been delayed one and half hours. A knot was found in the anchor; the centre coils had dipped deep into the sand and then clogged when hauled up.

Fine tomorrow? It is a red sky tonight – 'shepherd's delight'. Bass steers our windless course past the Needles. Home ahoy!

August 10 *Marmaris South Turkish Coast*

On board *Virgo*, a 2-masted, 75-foot, 47-ton ketch, built 1986 in Taiwan, registered as British in Southampton and owned by a Turk. A French crew of four completes this global provenance. A luxurious interior with generous double-bunks sports immaculate plumbing.

August 12 *The Bay of Ekincik*

A wasp plague over breakfast, but the hot northerly wind, the 'Meltem', had dropped. These sudden squalls result from low pressure over Pakistan and high pressure over the Azores; they prevail on this southern Anatolian coast through June, July and August.

We anchored last night in this small bay, poised for our visit today to the ancient ruins of Caunos. But this peaceful place with its surround of pine-forested, steep red cliffs is already threatened by future plans for a marina and hotel complex. We reach Caunos in a simple, canopied boat through a winding lagoon, banked with reeds and marshland. Our diminutive skipper plies us with boiled sweets and insists on anointing our sweaty palms with eau de cologne. Mercifully he has a cache of bottled water on board. Although only 8.30 a.m., it is hot with no breath of wind. We look out for the kingfishers, the hawks and the turtles; local sighting as proffered by our guide books, but no such diversions come our way.

The crumbled props of ancient Caunos, set high on the foothills of the Taurus mountain range, loom into view. A battlemented castle, an amphitheatre, the original harbour; their total abandonment is haunting, the remote setting a beautiful time-warp suspended between mountain, sea, and wooded cliffs. A local guide scoops us up in a tour (a motley crowd of Turkish, English, German, and French). He explains how the medieval inhabitants were struck down with malaria from the unhealthy marsh surrounds and were noted for their 'sickly, greenish complexion'. He himself proves a splendid specimen of improved twentieth-century living. A thatch of waved hair tops his handsome head (a pity though about the pot belly). 'We have famous fish farms here. We grow much cotton. It is easier than rice and fetch more moneys. We have fine honey and wild boars in the mountain woods.' Being an Islamic country they do not eat the boar, but their tourist industry encourages the sale of tusks. 'I love my fertile lands,' he smiles ingratiatingly at us. We feel poor and white before his burnished torso; he slaps his huge stomach as though it were a prized emblem of his native prosperity.

August 13 Fethiye

Fethiye is a dump. Re-built after a devastating earthquake in 1957, it fared better after a similar débâcle in 1856 when the ancient stones from shattered theatres, temples, and fortresses were judiciously re-employed.

The rock tombs, dating from the fourth century BC, have survived these past rigours. Tom and I take a taxi up the hill to check out the finely-carved tomb of Amyntas, which has dominated this harbour for sixteen centuries. Set proudly in the rock face high above, its Greek-styled Ionic columns support a triangular pediment, notched with a Greek key frieze. The unfortunate placement of a municipal telegraph pole alongside does not diminish its grandeur.

We ship a fresh supply of water from the quay, and Isabelle, our chef, buys a prolific haul of fish, lamb, fruits, and cheeses from the market. Tom and I argue desultorily with the kelim dealer at the Lykya Hotel; he has a pretty-enough rendition of the Tree of Life design. He wants £350. We offer him £250. On our tactical return, he has scarpered to the market. We let it go, let the anchor go, and sail through the afternoon at a spanking eleven knots. We anchor in the complete seclusion of the Gemiler Bay, where cicadas chorus shrilly in the pine-trees. We dine on deck in candlelight, no meltem wind disturbs the peace of a waning moon and silky sea.

August 14

We take the boat round the point to Ölü Deniz (the 'Dead Sea' harbour) where Tom and I book a taxi for the journey to Kalkan, a trip recommended by our friends in Istanbul and our captain, Pierre. '*La côte devient plus plate et un peu ennuyeuse. C'est maintenant plus intéressant la route par auto.*' Having travelled the entire coast road in 1983, I am conscious of how little one gleans of a country's colours, terrain, and tradition from a boat's eye view. The dramatic silhouette of the Taurus mountains and the scenic formation of jagged bays and inlets are beguiling enough, but our inland trip will be a stimulating contrast from the waves and sky.

But what a change in Ölü Deniz and its adjacent white arc of sand. Deserted in May 1983, but now heavily invaded with busloads from Fethiye on an August afternoon, four years ahead. Comments Pierre: '*Il faut venir au milieu de Septembre jusqu'à la première semaine en Octobre; puis c'est le temps encore parfait et moins de bateau.*'

As a pre-dinner cultural aperitif, Maxine persuades us to re-visit a patch of mosaic that she had discovered on our morning visit to the Gemili islet. It had passed the rest of us by. We fasten the dinghy to the rocks and follow her up through stones and bushes to a breath-taking vantage point over the surrounding islands. A small terraced floor of simple black and white mosaic and a toppled column of white alabaster with a cross inscribed in relief, suggest an ancient venue of prayer. There is little known of Gemili. Some suggest that it was a Byzantine settlement, subsequently demolished by earthquakes. Simple ruins of such a community are dotted all over, straddled by wild bushes and goats that tread gingerly.

During dinner, a grotesque gin palace (a breed of boat always dismissed by Pierre as *bidets*) encroaches on our ground. It churns its bulk into our little bay, promptly slinging its anchor across our own. Pierre's protestations to the surly Greek captain fail to budge the monster. We continue our dinner on deck while Isabelle calmy flames a lemon meringue pie to soothe our tempers. In the early morning, Tom clambers up the hill, camera in hand; using a wide-angle lens he captures this gross intrusion for posterity. Pierre compiles a report for the potential perusal of Lloyds of London insurance department. In the event of a meltem blowing up in the night, we could have been smashed in the bows.

August 15 Kalkan

Tom and I take our taxi from Fethiye to Kalkan. We halt at the ruins
of Xanthos and Patara; the former has a substantial theatre complex
with the usual stew of toppled capitals heaped upon the stage. A
handsome marble frieze that adorned a tomb – second century AD –
has since been removed to the British Museum. The plaster mould
replacement does not inspire. On to Patara where an imposing 'Arch
of Triumph', closely resembling our own Marble Arch, heralds the
entrance to the habitual line-up of agora, baths and theatre complex.
Situated beside the sea, Patara has been largely obliterated by the sands
of time. We stand in the theatre well and can only guess at the
architectural bran tub hidden under our feet.

    We arrive at Kalkan at noon, a charming harbour, forging bravely
ahead to accommodate escalating tourism. A newly-laid-out quay
boasts a generous supply of water taps. We lunch in an air-conditioned
hotel – completed a mere month ago. At 3.30, the *Virgo* makes her
majestic entrance with Anthony[1] and Maxine[2]. Following our indifferent report on Patara they elect to forgo their pre-planned sight-seeing
of the same. We wander up the steep, narrow streets from the harbour.
Pierre and Tony negotiate for kelims and saddlebags. We dine ashore
where we are seduced with fried mussels, spiced yoghurts, taramasalata
and succulent prawns grilled in white cheeses. White fish follows. It
is dull and we are full. A timely gaggle of geese and stray cats collect
below us, over the wall; they are handsomely rewarded.

August 16 Greece

We leave Kalkan and sail to a small Greek island; again uninhabited
except by elegant black goats that take up extreme positions on the highest crags, veritable 'Monarchs of the Glen'. We bathe in the clearest,
brightest turquoise sea and later disappoint Isabelle by returning our
swordfish steaks and our hot ratatouille almost untouched. The sun,
we explain. *Le soleil, comprenez?*

    In the evening we moor at another Greek island, inhabited, this
one – Kastelorrizo. A charming line of whitewashed houses with
variously-coloured shutters and elegant iron balconies. A fat lady with
'room to let', her yellow hair imperiously coiled, stands squarely on
her balcony and watches us anchor. We wander along the quayside

---

[1] Anthony Gray; specialist adviser on industrial development and technology.
[2] Maxine (née Brodrick), his lovely, vivacious, second wife.

heaped with fishing nets and old women smothered in black. Young men throw prawns and mussels on their flaming braziers. We are persuaded to indulge in their wares, and again ruin our diminishing appetites. Isabelle's dinner of cheese-stuffed pancakes, fillet steaks in a creamed pepper sauce, and îles flottantes proves the final dénouement to our digestive systems.

August 17 Greece

My forty-seventh birthday which Anthony and Maxine mark with an intriguing Turkish brass pen case and encrier. Anthony announces that he needs boiled eggs for breakfast to settle his stomach. A board meeting ensues regarding our future meals: two courses rather than four and less sauces. Isabelle enquires rather nervously about 'the birthday cake'. It is agreed that birthday cake and champagne can be happily contained in the lunch plans.

We set off for a further Greek island and bathe. A bottle of Veuve Clicquot swiftly follows, exquisitely chilled. We lunch more simply on grilled prawns and the anticipated cake, a rich, moist chocolate marjolaine. Isabelle explains that it is not perfectly set. Would we prefer it later in the afternoon? There is a unanimous decision to eat it straightaway; the risk of being haunted by a chocolate cake until tea-time, possibly even until dinner, is not to be contemplated.

We move on to the fast-developing harbour of Kas where I opt for bed and a boiled egg. The sun has taken its hold.

Kaş is an attractive, prosperous harbour; palm-trees shade the colourful streets, scarlet hibiscus and morning glory festoon the white-washed shops and houses. Tom introduces us to Serhan at the 'Anatolian Art Gallery of quality kelims and carpets'. His old house is cool with its ribbed wooden ceiling and polished floors. We settle down to a session of leisurely tea and display. The walls are hung and piled high with carpets and kelims; a cobbled courtyard leads off from his showroom; more an extended living-room, scattered with comfortable basket chairs; a loom, a guitar, and a backgammon board; a few black hens strut between the pots and beds of bright flowers. We buy a cicim, a blue, lime and tan rug with a handsome embossed design of the 'tree of life'. Recently woven in hand-spun lamb's wool, it cost £100.

August 20 Kale Koy Kekova Bay Turkey

The days drift by in sybaritic pleasures. Goats and peasants and the occasional precariously-placed Lycian tomb command our attention; the latter to be found dotted on hilltops of the remotest islands or incongruously parked in the middle of shallow harbour waters. Denis shows us a bay where natural springs of ice-cold water make for refreshing bathing, almost too refreshing. He then escorts us through the heat and stones and scratches of wild herb bushes to a deserted mud plateau; it is pierced in its navel by a medieval well. Goats and donkeys descend to sip delicately its pea-green contents. We congratulate Denis on his amazing 'fiefdom' and stumble back to his ice-cool springs in keen anticipation.

Pierre takes us to an excellent restaurant rejoicing in a galaxy of orange and red winking lights. A zealous generator alongside is almost drowned by a background whirl of taped Dervish dance music. We eat well in this thriving wood-constructed enterprise, built only last October. With a complement of some fifty customers, French, Italians and ourselves, it certainly has put one more deserted bay on the tourist map.

By day Maxine delights us with her tactical bargaining. She even manages to winkle an extraordinary crustacean delicacy from a wizened fisherman. Isabelle assures us it is a Mediterranean *cigale*, a sort of giant grasshopper with the tender, pink flesh of a langoustine. Once more Isabelle's epicurean talents are promptly revealed; more than can be reported of poor Franck, the under-deckhand (of Nantes extraction). An unfortunate mishap invades his morning on breakfast duty. At a stroke (when the final embellishments of eggs and more marmalade and fresh coffee have been hoisted up the hatch) the deck table collapses. We temporarily abandon poor Franck as he hoses down a viscous clog of honey, egg, and cornflakes. We have had a magical time cruising around the beguiling bay and inlets of these Kekova waters.

August 21 Olympus Turkey

We leave Finike harbour at 11 a.m. 'A dusty, ramshackle town,' as noted in Pierre's navigation bible, the *Turkish Waters Pilot*. However it has served well in replenishing toothpaste and unfamiliar suncreams. My own tube spurts a jelly so black that I fear for the boat's sea-covers. Anthony, in an attempt to relieve the tedium of motoring beside an indifferent stretch of coast, addresses his mind to the ancient history of Anatolia. His efforts are admirable, and he is soon in a position of unassailable knowledge with a captive audience. We are all initiated into the most precise outline of the emerging, the converging, and the submerging of Hittites, Hurrians, Lycians, and Assyrians. I repeat that his delivery could not be more precise and has the ultimate distinction of lasting a mere five minutes. But Maxine sees another bird and Tom (a Renaissance man himself) sees his watch-hand creep to noon and a gin and tonic. Our minds have remained seated in the face of Anthony's generous efforts to lift them from the mire of ignorance. My own has struggled to stand and in a tottering position has even caught the gist of this whole historical stewpot. Anthony helps me further by drawing an excellent map of the whole of Anatolia. Having established that the digits refer to BC dates rather than to mountain heights, I am marginally enlightened.

This evening our site-seeing takes on a dramatic turn. We beach at Olympus in our dinghy (Yamaha with remote control). An enthusiastic native with Mehmet emblazoned on his khaki shirt and a pistol slung from his belt pulls us ashore. The pebble beach is otherwise abandoned as the pale, clear water shuffles the white, grey, pink, and indigo stones, until the tip of a white scarf darts from a far cave; a group of peasant women and fishermen are keeping their distance. A backdrop of wooded cliffs plunges its guard around us as Mehmet beckons us through a screen of pink oleanders. To our right a flotilla of white ducks on a fresh waterstream quack companionably.

Having rounded up his loot for a tour of the ruins, Mehmet insists on decorating Maxine and me with sprigs of myrtle and laurel. Seizing the branches he makes us each a crown and presents us with herbal nosegays. Sporting headdresses some two feet in diameter that constantly entangle the branches around us like misguided antlers, and clasping our nosegays, makes for slow progress over the dishevelled stones. In no time I have landed in a helpless heap at the foot of a stairway. With hats and bones still intact we proceed through a remarkable mystery tour of finely-incised Greek doorways leading nowhere. A crumbling aqueduct, a posse of inaccessible Greek tombs, and the sensation that we are re-enacting exerpts from *A Midsummer Night's Dream*. A shambolic site of intriguing dimensions. I suggest that Olympus should be twinned with Stonehenge. On quick reflection Anthony feels that the Mayor of Devizes could not handle it. After almost two hours of musing and meandering in Mehmet's wake, the ducks loom into sight again; our starting point. The relief of Mafeking?

August 22

With our tour of Olympus fresh in mind, unsurpassed in its eccentric turns, the undivided attentions of Mehmet and the conviction that we had owned the place, we reach Phaselis in the heat of midday.

An extensive ruin, its broad streets, its theatre, its temple, and wide choice of baths and general recreation grounds clearly denote the luxurious modus vivendi of the Graeco-Romans from the sixth century BC. It also reflects the extent of the twentieth-century tourist boom. Again, remembering it on a May morning in 1983, deserted and strewn with bright wild flowers, I am now amazed at its crowd of visitors – the international world and its wife, variously clad in bikinis and sawn-off shorts.

We head on to Antalya which again bustles and bulges with a polyglot tourist invasion. An attractive old harbour with narrow streets winding up to the cliff-tops. There are kelim shops on every corner, with rugs draped and hung about the old stone walls and pavements. Calls to prayer reverberate through this timeless city at regular intervals. As Anthony observes, 'these Muslims never go to bed.'

October 16 Hardwicke House

Amazing devastation seen from the bedroom window this morning, the front lawn a battle scene of snapped willow boughs, the oak tree fallen – ripped up by its roots – the sumach torn down, a heavy terracotta tub, diameter five feet, upturned. Last night's savage winds cut a trail of disastrous damage from the Channel Islands to Humberside. Kent, Sussex, Surrey, and above all London took the brunt of the four-hour storm. Huge, mature trees have been tumbled from their roots in every street and square. Urban root systems are necessarily shallow and inhibited by inadequate ground conditions, circling in confined space rather than freely spreading; nevertheless the toll in the London parks is unprecedented. And Kew Gardens report huge losses to include rare specimen trees. They claim gloomily that it will take 200 years to fully establish their treasured scape of only yesterday.

A collision course of warm, humid air from West Africa and cold, Arctic air from the Atlantic caused the near hurricane, the worst and most violent storm ever recorded in Britain. Gusts of 94 mph were noted in central London. Meanwhile the Met. Office failed dismally in their non-prediction of this holocaust; lawyers believe they will be held liable for damage claims in the event of a future Court enquiry.

The furniture trade has certainly had a windfall; trunks of mature oak and beech will be selling like hot cakes. There is comfort also in that few people died in the storm, some twenty in all. How lucky it struck at night – from 2 to 6 a.m. – with people safe in bed. Indeed it could be argued that, if the Met. Office had given precise warning, panic may have set in; people securing their greenhouses and rabbit-hutches may have been fatal victims.

It was frightening to hear that wind thundering down the chimneys. We looked out at 3 a.m.; the trees were wild with the frenzied gusts and tugs; tortured renditions of Van Gogh's swirling cypresses. We feared helplessly for our willows and left the puppies, undisturbed, in their baskets. It would have been madness to honour their calls to nature in that frenzied dawn.

October 22 Hardwicke House

I rode through Richmond Park this morning; an estimated 700 trees were felled in last week's storm. But, apart from the dishevelment of broken branches littering the wooded areas, the damage seemed well-contained. The wide oak avenue dipping down to White Lodge and the sheltered space of Pen Ponds presented an intact front. A few casualties of beech on Test Hill. In this whole area of 2,500 acres, a toll of 700 fallen trees would only average a victim every three acres. However, in the *Richmond and Twickenham Times*, the Park's super-intendent, Mr Michael Baxter-Brown, says that the damage has been so extensive that the real level of destruction may not be known for many weeks yet. I am sure he is right (and pompous, too, they say). But a gentle ride on a calm sunny morning deluded the eye of any substantial havoc. The stags and deer nibbled contentedly on the unexpected accessibility of so much lush foliage, a timely alternative to the rutting season which they seem to have temporarily abandoned.

And the pickings are certainly rich for the cabinet-makers. Quality timber abounds. The Queen's nephew, Viscount Linley, who has his own furniture business, is reported to have already examined two prized walnuts and is now sizing up ten oaks at Slough. Disaster can leave serendipity in its trail, for some.

1988

Immaculate in his white jacket he hovers before our host Julian Byng. 'What have you there, Sobers?' Sobers balances a bottle of vin rosé in his long black fingers. Should he serve it with lunch today? The wine looks clouded, more rust than rosé. Sobers volunteers that it is an old bottle; indeed it has been at 'Laughing Waters' longer than him. 'And how long have you been with us, Sobers?' Nine and a half years, records the butler. On further investigation the whole case is pronounced off and a more dependable red wine, bought last week from Nick's Discount, is selected.

'Laughing Waters' was built by Julian and Eve Byng fifteen years ago, on a bank of wooded scrub set above the west shore. Today the arched and pillared walls of white coral stone and the cool verandas with their high wood-raftered ceilings are encrusted with bougainvillea and the vivid pinks and scarlet of hibiscus. A lawn of deep-pile emerald slopes to the sea. A streak of turquoise glitters through a screen of coconut palms, mahogany trees, and the feathered fronds of casuarinas and flamboyants.

The sun is up and heating fast by seven. Beach boys rake the fallen leaves from the manchineel grove that shades the soft white sand. Their red fruit would swell the throat; it is deadly poison and the milky leaf can sting. I am intrigued by the alien properties of these glossy green trees as explained to me by the wide-eyed boy. And how to spell this exotic species? He shrugs and rakes and repeats his warning. 'You asked a beach boy how to spell Manchineel?' Julian is incredulous, but agrees that the youth might have been flattered to have been equated with a superior education.

Early each morning we slice through the warm sea and gain the raft, our bodies browner with each dawn. William the Scottish Laird from Perth, Annie the champion golfer, Julian our finely-tuned host, and Eve whose beautiful eyes reflect the turquoise all around. Caroline[1] flashes past on her mono ski; we cheer her in her sprayed arc of triumph and moan when she flounders and falls. But where is our flamboyant friend, the Lord Lieutenant of Warwickshire, who sports his panama in the waves with its garnish of woodcock feathers? (He prefers to go out in the midday sun.) We begin to count the remaining

[1] Caroline, Lady Newman, whose husband, Sir Gerard, had died in 1987.

days; there is talk of snow back home. But now it is a brisk swim back to breakfast, to Gertrude's crooning over crisp bacon, her soft eggs sunny side up, the fritters with guava syrup, the paw-paws, and the sugar bird that skims through the arches to nibble on Tom's panama.

Outings to gardens are mooted and planned: Andromeda, the Flowers of the Forest, a visit to the Portvale Sugar Factory in St Thomas Parish. Yesterday we walked through the cool of St James's Church at Hole-town, an early seventeenth-century white stone interior, liberally adorned with memorial plaques of the first English settlers and a welcome escape from the heat and hustle of Nick's Discount, the supermarket, and the exhortations of 'Angry Annie' to drink a complimentary rum punch at her restaurant ('famous for ribs'). And there is an invitation to dinner from Stephen Cave, a descendant of the original plantocracy, whose family built the oldest seventeenth-century house on the island.

In the abating mid-afternoon heat we drive to Andromeda's Garden, an exotic profusion of tropicalia perched high above the foaming breakers of the east coast line. Planted thirty years ago by a reclusive Scot, the garden now bulges with an intriguing show of labelled exotica. A plethora of ferns – staghorn, fishtail, and rabbit's foot – and strange trees such as breadfruit, candlestick, mast, and screwpine, tumble and twist in strategic confusion. A glut of vivid flowers in outsize fanciful shapes lust after light and water. They make the warm air closer with their heavy breathing and they give no scent. There is something presumptuous about flowers of bright colour that have no fragrance. It is an exquisite display and William and his Countess Pamela, who are prone to orchids, are determined on re-vamping their Scottish greenhouses.

Tom sees a mongoose; the frogs bleep shrilly from the lily pool, and a young black girl prances at us from behind a pagoda plant, her long legs flying. Will we help sponsor her school trip to Canada? We fumble for dollar notes and she flounces off delighted. Minutes later William misses his wallet; general consternation ends in relief as it is tracked down to his backside pocket. With his nose and mind stuck in a *Duranta Repens* bush (Golden Dewdrop) he had stowed it absent-mindedly.

The sun is low over the sugar canefields as we drive towards home. Wide lands of waving pale green, where faint wafts of treacle – sweet and black – billow about where the cane is cropped. The smell thickens as we near the sugar factory, a complex of gleaming steel vats and drums and clanking shafts (made seven years ago in Derby, England). On entering the precincts the aroma becomes one remove from silage. A gallant with 'Leon Greenich' stamped on his tee-shirt guides us through the maze of machinery. The mystery of molasses is revealed. We see the juice bleed from the crunched cane, tossed and crunched, tossed and crunched into a sea of pulp and scum, and into a frenzied ferment of boiling syrup that cools to glass that is shattered into sugar. Leon unceremoniously scoops up surplus sugar from the factory floor and heaps our sticky palms. The crystal grains are light brown with a tinge of green. They smell strong and real.

The island of Barbados is twenty-one miles long and fourteen miles wide. For three hundred years it has subsisted on its sugar trade; through the centuries it has sustained the pain of slave emancipation and the competition of an expanding world sugar market. Today, strengthened by twenty-two years of independence, good housekeeping, and good rule, the island flourishes.

Tourism has proved an additional resource to sugar and the undeniable tolerance between white and black must be the envy of the Caribbean necklace; perhaps Barbados is the prized and envied pendant. Halcyon days? Driving from the airport, south of Bridgetown, at the start of our stay, we passed streams of schoolchildren, happy, healthy groups, bright-eyed and trim in uniform. What will become of them all? Will they be contained in Barbados? Emigration is already written on the wall – to America, Canada and the UK. Ronald Tree reflected on this same question in his book on Barbados. In 1949, tired from the war years and his extensive Anglo-American involvements, he built his distinctive neo-Palladian villa, Heron Bay. Set smack on the silver sand with a modest boundary of coral stone boulders, a variety of trees – teak, mango, mahogany, palms, and a small park behind – it must be the quintessence of architectural contemporary elegance. (Where the formidable Lady Salisbury, a regular guest, is said to have stuck solidly to her lisle stockings and tweeds in the heat of the February high season.)

We dine with Stephen Cave in his arresting house, St Nicholas Abbey. Built in the 1650s in the style of a Jacobean manor house, it is magnificently staged in a grove of mahogany trees with views of the east coast spreading below. Darkness has fallen, and we arrive to the stunning impact of its flood-lit façade, now painted cream with the window coining picked out in faint grey. The night is still and the garden a delicious profusion of tubs, brimful of flowers; bougainvillea, white begonia, and orange blossom cascade to the tailored parterres. A backdrop of palms and the habitual Douanier Rousseau jumble of ferns, banana leaves, and ginger lilies complete the scenario. A lion or tiger raising its head from the dense greenery would appear in place.

Our host leads us into his cool panelled rooms where we descend comfortably to earth with rum punches and New Zealand lamb stew.

He later ushers us into the old stables, where we sit in rows and watch a remarkable film, compiled by his father in 1934, of the St Nicholas Abbey estate. The women were filmed wearing dainty white hats and cotton dresses as they gathered up the harvested canes. Horses and cattle were instrumental in pulling the heavy cartloads and turning the cumbersome sugar mills. Apart from the ensuing demise of hats and horses, life on the plantation today seems little changed.

Back at 'Laughing Waters' we are greeted by the beaming night-watchman. He is poised by the spacious first-floor veranda and fondles his truncheon, or 'night-stick', as he calls it. We admire its milled head and leather strap handle. Is it made of mahogany? He assures me not, that it is made from the green-heart tree. I nod in complete misunderstanding; it is a different world.

In my hapless quest for scented blooms I am surprised one evening by a delectable whiff exuding from above the laughing waterfall in the Byngs' garden. Believing I was finally on the trail of some tuberose that had been encouraged to spill the beans by the afternoon's heavy shower, I sniffed like a dog at the hibiscus hedge and beneath the trees. But the elusive scent had flown. Whereupon Julian emerging from his bedroom, newly-dressed for dinner, asked me if I was enjoying an evening stroll. And I concluded that the scent that got away had been the pungent aftershave escaping through his bathroom window.

March 4 Hardwicke House

Last night we dined with daughter, Lydia; now removed to the blissful independence of South Clapham. We were encouraged to bring wine and sat ceremoniously sipping in her pretty drawing-room. She was cock-a-hoop with her new house (early Victorian, freehold, with an attractive front and good windows). Her trustees paid the asking price of £157,000 last October. An exorbitant price in the face of the Stock Exchange Crash – and yet still deemed a good investment. And her job? Her love life? For once the latter was non-existent. 'I am lying fallow – rotating my crops.' But the job! Her face crinkled with irrepressible glee. She was off on her first business trip – solo – to Birmingham; two nights in a hotel! And last week it was Brighton; she arranged all the shoots, the make-up artist, the positions. It was cold on the beach; the poor model froze, but her breasts responded magnificently. Oh! And the Bacardi Rum advertisement! She set that up on a tropical roof garden in Kensington. Lydia works for the Penthouse Magazine Group in Docklands; she is a graphic designer; a daughter of her generation.

March 6 The Cromwell Hospital

My brother Malcolm's forty-fifth birthday. We take him cake and champagne. It is eight weeks since he suffered a major stroke; a cerebral vascular infarction they call it; a clot on the brain. From a state of near-total paralysis and lack of speech, he can now talk again and move every inch of his body. Will he make it all the way? The doctors and nurses are amazed at his progress; his mental determination is phenomenal. He now stakes his 100% recovery on a smiling Barbara (Barbadian father, Scottish mother). She is strong and strict and full of jokes. She hoists him and pummels and bullies and cajoles him through six hours of intensive therapy a day.

March 26 Faringdon House Faringdon Berkshire

Visibility is good as we skirt Oxfordshire and veer towards Faringdon House. Green stirs in hedges and trees; ploughed fields are now ruffled with wheat. The Mercedes telephone buzzes and Tom takes the call in a lay-by. His travelling companion to Punjab is checking his passport number for visa formalities. They leave for India tomorrow at 6.30 a.m.

At Faringdon – a stunning early Georgian house and not too big – the vintage white Rolls stands at the front door; it will whisk the bride to the even more ancient church at the end of the garden.

The church is full of flowered hats and men with tidy hair. White jasmine and roses swirl around the wide pillars. A young man soothes a baby in the next pew with a bottle of orange juice.

The bride is late; twenty minutes and now thirty minutes. What has happened? The spectators become more subdued and the organist repeats his tune. Has her father missed his connections from America? Has the Rolls broken down? Perhaps our heroine, even now, is striding across the lawn in her gumboots? Or could she have changed her mind? Her mother and her groom look perfectly composed. 'Annabelle is always late,' murmurs a discarded swain seated behind us. But now she arrives! Supreme and radiant. *Honi soit qui mal y pense.*

We romp through two hymns and faultless marriage responses and arrive at the first reading from *The Prophet* of Kahlil Gibran. Ah yes – that fellow who exhorts the virtues of space in marriage – not to get in each other's way – to mature in separate consideration as do the cypress and the oak. One wonders if space has proved an advantage to the couples' parents. The bride's are divorced and the groom's also. In fact his dashing father (a Russian of distinguished descent) has re-tied the knot three times over.

An exotically-styled reception follows at the house; where young waiters, variously sporting a fez or a Cossack fur hat, offer us champagne and blinis. A lively steel band is encouraging dancing in a marquee; tables laid for dinner are grouped beside the incorporated lake and fountains. Are we supposed to dance already? Should we keep our hats on?

The bride's recently-acquired stepfather looks on with detachment. 'There's a smell of sulphur hanging about this place': his ambiguous statement is addressed to Tom who assumes that family differences are still smouldering.

Tom remembers the house from a visit thirty years ago. It is still a feast of eclectic taste and atmosphere; a dilettante's trove of things oriental and European, overlaid with that stylish clutter of English understatement. But where have all the pictures gone? Diminished by gambling, they say. The little bridesmaids and pages frolic with the family whippets, and, sulphur or not, a wedding is a wedding is a wedding.

Due to Tom's early-morning start for India, we forgo the dinner and the dancing. Apparently the festivities lasted to dawn.

May 23 Hardwicke House

'You are a star.' 'Such style and attention to detail.' 'Great panache.' 'Tom was in fine voice.' 'A brilliant idea.' 'Many fascinating and interesting people.' 'A hard act to follow.' 'Everything so pretty.' 'A wholly exceptional evening.' 'You have filled the house with such treasures and atmosphere.' 'Wonderful evening, totally memorable.'

And so it was. I am overwhelmed with such praise.

Two years ago it dawned on Tom and me that Hardwicke House would celebrate its tercentenary in 1988. Nothing daunted, we would give a party. Many warm baths became cold as I cogitated on how to proceed.

It was Thomas Tryon, a prosperous hatter (castor maker) from Hackney, who built the house in 1688, on land bought from Thomas Wigington. He and his wife Susanna, 'a sober young woman', felt the need for country air. Thomas Tryon wrote many books on sobriety which include: *The Way To Health; The Benefit of Clean, Sweet Beds; The Knowledge of a Man's Self; The Surest Guide to the True Worship of God and Good Government of the Mind and Body*. He also made time to travel to Barbados where he developed his trade in beavers. (Tom found these informative titbits in the *Dictionary of National Biography*.)

How to celebrate? We envisaged a dinner composed of dishes in

the seventeenth-century genre. Searcy's produced a fitting menu for
£32 a head:

Sparrow Grass

Excellent Fowle

Orange Cream Tarte

Tom opened the floodgates of his remarkable cellar. Between ninety
of us, we drank twenty-seven bottles of Château Léoville-Poyferré
1975, together with a white Sauvignon de St Bris 1986, Champagne,
and Fonseca 1963. A toast to Thomas Tryon was drunk at the close
of Tom's after-dinner speech.

We persuaded a flautist, a cellist, a violinist, and a harpsichord player
from the Royal College of Music to set the scene on arrival. They
arrived at 6 o'clock to install the harpsichord in the drawing-room. A
diverting rehearsal ensued of Handel, Purcell, and pieces by Vivaldi. I
scurried around in a half-dressed state, putting finishing touches to the
white table flowers in the scarlet marquee, and securing garlands to
the dogs' collars. Searcy's busied themselves with table-laying of white
damask cloths and napkins, silver plate cutlery and polished glass.

It was then that I discovered the dog meat. The stench! The habitual
cool of the backstairs had warmed in the sunny afternoon and
ten pounds of tripe was exuding a poisonous whiff. To the distant
strains of delicate quartet music, I set to in the kitchen, stuffing tripe
down the waste disposal. It stuck and it smelt; my arms were slaked in
fetid grease as I wrestled with the recalcitrant garbage. Tom and the
chairman of Searcy's tore into the kitchen. What was going on? That
smell! It had spread everywhere, through the marquee, all over the
garden. Dog meat? They had imagined it was a burst sewer. Armed
with room fragrance they rushed through the party precincts, squirting
furiously.

It was a fine, still evening; the wisteria over the fan balcony was
heavy with scent and full-blown honeysuckle clung to the wrought-
iron gates. We laid a Persian carpet before the front door and lit a
wood fire in the panelled hall. The music wafted our guests through
the marquee to the garden. Everywhere was sound and scent, colour
and flowers. A faint waft of cloves stole from the bay-tree where I had
hung pomanders.

Art historians and dealers, several owners of great houses, the Chairman of English Heritage, Lord Montagu, the President of the National
Arts Collection Fund, Sir Peter Wakefield, and Laurence Rich from

the National Trust all mingled together. In the event of this, our 'Anniversary Project', we had stipulated that guests pay £25 per head to any of the three above-mentioned Conservation groups. It would not take a mathematician to gauge that we raised a modest £2,000.

But it was the embryo of an idea we wished to launch, 'The Anniversary Project', by which house-owners would be encouraged to celebrate some landmark of their houses or their contents. A dated staircase, gazebo, or kitchen garden wall, a bust, or a barometer, or even the fact that one has owned a house for a decade. The excuses to celebrate on a simple or elaborate scale are legion.

A lovely happy party by all accounts with an excellent article by Vanessa Hannam[2] in the previous day's *Sunday Telegraph* anticipating the impending event. (The dogs and I were photographed in the hall as illustration.) How else to encourage others to follow suit? Will our party prove a one-off or a take-off? After nine years of Thatcher government, nearly 70% of Britons are now house-owners. How to consolidate our heritage? We have always been renowned as a nation of shopkeepers, our shops are fast being commandeered by Pakistanis and Egyptians. We must now become a nation of house-keepers. It has repeatedly been said that the country house is England's greatest contribution to the visual arts. In celebrating Hardwicke House's tercentenary we have tossed a ball in the hope that like-minded house-owners will start to roll it.

May 26 Hardwicke House

Today we received a letter from Major Spring-Smyth from Lyndhurst, Hants:

> *I was highly interested to see the article in the S. Telegraph about Hardwicke House . . . Hardwicke belonged to my grandmother, Alice Spring-Smyth for many years before and up to WWII . . . Christmas was always an occasion when members of the family would arrive complete with servants – another age! One uncle rode every morning; there was a stable by the garage; and another uncle had early breakfast with the children before departing for duty at Windsor or Wellington Barracks . . . my grandmother kept a parrot in a super old cage in the hall but it fell into disgrace after it had been taught rude words.*

---

[2] Author of historical fiction. Married to Sir John Hannam, the Conservative MP for Exeter 1970–97.

A bevy of bands have sent me their credentials; they look forward to playing 'Sweet Harmonies' from the seventeenth-century at any future anniversary parties.

My project and me, all geared up, but, for the moment, nowhere to go.

July 18 Hardwicke House

Traumatic weather, the heaviest summer rainfall since 1956; this last month quite appalling. The odd evening drink snatched on our garden seat can be counted on the back of one hand. Our white border of iceberg roses has been ravaged in turn by squalls and down-pours; unopened buds turn brown. Plodding through drizzle in Richmond Park one marvels at sheets of silver where pinpoints of rain cling to the wild grasses. (A heat-wave is predicted for August.)

The social season has romped through regardless. Ascot (mercifully free of rain) now allows divorcees into the Royal Enclosure; trousers are still banned. One pantalooned girl, in a successful bid to enter the hallowed precinct, squeezed both legs into one and dragged the other as a train. At Henley, sartorial strictures caused a near uproar. Fashionable (again) mini-skirts, a mere two inches above the knee, were not admitted into the Stewards' Enclosure. The Committee Chairman defended his stance: 'What is the next stage, if one doesn't have standards? You will simply get people stripping off to the waist if it is hot and Henley will look like Lords or Wimbledon – and God forbid we should get like that . . .'

The Queen was admirably prepared for all weathers when recently presiding over a tea party at Buckingham Palace Gardens, held as a celebration for the Grenadier Guards; we feared for our hats and silks on the open lawns. The Monarch was dressed in a straw hat and a mackintosh cape. We saw lots of friends; the sun finally came out, and the cape came off to reveal a blue silk dress. But the queue for the tea marquee was so daunting we took a taxi to a Bond Street café.

Lunches, drinks parties, and dinners ran their jam-packed course. Joan Haslip currently writing *her* biography of Madame du Barry was our guest of honour at a small lunch at Christie's. Had she seen the wax effigy of du Barry in Madame Tussauds? No? The thought of mounting to the Tableaux Section on the fourth floor clearly did not appeal. I assured her it would be worth the effort. There she has lain, Madame du Barry, for one hundred years, in a four-poster, her pearly bosom rising and falling, to simulate breath. Joan drew on her long cream gloves and vowed resignedly that she would fit her in with a dentist appointment.

The most significant global development this summer must be Mr Mikhail Gorbachev's proposal for a radical change in the way Russia is governed, namely to divorce the Communist Party from the stranglehold of government. The most fundamental volte-face since 1917? His programmes of *glasnost* (open-ness) and *perestroika* (re-construction) must, he insists, overrule the conservative attitudes of his opponents. His three-hour speech (on June 28) to the Soviet National Communist Party Conference has been described by a member of the Politburo as 'a huge step forward in democratisation . . . which would pave the way for the Soviet Union to become a free and open society.' Said Gorbachev, 'The people demand democracy, full-blooded democracy and there can be no compromise.' *The Times* leader swiftly denigrated his proposed reforms as 'Mikhail's Dream'. He is urging too much change too quickly, they argued. They condemned his sense of urgency and described it as 'the urgency of the last chance gambler rather than the confident bureaucrat'. What is *The Times* about? It has become increasingly left-wing.

Our police have also become uncomfortably officious. Some weeks back, my mind in neutral, I inadvertently drove over a red light in the centre of Kingston-upon-Thames. They squealed me down in the morning rush-hour traffic. Strutting towards me, chests thrust out, it seemed, with ominous intent, they barked, 'Get on to the pavement!' Thoroughly unnerved, I drove my car up on the wide paved area. They were furious. 'We want *you* on the pavement – not your car!' I explained that I was a harmless housewife and would they kindly approach me more graciously. A fine of £25 resulted. A second brush with the law ensued a month later. I was driving Tom home – in his Mercedes – from a charity dinner. We had been helping the Maharani of Jaipur to raise money for a drought-ridden game park in India. Unwittingly I made a wrong turn in Chelsea. 'Have you been drinking, madam?' A breathalyser bag was produced; I could not blow it up sufficiently. My heavy cold, I explained, and coughed convincingly. Despite Tom's exhortations that I was not fooling, that I did in fact have a bad cold, they reiterated, 'Two more attempts, madam. If you fail to comply, we must arrest you!' I failed miserably. An hour and a half later, in the dismal confines of Chelsea Police Station, I managed to raise the requisite puff. The result by the computerised test machine amazed us all. 'Christmas comes twice a year for some, madam! There's no alcohol recorded in your body whatsoever!' Greatly relieved, I told them that in the course of four hours I had drunk two glasses of champagne, three glasses of wine, and a tumbler of Perrier water. Had I eaten dinner? A four-course dinner, was it? They concluded that any alcohol had been absorbed by the food and that bodily fluids had dispersed the rest. 'You say you haven't passed water since 6 p.m. Well, madam, I expect you sweated during the evening.' I drew myself up in my sapphires and evening dress. Me? Sweated? Never! The swings and roundabouts of a democratic society?

August 7 Kuşadası / Pharmako Turkey

'The stretch of coast between Kuşadası and Bodrum is the least interesting and sometimes offers the roughest seas in the area. To get to Bodrum, take a taxi,' advises the magazine *European Travel*. We delay this unpropitious-sounding trip by taking a taxi to Ephesus. The site has been under restoration by Austrians for decades. Their special pride is the renovation of the Celsus Library, a towering white marble edifice, built in 135 AD by Julius Aquila in memory of his father, Celsus Polemeanus, a Roman governor of Asia. We stroll down the sloping marble street and marvel at the worn ruts of iron chariot wheels. The theatre, agora, and gymnasium are strewn in crumbling peace, surrounded by fields, and blackberry bushes. The sun beats down; the ruined range glistens against a blazing sky; we lose our taxi in the medley of fellow tourists.

From Kuşadası we finally set sail on our chartered yacht, *Virgo*, and moor for the night at Pharmako, a deserted Greek island. A stony shore slopes up through scrub and gorse where white goats wander. Four stone arches suggest remains of a Roman villa; a modest Byzantine church is poised on a peak like a long-lost beacon. We drag our anchor during dinner. The meltem wind has got up and we shunt to a more sheltered cove.

August 8 Didyma

We visit Didyma, a huge temple of the Ionic order 300 BC. It took five hundred years to construct and was never completed. Our heavy lunch beforehand of lamb and red wine at the nearby unattractive sea resort Altınkum precludes too much intensive sight-seeing in the heat of the early afternoon (90°F in the shade).

August 9 Gümüşlük

This evening we reach Gümüşlük ('silvery'). The bay has a narrow water-way approach through a hazardous clutch of rocks and islands; a peaceful village with a huddle of white villas smudged scarlet and purple with bougainvillea. The ruins of Myndus stretch beyond across the grass slopes. A minaret broods over all and wooden jetties lead to shaded eating shacks. Boys toss pails of sea water on the sandy floors to cool and clean. We eat simply – a white fish, white cheese, white wine. The coffee is bitter, refreshing. A ramble over Myndus follows the meal. The surrounds of scorched grass are straddled with olive trees, fig, and eucalyptus. A black bull prowls, his herd is rounded up within the crumbling walls of a farmstead. We come to a plateau where patches of dishevelled mosaic are woven into the soil and scrub, the blue deep gleams beyond. How can one begin to fathom the layered depth of arcane cultures that litter this land and sea?

August 11 Gökova

The bay of Gökova is a majestic succession of undulating peaks, tufted with pine and olive. Deserted bays of rose rock and silver slate are occasionally clamped with the white serried blocks of the tourist vanguard.

We eat well on board *Virgo*. Salad lunches, each plate a chef d'oeuvre of colour and graphic design. Sophistication is saved for dinner: Christophe and Franck excel themselves with their soufflé Grand Marnier and their incomparable crêpes suzette. Franck (last year's under-deckhand) has matured considerably. His general promotion is enhanced by a fuller figure, a broader grin, and a sartorial surprise a day. He wears braces on his downy chest this morning and a jaunty peaked leather cap.

We are moored by the islet of Alakisla, east of Bodrum. An evening stroll ashore. A narrow beach of shingle and valley beyond. Pink olean-der shields a freshwater pool; a frog leaps; a carefully-heaped cairn of stones denotes certain ownership. Allotments of stoney soil are planted with marrow and maize, faint vestiges of habitation. And now a squat stone rondavel; we feel constrained to keep our distance. Under a nearby tree, a levelled oblong of stones suggests a grave. Stones everywhere; some large and balanced; a fallen arch, a buttressed wall; and there a ruined room, where gnarled roots and trunks soar to a green canopy. The present and the past intermingle? A mystery. At sunset we are again bedevilled by the meltem gusting from the mountains. We anchor at the head of the adjoining, more sheltered bay and take a line ashore.

August 12 Bodrum

From a distance, the town appears a nondescript white scrabble notched to the shore line, the imposing Crusader castle a faint delineation against the backdrop of sun-baked mountains. A charming picture focuses with our approach. A rose-brick minaret and terracotta roofs rise from waving palms. The castle with its crenellated towers thrusts out its bulk and dominates the bustling harbour.

We lunch on a cool terrace, shaded with vines, on Doluca wine, tender lamb, and baklava pastries, oozing nuts and honey, at £6 a head. In the afternoon we cross to Kos (hoisting the Greek flag) to meet friends flying in from London. A different world, the island of Kos. Westernised, prosperous, an even flow of traffic with attendant horns and motorbikes. Cypress-trees, banana and palm are matured and lush with assiduous watering. A mere stretch of water slices between the muddied charms of Bodrum and the comparative order and sophistication of Kos. The news from London? A baby daughter was born on Monday to the Duchess of York? The eighth day of the eighth month in the year 1988, and pundits are suggesting the name, Octavia? A mini heat-wave has ended.

August 13 Datça

Sebastian's twentieth birthday. I hope his iced cake was delivered today; that Nanny remembered to post his birthday cards yesterday; that the blue elephant-printed pyjamas arrived in time. He will have had a happy day, with friends to tea. Our dearest Sebastian; who knows himself and, in his own special realisation, senses that 'in the dew of little things, the heart finds its morning and is refreshed'.

Datça, this evening's mooring, is a fishing harbour; small and sleepy with a quay of quaint shops. Red and blue awnings are spread with kilims. The 'Best Carpet Shop' vaunts its wares alongside 'The Silver House', 'The all kind of Leathers Gallery' and stands of rather frightful postcards. Two peasant girls swing along the sea front, their white headscarves and flowered pantaloons are conspicuous against the ramshackle mix of half-nude holiday-makers. They shoulder a bundle each and now stoop before a shop to lower their load and display. There is no sale for their gaudy lengths of cloth. With shrugs and twists of the back they are off again; languid with the insouciance of youth. Above the shops with their varnished fronts, tables are set on terraces; inviting recesses trimmed with iron balconies and fenced with slatted wood. Darkness falls. The eateries wink with coloured lights and vibrate with the muffled merge of voices, clinking glass and the pulsing whine of music fit for belly-dancers.

August 14 Datça, Simi, Bozukkale

The quay shops are open for Sunday trading. Tom bargains for a pair of late nineteenth-century scissors with silver handles from a plump lady in a tented sun-dress. The elegant long steel blades are inlaid with 18 carat gold. She regales us with quotes from Robert Browning and Shakespeare as we reach the price of £150.

We anchor for lunch in a bay off the Greek island of Simi. Palladian dolls' houses encircle the modest harbour, their ordered façades breathe peace and elegance; pale toast and ivory, with windows shuttered in cinnamon and emerald green. We stay three hours, bathing, wind-surfing, and diving from the deck. Pascal, our hostess deckhand, is revealed in her full Gauguinesque colour, with her coiled crown of dark hair, and a shocking-pink bathing suit. Her long brown legs go on forever.

An afternoon's sail round the point to Bozukkale ('Broken Castle'), a scape of limpid sky, the arid convolutions of a mountain range lost in haze and a dense navy sea. At the inlet of Bozukkale we drop anchor. The buttressed ramparts of the 300 BC fort stake their claim across the cliff, 100 feet above. In the falling night, we listen to Mahler's 5th symphony, Mozart, Tschaikowsky, and probe the Milky Way with binoculars.

August 15 Marmaris

A mist at sunset as we enter the bay of Marmaris. The mountains close in, strangely unsubstantive, like stage props crowding the sun. Distancing ourselves from Marmaris, we anchor in a sandy bay with palms. Franck ties the bows to a fig tree. In the pine-forested mountains above, white goats pick their way and peer. It is hotter here, further south, the sea like silk and shot with the reddening night. A flat-bottomed craft putters to our shore; a boy in a bandeau heaps it with bundles of bay-leaves. (An essential ingredient for the shish-kebabs in Marmaris restaurants.) A goat bleats and runs along the sand. Is he nibbling our shore line? No – it is a fig he stretches for.

August 16 Marmaris, Ekincik

Lunch on the shaded terrace at the Mati Hotel, arguably the biggest and the best in Marmaris; a budding complex strewn across the sand, pulsing with tourist business. Our meal is still a mere £6 a head.

At the bay of Ekincik, tonight's mooring, we take the crew out to supper. It is a steep climb to the one and only restaurant on the hill, the Ay Marina. We are treated to an amazing pudding display on silver trays balanced on glasses of red wine in a five-foot tier. Lighted candles are dotted between sorbets and fruits, a veritable fire hazard, which the waiters proudly navigate between tables and tasselled ceiling lights.

August 17 Göcek

At 7 a.m. we start for Göçek in the Gulf of Fethiye to honour an illustrious lunch date. We are guests of Haldun and Çiğdem Simavi on board *Halas* (Salvation), their renovated 1912 Bosphorus ferry. It has a handsome black body with butterscotch funnels, a crew of twenty-eight, and a keel of only two metres. Princess Margaret is their guest.

My forty-eighth birthday. Over breakfast our friends have presented me with an exotic pair of red shoes, grosgrain from Manolo Blahnik with a deep silk flounce on the instep – 'A Louis Quatorze!' pronounces Pascal.

What to wear for lunch? Casually draped, but as a concession to formality we cover our feet. Even our host Haldun greets us in long white socks; however Princess Margaret's lady-in-waiting redresses the balance, totally unshod. Drinks are served on deck. It is hot and languid in the lagoon. The necklace of peaked green islets gives an oriental effect.

The Princess joins us wearing a turquoise kanga tied above her bathing suit. Her thick brown hair is caught in a neat two-tiered roll with a turquoise plastic hairband set between. Her large eyes are even more turquoise, with enviably clear whites. Perhaps she uses drops. Her five-inch cigarette-holder must also ward off excessive pollution.

Lunch is announced. We walk down through the carpeted interior past alcoves of solemn elegance, where huge oriental lamps are set on small tables. The return trip to Istanbul must involve a mammoth stowing operation. Tom is seated on the Princess's right and later reported that he led the conversation. Halfway through the meal, a shawl is brought to cover the royal shoulders; the air-conditioning has proved too much for her slight figure.

Çığdem, always the perfect hostess, produces a cake and a candle. All sing 'Happy Birthday, dear Penelope'. The Princess turns in her chair and graciously acknowledges my plight. We take coffee on deck. Princess Margaret congratulates me on being a fellow Leo. And when is her own birthday? This Sunday? 'Yes, we are quite a clan – Mummy's was on the 4th, my niece on the 15th and then the little one the other day . . .' Would I like to come down and see her cabin? Three of us follow her through long passages to her room. She asks me to hold her sunglasses as she struggles with the lock. She is pleased with her large room and its low double bed. She discards her kanga and pads around unconcernedly in her bathing suit. Three pairs of her favoured white slingbacks are arranged neatly under a chair, an open wardrobe is stuffed with colourful dresses. 'Come and see my bathroom!' We all admire her basin of gold porcelain. (I would be terrified of the glass tooth mug cracking it). 'See you soon!' She waves us off as we decline her kind offer to use her lavatory.

September Hardwicke House

These last three months I have had bouts of depression. As usual I excused them to myself; you are tired; you need a holiday. I told nobody. The summer boating trip was imminent. That would cure it.

The first week of our holiday found me in a grotesque situation. The beautiful boat, the blue warm sea, the company of close friends and happy husband. Did I feel better? At the magnificent ruins of Ephesus and Didyma I longed to bury myself and my secret misery in the nearest Neolithic tomb. Beguiling and outwardly happy, circumstances cannot allay the monster. I rode it quietly, watched the waves with a sanguine smile and swam, sipped wines and ate up the crew's delectable cuisine, as did we all. I thanked my lucky stars that I wasn't in charge of the catering or the bilges, a sybaritic interlude with no decisions and no demands casts a balm on the mind. The depression[3] lifted in the second week. I was inwardly triumphant. I had kept my head and my guilty secret.

On my return home it soon seeped back, and stronger. One afternoon I lay on the sofa for three whole hours, rigid and tensed in a straitjacket of fear and dejection. The dogs knew; the next day the doctor knew. It is always a relief to come clean.

In the happy event of the anti-depressant pills providing the correct

[3] *The Nature of the Beast* by Ann Allestree; published in the Health Section of *Harpers and Queen* January 1993. *Ann Allestree describes her own journey through the dark waters of manic depression.*

chemical mix, you gradually sense positive thought-processes. You might even say something that smacks of spontaneity, or smile. Those dreaded dawn butterflies in the stomach die a little. You get up and dress with more conviction. Your previous inclinations to stay curled in bed in a darkened room lose their thrall. You know indisputably that you are on the way up, surfacing slowly but surely to sense the light and air.

It is a remarkable realisation to feel well again. It is profoundly satisfying. Your contentment and enjoyment of life appear more complete than ever. You are mentally revitalised to new dimensions of creativity; inspiration flows and your perceptions are heightened. Your mind is on honeymoon.

In retrospect, you conclude that any bad experience is a salutary experience; the next time round, you will knock it for six. There is always hidden treasure in the well.

September 8 South Lambeth

Dr Alain Presencer exudes the energy and enthusiasm to inspire rather than overwhelm, a temperate man on first acquaintance. At a house in South Lambeth we drink wine and nibble on salmon canapés. Dr Presencer briefs us on our trip to the Himalayas. 'When you reach Ladakh, you step back 600 years; everybody smiles in Little Tibet. The peasants are naïve and happy. They have known no other existence. It is a beautiful land, hauntingly beautiful.' From his pocket he pulls out a bone. 'A thigh bone from a child.' Putting it to his lips he blows a loud and musical report. He shows us slides of lakes, mountains, and monasteries. 'I can promise you amazing experiences and sights. And I warn you that the drive from Srinagar to Leh through the Himalayan ranges can be hairy; you will be quite safe.'

I make a mental note to add pills for altitude sickness to our collected heap of medicaments: pills for sore throats, sore eyes, sore ears and teeth, tummy upsets, protective sun-cream, lip salve, insect repellent, malaria pills, water purification tablets for bathroom use. Sealed bottled water, we are assured, is always available. 'But don't open you mouth in the shower.' Sweets to suck, digestive biscuits, dried fruit (shall I take a bottle of Justerini's good, ordinary claret?).

We are handed pamphlets, which include information on shopping in Kashmir. At Srinagar, our first stop, I would plump for saffron and shawls, a shahtoosh? 'A once-in-a-lifetime purchase,' the legendary 'ring shawl'. The fine wool is gleaned from the down of an antelope's throat; as he grazes a few precious strands are shed. The price for a shahtoosh is described as 'astronomical', but is not revealed. We shall see.

Sebastian and I set off in our group of fourteen people (under the aegis of 'Art Study Tours') next week. A trip to the Himalayas can change you, they say. Perhaps a case of long-held attitudes taking on new perspective?

September 16 Kashmir

We settle back luxuriously on the padded cushions of our shikara, a flat-bottomed craft, a cross between a punt and a gondola. Our steersman paddles from the stern; the blade of his long oar is shaped like a lotus leaf. We are crossing Lake Nagin to our houseboat moored on the opposite bank. It is a windless evening, calm and gold. The bearer dips his lean hand into the lake and sprinkles the lotus leaves. 'The waters of Nagin are so clean that the drops shine like diamonds,' he informs us. They roll like scattered blobs of mercury on the flat green saucers.

Muhammed, a smiling bearded houseboy in a skull cap, greets us on the steps of our houseboat. The cedarwood interior has large rooms carpeted in kilims. Ornately-carved walnut furniture, double-sized beds, and tiled bathrooms promise every comfort. The dining-table is already set for dinner with large white napkins furled in extravagant shapes and decked with marigold heads. Would we like a Kashmiri dinner? Lamb stew and saffron rice? First he serves Kashmiri tea; it is deliciously refreshing and scented with ginger and cardamom. Sitting on our balcony with its fretted balustrades, we are easy targets for the Shikari traders. In turn they draw alongside and extol the excellence of their jewels, necklaces of lapis-lazuli, yak bone, agate, and garnet, their drinks of fresh mango juice, apple juice, beer, and their exotic flowers. Every imaginable household adornment and necessity is paddled to the boat. Next the Ladies' and Gents' Barber calls. He finds a customer in one gentleman of our party. A chair is placed on the balcony and a hair-cut ensues for £2. The barber opens his black leather case to reveal twelve assorted scissors and twelve assorted combs. The trim even includes some judicious snipping at ears, eyebrows, and nose.

The following morning we are punted along the floating island waterways through Srinagar. Watermelons, pumpkins, and cucumbers are grown in abundance on these water-bound beds of vegetation, seemingly supported by a thick tangle of underwater weed. Kingfishers flash by tantalisingly as we wind our passage through the reeds. Women slap their washing on wooden steps at the water's edge. Ducks, chickens, cows, and dogs potter beside brick and timber houses where piles of logs are stashed in readiness for the harsh winter. Girls in colourful saris canoe their babies and shopping at a skilful pace through the busy water traffic, and a beautiful girl in scarlet empties her silver tea ewer from a bridge.

We visit the seventeenth-century Jami Masjid Mosque, which boasts 300 massive cedar pillars to hold it up, and the Shah Hamdan Mosque where we are greeted with 'no entry to women or Muslims'. We just manage to peer through its doors at the colourful papier-mâché interior. The narrow twists of streets are crammed with bazaars; the din of horns, bicycle bells, and horses' hooves adds to the frenzy. Vegetable stalls glow with glossy produce, red, green, and yellow (that inevitably turn up in a khaki stew at the table). The Kashmiris appear slim, with fine bones, straight noses, and glistening elliptical eyes. The majority of the women are unveiled, but a few Shi-ites (the fanatic Muslims) are submerged in black with protective face burkahs. We pass a Doctor's Inn, which offers 'pregnancy tests – cures by private arrangement', and a 'bone and joint' hospital, neither of which service is immediately in demand from our party. I make negotiations for a shahtoosh ring shawl and a reliable dealer agrees to call at the houseboat in the evening. He brings along three: one for £200, which transpires to be only half-size; another for £490 which appears to be the real McCoy; and the third which he claims is antique at twice the price. We take these prized pieces up to the roof terrace to view in a better light. I settle happily for the middle article; seven yards of the softest purest down of an ibex. He assures me that only seven are made in the year. A little boy with one eye espies me trading and pleads with me to buy his saffron. He clambers on board with his scales and weighs out 10 grams of saffron stamens for £8. Shopping in Srinagar is an expensive exercise.

An evening storm gets up. Lightning flashes across the lake and stabs the mountains which loom close and cowering in the dark evening sky. Wind chops the water and whips the canvas canopy off a shikara. We later hear that two women and a man have drowned. Anguished wailing pierces the night; dogs howl and the rain drums dully on the flat cedar roof terrace of our houseboat. The lake, now calm, amplifies each tortured sound to a tortured echo.

In the morning they find the bodies. They had clung together in death, hopelessly entangled in their sarees and the mesh of weeds of the forty-foot-deep Lake Nagin.

The sun is hot as we take shikaras through Lake Dal to the Moghul garden – Nishat Bagh (pleasure garden). A riot of water chutes, foun-tains, and brilliant colour is sandwiched between the towering Pir

Pinjal mountains and the lake spread out before. Ten tiered terraces of flowers, yellow marigold, scarlet salvia, dahlias, asters, and the rich magenta plumes of cocks'-combs make a vivid show of bold colour. Commissioned in 1633 by Asaf Khan, indigenous and scented flowers were originally planted, a more subtle display of lilac, jasmine and roses. We picnic under magnolia trees on fish curry and bananas.

September 20 Ladakh India

It is early morning. Today we leave Srinagar for our two-day journey to Ladakh, termed 'Little Tibet' – at the top north-east point of India, bordering on China. I walk first through the apple orchard behind the houseboat to thank our chef. His kitchen comprises a shed with a tin roof, a charcoal fire and a stone sink. A preponderance of large Nescafé and Birds Eye Custard tins are balanced on shelves, containers no doubt for curry and rice. To my alarm I notice tins of milk powder in his larder. Has he been mixing it with unboiled water?

We set off in a Super-Coach with anti-glare stained windows. We rattle through the river Sindh valley, where wedged slabs of rice fields and maize are in various stages of harvest. Women in bright sarees throng the road to the fields, balancing picnic baskets, water pots and samovars on their heads. Others are already threshing the stooks on stones. The rough road is lined with willow and poplar; walnut-trees and mulberry clump the fields giving shade to grazing sheep and cows. Strings of mountain horses loaded with sacks of winter provisions are led by Kashmiri Muslim nomads, the Gujars, to the warmer lowland pastures of the Jumma Valley.

At the village of Gund we stop and relieve ourselves under the camouflage of a maize crop. Hamid, our Kashmiri guide, tells us: 'The women in this village are brave. There are black bears in the mountains. The women go up in groups to collect wood, but you will see in these mountain villages many peasants who have lost their noses.' The Sindh river is a glacial churn of aquamarine with the coral plant bush clustered on its bouldered banks. The fruit berries resemble redcurrants. 'The local peasants claim they ease headaches,' says Hamid. I eat three in the hope that my headache from the steady climb in altitude will abate. Their sweet juicy promise is of no avail; an hour later I resort to Panadol.

We reach Sonamarg (golden meadow) at noon and eat a picnic by the river. Along with other lorries and buses we wait for entry to the formidable Zoji-la Pass (the Mountain of God), a narrow rough road built in 1962 after the Indo-Chinese conflicts. It took fifteen years to complete, with an average of one man per one kilometre killed in the attempt. Nothing could have prepared one for this horror in store.

Travelling between ten and twenty miles an hour our intrepid driver steers a course six feet from the edge. A fearful peep out of the window reveals a three thousand-foot drop. Our Super-Coach jolts and judders and sways alarmingly. I make frantic promises to God, all of which are ignobly swept aside with our safe arrival at our hotel in Kargil. Clean sheets, a bucket, a tap, a lavatory, and a hot meal of tomato soup and peppers stuffed with lamb and maize, all ensure a good night's sleep. Tomorrow we face the rigours of the Fatu-la Pass (lid on the mountain) at 13,475 feet.

September 21 Ladakh

'Ladakh means the land under the passes,' explains Dr Alain Presencer, our Canadian guide from London. 'You could also describe it as a cruel paradise.' We drive through an arresting landscape of azure sky, red sand slopes, and mountain peaks, the cool green and silver of willow and poplar, and the ever-present aquamarine skein of the Suru river below. He explains the seventh-century origins of the Stupa, an ubiquitous symbol of Buddhism. The descending layers of these squat pyramids are to represent the moon for spirit and light, fire for endeavour, air for breathing, and water for transformation from death to life. The central rungs are for steps of attainment and the bulbous base is for the earth and human advancement. 'You will also see many prayer wheels set in monastery walls. They are cylindrical, made in brass or painted wood, with scrolls of prayers furled inside. Be sure to twirl them clockwise as is the tradition.'

We pass through Shergol where a few houses dot the scorched stone valley. A monastery is perched on a rock and we see our first scattering of Stupas; clearly we are now in Buddhist territory. Hamid points out a herd of black dzos, a crossbreed of yak and cow. They have fat ferocious-looking horns and the tails of horses. They graze peaceably by a stream and are apparently harmless. At the next village of Mulbekh we see a famous eighteenth-century Buddhist statue. Standing eighteen feet high on a lotus-shaped base, it is carved on a rock. ('Carried by a Demon from Tibet'.) The left hand holds a ewer of holy water and the whole effigy is coated in a faded yellow paint. (Yellow is the Buddhist colour for peace.) Not the most inspiring piece of work to my mind. In a distant field, two young girls are winnowing barley with rakes tossing the golden spray high in the air, whistling a rhythmic tune through their teeth. They look jolly and decorative in their head-scarves and dangling earrings. I give them a tube of dextrasol (blackcurrant flavour) and they pose happily for a photograph. Our journey continues up to the Namika-la Pass (Pillar to the Sky). At 12,000 feet it can boast the original highest altitude for air flight. The surround of mountains resembles so many elephant hides with their wrinkled brown flanks. The bus twists and turns on and upward to Fatu-la Pass. At 14,000 feet we have now reached the highest point between Srinagar and Leh. We sniff the strong winds and gaze on this strange, lunar landscape. The soft blown shale is sculpted into dunes with the harder rock whipped into conical towers. The wind it seems has drawn parallel features to twin with Cappadocia. We stop for tea at Khalsi where we are mystified by dust-trails streaking down the mountain; at the base of each trail is stacked a neat square allotment of fodder. The peasants explain how they bundle herbs from the rocks on the mountain tops and slide them down to the village. They set great store by any animal fodder they can glean from their barren terrain. The flat roofs of their mud-brick houses are piled high with drying grass.

It is dark when we reach Alchi where tents have been set up in a vegetable garden. Very comfortable they are, too, with the added delicacy of lace curtains lining each interior. The night is warm as we sit over a candlelit dinner served by a shiny brown man in white gloves. (The tin plates and cutlery have been soaked in iodinised water.)

September 22 Alchi Ladakh

We are wakened by the raucous honking of donkeys. A gong announces breakfast as we hurriedly clean our teeth in tea. A huge meal is produced of stewed apples, fried eggs, toast, and battered cheese balls. Alain discreetly waits until the end of the meal to disclose that during the ninth, tenth, and eleventh centuries tuberculosis was rife in the area and the resulting sputum was used to good effect in mixing the vegetables and stone powders to a durable tempera.

We walk through the primitive village to the ancient monastery and admire the eleventh-century paintings; the colours have certainly stood the test of centuries, sputum or no sputum. The detail of work is formidable, miniature in style in Prussian blues and ox-blood reds with fine gold delineation. Every God and Demon of Tibetan Buddhism appears to be minutely chronicled. Brushes made from the yak's hair were used. How well that animal serves its country; its bones make jewellery, its hide the temple drums, and its tail makes fly switches.

As we peer with torches at this dark interior, an old monk limps towards us. Alain, who prides himself as an occasional healer, detects that he has a dislocated hip. He kneels before the old man and rubs the area of pain. In his yellow anorak, he rather suggests the Automobile Association man come to the rescue. We return to our encampment for another huge meal of crisp lotus roots, barbecued chicken, cream caramel, and a fruit salad overflowing from its own especially-concocted burnt sugar basket. We thank our bearers effusively and assure them that we have been made to feel as fêted as the old British Raj.

September 23 The Lamayru Hotel Ladakh

We wake to mountain peaks some 20,000 feet smothered in mist. The sixteenth-century Leh Palace built high on a sloping pinnacle broods over the town. It tapers up eight storeys in the typical caryatid formation of Tibetan architecture. The narrow sightless windows in the steep stone walls look desolate. The palace has been abandoned since 1834 when the Ladakh Royal family removed themselves to another in the neighbouring town of Stok. We pick our way through the primitive streets, circumventing open drains and good-natured grubby children, who clamour for sweets and pens. Peasant women with rosy, rough, tanned faces squat on pavements plying vegetables. They look jolly in their river-pearl earrings and their padded velvet top hats, knitting and chatting the hours away.

I spend the afternoon in my bed with eye compresses; they are red and sore from dust and altitude pressure. I reflect on the effects of altitude as our adjoining rogue lavatory dribbles its incessant dirge. (The cracked basin also has its shortcomings; it is impossible to wash one's hands without simultaneously soaking one's feet.) Headaches and sore congested throats are main complaints. We also seem to be divided into those who piddle every two hours and those who suffer water retention. Others have hinted at palpitations and heart flutters. The lack of electricity at night is another exacting challenge. You creep from bed to bathroom, where you clumsily overturn a glass jug of sterilised water, and return in search of a torch. You find instead a cigarette-lighter and espy the torch on a far table-top. You gash your shin on the bed-leg and make a mental note to put Savlon on the graze. Clasping the torch triumphantly you lurch again into the bathroom. Gingerly you pick up the shattered glass, relieve yourself, and return to the bedroom. You pour out a glass of bottled water and miss the rim; the table top is flooded, your watch is drowned, and your precious last packet of Kleenex is sodden. Your torch drops and rolls under the bed and you wonder why you are standing in the dark clutching an empty bottle.

September 24 Leh Ladakh

Ladakh is running with mud and mist after a night of heavy rain. It is unusual to have more than four inches of rain annually in this mountain area. It would appear this region has already had its quota. We set off for Thicksey Monastery driving through arid plateaus of brown sand, shale, and scattered boulders; it could be the Gobi desert. Roughly-cobbled prayer walls and stupas relieve the monotonous landscape, while the Indus river churns a brown and turgid course between.

After an hour on the road, the fourteenth-century monastery looms high on a mountain ledge, its blood-red façade conspicuous for miles. Harvested barley fields surround a village below. The rest is sand and an ever-receding range of mountains melted in mist. We climb the mount slowly and enter the inner courtyard. Some fifty monks, seemingly from the age of eight to eighty, are bustling around in grubby maroon gowns, performing domestic duties. One sits cross-legged over a Singer sewing machine. He stitches together bright strips of silk in preparation for their famous Mask Dance festival. Another slides his feet over the wooden chapel floor on skin polishing pads, which have been soaked in yak butter for this exercise. Two young lads are chopping wood in the outer courtyard where a donkey is tethered. It is bundled up with some load – the laundry perhaps? – and is led away. Dogs lie everywhere. It is a pleasant courtyard, edged with brightly-painted colonnades and a niched wall of brass prayer wheels. The balcony surround leads to the main chapel and the library and to a final flight of stone steps to the roof.

It is almost noon; a posse of monks with some grinning and skipping underlings leads us up to the roof. Whereupon two lads, maroon-gowned with heads close-shaven, position themselves behind the brass mouth piece of ten-feet-long copper horns. They blow measured, mournful blasts, the Tibetan Buddhist call to prayer as opposed to the Muslim muezzin. The village below looks totally dead and unmoved by this remarkable summons. It is too wet to work in the fields and the dzos have been taken into a shelter.

We are next invited to follow the monks to the chapel below and are asked to take off our shoes. It is dark inside. We range ourselves expectantly on carpet-covered benches along the walls. The wall-paintings and the sturdy cedar support pillars gradually take shape and colour in the candlelight. Baleful Buddhas draped in coloured prayer cloths lurk in dark recesses. Monks file in, each with his wooden bowl and his yak butter lamp. They sit cross-legged on more benches, draped with carpet runners. The drums of yak skin are thumped in rhythmical beat to time with the human heart. Bells, cymbals, and two more lads with two more copper horns achieve a cacophonous crescendo. Next there is chanting that rises and falls like soft wind. A monk with a two-litre brass ewer unobtrusively fills each bowl with butter tea; his brothers sip away between chants. One beside me pulls a blue plastic shopping bag from the folds of his gown. It contains tsampa, the staple cereal of ground barley. Carefully he pours a tablespoon into his bowl and works it into a paste, licking his fingers contentedly. A carnival atmosphere now pervades the ceremony. The cymbals and drums are silenced and monks talk together; a few still chant, some yawn, some even burp. Two lads beside me positively giggle and dig each other in the ribs. Their quiet life sentence has clearly not quelled their high spirits. Now a monk enters the chapel, carrying a small charcoal brazier. He scatters juniper berries over the coals and the sweet medicinal scent steals through the gathering. Again the horns strike up, next the drums, and more chanting. A grand finale of blasting of horns would appear to proclaim they have found the fox.

We shift our position and are invited to remain seated for the rehearsal of the Mask Dance. The central benches are cleared aside while some twenty monks draped in multi-coloured loose covers shuffle between the cedar pillars. They have donned gaudily-painted wooden masks with grotesquely deformed noses and huge, staring eyes. An aimless parade it seems, to the rise and fall of menacing music. We are persuaded that the all-pervading theme is the struggle of good Buddhists over evil infidels. After thirty minutes a sorcerer, in an authoritarian black top hat, vanquishes all demons with vigorous shaking of a perforated vessel. The monks file out in a dishevelled line. What next? The library? Would we like to see their library?

After a surfeit of strange sounds and rituals we sink on stools in a small cedar room. Wooden lockers brightly painted in the primary Tibetan colours of red, yellow, green, and blue line the walls. Each locker houses a thick, oblong parcel wrapped in coloured cloth and bound in ribbon. A monk takes one reverently on to his knees; he unwraps the block to reveal one hundred paper scrolls like so many lengths of ticker tape. Lost to the world and his assembled audience, he sways cross-legged as he chants out the Tibetan Script. On this peaceful note we extricate ourselves from Thicksey Monastery.

Continuing on our search for Buddhist culture, we set off for the seventeenth-century Hemis Monastery. It is set above a hidden valley, a tranquil pocket of waterfalls and willows. Founded by Shamunata, a handsome Mongolian, his impressive statue takes pride of place in the chapel. Complete with turban and beard his wooden core is lavishly overlaid with repoussé bronze. A solicitous old monk offers us yak tea. Will we come and see his kitchen? We proceed to a blackened, candlelit cave where a roaring fire is contained in the hollowed-out plinth of a stupa. A curtain of drizzle billows softly down the open chimney. The old man presides proudly over a vast three-feet-diameter pan of boiling water; a small pan with tea and yak milk bubbles alongside. With a gold and copper ladle he scoops the water into a tea pot. Methodically he rinses and warms the pot, ready for the treasured brew. We leave him surrounded by his trusted ladles, his ewers, and his brass spice tins.

Back at Leh, in the dark of the early evening, the rain is falling heavily. No electricity. Our laundry is returned by a house boy. It is damp and reeks of charcoal. Winter has arrived, he explains, and warms his hands on the charcoal burner in his bamboo basket. Dinner is served in the lobby. Buckets are placed under the dripping ceiling. Candles, rugs, and scattered cushions make a cosy ambience. The staff are cheerful and undeterred in their efforts to keep us warm and well fed.

September 25

Rain, rain, rain. The entire ground floor of the hotel is now two feet under water and top-floor bedrooms are leaking. Floods in Srinagar and Delhi, we hear, and forty killed. Breakfast of fried eggs, toast and jam, and tea is served in our bedrooms. 'Morning at leisure.' Now it snows. Lunch is set up in a first-floor bedroom complete with spirit food heaters. We slither up the snow-bound hill to the town centre and now thaw out in the Ladakh Art Palace, a veritable Aladdin's cave of native jewellery and artefacts. Silver-mounted conch shells, necklaces of agate, turquoise, lapis, and Chinese river pearls, painted masks, extravagantly spouted tea pots and beer pots, brass-turned prayer wheels, and bone-handled knives and swords sheathed in filigree silver, cram the walls and floor in a glorious clutter. The cloth ceiling canopy, fastened with drawing-pins, and embellished with gold dragons, dips and drips alarmingly as we browse and buy. In another den, I am tempted by a pair of pendant earrings of fresh-water pearls, turquoise and gold, six inches long, and tapered as darts with gilded hoops to encircle the ear. They would look splendid laid on an occasional table. But the price of 15,000 rupees (£200) stays my purse. 'They come from Royal Tibetan Family,' I am solemnly promised.

September 26

My mother's seventy-fifth birthday. Are they worried back home? They must have read of floods in Delhi and Srinagar? Here we have been cut off for three days. This quantity of rain and snow is apparently unprecedented. But the mountains slowly emerge through mist and cloud. Again we saunter through the streets. Slush, silt, and the accumulated sewage from inhabitants, cows, donkeys, goats, and dogs makes for cautious progress. The animals sniff dejectedly at the piled gutters and nibble on fallen willow branches; their soaked hair accentuates their mean bodies. Vigorous shovelling of snow and slush from the flat mud roofs proves another hazard for the pedestrian. The townsmen, variously covered in wool shawls, belted gowns, and fur-lined leather coats, are cheerfully putting their trade in order.

We visit Stok Palace. Built in 1811 on similar lines as the ancient monasteries, it is perched on a pinnacle of rock. A fertile apron of barley-fields and willows spreads below. The harvested stooks are capped with snow resembling so many iced coconut cakes. The resident Rani has fled to Delhi for the winter months. She has left just in time. Nobody could conceivably be persuaded to live in this flooded edifice. Oil drums overflow with muddy cascades from the roof and balconies. We squelch our way through the courtyard to the comparative shelter of the jewel room. The family collection of charm boxes, lockets, rosaries, necklaces, headdresses of turquoise, prayer hats, and children's party hats, evoke a more sophisticated environment. Two magnificent conch trumpets mounted in gold and silver repoussé are set in a glass case with the explanatory note: 'The conch is blown to summon monks to prayer and to invoke water and rains.' A redundant piece of equipment in the prevailing circumstances of this wet afternoon. Supper in the first-floor bedroom is enlivened by the guest appearance of a mouse.

September 27

The sun at last. Our flight to Srinagar is due to leave at 11.30 am. It is cancelled. Despite fine conditions in Srinagar and in Leh, there is hazardous weather, we are told, in between. The Himalayan range is notoriously treacherous in the winter months. I read with some alarm in my *Kashmir and Ladakh, A Travel Survival Kit*, that there can be as much as a twelve-day delay for flights out of Leh when the snow starts. Notwithstanding, an extra day in Ladakh is a bonus, especially with the novelty of sunshine.

Sebastian and I hire a car for the day at the cost of £20. The valley is alive with colour and sharp shadow. Peasants resume their interrupted harvest work, while the dzos and goats and horses graze over the stubble fields – a scene of pastoral peace in the wake of the flood. At Thicksey village we buy chocolate fudge and persuade a cook in a modest eating house to give us spaghetti. He tosses it in fried egg, tomato and onion and presents it, warm and oozing, in a plastic bag. We walk though fields, crossing rills and boulders towards the ruins of the Shey Palace. The air is keen and pure and the encircling mountain peaks are intensely white in their fresh shawls of snow. The distant willows blow golden like mimosa, as the wind twirls their yellow autumn leaves. We sit on stones in hot sun, struggling with our spaghetti and fingers. After a two-hour stroll we reach the four-teenth-century Shey Palace (Shey means shining light; the palace was originally reflected in an artificial lake below). It is a steep haul up the rough-hewn stone steps to the summit of the ruin which reveals the devastation of fallen mud ceilings and tumbled stone. We find two boys playing some form of draughts in a darkened cave. Can they show us the famous golden Buddha? They scamper off for a key and, leading us to a door in the yard, proudly indicate the appalling effigy, the largest Buddha in Ladakh. With bulbous head, eyes and lips it stands eighteen feet high, plastered in gold and copper sheets. Before it stands the gaudy regalia of a typical Tibetan altar: strips of bright silks, scraps of white muslin, burning butter lamps, plastic flowers and a jamjar of peacock feathers. Sebastian points irreverently at the Buddha and laughs. I think he has looked upon India[4] as a happy circus with everybody posing in fancy dress.

December 14 Hardwicke House

A swirl of cocktail parties steps up the pace of London these weeks before Christmas, together with Charity dinners, opera galas, concerts, fashion shows. Events to include a black tie dinner now cost £100 a

---

[4] Gail Jopling (to become Lady Jopling in 1997, with her husband's peerage) headed this trip under her Art Study Tours travel company. Michael Jopling often joined his wife's tours, contributing élan to the scene.

ticket. We especially enjoyed our Reception in the Captain's Room at Lloyds. (An ugly room in an ugly building.)

An excellent dinner of:

Filets de Sole Véronique
Noisettes d'Agneau Béarnaise
Pommes en Robe de Chambre
(a curious departure; I remember them as sautéed)
Oranges Oriental
Café et Truffes

And generous wines:

Veuve Clicquot 1975
Meursault 1985
Château de Pez 1976
Dows 1975

Two hundred Lloyds-orientated guests gathered to raise money for their own pet charity, 'The East India Club'. Tom was invited to auction off forty-four bottles of wine, a few days' fishing on the Test, and a day's fox-hunting with the Heythrop. Prices far exceeded Christie's conservative estimates; everybody was in expansive mood. Tom whipped up their good will, again and again, to a staggering total of £18,000. (He himself had donated a magnum of Château Palmer.) On the subject of record bidding, Picasso's *Acrobat and Young Harlequin* fetched £21 million at Christie's on Monday, November 28. A mêlée of continental bidders with fur-lined coats, cigars and breath laden with good-living and garlic were usurped by a diminutive Japanese. He was subsequently quite overcome with his exertion. A Christie's director found him a cold can of coca-cola and helped him slip through a side-door. Apparently he was buying for the Tokyo Mitsukoshi Department Store. It is a sensitive and beautiful picture, painted when Picasso, young and penniless in Paris, adopted his Rose period. You can feel the pain and the poignancy that seeped within. It is said that the Harlequin is a self-portrait. (Auberon Waugh afterwards noted in his *Sunday Telegraph* column, that he found it 'shocking' that Christie's should receive a commission of £3 million for arranging the sale!)

A spate of tragedies and violent crimes runs tandem with these seasonal diversions. A devastating earthquake in Armenia has resulted in a death toll of some fifty thousand. The Russians have proved themselves woefully inept at dealing with the catastrophe. Rescue workers from Britain, Europe and America were foiled in their attempts to give ready aid; inadequate air control from Yerivan airport to the scene of the disaster led two planes to crash, impassable roads delayed urgent medical and food supplies. It has shocked the world that the Soviet Union superpower had no available essential medicines or rescue equipment.

An appalling train crash at Clapham Junction, two days ago, has sent shock waves of fear and anger through the British public. (Cause: faulty signal lights. Result: 34 dead.) We are urged – 'Let the train take the strain'; to ease up on private car journeys to Central London; to use the underground. But the underground is rapidly becoming a no-go area. Two murders within six hours of each other were reported yesterday. Armed crime, with shootings and stabbings, is the standard scare today. The more prosperous a society, the more vulnerable to savagery, greed and vandalism. We need more police.

1989

January 28 Widcombe Manor Bath

Propped up with a delectable breakfast tray I am far too engrossed in the choice between home-made marmalade and confiture de framboises to consider the weather. But the pulled-back chintz curtains confirm that patter of steady rain. The Admiral's wife is up and dressed already. I hear her in the hall below commiserating over the cupids above the front fountain. 'Poor little things! They look so pathetic in the rain.' Rich wafts of sausage and bacon and the hum of husbands steal up the mahogany main stairs. I exercise and take a deep bath in a large carpeted room made larger with a mahogany chest, a wicker chair, a silk screen, a Regency fireplace and a fine selection of engravings and mezzotints. The additional niceties of bowls of pot pourri and a battery of bottles of this essence and that cream could keep one amused all morning in this room that is a bathroom.

We collect in the marble hall in tweeds and mackintoshes and an assortment of umbrellas. The American couple from Philadelphia look conspicuously smart in their Loden green capes. Mrs Philadelphia sports a matching hat that drips with feathers. The rain lifts and we stand and admire the 1728 façade of this elegant manor. Essentially Baroque and essentially unique. I am reminded of the fantasy picture of *Capriccio of a Netherlandish Garden*.[1] But Widcombe has the built-in advantage of local stone, with the 'grotesque' masks and decorative capitals carved in the durable coade stone. No amount of rain or wind can blur its intricate features.

There is a Victorian bow added to the west front that overlooks the dell below. It is sympathetically incorporated but to our mind the stone graces in the two niches would appear too small. Terraced grass 'salons', bounded by clipped beech hedges, descend to the dell with ornamental pools and fountains. The balustrades are liberally crowned with urns where blue and yellow pansies curl to overflowing. Pink dwarf cyclamen, snowdrops and the sharp green shoots of daffodils edge the gravel paths; aubrietia clings in juicy clumps to the walls. And do we see sheep below? Our host assures me they are Canadian geese and suggests that we now set off down the hill for Bath. But

[1] Attributed to Robert Robinson who decorated the main panels at Carshalton House (1696–1713).

first he must show us some eighteenth-century graffiti; on the east outside wall is carved in strident strokes: BURT IS A CUT PURSE AND KNAVE.

The butler who has doubled up as chauffeur is ready at the wheel of the Land Rover. The rain has accentuated the glow of Bath; its squares and crescents of gold stone, its cobbled alleyways. We browse through antique shops and the excellent antique market. Tom takes details of a glass-fronted late eighteenth-century bookcase; he has it in mind for Christie's dining-room; to fill it with Chinese porcelain. It is priced at £30,000. We both single out an Anglo-Indian ivory folder, inlaid with sandalwood, made in 1800. I buy it for £580 for his birthday. We do not linger; the butler must serve his other post. But in another shop a fetching blonde, apparently dressed in a grey riding habit and boots, engages us in her wares. Tom finally points out that her Regency overmantel mirror is hung upside down. She laughs and flushes prettily as the boys look on admiringly.

Back to a delicious lunch: smoked salmon is wrapped around creamed mackerel; ham is parcelled up in salsify and glazed with a cheese sauce; a succulent apple sponge is followed by cheeses, chocolates and coffee. The conversation eases and we disperse to the study fire, to the drawing-room fire, to the bedroom. Some play bridge or backgammon or sit with sleepy eyes beside the enormous wood puzzle. Our hostess relaxes with her tapestry and next cogitates over the seating plan for dinner. Local friends are invited, in a black tie. The old labrador looks suitably bored by the lull in activity and pummels large head and body into the middle of the sofa. I retreat to our room with the *Daily Telegraph* and inadvertently miss out on Nannie's tea party. Tom later reports that the Admiral was gently reprimanded for looking longingly at the chocolate cake before he had first eaten a slice of bread and butter.

February 27 The Oriental Bangkok

Our first visit to Bangkok. This legendary hotel is luxury and service personified. Once a favourite retreat for both Noël Coward and Somerset Maugham, and where the latter wrote his short story *Princess September* in the garden while recuperating from a malaria attack. Our room is in the new wing with a panoramic view of the broad Chao Phraya river below. The garden rustles with bamboos and soaring palms, banana trees, and pink and white orchids on tall, slender stems, a haven of secluded shade. We sip drinks on the terrace and plan our three days. Tomorrow we must see the Grand Palace, but today, our arrival day, we will relax. The humid heat cloaks us with a sensual lethargy.

The river calls. A steady traffic of tugs and barges, steamers and brightly-canopied pleasure boats, denotes an unhurried, purposeful life of its own. We take a ferry and sit swaying on heavy teak chairs as we cross over to an open-air fish restaurant. A bevy of diminutive pretty girls greet us royally. Demure and smiling, in high-necked white shirts and bright sarongs, they invite us to choose our lunch. Lobster and crab wallow sociably in huge tanks. Alongside, a display of silver pomfret, red snapper, and Indian halibut is embedded in crushed ice. We settle for tiger prawns from the charcoal grill and the recommended asparagus. A smiling damsel pins orchids to our lapels, while another hands us each a warm, scented cloth in a pair of tongs. The wine is opened with masterful deliberation, and finger-bowls of jasmine-scented tea arrive with our prawns. This whole operation is conducted with the maximum delicacy, much smiling and bowing, and earnest entreaties to enjoy our meal. A suggested dessert of egg threads in marzipan we graciously decline. All this smiling and bowing is catching.

A siesta in our cool, darkened room puts an end to the jet lag and the effects of heat and wine. It is dark when we wake at six o'clock; no lingering sunset delays nightfall in this equatorial land. We dine beside the river on yellow curry of chicken with coconut cream. Twinkling trails of fairy lights are festooned on swaying bougainvillaea and bushes of densely sweet frangipani. But Bangkok's renowned night life begs an exploration.

We hail a tuk-tuk (the standard open-air motorised rickshaw) and zip through narrow, dark streets, hair flying. Deposited in Pat Pong, the red light district, we size up the seething scene. Pulsating disco bars, flashing lights, and bodies jostling, drinking, dancing, and spilling over on to every pavement. The night air hangs above like an odorous blanket, steaming with curry, burning charcoal, and pungent joss sticks. A crowd of tourists – Japanese, Australian, German, Italian – stroll from bar to bar, where teenage go-go girls in various stages of undress cajole their prey to sip drinks, a mere aperitif to the pleasures they wish to impart – at a price. We step inside a bar where girls so young, petite, and pretty seem happily engrossed in netting their catch. Caught up in arms and laps or teetering from man to man, they sway and pitch their bare bodies in provocative abandon. A drawstring leaves their round firm buttocks exposed, but conceals the pubic hair. Others dance on stage, manipulating their bodies in amorous contortions around steel poles.

Finishing our drinks we again venture into a similar dive called

Lipstick. Here a girl and man with measured control are making love on stage, leisurely, artistically, inoffensively. They are followed by another girl who, with an engaging joie de vivre, succeeds in blowing a whistle and then a horn from the orifice of her vagina (an admirable feat of her stomach muscles). The next contender draws frenzied applause from the near-satiated audience for retrieving a twenty-foot string of orchids from her vagina, which she replaces with a lighted cigarette to emit punctuated puffs of smoke. Reeling with such sights and sounds, we call it a night.

March 2

Thailand is proclaimed to be the land of smiles. It is undeniably the white man's oyster. Be his status single or married, he is lavished with every overture and attention. Beguiling girls with flowers in their hair, their nubile little bodies snug in silk bodices and sarongs, kneel before him to take his drink order, to measure for a pair of trousers, to pin an orchid to his lapel, his laundry, his pillow, to massage his mind and body, and so totally enslave his attention that it may effortlessly indulge in theirs. I do not suggest that a woman does not enjoy the same attentions. On the contrary: I have had my share of smiles and orchids. Seamstresses have run up silk dresses and shirts overnight and my pillow has been adorned with quotations from Bob Dylan and Cervantes: 'I'll let you be in my dreams, if I can be in yours' and 'God bless the inventor of sleep, the cloak that covers all men's thoughts'. The unassailable fact is that the Thais are a genuinely charming race, bred for pleasure, it would seem – their own and others'.

The manager of the River Bootery talks as we sample his snakeskin shoes. 'Thailand is a happy, organised country. But her proximity to Burma, Laos and Cambodia is an ever-present threat.' What about Bangkok traffic? (It is even worse than London.) 'Yes, this is bad, very, very bad, and we cannot ease it with an underground system. The souterrain is too moist.' We tell him how clean we find the streets, cleaner than those in London, and that we see everywhere big, expensive cars: Mercedes, BMWs and Volvos. Warily he concedes that Bangkok has become prosperous, with tourism the prime boost to the country's economy.

Three days in Bangkok, where we have seen so much and yet so little. The floating river markets, Chinatown, the crocodile farm, the cruise up-river to the ruins of Ayutthaya, the former capital; all these sights we have had to put in abeyance. However a pert little guide, whose unpronounceable name translated as Rabbit (she was born in the year of the Rabbit), took us round the Grand Palace and the Temple of the Emerald Buddha. Despite the cool marble courtyards of this square-mile Royal City and the shade thrown by the deep eaves of the pagodas, it was an excruciatingly hot morning's sightseeing, producing a staggering impact of brilliantly-coloured tiled walls and glittering mosaics. One monolithic Buddha was totally faceted with gold leaf. I wondered if he could become dulled and stained in the monsoon. Rabbit, seeing us wilt in the face of such overwhelming splendour, scuttled off in search of coca-cola. We propped ourselves against a marble parapet, sipping and dripping simultaneously. My linen skirt was soon blotted with a map of Australia. We recovered ourselves and entered the Temple of the Emerald Buddha. Rabbit pointed out that we should first take off our shoes and that the Buddha was in fact made of jade and not emerald. On our entering the beautifully-painted cool interior, an official gentleman asked me to remove my straw hat; a strange Buddhist rule considers a hat an affront. The Buddha was set up high on a gold altar and draped in a cloth to the neck, his winter dress, explained Rabbit. It was necessary to visit in the summer months to see the Buddha unclothed, she added helpfully.

Out in the sun again, we strolled through the marble precincts of the exuberant palaces and temples. Huge porcelain water jars, swimming with orchids and floating lotus, were positioned beside stairs and terraces. Bonsai and ebony trees, potted in marble urns, lined several parapets; their crippled black branches burgeoned leafy balls. We left through an avenue of tamarind trees, symbolically clipped in the pyramid outline of the Throne Canopies. Rabbit, whose services we had booked for the whole morning, next took us to see Jim Thompson's house. Thompson was an American who introduced Thai silk to the world. He lived in a charming teak house on stilts, alongside one of Bangkok's many canals; in fact it is seven teak houses on stilts effectively knocked into one. (He disappeared, mysteriously, in 1967, while on a visit to the Malaysian Cameron Highlands.) The cool dark interior was a soothing antidote to the heat and pomp of the Palace quarters. Again we were asked to remove our shoes; the teak stairs and floors are kept meticulously waxed. We wandered through little rooms that bulged with Thai and Asian artefacts and an abundant store of blue and white bowls. It was all very quiet and very tidy. The canal below looked clouded and khaki, but did not smell. It was overhung with flowering trees that appeared alive with cackling birds. A marmalade cat sat by the front entrance and Rabbit confirmed that it was not of the Siamese variety.

Today we lunched with Professor Victor Sassoon. He made his life in Thailand, over forty years ago. Before his retirement, he taught

English at the Chulalongkorn University, Bangkok. We took off our shoes in deference to the gleaming teak floors of his modest home. We admired his elaborately-carved door architraves, his shelves and shelves of faded multi-lingual books, and a brand new motor bicycle which his house boy had seen fit to park on the front veranda. The professor proudly guided us round his 'pocket garden'. Did we know this hanging orchid? He dangled a trailing pink bloom before our noses. What smell did it remind us of? It was strong and exceptionally sweet. 'It smells of strawberry jam,' declared the professor, as we fumbled for a more fitting analogy; perhaps it reminded him of England. We next admired his copper pod trees; a light breeze had whipped the top branches into a froth of yellow flowers. Shade, water, and colour are the priorities of a Bangkok garden. We slowly advanced on his lily pod, the pièce de résistance. Here his prized hanging heliconias waved red tails and a rare variety of banana enfolded mauve flowers in huge green leaves. We next repaired to his study, which had been converted from a garage. It had subsequently been flooded by the lily pond with many books ruined. Nothing daunted, the professor had raised the room two feet off the ground; in doing so he had rendered the existing French windows an obsolete exit to the garden. (Men on their own make do with such shortcomings.) We talked of our visit to Jim Thompson's house. Had the professor known him? 'I knew him well; he was a charming, highly intelligent man.' And his sudden death? The professor did not attach much significance to his friend's mysterious disappearance; he preferred to assume that he had gone walking in the jungle terrain and tumbled down a hole. And had he known Somerset Maugham? Indeed he had, an arrogant man in his opinion, and yet strangely insecure with his stultifying stammer. 'He visited the university on a few occasions. I went to great trouble to spell out the complicated names of the Thai professors who had entertained him, gave the list to his secretary, Alan Searle, in the hope that Maugham might write a few letters of thanks. He never did. He had not one ounce of charm.' The professor paused and added as an afterthought. 'Do you know? He told me that he considered *Cakes and Ale* his best book. It was too terrible to hear him stuttering and spitting out that one title, when he had such complete command of the written word.'

Over a simple lunch of yogurt-dressed prawns and pineapple, the professor talked of his disinclination to make the pilgrimage to England, to visit his ageing relatives. 'They can all come over here whenever they want, have the run of the car.' I agreed that he should not feel bound to make any altruistic journey home. 'Only go if you feel compelled,' I cautioned him. 'What sensible advice!' He beamed, the ultimate self-contained bachelor. And how was Queen Sirikit? 'Not well.' The professor frowned over his plate of prawns. What was the trouble, we wondered? Her glamour and sweetness were legendary. She had been the darling of the British press. Continued the professor: 'Some sort of allergy has made her over-dependant on drugs. She went to America for treatment, but it was not successful. She sometimes appears in public, but looks dazed.' More a psychiatric disorder than a physical one? The discreet professor would not be drawn. And her family? 'King Bhumiphol is a marvellous chap, now aged sixty-two. He does prodigious work for the underprivileged, always in shirt sleeves calling in on the deprived villages up north. Their eldest child, a daughter, has opted out, married an American and lives in San Diego. As for the Crown Prince, he has now acquired three illegitimate children, whom he promotes alarmingly. The younger daughter, whom I taught, makes more sense. But she has become awfully fat. On the other hand she is a responsible figurehead and is involved in public work.' We were off to Phuket? 'The new hotels are getting a stranglehold on all the beaches. Get William Warren's guide book. You are seeing it all just in time.'

March 9 Phuket Thailand

A small paradise island off the south peninsula of Thailand, where the Indian Ocean laps the pearly white sands, faithfully bears out the fulsome panegyrics of the guide books. The succulent seafood and exotic fruits are served by the habitual line-up of engaging nymphs. In figure-hugging silks, they bow and smile before us, their finger-tips touching lightly in greeting. This charm of the Thais and their desire to please is an endemic phenomenon. Will this future invasion of tourists take their smile away?

Jerking in a jeep over scenic dirt roads, we have traversed the whole island bar its mountainous middle. A glut of impenetrable jungle cascades down the slopes in a profusion of waving coconut palms and wild banana. Crops of pineapple are cultivated at sea level, each fruit set up on its ramrod stalk, a gold casket shielded in silver leaves. There are cool glades of rubber-trees, where a half-coconut shell is attached to each trunk to catch the sticky white sap. And, beside livid green rice paddies, water buffalo wallow. Simple villages straggle the narrow roads made up of modest bungalows with roofs of coconut thatch and bamboo, some set on sticks, others more recently built, with tin roofs and verandas. The few shops display a variety of local fruits, enticing pyramids of oranges, grapes, and mangoes, clumps of small green bananas, and water melons; oozing ruby-red with juice. Each modest homestead has electric light and television run on the communal generator. Second-hand motor bicycles are propped by each door and more often upturned with the whole family engrossed in any repairs.

The north of Phuket is less populated and commensurately lush with crops and jungle. Driving one afternoon through the green shade of rubber-trees, we found the Tone Sai Waterfall. A six-year-old girl adopted us and nimbly led us up the cliff side to find its source. She darted ahead, indicating rock foot-holds and the sturdy roots of trees. Higher and higher she beckoned us; we were crowded in by towering tropicalia: huge, exotic ferns and palms had sprung a dense screen beside the trickle of water; everywhere the whirring and shrieks of unseen birds. We watched out for snakes and dreaded our descent. Yelping with glee our little leader reached the grotto and with water tumbling behind her she danced an exultant fandango on the glistening boulders. Finally she rinsed her black hair in the crystal pool with evident gusto.

After such daily excursions, we returned thankfully to the cool and comfort of our hotel, the Dusit Laguna. A vast low-spread hulk, it is set back from the pounding sea with a glade of casuarinas between. Here an army of amiable village women, with cane mats and baskets of emollients, daily accost us with their massage services. Lying beneath the waving, feathery leaves I have relished these sessions where every bone and muscle is expertly pinched and prodded, pulled and pummelled. Sturdy bare feet are pressed down on back and buttocks, as though to plant one into the very ground. Unctuous oils of camphor, menthol, and coconut are intermittently rubbed deep into every pore.

On the subject of massage, Tom prefers the indoor variety. Together we sampled the renowned massage parlour at the Pearl Hotel in Phuket town. Seated in tiers behind a glass screen were a gaggle of smartly-dressed pretty girls. They rather resembled a school group and smiled at us encouragingly. The more mature Madame of the establishment intimated to us to make our selection. We chose four and fifty-nine. (The disparity in their numbers rather suggested that more girls were hidden away or that they had not shown up for afternoon school.) We were led away to a large room, equipped with an outsized bath and two rubber lilos. Would we first like iced lemonade? There was great activity as we prepared ourselves for this bodily onslaught. A huge bar of 'baby care' soap was first grated, the bath was run and the soap flakes scattered and fluffed up in the bubbling bath. We all undressed and soaked companionably in the huge bath, sipping lemonade. Our pretty pupils then directed us to the lilos where, in a frenzy of flailing limbs, flying soapsuds and rising steam, they massaged us with their entire bodies. This traditional scrubbing with the pubic hair is a pleasant-enough innovation, but I had to restrain my girl from nibbling my nipples. Tom placed no such embargo on the attentions he was enjoying. 'When in Rome, when in Rome . . .' he warbled merrily from the confines of his own lathering lilo. We capped our libidinous afternoon with a drink in the neighbouring town, Patong. There, the grinding jaws of tourism have pitched a solid crush of go-go bars along the two-mile shore line. Patong has consequently become a comparatively seedy resort where every visiting man is encouraged to drink and procure to excess. Such dives as the Patong Palace, the Banana Moon, the Kangaroo Bar, and the Swiss Garden ('good location, very safe and clean rooms') belt out music all day and night. Alluring girls in skimpy dress strike a languid pose on the bar stools. They tease the chained monkey or the parrot in the cage and wait, listless and pouting, for the evening trade. Iced drinks, whether soft or potent, travel under such seductive labels as Phuket Dream, Pink Coral, Laguna Sunset, and Bang Tao Flip. Delicious concoctions of blended fruits: pineapple, tangerine, coconut, and banana are laced with rum and curacão and whipped to a froth with white of egg. At the Golden Beach bar we ordered two Bangkok Blessings and were rewarded with hollow pineapples, brimming with juice, and pierced with orchids and drinking straws. It was pleasant to watch a bemused world stroll by, to sip and sweat and speculate. Across the street stood a 'blood and urine' clinic which seemed to be doing rather more business than the bars. Worried-looking young men in shorts went in and out.

AIDS has not yet become a byword in the Orient. The *Bangkok Post* still spells it out as Acquired Immune Deficiency Syndrome. This very week journalists from the world over have been busy reporting on the AIDS Conference hosted in Bangkok. Representatives from thirty nations have attended. One expert did not mince words: 'While the rest of the world reels in the face of AIDS, Pattaya's party rages on like a blind idiot in the path of a speeding train.' Another claimed that in the whole of Thailand 'only 300 cases' had been recorded. The Thais are an essentially tactile people: to give pleasure with their bodies is a traditional element of their breeding. The much-vaunted Cleopatra and Darling massage parlours are exclusive-enough establishments, where there is no arbitrary dividing line between no sex, sex, or more sex. For the Thais sex per se is an intrinsic embodiment of life, a pleasurable and edifying exploitation of the body function. *Que serà serà*. But beware the body.

March 27 Renishaw Derbyshire

Easter fell early this early this year. We spent the long weekend with
Reresby and Penelope Sitwell, at Renishaw, in a house party of ten. A
consortium of local friends were invited to dinner on Saturday. Tom
forgot his black tie and borrowed Reresby's. It was fortunate that he
had not forgotten any other sartorial necessities as our host has now
become an extra-large model. Darling Reresby; beatific and brimful
of anecdotal wit. His self-sponsored tours of Renishaw are an ongoing
feature for every guest. 'No, Reresby! It's time for lunch; Osbert's
study will have to wait;' and Penelope successfully herds us to table.
The house has been transformed by Penelope's recent decorations.
Her novel treatment of the drawing-room floor is a sensational triumph. Like any large, high-ceilinged room of late eighteenth-century
proportions it has always posed a carpet problem; the bare oak floor
has now come into its own. It was first sand-blasted and then marked
with a compass in a stylised motif of circles and corollas. The design
was stencilled in with lime-green and chocolate and finally sealed with
several coats of varnish. The resulting floor is vibrant with pattern and
colour; a striking alternative to any faded carpet. Penelope said she
had cribbed the idea from Russian palace interiors; perhaps she has set
a trend.

Meals were served in the dining-room with family silver brought
up from the safe. Maids in white aprons were recruited from the
village. Meals of time-honoured English tradition: roast beef and Yorkshire pudding, kedgeree, boiled gammon, soups, smoked salmon and
rich, rum cake, swathed in an involucre of thick, sweet cream. The
Sitwell family portraits by John Singleton Copley and John Sargent
are lit to advantage in this coral room. Coral silk curtains, deeply
swagged, smudged coral walls and a set of twenty eighteenth-century
chairs with coral leather seats.

There are some nineteen bedrooms at Renishaw; each one is gradually redecorated, with four-posters glimpsed through every door. We
ourselves are in 'Blossom's' room: 'Blossom' so named by a disenchanted Dame Edith; he was Sir Osbert's special friend. From the
faded photograph on Sir Osbert's desk he resembled Benjamin Britten.
The room is now draped and flounced in green and pink chintz. A
gilded rose is fastened to the pink domed tester of the bed, where we
luxuriate below on plump, pink pillows.

Easter day was mild and sunny and set the birds singing in tremulous
trills and chortles by the lakeside, where trespassers are deterred by the
sign: 'Please do not tread on Mr Sitwell's snakes.' I walked up the
steep grass hill to the ha-ha. The house looked resplendent in the sun

with the flag flying and with Reresby's fountain spewing to the heavens. Tom took some photographs and planted me in a stream of daffodils beneath the 200-year-old lime avenue.

The leisurely weekend passed in sight-seeing trips to ancestral homes, games of bridge, talk, drinking, snoozing and reading; mostly newspapers. Sorties into the garden were an obvious diversion. Nobody could fail to admire those descending terraces of Italianate green salons; those parterres and pools and the statuary; the whole elaborately hedged around with topiary. (The garden was conceived and laid out by Reresby's grandfather, Sir George Sitwell, and is now finely matured.)

Under Penelope's direction still more plants and vistas are continually developed. She called us out on the terrace one night. Could we smell the coal dust? A biting, sharp whiff was carried on the soft wind. It smelt like tar and made the eyes smart. 'We won't smell it anymore,' said Penelope nostalgically. 'They are closing down these mines next month. The dogs will miss it! The moment they smell it from the M1 they bark and know they are nearly home.'

On Easter morning a few of our party went to church. The little Norman church of Eckington positively bulged with blooms and bodies. The narrow approach road was so crowded with cars that a farmer, in a fit of benevolence, let us park in his field. Village people still like to say their prayers.

Calke Abbey, Kedleston Hall, Chatsworth, Sudbury Hall. In the Derbyshire Dukeries you are spoilt for choice. Kedleston, newly acquired by the National Trust, was comparatively empty of pictures and furniture. But the massive pomp of the coral-veined alabaster columns is an astonishing tour de force; the epitome of eighteenth-century grandeur. (Local alabaster, too.)

Beetling back on the motorway we were too late for Sudbury and walked instead in the garden; the sturdy Carolean façade with its diapered brick formation emanates aeons of history. One senses strongly the parade of seventeenth-century souls that lived and passed through its walls. Half-close your eyes and you can see shadowy figures parading by the lake; women in gem-studded stomachers and starched white ruffs on the arms of men, sombre and attentive in their black chimney-pot hats. And, finally, the incomparable Hardwick Hall. Set high on the hill with its famous fenestration facing the setting sun, it flashed magnificently as we drove past below. 'Hardwick Hall – more glass than wall.' It had looked like a badge of blazing diamonds.

June 5 Parkside Hospital Wimbledon

Lying in wait for one's recalcitrant bowels to open is the height of ignominy; but it is apparently the one event that endorses a quick recovery. My operation on Saturday afternoon was a mere snip; the removal of two 'piles' from the rectum; a haemorrhoidectomy. But the effects of a general anaesthetic and subsequent pain-killers induce a languor long after the event; one's nearest and dearest appear and recede in a mist of smiles and flowers; news of the outside world bears little consequence compared to that stern, staccato sting in the bottom. But all such subjective triviality is swept aside in today's shock horror reports on the Peking massacre.

For seven weeks the world has focussed on the Chinese student demonstrations in Peking's main Tiananmen Square. 'We have to change the political system!' It has been a peaceful and polite demonstration with many students waging a hunger strike. The Peking Medical College Hospital instigated a sympathetic service of ambulances and beds for dehydrated victims. After forty-eight hours' recuperation the students would race back to Tiananmen Square cautioned by their doctors to 'drink a little milk'. Two weeks ago the scene turned ugly; from this unprecedented triumph in which the whole country embraced the students' exultant thrust for democracy, winds of hostility set up a murmuring.

'The People's Liberation Army will enter Peking to restore order,' announced the Premier, Mr Li Peng. The students, boosted by the increasing crowds of more young people, set to with a will to defend their precious ground in Tiananmen Square. By the simple act of linking arms they warded off the initial military intervention. Others let down the tyres of army trucks and sat fearlessly in their path; they sensed correctly that the soldiers were reluctant opponents; that they supported their cause. Mr Li Peng's clamorous command for martial law went out with a whimper.

But the carnival in Tiananmen Square had to be decisively quashed. Knives, clubs and bloody killings brought a hideous end to this coherent challenge of a youth movement that had fanned the admiration of the entire Western world.

Today thousands are feared dead; crushed by tanks and blasted by gunfire, their bodies piled high and burnt without trace. Mr Li Peng has had his revenge at the irreparable expense of his students' blood through the dubious loyalty of the People's Liberation Army. The frail figure of the eighty-four-year-old Chairman Deng Xiaoping is hors de combat in hospital with cancer of the prostate. The world expresses outrage that such an exemplary demonstration should have ended in this blood bath. And Britain is now beleaguered by panic calls from Hong Kong. 'How can the British Government ever return the people of Hong Kong to such a régime?'

It was in October 1980 that I myself stood in Central Peking. 'Democracy Wall' was boarded up. Why? 'The people served too many complaints,' explained our young guide. 'We have too many old men at the top'; *plus ça change* . . .

The world press can only speculate, today, on China's immediate course. Civil war between rival army units? It is sad that with all their restraint and co-ordination the students never adopted a leader; an articulate flesh and blood embodiment of their democratic ideals. In marked contrast to the present Chinese predicament is the cautious victory of Poland's Solidarity movement over the acting Government's Communist candidates. It look Lech Walesa, the Solidarity leader, ten years of pain and patience to bring his democratic reforms to such an ordered triumph. He now warns his euphoric supporters to keep cool; too much emotion could prejudice further elections. Communism, the world over, has become an anachronism; a shambling weed, watered by bigoted old men. The painstaking approach of Lech Walesa to dig at the roots has proved more effective than the exuberant heroism of the young Chinese students.

June 6 Parkside Hospital

A wet morning. Things start early in hospital. The clink and clang of the medicine trolley is a reliable alarm at 6.30 a.m. In comes the pretty Singaporean nurse with pills and a thermometer; the girl from Ghana with breakfast (prunes and bran, more prunes and bran), and the pink English nurse with salt for the bath; to soothe and soak the sore, sore bottom. And now the lady from the kitchen with the menus for the day. A blackbird, its wings congealed with rain, pecks furiously at the green sisal matting that covers my veranda; he needs wet grass and worms. Now if he had been a robin . . . day after day I would feed him with milk and gravy; milk and gravy out of the white hospital saucer with its thick gold rim.

I think back to May; a month of crowded pleasures when the sun shone steadily. Temperatures in London topped 84°F; the warmest May in London since records began in 1833. And when Suzannah married her military man. Southwell Minster, Nottingham, enveloped a packed congregation between its cool Norman arches. On the dot she came; glorious and happy and trim, caught in veils of white and the rich sheen of satin. Handel and Mozart, prayers led by provosts, a

Shakespeare sonnet, an address and a blessing, hymns of love and alleluias wafted Suzannah on the arm of her groom; out to the sunlight and to their new life beyond.

First to the reception on sloping lawns; Suzannah's rose-brick Georgian home behind and her father's orchards stretched beyond were flooded with sun and colour. The band of her husband's regiment. The Queen's Dragoon Guards, thumped merrily away beneath a brightly-striped awning. In broad-brimmed hats and sparkling silks, girls laughed and talked and promenaded. One lingered in the ha-ha . . . as the afternoon drew on we sank on scattered bales of straw, until Suzannah should reappear. There she goes! Radiant in her going-away carriage — a newly-painted steam-roller!

Next we coasted along country roads to Rutland and spent the night in style and luxury at Hambleton Hall. The solid Victorian house was recently converted into a country hotel. The words '*Fay ce que voudras*' incised above the stone front door portended an indulgent stay. A wide gravel terrace overlooked a descending, tiered garden; fields sprayed with buttercups and clotted with may sloped to the lake below. We lingered over a bottle of champagne. The evening was thick with wisteria and the powerful scent wafted from huge vases of lilies. Acclaimed as the best hotel outside London, we could only agree. An exquisite dinner was master-minded by the young English chef, Brian Baker. The rooms, decorated by Nina Campbell, combined a recherché and informal comfort. Despite the exceptionally warm night, it was an ultimate pleasure to see a fire smouldering in the hall grate, as we walked up the wide oak stairs to bed.

Wending our way home through Northants on a cross-country course, we marvelled at the lush green rolling tracts of unspoilt country, now wooded, now streaked sharp yellow with rape. Hedgerows shimmered white with hawthorn, and villages of weathered gold stone sprawled in gardens beneath the old church spires; through Cropwell Bishop and Stragglethorpe, ancient villages with names to evoke Trollope, past the White Swan and the Old Post House and J & C Cockle & Sons, purveyors of meat, game and poultry. We stopped for lunch at the Spencer Arms, with a visit to Althorp in mind. The seventeenth-century brick façade with its original E-shape formation was refaced in white stone two centuries ago. The house today has forfeited its original distinction and the garden is of no account. 'Keep off the carpets please.' A ringing command from a side-room and every one of us skips off the Indian carpet that covers the central oak hall. 'Off with their heads' could not have dispersed us more quickly. Raine Spencer, the present châtelaine, is formidably possessive of her newly-decorated rooms. A perfectionist, an arch contriver, she is also an acknowledged born organiser. We are guided through the main saloons where colours leap to attention. A drawing-room, with curtains drawn to protect the coverings, reveals, even in the subdued light, a hotbed of variegated salmon-pinks. An adjoining room is more muted with oyster walls and lime silk sofas. (Everybody is agreed that Althorp was distinctly shabby before Raine came.) She has drummed up further public interest with her fashion jewellery shop, the tea room, the wine shop, and the hiring out of the re-decorated State rooms for meals and weddings.

We find her prominently perched between little red-clothed tables that groan and glitter with trinkets, cut-glass, and Victorian china. But of course she remembers. On this hot Sunday afternoon it is an obvious diversion to lead us to the converted stables for a cup of tea. She looks cool in her blue and white tent-like dress; her pink and white skin is commendably wrinkle-free and her smooth white hands taper in perfectly-manicured nails, varnished in bright cerise. Last week she was sixty years old. How awful that we had not been invited to the ball. They even had flares lining the drive – and Princess Diana came. (According to later reports, Raine's dress was black and heavily plastered with red poppies; she took up more than her fair share of the ballroom.) Now she talks of 'John's grandsons'. (Of course they are just like any little boys.) 'We have a holiday place in Brighton. They enjoy that. They taunt me by the swimming pool. "Look at me, Auntie Raine! Look at me!" I don't take any notice of course.' Lord Spencer is passing through the stables and is immediately harnessed. He sits dutifully bedside us round the little tea table. A charming, gentle man, his voice only marginally impaired by his stroke. So we had stayed at Hambleton Hall? He was taking Raine off to a good food guide establishment at Chagford in Devon later in the summer. 'She needs to get away from all this hard work and worry, you know. And now I must go and look after my people in the wine shop.' Finally extracting ourselves from Raine Spencer's exuberant outpourings, we visit the modest Lord in his place of work. He stands behind a broad counter of white marble – made up from the old bathrooms, he tells us proudly – and the wine storage shelves are made from the elms struck down in the hurricane. We buy a bottle of his house champagne for the princely sum of £14. He wraps it in tissue and his man puts it in a bag. 'You are very kind,' he nods courteously. We walk away from the house precincts, touched and bemused that the father-in-law of our future monarch plays shop in his stable-yard.

June 7 Parkside

Tom calls; every day he has come. He brings a menu for the annual dinner for the Grenadier Guards, held at the Savoy. The Queen and Prince Philip were there; the latter made an incoherent speech about dying elephants and then commented on the abysmal level of conversation that he had encountered during the evening. (Perhaps they should include some women guests in the future.) A menu of 'Le délice de cailles en chemise' preceded by a fatuously described 'La rosette de saumon d'Ecosse fumé Savoy' concluded with a tulip sorbet and cheese soufflé. The Regimental band accompanied the banquet with waltzes and serenades; a little Mozart Nachtmusik was sandwiched in between.

I reflect on the care and comforts I have enjoyed in these six days. Pain has been modified by such pleasure as clean sheets each day and nutritious meals winged on trays; sole in white sauce with eggs and prawns; a stuffed aubergine glazed with cheese; steamed apple, a passion fruit mousse, a gooseberry fool; accompanied all the way by Highland Water from deep below the Ochil Hills.

June 7 Hardwicke House

The last day of May, this year, was proclaimed as Eton's June 4th. The wind got up as we gorged ravenously on Valerie's picnic lunch. We were settled with chairs and tables in the Agar's Plough carpark. Time to move off and we hurried past the cricketers, who seemed to be drawing far less attention than the wet bobs. To the Procession of Boats! We stood on chairs on the cropped grass bank of the Thames; a secluded corner of Eton where the Carolean bricks of Upper School rise intact and upright behind. The boats are now a hundred years old. And are sedulously preserved for this one annual event.

And there was nephew Mark! Perilously tall in his long white ducks, he stood in his skiff, his oar up-ended with the rest of them. With balance secured, each eight doffed their straw hats; hats lavished with flowers from mothers' gardens; lupins, red roses and marigolds were shaken and tossed to the water. It was the Duke of Wellington who pronounced 'The Battle of Waterloo was won on the playing fields of Eton'; perhaps the water running beside them, strewn with vivid petals from the Procession of Boats, could inspire a second Monet.

August 7 Forest Cottage Ashclyst Forest Broadclyst South-East Devon

Mr Mitchell is tending his runner beans at the bottom of his cottage garden, our cottage garden too. We were staying for the week, sharing with him the silent depths of Ashclyst forest, the thatched roof, and the diminishing water supply. Mr Mitchell protects his bald head with a knotted handkerchief. The sun sinks behind the oak-trees and a tremor of cool darts through the forest. Mrs Mitchell, who holds herself and her head of immaculately-waved grey hair with the dignity of a duchess, stands a little apart from Mr Mitchell and his runner beans. They make small, intermittent exchanges and sniff the air. They have lived in their end of the cottage for fifty years and clearly depend on each other's company. Each evening Mrs Mitchell joins Mr Mitchell at the bottom of the garden.

My mother sits in a deckchair under the damson tree. She strings some beans for our supper. She brought them from her Hampshire garden, she brought her stringer too. Taking up residence in a cottage concentrates the mind on every favourite household gadget and necessity – the electric orange-squeezer, the diabolically sharp potato-peeler, the teapot for one, the bedboard, and even the scented drawer-liners – a host of travelling toys, which only too often are lost in transit or left to the benefit of the next let.

There is a gentle tap on the kitchen door. Mr Mitchell stands before me, divested of his handkerchief. 'Not too many hot baths tonight,' he advises cheerfully. We have not had a hot bath for two days. And now my cold tap has cut out, defiantly retching and squawking like a sick dog. He will get through to the National Trust and have a tank of water delivered tomorrow. Never has he known the well so low. He showed it to us this morning. Prising off the iron lid, he motioned to us to peer into a dismal level of two feet of water. The surface was dusted with flies and dead leaves. 'They don't worry,' said Mr Mitchell, 'but the worry of it is that this here well is gravity controlled-like.' He had seen many changes in fifty years too. The woods weren't what they were in them days back; they had foresters in horse-drawn carts and all a-scything and a-trimming up and the chopping up of all over.

Ashclyst Forest was bequeathed to the National Trust together with the entire Killerton Estate by Sir Richard Acland MP in 1944. The Aclands, an old Devon family, who minded their estates and their seats in the House of Commons, built their family home Killerton House in 1777–79. Originally it was intended as a half-way house to a larger, grander establishment; the final house was never built. The house today acts as an excellent repository for the extensive costume collections left to the National Trust; they pose a redeeming feature for the rather ordinary and sparsely-furnished rooms. The National Trust, now nearing its hundredth year in existence, is always keen to acquire good land. The Killerton Estate includes a thousand acres of park and woodland and some twenty farms, liberally dotted with cottages, which are now let to holidaymakers.

We were more enamoured of our visits to Knightshayes Court and Castle Drogo; again Trust properties, but still imbued with the love and taste of their former occupants. It never necessitates centuries to instil a sense of life and beauty in a home. The terraced gardens of Knightshayes were framed with ornamental stone seats, fountains, urns, and statuary, and everywhere a profusion of flowers and scents. We rested in the shade of a fine cedar-tree. A canopied pram was wheeled by on the terrace above and gardeners outbid the hosepipe ban with wonderfully ancient watering-cans. The red stone Victorian mansion, set up high above woods and farmland, dreamed on, in a time warp of its all-pervasive past.

Now, a tap on the front door. The wife of the MP for Exeter and her son have arrived for supper. Vanessa looks exquisite in her shirt of white Honiton lace. She scampers up and down the narrow stairs, exploring each room with shrieks of delight. But how had we found this gem of a cottage in the middle of a wood on her very own doorstep?

In candlelight we eat our rack of lamb and my mother's glistening nectarine tart. The evenings are drawing in. It is nine o'clock and dark already. A strange quietness out there in the woods. No birds sing. Now a faint rustling. The dogs stiffen; hackles up, they sniff the silence. A patter on the window. Raindrops. Blown from the branch of the damson tree. We run to the crude wooden porch to see rain at last. A dense and sparkling curtain is teeming off the eaves. We breathe in that pure, wet air and wonder at the magic of a heavy fall of rain.

September 7 La Musardière Millau France

Madame Gisèle et son équipe vous propose. Madame keeps a renowned table in her eighteenth-century mansion. La Musardière in the provincial valley town of Millau. This south-west area of France boasts a dramatic terrain with sheer 3,000-feet gorges flanking the wide Tarn river and densely-wooded hills that slope steeply to fertile valleys and pastureland.

The famous Roquefort cheese has its provenance in these hills. The small town with its cool caves is wedged in a curved range of sheer cliffs, and a conducted tour reveals that the silky white cheese with its matured pockets of blue-green powder is made from ewe's milk and that twenty-five pints of ewe's milk are needed to make a cheese weighing six pounds.

Warm clothes are advised for visiting these draughty caves. Our guide, a fresh-faced pretty girl – a Roquefort-raised product? – wears a capacious tweed cloak to her ankles. An old lady amongst the party firmly ties a thick mob cap under her indeterminate chins. Our girl warms to her subject and concludes that cheese from the ewe is the whitest and purest of all. We finally pass through the chamber of the 'second ripening' where the aroma of imminent maturity from a thousand 'loaves' catapults us into the warm sunlight.

Madam Gisèle warmly welcomes us back to the evening performance of her dinner table. *Vous avez passé une bonne journée, Monsieur et Madame?* In deference to the day's outing we settle for crêpes Roquefort. We are served by a trim head-waitress of middle years, whose generous application of eye make-up resembles a Caribbean sunset. Two dining-rooms doing a brisk trade lead off from the marble hall where cumbersome pudding trolley stands unceremoniously in the hall, giving prospective diners a tempting eyeful as they descend the wide curved staircase. The walls of the high-ceilinged dining-rooms are generously padded with apricot silk, now worn and faded. Tell-tale flakes from the white cornice appear poised for an untimely descent on to dinner plates. It is evident that some years have passed since Madame has suffered the decorators. Her garden and park have also seen trimmer days with last autumn's leaves haphazardly cornered in their drifts of decay. Perhaps Madame Gisèle, aware of her advancing age, and the debilitated elegance of her hotel, is coasting her enterprise to a finish? And yet her eager patrons would goad her on and on. With her captivating smile and spirit, she rises again and again to take each insistent call.

We have lunched in the fifteenth-century Château de la Caze, which looms steeply from the Tarn. The bouldered mass of the gorges envelop it in a chill, quiet gloom; a shivering screen of almond-trees and poplars line the water's edge below. An alsatian is curled up in the cobbled hall. Two cheerful maids, rubbing up brass pots and jugs and fenders, motion to us not to be afraid. (The alsatian is an ubiquitous household pet in France and is appropriately docile.) We later visited the Château of Sévérac set high on its hill. How the scene has crumbled. Originally an eleventh-century fortress it became a handsomely-developed stone palace in the seventeenth century with richly-furnished pavilions, galleries, massive staircases, and vast windows. After the owners fled with the French Revolution, it lay neglected until fire destroyed the main wings. Today an old woman sits in the open courtyard knitting impassively. She oversees the few visitors and the few boxes of scarlet geraniums precariously perched in the gaping windows. The sleepy village below was animated in contrast. We watched little groups of peasants pottering in their neat allotments of beans and cabbages, lettuce and pumpkin.

Medieval foundations abound in this sparsely-populated Aveyron area of France. The small stone villages can often boast a twelfth-century church in moderate repair. Seeing these great tracts of rolling plain and wooded hills I recalled the story of the 'wild boy of Aveyron', the deaf mute who had run naked in these woods until at around age of twelve he gave himself up at an isolated farmstead on January 8, 1800. He became a cause-célèbre. But years of training and tuition failed to properly tame him or enable him to talk and he died aged forty in the Paris home of his devoted care-taker, Mme Guérin. He must have longed to return to these Aveyron woods. An excerpt from his doctor's diary reveals the boy's passionate reaction to nature: 'If a stormy wind then chanced to blow, if the sun suddenly came from behind the clouds brilliantly illuminating the skies, he expressed an almost convulsive joy with clamorous peals of laughter, during which all his movements backward and forward very much resembled a kind of leap he would take, in order to break through the window and dash into the garden.' Or, 'when on a beautiful moonlit night, the rays penetrated into his room he rarely failed to waken and go stand in front of the window. There he remained, according to his governess, for part of the night, motionless, head high, his eyes fixed upon the moonlit landscape, carried away by a sort of contemplative ecstasy, whose silence and immobility were only interrupted at long intervals by deep breaths, nearly always accompanied by a plaintive little sound.' His tragic story, as recounted in Harlan Lane's book *The Wild Boy of Aveyron*, inspired Truffaut's film *L'Enfant Sauvage*. Today the many training methods of the handicapped are directly attributed to the close observations of this boy's behaviour. We ourselves realised how easily he could have sustained his life in these woods and hills, with its plentiful supply of fish and game, with truffles perhaps, and nuts and mushrooms, at his daily command. And clustering every lonely lane we saw blackberries, figs, apples and grapes, all ripening in their wild abundance and unpicked.

September 11 Le Grand Ecuyer Cordes-sur-Ciel

Relinquishing our tenuous hold on Madame Gisèle's charming attentions, we have been spending a few days at Cordes-sur-Ciel, near Toulouse. Here at the Le Grand Ecuyer, once the Gothic shooting lodge of
a Comte de Toulouse, a dapper chef of the first league holds sway.

We dine between walls of heavy, dark panelling and rough-hewn
stone in an expanse of frothing white lace tablecloths, fresh flowers,
and candlelight. The young waiters are trained to a high degree and
deliver well-rehearsed panegyrics on each dish set before us: *Pour
Madame, la terrine ris de veau aux olives et artichauts et pour Monsieur, la
salade coquilles St Jacques*. The chef, Yves Thuries, distinctive in his
toque blanche and gold earring, bows an earnest passage from table to
table. The young waiters let all such formalities slip each morning as
they take turns to smoke surreptitiously in the terraced herb garden
beneath our windows, snatched moments of space from the kitchen,
on the pretext of more sage and thyme and rosemary.

From this medieval village, which curls and twists through its high
mountain of rock, we have a panoramic view of the chequered fields
below of harvested corn and crops of maize, sunflower, and ripened
vine. Cows and sheep collect in somnolent bundles beside the scattered
farms. The evenings are quiet and the air is motionless as we sit on
our roof terrace and strain to hear the hush of each dying day. A dog
barks in the far distance; doves croon and croak on terracotta roofs
and the church bell chimes the hour and then the half-hour. Only the
swallows darting to the eaves above with the plaintive whip of their
whirring wings hint at urgency.

In order to offset Yves Thurie's superb cuisine (specialities: *oeufs de
caille au foie gras en cocotte, filet d'agneau en croûte*), we forgo breakfast.
Seulement les deux cafés et absolument rien à manger. We also eat a
simple lunch. Today we cruised through country lanes to the village
of Marsac and took pot luck at the roadside Hôtel de la Poste. We
stepped into a scene worthy of Emile Zola's *L'Assommoir*. Three strap-
ping workmen, their bulging stomachs hoisted in blue dungarees, were
bent low over soup and a jug of the local Gaillac wine. They growled
and slurped, intermittently slapping each other's thighs and gesticulating
to the good-humoured waitress. In a quieter corner a large party of old
ladies chuckled over their crème caramel. They also seemed to be
enjoying their fair share of Gaillac wine and finally rose from their tables,
swaying on sticks and skinny legs, their hairpins all awry. Edwardian gas
lamps, attached to the dark green anaglypta walls, with fancible brass
supports, gave the whole convivial scene a period dimension. We ate a
simple meal of boiled beef and peas, but found the Gaillac red wine

rough and sour on the palate. (A far cry from the white burgundy that Tom selected at last night's dinner from the propriétaire de Puligny-Montrachet, Domaine Leflaive; it even drew praise from the fastidious sommelier: Pas beaucoup de nez, un vin discret.)

Albi and Toulouse are rose-red brick cities that again boast medieval foundations. Their five cathedrals and their web of narrow streets and timber-framed houses evoke historical time-warps despite the heavy industrial encroachment of today. The Musée Lautrec at Albi is fascinating. Housed in a gothic fortress beside the Cathedral it is a permanent exhibition of all this artist's known works. How poignant that a crippled man should capture so triumphantly the zest and extravagant drama of others. His cane is displayed in a glass case; it lies unscrewed to reveal the fitted glass tube which secreted his cognac, an ingenious device that effectively cheated his doctors.

And the Cathedral at Toulouse is especially remarkable for its fine eleventh-century Basilica. Seven figures to represent God and apostles and angels are exquisitely carved in marble bas-relief. There is an immediate appeal in those faces with their pronounced under-lips, their intricately-coiled hair, and the cheeky pose of their rather stubby right hands (two fingers point to the sky, an almost 'up you' gesture).

We conclude our sight-seeing of Toulouse at a small restaurant La Belle Epoque. A large unframed oil of a voluptuous nude was optimistically suspended above a radiator, while from one of the huge bell-shaped crimson light shades water dripped into an ice bucket. Notre voisin, explained the pretty waitress. His bath had overflowed.

October 31 Hardwicke House

We were in Istanbul last week when the Western world broke the news of Nigel Lawson's resignation; with Turkey's own inflation at 80% our political troubles seemed comparatively negligible.

At the Yildiz (Star) Palace, the Anglo-Turkish Antiques Fair and Auction was busily setting its stalls. Christie's, Sotheby's and Spinks were among the exhibitors. Ottoman silver incense-burners, coffee-pots, oval trays and sherbet cups, Iznik tiles and dishes, and gilded Koranic scrolls made a colourful show that rapidly assumed bazaar proportions. The only misfortune of the enterprise is that the Turkish Minister of Culture will not grant his country an export licence; artefacts will merely regurgitate on their home terrain. But, if communications are forged between a fast-developing country and the International market, they must be a good omen for a future, more profitable exchange. It was twelve years ago that Tom first visited Istanbul –

to sell the name of Christie's and to investigate this whole auction phenomenon.

The weather was golden; the afternoon sun lay low and cast long shadows in the open courtyards of mosques. The summer tourists had gone, leaving old men and stray cats to accustomed corners. Out on the streets the ubiquitous bustle of Istanbul scooped you up inexorably in its smells and noise and incessant activity. No man has the time nor inclination to stand and stare; he would rather shine shoes, roast chestnuts, spin tops, sell pomegranates and figs, bread, and buns, and huge pyramids of sticky whorls of dough, steaming honey. The fumes from the jolting, solid traffic, mingled with the putrid reek of rough tobacco, propel you along the jostling pavements. Presiding above in majestic oblivion were those sacred domes, although the Blue Mosque appeared to have one fragile minaret cradled in scaffolding.

We dined each night with Çiğdem and Haldun Simavi in their spacious yali beside the Bosphorus. Çiğdem, a petite and beautiful blonde, is the moving force behind the Istanbul Fair. By her subtle persuasion and her rich husband's financial backing she had set this show on the international road. There was nevertheless grave concern over the non-existent fire precautions in the predominantly wood-built Yildiz Palace. Standing beside an English girl one evening, admiring her decorative stall, we smelt a distinct singeing. She whipped round as I slapped her long blonde hair in the nick of time; it had caught a candle. Çiğdem dispelled all dark thoughts as she presided over her glittering dinner table, set with a sea of flowers and glinting silver and glass, and laid for twenty guests. A stream of waiters, monitored by her minuscule maid, Fatoş, served us with every variety of smoked fish and exotically stuffed leaves, kebabs with wild rice, and honey-soaked wedges of pastry.

The Iznik exhibition at the Palace of Ibrahim Pasha was a compelling agenda in our short stay. We went twice. Magnificent bowls and dishes and jugs sent in from all Western Europe were mounted importantly in glass caskets. The exhibits were lit individually and glowed in bold relief against the darkened interiors of the rooms. The azure blues and turquoise and brilliant rust-reds adorned these treasured polychrome pieces, in the traditional designs of the serrated saz leaf, the trailing hyacinth, the carnation, and the tulip; delicate wave and wind scrolls licked the wide rims of huge charger dishes.

And we called on Durusel, the renowned carpet-dealers. Staggering under the weight of our Bessarabian carpet, lugged over from London, we heaved ourselves into the head office. Could they repair the black threadbare field? After ominous shaking of heads and much muttering, they agreed to repair it at some considerable cost; it would take three women three months. The carpet, measuring fifteen feet by twelve has covered our drawing-room floor for ten years. It is a vivid expanse of colour, with its deep floral borders in excellent repair. The dealers explained to us that the corrosive black dye, used on the wool of the background, had finally rotted the strands. We originally paid £5,000 for the carpet; the repair will now cost around £1,600. It would be impossible to get the job done in London.

With our carpet mission achieved, we took a taxi to the fishing village of Tarabya (as in therapy). Our friends Emŕe and Aylın Gönensay live perched high above this Bosphorus harbour, a peaceful retreat from the hustle of Istanbul. Over drinks, in the substantial clutter of their home – the heavy brassware, the boldly-carved dark wood armoires, and bulging bookcases – Aylın spelt out her disgust with Turgut Özal. She described him and his wife as 'peasants'. 'They have allowed pitches of prize land along the Bosphorus to be built on by their friends.' I told her that we had seen the President on television and thought how ill and fat he looked; perhaps he would sink under the strain of his new Presidency? Aylın replied darkly, 'We say in Turkey – "a bad seed stays around". ' Would she prefer Mr Demirel to lead a Communist party? 'Oh no, but he was the more distinguished man.'

Emŕe took us to lunch at a fish taverna on the edge of the Bosphorus at Ortaköy village. Here it was that the first Bosphorus bridge, stretching in a gentle arc to the Anatolian shore, was opened in 1973. We sat under plane trees, where the autumn sun dappled the cobbles. Scouring kittens darted between the tables; I was fearful for my expensive cashmere skirt as they hovered for fish bones. A horseman trotted to the water's edge; he made a striking figure in his astrakhan hat and leather boots and breeches. 'Oh, he's mad!' exclaimed Aylın. 'He's a regular sight all over Istanbul!' Aylın knew everybody and table-hopped with unabashed abandon. We were finally introduced to the sister-in-law of the local bank manager. Emré ordered a delicious meal of stuffed cabbage leaves, pulped aubergine, pickled sardines, grilled halibut, and a bottle of Cankaya white wine. Aylın later assured us that the bank manager's sister-in-law kept family silver stored in black bin bags. Everybody who is anybody along the Bosphorus stores their silver away from the tarnishing damp air. Stored silver is a main criterion for social acceptance in Aylın's book.

Before we left Istanbul we paid our customary visit to the Chinese porcelain collection at the Topkapı Palace Kitchens. What richness is heaped under those brick-domed vaults and funnels! The celadon ware, the Imperial yellow, the blue and white ware with grinning dragons and tropical birds and the gowned figures with beards and moustaches and ladies in peignoirs and piled-up hair. The *Imari* Japanese porcelain, exhibited alongside, looks florid in comparison; the blues and golds and corals appear smothered and confusing in these overworked designs. (*Imari* so-called after the southern port in Japan from where the ware was imported during the seventeenth, eighteenth and nineteenth centuries.)

And lastly to the Baghdad Pavilion, the most elegant and beautiful corner in the whole Topkapı Palace. It was conceived in 1639 by Sultan Murat IV, to celebrate his Baghdad campaign. Exquisite tiles from the period line the walls, while outside on the white marble terrace there stands a gilded baldachin. I stood there reflecting, high above the confluence of the Golden Horn, the Bosphorus, and the Sea of Marmara. What strange, sad lives and customs had weaved their passage through these stones and waters.

November 16 El Albany

Albany's Rope Walk is a melancholy passage on a cold winter's evening. Footsteps reverberate between the dimly looming hulks of garden urns and shrubs and seats. El Albany lies at the far end of the walk, on the ground floor. This conveniently precludes a further climb up a curved flight of steep, stone steps. Miles Jebb[2], to whose chambers we have been invited, swings open his heavy black door. 'We are in candlelight,' he announces gravely.

A power strike? No, he has friends from the Zimbabwe bushveld dining; in deference to their civilised habit of life sans electricity, he has tonight consigned his drawing-room and dining-room to candle-light. The high, corniced ceilings are lost in the enveloping glow of a log fire and candelabra positioned on side-tables and marble mantles. Huge, gilded wall glasses reflect the incandescent scene. We meet the English Lord who divides his time between Zimbabwe and London and his well-built wife, a one-time ballerina. The deft turn of her head and the precise positioning of her still-elegant feet and ankles convey her youthful talent.

We drink champagne out of silver tumblers and soon embark on Miles's carefully prepared dinner; a pink fish mousse from Fortnum and Mason, and roast partridge with an arduous choice of vegetables. Miles, an historian, has just completed his comprehensive history of East Anglia and is now exercising his mind on the Oxford Colleges.

---

[2] Succeeded to his father's title in 1996. A former athlete and alpinist, Miles Gladwyn is now an inspired writer on walks through England and France.

He is also an inveterate walker, leading and lecturing his touring companions through the Alps and the Tuscan hills.

After dinner, the ballerina and I take turns in Miles's bathroom; its meagre confines with its scrubbed plank floor are magnified after the cosy ambience of his candlelit rooms. A black sock dangles dejectedly from his laundry basket and a reeded chair (as featured in Van Gogh's more scanty bedrooms) stands by apologetically.

Back to the fire and those deep comfortable seats which all bachelors set great store by, where Miles is discussing Macaulay and Milton. Yes, Macaulay – Thomas Babington – lived in these very chambers from 1841 to 1846. Miles believes he wrote his *History of England* in these rooms. A sense of awe and reverence steals through the shadows and the silence. To think that Tom Macaulay had embraced our whole country between these walls and re-assembled it in words – and then a younger man than us!

'I would like to recite a little Macaulay,' announces Miles. He is prone to poetry recitals. He promises some Milton too. We sit in bemused anticipation. 'I think I will stand,' adds Miles abruptly. He jerks his stick-thin body from the chair. The flames falter. He stands remote and pale, his sharp ascetic features drawn in sacred concentration. He cuts a most romantic figure. His brown velvet suit, his tie of pink satin and the glint of his brocaded slippers are the stuff of theatre. Next – in the measured tones of one who knows and loves each word:

> 'By those white cliffs I never more must see,
> By that dear language which I spake like thee,
> Forget all feuds and shed one English tear
> O'er English dust. A broken heart lies here.'

1990

Nothing prepares you for the blatant beauty of the Goan beaches. This idyllic 82-mile shore line gilds the south-west coast of India. Dense groves of coconut palms screen the sloping sand pounded through millennia by the Arabian Sea.

Golden Goa – the paradise port possessed and plundered by the Portuguese in 1510. Her coves and natural harbours became a prestigious link in the Arabian trade routes and she got rich quick on such sumptuous traffic. But she forfeited her Hindu temples in favour of the distinctive white stone Baroque churches which survive today, glorious white elephants richly caparisoned with the trappings of their colonial heyday. The Goans complied to Catholicism with that religious tolerance endemic in the Indian people, and the Portuguese had a fabulous run. Their luck and loot lasted a hundred years before thieves broke in and the British and the Dutch became contestants for the prize. Worse still, malaria rising from the steaming marshes of the Mandovi river turned Old Goa into a ghost town. In December 1961 India finally reclaimed Goa after 450 years.

A light tap on my shoulder. I look up from my perusal of Goan history. Silhouetted against the sea, standing before me in the shade of my palm umbrella, is a small girl, all black arms and legs in her skimpy pink dress. She balances an outsize basket on her little head.

'You want pineapple, lady? Mango? Banana? Where you from?' Her name is Yumaima. Is she not at school today? 'I go school six years. It is enough. I learn English.' She is ten years old. She sits beside me companionably and displays her wares. I do not need a pineapple today; another day, I promise her. Her bananas looked well past their best; perhaps they are earmarked for her lunch. She reveals to me the mystery of the gold stud in her nose. She pulled up her nostril to explain the workings of the internal screw fitment. A German couple saunter by on the hot sand.

'Hello, Yumaima. Are you coming to our villa to have supper tonight?' They are very persistent, but Yumaima is adamant. 'I ask my mummy. My mummy does not like me to go any place where there is television.' She turns her attention back to me. 'You like pineapple tomorrow, lady? Promise?' She hoists her basket on to her head and sets off briskly down the sand. With her top-heavy cargo supported by her thin little body in its bright pink dress, she has the appearance of a psychedelic mushroom.

My peace is again interrupted. A young man selling t-shirts has invaded my pool of shade. Again I postpone any purchase and I suggest to him that he has a good life. He squats beside me. He is called Fernandes. (Such ubiquitous use of Catholic names – Luis, Rodrigues, Pedro, Magdalina – is the legacy of the Portuguese colonisation.) 'Trade is good in the winter months,' explains Fernandes. 'The tourists come for the season. Now we make our money. We save well. There is no money in the summer rains.' Are they awful? I ask. I have visions of village dirt tracks running with red silt and water pouring though wind-battered palm groves. 'It is not so bad. The rain harvest is a busy time. We collect the rain from roofs, courtyards, and any catchment areas. And the village supplies portable water from tanks and ponds.' India's perilous water supply system does not improve. Does Fernandes dislike the summer rain season? 'We like it after. The rice fields and grasses come green again. You come October, November. Now is too dry, too hot. It is the end of season. Business no good. You do business tomorrow?'

My attention is next enslaved by the exquisite parade of three Goan beauties, painted scarlet, pink, and saffron against the sea. Their sarongs swirl seductively as they glide over the sand, coconut baskets balanced on their black braided heads. With a twirl of their bangled arms they prostrate their pineapples before yet another unlikely punter.

I plunge into the sea for cover. It is blood heat but refreshing nevertheless. The waves thunder and froth in some quarrel with the moon. I jump and tumble, relishing the pummelling foam, but dare not swim out. I see a young girl in a peacock sari sitting becalmed in the toffee sand; girdled in the fizzing eddies of the sea, she smiles, enraptured, her blowing black hair caught loosely in a silver slide. It is a joke to see Indian women dabbling with the sea in saris. The more sodden they become, the louder and happier they squeal. Up the steep red steps to the flower-crammed garden of this celebrated Taj Hotel. Two small boys bare white teeth in a wide smile. They stoop over the path, sweeping puce petals from the bougainvillea into plaited baskets. Past the dazzling coral-tree, where the black-headed mynah birds cackle, scattering petals and pollen, and the pagoda-tree, where each golden-eyed waxy cluster pulses with overpowering scent. Theresa, in her gold cross neck chain, presides proudly over her sea-food stoves. Her tables are set alongside, high above the sea, on the breezy garden terrace. Her voluptuous display of fresh lobster, langouste, tiger prawns, mussels, and white pomfret is replenished each day. Each tiger prawn is as fat as a croissant. This abundant yield of the sea is astonishing.

We follow our siesta with an evening walk, along the seven miles of beach. Villagers and dogs emerge from the grassy dunes and palm groves beyond. Little girls prod the wet sand for mussels and everywhere sand crabs, as transparent as wind-blown fluff, skitter from hole to hole. The horizon reddens as the sun sinks fast. The translucent sky is brushed with gold and rose and lavender as the sun slides swiftly through the sea. Yesterday evening the wind was high and the palm-trees jangled their fronds like sharpening knives. The swollen muscles of the sea boiled in the hot copper light and the waves were seven feet high. Up and up they reared, curling in thrilling green glass tunnels, to shatter in thundering foam.

March 14 Goa

It is early morning. We drive hastily through the jumble of villages down to the banks of the Mandovi river. The stone farmhouses are painted white and pink and lemon, with red tiled roofs. Windows are shaded with tin awnings or shuttered with plaited palms. The red sandstone boundary walls, rounded by the summer rains, encompass the smallholdings of goats, cows, and chickens. Each village well swarms with women as they slap the family wash on stones. They must be quick for the string of cows will soon crowd them out. Through the trees a lagoon is ablaze with the early sun. Two boys are silhouetted in a gondola. Their agile bodies swing their craft through a drift of pink water lilies. Such uniquely beautiful vignettes of India, en passant, redress the grim ravages of others. We near the ferry crossing, a picturesque service soon to be superseded by a handsome new bridge ('Fitter feared drowned; he fell into the river Mandovi this morning while working on the ninth pillar of Mandovi bridge,' we read in yesterday's daily newspaper).

'You see old Goa in the cool morning air, lady. Now we cross with ferry.' Our driver accelerates his jolting 1935 Morris Oxford up the ramp. We squeeze on to the deck between mothers and babies, bikes and bananas. Squeals and shouts, everywhere the reeking stench of fish and petrol. We judder slowly across to the landing stage of Panjim, Goa's capital, a prosperous, pleasant, white stone town with its glistening white Church of the Immaculate Conception enthroned high above, up terraced steps. We proceed through the town where businesses proclaim their hereditary Portuguese affiliations – Fernandes – Braganza – de Souza – Durrante. We note that 'Yummy Ice Cream' is liberally advertised, along with 'Panama cigarettes – good to the last puff.' The Souvenir Shop, The Primary Health Centre, and 'Here, well stitch apparels' suggest an evenly-balanced economy.

Our driver now indicates an old Goan church. Seen across a broad stretch of brilliant green paddy fields, it positively glitters in a soaring baroque façade of white lime-washed stone. Two huge bells swing gently in the twin towers. We are the only visitors. A dog sleeps in the aisle, sandy-haired with a foxy head, and a panting pink tummy blotched with black. It is hot outside and the pink marble slabs of the aisle are a perfect refuge. This church is called *Mae de Deus Saligao*. We find the fussy Gothic interior disappointing. The barrel-vaulted altar ceiling adds a ludicrous touch; it is painted bright blue, complete with fluffy clouds and pricked with gold stars.

Our driver takes us next to the heart of old Goa, where the chapels and convents, churches and cathedrals are grouped in a three-square-mile area. It is hard to imagine the sixteenth-century scene when a rich town bustled and seethed with commerce and sumptuous living. Malarial plague and the subsequent battles between Dutch and British invaders desecrated the old city. Today the churches alone bear witness to their ghost town. Symbols of sacred survival, they stand, proud monuments to their powerful past. Old women crouch over their landscaped garden surrounds weeding in a timeless solitude. We wander through the cool marble and stone interiors. The main high altars reach some 150 feet, boiling with gilded baroque carving and resplendent twisted columns. An exuberant mix of Hindu gods tumble along with Catholic saints. These churches have become treasured showpieces, their shining white-washed façades and towers and cupolas are zealously maintained. But with 70 per cent of the Goan population now reverted to Hinduism, their local patronage has dwindled.

It is midday and 95°F. We gain our Morris Oxford gratefully; it is hardly the best antidote to the blazing outside, but rumbling along through the coconut groves it generates some breeze. At the ferry quay sticky boys with sticky hands force cartons of mango juice in our hands. We pay them too much and are immediately rewarded with a heap of t-shirts barring our way.

March 17

Rosita's massage is the ultimate luxury. Her minuscule appearance belies the strength that steels her long, thin fingers. She slavishly sculpts each muscle and then punches her hand-work in a frenzy. I roll off the hard bed, gleaming with coconut oil, feeling like a choice joint ready-basted for the oven. Rosita is from Bombay. She speaks excellent English. I congratulate her on her colloquial vocabulary. 'I read much Agatha Christie and some P G Wodehouse. You enjoy your holiday here? You are 'unvinding' OK? It is vital to unvind.' I promise her my Agatha Christie, *Sleeping Murder*, before we leave tomorrow.

On the beach I have a final rendezvous with Yumaima. Our protracted bargaining over her pineapples has left her distinctly in the advantage. On the other hand, I have avoided a deal until now. The agreement that I finally buy her pineapple for 25 rupees, the equivalent of £1 (pineapples cost 2 or 3 rupees in the local market).

Yumaima stands four square on the sand assiduously mindful of our appointment. She swings her basket to the sand as I triumphantly present the 25 rupee note. She looks marginally mollified.

'Why not you have this one, for 30 rupees?' We finally select the one that she should give me. 'You want eat now?' A large knife with an evil black blade is produced. She smoothes some crumpled cloth on to the sand and with great determination carves up the juicy fruit into very plausible slices. Her elder sister arrives. She is beautiful in a green sarong with a string of fresh marigolds tumbling through her hair. 'You want?' I ask her. The pineapple is largely despatched between Yumaima and her family. Yumaima concludes the operation by picking her excellent white teeth with the point of her unwieldy knife.

March 23 Hardwicke House

Labour's historic by-election in mid-Staffordshire today sends spasms of fear for Maggie Thatcher's credibility. Her grossly mismanaged Community Poll Tax Bill has cost her dear. Local councillors throughout the country have been knocked sideways by unprecedented and violent demonstrations. Perhaps all the television screening of the recent uprisings in Eastern Europe has sparked the venom of our own 'people power'. Maggie's pragmatic conception of a revised Poll Tax may well be ultimately viable, but it has been far too harshly implemented. She is in real danger of disaffecting both her Cabinet and her many supporters. Has she become an electoral liability? Or is this latest show of desertion, this conceding of a 14,654 Conservative majority to a Labour majority of 9,000, merely a mid-term election protest?

Last week Tom had a drink with John and Guinevere Tilney. Guinevere is a shrewd observer of the scene.

'She should go now,' opined Guinevere. With the Cabinet endemically disenchanted and her ruinous Poll Tax policies, she is certainly entrenched in trouble. 'There is one person who can still influence her,' continued Guinevere, 'and that's Denis. He has urged her already to leave through the front door, her head held high, rather than bowed and beaten through the back. And Margaret said to him – "But there is nobody to follow me." To which Denis replied – "Balls!"'

April 15 Orchard House Plymtree East Devon

A blustery wind tugs at the blossom boughs, and the lawn, green and juicy from heavy rain, is speckled with flattened petals; primroses, daisies and dandelions are clumped along the garden hedge. Vanessa, wife of the MP for Exeter, fries sausages, eggs, kidneys and bacon. The agreeable smell of breakfast spirals up the cottage stairs, to encourage the party for church. Vanessa has already tied back her hair in a lavender silk bow.

We sweep along the bending, rain-washed lanes to Clyst Hydon church. It is as wholesome as home-baked bread or worsted flannel; garden tulips hug the pulpit and a fresh-faced vicar, generously draped in a yellow taffeta chasuble, presides at the altar. The bell-ringers conduct a crazy fandango as they juggle the silent ropes; it is disappointing that the cause and effect of campanology can never be appreciated from the aisle. We admire the stained-glass windows; each pointed incision and curve and roundel, a flaming jewel in the sun. A native young man (with piercing blue eyes, a ruddy complexion, a beard and plus-fours) reads from the Gospel of St John. Our small congregation copes manfully with several unfamiliar Easter hymns. It is a reassuring country scene. And every child is given a chocolate egg by the jovial vicar, standing in his porch.

On our way back to Plymtree we speculate on the Easter activities of 'that other house party', grouped in a medieval farm house, four pot-holed miles down a valley. A stunning venue, where we had all dined last night. A pair of retired professors (of Arabic studies) had flanked our hostess; a talented artist with flaming hair and knee-high boots. She was particularly delighted to see us; we were late. The MP for Exeter had been driving. To find the right turn, down the right lane, in the right valley was a hapless task; a diabolical responsibility. The rain had sluiced down and the windows had steamed up. We all felt helpless to help such an admirable man. The MP for Exeter had lost his way. With sound pragmatic strategy he had finally turned back to Cullompton and started again.

It had been quite a dinner party. We had especially enjoyed the novelist; a towering man with a big head, who wrote in the vein of a woman. 'I write under Emma B . . .,' he assured me. He had also acted with the Royal Shakespeare Company; writing novels in a Devon valley was apparently a more lucrative alternative. Our hostess's table glittered with fine Edwardian cut-glass centre-pieces and each wine glass flaunted a gilded vein. Two stout maids in black with white aprons served us a delicious dinner; it included ramekins of baked seafood in cream and a huge chocolate mound of crunching texture, which the maids insisted on carving up themselves. Such indulgence at the elegant dining table and the prospect of sitting again by the fire in the beamed stone hall imbued us all with total satisfaction.

Our post-prandial content was suddenly interrupted by the arrival of Samantha, the sixteen-year-old daughter of the house, and her student girl friend. Slapping their patched jeans for packets of cigarettes and flinging long wet hair off their faces they gained the fireplace in a type of staggered lope. Samantha next helped herself to a dribble of whisky in her mineral water. What would mother think? 'That other house party' will need plenty of dextrous manoeuvres between the talented hostess, her mock moronic daughter and the two austere professors, to complete the weekend on an even footing.

Here, the Under-Secretary for the Department of Employment, the Rt Hon Patrick Nicholls, has arrived for lunch. He and his wife exude a bright capability. He talks rapidly and informatively and clearly lives to work. He also looks utterly exhausted; his pale and handsome face is illumined with a round-eyed anxiety. Certainly it is an anxious time for all politicians; no seat is comfortable. To support their leader or swap their leader? The MP for Exeter (whose twenty-year tenure may soon be rewarded with a KBE) is obviously a full supporter. But younger ministers are restless; they see Michael Heseltine (the member for Henley) as a charismatic new image-maker; a winning horse for the 1992 election. The MP for Exeter calls for order at his lunch table and makes an emphatic statement: 'Maggie will tough it out; win the next election and ease in the successor of her choice; John Major or Chris Patten.' But what about Heseltine, we all demand? The stoic member for Exeter continues: 'If Heseltine pulls a fast one and slips into her place she will fight him and get him out.' We are all confounded by such pre-ponderables. The ultimate conclusion is based on economics; Maggie Thatcher's fourth election victory, or her downfall, will entirely depend on the current state of the balance of payments, or on interest rates. The balance of power will hang on the pound?

April 30 Half Moon Cottage Manaton Dartmoor Devon

Jeanne du Maurier is the youngest daughter of the legendary stage actor and manager, Sir Gerald du Maurier. She played hostess to Beverley Nichols two or three times towards the end of his life. Ten years on and intrigued to see for myself this west country retreat, I set off down the M4 one sunny April morning, arriving at Half Moon Cottage, Manaton, in time for tea.

Daphne du Maurier's autobiography, *Growing Pains – The Shaping of a Writer*, reveals Jeanne du Maurier as the adored younger sister, the invaluable caddie to Daphne's triumphant Prince Hal, a Little John to her Robin Hood. The two sisters, aged seven and four, would forage in their Hampstead garden for suitable props and venues to enact Daphne's mise-en-scènes. The wheelbarrow particularly excelled in its service as a death-cart. Daphne's shrieks of 'Bring out your dead! Bring out your dead!' were the cue for Jeanne to hurl all the teddy bears from their bedroom window. Daphne's autobiography also describes Jeanne as an accomplished pianist, a painter, and a drawer. As a member of the WRA (the West of England Royal Academy), Jeanne had worked alongside Ben Nicholson and Barbara Hepworth, at St Ives. And in *Old Maids Remember* Angela, the eldest du Maurier sister, alludes briefly to Jeanne's ménage in Devon: 'Jeanne, who lives in Devon with a friend and has five horses, seven dogs, five goats, a cat, birds, poultry, pigeons, heaven knows how many acres of ground, as well as her enchanting thatched house.'

It was a gratifying scene to come upon. There, on its apron of lush green, stood a Devon 'Long House', newly-thatched, with an old church tower soaring up beside; the broad sweep of Dartmoor lay beyond. A peke, a pug, and a papillon eyed me quizzically from the open front door. ('Jeanne, my youngest sister, goes in for pekes and pugs.') Strains of Berlioz's *Flight into Egypt* filled the house as Jeanne du Maurier's lifelong companion, Noël Welch, stepped out to meet me. She reminded me that Jeanne had lost her memory, and that, like many older citizens, she found childhood a more conducive focal point than the present.

The three of us sat in the long hall where the whitewashed walls were four feet thick and the stone-flagged floor smoothed down since Domesday. We sipped tea at the oak dining table and ate sponge cake. 'Why exactly are you here?' asked Jeanne. Her enquiry was friendly but perplexed. Her still-life oil paintings of flowers intermingling with violins combined in a Chagallesque effect across the walls. A Bechstein grand piano was positioned by a window overlooking the green.

'Beverley must have enjoyed your piano,' I ventured. 'Did you all have musical evenings together?' Jeanne, a spare and gentle lady with anxious, wide eyes, slowly shook her head. 'He was Angela's friend you see. Angela brought Beverley to our Hampstead house – Cannon Hall. My parents gave these huge Sunday lunches and then there was tennis and cricket. And then Angela's friend, Betty Hicks, the daughter of Seymour Hicks, the actor – it was Betty who brought Beverley here when he was ill.' Did Beverley have a favourite walk? A seat in the garden? A view? Noël interjected that Beverley and she had had different views on the garden, but that she had been interested in all he had to say.

Next I was shown Beverley's bedroom. It was bright and spacious with a handsome mahogany cheval glass, a capacious brass bed, and rugs thrown over the bare polished boards. 'I don't know if he liked the room especially,' continued Noël. 'I am afraid he was always bumping his head on our low door frames; he kept urging us to dangle posies from them.' We came next to the small conservatory. I admired the two cockatiels in their elaborate birdcage; miniature crested parrots with scarlet cheeks. 'But Beverley couldn't stand them. He could not bear their screeching call. The sight of any caged bird drove him hysterical. He had to leave the room. He wasn't well, of course. But he was very highly strung.' Noël led me out into the garden.

Trim grass terraces of boxed rose parterres, herb gardens, and a marked penchant for purple Black Knight tulips sloped up to the moors. Low stone walling and gravel paths nicely divided the precincts along with cypresses and glossy pyramids of clipped box. I admired the rocks that lounged on the grass in rugged abandon, like so many cowering animals ready to pounce. Jeanne and Noël had attempted to soften their gaping crevices and bald flanks with a fuzz of herbs and heathers and trailing aubrietia. 'Beverley didn't approve of us planting up the rocks. He felt all rock formation should be left to their natural heather habitat. Really he would have preferred the whole garden left to the moors. He had no love for the style and order that we have achieved. And then he went and over-pruned my lilac.' Noël's voice was rueful. Slowly it dawned on me that Beverley had not been the easiest guest. 'Well, he was ill, you know. And he was Betty's friend of course.'

Beverley pottering round the lovely old house and garden, in the unlikely company of three women and three dogs, could never have been in his element. Noël waved to the beech woods that linked the garden to the moors. The gorse and bramble had been cleared and the ground was drenched in bluebells, wave upon wave of Côte d'Azur blue. 'That is where Beverley was happiest; just wandering though the bluebells.'

May 25 Quiberon Brittany

Our last day, I walk from the Institut Thalassothérapie over the rocks and rounded grass banks to the 'baie de Quibéron'. A dull day, with the sea pocked and grey. I recall those captivating clear waters off the

Bahamas on this same Atlantic ocean. What a contrast! A month ago
we were there, staying with friends, within the manicured confines of
Nassau's Lyford Cay. We took a fishing boat and saw dolphins; black
mottled lumps deep in the blue glass sea, when up they frolicked for
air. That sea defied description; striped in navy ink, then turquoise, it
lapped the blinding white coral sands, its clear, cobbled water, cut like
glass sand veined in flickering sunlight. We took two barracuda back
to the three black maids. They stood laughing in the garden in stiff
white overalls. And their teeth flashed white and they rang a little brass
bell for lunch.

There are no such exotic displays on this shore. How good this air
is! It is blown over freshly-drenched seaweed and slime. Gulls scream
and shells and weed are precisely deposited in each pristine cove.
Everywhere there is muted colour, not those brilliant daubs of distant
climes, but the pastel frailty of wild pink columbine and clover, sprays
of pale mustard, long grasses flushed with sorrel and the gold dust of
lichen on the rocks.

One last look at Quiberon. There is a predominant penchant for
poodles and alsatians on the promenade, the extremes of French taste!
The stuccoed villas face the bay with arched windows quoined in
stone, slate roofs, and painted wood balconies. They present a pleasing
understatement with façades of ochre, greige and écru, and a hint of
almond pink. And, oh, those *Galettes Bretonnes* again. I hurry on to
stand *bouleversée* with lust before 'L'épicerie, pour fruits primeurs'. The
sweet freshness of strawberries, melons, cherries, of radishes and cress,
is overwhelming – the elixir of excellence. And each cherished produce nestles in its plaited reed basket, tucked around with ferns.

August 14 The Keswick Hotel Cumbria

Three years since our last visit. This time Sebastian and I have brought
the two labradors Tobias and Joss. We left home at 9 am, arrived at
3.30. Insurmountable difficulties in cajoling the dogs to squeeze
through the Victorian glass heavy swing-door. We failed. The obliging
hall porter dismantled a brass rod to open it up. I have since located a
garden door to ease our comings and goings. The hotel has visibly
prospered. A croquet lawn as smooth and green as a billiard table and
a well laid out sunken flower garden are pointers to a discerning
clientele. But Joss disturbed a rabbit in the rose bed and Toby sicked
up a ginger nut biscuit in the bedroom, too hot for his tender palate.
Hotel life is a whole new experience for them.

Our walking guide, Frank, an ex-English language and literature school teacher from Oxford met us in the bar. He discussed walks, boots, dogs, picnics, and did we mind heights? He told me that one person a fortnight is killed walking or falling in the Lake District. I merely feared for Bass's septic toe and for my suspect corns. I swore that the dogs would not chase sheep; a rash commendation. They bay incessantly in the surrounding fells. And how green is this country of wooded hills and lakes and mountains. Compared to our scorched south, it is an oasis.

We are now two weeks into the Gulf crisis. President Saddam Hussein has effectively turned the world into a hive of intensified air, ship and troop deployment. President George Bush, his spine and resolve soundly strengthened by Maggie Thatcher's support, has initiated a defensive blockade and sanctions on Iraq's oil and food trade. Argument and conjecture are rife. The French, true to their endemic duplicity, sit on the fence; they criticise and prevaricate. The Jordanians argue that any American aggression against any Arabs only serves to reaffirm their alliance with Israel. Germans judge Arabian strategy as a law unto itself. Where does compromise fit in? King Hussein of Jordan, friend of the West, friend of Iraq, emerges as the only viable 'go-between'. And through these hot and humid August days we hear chilling tales of rape and pillage; wild Iraqi soldiers on the rampage through the newly-annexed Kuwait. Today marks the death of the first Briton; he was shot while attempting to escape by car to the Saudi border. It is ghastly to speculate on the unknown and as yet unrecorded atrocities there must be going on in Kuwait at this time. There are many Britons and Americans already detained at Saddam Hussein's pleasure, in Baghdad.

August 15

A morning of gale-force winds and heavy rain. The dogs slept well after their long journey but woke at 4 a.m. They nuzzled me plaintively, persistently. I took them through the long carpeted corridors, down the wide main stairs and into the garden. A repeat attack of acute diarrhoea (as sustained yesterday in the back of the car) was not to be contemplated.

Frank meets us at 9.30 as arranged. We set off down the Penrith to Keswick disused rail track in the direction of Threlkeld. The rocky bed of the river Greta foams and tumbles far below. The dogs go mad and leap in frenzied joy through the spray and froth. I fear for their lives, their necks, their sanity. In a day of ten miles' steady walking, they scramble through more fences, jump more walls, sight and sniff more cows, sheep and rabbits than they could ever dream of. A pale, shy sun splashes the fells and everywhere fresh cascades from the heavy night rain toss down the mountains, monumental mountains older than the Himalayas, claims Frank. How old? Four hundred and fifty million years old, says Frank. A geologist told him. We eat our egg and bacon sandwiches in the porch of a typical Victorian stone Lakeland church, the chapel of St John's-in-the-Vale. It has a cosy panelled interior of well-polished pews, suggesting regular use. I leave our few surplus bananas in the vestry. 'Notes of Interest to Visitors' suggests that there was a place of worship here from the thirteenth century. The dogs lounge respectfully in the immaculate graveyard until we set off down the fields, in the shadow of Walla Crag, to Derwent Water and Keswick. Bass and I later indulge ourselves on enormous slices of chocolate cake at Johnson's tea shop; it was a sumptuous conglomerate of sponge and cream and fudge chocolate icing.

August 16

The early morning Cumbrian news reported a man killed off Buttermere yesterday; he fell from his mountain bicycle. And a young woman was threatened by a man armed with a gun and, more ominously, with a Swiss Army knife, the four-inch silver blade at the ready. She had been walking alone along the quiet road between Hawkshead and Satterthwaite. 'Women walkers are advised not to set out alone.'

Mercifully, our feet are not sore. However, a change of shoes is always a good precaution. Sheets of rain batter the solid plate-glass window, more gale-force winds. We set off at ten o'clock and take the car to Buttermere. Toby is taken short as we descend a steep, desolate hill; he sicks up his breakfast on the floor of the car. I mop up with Kleenex in a howling wind and hail, and proceed down the valley to Buttermere. The weather steadies and we climb over the fells to Crummock Water; a magical walk through this 'Hidden Valley' of chuckling streams, lush grasses, and wild flowers. We keep the dogs firmly on the lead; sheep are everywhere. This is essentially sheep-farming country where a dog seen chasing them can be shot. But Joss breaks frees; it is a choice of his life or mine as I am nearly pulled down a sheer drop. He has a joyous skirmish putting up beasts from the thick forest of ferns. Crummock Water is choppy in the wind; it is grey, transparent, with rounded flat slates. The dogs have a boisterous swim. Toby ruins everything on an ecstatic roll in the soft grey shingle. At the sixteenth-century Kirkstile pub by Loweswater we eat Cumberland sausages and jacket potatoes. On return to Keswick the dogs wolf their 'Pedigree Chum' as dispensed from the boot in the hotel carpark.

The 9 o'clock news

Mr William Waldegrave, the Under-Secretary to the Foreign Secretary Douglas Hurd, is becoming a familiar face on our TV screens. (His boss is still away on holiday.) With a grave clarity he attempts to decipher for his viewers the bewildering issues of Arab strategy. He conjects and comments and is ultimately in no position to convince anybody of anything. The news tonight is that King Hussein of Jordan has patently failed in his attempt to mediate between President Saddam Hussein and President George Bush. The King is clearly fearful of his Iraqi neighbour; he is at his mercy on both military and material grounds. The other development, described by Mr Waldegrave as 'grave and sinister', is that all British and American expatriates in Kuwait have been ordered by Saddam Hussein to converge on the Regency Palace Hotel. It has only two hundred rooms. There are four thousand Britons and two and a half thousand Americans. Will they next be herded off to Iraq? There is talk of them being strategically positioned by oil stations; to be hostage pawns to deter any Western attack. Meanwhile the forces of the allied world are now massed around this cockpit of war, all dressed up and ready to go. The lull before the storm?

August 17

My fiftieth birthday. Bucketing rain at 5 a.m. when I take the dogs down to the garden. They relieve themselves on the croquet lawn. A 9 a.m. forecast of showers and sunny intervals. We clamber up through woods to Borrowdale. Joss snaps his collar and I bash my shin on a rock; a stain of raspberry jam oozes through my thick white sock. We reach the hamlet of Grange where we opt for lunch in the tea shop with its slate-slabbed floor. The good lady prides herself on making voluptuous Cumbrian cakes, carrot sponge, orange and lemon sponge, ginger and pineapple sponge, well-buttressed and blanketed with soft thick icing. She is prevailed upon to take in the dogs. She accepts our assurance that they are guide dogs; she is always agreeable to shelter guide dogs. Would we bundle them under the table? Peg their leads under the table legs? We plan a bigger and better walk tomorrow – above Grasmere. The combination of a good lunch, damp clothes and leaden grey skies bulging over the peaks puts an honourable end to today's enterprise.

Back at the hotel a beaming receptionist is framed in an enormous basket of pink and white lilies; two enormous bouquets, one from my mother, one from Tom. 'We have to congratulate you on a birthday?' Later at dinner, after Sebastian and I have gorged ourselves on roast pork and the Austrian chef's exquisite Bavarian lemon torte, the head waiter makes an ominous announcement. 'We have something to give you.' The lights are dimmed as the waiters parade a huge iced cake with five pink candles. The few guests lingering in the dining-room join in the chorus of 'Happy Birthday'. Inscribed on the cake is 'Happy Birthday darling. Love from Tom.' It is suitably rich and delicious.

We stagger upstairs to see the 10 o'clock news. Today an Italian touring group has taken over our corridor. They beam at us from their pasta-pale faces and scraped-back hair buns. They admire the dogs, patting their sleek black fur with podgy heavily-ringed fingers. Last night we almost collided with a group of Japanese; they threw up their heads and hands and scattered like stricken birds.

August 18

The mountains are serene and majestic in sun again. It is 6 a.m. The dogs scamper through the garden. The low golden light rises and shapes every contour by the minute. By 7.30 am this lake-land universe is ablaze. We drive to Grasmere and to Elterwater, a bowl of peace, green fields and sheep and streams. We climb up wooded slopes to the foothills of the Langdale valley, crossing the rushing mountain rivers over sturdy plank bridges. The dogs now adept at squeezing through kissing gates and clambering over stiles and ladders have to be restrained. They are crazy for these weltering waters, these roaring phenomena of rock and foam and spray. We lunch on pâté and salad at a slate inn. The Three Shires, built in 1872, effectively straddles Cumbria, Westmorland and Lancashire. It is hot, we sit on garden benches and spread our legs. Walk resumes past cottage gardens crammed with scent and colour, yellow and scarlet snapdragons and purple sweet pea. We branch off into the hills. This is remote, rugged country, unreal in its beauty. We cut through a rock and slate farm holding, it is neatly wedged in a sheltered hollow with a huge stack of winter silage ready stowed in black bags. Sheep and silage; silage and more sheep; at the standard price of 60 pence per 2 kilos (one sheep's yield) of wool, the farmer lives to exist rather than spend. Says Frank: 'It makes you sick when you see the price of a sweater in the shops. This poor bloke has to give over the wool to the shearer in payment.' Our farmer rounds the corner of his barn. 'How do?' He then proceeds to holler for his goats. He stands on a grass knoll swinging a bucket, 'come on then! c'mon then.' On a sunny August afternoon it looks the stuff of fairy tales.

The 9 o'clock news reveals that the British and Americans persist in effectually condemning the Iraqis for every fresh outrage. It is now established that a number of British and Americans have been taken to military installations and oil stations; purportedly to save such strategic spots from Western Allied air attack. Hostages have in effect become 'human shields' or 'sand bags'. And Douglas Hurd reiterates his now familiar condemnations: 'outrageous, revolting, totally unacceptable, illegal, repulsive, repugnant.' Etc., etc. Words, words . . . (rather jaw, jaw than war, war). Remaining Britons and Americans have again been ordered to move to three large hotels in Kuwait. If they stay in their homes, 'They will be rounded up.' President Hussein has also put babies on the mat. 'Any US and British babies will suffer the same food shortages as Iraqi babies.' The US, it is just reported, have shot across the bows of two Iraqi boats. The US are clearly on the brink of war. In the opinion of the Western world, President George Bush has handled the events of the last two weeks commendably; he is even dubbed 'From Wimp to Warrior'.

August 19

A wet day. We have also awarded ourselves a rest day from all tread and trudge. We make a leisurely start and drive through the rolling hills of Penrith and up the steep winding Moorland pass to Alston. A thick hill mist and the dogs grunt ominously in the back; are they complaining of altitude sickness? We have lined the floor in newspaper in anticipation. Snug in a dale lies Alston, a quiet, cobbled town straddling the hill. Alston's principal attraction is the little Victorian steam railway that runs along the South Tyne Valley to Gilderdale. At 875 feet above sea level it claims to be England's 'Highest Narrow Gauge Railway'. An eight-year-old boy explains to me the machinations of this belching and puffing and hissing engine. Gaseous heat from the burning coal is pumped through pipes into the boiler. The water bubbles furiously, as in the inside of an electric kettle, and our steam engine is propelled into action. 'I love all trains,' the boy confides reverently. 'My father is an ambulance-driver.' On board, Bass and I sit opposite a grandmother from Penrith; her five-year-old grandson is squeezed in beside. His angelic blue eyes observe the passing scene from the luxurious shelter of his grandmama. 'We nearly lost him you know; he was born with all his intestines hanging out.' The boy blushes at such intimacies being bandied about the entire railway carriage. 'Yes, we very nearly lost him,' continues the grandmama. 'There were ten cases in Newcastle infirmary, all just like him.' I long to tut-tut and speculate on such a distressing coincidence. Something to do with the water perhaps? Or certain pills taken during pregnancy? Rough driving up cobbled hills? Too much black pudding? Cumberland sausage? Or even that renowned 'Death by chocolate cake' at the tea rooms by Wordsworth's Dove Cottage? But the child's evident discomfort at such confidences stays my tongue. On the return journey from Gilderdale, the garrulous grandmama is manoeuvred by her little hero to another carriage.

August 20

A serious climbing programme. A bright, blustery day with wind and cloud and capricious sun patches that stamp fell and mountain. Exhilarating air and light. We drive to the south end of Ullswater and park the car at Side Farm by Patterdale. Side Farm is an admirable riding establishment where docile mountain ponies are tethered, saddled and bridled, ready for the mid-morning hack. A medley assortment of riders from the age of seven years to seventy are mounted in various degrees of unsuitable attire. One wonders how they stay on board clambering up the narrow-ridged flanks of the fell beyond. We pass hurriedly through the stable yard; unfortunately Joss disturbs a hen which squawks with quite unnecessary fuss between the ponies. However, no one thing stirs; horses and riders are long inured to any untoward farmyard behaviour. We climb in a steady zig-zag up the rock and shale flank to a grass summit 2,000 feet up. Severe gusts of wind and the sudden fear that I have lost my car keys promote a rest and Kendal mint cake all round. We flap our jackets as the wind whistles pleasurably across our sweating backs. A superb view of the Ullswater Valley, a far distant bowl of green criss-crossed with walls and hedges and dabbed with white farmsteads. The long coil of the lake to our right and to the left a glimpse of 'Brothers' Water Tarn' so named in memory of the two young men who drowned in 1790.

August 22

More ravishing views: fells, mountains, and lakes unroll before us as we climb up from Rosthwaite village and over the hills to Watendlath Farm. We photograph a lone fisherman in his dinghy on the tarn and the gaggle of white geese on the green sward of grass. On and up the rocky summit of Joppelty Howe. The dogs do sterling work pulling us along on their leads. But a surprise sighting of a sheep can yank one suddenly off course. We eat bacon sandwiches and fruit cake in our heather eyrie and speculate idly on the world of Rogue Herries spread below. Did Judith Paris and cousin Francis Herries pound these same rugged hills with galloping hooves? And did their redoubtable author, Sir Hugh Walpole[1], pace these very paths?

We drop down through oak woods and tumbling mountain streams to Lodore Farm and tea with home-made scones. Exceptionally good they are – light and fluffy, dolloped with fresh cream and blackcurrant jam. 'The farmer makes them first before he goes out to the fields,' Frank tells us. 'A Belgian lady I was guiding found them so tasty she asked the farmer for the recipe, "dirty hands and lots of flour" is all he would tell her.' Frank knows all the farmers and their wives, 'the goings on'. In the winter months there are social evenings and village hops. 'My good friend, who owns the home-made meats and cheese shop in Station Road, Keswick town. You know? His wife has just run off with the milkman. And the milkman's wife only dead since January!'

This evening we take ourselves off to Moot Hall in Keswick Market Place, to a lecture and slide show on *The Ice Age in the Lake District*. (This necessitates an early rushed supper and no compliment to the chef's Braised Beef Cumbrian Style cooked in Local Ale and Deep dish Apple Pie with Cream.)

Why are the Lakes there? How were the mountains made? A cherubic, white-haired Dr Cockersole talks with his slides. It is hard to keep awake after the fresh air and exercise; the man behind snores openly. Again we all assume the mountains and lakes evolved volcanically 450 million years ago. The doctor's confident knowledge sounds more impressive than plausible. The subsequent Ice Age, set by Dr Cockersole as recently as two million years ago, submerged the craggy peaks and blunted them with glacial crusts and friction. Today's landscape was largely moulded by ice and tumbled glacial debris. Nobody is in an agile enough state of mind to question Dr Cockersole, let alone contradict him.

---

[1] *The Herries Saga – Rogue Herries* 1930, *Judith Paris* 1931, *The Fortress* 1932, and *Vanessa* 1933 – evoked the drama of Cumberland's wild and rugged beauty – and romance.

September 19 Moscow

In Moscow it poured, a chilling relentless rain. But plenty of glitter and riches in the Kremlin's recently restored buildings to offset a grey morning. These nineteenth-century State apartments have now become the major storehouse of Russia's priceless Imperial treasures and objets d'art, a plethora of silver work, gold and jewels, crowns, textiles, and resplendent royal carriages is liberally dispersed through the Emperor's study, the boudoir, and the State dining-rooms and drawing-rooms. It is a staggering glut of loot, exhibited for the first time since the Great October Revolution of 1917. Lenin would surely approve; his dictum for preserving historical monuments and heritage has been studiously borne out across Russia: royal palaces, cathedrals and monasteries, and every notable architectural endeavour, are earmarked for restoration. But Lenin's own tomb in Red Square is poised for demolition, we learn.

From the lugubrious confines of the old National Hotel we set off each morning with our guide, Marina, a pink and milky maid with a generous smile and some hapless lover shored up in south Wales. Perhaps the newly-functioning churches afforded the liveliest scenarios. Whole families crowded churchyards and graveyards to be swept up into the warmth and rich comfort inside. Chanting monks, candle-light, incense, and crowns – six crowns held above three couples – marked that bizarre and colourful marriage ceremony of the Russian Orthodox Church. In the porch, meanwhile, there rested two flower-bedecked corpses waiting their turn. Outside again the young and old chattered and laughed; the scene was as animated as a market place. And wizened women in black begged successfully with patient persistence. Wet days in Russia can clearly be happily contained orientating yourself around a functioning church. But, in his book *Journey into Russia* (1964), Laurens van der Post takes a jaundiced view: 'They make me sick,' a Russian friend told me. 'That's what the churches do to people. Those women have no need to beg, for the state takes care of all. It's just greed. And I bet you all the time the priests are eating caviar and drinking wine all day from the kopecks collected by those filthy women.'

The subsequent wonders of the opera house with its superior red plush armchairs, the spotless metro with its 1930 grandeur intact, St Basil's at night with each dazzling dome a fairy jewel, and the Moscow State Circus, where a fair share of flesh and talent engrossed a full national house, did not disappoint. Visits to Kuskova, the nineteenth-century pleasure park and mansion built by Count Sheremetiev, to Zagorsk and its fourteenth-century monastery complex, and

to Kolmenskoye, the favourite summer residence of the Tsars, all make
for rare kaleidoscopic recall. The beauty of the Kolmenskoye cathedral
is particularly haunting; the conical stone tower looms in silhouette
against a clear untrammelled skyline, high above the Moskva river.

Meanwhile the British Embassy – that stronghold of solid Victorian
Gothic – the sweet national champagne, the judicious Intourist hand-
outs of vodka, caviar and smoked sturgeon, the black bread, the brown
bread, the comparatively good choice of bread, and the absurd onus
of clutching your own bath plug have not changed in twenty-five
years. But today's begging in the streets smacks of a new-found freedom. The boys who pester you with watches, postcards, spurious
money exchange, and black market caviar, are the vanguard of a
changing creed; yet their clumsy crawl to consumer capitalism is to be
applauded. Girls of the night are also overlooked by the authorities;
they are even purported to be well-born; and many are undeniably
pretty. Russian youth still blooms in this time of stringent food shortage, but the old look tired and grey. What is it all about? It used to
be about the 'Nyet' phenomenon; saying 'No' to fellow subordinates
and more particularly to foreigners gave them a valid stand, a rightful
place in the Comintern conviction cycle. In the all-pervading fog of
Perestroika these old-age pensioners have lost their way. (We heard
disturbing rumours; but Moscow is a labyrinth of disturbing rumours;
they spread like a virus here. It is said there will be renewed Jewish
Pogroms throughout Russia. The murder, on September 9 past at
Zagorsk of Father Aleksandr Men, the prominent Jewish Russian
Orthodox priest, has refuelled anti-semitism in Soviet society; to an
alarming degree.)

September 20 Kiev

The autumn sun filters through a screen of chestnut-trees. We stand
in a small grass clearing. It is moated around and supports a central
grim monument, a group of Jews, young and old, victims of the Nazis.
The tumbling girl is caught in bronze and pain; her slim, sweet life
wiped out by guns at Babi-Yar, this seat of Huns. It was in the ravine
nearby that a quarter of a million died, each shot on a narrow ledge
and then toppled to a bath of blood. September 1941, 'All Yids to
report with warm clothes and valuables.' It had sounded almost
friendly, like 'bring a bottle'. And then a rumour had spread; they
were being sent away to Palestine . . .

Kiev has a natural luxuriance. Thickly-wooded banks plunge steeply
to the Dnieper river. This rippling swathe of green and red and russet

is studded with gilded cupolas and the fanciful contours of Rastrelli's eighteenth-century baroque façades. From the marble balcony of St Andrew's church you have such a view. But the monuments to post-revolutionary art are clumsy imposters; the monolithic aluminium figure of 'Motherhood' and the 'Arch of Friendship' must be condemned on their size alone.

We amble through the ancient precincts of the tenth-century Pecherskaya Lavra Monastery, a complex of jewel-like churches with exquisite painted interiors, clustered on a cobbled hill. Our guide, Natalya, looks pale and tired. She has seen fit to wear high-heeled slingbacks for this morning's tour; the cobbles are an added hazard. But she talks of more weighty matters – her two young sons. How can she explain to them that Lenin is finished? That Stalin is disgraced? That Gorbachov is good when he gives no potatoes? 'We are a tired and disillusioned people.' She goes on to disclose that there has been a significant increase in cancer and leukaemia since the nuclear explosion at Chernobyl. And again we are struck by the ubiquitous pallor of the man in the street. Had we noticed the cupolas? 'Here in Kiev the cupolas are shaped as pears. In Moscow you have the onions.' Two young monks in black gowns walk by. They are overweight, pasty, with unkempt beards and hair. Too much Chernobyl? Or too much caviar? Young Martynov (formerly of the Cossack Grebensky Regiment) would surely have cut a more imposing figure. His four-year sentence was served here in this monastery (1842–1846) because he had shot dead the poet Lermontov in a duel.

September 21 Tbilisi Georgia

Lenin's fall from grace is pursued even more keenly in Georgia. Through centuries of effective independence from Moscow, induced not least by their formidable Caucasus mountain range, the Georgians have heartily despised the Soviet system. 'You see? Lenin is gone from our Liberty Square. Just last week!' Our guide, Nana, flashes her wide blue eyes on the bare grass precinct. 'No, it is now two weeks that he came down. You see how the new grass is grown?' In the nearby Rustaveli Boulevard, Nana lowers her voice. She speaks tensely. 'Just here, before the Georgian State Supreme Building, we had sixteen dead on April 9, 1989. Fourteen were women. Just a peaceful demo by the Georgian Nationalists and then police beat them to death. Things have been falling downhill since November 1988. The authorities have many worries at this time. I am frankly surprised how things can still work in Georgia.'

Things are certainly not working too well at the Hotel Iveria. Reasonably immune by now to the prevalent rogue conditions, we do not complain. The basin with multiple fractures is suspended on some lopsided support. Any rash filling with water and it lurches down the wall. Feet, beware! However, the lavatory flushes and with conscientious removal of all lingering paper the system is viable. But a row of bulging tiles above the sitting position appears imminently targeted for the head. A slipped disc threatens with each rotation of the awkwardly-positioned lavatory paper. Hair-logged plugholes are more quickly dealt with. Any vigorous pulling on sticky drawers can result in the whole chest toppling on to its assailant. Reported sightings of mice and cockroaches are best put out of mind; a full night's sleep is a survival must – but midnight telephone calls from the black market caviar pushers, or indeed from any type of moonlight pushers, are regular threats.

A stroll through the old quarter of Tbilisi (town of Hot Springs) reveals quaint timber houses, their wooden verandas and deep eaves are indicative of the summer heat. Umbrella-pines, acacia, and maple line narrow cobbled streets and the wider boulevards. Straddling the hills above the town is the fourth-century fortress and spread below this vantage point is a hodge podge of Eastern, Mediterranean, and European architecture. Conical steeple towers and rose-brick Romanesque walls compete with the minarets of a blue-tiled Iranian bath house and Turkish-style balconied houses. The outsize twentieth-century revolutionary figure of a Georgian woman soars incongruously on the hill-side. She holds a barrel of wine in her left hand and a sword in her right. But her flourishing girth and stance have done little to encourage the recent wine harvests.

The simplicity of the sixth-century Georgian churches is refreshing when compared with the later busy Byzantine decoration of the Moscow and Kiev interiors. No magnificent frescoes or mosaics adorn these lofty stone Georgian walls. Shafts of sunlight splintered through their slitted conical domes are their sole gilders. But on their sturdy outer façades you see striking stone relief carvings and extended line narratives of flora and fauna that suggest a Seljuk hand. At the sixth-century church of Jvari (The Cross), eight miles north of Tbilisi, there is an especially beautiful stone relief. Set on the tympanum above the south door, two angels with outstretched wings support the Georgian Cross. Comments Michael Pereira in *Across the Caucasus*: 'The twin angels supporting the cross on the tympanum over the south door seem literally to float in the air; at any moment, one feels, they might detach themselves from the stone and soar away up into the sky.' Perhaps this Georgian Church of the Cross is the most memorable,

the most evocative of them all. Rooted for centuries on its sheer
pinnacle it commands a bare and windblown hill with the confluence
of the Kura river and the Aragvi far below. Who has not sought the
shelter and solace of these honeyed rough-hewn stones? Love and
guidance from its wooden cross? Inspiration from its very survival?
Nana urges us to light candles. 'In the Christian Orthodox Church
we always light candles. If you light candles it means the church is
always alive.'

September 22

At this evening's service at the Sioni Cathedral, the seat of the Patriarch, we light candles again. Hefty bell-ringing in the campanile draws
an essentially local crowd. Young girls dressed more for the fairground,
children, babies, bearded men, and grandmothers line the walk
between the Patriarch's front door and the church porch. A row of
white doves roots in the eaves of the Patriarch's brightly-painted
wooden house. Here he comes. A red-flowered carpet runs from door
to door. He walks slowly through his rose garden and descends the
steep steps to his people and his church. A modest, middle-aged man
in black, a pale face and hand raised in acknowledgment. We are swept
up into the rich medley of sounds and smells and colour that is a
Georgian Orthodox service. Generous vases of red gladioli, red roses,
and dahlias are propped haphazardly beside pillars on the marble floors;
red – the colour of murder and mourning. Young girls crowd the
candles with their glistening, dark, elliptical eyes transfixed with love
and hope and fear. One wonders how the modest patriarch begins to
cope with such hot-blooded maids. The thin re-cycled candles keel
over like half-cooked spaghetti under such fiery demand. Their precious congealed droppings are scooped up into enamel buckets.

September 23

The eleventh-century monasteries, Alaverdi and Ikalto, are two more
treasures from Georgia's rich architectural heritage. Situated near the
fortress town of Telavi and forty miles to the north-east of Tbilisi,
they are almost cushioned against the Caucasus range. The beauty of
a monastery must surely be enhanced by the evening light. The setting
sun weaved rose and amethyst across the chiselled mountains and lured
them closer. We sat on toppled stones in the dishevelled precincts
amongst the peace of butterflies and brambles; a cricket trilled with

some special inner conviction under the walnut tree. Inside Alaverdi stood massive pine trunks; this primitive scaffolding shores up such gems for better days and restoration.

September 24

'To be born British is to win the lottery of life.' So quotes an enlightened camp follower over breakfast. Bons mots, suggestions, and counter-suggestions flow. It is a free day. We are thrown on our own haphazard resources. Our long-suffering guides have taken leave of their senses. We wish them a well-earned day of peace and quiet.

Plans for the free day were first mooted last night at dinner. The dining-room, which the lady of title compared to Intensive Care, owing to its oblong, white, totally disembodied aspect, made an excellent forum. A suggestion that the ceiling water-sprinklers were bugging devices was summarily quashed but the shapely leg straddling the veranda from the room next door took longer to contain. The beautiful girl claimed she needed her cigarette lit. It was finally the harbour master who had assembled the most plausible package for a picnic party; a twelve-mile drive to the south-west of Tbilisi would bring us to a clearing in wooded slopes by the village of Khodzhori. The harbour master also envisaged a five-mile walk back down the hills to Tbilisi after lunch, for those who felt inclined, of course. At this juncture the prince stepped in with an alternative. How about a boat trip up the Kura? But the severely-dwindled Kura was considered an inadequate conveyance for the party. The prince promptly switched his alliance to the picnic and got out his Baedeker. It transpired that Khodzhori was 4,370 feet, that it cost 'eight roubles by phaeton' and walking was not recommended.

At 11 o'clock, the sun is high in a gin-clear sky and we are ready, assembled before the hotel, before the harbour master, complete with our picnics. The harbour master has discarded his familiar yachting cap for a sun hat. I should explain that our hero has no essential nautical attachments except for his navy cap and matching waterproofs; he just looks the part. Today it is a different story, the harbour master is assuming his rightful role as a military man and as properly befits the son of this century's most distinguished Field Marshal, viscount Montgomery of Alamein. The harbour master, who holds his own renowned military record, is in his element. 'Come on, troops.' We wait, cabbage-like, complacent; somebody else is in charge. The lady of title sports a bold flowered sun-dress; at least she won't get lost in the woods. The historian has strapped himself in with binoculars, a camera, and a large Selfridges carrier bag. The MP for Westmorland and Lonsdale makes a brief appearance, his long legs bared to a startled world in the shortest of shorts. If only E M Forster might join us to take up the tale.

It is 11.40 and the harbour master is running into difficulty; the mustering of six taxis to transport us twelve miles up the hill is proving an incomparably tricky exercise. The MP removes himself and his spectacular legs to the roof garden for 'some quiet reading'. Perhaps in his capacity as an ex-chief whip he judges the situation as irredeemable. There is timely intervention from a camp follower. (She has already proved herself a dab hand with the Black Market in extracting proper caviar at proper prices.) Our heroine has successfully commandeered a large orange van. It will take half of the party up the hill to Khodzhori. The ominous dent on its rear is overlooked on the strength of its being bright orange anyway and surely impossible to hit a second time round. The rest of us follow in yellow taxis, winding up the steep hill, through pine-woods. We converge by a clearing, the proposed picnic venue. The harbour master is clearly delighted by our intact complement on this first leg of the free-day celebrations. 'We will now proceed in column.' But his command is thwarted by the discovery that we have no drinking glasses. The resourceful van driver announces that if he were given a packet of cigarettes – preferably Marlboro – he would collect glasses from the village. Arrival on the top of the hill also confirms that it is far too steep and too far a walk back to Tbilisi.

The party spreads out in the woods for an alternative ramble before lunch. The lady of title identifies – quite correctly – Solomon's Seal among the brambles; anemone and primula also come to light. The historian who in a concession to this pastoral dalliance has donned a black fez, as worn by local shepherds, identifies the spindleberry tree; ash, hornbeam, and birch are swiftly added to this veritable arboretum. Our other distinguished writer mumbles a curse through his lips jammed with top soil and sticks; the dry branches come away in our hands as we lever ourselves up the steep wood-side paths. I am reminded of Lermontov's *Princess Mary*: 'There was a sudden loud rush of stones under our feet. It was Grushnitsky – he'd missed his footing when the branch he was holding broke. He would have gone sliding down on his back if his seconds had not supported him.' A sudden shot – 'Mortar fire!' raps the historian, his nostrils flaring. Stock still he stands. At a sweep he recalls the entire fifteen hundred years of Tbilisi's bloodied history. The sackings, the sieges, the pillage. We walk on and come upon a pen of pigs, a cow, and an awesome heap of rusted caviar tins. We are not the only picnickers to have found Khodzhori.

Back in our clearing we re-group around log tables, digging and scraping at dried ducks' breasts with dirty fingernails. Despite the Hotel Iveria's stoic attempts at a picnic we welcome the prince's prosciutto, the Danish countess's cheese, the harbour master's toffee Rolos and a generous camp follower's tin of Harrods Dundee cake. It is story time and each embarks on how he met his spouse. The prince claims that he initially courted his future wife with the bait of a gun in his shoot. Others compete with equally fatuous tales, but it is the Danish countess who wins the day. She astounds us all. Her prospective father-in-law had discovered her in a crumpled heap of scarlet taffeta on his drawing-room sofa. His son had proposed to her that very dawn. Reluctantly we pick our way back through the wood to questionable civilisation, when the prince stumbles over a long cleft stick. 'On such sticks I would balance my sword and roast meat.' A fitting observation with which to end a day in the country.[2]

September 25

The Georgian Military Highway is romanticised in paint and prose down the centuries. It has been the main link between Georgia and Russia since the second century BC, The present road is 237 km long and was constructed in 1817. The green Kura river swirls alongside, its banks sheltered with pine and poplar. Beneath the sheer summit of the Jvari Monastery, its distinctive dense water merges with the silver white flow of the mountain river Aragvi. Cows graze on the rolling plains, eagles with striped wings hover, vineyards sweep up to foothills, and caves appear on wooded slopes, huge gold stone boulders with gouged-out predatory eyes. We approach Ananuri and its cluster of sixteenth-century churches. They straddle a lake. Distant mountain peaks are clearly delineated as they fold into the horizon. Blurred in rose and copper-brown they exactly reflect Prince Grigory Gagarin's nineteenth-century watercolours of this lake and mountain setting; these old brick domes; these grassy nooks where wild flowers coil and fat hens peck and strut the graves. It is a place apart; the stuff of dreams, and there incased in stone are more flying

[2] The harbour master – David Montgomery
The MP – Michael Jopling (Minister of Agriculture, 1983–1987)
The prince – Yuri Galitzine
The distinguished writer – Peregrine Worsthorne
The historian – Alistair Horne
The lady of title – Amabel Lindsay
Our heroine – Janet Berens
Our brave contestant for the water massage – Colin Campbell.

angels and even a deer with an outstretched neck, who nibbles grapes.

Higher and higher to the cool and the green. The Aragvi runs dry on its tumbled bed, a winding white scar through shale and rock, by terraced swards of emerald where sheep and goats graze, conical haystacks, red-tiled farmhouses with wooden verandas, cottages, orchards, and beehives. Up and up. Beguiling, absorbing, and everywhere slabs of terraced green, webbed with mountain rills like the silver scribbles of a snail. We stop at the hamlet of Mleti where stern hill-women, wrapped in wool and wrinkles and bright scarves, sell us apples and grapes and golden crêpes. Then on to the Krestovaya, the 'pass of the Cross'. Lermontov refers to it in his story *Bela*: 'The road was certainly dangerous. On our right were piles of overhanging snow, looking as though the first gust of wind would send them plunging into the ravine. The narrow road was partly covered with snow. In some places it gave way under our feet, but in others it had turned into ice by the sun and the night frost. We found the going difficult enough ourselves, and our horses kept stumbling. On our left yawned a deep chasm down which a torrent flowed, one moment vanishing beneath the crust of ice, the next leaping and foaming above black rocks.'

At 9,000 feet on a sunny September afternoon the scene is not so ominous. A hideous vantage point stone veranda crudely studded with mosaic is the only balking point. The minister remarks that he has never seen such beauty alongside such ugliness. With binoculars we see a nineteenth-century Cossack fort nestling on its own bluff of rock in the valley below. Bathed in golden light with a huge sheltering tree beside and what crapulent Cossack would have sat in its shade? Fingering his long mustachios, drinking, listening, waiting for trouble, for action, for death? And we see avalanche tunnels and wood-paling snow walls. The sun goes in and predatory birds are wheeling and screaming.

The mountains hover all around, a grim, serrated convoy where no ice-cap ever rounded those sharpened peaks. Shawls of snow are cradled in their craters, and Mount Kazbek, their king at 14,000 feet, is cloaked in white. The mountain road descends through red rock and soil; this local oxidised iron terrain results in the spectacular 'blood snows' of the Caucasus.

A huge herd of sheep blocks us in; they have come down from the mountains to be clipped. Now the long-haired black goats and laden donkeys escort them back again up to their pastures for a final graze before winter's white-out. These dark-skinned shepherds look fit and proud. They have their livestock, their fief, and their fine chow dogs.

They know their way. They have their rhythm. They are in step with their rich earth, their wind and snow and rushing waters. Marina II, our guide from Lenigrad, concedes that rural Caucasian life could be a tempting alternative to the exigencies of urban reality. She needs little encouragement to expound on the shambles of her society: 'My country is on its knees. We have nothing to sell. And we have nothing to spend our money on. Even tourism will lessen. Hotels built twenty years ago now fall into disrepair. The upkeep of our hotels? It does not exist. A plumber? An electrician? They would be paid 90 roubles a month. They do not exist. We would like local government systems to organise our food production. But the Party bosses dislike change. There are antagonisms everywhere.'

The evening sun is locked behind the mountain range as we pull in at Vladikavkaz. The famous Terek river variously described by the School of Caucasian writers as 'resounding Terek'; 'bright and shining as steel'; 'blackening with rage'; 'roaring Terek'; 'mighty Terek'; 'its wild and troubled waves raging like infernal spirits', conducts itself in a perfectly orderly manner below our bedroom windows. This hotel is to be recommended. The manageress greets us in the hall with positive recall of our booking. She is pretty and young with a lovely figure. Her long black hair is caught in a brilliant and tumbles over a well-laundered shirt. Her beds and wine and table are above standard reproach. Her meat dumplings are swiftly followed by three-foot steel daggers brandishing chunks of roast pork, and a subsequent ice cream dusted with nuts helps cool the palate. Our indulgent manageress complains that tourists only stay for the one night in her good hotel. Why do they not stay longer? But Vladikavkaz (Dominion over the Caucasus), guarding its indisputable peer position through to Georgia, holds no interest to the culturally-bent, although the disused nine-teenth-century Sunit Mosque on the left bank of the Terek, with its Egyptian-style twin minarets and its gilded cupola, is decorative enough. Perhaps the mosque could be made a 'functioning' mosque? The engendered crowds would then repair to the well-appointed Vladikavkaz Hotel to celebrate weddings and funeral wakes.

September 26 Pyatigorsk

A pleasant drive on another sunny morning through the arable plains of Ossetia. The wide grass verges are shaded with poplar, pine, and birch. A wooden bench, apple orchards, a dog in a stream, white ducks, cows, it could be *plein-air* Clausen, his *Girl at the Gate*. Vast crops of corn and maize are interspersed with fields ploughed up for winter wheat. Brightly-kerchiefed women and children glean the stubble where a herd of horses graze. Thomas Hardy! we cry, but pure scenic spin-offs are precious reward for the breakdown of machinery that has cost them their bumper harvests. And why did not the Army help? (Troops recently returned from East Germany and Afghanistan are no longer heroes. They are disillusioned, thrown off their ladder and disorientated.) Why did they not put the soldiers in the cornfields? Marina II attempts to soothe our exasperation. She assures us that all soldiers are now billeted on the equally momentous potato harvest. The minister, in his added capacity as a Yorkshire dairy farmer, comments on the scene spread before us. 'Despite their abundant resources the USSR is still the biggest food importer in the world; five years ago their Ministry of Agriculture talked of privatising the farms, but the Stalin years had snuffed out the necessary entrepreneur faction . . . the quality of management is the crunch . . . you can discern differences here in each collective . . . you see some areas tended efficiently, with love and care . . . the State collective does not encourage love and care . . . the quality of production and distribution can only be improved with competent management . . . the cows and sheep look healthy.'

We stop briefly to stretch our legs. A short walk from the road looms an awesome war memorial. Four fighting Russians, their stern profiles set in stone, a swarthy moustachioed Cossack in his hat, a soldier, a sailor, and a partisan, it marks the spot where the Nazis were finally defeated and barred entry to the Caucasus in December 1942. We arrive at Pyatigorsk this afternoon.

Lermontov in his *Princess Mary* records: 'I arrived in Pyatigorsk yesterday and took lodgings in the outskirts, high up at the foot of Mashuk. When there's a storm the clouds will come right down to my roof. When I opened my window at five this morning, the room filled with the scent of flowers from the modest garden outside. Branches of cherry blossom peep in at my window and the wind sends showers of white petals on to my desk.'

So he described his digs which he took for the season in spring 1841. We now stand in this same little whitewashed house where jays peck at the newly-thatched roof. The garden is still modest. Acacia, walnut, and horse chestnut screen its secrets. A 'petit Trianon' of cottages it is, with their quaint wood verandas and balconies. And there is still the scent of flowers, beds of petunia, roses, and marigolds are caught behind a wood-paled fence. Lermontov only lived here for two months, the last two months of his life before his fated duel with Martynov. Our guide, Lilia, is a well-built girl, a buxom brunette, draped voluptuously in a purple blouse. She shows us examples of

Lermontov's watercolours and drawings which suggest that he had the makings of a considerable artist as well as a poet.

We walk down the terraced hill. Pyatigorsk is lined with terraced hills. The valley is lush with trees and springs of water. In Lermontov's words, nearby Mount Mashuk: 'towers like a shabby Persian cap . . . while along the horizon stretches a silver chain of snowy peaks with Kazbek at one end and the twin summits of Elbrus at the other.' We pass by the towering black marble statue of Lenin. A hooded crow sits on his head, a halcyon perch. The historian's wife would like to see Lenin replaced by Lermontov on his horse. The evening sky is clouded and the mountain blotched. Night falls early with thunder and lightning. On such a night Lermontov died. His friend Mikhail Glebov, a member of the Life Guards, later described the scene to his friend Emilia Verzilin. She records: 'what eerie hours he spent, having remained alone in the forest, sitting on the grass in the pouring rain. The head of the dead poet was resting on his knees – it was dark, the tethered horses neighed, reared, pawed the ground with their hooves, the thunder and lightning was incessant it was frightening beyond words. Glebov wanted to lower the head carefully on to his greatcoat, but this movement caused Lermontov to yawn convulsively. Glebov froze motionless and remained so until a police cart arrived in which poor Lermontov was carried to his lodgings.'

September 27 Pyatigorsk

I am lured back to Lermontov's house. It is empty. I walk slowly round the minuscule rooms. In this very hall they laid him. Flowers crammed the house and friends passed through for two whole days. His pistol and gun and dagger hang on the same wall today; in this same, very same hall where . . . Lilia steals up. 'Where did they put the body?' I asked. Lilia positions her sturdy frame squarely in the little room; 'Lermontov is rested – just here – on the long dining table,' she turns to demonstrate the exact posture of his head and body. 'His head is turned to the north. And the painter, Shvede, stands to paint the death mask from this opposite corner. Lermontov wears his white shirt. He dies early evening on July 15, 1841.' Sensing my yen for morbid detail, Lilia adds crisply: 'It is a hot night and very many flies. Lermontov's servant, he stays by him to keep away the flies, and he catches the blood drops in a copper bowl.'

A few of us are seduced by the Sanatorium on the hill. It promises massages of every variety and mud baths. An enormous pile of concrete, built 1974, it hardly looks inviting and a brief encounter with matron, resplendent in a white overall and a Maginot line of gold-capped teeth, is positively intimidating. Our blood pressure is taken with near strangulation of the arm and a warning that any mud treatment is potentially ruinous to the heart. It is only possible to have half the body treated with mud. I opt for below the navel. We are led through a labyrinth of green passages that lead on to rooms and rooms of empty white-curtained cubicles. And there, cowering behind a potted plant, we see our one male contestant for the underwater massage. How is he getting on? He is in a state of near apoplexy. 'Some crazy nurse saw me stripped down, waiting for her in the water tank and ran screaming out of the room! I thought I was going to be arrested. She then told me to put my pants back on. I refused naturally.' 'What happened next?' 'Oh, in the end she flashed a tap over me for fifteen minutes. I am now supposed to be resting.'

We continue down the passage towards a fearful smell, which can only be described as a fruity mélange of manure and silage. We enter the chambers of the mud bath with some trepidation. In a dingy, tiled barrack-like room we each lie on a narrow bed. Next, hot poultices of the evil-smelling mud, packed in lint casings, are slapped on our offending parts. It is not an invigorating experience. However, some of us, who later opt for a straightforward body massage, report back favourably.

Pyatigorsk in its continuing capacity as a health spa is taken seriously by the Russians. Sanatoria, sulphur springs, and infusion centres are liberally dotted about the town and surrounding hills. Rows of capacious bottoms, spread on stools, with heads bent over basin-inhalers, are a droll and common sight. From behind, especially if you are waiting your turn in the queue, the scene suggests an attack of multiple vomiting.

Other drinking establishments offer gargling facilities and sulphur tastings from the different springs. Lermontov's dandiacal accounts of Pyatigorsk society are hardly evoked today.

September 28 Moscow

Our accompanying British guide, Kathleen Berton-Murrell, author of *Moscow, An Architectural History,* has lived in Moscow for the past eleven years and has travelled extensively throughout Russia. Her grasp of Russian history, literature, the arts, the religions, and present-day politics was to our infinite gain. Grouped in bars, buses or on hotel landings, an hour with Kathy never failed to educate and enthral. Her delivery and her gaiety were infectious.

On this last night we take a drink with Kathy's friends, a British woman married to a Russian philosopher. We crowd into their modest Moscow flat, armed with an assortment of wines and spirits. Rammed up against the kitchen sink, the bed, the bookcase, the bath, we all fit in somehow. The small square rooms are glorified orange-boxes; the stone stair approach with smashed windows is a sober indictment of urban upkeep.

Clearly our hostess is a highly intelligent, charming woman. Does she see herself and her husband as the vanguard of a brave new Soviet world? Or will they subsist − forever amber − in their orange-boxes? She certainly concedes that there is a grave national crisis in confidence. And I am haunted still by the little old waitress in Tbilisi. Early each morning she sweeps the dining-room with her willow whisk; from side to side she sweeps with acceptance etched deep in her pale, tired face. She does not smile; she does not look sad. Again in the evening she is there; her willow whisk, to the right, to the left, like a blind man with his stick.

December 5 Hardwicke House

The park glitters this morning; crystal-sharp in a hard white sun. We canter cautiously, Miranda and I. The air is champagne in a frosted bowl. But she is scared of the logs; round corners behind bushes they cower, like crippled dinosaurs, ready to pounce, mounted cannons ready to fire. 'There's a good Miranda, they won't bite you; they are not going to move.' I anticipate her every shy, interpret each snort, her stiffening neck, the pair of us vie to sniff out trouble first. With a sense of achievement I finally dismount in the stable yard. We have had our moments, Miranda and I.

Christmas in three weeks. As usual we wait in vain to be engulfed in waves of Christmas nostalgia, to be swept up in the compelling magic of childhood conceptions. Next week I will coax the spirit with a thick, blue, scented spruce. Smells and colour, spiced candles, wrapping paper, a wreath on the door, candles − it will come, it will come.

And there have been parties through these long dark nights. At Sotheby's an evening view, room upon room of divertissement, less cluttered now that they have extended their rooms, far less cosy. Christie's on the other hand has elected not to give a Christmas party this year. Shame. Then there was that modest ballet performance, sponsored by Asprey, by the English National Ballet School. We were a private audience of one hundred, sipping champagne in the high-ceilinged practice rooms of Markova House. Mirrored walls and exercise bars reflected the scene. Cocker spaniels scoured the skirting for explosives. Princess Diana arrives, simply dressed in a green wool dress to the knees. She smiles and weaves a pretty passage through the guests. Smiles and pleasantries, smiles and pleasantries. Tom steers her to the Asprey table. She is friendly, gracious, relaxed. She drinks sparkling water. I wish she would grow her hair, the cropped style she has now adopted leaves little scope for chic or variety. Sometimes she has a fringe bungling her forehead – so ordinary. She has broad shoulders, a big tall girl, exceptionally photogenic, the press promotes her glamour. (Later in the week she flew off to Japan and was resplendent in tiaras and ballgown, diamonds and pearls.)

The Royal Academy showed Monet's atmospheric series of Rouen Cathedral, his haystacks and the Thames bridges, the bridges blurred in foggy dawn, the stacks in snow and summer sunsets, the cathedral ablaze in a high gold moon and then quenched dim in dusk. An evocative show of contrasts in light and shade; to recall again W B Yeats: 'the heavens' embroidered cloths, enwrought with golden and silver light, the blue and the dim and the dark cloths of night and light and the half-light.'

And there was that Service of Thanksgiving. Paeans of praise for an old friend, an accomplished cricketer. (His age saved him from service in the Second World War; competition in the athletic field thus substantially reduced.) Is that a sour observation? Three wives, but he is the ultimate hero. The devoted father, friend, brother, husband. The noble Group-Captain, slim and erect at the pulpit, eulogizes our friend. In half-audible tones he promotes the prolific achievements of our dear departed through a full twenty-five minutes. It is comforting that, in death, one's friends, if not one's God, are magnanimous.

1991

The venue for tonight's party is a substantial Regency house set on the river a mile away. A '60th birthday' party? A 'concert'? Josephine sixty already! Her Austrian husband, Prince Rupert, who masterminds the finances of singer Mick Jagger and his Rolling Stones, could indeed be a candidate for the advanced sixties. He is a convivial man, wreathed in smiles and charm and an indecipherable circumference. But Josephine with her Junoesque good looks and disciplined contours does not suggest a woman of sixty. In a recent press article 'a woman of 56' was defined as a 'crone'. (In the *Oxford Dictionary* a 'crone' is dismissed as a 'withered old woman; old ewe'). It makes the blood curdle. Let us conclude that the outward appearance can confound the years.

A concert? Presumably the Rolling Stones will be the star performers? Mick Jagger? Jerry Hall? Elton John? Princess Margaret? A razzmatazz to end them all? A marquee? A buffet? Too many to be contained in a seating arrangement. We are asked for 7.30 in black tie. This early start to the proceedings must surely ensure that we arrive before Princess Margaret. We must go by taxi; the narrow approach to the house precludes all parking and turning. What a jamboree to liven up a damp and war-weary January evening. With a marquee in mind I regretfully discount my Christian Dior scarlet silk with its topless shoulders, though its trim of black cock's feathers might have competed well with any glittering extravaganza of Jerry Hall's wardrobe. Something warmer would be more prudent. Tom chooses for me the long black figure-hugging jacket with its bouffant red skirt in preference to the ink-blue frothing ostrich feathers.

Solemnly, in a local taxi, we set off on the one-mile drive. We are surprised to find the approach quite clear; the house decked in light glistens like an uncut wedding cake. 'Please enter by side door.' Curiouser and curiouser. And there is Rupert beckoning us in to the spacious hall – the grand piano, musical stands, gilt chairs, and more gilt chairs. The nucleus of a small audience is already in place considering its position. We see Penelope Sitwell; she smiles quizzically from the elegant confines of her black velvet bodice and her puffball skirt. More elegant women, and here we have Sir Hardy Amies, silver-haired, precise and chiselled; next a distinguished interior designer, and there the venerable publisher Lord Weidenfeld. Beleaguered by embonpoint, he is not easily contained on a gilt chair. (Two days later he was escorted out of Wilton's in a commodious wheelchair; he had come over queer at the lunch table.)

Tom and I sit to the back of this assembly, sharing a niche with a spectacular vase of lilies. The family nannie sits immediately in front of us nodding her vigorous grey head and regaling with her musical preferences the bearded young man at her side. He had been her baby and his mother Josephine had been her baby. A glance at the programme reveals that the performance is a family exertion bolstered by professional talent. Josephine will play the piano in the Handel Partita; her second son (another baby) will play Chopin Études and Nocturnes; and an acclaimed violinist and his Chinese lady accompanist will play the Chaconne by Bach. Our previous conjectures at the evening's entertainment could not have been more wide of the mark.

An air of knife-edge anticipation prevails. Even Nannie's staccato observations are quelled to grunts and whispers. Will Josephine sweep down the stairs in full evening dress? Down the imposing iron banister to the black and white marble hall, where huge carriage lights hang from ruched silk sleeves and voluptuously swagged lime curtains drip with tassels? A hush as Rupert steps into the pool of light beside the grand. Like that sombre man in the dark suit who parts the heavy red curtains at Covent Garden with bad news, Rupert clearly has bad news. Has Josephine lost her nerve? Caught her fingers in the wardrobe door? Fainted at her prie-dieu? Overslept? 'I have to tell you, with great sadness, that our leading violinist will not be with us tonight. We heard at lunchtime that he has flu.' Phew! At least he has not been thrown from his motor bike and smashed a violin. His mother has agreed to take his place.

Josephine rustles in from the adjoining drawing-room, her blonde hair piled high in a chignon. She looks serious in spectacles and long black taffeta. We clap. There follows that cruel expectant silence. Will this self-inflicted enterprise stand up to the exacting scrutiny of her friends? Suddenly the marble hall is swaddled and swept with sound. Josephine, the Chinese violinist, and the elderly mother romp merrily through the Handel; an excellent performance to the untutored ear. Now it is Chopin with Josephine's son. His ascetic beaky profile looks the part as he ripples through his devoirs. Nannie must be proud. We finish with Bach and the Chaconne, a frenetic feat by the Chinese violinist, her violin dispatching the most rumbustious sawing and plucking and chopping to emit the desired effect.

February 15 Hardwicke House

The glut of media coverage of the Gulf War can dull and sicken the layman's attention. Now, in the 28th day, the bombardment continues. Rumours of an imminent Allied ground war initiative. What to think? What is wisdom, time and hope? The price of victory? The cost of its dogged pursuits? Allied casualties will be markedly more heavy with a ground offensive.

There is another reason why my personal interest in this war has waned; it has been superseded by the sudden shock and sorrow of my brother-in-law's suicide. His tragic tumble was meticulously planned, it seems; members of the family recall the last time each spent with him; a drink together, long talks, lunch, a walk, a supper. Last moments loom in the memory with renewed significance; of no avail. They can prove nothing even as suicide can prove nothing.

They found his body in the hired car with its small exhaust pipe. Deep in the woods he had driven: into the woods on the Cliveden estate that he knew and loved so well. An empty whisky bottle, a pad of paper – blank – and the siphoned fumes. Snow fell heavily after his death. 'It is a blanket of peace,' exclaimed his wife, Valerie. It stayed with us through his funeral service and his burial, a harrowing moment this last. The coffin, carpeted with flowers, is lowered into the deep cavity, lurching on its straps. The formidable, jagged heap of displaced soil is piled alongside.

Poor, troubled Dickie: trapped in the bewildering black tunnels of mental pain, he took his life. A lovely wife, two stalwart, handsome sons, he left behind, on the brink of their adult life. We are incredulous as we withdraw from the shock, tired and heavy, drawn and nauseated.

His wife and mother, his two sons; they still expect him through the door.

February 27 Hardwicke House

And another subsequent suicide; Nicky Phillips, owner of Luton House. He inherited the estate and legendary contents from his grandmother, Lady Zia Wernher, in 1977. Nicky was a striking figure, tall, dark, and handsome, with a facial bone structure to reflect his distinguished Russian forebears. His grandmother was the elder daughter of Grand Duke Michael of Russia and the maternal great-grand-daughter of the poet Pushkin.

Found dead in his car . . . parked with engine running . . . in a garage . . . near a shooting lodge . . . 200 yards from the house . . . aged forty-seven.

This last December I sat next to Nicholas at a dinner party. Our hostess was Tania Illingworth (née Tolstoy), blonde with ravishing blue eyes and a descendant of the renowned Count. Nicholas, on my left, was monosyllabic, mild, withdrawn. Was he dull, depressed, or naturally detached? He certainly lacked the sparkle of his Czechoslovakian wife Lucy[1]. She had just returned from a trip to Russia with Tania as her guide. Lucy had plans to expand the exhibition of Russian treasures at Luton House. Will her energies extend to running the estate until Edward, son and heir, inherits? He is still a child.

March 6 139 Randolph Avenue Maida Vale

I regret not telling Princess Maria, that I eat only a small lunch. Elegant and undeterred, she hovers by her oven, pulling, lifting, sliding, juggling casseroles, appetising stuffed cabbage, Polish-style, and teasing pastry parcels. I sit helplessly in the corner of her pretty kitchen, bright and spotless, in a flood of sun. Purple crocuses bloom on a patch of grass beyond.

'How is your vodka? My dear child – you must not sip your vodka. That is pathetic. Did a dashing Pole never show you how to toss back your vodka? So! And again!' She refills my glass.

We eat our herring companionably. 'I give you a typical Polish lunch. A little more sour cream? Of course this Maida Vale is not the same as Little Venice. How spoilt we were in Warwick Avenue.' Married over fifty years to the Polish prince Jan Sapicha, now widowed, she looks remarkably young and handsome.

'In Poland I feel invigorated. This last visit I returned to my father's estate near Warsaw. He had a fish pond business. It is not so important an estate, some 400 hectares. The government have kept it these last fifty years.' And the elder son? The charming Adonis who married the Brazilian princess? 'But you know that he has divorced his Brazilian bride? and you know . . .' A sharp intake of breath, a lowering of the voice. 'He has become a priest! A Protestant. My son is now a reverend!' I am amazed and mutter disbelief in the face of his own new faith. 'It is disappointing,' concedes Maria drily. She is a master of acceptance. She is the most admirable and unforgettable woman. 'And the estate is in bad repair with four families running over the house.' Would she like to live on the family estate again? 'I feel my roots are

---

[1] Maria Lucia, née Czernin.

pulling me back to Poland. I would like to find a small flat in Warsaw. The family here, they can come and visit me in Warsaw. I am tired of their problems.' She concludes, 'We all expect too much. We should never expect anything.' She endows these words with the weighty wisdom of a lifetime's experience.

There is a light step on the stairs. The Protestant son is framed in the door. I might have expected a black-cloaked figure to resemble the actor Gérard Depardieu, but no; he stands tall in a smart grey suit and a cheerful tie, more like a banker poised for Geneva, Zurich, Paris, Rome . . .

'Would you like some pudding, dear?' His mother is his mother is his mother.

March 27 15 Harbledown Road Parsons Green

'Patches of poppies! Patches of poppies! Sound the "S", darling! Like a "Z", darling! Put plenty of puff into the "P". Remember! Plosives and stops! Plosives and stops! Stops, darling? Lip stoppage of air . . .' The telephone shrills and Yvonne Wells, elocutionist élite to the English National Opera, the Royal College of Music, the Old Vic, sweeps out of the room. 'Carry on, darling, practise your "Fetch the fresh fish from Framlingham" and then John Dryden's Heavenly Harmony piece.' I hear her articulated and perfectly-pitched tones in the adjoining room. Her front room is a cosy womb of mushroom and pink thrust with strident male bronzes mounted on mahogany plinths. Rich Turkish rugs lap up to the heavy mouldings of Edwardian commodes and cabinets. A gleaming, gnarled conglomerate as rich as Charbonnel's chocolates.

Yvonne returns and eyes me quizzically as I rise to my feet. Something brisk in her manner evokes that long-buried reverence of the schoolmistress; then, as suddenly that ubiquitous 'darling', as delusive as an elision, redresses the scene.

'Tell me, darling, why are we here? Has the husband a hearing problem? Mind you, we can improve on your delivery. Much more bilabial activity needed. Lips, jaw, and tongue must combine in better attack and clarity. Exercise those lips. Sneer, pout, relax and chew. Excellent! Now the tongue. Wag it for me. Point it out and in and out – rrrroll it rrrround and behind the teeth. I will now hear you read my favourite piece, 'The Faithful Wife'. Stand, darling. Posture! Breathing!' Yvonne Wells's chosen poem starts on a more suggestive level than it concludes. I wade down the plaintive page.

'I am away from home . . . I left the forsythia half yellow . . .

Adultery in the heart, life is so short . . . you are middle-aged now, as I am. Write your notes up, fix the rattling window, keep your marriage vows, as I shall.'

Yvonne's front room falls silent with unmitigated regrets. What lost opportunities! Yvonne sighs richly and asks me to read the piece again. 'Pay particular attention to the clear "l's" and the dark "l's". 'She sits upright in anticipation on her pink velvet tub chair. It occurs to me that we might even indulge in a third round if she were to read it to me.

She tapes my effort; my voice sounds appreciably lower. It was in the 1950s that the high, light voice was fashionable, she explains. Julian Slade's *Salad Days* and the Coronation of the Queen set the pitch. But she categorically condemns the state of spoken English today. She insists that it has been in decline for thirty years. Of course, she adds, if we were to imagine Queen Elizabeth I walking into the room, she would talk in the strangest vowel glides and junctures. I suggest that Queen Elizabeth's lack of teeth and consequent habit of keeping her mouth shut tight might have some bearing on this shortcoming. 'I would not know, darling.' Yvonne cuts an imposing figure on her chair beside me. She is a handsome woman. Her bright vivacity generates her mind and body to a crystalline sparkle. Our one-hour session is nearing its end. She smoothes her blue and white print dress over well-built knees. 'Take regional accents and you must believe me they have all lost their purity, darling. It is a sad fact. Too much ethnic involution; Indians in Leicester and London criss-crossed with every nation that ever saw the light of day. However in Glasgow a bráss báth is still a báss báth. We both shout the short northern "A" with relish.'

I stand up to go. Yvonne stares up at me closely with a look of sudden revelation. 'Tell me, darling, did you ever have a regional accent?'

April 28 France

The A26 from Calais is swift and smooth as silk. Smart road furniture, that sign for priorité à droite (the yellow diamond with the white and black border; it is stylish, a bright bold statement; it is Mondrian. These Péage autoroutes are a commendable force to contain the breadth and length of this spacious country. No road jams here. No protracted repair works. No graffiti. No vandalism. And no litter tossed at central barriers or caught flapping like torn underwear in trees. Those littered banks that defile the M2 run-up to Dover. It makes you shudder. Here, in the Marne valley roses are trained to mask road barriers and fledgling trees are nurtured on every bank. I grieve for Britain's sloppiness and yearn for France's *soin*. Is it a sign of middle-age to be ashamed of one's country?

Mists rise from the wide, flat expanse of the valley. Soft shawls of steam hang low above plough and plain and swards of woodland. As we approach Dijon, the shimmer of yellow mustard fields is a vast fieldscape; no hedges to blur this chequered land of Northern France. From Dijon to Beaune along Route N74 (Gevrey Chambertin, Morey-St Denis, Nuits St Georges) '*Ses grands vins! Les grandes caves!*' These stone Burgundy villages, where each sober façade is etched in cream shutters. Vineyards sweep down to the road from the low crest of wooded hills, a most remarkable stretch of viticulture. At Nuits St Georges we sip a glass of chablis, huddled on a windswept corner of this modest town. It is our twenty-sixth wedding anniversary. We lunch at Beaune in the central, cobbled square. The surrounding old tiled roofs are clotted with moss, as though draped with rough, soft tweed.

April 29 Dieulefit Rhône Valley

Le Poët-Laval is a medieval village, high on a hill above the rich Rhône valley where they shape up stones and slabs in extensive restoration, cream and crumbling age-old stones; a ruined tower, a temple, both open to the skies. We pass tumbling tails of purple lilac, banks of wild iris, troughs of deep blue pansies. In the evening quiet, the mating calls of doves. Night comes, then the barking of distant dogs. A full moon floods each tower and rampart. In this retreat we find Les Hospitaliers, described as 'one of the best hotels in the world'.

France is exquisite in spring. No British. The few Germans keep to the hills. Villages hug the folds of twisting mountain roads. Snow-crusted peaks hover high above mustard fields, the frail green of opening buds and tracts of coiled rich plough. At 3,000 feet and 44°F the scene is stark with shale and scrub. A ruined castle frowns from its wind-scoured pinnacle. The lush valley is cut through with the ice-green mountain river Drôme. Here cows are chocolate and sheep are white as they graze on cowslips and poppies. We reach La Petite Auberge at Die, our proposed venue for lunch. It is *fermé*. It is '*L'Hebdomadaire*'. (Recourse to the dictionary reveals 'annual holiday'.) We drive on to Crest; a brooding Romanesque rose-brick castle presides over this medieval hill village. We eat at the Porte Montségur restaurant, built into the sprawling ramparts. Tom chooses pigeon doused in a rich demi-glace of wine and herbs. My foie gras de canard aspires to be as rich and silky as any foie gras de canard. We drink a red Burgundy, Crozes Hermitage, 1987.

We follow dusty signs to Atelier du Poterie de Grés (Sculpture – Raku). Through vineyards and apricot orchards we climb, to the hills above Nyons and Venterol and olive groves beyond. More vineyards, soft vale upon vale, each sturdy vine a candelabra flamed with the first green shoots, each squat gnarled limb outstretched and fired with the evening sun. Twisting and zig-zagging through a narrow track we come upon a scene straight from Marcel Pagnol's *Jean de Florette*. A modest stone house dappled with the shade of lime-trees; rams and bears and lions sculpted in stone and terracotta peer haphazardly from clutches of wild iris and yellow broom.

A simple showroom within, where cats curl in the local pale grey glaze, and a ram, a tortoise, a lion, and an owl in every size and persuasion. The potter's wife is English and forty. We eye each other narrowly. She likes us. Would we meet her husband and assess her Dresden coffee service? We follow her down rickety wood stairs to the studios below. The air is stiff with grey dust, the floors deep in wood shavings, toppled pots of paint, and the other accoutrements of an idiosyncratic workshop. An assortment of unbaked big bears and little bears wait their turn in the rubble for the kiln.

Jill Ratel's husband, Dominique, is half-French, half-Danish, a serene good-looking man. He sits authoritatively behind his wheel. The Dresden coffee service – eighteenth- or nineteenth-century? That is the question. They lead us to the garden, down steep stone steps smothered in wild mallow. We enter a small sitting-room; dark and tidy, it feels dead after the congenial clutter of the studio. The Dresden coffee service with its fanciful cake plates is pronounced nineteenth-century and not to be sniffed at. The hand-painted pieces are ranged on a low table when a burly, brindled dog thrusts into the little room, an alarmingly large dog, suggesting some variation of a rottweiler. I am appalled. He noses towards us. Will he smell my fear? He is swooshed out by the potters; his tail could swipe out their entire Dresden inheritance. A scuffle at the door and two little boys (Algerian, adopted?) appear. 'Our two sons,' beams Jill and under no visible compunction to explain. Again the rottweiler bundles in behind. The sturdier of the two boys hurls his entire body over the dog's broad rumpled back. He tells me with fearless conviction that he wants to be a '*chasseur*'. His brother, taller, slender and with a diffident manner, assures me he will be a '*jardinier*'. Says his mother, 'he is the dreamer'. She shrugs in mock despair as she indicates his pullover slipped on back to front.

Encouraged by Tom's undeniable ability to value Dresden, the couple lead us on to a poky dining-room. What does he make of this glass-panelled cupboard? It appears a rough rendition of Art Nouveau. The carved and nosed wood-scrolling embraces the two glazed doors. Their glass panels are an opaque beer bottle brown. It looks crude and utterly original.

Tom is lost. What an extraordinary object to be confronted with. Dominique believes it has been made by Gauguin. Some crazy supposition? He explains how his Danish grandmother was engaged to Gauguin's son. The marriage never materialised, but the cupboard did. Tom is suitably astonished. Have they more Gauguin memorabilia tucked away? Drawings by the *grand maître* of his family are produced with faded ochre photographs. Tom adjusts the focus on his Canon camera and in the fading evening light records the assembled finds for Christie's. He tells our friend that their cupboard could be worth £30.

May 1

South of Montélimar, the flat fields beside the Rhône are cushioned with lavender, soft rounded clumps of green, hugging the soil like hedgehogs in convoy. Soon now each bundle will burst in a spray of blue and purple.

To combat the ruinous effect of exquisite French food, we stick to our ruthless rule: *'Rien à manger pour le petit déjeuner!'* A stroll through cobbled streets before lunch, a wander through ruins or a church and you are faint with hunger. You can pass by any attendant beggar with impunity.

We celebrate the revived appetite at L'Escalin, a modest farmhouse notched into the foot of a medieval hill. The village, La Garde Adhémar, crumbles the rounded summit. In our paved courtyard shaded by lime-trees we are promised *'le calme et la gastronomie'*. A sudden gust of the Mistral and a blonde maid flies to the fringed *parapluies*. A purple patch of cloud billows past the orange roof. Now all is calm; a blue and golden peace, warmth in the dappled sun. We select a feast from the absurdly priced 100f menu:

Terrine de langouste et foie gras au Sauterne

Millefeuille de saumon aux morilles

The meal which embraces a comfortable three hours certainly fulfils its promise of tranquillity. We notice the local patrons are happily accustomed to the protracted arrangements. But even the most dutiful grandchildren are rolling between the table legs in the final lap of such marathon feasting. Requests to the blonde to bring us more wine are met with flat uninterest. It transpires that her duties are strictly confined to the table-setting, that she is of halting intelligence, and that her sister is in overall charge. As the two sisters are identical twins it is an awesome hazard to target the right one.

We walk up the winding lane to the village above. Sheep graze the sloping flanks of long swaying grasses and wild cyclamen. We breathe deeply on the cleansing tang of fresh grass, fresh flowers and fresh air; the cuckoo's call is a clarinet on the wing. We gain the cobbled square with its twelfth-century St Michel's church, a simple white stone building village with narrow streets shaded by their walls. There is a sale of local produce in the square. (The proceeds are in aid of a fierce local protest at the threatened route of the '*train grande vitesse*' through this peaceful valley.) Trestle tables set with crisp white cloths are stacked with white cheeses, white asparagus, olive oils, and honey from the forests, honey from the lime-trees, from 'toutes fleurs', and lavender. The honey-seller presides over a large glass case in which a dripping comb is set upon by bees; his village audience looks on reverently. We sit in the pristine simplicity of this sunlit square; to collect idle thoughts is a luxury in time. The church beside us with its conical dome and its stone friezes recalls the vernacular of Caucasian churches. The simple dark interior with its disproportionately high-vaulted ceiling is pierced with brilliant stained-glass slits. In the nearby Chapelle-Musée it is described in a nineteenth-century manuscript: *Dans cette église Oh! Qu'il fait bon prier. On se sent ici Heureux à l'ombre des piliers . . .*

May 3–7

Chez Pic at Valence, the redoubtable Paul Bocuse, and Léon de Lyon: no visit to France can ever be quite complete without sampling the ultimate in her cuisine. In these establishments where standards and traditions are unrivalled, we detect no fall from scrupulous perform-ance; though a diminished clientele reflects the ricochets of recession.

Next through the vineyards of Meursault, Puligny-Montrachet and Volnay, those few prized slopes on which the world depends for its exigent supply of Burgundy. The drystone boundary walls straddle the higher slopes and below on the plains small villages with churches and Gothic steeples cluster protectively. We draw up at Le Montrachet Hotel for the night. Our pristine white bedroom opens on to the Place des Marronniers, a lush green square where shivering chestnuts are clipped like lollipops, croons of mating doves stroke the summer air. An elegant surround of cream stone houses with slated roofs suggests a Cotswold village.

I opt for an early night, a book (James Lees-Milne's entertaining *The Bachelor Duke*) and a bottle of Evian. Tom is not pleased at making my excuses to the proprietor; nor does he find the prospect of navigating another heroic meal any more beguiling.

Three weeks after our encounter with Dominique and Jill Ratel we were at an evening view in Christie's Great Rooms. Noël Annesley (deputy Chairman) came up to me, slapping his pocket. 'Tom's photographs of that strange cupboard are excellent! We think it might be by Gauguin's son. And the drawings all look genuine. We are sending out Guy Jennings to look up your friends. Does Tom often stumble on windfalls down French country lanes?'

On June 17, Christie's 'Impressionist' director, Guy Jennings, returned from his trip chez Ratel, and wrote the following letter:

'Dear Mr and Mrs Ratel, it was a very great pleasure to meet you last week and to see your fascinating group of Gauguin drawings.
I have considered carefully their values in the light of the similar drawings by Gauguin and, bearing in mind their current condition, I would expect them to fetch the following at auction

Heads & Hands	£5,000 – £7,000
Studies of Cows	£2,500 – £3,500
Child in Bed	£8,000 – £12,000

Guy Jennings refers to the other item with little enthusiasm:

The cupboard is a wonderful object but not easy to value and, for the reasons I expressed at the time, I would not expect it to be very valuable at auction.

May 18 Luton House Bedfordshire

We accepted gladly Lucy Phillips's kind invitation to attend the consecration of the recently-restored St Nicholas Chapel at Luton House. We all applauded her spirit. Her husband Nicholas's devastating suicide a few weeks previously was not prejudicing her projects for Luton House. A selective viewing of her newly-assembled Russian rooms was also promised.

Approaching Luton House through the suburban tangle of the North Circular Road and the hideous accretions of Luton town itself, you marvel at such improbable juxtaposition. The handsome gates that terminate a particularly vile 1930 terrace open on to the rolling green vistas, lakes and wooded parkland as initiated by Capability Brown. The house itself, though comparatively small, is pretentious, an ill-conceived mélange of sombre Victorian and grand pilastered Adam. Glazed and mirrored double doors open on pale marble halls and sweeping staircases. The long wide corridors are flanked with tapestried canapés and gilt consoles; brightly-lit ormolu ceiling lanterns induce a nostalgia for palatial European turn-of-the-century hotels. We pass through Victorian lugubrious anterooms to the Chapel and group ourselves on a marble floor. A certain apprehension sets in; will we be standing here long? It is cold, this little chapel. The walls are hung with richly-coloured and decorative paintings of the Russian Royal families. Newly-commissioned icons mask the altar rail, startling in their bold colour and gilding and unattractive to us heretics. A Russian choir, ranged on the gallery above, leads the soft mesmeric chants.

The Bishop, the Most Reverend Anthony of Sourozh, and his black-gowned, bearded retinue parade the corporal cloth with the holy relics up the little aisle to the Sanctuary. Much sprinkling of holy water around the screen of newly-painted icons, a generous tossing of incense (East Indian orange spice?) and a surreptitious stomping of feet and shifting of position on our marble floor. With a final deep-throated invocation to 'Christ, His all pure Mother . . . the holy Tsar and martyr Nicholas, and of the holy martyrs Alexandra, Alexis, Olga, Tatiana, Maria, Anastasia . . .' the Chapel of Saint Nicholas is undeniably conse-crated.

Those of us who have not already crept away to perches along the corridors shuffle from this hour-long vigil as if in a dream. In Lucy Philipps's newly-presented rooms of Pushkin memorabilia and Fabergé treasures, the talk is more topical. Why did Nicholas Phillips gas himself in the Stable Wing? He lost £50 million? (Some would even put it at £100 million.) Lost in his industrial development 'Capability Green'? He was a pronounced depressive? 'It was a shame,' declared the pretty young blonde. 'It was his sense of honour that killed him.' On this assumption of heroics, nobody comments.

The conversation veers to the Orthodox Russian Church. 'It was a shambles at Easter, you know. The Russians have forgotten how to conduct their own church services.' Interjects another Anglo-Russian, 'And they have totally forgotten how to cook their traditional Easter cakes and 'Paskha' [a type of rich curd cheese mixed with candied fruits and almonds; taken with a crisp saffron crust].' Suggests a third,

'You would think in their renewed enthusiasm they would have looked in their old cook books?' 'Oh!' A handsome beauty with soothing Slavic tones ends the exchange. 'I expect they were burnt long ago.'

We stride through the several sets of mirrored doors and find the body of the party complete with band and wines and canapés and cake. We are stationed in the huge brown drawing-room, an ugly room. In a corner stand the extant Grand Duke Vladimir of Russia and his Georgian wife, Grand Duchess Leonida.

June 30 Hardwicke House

Rain and recession have cast a blight on our archetypal summer season. And if Ascot's Royal Enclosure is less full and if White's tent leans more on corporate entertaining – 'honi soit qui mal y pense' – the show will go on to the tune of change and compromise. For every loser there is a winner, the 'name' in Lloyd's who has floundered over his insurance demands (a net loss of £50,000 or more in many cases) is paired with another who bags a respectable cheque. But has Lloyd's lost its credibility? Has the integral gentleman underwriter been totally superseded by his greedy younger brother? Is there complacency in the ranks? An economy of truth and manners? Are future directors to be steered by fingers in the till or on the tiller? Would Lloyd's now appear a cottage industry in the face of the multiple global disasters commensurate with our modern age? 'For whom the Lutine bell tolls', wrote Bernard Levin in his damning piece in this week's *Times*.

But the erratic British rainfall is steadfastly immune to change and compromise. (What a fiasco of a summer we are enduring.) Is it not time to adapt contingency measures? Huddling under rugs and umbrellas at Wimbledon's Centre Court, one feels ashamed; ashamed that these international stars are held to ransom by the British rain. The first week of the tennis tournament this year was a wash-out. As they waited in the wings, these young players became champions of black jack, backgammon and bridge. Something must be done to shelter the Centre Court. A sliding roof? Indeed, should not Wimbledon be totally redesigned?

White's tent at Ascot, with its white silk lining, is superbly self-sufficient, whatever the weather, and it has the added convenience of betting facilities on the premises. It is a sight to relish, club porters in livery tending members and their wives *en grande tenue*. Top hats, some black silk, some grey rabbit, are stacked neatly on a rack; umbrellas are stowed and annotated. You are reminded of those Victorian paintings by George Earl, 'Going North, Kings X Station' and 'Coming South, Perth Station', the platforms crammed with life and luggage as the gentry and their retinue of servants, gamekeepers and dogs set off for the Shooting Season.

Meanwhile, Glyndebourne, another major adornment to the season, has looked to its laurels. In 1989, family Chairman George Christie launched his daunting project for enlargement of the theatre. A mountain of money to the tune of £32.5 million is being steadily realised; the magical power of 'corporate supporters' has been largely instrumental. (A curt line of self-satisfaction from Sir George is included in his 1991 programme foreword: 'Given that our corporate supporters have already pledged an enormous percentage of the capital cost of the rebuild, I can see no justification for any persistent and groundless carping about the Glyndebourne audience being corporately weighted.') And there are those who would wipe out the black tie (de rigueur at Glyndebourne since 1934, the year of its founding by the singer Audrey Mildmay and her husband John Christie).

July 7 Hardwicke House

Last Tuesday, as we dined sumptuously in the gilded candlelit splendour of the Goldsmiths' Hall, our host, Sir Edward Ford, turned to me. After a long life of private service to King George VI and subsequently our Queen, his words had their own sombre value: 'We are heading for the demise of unjustified privilege ... The Queen has been called upon to pay her taxes.' He also divulged that, on a rare visit to the Beefsteak last week, the political journalist, Frank Johnson, cheerfully predicted there would be no more Old Etonian Prime Ministers. The purges of recession are palatable in comparison to this undermining of the establishment. We savoured the endangered scene before us; the gold and glitter, the Prime Warden resplendent in his scarlet gown and medals, and the worshipful company of Goldsmiths. Each lady guest was given a handsome silver Apostle spoon, a generous chip off the old block. We drank champagne, Cockburn's special cuvée NV, Château Plince 1982, and Sandeman 1963.

The sole Balmoral and the fillet of beef Richelieu lent a regal touch to the menu together with the gleam of soft gold, the Lamerie Cup and dish and ewer, the Paul Storr candelabra, and the gold-plated surtout de table with a mirrored base to represent an ornamental lake. (This last, a feat of indeterminate ugliness that stretched down the centre of the table, was masked with ferns and roses.)

The Sainsbury trio have triumphed. Under their ample auspices and an inspired choice of architects, the American Robert Venturi and his wife Denise Scott Brown, the Sainsbury Wing has evolved; an adornment to our national heritage and a prize dimension to our National Gallery. John, The Hon. Simon and The Hon. Timothy MP each invited 200 guests to an inaugural dinner. (Indisputably black tie.) Their respective invités encompassed the great and the good from all walks of life; it was an exceptional party. Princess Margaret headed a small Royal contingent; she swept to her seat in a peacock-green cloak, her piled hair as smooth and polished as a chestnut; her ex-husband the Earl of Snowdon looked pale and diminutive seated in a diagonally opposite corner of the room. (At a subsequent small country lunch party he made unfavourable comments on the lighting effects of the new gallery.) For those of us uninitiated in the finer points of architecture and lighting, the building was superb. The spacious entrance hall with its curved stone walls, a fine flight of stone stairs, the rises rough, the treads polished. On the stone wall alongside are incised the names Mantegna, Bellini, Leonardo, Raphael – all to prepare you for the riches to come. A warm, Renaissance-style grey is the prevailing background colour on walls and arches. The recessed ceiling lighting is unobtrusive, geared principally to daylight effects. The space conveyed by the uncluttered hanging of pictures and the peace induced by the aisle of rounded arches both soothes and stimulates. Edwin Lutyens, already credited as a source of inspiration to the architect, would have approved these arches; he always insisted that 'one cannot tinker with a round arch' and that God did not make a rainbow pointed.

This newly-hung collection of two hundred pictures dating from 1260 to 1510 are Italian in the majority with a few French and Flemish. They are predominantly religious and are in sympathy with their new church-style accommodation. Grey marble (pietra dura) was imported from Florence to line the arches and to make up the bold Doric pillars that secure the corner walls. These solid structures are polished smooth as satin. But it was in the Piero della Francesca room 66 that irresistibly my eye was caught: the glorious tableau 'The Baptism' distinctly portrays a young man scantily clad in Y-front pants, in the act of stripping off his white sweatshirt. I should add that he is not the central figure of this magnificent masterpiece. From the copious widely-favourable reviews of this new Sainsbury Wing there must be one observation that strikes a special chord in most of us: Richard Dorment's review in the *Daily Telegraph* included the line, 'I look forward to the rainy winter afternoons when these galleries will be islands of calm and peace in the heart of London.'

There were many more parties to keep the Season afloat. Parties that dodged the rain in gardens of Elizabethan topiary, pleached hornbeam walks, avenues of sharp sweet limes and the tumbling profusion of pastel roses and the seclusion of a slate-laid veranda with cool tubs of lavender and the scent of swaying lilies. But it is Colin Haycraft's leaving lunch party that clings to the memory; Chairman of Duckworth since 1971, he was relinquishing his long-established premises at the Old Piano Factory in Camden for new offices. A motley assembly of professors, authors and publishers converged on the scene – dirty, dark and desecrated in its recent abandonment. And where was Colin's wife? The legendary satirist Alice Thomas Ellis? (I had been told that she takes up her corner and guests make their obeisance.) Colin manfully dispensed drink and cake and sandwiches, he hid his disappointment at her non-arrival with aplomb; she rarely came to his parties anyway, despite the proximity of their Georgian terraced home down the hill. 'If anybody sees Anna in the street, just ask her if she lost her way.' Later we saw her. As the party dwindled, my brother Stephen took me to the Haycraft home.

There she stood, the indomitable author of the *Spectator*'s 'Home Life' column and other acclaimed literary gems. She stood propped by her bottle-green Aga, a luminous white neck with head held high, the rest swathed in black crêpe to reveal a generous décolletage and sturdy maternal arms. A beautiful face in which eyes glittered in triumph over tragedy, one sensed a mind and spirit finely chiselled by perception. She blamed her absence from Colin's party on a sore bottom; a recent trip to Poland. We did not stay long, seated like voyeurs of 'home life' at the scrubbed pine kitchen table. It is there she sits to write in a minute neat hand that runs without correction.

July 13 Widcombe Manor Bath Somerset

A neat, incisive man with sparse strands of hair carefully combed, and shoes well polished. His talk succinct and deftly sprayed with wit and anecdote, he is a past master of gauging his audience, holding the attention with that timely delay of dénouement. He is Kenneth Rose[2], the exponent for thirty years of 'Albany at Large' in the *Sunday Telegraph*, the biographer of Royalty and other superior persons.

We are grouped in the drawing-room, drinks in hand, waiting for James Lees-Milne[3] and his wife Alvilde to arrive for lunch. Kenneth bemoans the length of Bob Boothby's new biography by Robert Rhodes James. He has been reviewing it all morning. 'Far too long;

[2] In 1997, Kenneth Rose received his CBE.
[3] In that same year, James Lees-Milne died.

nearly 500 pages. Good biographies are never long.' At breakfast his proof sheet of tomorrow's 'Albany' column had arrived. 'Rushed through the night on the Bath train,' he assured us with a certain relish. He handed a slip to Tom who gave it a cursory glance.

The crunch of gravel and our hostess, the Hon. Mrs Robin Warrender, stiffened a little and stowed her glass. The dogs preceded her to the small marble hall with that exquisitely-turned mahogany staircase. Oh! The sadness of the grey, cold day. Alvilde Lees-Milne is a gardening expert. She steps briskly to the bowed French windows and looks out with satisfaction on the manicured terraces of velvet green, gravel walks and urns and ponds, clipped corridors of yew and beech, secluded seats and a brace of sphinxes with their snubbed noses buried in santolina. Alvilde, an indeterminate shape in her long loose skirt, now gazes intently at the exuberant foreground of pink and apricot roses, the spray of pale potentilla, the blue flurry of silesia and lavender and campanula and everywhere the elegant eighteenth-century urns in a halo of geranium and verbena.

James Lees-Milne is in stark contrast to his plump, ebullient wife. A tall and elegant man with a long spare body entombed in tweed. He looks grave under his fuzzy rim of grey hair and a shade distrait; his erudite mind on a more compelling foray than the immediate conversation? Or has he just sent his cufflinks to the laundry? We later all agree that James Lees-Milne OBE should have been better honoured for his life-long commitment to the National Trust and his prodigious literary and architectural output. 'James wrote miraculous books on architectural history,' Kenneth's stout affirmation breaks the conversation and it occurs to us that he, Kenneth, might like a knight-hood also. But he is now bent on decrying the Garrick Club. 'Too many actors . . .' He repairs to an afternoon nap with Bob Boothby.

The climax of this harmonious weekend evolved and was immedi-ately dissolved around today's breakfast table. The *Sunday Telegraph* arrived with my beautifully-appointed breakfast tray. I turned straight to Kenneth's 'Albany' column. And there it was! A blunder! Kenneth had blundered! I shuddered for his despair and angst. (It is remarkable how often you perceive blaring inaccuracies in print if the subject is known to you.) Kenneth referred to Ditchley, the house bought by Ronald Tree in 1933: 'Whose American wife, Marietta . . . used her own considerable taste to restore the dilapidated house to its eigh-teenth-century glory.' Marietta married Ronnie Tree, as his second wife in 1947. It was of course the redoubtable decorator-designer, Nancy, his first wife, who did the stylish honours at Ditchley. I alerted Tom to the mishap as he went down to breakfast; Tom alerted our host. After broad deliberation, Robin ruled that nothing should be said to Kenneth for fear of upsetting his entire Sunday, and everybody else's.

July 27 Udny Castle Aberdeenshire

Glorious sun in north-east Scotland. Like prisoners in *Fidelio*, we step out to a hidden paradise of walled gardens, green cool salons, hedged with yew and sunken courtyards of pools and roses.

'*O welche lust!*'

Maggie's kitchen garden is a brilliant stage of order and colour. The tenderest fruits are splayed on brick walls – apricots and white-fleshed peaches. Sturdy greens are locked in soil. Scarlet nasturtium streams down the tall yew divides, with fine iron gates closed on the park beyond. Blackcurrants, redcurrants and white, and the broadest beds of strawberries, tautly netted, the juicy red noses poke through billowing straw. (Always best eaten warmed by the sun; each tooth is drenched in the sweet red nectar.)

The Scots make hay with their elusive sun. A cricket pitch is hurriedly mown in place; a tennis net is set up on the front lawn; neighbours converge on the action; al fresco meals are cooked on the barbecue. And birds' mess – untended through a sodden summer – scrubbed from garden chairs and tables. Everywhere there are pleas to everybody to visit gardens, as never seen in sun before.

July 28 Esslemont Ellon Abderdeenshire

A note flaps on the iron-studded castle door: 'Walk through the wicket gate in yew hedge. Pass greenhouse on your left, turn into rose garden with the weeping pear . . .'

From the imminent severe contours and the blunt green surrounds we enter another world. The wicket gate opens to a fantasy of flowers and secret vistas. We meander down paths, through grassy closets, Alice in Wonderland would feel at home.

A sudden squeal and our hostess, Rosemary Wolrige Gordon, streaks down a distant border, her low-scooped sundress topped by a scarlet hat, and two old labradors tearing close behind.

'I'm getting borage for your Pimms!' She shrieks through a screen of flame crocosmia. Next we come across her Captain, Robert. In a frail greenhouse with an outer layer of wilting Russian vine he has his drinks table well in order to include a generous stock of gin.

'Did you see the Bishop of Durham on his way? And Lady Aberdeen with her granddaughter, Alice?' It transpires that Lady Aberdeen of Haddo House is bringing her house-party, the notorious Bishop and his wife, Mrs Jenkins, and a certain Mrs Bruce. Rosemary rejoins us, clutching borage to her bosom.

The Bishop startles us as he rounds a bush in an aertex shirt and freckled forearms; he is relaxed and agreeably non-committal. The sun is a sedative to provocative thought. He merely proclaims that the Government is living in the nineteenth century. Nobody disagrees. It is Alice who now takes the floor. Alice is a down-syndrome girl of nineteen; a happy, squat girl, she has a ready smile and a remarkable intelligence. We talk of dogs and horses. Which animal does she find the more intelligent? The horse? Why? 'Because he neighs when he sees you coming; the dog just wags his tail.' Does this garden remind her of Alice in Wonderland too? Now Alice recalls the scene of that other Alice falling asleep on a summer day, as her sister reads her a story. Whereupon, the Mrs Bruce, a handsome, substantial lady in nasturtium linen, comments: 'This could all be compared to the Mad Hatter's Tea Party!' I ask Mrs Bruce what moral lies behind that tea party. 'Oh! Getting on with strange neighbours,' she says airily.

Our valiant host is in and out of the stifling greenhouse, attending to the Pimms, perhaps he allows himself the odd gratuitous sip.

August 22 Chillingham Castle Alnwick Northumberland

Sebastian and I drive an hour through rugged inland country. Harvested cornfields, woods, blue distant hills and purple peaks and moorland, stretching high above and beyond, an arresting country with capricious contours. At Chillingham we leave the car by the thirteenth-century parish church of St Peter. The dark woods behind, thick with beech and oak and fir, are forbidding. But the snug interior of St Peter's is cheerful with flowers and freshly-made Seville marmalade at £1 a pot. Sir Ralph Grey (died 1443) and his wife, Lady Elizabeth, lie prone in the Lady Chapel, their upturned patrician profiles an admirable gift to posterity.

Up a sloping dirt path we find the warden's cottage. Two tickets to see the White Cattle? The warden's wife looks doubtful. 'If it rains, mind you, they go back in the woods and you have to come back another day.' She points us to the steep rocky track up through the woods. 'After a mile you will find the warden, in his shed, waiting.' And the cattle?

The Wild White Cattle of Chillingham have existed for at least 700 years with a fiercely-maintained independence. Continuous interbreeding has carried no ill-effects; each calf is pure white with the rare distinction of red 'fox fur' lining to the ears. The warden is a lean and lanky man. He walks us through a field divided by a fine row of ancient beech-trees. We adjust our binoculars. A cluster of sheep on the hill beyond? 'People always think they look like sheep!' The warden sounds bored and disparaging. He jerks his head, 'Look to your right!' In a dip barely ten feet away, sit three bulls with their backs to us. Their hefty rumps and widely-splayed horns look most alarming. 'They won't hurt,' says our cavalier warden. 'They have been fighting each other all morning, now they're taking a break.' We approach the hill and the 'sheep' metamorphose into cattle. Our friend urges us to note the red lining to the ears and the distinctive lyre formation of the female horns. How many are there? 'About fifty all told. They dropped down to just eight cows and five bulls in that hard winter of 1947. We had snowdrifts of forty feet in the park, then the Foot and Mouth outbreaks in 1967 stopped just two miles off the park. We can't trust to fortune again. A reserve herd has got set up in Scotland.' On the horizon behind us we see more visitors nearing the three imperturbable bulls. Our audience with the intrepid warden is up. Back at his shed an original letter form Charles Darwin is printed on a beam. The ink is unsmeared, despite this rudimentary shelter, open to the winds. (He thanks the renowned Chillingham estate for sending him a skull from their famous White herd.)

We have a lunch date at the School House, on the estate. Our host, Henry Potts[4], has also invited Sir Humphry Wakefield, present owner and inveterate restorer of Chillingham Castle. Victoria Wakefield, Humphrey's sister-in-law, joins us from her family home at nearby Howick Gardens. She is a keen gardener and admires Henry's bright clumps of colour; a collected profusion includes blue agapanthus, flame crocosmia, phoebe and lavender, that crowds his borders and screens the sun terrace with shade and scents. The idyllic scene of sunhats, wine and horticultural exchange is soon shattered by an irate tractor driver; the sudden intrusion of cars has barred his entry up the lane. Next, our labradors are seen spraying Henry's lettuces. (Henry's vegetable garden is second only to a Beatrix Potter model in all its exquisite order and prize produce.) Tobias and Joss are promptly locked in the car; their disgrace is doubly reprehensible after the trouble Henry had taken in giving them an enormous bowl of water; an unfortunate return. The five of us lunch in Henry's brilliant pea-green kitchen; a

[4] Exhibits in Fine Art Fairs across the country and in London; an enviable collection of architectural drawings and paintings of period houses.

home-grown, home-cooked lunch, with the crowning achievement of an apricot pie.

We spend the afternoon wading pleasurably through Humphry's ongoing restoration of Chillingham Castle. (He bought it seven years ago when it had lain abandoned since 1933.) The thirteenth-century foundations appear to have stabilised with the seventeenth century; the inner stone quadrangle is adorned with pillars and statues in various degrees of disrepair; dungeons curl off into the damp and dark beyond. A flight of stone steps leads up to the Great Hall while a central inner turret of stairs winds to salons and bedrooms above. The castle is restored rather than decorated. The public are pouring in. Two electricians with a clutch of cable say they are having a field day in such virgin territory. Over a cup of tea in the vast servants' hall, we meet Humphry's gardener; a pretty girl in jeans called Isobel Murray. Victoria is on full alert; she and Isobel have exchanged notes all afternoon. The Italian Gardens, as laid out by Windsor Castle's mentor Sir Jeffrey de Wyattville in 1828, are now faithfully re-established. Humphrey, his racing mind sharpened on a million points, ushers us out to admire his faux-lead urns and statuary. 'But I'd like to show you the lake!' he exclaims. His energies seem hell-bent on a sprint through the woods. I dissuade him. Sebastian and I wander through the trees to the wooden bridge and lake beyond. A slab of silver with green and gold lies tremulous in the evening light; no leaf stirs, no reed, no bird, no fish. Humphry's lake is locked in the still of the evening. A single scarlet rhus bush reflects its ruby badge, a bright talisman to his endeavour.

September 6 Halas Göcek South Turkey

Breakfast under the deck canopy: fat black olives, white cheese, tomatoes streaming juice, the stickiest jams – peach and fig and cherry. And would we like pine honey this morning? Or orange honey? Earl Grey tea? Or 'English Breakfast'?

'Today, we will sail,' murmurs our hostess. The canopy flips encouragingly. Idly we gaze on blue, blurred mountains and sniff the pinewoods that circle and crowd the sea. We are cocooned in the peace and warmth of this sapphire womb, in this intimate, stylishly-contrived harbour that is Göcek.

Our stately vessel, *Halas* (Salvation), is a sumptuously-converted steamer built in 1911. For fifty years she ploughed the Bosphorus from shore to shore, laborious and slow, laborious and slow; passengers groaned to see her come. Now she is so heavily endowed with chattels and bibelots and the elegant trappings of a rarefied life that she is spared any active service. 'We will sail . . .' indicates we will transfer to the three-masted schooner *Melek* (Angel) and chug between the myriad islands of Fethiye, those emerald corrals of pine, black goats and donkeys; each the exclusive playpen of a rich man and lapped by indulgent deep, blue waters.

Our hostess Çiğdem (Simavi), diminutive and beautiful, exudes a false languor. She manipulates her crew, her guests, her family, her wines and food, and her fax with sleek command; she is shot with steel. The tilt of her pert profile and raised slender hand, an imperceptible murmur and instantly more bread and wine appear, or more light, more shade, more speed, more peace, more anything.

Melek under sail is a myth. It is years since her sails were unfurled; there is a fear that mice have nibbled right through. Her top decks are glossed in banana-cream. On the lower open saloon deck, deep sofas are piled with soft, large cushions, wool rugs, magazines. In such comfortable clutter you are persuaded to curl up for hours. Lit up at night, *Melek* is superb; her 200-foot black hull is lost to the sea, with her masts and rigging exquisitely webbed against the arc of the night sky. Ethereal, detached, a puff of gossamer on a black velvet screen.

We are nearing Belma's island. Belma is Çiğdem's sister-in-law. Belma is pretty, pink and plump. She wears a pink dress and has curly, copper hair. Her house accentuates her pinkness by being pink outside. She ushers us inside; blinking from the sun we still see pink. The garden chairs and tables used to be white; but their whiteness glared so aggressively that they were also painted pink. Everybody agrees that pink is perfection. We eat lobster on Belma's sloping lawn which is green.

September 8 Antalya to Termessos

A comfortable night at the Marina Hotel; a sophisticated reflection of ten years of tourism. An elegant plant-festooned courtyard with a pristine pool and dining area surrounded by comfortable cane chairs, crisp linen, flowers, and candles. Waiters in black tie give impeccable service in impeccable English. They flourish matches and menus with timely aplomb. Atatürk would have been proud. His urgent exhortations to his countrymen to join the international bandwagon have now materialised; a triumphant emergence through fifty years of pain and progress. (A leashed brown bear rises on its haunches in the street outside. Old traditions die hard.)

Leaving the coastline and its sensational beauty, unspoilt still, we drive to the foothills of Termessos. Here the mountains rise to 3,000 feet. The original King's Road (Kral Yolu) is reduced to a rocky dirt track. But was it ever paved with gold? Up through the steep wooded gorge we climb high and higher, where the wind whines and lopes through birch, pine, and ash and hollow crags and quarries. We soon gain the stronghold settlement and potter through scorched scrub and thistles, through stillness, bees, and butterflies.

Monolithic windows and temple doorways gape on burning blue sky to the distant peaks and tumbled valleys of millennia. Here in 500 BC the Termessians claimed their pitch. A fierce and warlike band from North Pamphylia, they survived on olive crops and honey. Today the toppled agora and gymnasium, the remarkably intact theatre (to seat 4,200), stand witness to a pleasurable, though precarious, life. This unique blend of position, ferocious possession, and plunder held fast for ten centuries. Not even Alexander the Great could breach this bastion. In 333 BC he had massed his army on all approaches and stormed the city gates. The heavy walls and portals crashed down on warriors and horses, hurling them to death. After several days of fruitless fighting, Alexander, depleted and humbled, bayed to the impassive mountains: 'Let me be. I still have a long way to go. I cannot permit my armies to be decimated before a falcon's crest.'

Through the blue and gold of this serene summer morning, Termessos is haunted still. In the Necropolis each toppled tomb has a story none now cares to know; a ransacked parade of death and dignity and dreams. 'What's it all about? For a thousand years our people fought and built and lived and loved!' Termessos is a shrine to man, to his motivations and his meaning, his victories, his struggles, and his final defeats, his surrender to the march of time, to the ravages of nature and her green embrace. His dust returned to the dust of all before.

Back in the valleys we drive through apple orchards, vines and olives. Black cows and black goats sleep in the shade of the mountains by dried river beds nursed by wilting willow. 'The rains come December.' We skirt a vast lake; Egridir (he is spinning), and find a solitary café on the shore. A bottle of red Doluca on a red gingham check cloth, scarlet tomatoes, omelettes and a bowl of lapping blue before. Three more hours to Konya, through the stubbled steppes of Central Anatolia; a blanket of faded gold thrown over miles, here and there barred black with burning. We approach Konya through the evening sun; huge, rounded grazing slopes undulate and dip to the town below. The encircling rocks glow red and pink and aubergine; precursors to Cappadocia.

September 9 Konya

Konya in the heart of the Central Anatolian plateau takes a back seat in the tourist stakes. The city's traditional charm and intrinsic identity is preserved accordingly. A shrine of Islam and of Persian twelfth-century Seljuk architecture, Konya boasts an exquisite mosque – the Mevlana Tekke. Today, more a museum, to the Whirling Dervish creed, the vaulted interior is cluttered with the tombs of renowned performers. Their sculptured silk turbans and long white winding scarves are placed on board each chest. A rich variety of coloured lanterns, enamelled, gilded and exuding burning spice, hang in festive profusion. Open manuscripts of the Koran, leather-bound tomes, and brocaded textiles suggest an exclusive and secular museum. Outside, an elegant marble fountain is crammed with dunked feet and faces.

It is a dusty town, set in its loop of distant mountains. With the evening calls to prayer we are pleased to sink in a bath; a genuine zinc bath, deep and wide. This best hotel is cheap and clean; supper is adequate – white fish, white rice, white cheese, white wine.

'Ankara has passed us by with any money hand-out,' confides a rug-dealer. He sells us a silk cotton Soumak (woven yesterday) for £200.

September 10

Each morning our driver, Sabu, scrumples his newspaper and rubs the windscreen clean. We reach Göreme early evening. That quiet, green valley, as remembered in May 1983, is now scarred by a long, hot summer and a tourist invasion. Germans crowd us everywhere as do the French. The grass is scorched and balding in the dust. And are the frescoes faded? Listlessly we sit sipping apple tea. (Contemplating Cappadocia at the end of a long day is not to be recommended.)

September 11 Cappadocia

The road to the Ihlara valley is a familiar panorama of arable plains of wheat and sugar beet; hills swell up at the village of Selimye and loom and tumble into abandoned gorges. At Yaprak Hisar (leafy fortress) the rising mounds of lunar strata are streaked red and black with rock and basalt. We pass red-brick farmsteads, horses, cows, and donkeys. Poplars ruffle streams, girls and grandmothers steer laden donkeys. Pretty young women, poised and sturdy, with warmth in their black eyes, wear full bright shirts; white, soft scarves tucked under chins like balaclavas.

In the heat of the mid-morning we stumble down four hundred steps to the floor of the valley. The Melendiz river is shrunk with sun; like a restless green snake it winds, blue butterflies, one sleek donkey. We are alone in the Ihlara valley; yet it teems with life. These Byzantium rock churches still emanate a living fervour. Scooped-out lairs of secret worship once provided escapes from religious persecution. Little rounded naves and altars. Extant shrines since one thousand years! How to restore these primitive frescoes? How to save and secure them? Mercifully there are countless hidden churches in this valley preserved by inaccessibility. (French voices we hear today, no Germans.) That steep descent does not ingratiate itself with their bulk, and boulders by the riverbank are crazily poised in barriers of embrace. The English? They race like lemmings to the sea and sand and tiger prawns and yachts.

On a single veranda balanced high on the edge of this rock valley, we eat grilled chicken and drink the local wine. (The red is dyed, they say.) The dispirited waiter bemoans 'slow season' induced by the international recession. 'Many few tourists this year. Many, many few.' We assure him he will soon be rich and busy beyond compare; package tours have now permission to land jumbo air-buses at Kayseri! This trickle through Cappadocia will soon be a watershed! We leave our friend weighing up the perplexing alternatives of prosperity or peace.

The rustic mores of these valley villages recall Georgia and Ladakh. Squat stone cottages, their flat roofs smothered with hay; red and yellow peppers and bundled herbs, cluster eaves and windows; courtyards are heaped with walnuts for shelling, pearl onions, and chopped wood; the colourful family wash stretched to dry on the stone wall; the tethered donkey, the screech and cluck of pecking hens.

Güzel Yurt (beautiful land) is a web of winding alleyways, where far below I see a settlement scooped out of rock – a cave with a blue-painted door and two windows, a courtyard with gouged cavities for wood and fruit and vegetables. I lean on the rough wall above and stare down shamefully. A boy darts out and eyes me sharply: 'Kiz,' he yells to the nether regions. ('Kiz' means girl as opposed to 'Kadın' for woman; I am flattered.) His older sister now appears. She is pretty and welcoming. 'Buyurün!' she calls up to me (welcome). I walk down to them across the rocks. She speaks no English. I admire her courtyard, her long billowing red skirt, her naked feet and slender brown toes, unblemished in their film of dust, her black, bright eyes and ruby cheeks. She insists I enter her large seven-foot-high rectangular rock room. It is painted sky-blue and strewn with bright rugs. I prise off my dusty shoes before venturing on this immaculate scene. The only item of furniture is a large black and white television. The reception is excellent and the girl's father is engrossed with the flashing screen. Her mother works in the fields, she tells me. In between our halting confidences my little friend repeatedly promises me tea. Finally I take my leave. The enthusiastic offers of tea never materialise and I fear that Tom might think I have gone native. ('Watching TV in a cave?' He is incredulous.)

September 12

We head for the Soganli Valley and the eighteenth-century Keşlik monastry along a quiet country road with the familiar strings of donkeys and peasant women ferrying sacks of corn and pumpkins and sugar beet and babies. At Mustafapasa old men in dark suits and trilbies sit and stare and drink sweet tea and raki and fling dice at backgammon boards. Here is a village of Greek provenance where the nineteenth-century carved stone façades denote that characteristic and elegant reserve.

The valley is cool and green and rustles with fig-trees, pistachio, poplar, and willow-trees; the sun has bleached the hot plains white. In spring this land is emerald. Refreshed from heavy snow and tumbling water, it is re-stitched anew in a tapestry of flowers. Here we are enveloped by tufaceous rock forms – the pink and ochre flanks, the red and mauve and black – a crazy cavalcade of that hapless volcanic cavorting of 4,000 years ago. And, in these sprawling, pyramidal tufa ranges, many eke out their lives and home today.

At the monastery a watchman steps out from the shade of a fig-tree. ('He no busy. Afternoon come busy with big buses. He show treasure He speak German, Japan, Italia, French. Yes, he speak no English.') He abandons his makeshift desk, a rickety table with a rug thrown over and leads us up a grass path. A straggle of stone and rock with gaping black orifices that lunge to the bowels of the mountains confronts us. This eighth-century monastery reveals the most credible illustration of that arcane and flourishing community life. The refectory with its sunken groove for the long plank table, the stone bench seats beside, the smoke-blackened niches for the oil lamps, and the scooped storage alcoves for wines and food, all denote a certain convivial good living. The kitchen with bread ovens and arched ceilings, blackened from centuries of roasting and baking, is joined to the refectory by an underground passage; today it is blocked by a millstone. An adjoining frescoed church appears totally blackened also. Had the excessive catering demands of the day requisitioned it for extra roasting? Our watchman is shocked at such irreverence. These frescoes were blacked out by iconoclasts, he insists, and leads us, hastily, to another church, where a colourful frolic of dragons and serpents and pendulous bunches of grapes busily assist a flight to Egypt and the Angel Gabriel. Our appreciation of frescoes now suitably redressed, we are rewarded with the wine press and the cellar. The arched alcoves in this porous volcanic stone generate the perfect temperature for wine storage.

We stumble out into the midday sun and admire our friend's vegetable garden. Another bequest from the eighth century? He hands us sprigs of mint and proudly indicates his swelling pumpkins, his apricots. Will we take his black grapes? He reaches to a vine which has entangled itself with an apple branch. We leave him, mute and diminutive in the shade of his fig-tree. Is he bored and lonely? He is shocked (yet again) at our stupidity. With all this quiet and loveliness? He straightens himself with an air of resolve and reminds us – 'Afternoon come busy with big buses!'

September 13 The Hilton Istanbul

We fly from Kayseri to Istanbul. We liked Kayseri; a prosperous, industrial city with sturdy black rock avenues, cushioned by parks and trees and flowered parterres. 'Many snows make green city.' And many jumbo air packages are poised to make an extremely rich city. (Today the modest airport could barely cope with a mere thirty people.)

Istanbul, 4 pm: the Bosphorus trails a sash of blue below our window. It lures us outside to the streets and smells of evening. Taksim Square and rough, rich whiffs of tobacco, shoe polish, sweet buns and sweat. Down many steps, narrow alleys with cheap, bold, little shops, down past stern nineteenth-century somnolent villas with grimy walls. Now we reach the hectic mêlée of the Galata bridge where salt breezes joust with whiffs of mackerel, baking sweet-corn and walnuts and the vendors' yelling. Between the bulging cartloads of grapes and peas and figs and apples, eddies of garish litter dance in the wind. A rumbustious, jostling scene where people still shout and sweat and sell and bargain and live through another day.

December 20 Hardwicke House

It is refreshing to read the obituary of Henry Harpur-Crewe, 'the squire of Calke in Derbyshire'. 'This shy, private man . . . his brother Charles died suddenly while setting mole traps in the park . . . His only confidant was his head gamekeeper, one Agathos Pegg, who would accompany him in his pursuit of birds and butterflies.' No motorcar or bicycle was allowed in the grounds. 'Visitors had to park at the gates and were then collected by carriage.' Henry's heir is his sister, Miss Airmyne Harpur-Crewe.

The recession has bitten holes in every purse. Few private parties this side of Christmas but plenty of corporate ones, charity dinners, balls, and concerts; evening views at museums and art galleries: all to advertise and to cajole; to lure patronage from its substantial hearth and to part promptly with its fortune. Tasteful, delectable bonnes-bouches on silver trays, Californian champagne, the glow of generous gilding, rich paintings, covetable old glass and porcelain, more canapés and wine and smiles and slick exposés on this rare piece and that and the pure glass grandfather clock to end them all.

It was such an evening when Partridge's Fine Arts, Mallett, Richard Green, and S J Phillips, the antique silver and jewellery dealers, held an open evening in New Bond Street on Wednesday December 11. A pub crawl? A street party? It was a fascinating scene, reminding one of that game 'Sardines' when all are lured to a secret, prized place. Clearly S J Phillips held the accolade. Their door opened on a scenario of full-length furs and chic coiffures crooning over glass vitrines. Men in tweed coats cast a wary eye over this sumptuous spread of stones. Everywhere, before, beside, and above, the glazed coffers pulsated with the coaxing cascade of jewels – pendant necklaces, chokers, cameos, stick pins, cluster rings, jewelled combs, étuis, earrings, brooches, and bracelets. Rich flairs of colour sparkled in cabochon amethysts and emeralds and rubies, enveloped by diamond circles and diamond bombes and diamond 'half-eternity' rings.

Martin Norton, the arch octogenarian Godfather of this rich man's parlour, retreats to a corner, quietly curling his generous lips. And now he comes forward and sits in the raised chair (where the man who polishes silver sits by day), set in the middle of the room like a throne. His two sons and his nephew – charming, good-looking 'boys' in their fourth decade – man the treasure troughs with a flourish. They pronounce and probe and flaunt and fasten round necks and wrists until whims are resolved. The sleek, susceptible heads nod and turn, reflecting from side to side; their men feel hot and trapped in their tweed and cashmere and lapsed hair-cuts. The Godfather beams at this evening's clientele as a seasoned fisherman would appraise an exceptional catch: the Tavistocks, the Spencers, the Knight of Glin, and the statuesque Lady Wimborne (who once adventurously observed 'you never know who will come out of the lift'). Martin Norton prattles indulgently: 'He's a nice boy, Robin, a nice boy. We had a nice little evening with him and Henrietta last night.'

In the end small room that displays the Russian objects, with his bulky back to this scene, sits Earl Spencer. An empty table with a white damask cloth supports him in his vigil. Raine, rigged fore and aft in flounced black taffeta, her hair in sculptured waves, bounds up and kisses him good night. 'She's off to the Garrick,' he explains to me with a rueful smile. 'The only woman at some committee dinner, you know.' I sit beside him. He is always the most gentle and humble of men, all pink and white and mildly befuddled in his black tie. 'Where will you have dinner?' I ask him. 'My man will take me to my club. Perhaps I will even pick somebody up here.' We both laugh and again his smile is rueful.

1992

Dark fell early last Friday, with a grimy fog sprawled over the moon. Despite the murk first impressions of Buscot Park were grand enough. The drive swept up through a park of winter-stripped lime and oak-trees, swirling to a halt before the gold stone façade. An imposing flight of steps led to the glazed front door, a happy substitute for the original heavy Victorian porch demolished by the 2nd Lord Faringdon in 1934.

We rang the bell. The empty hall blazed with light and gilded Regency pieces in the Egyptian taste. We walked in, to silence. Massive porphyry pillars met the ceiling in a crunch of white-icing Ionic scrolls. A light step and our hostess, Sarah Faringdon. She ferried us along a broad corridor of waxed flagstones to a library. The scent of white hyacinth and jasmine, a bright fire, deep sofas and book-lined walls were the perfect antidotes to a fog-bound journey from London. A mournfully pretty woman peered up at us through a tent of red hair. She got up stiffly from a stool to be introduced by Sarah as her cousin. The Carew Poles from Cornwall were also staying.

The Pre-Raphaelite Room was designated to Tom and me, together with an elegant dressing-room en suite, and two large bathrooms. 'There are sixteen bathrooms in the house,' said Sarah. We try to use them all to circulate the water. By Sunday it should be running clear instead of all whisky-coloured.'

I was reminded of eighteen-year-old Maud Sambourne, when expounding the luxuries of Buscot in 1893: 'My own darling Mother oh my goodness what a place!!!!!!!![1] You never saw anything to equal it under the sun – no never because I never have!!!!!!!! My room is much too much for me to describe – Electric light all over my room and I have amused myself by turning it all on at once. It's on over my bed so that I shall be able to see to read and no trouble striking a match.'

Five years later Maud married Leonard Messel. Their son, the stage designer Oliver Messel, was destined to create the theatre in Buscot's east wing.

For all the elegance and high-ceilinged grandeur of its decorative

---

[1] From Shirley Nicholson's *A Victorian Household, based on the diaries of Maud Sambourne* (published 1988).

rooms, Buscot is essentially a family home where children, friends, and dogs feel easy. The front façade, well-mounted on its hill, blazed gold in Saturday's sun; the distinctive, cream-painted lambrequins glistened above each window. The pellucid sky of that winter afternoon, with a faint moon wavering through the cedar-tree, cast a gilded tableau.

We were sixteen for dinner in the unashamedly scarlet dining-room. ('Looks like an Indian eating house,' said Charley, the 3rd Lord Faringdon.) We were to change. 'Black tie' is now interpreted by most women as short cocktail dresses. The men and the maids and butlers looked the more distinguished in their black and white. Mrs Carew Pole was neat in black all over. A petite, good-looking woman, she is a sometime lady-in-waiting to the Princess Royal. But with her spectacles and her total lack of make-up, she makes little of her appearance. Her Royal commitments have perhaps inured her to fade into the background. The mournful cousin, meanwhile, had scooped and twisted up her Titian tresses into enviable coils. Her flounced white voile bodice even hinted at a romantic turn. Our hostess, an English beauty, and often compared to the Princess of Wales, wore a fuchsia silk dress with black spots. I wore the red velvet. With its low scooped neckline, my thermal vest was exposed at the cleavage; I doctored it with a spray brooch.

The talk was light and spontaneous; it had been a good day. The hounds had dispatched the fox; continuous reports from the shooting party on the Buscot lakeside and the west walled garden had proclaimed a good bag. From silver gilt salvers and tureens, we were served Coquilles Saint Jacques, roast quail, and a delectable chocolate rum mousse parcelled in a brandy snap. A sudden silence – Czechoslovakia has got the definitive bomb? Charley Faringdon let slip this momentous crumb. Douglas Hurd, Foreign Secretary, had been dining last weekend. He had pronounced Eastern Europe flush with fatal hardware, one liberated satellite scheming against the other? What price these new 'democracies'? What cost to Western Europe?

The lady-in-waiting later spied the Rt Hon Nicholas Ridley's signature in the visitors' book and beside he had written, 'on the eve of Maastricht'. 'Oh! Typical!' she cried. 'Nicholas attracting attention again!'

We slept late on Sunday morning waking at 9.15. The shuttered windows and the bed, sheltered with its draped tester and deep pelmet, were custom-made for a lie-in. On the stone stairs down to the breakfast room, I passed the cousin. She looked exceptionally grave; her hair scraped back and covered with a scarf. 'I am going to church separately because I have become a Roman Catholic.' I headed for the laughter and the eggs and toast and sausages. Convivial talk, every conceivable Sunday newspaper, duplicated. No mention of church. 'I need to shake up my liver,' said the lady-in-waiting and she and I set off in wellingtons down the radial grass avenues and past the hump-backed bridge, through the Harold Peto water garden, to the lake beyond. In the walled garden greenhouse we found our host. He was tending his box hedge culture; the clippings from the garden are re-potted and nurtured and mailed on order all over Britain. The Buscot box hedge has cornered a market. In his capacity as deputy Chairman of Cazenove & Co., Charley Faringdon runs his estates with an austere hand.

Sir Hardy Amies, the ultimate dapper octogenarian, came to lunch. He wore a charcoal flannel riding coat. I sat on his left. What did he think of fashion today? Those skirts slashed to the navel, met by necklines scooped to the navel? A travesty of all elegant conception? Was it not amazing to remember how twenty years ago we went to Covent Garden operas in long dresses of chiffon trimmed with marabou, in silks and velvet? The men in black tie, naturally. 'But we are in a different generation!' Sir Hardy licked his thin lips. 'And just imagine the shock and dismay in 1805 when crinolines were abandoned for those flimsy Napoleonic décolleté tunics!' (In today's *Daily Express*, Sir Hardy is featured: 'Style King Hardy puts on a bold front . . . Royal designer Hardy Amies took the plunge yesterday. With this stunning evening dress the grand old man of British fashion, now aged 82, used a gold and silver brocade for the décolleté top and daringly split skirt to provide a glittering end to this year's British couture week.' He has indeed kept abreast with the generations.)

The end of a great weekend. Charley, himself, helped Tom down with our cases; the platoon of the weekend staff had left. Back to the grind, not least for our beatific host, who dives into the underground each morning like all true stockbrokers.

January 31 The Shangri-La Hotel Kuala Lumpur Malaysia

In twenty years Kuala Lumpur has launched more skyscrapers than any capital in the world. From the terrace of a Chinese temple, set high on a hill, these stylish sentinels are seen to advantage, plunged deep into the cushions of this jungle city. Slender decanters of steel and faceted glass, blue, gold, and lustrous, suggested a kaleidoscope. Others are honed in stone with Islamic fretted arches, each obelisk a different statement, curved or angled, seductive or sharp. The skyscraper is a perfected art form in Kuala Lumpur.

This contrasting clog of high-rise and crumbling Edwardian stucco, of grandiose Victoriana and shanty settlements, is buffered with jungle sprouting up between. Grassy backyards are strewn with cockerels, ducks, and children. Patches of maize and banana, palm-trees and rain-trees, and hibiscus hedges spotted red and yellow all redress the city to its jungle roots. A waved screen of distant forested peaks sweeps round the city. What is it about Kuala Lumpur that is so appealing? Conceived one hundred years ago on a malarial mud bank (the name means 'muddy estuary') it fast became a lynch-pin of trade connections and the cultured mores of Chinese, Thais, and Indians. Today the population comprises: 60% native Malay (Sons of the Soil), 30% Chinese Malay, 10% Indian Malay. (There is a tacit acknowledgement that the Chinese run the place.) Perhaps Kuala Lumpur's prime appeal is its people; their exuberance, spontaneity, and smiling desire to please is infectious. With their fastidious attention to detail and their astonishing computer technology they will sweep the West all before them. 'Go East, young man.'

February 1

In our London *Daily Telegraph* (edition Thursday 30.1.92) we read the astonishing report: 'An 18-year-old Romanian girl, declared "clinically dead", regained consciousness while being raped on a slab by a Bucharest mortuary attendant, it was reported yesterday. Police arrested the shocked rapist but the parents refused to press charges because their "daughter owed her life to him".'

An afternoon thunderstorm; one inch of rain thrashed down in thirty minutes. The open street drains had a transfusion and every gutter gurgled. In the cosy exhibition rooms of the National 'Negara' Museum, we gloated on stuffed reptiles, mammoth species of the jungle and weapons spanning four hundred years. The sword-hilts and scabbards, inlaid with ivory, silvered enamel and fruit-woods, were a rich art form of the old Malay culture.

We talked tentatively of a stay in the Cameron Highlands.

February 2

The after-breakfast malaria pill stuck stubbornly in my gullet. It would dissolve of course. It didn't. A pot of jasmine tea induced sweating and nausea. I returned to bed. Fatal. In the horizontal, all hell let loose. Burning chest pains, wave upon wave as if fanned by bellows. I writhed and whimpered. The doctor came. Angina? Coronary infarction? No soothing pill given until patient's condition diagnosed? Blood pressure? *Orl korrect.* He advised on an electrocardiogram at the hospital. Straightaway. A wheelchair was provided to take me down in the lift, across the acre of marble lobby of the Shangri-La Hotel. (The pretty girls at the reception desk waved me off uncertainly; to smile or not to smile?) I hunched my shoulders. If I could not nurse the pounding bellows in my breast, I could at least cosset the heart. I stepped from the chair to the car with an economy of effort.

The hospital Tawakal; an aquarium brightens the dark hall. Yellow children wriggle between grey grandmothers. Flat on my back behind a screen, flex and tape and nozzles are strapped and stuck to my body. Trussed up for electrocution? 'Now, now, you will not feel a thing!' With my ECG as steady as a plumb line, I was out of the faulty heart contest. A nurse sat me up to water and a pill – for the gastritis of the oesophagus? It cooled the burn. Pills around the clock; pulse and pressure; a night in a clean quiet room. Nurses – smiling, petite, immaculate – a nun, an Indian cleaning lady with a feather duster and spotless white gloves; a supper tray of Chinese fried eggs and a hot chocolate drink. The young doctor explained: 'The body has its weakness. Your condition is due to reflux of the oesophagus; your sphincter muscle let slip acid from the stomach. Your oesophagus has no appropriate disposal system; it complained bitterly . . .' He admired my amethyst ring, 'the birth stone for February'. He had fond memories of London, Hammersmith Hospital and his rooms in Westbourne Grove. He finally urged me to eat Satay sauce if I got the chance; a rich mix of peanuts, chilli, and coconut milk. In view of my gastric incompetence his recommendation could have been imprudent.

February 4 The Cameron Highlands

A general exodus from KL. It is the Chinese New Year holiday. *Kung Hee Fatt Choy!* The year of the Monkey now succeeds the year of the Ram. The lobby at the Shangri-La is tastefully crammed with decorative monkeys and orange trees; oranges for gold and prosperity. Chinese soothsayers predict a year dominated by water and the speedy downfall of Boris Yeltsin, George Bush, and John Major in that order.

We set off for the Highlands with a beaming young driver in his air-conditioned Mercedes. There are nine states in Malaysia. We head for Perak, an hour's drive from Kuala Lumpur. It is a tin state, rich in red soil, rivers, and tin. The main trunk road is flanked with dense coconut groves. Acre on acre of arched fronds shine metallic in the blinding sun and shade; their sturdy trunks pace out the cool green tunnels. Distant mountains hover in a blue fog above this canopy of green.

Through each village booths and bright umbrellas line the road. Coconuts, unripened, palest green, hang in nets for sale. We pass a smattering of simple farmsteads and village homes, cream stucco bungalows with tin roofs and tiled roofs, red from the natural soil. We see no animals, no cow or horse or donkey. A few hens we do see and a handful of dogs foraging by the roadside parking bays. The Malay population is predominantly Muslim and eschews domestic animals.

The switchback hump of mountains looms closer. Thickly-forested and dabbed with cloud they soar from 4,000 to 6,000 feet. At Tapah, a prosperous hill town, it has been raining. The main street and its colonnaded arcades are potted with red puddles. We take a sharp right turn up the winding road to the Cameron Highlands. Now you sense the thrust and press of the jungle; thick growth and ferns and fir and the sense that eyes are on you. Streams course down in the interior gloaming. On the distant flanks of mountains, waterfalls glint from the inky depths like swords.

Beside rivers and clearings clusters of thatched homes on stilts denote the remaining settlements of original tribesmen. At 3,000 feet we see the renowned tea terraces, cloths of emerald flung far and wide over these undulating plateaus of the Highlands. It was in 1885 that the Scotsman, William Cameron, on a government mapping survey, reported 'a fine plateau with gentle slopes shut in by mountains'. The Chinese tea-planters moved in and for over a hundred years these Highlands have developed into the market gardens and golfing resorts of today.

High up the mountain range at Ringlet Village, the police have set up a road block. Slim, smart men with guns and peaked hats are after drug-smugglers. 'Dadah' is the collective word for drugs in Malaysia, an infantile connotation in direct contrast to the death penalty incurred. 'Dadah' is currently being secreted across the borders in the hubcaps of cars. The criminal smuggler follows behind the innocent party and his unsuspected load. At the smuggler's convenience the caps are dismantled and the loot retrieved. Alternatively, the innocent carrier is caught by the border police and charged. The police them- selves have taken the precaution of removing all their own hubcaps.

Our mountain climb ends at 'Ye Olde Smoke House' near the mountain town of Tanah Rata. The telephone lines having been out of order from Kuala Lumpur, we have not booked. 'No problem, Sir, Madam. We have the suite for you. £100 a night, to include cooked

English breakfast!' In the event, the food is so lousy that full English breakfast is our staple diet round the clock. (Breakfast itself was to be accompanied by the sound tracks of British Regimental marches, Richard Dimbleby's commentaries on Royal Circumstance, and Highland Bagpipes.) We pass through the pseudo Tudor Hall with its blackened beams and latticed windows, its red-shaded wall lights and red plush seats, and armchairs flounced in cretonne. Fifteen vases of roses and carnations embellish each surface of custom-made oak. Tables, chests, and dressers are set about with brass and silver jugs and bowls and warming pans. This phoney pastiche of an English country inn is affecting.

Up red-carpeted stairs to our suite, where no less than three vases of scarlet viscose roses await us, along with a wardrobe with insufficient hangers, a bathroom with no waste bin, and a presumptuous-looking four-poster with no under-blanket. Lamp flex coursing across the room under cover of rugs gives me a fear of faulty wiring. I earmark our escape route through the window on to a pitched porch, to a lush bed of salvias below.

In the garden we sniff the promised clean mountain air over a cup of hallowed Cameron tea. (The first pot had to be sent away as the water was not boiled.) The garden is a glut of colour; hedges of scarlet and pink poinsettia, hibiscus and purple heather, yellow, red, and pink iris are clumped lusciously, their voluptuous throats flopped open. Orchids everywhere, hanging and potted, grow in a proprietorial profusion.

February 5

Low cloud under a pallid sun. We set off from this saucer of trim green into the jungle through a narrow footpath, an innocent incline, a gentle preamble when, suddenly, a steep drop. Roots and severed branches and the reassuring gravity of our bottoms ease us down; then we claw our way up again. This switchback trail has us in its thrall. It is early afternoon. The silence of death, siesta, sleep engulfs. A bird trills. A dab of fleeting yellow flits through the trees. We marvel at the deep, thick mattresses of moss and rest back on the accumulated folds. A crackle of twigs, then sharp, running steps. A native hurtles past. He has a blowpipe on his shoulder and a quiver of arrows on his back. We don't exist and unseen animals wait for the dusk. We fumble on through this green quiet world, through its crowd of beech and oak with palms thrown up between. A cluster of banana-trees and ornamental fern spells water. We cross the stream which would rise rapidly in rain. The profound density of this jungle! One step from the path and you can tumble sixty feet. Two steps and you are lost. We remember the salutary fate of Jim Thompson, the American Thai Silk entrepreneur from Bangkok. On March 2, 1967, while on holiday in the Cameron Highlands, he stepped into the jungle for a pre-dinner stroll and disappeared without trace. A tiger? Kidnapped? A fall? The jungle keeps its secrets. We grapple and slither. How much further? Three hours already. The map shows a market garden at the end of all our pain. On a little, on a little – and there! Plump lettuces and space and air as we tumble from the womb of the jungle.

February 8 Kuala Lumpur

Omar Arsagoff, son of the ex-Saudi Ambassador to Singapore and married to the daughter of the deceased Sultan of Perak, King of Malaysia. We drive to the neighbouring state of Selangor. Omar's diminutive bodyguard eats and sits and proceeds everywhere by his side. Omar is widely travelled and has an articulate grasp of global shenanigans: 'So Germany is after you again. Germany neutralises France; she ingratiates herself with Russia through her East Germany. She will thrive on this transfusion of new labour force.'

He fears for his adopted Malaysia and its inevitable escalation to a more material society. 'The value of the fully extended family is still integral to our society.' And will Malaysia be a future playpen for the Western world? In today's *New Straits Times*, the headline was '130,000 hotel rooms needed . . . at least 20 million foreign tourists to Malaysia in the year 2000.' Omar at the wheel of his prized new Japanese 7-seater auto looks a shade sheepish. 'You know, we have to join it. I am myself building a hotel on the east coast.' His car phone trills. 'Yes? Yes? Yes? I said yes.' This perfunctory call refers to Omar's order for eighty hotel beds. 'Where do I get eighty beds?' He throws up his hands. 'London,' I suggest unhelpfully, 'or Singapore?'

What about Malaysia's wild life? 'Yes, there are tigers in the Cameron Highlands and in the state of Pahang. Elephants stay in the south. But their territory is being eroded by our programme of fast development. All the species are threatened as they turn about in ever-decreasing circles. If we deprive them of space and game, they will forage in the villages.' I tell him of the wild boar reported to have gone 'shopping' in a Jakarta supermarket this week. 'Oh yes? Did he attack?' 'Apparently not. Pandemonium broke out when he approached several customers and rubbed himself against them.' We all squeal and shudder, including the bodyguard.

Selangor is approached through a marble arch and avenues of flowering trees and red hibiscus. On the near horizon a sizeable stadium is being built for the 1994 Commonwealth Games. The emerging chassis resembles a crashed airbus. Beyond, clearly delineated against a storm-grey sky, the Sultan's newly-erected mosque swells up supreme. The dome is of deep blue faceted glass in imitation of lapis lazuli. Who paid for it? 'The Sultan of course; he is rich and generous and getting old. And he likes young girls. I had an Irish girl in London, Annette. Annette with the green eyes. I introduce her to the Sultan and we all dine and dance. Annette does not care for the advances of the old man and suggests that he give her a ring in the morning. The Sultan turns to me in all earnestness and asks me, "Does your lady friend prefer diamonds or emeralds?"' The storm breaks with a spectacular St Vitus's dance of pink lightning above the Sultan of Selangor's mosque.

February 9 Kuala Lumpur

Sharmini Tiruchelvam has yet to seize upon the ultimate hair-spray. The ninety per cent humidity is anathema to her long thick hair; the dark curls hang limp and frayed. And now the airport controls have banned all aerosols! Her precious London-imported hair-sprays are condemned as ozone-hostile. 'All nations must do their part to save the earth.' Sharmini sighs dramatically with a lift of the delicately-arched eyebrows.

Painted in 1956 at the age of eighteen by Pietro Annigoni and subsequently each year for a decade, Sharmini is used to adulation. Annigoni pronounced her 'the most beautiful woman in the world'. This legendary tag promoted others to touch the hem of her renown – Picasso, Augustus John, and de Chirico, to name a few. Today, in her early fifties, her caramel skin retains its luminescence; her deep-set sparkling eyes and the full, firm lips are in constant thrall to her lively mind. Her entire persona smacks of talent, the musical, literary, and artistic strains nicely balanced with a medical training and a daunting self-sufficiency – she needs nobody. This arresting impact detracts from the downfall of her lower body. Not even the billowing shield of her sari can disguise the haphazard ballooning of her bottom. The precise agility of the mind, the regal set of the head and shoulders are at wide variance with this 'toby jug' support. 'I am the biggest person I know!' shrills Sharmini. 'Push me right over and I bounce back.' She gladly settles for a chocolate milkshake before we set out for lunch.

And we plan her illustrious dinner party to be held in the private room of the Shang Palace restaurant, Shangri-La Hotel. We will have:

> *Braised crab claw meat and bamboo pith soup*
> *Baked lobster with sliced ginger and spring onion*
> *Fried boneless chicken with lemon sauce*
> *Steamed Soon Hock fish*
> *Eight fairies conference*
> *Fried rice Yong Chow style*
> *Red bean paste*
> *Chinese pancake*

'And they will drink brandy and iced water, the best brandy.'

Sharmini's friends are drawn from the nine Sultanates of Malaysia. We wait in the bustling lobby at the appointed hour. They arrive in twos and threes, informal, the men in open shirts, the ladies in long bright silks, except for the dashing Tunka (or princess), from Kedah state, who displays her legs in a black satin miniskirt. Her features are sleek and Thai as befits this north border state. A younger beauty with raven curls swings diamond hoops from her ears; she is the daughter of the next King (from the state of Negri Sembilan). Her husband has sharp, handsome features. Sharmini effects the introductions with aplomb. She reminds me that the little lady in green with the wrinkled Simian features is the most revered aristocrat I could ever hope to meet, and the lady beside her with the muddy complexion and clumsy nose is apparently the second-most distinguished in the land. It is a congenial party. The King's ADC, sitting on my right, intimates that the King is anxious to play golf at Swinley Forest and to sample steak and kidney pie. ('Oh! He has such airs and graces this King. In two years we have a new one. You will enjoy him more.') Clearly Sharmini will not be a candidate for the golfing party.

April 8 Hardwicke House

Brilliant sunshine and warm air, a surprise spring day. Blossom, birds and daffodils and the saturating scent of wallflowers circle the house in a whirl of colour. But on Monday morning it blew wet and cold, fitting for a funeral. Prince George Galitzine's funeral. Described in one obituary as 'sprightly', he was on his toes all his life. Born 1916 in Tbilisi, Georgia, in revolution-torn 1917, he was soon packed off with his illustrious and impoverished family on a boat for France. Paris proved already crowded with White Russians and so on to London, which was not. George's own family settled in London where their cousins from our own Royal family kept up a close touch. George crammed his life with forays into bygone Russia, guiding art study tours through St Petersburg, Moscow, Kiev and the whole gamut of that vast comintern. He became a loved and revered figure in today's Russia; long-locked doors to his family palaces were spirited open and the select tourist found himself initiated in fine, unchartered territory. George, always indefatigable, and his lovely, vivacious wife Jean enhanced the London scene. He gave numerous talks pertaining to all things Russian and compiled beautiful illustrated books.

But, five days before he died, we heard him speak at the Guildhall; he was hosting a large dinner in aid of Russian Youth Clubs. His voice was low and more husky than ever; his delivery laboured and rambling – reminiscence overspill and too long. On my right sat that agreeable, aquiline Jugoslav, Vane Ivanovic. He murmured in my ear, 'When Lloyd George heard Harold Macmillan make his maiden speech he said to him, "Find a point, young man, and stick to it."' George's battery was running down that night. Five days later he died.

His funeral at the Russian Cathedral in Ennismore Gardens was attended by his family, friends, and HRH Prince Michael, our bearded look-alike Tsar Nicholas II. As we perched on chairs or simply stood, a smiling young girl handed us each a candle, which we lit, one from another. It was an awesome responsibility to hold it firmly and still; after thirty minutes I blew mine out, in fear of my mink muff. Several obliging neighbours offered to resuscitate my flame and, when I declined, I think they judged me a heretic.

In the dim, grey of the cathedral interior I had not at first appreciated that George's mahogany coffin was open to the winds. I realised only when I saw Jean, pale and elegant in her black draped shawl, peer and bend anxiously over the top end at George inside. She bent nearer, patting his head, and kissed him, as though settling a baby in his pram. Georgian chants from the gallery choir lulled us into meek submission and peace. The priest, solemn yet splendid in his brocade chasuble and mitre, swung the incense-burner. To and fro, to and fro. Both George's head and Jean standing alongside were smothered in the scented smoke. The congregation of the many faithful then filed past George, crossing themselves, touching his hand, and kissing his forehead. This took some time.

Jean, regal in grief, finally reasserted her conjugal rights with a last, long kiss. The lid of the coffin was then placed on top of George, with admirable precision, and thumbscrewed down by the undertaker.

May 2 Sicily

We touch down at Rome airport. The gold puppy retriever peers out from his wicker basket. Did he enjoy his flight? The security officer pokes through bags and sends my face-powder flying; his navy suit is sprinkled pink. We are lost in acres of marble floor space and crave a loo and coffee. Now I have lost my ticket. Horror! Painfully we plod this marble area, retracing steps. There! Face down, a strip of innocuous white, unclaimed, mine. More anxious shooting pains. Money? Passports? We slap our pockets, dig deep, scrabble, search. Where are the travellers cheques? Those red embarkation cards? Only one passport?

From Rome to Palermo. No sign of Mount Etna and her torrent of lava; just ten days ago, the flow of molten rock gushing from her side was plugged with concrete blocks. The village of Zefferana, in direct line for a lava take-over, raised hands and hearts in thankful relief. Will we see this congealing, steaming flood? Spent and spurned like a stale pudding?

We drive through the wet green country in a nine-seater pillar-box-red Land Rover. We are fellow walking companions, neat and fit and ageing, with short hair and short sleeves, five men and five women, all apprehensive of our untried breath and bones and blisters. A cloud mist lounges on mountain peaks; the emerald slopes are jagged with rock. Black cows, sheep, and lone stone farmsteads are pinned with a single pine. We pass orange-groves with ripening fruit, white blossoms, olive-trees and pink judas, there are few people, fewer cars – a volcanic, fertile land, sombre in swirling mists, sullen in its somnolence and in its poor regard for good property development.

Up the winding hill to Enna, the original stronghold crag town of Sicily; a medieval fortress of cobbled roads and alleys, each rounded stone hand-hewn from rock and laid in loops, now rain-washed rose and tan and black, to a bright-lit restaurant for local fish and good wines – Corvo and Pignatello. A pyramid of fresh-picked lemons and oranges smothered in their glossy leaves decorate our table. Back up the cobbled dark street, still soaked in mist and running gutters, we return to our modest hotel the Grande Sicilia.

May 3 Enna Sicily

The Gothic-Baroque cathedral is strangely deserted for a Sunday morning (but its nearby street market does a good trade). Inside is an impressive aisle with massive Corinthian columns made of black rock with polished bases of basalt. The ceiling is coffered, intricately-carved, ungilded wood like dark, rich chocolate. A total absence of tourists in Enna is refreshing.

We set off with boots, bandages, water-bottles, sunhats, binoculars – as befits our needs – to walk. Over hills, down valleys, through dust tracks and Roman causeways, over streams, mountain flanks of loose shale, and tumbled rocks. Each grass valley, bank, wooded dell, and rock-faced slope is spread with wild flowers in a profusion of brilliant blue, red, pink, yellow and purple. The rich, red rash of sainfoin on distant hills, the clumps of lemon-scented gorse, orchids, iris, gladioli, and sweet peas, all wave bright petals from long grasses and silver santolina. These first six weeks of Sicilian summer are a botanist's paradise. Butterflies, in all the rich markings of a Hermès scarf, flit and flutter between, and little lime lizards dart for cover.

A picnic lunch in a gorge of tufa catacombs: salami, cheese, salads, honeyed rice cakes, and Corvo for those who can trust their head and tread. I watch three ants swarm on to a bread crumb. They scurry sideways, bearing it aloft as though transporting a prized mattress.

Piazza Armerina and its Villa Imperiale promises a cultural after-noon. An astonishing display of mosaics set between a vast structure of floors, bounded by marble pillars, and recently excavated, show remarkable narrative portrayals of daily life from 300 to 500 AD that are explicit and tactile. The subtle working of form and light and shade adds an alluring dimension. The 'Room of the Girls with Bikinis', and the jumble of legs and drapes in 'Bedroom of the Scene Erotic', incite endless speculation. Bikinis in 300 AD! Life in this luxurious hunting lodge-cool summer house was clearly geared to *la dolce vita*. If only the floors could talk.

May 4 Enna – Gangi

Through a rolling landscape we walk to the fortress town of Gangi. Mud everywhere wedged on boots makes heavy boots heavier; fear of blisters; hot sun on the neck; sweat on the back; relief winds on the rock summit. Skylarks and nightingales; sheep and persistent clinking bells from a herd of cows; the chestnut mare, her forelegs tied with sisal, and her foal beside. Wild flowers superb; blowing above a milky froth of clover, we see marigolds. In an almond grove we lunch and doze.

The rose-stone cobbled alleys of Gangi zigzag to the Duomo. Old men chatter in a row, perch like birds along the Duomo wall; sharp-featured, neat, diminutive, parcelled tight in suits and caps, their sturdy ladies stump the streets with baskets, blank in black; in peaceable anticipation of the next church service and a suitable soup for supper.

May 5 Hotel Miramonti – Gangi

The world starts and ends at the Hotel Miramonti, the yank and lurch of lorries up the hill, the screech of brakes and bikes and boys, and ruddy-faced men with ringlets yelling and laughing raucously from the gas station below, the café, the bar, and those unexplained bullet holes in the vaulted ceiling, with its meticulously restored göbek[2] in the church down the hill.

I jam my basin with mud and stones in an attempt to unclog boots with nail scissors. Our innovative tour manager pierces this impasse with a steel coat-hanger, a reassuring gurgle results.

May 6 Gangi Geraci Siculo

We leave Gangi at 8.30 a.m. and the young Lotharios with their Byronic curls, their spitfire bikes, the old men in a row, the nymphettes tossing dyed blonde manes, the patient loaded donkeys, the sad and dirty crumbling corners of the new walls, ugly and half-erected. High above in the duomo of San Nicola those black limestone pillars dismiss the centuries with their proud survival. The sun is faint in the steaming, secret valleys. Muddied arteries meander up through wooded slopes of olive, oak, cork oak, beech and eucalyptus. A nightingale, a cuckoo and a shepherd's holler echo over the hill. We cross a medieval stone bridge to a field beyond of yellow tulips and more orchids, cyclamen and a shower of buttercups. We pass small stone holdings with their corrals of stone walling, fuzzed with spiked thorn, effective sheep shelters from winter wolves. This succession of wooded slopes and interfolding valleys, these foothills of the Madonie mountains, are as old as time, the rooting ground of the Aegean Greeks, the century-long 'Golden Age' of Sicily, 400 BC, their Roman successors and the first invading dawns of Byzantine, Moor and Arab. This landscape, little changed since Plato, Cicero, Saint Peter, and Saint Paul passed through these volcanic bright green hills and fields.

In the afternoon we gain the sprawling fortress town of Geraci Siculo. The eleventh-century Saracen castle sprawls its ramparts overhead. We drink from the fountain in the square; the cold *dolce acqua* spews in a bow from the stone lion's mask and tastes of minerals and iron.

---

[2] Göbek – Turkish for belly or navel. In this case, a decorative ceiling light fixture.

May 7 Piano Zucchi

Last night spent again comfortably in a mountain inn, '*Lontana da Smog e Rumori*'. We are promised another view of Mount Etna but visibility does not comply. These Madonie mountains, 4,748 feet at the main ridge, mark the original eruption of Sicily before Mount Etna's dominating summits were yet to evolve. Wild peonies, we see, white and pink, and ancient ilex-trees blotch the green mountain slopes with shade. The scene is softened with silver pear and white blossom and the grey fuzz of olive. Cliff faces, sheer and tumbling, inked with scrub and hollows, invoke the romantic landscapes of Claude and Girtin. On a distant plateau we see herds of red deer and the idyllic setting of the hamlet in the fold, our venue for the night, Piano Zucchi.

Our host of the inn, Salvatore, is economical with his hot water; neither does the pile of accumulated ash in the dining-room make for cosiness. Salvatore complains that lighting the fire makes his entire establishment smell for days. His be-ringed and be-ribboned son serves us an agreeable meal, cooked by Signora Salvatore; a thin herbed soup, wild asparagus (another expedient economy) incorporated in a pancake, and spaghetti tossed in the herbs gleaned from the rocks and hedgerows.

May 8 Cefalu

We proceed down to sea level through rocks and steep grass slopes. The musky scent of gorse is everywhere. We find a mauve pink butterfly orchid and compare it with book illustrations; it is hailed as the rarest and most ecstatic finish to the week's findings.

The cobbled streets of Cefalu slant to the sea. We drink espresso and arancia fresca by the harbour rail; obliquely opposite sits a row of garrulous, moustachioed Sicilians, their backs to the sea. And not twenty feet away on the sandy shore below lies a slim, dark-haired beauty, her long legs and body bared, save for a black monokini. You would think the men would face the other way. 'Oh! If she were blonde and buxom they would be fainting in the aisles all right.' We buy gorgonzola and parmesan and see the Byzantine Christ high on the Duomo altar; the wisp of hair escaping from his widow's peak is a masterpiece of mosaic dexterity.

Dust and grit and detritus eddy in sea breezes and crumbs from the tourists' tables and from the crumbling poverty that is much of Sicily. The rasp and rev of bikers hurl at hair's breadth past bodies, bags, and baskets. The Duomo at night is a vision; an opera set. The twelfth-century fortress façade with its twin towers has survived the centuries intact; an avenue of magnificent seventy-feet palm-trees frames it proudly: an understated monument of love in strong, white stone. At midnight, the nearby café-owner sweeps his floor and his patch of *pavimento*. He stacks his chairs, turns off his aranciata machine, his cappuccino tap and his gelati paddles. His domain blazes in the darkening piazza like a peepshow in the fairground – green, yellow, red and gold – lights out.

May 23 Venice

We were running late for the Corsini wedding. Air traffic control in Italy confirmed a two and a half-hour delay. The best-laid travel plans are easily thwarted. We finally touched down at Venice at four o'clock; we were due at the Basilica dei Frari at five. Our water taxi bounded through green water lanes marked with asparagus piles. We made a more sedate entry up the Canal Grande and were ceremoniously decanted with cases and hat-boxes at the canalside entrance of the Bauer Grünwald Hotel. A lightning change of clothes and the taxi eased us further up the back waterways to Santa Maria Gloriosa dei Frari. It was 5.45; the service, half-way, was in full swing, and my emerald ostrich feathers unruffled.

It was crowded, though cool, in the Basilica. The lofty, Gothic vaulted canopy with its rose-brick webbing could never succumb to stuffiness or heat. We eased our passage down the taffeta-congested aisle; some of the women sat on benches alongside, where they flaunted, to advantage, their elegant jewellery, lissom legs, hair and hats, and patrician profiles. They chattered freely, gesticulating with be-ringed fingers, and took little note of the marriage proceedings. The rest of the congregation stood; they had been standing for three-quarters of an hour and the service was set to continue for another three-quarters of an hour. Little singing; little organ music; much talking and reciting in low voices and then again in high voices. The ladies on the sidelines continued their deliberations in blithe oblivion of the solemn inductions between Duccio Corsini (Duca di Casigliano) and his Clothilde. The handsome couple stood tall, facing the altar. Their stage was woven round with waves of white lilies and marguerites and pyres of white and pink rosebuds. The awesome red and gold sweeping strokes of Titian's *Assumption* were suspended above them.

Suddenly a clap of hands and everybody clapped as though a wind-buffeted plane had landed safely. The altar precincts took on the properties of a cocktail party as the two families converged, with much kissing and chatting and hoisting of sleeping tots and babies, to sign the register. We pressed back from the aisle as a beaming Duccio Corsini and Clothilde preceded an indeterminate line-up of relations; the older ones tripped over a curled-up edge of sisal matting, which nobody seemed capable of fastening down.

We fanned out in the Campo dei Frari, a mellow little scene in the evening sun; below the bright canopies and blinds and blistered shutters, a face leaning out of every window and washing on every wall. Then shouts to throw the groom into the canal? Instead the bride was tossed three times, high above the little hump bridge and caught in a cradle of arms. Her poor oyster satin, pearl-beaded dress! (And I hoped she was not already pregnant.) The happy couple recovered themselves in a scarlet velvet-lined gondola that removed them to the reception further down the Canal Grande.

At the Pisano Morita, a substantial, privately-owned palace, we were greeted by the bride's mama and Duccio and Clothilde who professed amazement to see us *da Londra!* (There was nobody else *da Londra.*) We wandered up and down three floors of stone and marble, baroque mirrored walls and boiserie, and huge Venetian glass chandeliers (furred with grey dust) where ivory candles burned and guttered in the breeze from the Canal Grande. Pyramids and platters of canapés and everywhere oranges and swags of white blossom festooned dadoes, arched doorways, and stairs. Balconies overhanging the Canal gave cool relief with a view of the palaces on the opposite side. We watched the pageboys on the red-carpeted jetty below, angelically dressed in saffron satin and peach and duck-egg blue, duffing each other up; kicking and wrestling, getting hotter and angrier under their muslin collars. At last we found Giorgiana, La Principessa, the ebullient and vivacious mother of the groom. A small sturdy lady, dressed in buttercup yellow under a wide blue hat. She looked brown and well. 'Last week only, I was in Spain taking a group . . .' Tom asked her if the happy couple had known each other long. 'Oh yes, two years. You know, I never encouraged it, as I did not know the family.' She then proceeded to introduce us to the bride's father – *un avocato* – who seemed eminently respectable.

June 14 South Mead Queen Anne's Road Windsor

Cecile walks stiffly through the long drawing-room into the sun. Shall we sit out or in? Too hot in the garden? The garden chairs and umbrella are hustled to the shade.

Our hostess, Cecile Grandy, erect and finely-drawn from years of arthritis is a distinguished, pretty woman. 'I'm the cook,' she says nervously. Sir John Grandy, Marshal of the Royal Air Force, pours another round of champagne and takes up his stand by the front door. A handsome equerry, the commanding officer at Windsor of the Blues and Royals, steps through the French windows: 'HRH is on her way – she left Windsor Castle five minutes ago.' John nips out for a second glass to sustain his watch. Sir Hugh Dundas, another holder of a distinguished war record in a Fighter Command Squadron, and his wife complete the small party. The lime-trees sough and sigh and float their scent across the lawn.

Framed in the modest conservatory and its retinue of bird tables, watering cans and plastic pots, she pauses; diminutive in a yellow scooped neckline and puff sleeves. A round of curtsies and 'ma'ams' and we women re-settle ourselves on the white garden chairs. The men stand awkwardly. Four more chairs from the kitchen are soon produced.

Princess Margaret chats vivaciously to the handsome equerry and to Cecile – 'What a pretty garden!' 'We are on the Crown Estate, ma'am.' 'Ah, this estate is one of ours?' (Waiting in the shade of a horse chestnut-tree, prior to our over-punctual arrival, Tom and I had remarked on what a badly-designed set of houses they were too.)

Cecile motions us to lunch and iced borscht soup. The princess talks happily with Sir John; handsome, lean and fit; in his seventy-ninth year, he was always a favourite with the ladies. The equerry on my right talks of his pending trip with his troops to Pembrokeshire. 'I lay on all these outdoor activities for them when all they want is a "leg-over" in Tenby.'

The serving woman, who must also be in her seventy-ninth year, does a valiant job; single-handed she squeezes her girth round the small room, wielding a precarious pile of dirty plates. Princess Margaret takes a fork to Cecile's light concoction of avocado and chicken in a velouté sauce. She declines the pudding, a banana ice cream. She has eaten nothing and drinks less. No wine, preferring a tumbler of gin and lemon barley, which she lowers beneath the table to express her disaffection at the mention of certain people. Tom, sitting opposite, talks to her of our necklace cabinet, designed by her son, David Linley. 'Tom and Penelope live in a lovely house on Ham Common, ma'am, a palace,' interjects John Grandy. It is an obvious relief when the banana ice is cleared away and the royal cigarette-holder can come into action. She looks pretty, even glamorous, her whittled waist is accentuated by a boned bodice, her bosom up-thrust to advantage.

We ladies leave the dining-room. Again the perplexing choice, coffee in the garden or in the cool drawing-room? Princess Margaret sniffs the hot, cluttered conservatory. 'Let's be in the drawing-room,' she says and makes to move in the tray of coffee cups. 'No, ma'am, you must not lift that, let me.' But I am clutching my bag and sunglasses; she deftly takes them from me and puts them aside as I grab the tray.

If we had expected an insider's dissertation on the marital traumas of Prince Charles and Princess Diana we are disappointed. Princess Margaret is the perfect guest: charming, vivacious, and tactfully inconsequential. A policeman is called to escort her back to the castle. As she left the drawing-room, she paused at the door with a smile, sweeping the room with her lovely eyes, checking that we had all been accounted for.

July 14 Çırağan Palace, Istanbul, Turkey

A blaze of gold with every chandelier a festoon of diamonds hanging there; the twenty-foot windows are framed in pilastered, ice-white marble; the fabulous façade comprises every Moorish, Gothic and Baroque caprice, stretching 200 yards along the Bosphorus shore. This late nineteenth-century Çırağan ('torch') palace, once famous for its parades and parties, has been recently restored. Since 1912, when it was ravaged by fire, it has stood, a blackened landmark; a file of abandoned pillars open to the winds and flaming sunsets, where rooks have swooped and cawed through eighty years.

The evening air is soft and scented; white lilies, white roses and frangipani are bunched in urns up the palace horseshoe steps. Behind us, the Bosphorus. Guests, arrive by speedboats, by helicopters; guests, more guests. The terraces are crowded. Handsome women in haute couture taffeta, with bold décolletage, are heavily jewelled and tanned and lacquered. Ayşegul Nadir swivels through the crowd. Tom jokes admiringly, 'Ayşegul, my dear . . . you have more jewellery tumbling down your back than most women have on their front.' Ayşegul – a celebrated Turkish beauty, twice divorced from the dishonoured Polly Peck trader, Asil Nadir – pats her emerald pendants reassuringly; her shapely shoulders soar from a snugly-swathed bodice and a tent of sumptuous shot silk (Anouska Hempel). Her hair, a contrived tangle of wild, dark curls, her eyes elliptical – she is a knock out. 'Penelope, you have nice earrings too . . .' (My pendant diamond and sapphires – bought twenty years ago at Christie's.)

We stroll along the gravel terrace; a quintessential English couple heads toward us. Our ambassador Sir Timothy Daunt – tall, distinguished, reserved; fluent in Turkish, they say – and Patricia, his vivacious, clever wife. The bands strike up and coloured laser beams are honed on the central balconied palace wall. The occasion for this

congenial pomp and ceremony? The renowned Koç family are marrying off the third generation. Mustafa Koç – the eldest grandson of
Vehbi Koç, founder of the Koç Holding empire – marries Caroline
Giraud, daughter of a prestigious Levantine family from Izmir. Mustafa's father and mother, Rahmi and his estranged wife Çiğdem, are
briefly reunited in this civic balcony scene. Mustafa cuts a proud figure
beside his ravishing bride – described as a 'swan' by the press – her
auburn hair swept back and gleaming in a froth of white silk flowers.

The night is upon us; a moon as full and fat as a ripe camambert is
poised low over the Bosphorus. Atatürk's renovated yacht, the
Savarona, (now valued at $75 million), sits seductively on the waves,
looped with fairy lights from her masts and bowsprit. What a setting
for a pledge and a promise!

Was it only ten years ago that Istanbul ran with mud and had no
hot water?

September 13 Veryan in Roseland South Cornwall

A sad summer (the wettest August in years). A summer soured by
the unprecedented, intrusive media reporting on the Royal family; a
summer shadowed by the ominous portents of the Maastricht Treaty.
The media and 'Maastricht', ironically honed on the same target;
the dissolution of British Sovereignty? The bones and guts and
growing achievements of Britain; her historic hierarchy; all now stand
to be homogenised by the heavy plough of a federal Europe. This
cannot be! Has John Major (whose prime pledge was to create a
'classless' society) gone off his grey head? He doggedly persists with
his 'yes' to 'Maastricht' and he fairly predicts a 'yes' vote in the French
referendum on this coming Sunday, September 20. He has ruled out
a British referendum over 'Maastricht'. The Prime Minister has effectively pitched Britain's democracy against his own prestige and self-
aggrandisement; he urges us to fall in with the bandwagon of the
Bundesbank; to fork out yet again for the Germans. The tactics of
political tactics! Imagine the cunning interplay and chicanery of an
ill-adjusted federalist Europe when muzzled Nationalism runs amok?
No sooner are the manacles of Communism confounded than we
stoop to pick them up again.

And if the French vote 'no' to 'Maastricht'? They will give Europe
twenty-five years' reprieve from Federalism? They will at least open
up the trading markets.

Such boiling contentions are soothed by these misted Cornish head-
lands; the enduring landmarks, the Lizard and the Manacles; the sea-

swept beach at dawn, the grey claws of hunched rock and cliff; warm pools and weed and shells and a pulsating, exquisitely marked jellyfish, screwed up in sand. Harbours, bobbing boats and buoys and tankers churning on to Falmouth; fresh crab salad with surf and waves below, cobbled quays and village greens, sugar-iced cottage walls, thatched roofs and snug, grey Anglo-Saxon churches. Your medical prescription from Truro will be stored at the local post office; the post van will deliver your milk, and your neighbour will walk your dog, take your grandmother to church, feed the baby, buy the bread. The established mores of these Cornish coves are precious and proven.

The Maastricht Treaty? A federalised Europe? 'The Brussels Book of Rules'? Our way of life, our historic symbols and personal directives are fatally threatened. Already there are absurd inroads to our privacy and existing fabric; lunatic strictures on the correct curve of a cucumber; the banning of village fresh-fish vans, the banning of home-made jams; of custard tarts, the wholesale banning of butchers' shops – all in the name of 'European Community Directives' standards. Finally the Walloons of Brussels have seen fit to ban the pink food dye – 'canthaxanthin' as used in sausages and flamingo feed. ('The day the flamingoes at Buckingham Palace turned grey . . .')

It is time John Major stopped contemplating his navel. He is pushing his luck and the country too far.

November 27 Singapore

A distinctive bien-élevé air hangs over Singapore. The veteran Prime Minister, Lee Kwan Yew, has banned chewing-gum. Each street and stick and stone, rinsed and polished, recalls the old military command: 'If it stands still, paint it! If it moves, salute it!' Each angle and esplanade is cushioned in a blaze of well-trained tropicalia and everywhere fountains tumble and orchids blow. Computer literacy and high technology all the way to the bank. Crime? Unemployment? Vandalism? The curses of our Western ways have no platform here. Singapore is the ultimate bastion of good behaviour, progressive attitudes, and prosperity. Her people are fastidious and full of grace. Her renowned airport is a gleaming labyrinth of dovetailed steel and glass and marble, where dazzling shops and sumptuous rest-rooms with shaded lamps, deep sofas, fish tanks, and flowers, soothe and pamper the most world-weary traveller. Would Somerset Maugham have been seduced? His junketing around the South China Sea spawned a crop of evocative stories. Such art and eccentricities of travel have long been subjugated to comfort and speed.

Yesterday we lunched with His Majesty the Sultan of Johor and his
Sultana, a serene, grave beauty, dark-haired with long slanting eyes, a
daughter of the Sultan of Kelantan. From that northern State on the
east Malaysia coast, with its fleet of gaudy fishing boats, its prized batik,
and silvercraft, she came south to the sultry Malacca Straits and the
lights of Singapore beyond. The birth of two sons and eight daughters
and a husband renowned for his irascibility have taken little toll on
her – she is fifty-two.

The Sultan's ADC is detailed to collect us from 'the Pride of Johor
Bahru', its singularly ugly, newly-built Puteri Pan-Pacific Hotel. After
cursory introductions he removes himself and his portable telephone
to the nearest pillar where presumably he relays an okay to the palace.
We are driven through neat roads of white villas, palm-trees, figs, and
scoops of distant sea. A high pair of iron gates and we wind up the
drive to the Sultan's Palace (built 1938) and set square on its man-made
hill. A pretty girl in immaculate jeans ('I am daughter no 6') apologises
for the haulage lorry that bars the head of the drive; we walk the last
few yards companionably. 'My father is replanting trees moved from
his town garden.' She leads us through spacious high-ceilinged rooms.
Soldiers hold guns to attention as we pass through the arched colonnades. Substantial and colourful vases and jars of every Eastern and
European persuasion flank our passage. In a central room with two
gold damask chairs at its head, No. 6 daughter indicates we sit at each
right angle. The audience is about to begin. We wait expectantly
alongside forty other empty chairs.

The Sultan of Johor enters the room with little ceremony. We bow
and curtsey respectively. Our hero straddles his long thin legs over his
cushioned seat; his black buckled Gucci shoes are fastened to the floor
throughout our thirty-minute preamble. A heart-shaped diamond on
a chain flashes through his open-neck t-shirt. Having just studied his
official state photograph that hangs in the Puteri Pan-Pacific, I am
surprised at the real macoy. Here we have a wizened face with fuzzed
and thinning grey hair. The state portrait in 1984, as the handsome
ruling King of Malaysia, has him in his 'titfer' and full military regalia.

He talks exclusively to Tom in a high reedy monotone. Yes, there
is a market in Malaysia for Asprey; Tom must come again. Next time
they must play golf. 'But you must first understand, I never play for
money. I have a passion to win at everything. No, I cannot even play
for your golf balls. You see,' he adds sanctimoniously, 'I may be playing
a man who cannot afford golf balls. You sell watches at Asprey? I have
this Rolex but it is bashed up and I keep drowning it in the pool.
What watch do you wear?' Tom laughs nervously, 'You see, sir, when
I travel I wear this Japanese Swatch; waterproof and costs nothing.

When John Asprey sees me wearing it he is very cross; however, sir, I am happy to wear it with you because I know you understand the logistics.' The Sultan beams. Footmen in white tunics and fezes filter in from the aisles with silver salvers; gold-rimmed glasses are proffered, of coca-cola on the rocks. The Sultan stirs in his chair and we all rise at the approach of Her Majesty.

She sits in the throne chair beside her husband. 'We have met before?' Her warm and accessible manner is immediately endearing. Now she flicks her hands at a distant footman and then whirs them vigorously; the over-zealous ceiling fans dwindle to a stop. We follow the Sultana into the dining-room through heavy teak doors mounted in ormolu into another vast room emblazoned in gilt and glass and the Johor royal colours of buttercup and deep blue. The Sultan stations himself at the head of the long glass table with the Sultana on his right and Tom on his left. The Sultana motions me to sit on her right and charming daughter No. 6 steps in on my right. A file of six moustachi-oed young footmen surrender their silver salvers to HM. Plates are piled with pungent curries, rice, and watery vegetables. The Sultana leans towards me. 'This next one is our national speciality, fish head curry.' The shell and bone left on our plates make an interesting study. No. 6 is a happy scion of her mother. A retroussé nose and long, slim neck add distinction to her; her dark eyes and hair gleam with health. She loves history and reading and computer technology. She is reading Antonia Fraser's tome on the wives of Henry VIII and assures me that Anne Boleyn is a bad lot.

The Sultan mellows away to Tom; the famous histrionics are not for us, it seems. Crème caramel is served in wine glasses. The phalanx of glass candelabra down the table must stand six feet high and the silver-worked palm-tree set before me is hideous. The footmen straighten their backs in their brass-buttoned tunics as we leave the room. The heavy doors close behind us when His Majesty remembers his half-finished tumbler of coca-cola. The Sultana motions me to the powder-room which is crammed with every scent and emollient and gew-gaw. A guard is stationed outside to return me to her Majesty. Would I like to see the family photographs? We walk the length of the drawing-room past console tables laden with framed brides and military consorts – our Queen, the Queen of the Belgians, Queen Sirikit of Thailand. How is Queen Sirikit? Still not well? 'She has a hormonal disorder. She has swollen up. I feel so sorry for her. She has such a big palace to run. This is our daughter with her husband the Crown Prince of Pahang, and here, our other daughter, married to the younger son of the Sultan of Selangor.' This prudent intermarriage between the Royal families of Malaysia would appear exemplary. These noble young marrieds beam confidently from their silver frames. 'Come into the garden and see the sea!' She breathes deeply. 'This time of year, it is cool. The monsoon season is my favourite season.'

Lunch with the Sultan of Selangor had been a less formal occasion. One hundred guests were invited to a house-warming of the newly-built Golf Palace. The vast teak-lined, mirrored rooms swarmed with silk sarongs and kebayahs; brilliance and jewels emblazoned upon all. This Sultan is a man in a hurry. Armed with a beautiful new wife, younger than his own daughters, a vast mock-Palladio golf club, built within the year, he promotes an infectious joie-de-vivre. Reports that tapioca crops in surrounding villages have been ravaged by wild boar did not dim the celebrations. (This invasion of wild life from extended golf courses and express roadways is upsetting the animal apple cart.) The whole of Malaysia has gone golf mad; jungle is cleared at a stroke and red mud swamps are laid with New Zealand turf in a trice.

Clutching coke and orange juice we passed through rooms of monolithic chandeliers, brown furniture, and pink, squashy leather sofas. A portrait of the recently deceased first Sultana gazed down the length of the main reception room, her pale little face pinched with pain. Before taking to her wheelchair she had lectured on domestic science in Kuala Lumpur. As wife and consort to the Sultan of Selangor, she had been renowned for her Palace table.

The present Sultana looked too ethereal to eat, let alone cook. She smiled at us helplessly as she teetered by on pink stilettoes, her tall body trussed in a tube of sky-blue silk. The affable Sultan, casually dressed in open-neck shirt, led his party on to the pool terrace. Lunch tables had been set under umbrellas. A pair of blue and gold macaws screeched in their cage set beside the royal dais. An elegant white cockatoo set free to flit and flutter maddened them. A lunch of spiced meat and chicken, grilled and doused with the favourite satay sauce, a sugar-salt mix of crushed peanuts, chilli, and coconut milk. (Hot food is an acclaimed antidote to a burning sun.) The Sultan and bearers filled our glasses again and again with iced water. 'You like golf?' A member of the Royal household sat beside us. (He had qualified as a surgeon at Guy's in 1947.) 'This golf course is the first night course in the world. It is like daytime play with our fine lighting system; we have 27 holes. People like to work all day and play all night!' (And in the London *Times* 'City Diary' we have already read: 'A new golf club in Malaysia has imported 120 Indonesian women to act as caddies . . . it is not unusual for the girls to take their tops off . . .') The Sultan of Selangor is a serious spender? 'Oh, the Sultan thinks big! You have seen his new blue mosque? It is bigger than your St Paul's.'

December 9 Hardwicke House

The Prime Minister's announcement, today, of the official separation of the Prince and Princess of Wales was marked by an eclipse of the moon. We were dining with the Tanlaws[3] in Brompton Square. At around ten we spilled on to the pavement to see a silver moon swiftly erased. Strange to tell: there was an eclipse of the moon at the time of Edward VIII's abdication, December 1936.

December 10 Hardwicke House

Sir Eric Penn, former comptroller of the Royal Household, brushed past our table in the crowded Poissonnerie restaurant. Tall, handsome, and eminently distinguished as he approaches eighty, he looked pale and harassed. Tom stood and called to him, 'Dear Eric, there is bad trouble in your old shop. How are you?' He replied, 'It is appalling, I cannot even contemplate . . .'

December 26 Hardwicke House

Christmas Day, Boxing Day, the house ablaze with scented candles, champagne and roses, tartan bows and log fires, spruce and spice, smiles and screams and excitement; like a runaway train is Christmas. Then all is sudden silence and dirty plates; dishevelled sofas and contorted rugs; a heap of tinselled debris, dismembered crackers, presents half-opened, presents unopened. Exhaustion and dying flames and flowers and voices. 'A lovely day, darling, you must put your feet up.' 'Wonderful lunch and wines and presents. We can't think how you manage.' 'We must go now, we have to drive 200 miles to a Christmas dinner.'

If there is joy in our Christmas it is in the preparation, the decorating, the burnishing of favourite chattels, the buffing of brass and glass and silver, the perfecting of a performance. But the dawning of the day, its rush and banana-skins, the bottle of water that slipped from hand and bust the Georgian wine glass, the sausage meat stuffing forgotten and untouched, as it lay in its roasted womb; sparks from the fire and warning smoulders and the over-zealous tidy one who banished my new black kid gloves to the bin.

[3] Simon Tanlaw, created a Life Peer in 1971, is a prominent member of the Liberal party, and adviser on alternative energy strategies. Rina, his second wife, is the daughter of the late Tiong Cha Tan and Mrs Tan.

On, on with the show; for lunch on Boxing Day we have Malaysians. (The ADC to the King extant telephones his good wishes. But what was he doing in London boxed up in Notting Hill Gate? He had to be asked . . .)

Cold pork and gammon for lunch? Muslims? Salmon is hastily sliced; the butter for thin bread is too hard to spread.

'Do you mind dogs? Labradors . . . very friendly.'

'If your dog touch us we have to wash seven times over.' We are silenced. As labradors have an unfortunate propensity to lunge at the private parts, the mind boggles.

The ADC's khaki face creases amiably, 'You serve an excellent smoked salmon.' He masticates with relish. I am embarrassed by the glob of butter on his bread. (As long as Nanny keeps the dogs shut away in the nursery – then after lunch I can move them to the sitting-room – soothe them with *The Marriage of Figaro* . . . The ADC to the King of Malaysia must not be alarmed or discomfited – The Asprey account is at stake . . .)

1993

January 1 Chilworth Manor Nr Guildford

Lady Heald is indefatigable in voice, spirit, and cyclamen-pink. Widow of the late Attorney-General, Sir Lionel, she is hosting a small lunch party; on Christmas Day she sat down twenty-six to include her grandchildren and great-grandchildren. Her emerald lawns and white panelled drawing-room are awash with winter sun; it slants through the old avenue of . . . lime? Oak? In the dining-room a celebration of glass and silver on white linen quivers in prisms of light. 'I am a dull, conservative type,' cautions the man on my right. He is handsome and charming. On my left a more professional charmer, a military man. 'I fought my five years in the war, only five out of twenty in my class at Eton survived, but it was as good a way as any for a young man to spend his time. Very comfortable we were, always dog-tired. I am reading this book by General de la Billière; the Gulf War hero. Funny name de la Billière, sounds like a piece of lady's underwear, bustier? Billière?'

'Prince Charles should have gone to Eton!' Lady Heald's ringing summation bounces off the silver down the entire length of the lunch table. 'That stupid Prince Philip sending him to Gordonstoun! I am told it is an appalling place. He never met anybody up there. At Eton he would have found his milieu.' In the face of a discredited monarchy and a jejune government, are the playing fields at Eton the last bastion of British rank and order?

January 19 Hardwick House

As Bill Clinton takes up the cudgels for the 42nd Presidency of America, the British Monarchy crumbles. The Royal family has barely sustained a six-month siege on its privacy. Its defences are down and its administrations confounded. That long-hallowed veil of mystery has worn a little thinner with each decade; that timely tweak from the Princess of Wales goaded the media to rip it away. Has she unwittingly instigated a streamlined workaday force more suited to today's social mores? For forty years the Queen has presided admirably over the rich ceremonial and trappings of royal life; today's priorities and pleasures are changed. The public likes fast food, instant sun, home videos, disposable nappies, hair-dryers, and husbands. The old anticipation and mulling over of tradition and glorious pageantry has shot its bolt. Contributory factors? A rampant and outrageously intrusive press: the provocation of young royals by their spoilt, puerile, and sexually unwary behaviour; inept advisors in the Palace; the unheeded passing of time and relevance.

Has the Monarchy become a phased-out cottage industry? Where did the Queen go wrong? (Some British aristocrats, whose lineage is rooted far deeper than the Royal family's, must be tempted to dismiss them as 'little people'.)

Every glittering facet of the Royal family is now under probe and speculation.

Will Charles and Diana finally divorce?

Will Charles come to the throne?

Does he want to come to the throne?

Will he remain unmarried?

Will he remarry?

One weekend story read: '. . . at the height of the separation drama Charles found the pressure almost impossible. He once broke down and said he could no longer cope with this ghastly country!'

Will the Queen promote Prince William for a new lead?

Will Princess Anne step in as the Princess Royal Regent?

(She has sustained her image and public respect through hard work and a circumspect life style. Her new naval commander husband would be an excellent consort.)

Princess Diana? The world is her oyster still. She must continue to build her life outside the Palace corral. A little more humility could do her proud and a real man next time round.

February 24 Hardwicke House

We have fast become a crime-wise nation. Danger lurks even by the country kissing gate where long grass hoists a flag to rape. No London subway, street, shop, bank, garage, or home is safe from the lawless tentacles of pillage, rape, and murder. Last week a two-year-old toddler in Merseyside made history. Bored with the butcher's queue, he wandered from his mother's side, in a trice he was spirited away by a pair of ten-year-old boys. Hours later his body was found mangled on a rail track. To simulate an accident? The two minors are charged with his murder and constitute the first such case in this century. We have to thank computer technology for catching the two miscreants on the video screens of the shopping arcade. Such bland intrusion into privacy can sometimes serve us well.

Despite media-overdrive on murder, child abuse, wife-bashing, rape, geriatric mugging, vandalism, and burglary, London still falls behind in world crime statistics. Rome is judged the most dangerous city today, where one person in sixty-four is a victim of violence. Los Angeles, Miami, and Berlin are hot contenders for danger. Paris (1 in 140) and New York (1 in 166) are also precursors to London (1 in 178). Tokyo sits smug as teacher's pet, with one Japanese in 2,332 singled out for harm. (It could be worth staging a fall from grace for posterity.)

Clutching my bag through Carnaby Street I walk purposefully to a lunch date with Selina Hastings (biographer and literary editor of *Harpers and Queen*). I arrive early at the modest restaurant in Lexington Street. The sunny morning, the bustle of the cobbled streets, garish with lights and grimcrack trade, bejewelled noses and frazzled hair and jeans, lure me through the mêlée to Greek Street to Au Jardin des Gourmets and L'Escargot, a favourite venue of thirty years past. But where is the mural of flowers and shutter boards that clasped the diners in a bower? Au Jardin was re-furbished in January, the waiter tells me. It now resembles an executive suite, a dentist's waiting-room with pseudo-leather bucket seats and powder closet lighting. And L'Escargot? What a travesty! Vegetable soup and grilled plaice on the menu of today? It is a sad and empty scene engulfed in green. Back to Frith Street where towering flambeaux tempt me inside L'Epicure. The same tables. The same crêpes suzette being flamed at your side. And then a curious shiver as I recognise the headwaiter from 1957.

Back at The Lexington, Selina and I are tucked into her corner table. She looking fresh and pink and young, untouched by the trammels of domestic life? Yet harassed by her publishers. How is her biography on Evelyn Waugh? 'We are in our seventh year.' Her next candidate is the novelist Rosamond Lehmann. How to begin these undertakings? 'I wade through mounds of letters and material, year by year and month by month. Gradually my own opinions are sifted and evolved, one foot in front of the other.' Writing a biography of somebody so minutely analysed by others must be one long process of elimination.

As I walk through narrow streets to that pulsing artery off Regent Street, I wonder at the ostensibly innocent face of Soho. Even that brazen callgirl in the black doorway looks more ready for aerobics than flagellation. Perhaps it is all a question of being in the wrong place at the right time.

March 21 Manila The Philippines

The bouquet of orchids is so pendulous and so rotund that it is wheeled to our room on a trolley. The diminutive bellboy clasps the arrangement manfully to his white tunic and staggers to a side-table. (When two days later we tried to airlift it to Singapore we found each bloom had been docked and inserted in a plastic phial of water, in turn inserted in a hollow twig, the whole artfully masked in moss. By such innovative deception is dimension achieved. A national Philippine characteristic?)

The Philippine Islands are spattered on the South China Sea, etched on the map like some skeletal grasshopper. Fragile and vulnerable on their volcanic bedrock, they are perennial prey to fire and flooding. Here in Manila, a sprawling concrete concourse of stern façades and belching traffic, the overall and sinister Chinese whispers of kidnapping and torture are blamed. The spasmodic eruption of volcanoes and earth tremors are equal turn-offs. But these black rock city walls conceal some friendly modernised interiors, gleaming marble flooring, and richly-carved ceilings. You step back in time at the luxurious and renowned Hotel Manila.

At the mouth of the stinking Pasig river we wander in a haze of heat and jet-lag through the precincts of Intra Muros (within the walls), the sixteenth-century fortressed city of old Manila, a restored but diminished complex after centuries of attack by the Chinese, Portuguese and Dutch. At Fort Santiago, the vantage point on the harbour bay, there was a final watershed of bombs from the Japanese in WWII. I step down shallow stone stairs where a small arch gapes, black and void; it leads to dungeon cells. Here the WWII Filipino prisoners were rounded up, wave upon wave, to drown in the rising tide.

'On a green hill far away' and high above the city wall lies the American WWII Cemetery. A monument of light and air where frangipani trees (the white flower of mourning) and the yellow flowering acacia rock their fragrance through the white stone colonnades, where birds and the sun and moon flit through each arch, inscribed with name after name. The acres of green rounded slopes are stabbed with 17,000 marble crosses: the American thousands who died defending the Philippines from the Japanese.

March 22 The Malacanang Palace Manila

We crawl through the dusty suburban tentacles of Manila. Our driver explains: 'We have three main problems: political stability; peace and order; power energy and infrastructure.' It all takes time, we assure him. 'Last week we had a ten-hour black-out. So many outrages; so much production loss. And we have no tourism.' We arrive at the Malacanang Palace which sits like a delectable Belgian white chocolate by the waving palms on the Pasig river. *May Lakan Diyan* (here lives a nobleman). Built by a Spanish aristocrat in 1802, on rich and solid lines, a colonial pillared façade with much marble and carved wood ceilings within.

Two young men in jeans are busy in the front marble hall meticulously re-gilding foliate scrolling on a wrought-iron screen. (Above them a pair of suspended glass lights are blurred with dead flies heaped on their shallow saucers.) We are led up the red carpeted stairs to the former residence. Imelda Marcos's king-sized bed is flounced and draped in ivory muslin woven from 'our best pineapple fibre'. (It looks lustrous.) Her shoes and lingerie? Now confiscated from public view? Caused too much comment? 'The subsequent President did not like.' The oval ceiling is elaborately carved in heavy dark wood. Her own collection of Indian furniture, inlaid with mother of pearl and ivory, stands, stilted and uninviting in the adjacent salon. There are no outside windows in these rooms. Imelda's former rooms – dark, secret, womb-like – her retreat from the hostile world that she provoked around her. Ferdinand Marcos's rooms ensuite are open and light in contrast. Cool from the breezes of the Pasig river below with waving palms and an open sky; pleasant rooms conducive to talk and thought, a regular rendezvous for the President's men.

March 23 Forbes Park Manila

Tonight we dine with Jaime (the former Philippine Ambassador to London) and Bea Zobel de Ayala. (It was Jaime who sent me the stupendous orchids.) Over breakfast we have devoured Jaime's dynamic dictates in the *Manila Chronicle*. His stark prognosis of the state of his country is stirring stuff. Jaime Zobel, from one of the world's richest families, is a respected entrepreneur and industrialist on a vast scale.

The economic outlook for the Philippines is poor; the future looks tough. The two salient forces for progress today are new technologies and exchanges with the 'Tiger Economies' – Korea, Taiwan, Hong

Kong and Singapore. They thrive. Japan is now the world's leading financial power and the most innovative in high-tech. (Compared to our previous conversation with the driver, Manila's painful plod to posterity has clearly hit an all-time low.)

A maroon Mercedes – the latest make – swoops us through the wide dark roads of the exclusive residential area, Forbes Park. Substantial villas brood behind high walls; the car sweeps into Jaime's drive and forecourt. Soldiers ring the garden. They slip in and out of shadows and nurse their guns and holsters. Manila is under siege in fear of kidnapping, of torture, of death. A band of Filipinos (and retired military police with their guns still stowed are even impugned) have been clawing at the rich Chinese community. Their jealousy is rife. The power and progress of the Chinese in Manila has precipitated a peevish bed of crime.

We are siphoned through rooms with broad views and verandas on to the garden. Brown men in white gloves hand us drinks and sea food canapés in warmed napkins. The soft-lit rooms are comfortably padded with low sofas and benches covered in chintz. Ancient porcelain, rare books, and splashes of modern art reflect the selective tastes of an old-established family. Jaime and Bea have seven children. 'My daughters have married Spaniards,' explains Bea, herself the daughter of a Spanish admiral. 'We spend our summers at Soto Grande and the young, they all meet up. It is not so surprising.'

She leads her guests to a swagged canopy in her shadowy garden. Parchment lanterns swing from huge acacia trees, and orchids, pink and sweet-smelling, trail through tropicalia. There follows a five-course dinner – wines and flowers and embroidered linen. It is eighteen years since we last met. From 1970 to 1975 Jaime was the Philippine Ambassador; aged thirty-six he was the youngest-ever incumbent at the Court of St James. 'The youngest ambassador of all and undamaged,' recalls Jaime whimsically. 'But I shut away my medals into little boxes long ago.' Slim, dapper, and an enthusiast, he aims to revamp metro Manila's business concourse with strategic real estate, fully-powered infrastructure and telecommunications. 'I am an industrialist,' he asserts firmly.

March 24 Singapore

Nina's house, an elaborate colonial villa plunged into palm-trees, rests high on a hill. Singapore, black and pulsing far below, pin-pricked with lights. Nina, luscious in swathes of oyster satin and a bodice of encrusted sea pearls, glistens between thick tumbling black hair, wide eyes, wide lips, white teeth and jewels. She is an inveterate hostess. Indian, rich, and cosmopolitan. (Husband Rajan is big in food stuffs.) We sip Roederer Cristal champagne from magnificent flutes and eye the spacious white room with high ceilings and windows and walls cushioned with succulent fronds in priceless porcelain. Great arcs of stiff sweet lilies and bright orchids, and raw art is thrust beside old books, bronzes and a phalanx of glass. Glass everywhere, glittering, reflecting diamonds, flared with lights. A low table with sphinx supports and a candelabra that flutters in the evening breeze. A headless torso astonishes in a corner. Nina has slung emeralds as big as quails' eggs around the neck. Are they real? The fastidious man from Sotheby's cowers before this whole flamboyant scene. 'I should not imagine so,' he mutters. 'On the other hand . . .' He looks suddenly suspicious. They look superb. Nina glides towards us, a white chihuahua nestling in her pearls. 'Oh that? It's acrylic you know.' But did she mean the necklace or the torso? (Travel provokes endless unanswered questions.) She wafts us through to an Italian-Indian dinner set on more waves of sumptuous glass.

March 25 Kuala Lumpur

Hari Raya (the Muslim New Year) and the end of Ramadan and fasting is a celebration day when families hold open house and the Sultans open up their palaces. At the Istana Kayangan the expansive Sultan of Selangor (who next week celebrates his sixty-seventh birthday) rolls out the royal yellow carpet. He cuts a striking figure in cream satin with a sarong of rich brocade tied across his hips in the manner of a bath towel. He wears his songkok – a type of fez – at a jaunty tilt. His twenty-three-year-old second wife stands tall and serene beside him. She shakes hands, smiles, stoops, and straightens. One day she could be Queen – a dowager – the mother of his children? (She is younger than his own.) The scent of lilies swirls through the rooms where pungent curry is served and cakes and orange juice and tea. (It is a Muslim feast.) Each man is resplendent in his high-buttoned silk pyjama suit and songkok. Vivid, garish colour rules the day, men in purple, orange, blue, shrill green, and shocking pink. Each waist is firmly bandaged with a brocade sarong, 'for fear we seem to wear our pyjamas'.

We sit in a cool, wood pavilion, with the flower garden, lawns, and terraces all around. I sit between two princes. The Sultan's son Prince Suleiman is affable and fleshy with a croquet hoop moustache. Married to a daughter of Johor, he is openly concerned at the newly-revised legal strictures on the Sultans and their families. The unpopular Prime

Minister Dr Mahatir is corralling the Sultans into his grand centralis-
ation scheme for Malaysia. His aim is to annihilate their influence in
politics and in trading and to make any extravagant, bad, or quixotic
behaviour accountable to law. All previous immunities are effectively
now quashed. (It is the demise of unjustified privilege that sweeps
through the entire world.) In between mouthfuls of cake and curry,
Prince Suleiman dabs his dewlaps and expostulates roundly. His podgy
fingers, trapped in silver knuckle-dusters, pat the table top. He says:
'We have the French Revolution, the Russian Revolution, the stripping
of the Maharajahs, the Iranian Revolution, the fall of the House of
Windsor? And now the muzzling of the Malay Sultans. But we are a
body of nine and the people of our nine states do not want centralis-
ation; they want their ethnic customs and geographical distinctions.'

Clutches of balloons bat listlessly on the ceiling, some shrivelled.
Children run in and out in various degrees of fancy dress. They sit
quietly for a moment with their cakes and juice and dutifully admire
the blue and white iced masterpiece of the Sultan's mosque. Is it
edible? The brittle domes and minarets do not invite a prod from
sticky fingers. Plump Prince Suleiman looks far more alluring. They
slip from their chairs and run up to him in turn to bow and curtsy
their thank yous. A continual stream of well-wishers sidle up to stoop
and press the royal hand.

March 30 Kuala Lumpur

Tom is disconsolate; all this protracted patience. For what? A telephone
call from the Palace of the Sultan of Pahang! An audience we crave –
will it elude us? The days run out; but this very afternoon a call is
expected. Our case has been handled like eggs; coddled in all the
delicacies of an auspicious introduction.

A thunderstorm shatters and rumbles around us. From our cosy eyrie
on the twenty-third floor we gaze on the frantic dance of lightning, at
the sluicing sheets of rain. An exhilaration takes hold. After rain, more
sun and steam. We plunge into Chinatown, the covered market, and
the winding streets, the evening air thick with foods and frying fat.
Black woks sizzle with fish and glass kiosks groan with unidentifiable
bits of unidentifiable animals, curried and coated in khaki. It is rush
hour and full of the roar of traffic, the shouts of young people set free
from work . . . Indians, Chinese, Malay, thrusting in a tangled weave
of saris, sarongs, and jeans. The strains of a banjo as a yellow young
man with long black hair sings of love in English. Seasoned crones
are clustered in a corner, stern, imperturbable, their fief stapled with

umbrellas set on stands. Wide wicker baskets are heaped with preserved ducks' eggs with orange yolks, the tropical harvest of starfruit, breadfruit, papaya, mango, guava, and jackfruit; better admired than eaten. Young girls flutter like moths to the 'gold' booths, the twinkling vitrines wink their wares. 'Milky Way Jewellery.' 'Golden Star.'

April 1 Kuala Lumpur

'Chinese submarines deployed at Spratlys.' As reported today in the *New Straits Times*. Patrolling? Prospecting for oil? The South China Sea is shallow – a sitting duck for oil-diggers. These outcrop islands are contested openly by Taiwan, Hong Kong, the Philippines, Thailand, and Malaysia. Are we approaching the foothills of a mounting disaster? Is the Far East a new danger zone about to happen? (Malaysia claims twelve of the Spratly Islands.) Asia today is a flourishing arms market – wooed by Russia and America with cut-price arsenal. 'Our intention is strictly defensive,' asserts the Malaysian Defence Minister. Nothing to do with the Spratlys? China desperately needs oil fast to fuel her escalating economy; her mounting focus on the Spratlys sends tremors through the Pacific Rim.

April 3 Istana Alam Shah Klang Kuala Lumpur

It is 9.30 am and we sit in rows, on high-backed red velvet chairs. We are encrusted in jewels and brilliant silks, the men in particularly exotic headgear, each fez of a different brocade and caprice as befits the wearer's geographical state. Seating of subjects is effected with much chatting, rising from seats, cheerful salutes, and shoulder-patting. The throne room is ablaze with chandeliers, reflected in mirrored panels. The sun pales in significance. We wait in a womb of scarlet and yellow, and leaf through our yellow programme; 'yellow is the Royal colour in Malaysia', substantially illustrated with the Sultan of Selangor and the Crown Prince, both in yellow. Various medals deployed on yellow ribbons will soon be awarded. This is a Royal investiture.

A gilded throne is set on a dais between two gold cabinets. Swags of yellow satin clasped with finely-carved screens and gold filigree flank this shrine of anticipation. Now silence – a shuffle, a rustle of silk – we stand. The Sultan glides to the throne, a pillar of yellow silk, his fez billowing with peaks and pleats, secured by a double clutch of diamonds. His entourage disperses as he takes his throne to the sound of trumpets and clashing cymbals. The band, discreetly posted outside in a palm grove, is quickly outdone by cannon fire. How many shots? (It is the Sultan's sixty-seventh birthday.) A complement of twenty-one explosive shells rattles the chandeliers. The Sultan attends to his citizens oblivious to fire and fanfare. Two guards proffer each medal to the Sultan on a yellow velvet cushion. The Sultan has a practised touch; yellow sashes are placed firmly over shoulders and around necks. Finally he hands a scroll to each Justice of the Peace and the ceremony is concluded.

The low white palace with its gilded cupola and balustraded terraces is en fête for the Sultan's birthday. Yellow carpet careers up and down steps and stairs, through reception rooms and verandas. The band belches out such golden oldies as *O My Papa* and *You Are My Destiny*. The clamour, the dazzling kaleidoscope of gaudy tent awnings, sarongs and pantaloons, and floating chiffon, punches the sun and heat to a frenzy.

Silence, and the Sultan descends from the palace terrace and walks majestically to his air-conditioned veranda; his Sultana and the ebullient Suleiman follow behind. The Sultan arranges himself and his yellow finery in a yellow chair. A flotilla of pretty girls, demure in white, form an arc before him. (Perhaps from such a group he singled out his present young wife?) Now the Mullahs take over, their mournful calls to prayer well-amplified. Behind us in the serving tents, the clink and gurgle of orange juice being poured into glasses, the clatter of kettles and cups, the whiff of tea and cardamom and curry. The Mullahs draw breath, a pause to sip orange and some innocuous pink fluid which defies detection, and to chew on glutinous sweetmeats of bilious green and magenta and royal yellow.

'It must be over 100°F,' mutters Tom, as we all form up on the vast grass pitch to press the Sultan's hand. Some 600 people, Tom reckons, and now 599 as our colleague dives into the nearest rose bush to be sick. (He has been complaining all day of wearing too heavy a suit.) The Sultana teeters behind her husband in her green stiletto heels. This afternoon she wears a fitted green brocade jacket over a long skirt, a tall obelisk of green, she seems, with a veil of fuchsia chiffon, stitched with silver arabesques and gold. We have never seen her hair or ears; all adornment is confined to the elaborate silks of her gowns and headdresses and her determined penchant for stiletto heels. The Sultan is upon us, lustrous in his smiles and yellow silk. 'Ah! We have a fiery sun for you today!' He expresses concern for our colleague whom earlier he saw being whisked away with a glass of water in a Mercedes.

An essentially Muslim show of tradition and deference and affection for the Sultan and his family. (And yet he had commissioned from

Asprey two guns, disguised as walking sticks with hilts of gold and
emerald and diamond.) For today he rides a gentle Malay sea of round
brown smiling faces, not one centralist or Chinese in sight.

April 21 The Blickling Estate Itteringham Norfolk

I love this north Norfolk. We are snug at night in our National Trust
Cottage at Itteringham, a hamlet on the Bure river, sheltered by
oak-woods and chestnut and spread around with spongy fields and
dykes, black mud and streams and raging sunsets. Our newly-converted
cottage is flush with whitewash and pine and provençal floor tiles. The
kitchen boasts a micro-wave oven, but such advance is readily
redressed by no telephone. A young family has rented the other half.
Baby Imogen drools placidly on the patch of grass beside the washing
line of flapping rompers, towels, and daddy's shorts. Her older sister
Kate is bright-eyed with an insatiable desire to pour out newly-culled
information and to fill up with more. This evening we had an exemplary peroration on water tables. She finally thanked me for *Jane Eyre*.
Aged eight she is happily into the second chapter.

Blickling Hall exhales history, intrigue, and that distilled purity of
age. It remains a glorious statement of brooding plum brick furbelows,
gables and turrets and ornamental chimney-stacks, to compare with
Hatfield House and Hampton Court. Its lakes and lawns, topiary and
parterres enchant, with the sweep of woods around. And those purple
pouches of aubrietia entangled in its eaves surprise and delight as you
approach.

Did Henry VIII court his Anne Boleyn in these water meadows?
Her father, Sir Thomas Boleyn, was only too happy to press his suit
through the King's ardent pursuit of his second daughter. But the
romances of the Tudor and Jacobean years were curtailed through the
centuries. Solemn, single men and long-term widows have left their
stamp of austerity and gloom. Fine Jacobean ceilings with stalactite
finials preside over brooding rooms of indifferent furniture and pictures. The Long Gallery, the Brown Drawing-Room, where 1930
tastes for sad, soupy greens and cream dominate. The invasion of the
RAF in WWII was another blow to grace and order. Blickling became
the local officers' mess. Nights off-duty were enlivened by bashing
through to sleeping state-rooms, orgies of vandalism, and the smash-
ing-up of old crown glass windows. Back in September 1772 there
comes another disenchanted report from one Lady Beauchamp Proc-
tor: 'We were afraid of being too soon but on sending our names were
admitted. We found they had breakfasted and my Lord's horses stood

at the door, though the servant told us he was gone out. We saw no other trace of her ladyship than two or three workbags and a tambour; I believe we drove her from room to room but that we could not help. We saw only the old part of the house, over which a very dirty housemaid, with a duster in her hand, conducted us.'

Blickling is history, a resilient gem in the National Trust's cap.

April 22

As an antidote to culture, Sebastian steers me to the Northern Norfolk Railway. We take a vintage coastal steam train from Sheringham to Holt, past sea shores, golf courses, woods, and half-dismantled tracks. These village platforms evoke nostalgia with Victorian trunks, hard leather cases, weighing machines, and familiar old adverts: 'Spillers Shapes for Dogs', 'Wills's Gold Flake cigarettes', 'Mazawatee Tea'. These period sets are used regularly for Agatha Christie 1920 detective thrillers, but the stench, the shunting, the jerks and chunting, the shouts and hoots and creaks and jolts, the guard in his hat with his flapping flag, the hiss of steam, and the putrid smoke give me no sharp thrill of nostalgia. It was only thirty years ago that these relics played a humdrum role in our daily lives.

Sebastian graciously concedes the afternoon is mine and prepares himself for a stolid tramp through Felbrigg Hall and its walled garden (where the eighteenth-century octagonal dovecote provides prized manure for the roses). We approach through a long wooded drive; the flintstone parish church, with medieval foundations, squats in the middle distance of a ploughed field. Two black labradors and a tractor bound before it, to and fro. The first village of Felbrigg passed away in the Plague, they say. The parish register records a heavy toll in the summer of 1550. The hall is a bleak façade of eighteenth-century limewash that crumbles from the red brick and flint wall. This main south front shows modified characteristics of Blickling and contrasts uncomfortably with the adjoining 1750 red brick west front with its tall sash windows. The subsequent east front, built in a medley of Victorian, Gothic, and Flemish flourishes, adds to the confusion of age and styles. Roger North, a contemporary writer, in his essay *Of Building* says, 'Mr Windham's at Felbrigg, where is added to an old house, a stately apartment . . . the whole so different from the rest of the house, that I am not, though the generality are, pleased with it.'

It is nevertheless fascinating to see such demarcation of style in the space of fifty years. Inside, Felbrigg does not disappoint. Its outer mongrel packaging conceals a feast of fine plaster ceilings, fine furniture gilded and inlaid, sumptuous wall glasses and silk damask walls clustered with gouaches and oil paintings. There are four-posters in the Red Room, the Yellow Room, the Rose Room, and the Chinese Room, all lavishly festooned with chintz or silks. Day beds, sofas, and chaises longues, en suite, and intimate writing tables, dressing tables, and gilt pier glasses that exude memories of lives loved and lost.

I am in the Book Room looking through the window over the porch to flat fields and sheep, old, gnarled chestnuts and oaks. The sea is two miles beyond, shielded by the Great Wood founded three hundred years ago. Time stands still. A National Trust caretaker talks softly in the corner about a young man lost in the Great Hall and wanting to go home. I find Sebastian by the east wing. He has made friends with two young men up ladders, painting the drainpipes in the National Trust dark green.

May 1 Hardwicke House

A grey afternoon, too cold to open the balcony French windows; the heavy swags of wisteria sway their scent on the back of the wind. I sit on the sofa pen-pushing with half a mind; Lydia is in labour. When will we hear? 6 o'clock? 10 o'clock? Midnight? Tomorrow? The telephone! Rupert's voice – amused, tired – 'Hello, Grannie! Luke was born at 3:15 pm.' On subsequent inspection Luke appears the perfect baby – long fingers, long legs and such thick, long blond hair that he has a parting. Said Lydia's old nanny on peering into his swivelling blue eyes, 'That child has been here before.'

May 5 Hardwicke House

Tom has been made redundant from Asprey plc. He is shocked, surprised; not altogether sorry; relieved rather.

May 8 Barnsley Cirencester

A ravishing morning with bright sun and boisterous north wind; we amble through radial rides between beech-hedges, rich and green and regimented. A strategic statue is poised at each apex. Barnsley is Charley and Sarah Faringdon's summer home. It is a grand diversion to have a house for each season. 'Today we lunch in the Winter

Palace.' And this arrangement gives the resident dining-room a rest and time to lay up for dinner.

At Barnsley, a cornucopia of Baroque Italian ceilings and Nash embellishments overflow into the garden. Sarah heaps luxurious and cosy accoutrements round her guests . . . roaring fires and flowers and piles of new books and papers and more flowers. 'I love white flowers; they look best in these rooms.'

From Barnsley we drive through green lanes frothing with white chestnut candles through many stone Cotswold villages to Buscot. Set high on its hill, where winds buffet and scorch, the front lawns look bald. Charley leads us to the orangery and doffs his chef's apron. We sit beside his brazier and sip sparkling rosé, marvelling at the red juicy steaks exquisitely branded and cooked within five minutes. (I am alarmed at the wind and flames and hold back his billowing apron.) Sarah produces hot baked potatoes from the Land Rover. From brazier to orangery – never has meat tasted better. Now the brindled lurcher barks with anxious, amber eyes. 'The public are on their way up the drive.' We pack up and take a quick look in the house. The rooms look doubly important and unfamiliar, penned off with cord for public view. Tom takes a photograph of the dog Caspar, on the wrong side of the rope, rammed against a gilded Egyptian banquette, bristling with sphinxes[1].

Back to Barnsley, where every era is reflected. I revel in the capacious 1930 zinc bath, the mahogany lavatory with its ferocious flush, the defunct in-house black telephones, the porcelain bell-pulls, the fanned cream card in empty grates, the bois-clair bath water, the outsized brass locks on every door, meals with garden vegetables from an unseen cook and unheard kitchen, the final sinking into white linen and a four-poster bed. At 2 am this sense of timeless luxury is redressed; a visit to the mahogany lavatory at the far end of the passage incurs much groping around the bed posts and protruding sofa, a crash with a writing desk, a marble-topped commode, a stool and a frantic fumble for a door knob, a light . . .

May 9 Barnsley

In driving rain we bounce round Charley's newly-planted arboretum in a Land Rover. I am reminded of *Oh! What a Lovely War*. Rows of slim baby trunks prick the long wet grass as far as the eye can see. Each specialist tree is shouldered by an alder or beech; this lesser stock

[1] Caspar, the lurcher, to be finally enshrined in bronze and put on display by the sphinxes.

acts as a decoy for feeding birds and rabbits and ensures a straight trunk. In time they will be felled for sale and firewood to leave the specialist trees, three of each variety; one for keeps in prime position, one for sale transplant and one for use in large cabinet-making. Charley is agog with enthusiasm – leaping in and out of the Land Rover in rain and sopping grass. We follow him and get soaked feet. 'You see this Chinese red bark birch? And now see it here on the map! We have brought over a lot of trees from China; they have lime soil like ours.' A helicopter drones overhead.

'There goes the Monarch. He likes my arboretum and zones in with his weekend house parties to have a look; not in wellingtons and sweaters, you understand; he likes to be asked to lunch.'

May 17 Hardwicke House

Sir Anthony Tennant, the new Chairman of Christie's, comes to dinner – black tie, ten round the table: silver candelabra; roses; lobster; duck; bombe cointreau; two pretty maids and Château Palmer 1970.

Anthony Tennant arrives, clutching today's sale catalogue, with the colour entry of a nineteenth-century gilded German calculator. It was valued at £20,000 and was sold this morning for £7.7 million. On his second day in office, Sir Anthony is cock-a-hoop.

May 26 Hardwicke House

This evening the opening of David Linley's new furniture shop at 60 Pimlico Road. Everything has come together for him, a lovely fiancée, Lady Serena Stanhope, his burgeoning career, the prestigious new premises, and the publication of his book on classical furniture[2]. His mother, Princess Margaret, diminutive in lavender satin, smiles proudly. (We missed her cutting the white ribbon. The rain, crowds from Chelsea Flower Show, security police, and police directing traffic, and misdirecting traffic, caused chaos.) Tom talks to David's father, who as the young Tony Armstrong Jones, forty years back, set up shop himself in Pimlico Road. Lord Snowdon, today, is worried that his son has bitten off too big a property, but as a parent what can one say? Tom asks him if David has managed to sell off his old shop at No 1 New Kings Road. 'I haven't dared ask.'

It is a great opening party with bright young aristos and artisans,

---

[2] *Classical Furniture* by David Linley. Dedicated 'To my mother and father' (published 1993).

crowded in a sporting clinch, steering glasses of champagne and bodies through more champagne and bodies and much noise. And, closeted in a modest first-floor room, Princess Diana holds vivacious court to a ring of girl friends, her fair curls and rosy face offset by a severe black suit and her trademark shapely legs.

David Linley's distinctive pieces of solid and inlaid woods – ebony, walnut, Swiss pear, burr elm – edge the rooms. Bookcases with pine-apple finials and ebony obelisks; mirrors, and desks are all full of unique quality and finish. His style would look well in the Malay Sultan's parlours.

May 31 Hardwicke House

'The Government isn't working': a caption in *The Times* in January. Four months on and we continue to have a divided and downtrodden Cabinet. John Major's sacking of his Chancellor of the Exchequer – Norman Lamont – has done little to boost national morale; rather it suggests one remove from his own exit. As he doggedly clutches at the coat-tails of each fresh disaster he survives the ride with a shrug and a grim grin and a dollop of more grey platitudes. But we want political acumen, authority and proper peers; an aggressor, a chief, a leader, a man who stands up. When will he be ousted? This autumn? Or 1994? Before the next election for sure. He will never resign.

June 1 Hardwicke House

Tom lunches with Anthony Tennant at Christie's; alone, in Anthony's office, perched at one end of his desk, with a decanter of claret. Would Tom now consider acting in some advisory capacity for Christie's? In the Middle East area/the Far East?

June 11 Hardwicke House

Tom's last day at work; John Asprey suggested they play golf sometime. 'What will you do now?' he asked, grinning. 'I will lick my wounds and do some thinking,' replied Tom and turned on his heel.

Oliver Hoare rang this evening; he asked Tom to look out for any Old Masters; money no object. And then Simon Tanlaw; did Tom ever regret leaving Christie's? 'No – we all reach our shelf life; and Asprey was an idea that did not work out.'

June 27 Horris Farm Nr Newbury

Lunch in a Berkshire cottage garden; six of us; non sequitur conversation in the hot sun, sipping Pimms. Parkinson? Michael Heseltine? Not possible! and his friend Michael Mates resigned from the Government! (Mates is a dab hand at rearing Heseltine's precious pheasants' eggs. Somebody suggested he should now slot in as Mellors in the first TV instalment of the present production of *Lady Chatterley's Lover*.) Is Clinton off his head? Gone and bombed Intelligence Headquarters in Baghdad? Who cares? Anyone read Shirley Letwin[3] in today's *Telegraph*? An edited lecture is reproduced, expounding her theory that Maastricht is a ruse to centralise Europe into a pulp of a newly-abridged Communism for the Capitalist.

The dogs, under sun; panting, flopping, snoozing, sighing; the blood-red rose, wilting; clasped to the wall by purple foxgloves. 'We have to go,' says Susie mournfully. She wrenches herself from the table. (They have animals in Hereford.) 'We have to feed the sheep, the ponies, the pheasants, hens and birds and bees . . .' Husband Esmond Bulmer (MP for Kidderminster 1974–1983) advises Tom: 'Tell your story of the Asprey Board to the Council of the Stock Exchange.'

July 6 Hardwicke House

A press release from Asprey: 'The Sears Retail Group – now under the new Chairman – Liam Strong – are to sell their entire 25% stake of Asprey shares – worth £92 million.'

July 14 Hardwicke House

A mother dies. Your own.

What did they say? You will feel old, alone, orphaned, depressed, tired, lost, a daughter no longer. 'Take *Quiet Life* pills from the health shop. They are big and pink.'

She died some six weeks ago prone on her bed in a beautifully-appointed nursing home. She never did get to see the elegant Victorian Gothic day rooms, the blue Soames room, and the peach Fleur, to evoke *The Forsyte Saga*. (The house was built in 1860 by Galsworthy's father.)

---

[3] Mother of the Rt. Hon. Oliver Letwin, the Conservative MP. Shirley Letwin died 1993.

Patient, polite and modest in all her requirements, she endeared herself to the masseuse, the hairdresser, the chiropodist, who would seize her feet even as she slept. The day lady in her flowered overall brought her ice in a glass goblet, bottled water, boiled water, pepper-mint water, freshly-squeezed orange.

We sat on her bed and gazed together on that belt of blue above summer trees. 'One evening I saw a nightingale; he had a cream tummy.' 'And did you find the Chanel No 5 in my medicine cup-board?' (Some thirty untouched bottles, amber with age and sediment.) 'And did I tell you? These two faith-healers stood on either side of my bed. Each took a hand. They saw indescribable beams of light around me. There was a message for me: "All will be well but not as she expects" .'

Her hold on life became more tenuous each week as prospects faded. Dimmed with drugs and ineluctable pain; water swept the system with swelling and despair. In turn we are drawn like moths to the flickering light; our mother wrapped in morphia and peace. How do you feel when your mother dies?

I looked down on her fragile head, the frayed white curls, the delicate nose, the closed cornflower eyes, the compliant lips. She cast her hand on the sheet, scrawny in near-death. I grasped it. 'How did you know I was here?' 'I just did.' She breathed. Ten hours later she was gone.

July 28 Hardwicke House

Tom collects mother's ashes from J H Kenyon, funeral directors, Rochester Row. Our officiating friend, the senior undertaker, sits at his desk in a bright yellow shirt and flowered tie. 'Hello, Tom! Here we are. When you open up this cardboard box you will find a pink plastic canister with the ashes inside. When you inter, don't discard the canister any old how; it is recognisable. Wrap it up well – there's a good man. What a morning!' He puts hands to grey temples. 'We have missed out on Margaret Argyll; she's gone to Kensington branch.' 'Perhaps she could not afford Rochester Row?' 'Oh! Tom! We have all the G and Gs here; so convenient with the Houses of Parliament just up the road. No, no, Frances and Brian would have paid up.' (Our friend is commendably familiar.) 'Lot of trouble up in North London this morning. Funeral party with no cremation documents.' The telephone trills. 'No! No! No! On no account. You cannot cremate without signed documents! If you go ahead you could end up in prison!' Outside the office there are more shrill voices. 'A pair of gays,' explains our friend. 'I have buried ninety-nine of them and this one will be the 100th. No trouble catching anything, you understand, Tom, but we never embalm.' In order to alleviate the stresses and above all disappointments of our friend's morning, Tom throws him a potential palliative. 'Er, my aunt Mrs William Vestey is near death; perhaps we could call upon you . . . in the event?' 'Ah, I well remember handling Lord Vestey, yes, that would be most acceptable, Tom.' 'I can't say when exactly,' continues Tom, 'but any day soon, or night, for that matter.' 'Oh, indeed, Tom. Few people die in office hours; only eight working hours to die in which leaves sixteen at large. Most people die between midnight and 3 am. Of course we have our all-night collection service extra charge.'

August 27 Prince William Sound Gulf of Alaska

How to convey this phenomena – Alaska? This vast, impenetrable guard of granite peaks, these petrified glaciers and frantic falls, the deep belt of spruce and mournful hemlock that ruffs each lonely shore. The silence, a heavy silence, weighted with canny forces. And the secrecy, all teeming life is here – the sky, the sea, the forest – all nurse this hub of harsh existence, a self-sufficient existence to outwit any man. Space, horizons, and white frozen peaks flung open to the sky.

Churning through green fjords we train binoculars on bank and mountain slope, spit and islet. Is that a bear? A walrus with ivory tusks? Otters? There, like a golf ball caught in the web of hemlock trees, a bald eagle with a white feathered helmet? Look out for white goats. Such sightings, as flaunted in our travel guides, we expect to see. But Alaska screens her secrets. As you pass from the pampered confines of a cruise boat (800 feet long, passenger capacity – 1,500; with one week's supply of meat – 7 tons; coffee – 4,500 gallons; wine – 1,200 bottles; and flour – 6 tons) you pay the price of audience overkill; your prey is cruise-cred.

But at the Captain's Welcome Dinner there was a furore. A whale? A whale! Spray spewed high from some orifice and with a walloping cavort and lash of his forked tail he was gone. The navy sea of the Summer Strait quickly smoothed its lap for the evening sun. We were eating chocolate soufflé at the time. Stray viewers edged back from the window to their tables, clinging to spoons and forks and half-finished mouthfuls. (Subsequent soufflés included soufflé au Grand Marnier, soufflé au vanille, sauce chocolat; they were unaccompanied by whales, but rose admirably, to be dusted with icing sugar.) Their reliable consistency suggesting a fair scoop at the six tons of flour. The remainder being largely bagged by the Victoria Grand Gâteau, Grand Gâteau

Napoléon, Gâteau Saint-Honoré, and the time-honoured Baked Alaska.

We boarded the *Star Princess* (P & O Steam Co., London) at Vancouver. Set between spectacular mountains and seaways and islands, Vancouver has become a vibrant, prosperous city, 'Hong Couver', and its dazzling glass skyscrapers is being rushed by the rich Chinese, in anticipation of their Communist clamp-down in 1997 (they will soon have appropriated the entire Pacific). But we enjoyed this oriental dimension; walking down wide elegant streets to the sea we found a sophisticated Japanese restaurant at the harbour's edge.

Our first port of call, Ketchikan, we reached in thirty-six hours and 574 nautical miles. A rustic stronghold of original Indian settlers, it has a flourishing timber and wood-carving industry. With a prodigious rainfall (only twenty-five days' sun per annum), it is an area of steaming mountain rivers, much salmon, waterfalls plunging into mists, and gloomy spruce forests. An obliging Indian family danced and sang for us in a cavernous log barn; they showed us their painstaking craft of carving totem poles, many of which were explicitly sexual. We were glad to be warm and dry on board again. Our Italian cabin steward promised more blankets. (He was homesick for Venice.)

Tuesday was Juneau with a word of advice from our guide: 'If by chance you come across a brown bear, lie down and play dead. For black bears you should shout and sing.' Any such allusion to black bears, goats, and porcupines again drew a blank. Our guide further pointed out that the mountain melt-water thrashing through the near forests and valleys was thick with glacial silt. The salmon had turned tail for clear waters and any bears had followed their lead. (This rushing opaque water resembled the pale clouded green of iced Pernod.) We headed on to the Meldanhall Glacier, 12 miles long, 1.5 miles wide, disgorging into a 200-feet-deep lake; it was a must. One of the many 'rivers of ice' formed 3,000 years ago during south-east Alaska's Little Ice Age, it edges forward at an average of two feet a day. Muffled reports like distant thunder heralded a spectacular cloud of snow; the glacier face had 'calved' and sent another iceberg skimming down the lake. This churned-up motorway of snow looked in need of a good scrub. But winter snows would soon blanket the striations of rock and dirt, ground up from its passage.

As the *Star Princess* cut her level wake through island passages, channels, canals, and fjords, we lolled in shipboard luxury. But the icy, rarefied air induced lethargy and a dulled appetite. The top deck's bubbling warm steam tubs tempted a few; exercise bicycles in the basement gym did a desultory trade. My mother-in-law and Sebastian would take up their post-prandial position in the 'window of the world' lounge. A scan through binoculars at the passing scene encouraged digestion and a doze. A mud-massage under the brisk attentions of Adrienne was an alternative. A fresh, pretty redhead from County Kilkenny, Adrienne stood poised above my prone, naked body with a glob of black mud on a pallet knife. 'This will be cold, very cold.' 'Aaaargh! Can't you warm it up? Put it in the sauna for a few minutes? Ay-yay-yay.' 'That's one leg, you'll soon be sweating in your paper bag.' She trussed me up in foil and towels and left me to cook in the oven of her small dark cabin. I dozed until Adrienne peeled off the steaming paper and hurried me off to the shower to disgorge myself of sweat and mud. It took much time and clawing with blackened nails. Adrienne talks to me about the crew bar. 'I am new, they all want to know – the stewards, Italians, all gay, I'll have you know, I met this guy from Security. He's Italian. Gay? Oh no. He's thirty-eight. Married? Oh no. He has one eye blue and one eye brown; we were in the 'windows' last night until 4 am. And today he comes down with his hat on to check our security. He asked about a manicure! But you are right. I will take care. By Anchorage I will be worn out and flat and regretting everything.'

My eighty-year-old mother-in-law's trip via sea-plane over the Juneau ice-field sorted the men from the boys. 'You and Bassie would have hated it,' she says. 'Single engine, single pilot. He wound the landing floats up and down by hand. The ear-phones were so filthy I thought I'd get lice.' But was it amazing flying through the mountain chains? 'Air pockets sucked us sideways as we flew past the gaps.' I shuddered, happy the woman who knows her limitations. 'And then we had lunch at this remote mountain lodge; a salmon baked in apples and a honey marinade. The room was stuffed with hunting gear and dog sleds and harnesses, and all immaculate and highly polished and privately owned.' Did she see any animals in this recherché retreat? 'After lunch we strolled on the edge of the rain forest. We saw an eagle's nest and a baby eagle and a brown bear.' A bear? No! 'Yes, apparently he likes the smell of the salmon bake; the lodge has to be careful to seal down the dustbin lids. He was sniffing and stamping about one hundred yards from us.' What adventures! 'On the trip home the pilot pointed out walruses sprawled on the rocks.' And did they have ivory tusks? 'Oh yes, ivory everywhere.' How I admired her trepidation. I deeply envied her the experience.

It was dawn as we sidled up the narrow creek to Skagway, the black green water hemmed in with fir and towering snow peaks. A swarm of fading stars and then rounded, rosy clouds. The Chinese deckhands hosed down the decks. Smiling, fit, and nimble, they will inherit the earth.

A resident guide drove us through the clapboard-fronted main street of Broadway; a colourful, tatterdemalion line-up of saloons, bars, hotels, and eateries. The gambling dens and brothels of a frontier town one hundred years ago are now superimposed by gift shops, fur traders, and the Skagway Trail of the '98 Museum. It was the Alaska Gold Rush of 1898 that shot Skagway to fame and villainy. While demented fortune-seekers stampeded through the Canadian goldfields, Skagway made hay. Profiteers, prostitutes, gold, guns, and shoot-ups fuelled the freezing nights. In 1900 the gold dwindled and the lethal party was over with a trail of death and debts and debris. Our guide shook his head sanctimoniously at the horror of it all. 'My wife and I might take a peek maybe at Soapy Smith's grave.' The eager voice at the back of the bus was given directions to Skagway's Gold Rush Cemetery. 'You'll find his killer, Frank Reid, along there and a whole gang load of lawless heroes. Watch your step.'

We drove along the White Pass road up the river valley with the Canadian Yukon mountains on the horizon. 'See in the forest there? That path? Dead Horse Trail they called it. We're in Tormented Valley now, coming up to Dead Horse Gulch on the rise. Over there you have Bridal Veil Falls. Isn't she just darling?' The said cascade frothed and tumbled down a distant mountain. This was a cruel and treacherous terrain where men and dogs and horses dropped dead in droves. 'The Gold Rush left a lot of unfinished business,' concluded our friend. 'Still a lot of bad feeling around. And ghosts, ghosts everywhere. You can come over real queer in the Red Onion Saloon; there's this certain electricity hangs out over Skagway. Watch your step.' We strolled back to the Princess for broiled sea bass fillet, lemon wedges, and steamed potatoes. Should we have given the Red Onion a whirl?

Friday promises a glut of glaciers (pronounced glayshah). Glacier Bay is an eye-trainer, with hefty ten-mile glaciers churning their switchback course through the mountains, to lunge at the sea in a solid front of ice, a mile wide. The bay evolved through two hundred years of retreating ice as land and sea were carved out from the centuries of an old ice-field. This morning we take a north-west course across the Gulf of Alaska to College Fjord, another glacially-carved valley. We pound down this spectacular cul de sac of snow peaks and iced plunges. Strangely-shaped icebergs – a bear? A cloud? A horse? A bust-up Cadillac? – skim past our bows. Some are grimed with dust from the glacier's earth-pounding passage; others are translucent, blue like sculptured glass. Why are glaciers and icebergs blue? (Not such a silly question. One disorientated passenger, his eyes on the skyline, has already asked the Captain, how high are we above sea level?) Glacial ice is a mineral and has a crystalline structure – as in compressed snowflakes. When we look at glacial ice we look through myriad crystals. As light strikes the ice surface, all colours of the spectrum are absorbed except blue, which is reflected back.

The engine falls quiet. The *Princess* is in plumb position up against an ice wall, rather too near this mother of all glaciers, we feel, and make weak jokes about the *Titanic*. We crowd the bows with our American friends in their loud jackets and snazzy peaked golf club hats. They are all agog and happy. 'Watch it, fellas! Hear that one? See it calve off?' Incredulous cheers as the ice cracks resoundingly and tosses another chunk at the sea. The engine starts and we appear to head even closer to this waiting wall of ice. What is the Captain up to? 'He is turning,' suggests my mother-in-law, hopefully. The pristine green water of the U-Fjord turns muddy as the Captain sees fit to reverse instead. 'Are we all right?' We shout at two official uniformed men on the bridge below. 'The Captain knows what he is doing!' They roar in rich, baritone Italian and remove themselves from sight and provocative passengers. A helpful American assures us that we are near one half mile away from the glacier. 'It is all one helluva illusion.'

August 29 Anchorage to Seattle

Noon flight to Seattle in a blazing sun over a sensational range of coast mountains, pinnacles 3,000–4,000 feet, blotched with snow; streaked with iced arteries. Miniature lakes suspended high between precipices like sapphire pendants clamped in rock. Peacock waterways and islands, bald with distance and dirty green. Intense light and shadow, compressed in every soaring shaft, hangs dense and tangible and blue – Alaska's evanescent farewell.

September 23 Loch Gleann Na Cloiche Sgoilte (Middle Glen) Ardgour Estate Argyll

The keeper spurns my string riding gloves; too conspicuous. A second cursory glance and I am judged a suitable stalker, a cobbled obelisk of mud and khaki camouflage.

A seven-mile juddering stint in a Land Rover and we near the head of the glen. Range on range of hills and mountains lock in the low sun and roll towards Ben Nevis. (At over 4,000 feet it is the highest peak in Britain.) Moor and slope are singed soft gold; chips of granite glint like scattered diamonds in their shafts. We approach the chosen mountain of the day through bog and squelching couch grass. Within five minutes my boots have taken water.

We climb into blazing ether, shuffling through gentians and cushions of scarlet and gold moss and lichen as luminous as jade. Head-keeper Allan is a practical pacemaker. After fifteen minutes we stop and survey our minimal progress. Mountain streams twist and froth below. Safe to drink from? 'You can read a newspaper through the water, it's that clear. Drink where the water is running.' We nibble on our pieces – food picked from the home larder. It is good to sink teeth into Lucinda's[4] six-month-old wedding cake mid-morning up a mountain-side. Allan remarks, 'The Germans love this gold autumn light and rusty colours; they call it the *Hirschbaum*, the stag tree.' Does he take out many Germans? 'Quite a lot. My grandpa and father were paid to kill them, now I am paid to look after them.'

Clouds, spongy with rain, lump on distant peaks. Far below, a small loch is plunged in gloom, a slab of slate, as dead and cold as armour. "That Loch? Lochan Dubh it is. "Black Loch" .' And now the sun darts out and chivvies it to a sullen pewter blue. Somebody sees an eagle, two eagles. They appear black and unremarkable on slow, flapping wings that span seven feet, Allan assures us. We marvel and then the second keeper, Alistair, finds a frog. We marvel again. How does a frog land up a mountain? The birds ... they fly the spawn to mountain pools.

Allan hoists his binoculars and points out a stag on a distant ridge. They sit at ease, regimented in a spaced-out garrison, erect and still as stone, silhouetted like cannonballs. Early in the afternoon the first viable stag is discounted, he appears to have acquired a defensive entourage of two sheep and two hind. In the event of a shot they would have 'spooked'. (Alistair's succinct word for racing down the hill in a blind panic and disturbing any likely herds in the vicinity.) Allan spots a herd further down and marks a stag; it is easily identified through its one missing antler and a danger to his peers with such a one-pronged weapon. He proves a satisfactory target for the day's cull.

Allan explains between eyefuls of binocular how much easier it is to select stags for culling than hinds. 'With a hind you must consider whether she is in calf or has a young one dependent on her. A stag and his age and condition are easy to assess. On average we cull thirty-five stags a year and one hundred hinds.'

We separate and crouch by knolls and rocks, wedged in the mountains. My host Raymond[5] and Allan squirm off for a good killing

---

[4] Lucinda Butcher (née Allison); aunt to the author's grandchildren, Luke and Jemima.
[5] Raymond Allison (Ray) and his wife, Pauline. Grandparents of Luke and Jemima Allison.

position. I am glad I am not a man and sink teeth into the last of Lucinda's icing and marzipan.

The shot rocks through the peaks and valleys; like a bomb it sounds. Now the echoes rolling in one long rambling lament. Alistair sets off down the glen to collect the hill ponies to haul the carcass home. I am detailed to help Ray with his stag. We find it slumped on its stomach with a broken neck and foreleg, a bullet through the heart. We roll it to a better position for gralloching. I plead total ignorance at digging through blood and viscera up to the elbows. 'Just hold the legs apart – wider – and keep absolutely still.' Raymond slits above the sternum with a favourite knife we later nearly lose. I watch in mute thrall as bladder and liver and the intestinal sausage bulge out into Ray's bloodied arms. The sun is still warm; flies collect feverishly. Ray straightens and looks around for water to wash in. (And, when daughter Lydia stood at the altar with his son Rupert, little did I imagine that I would ever be halfway up a mountain gralloching a stag with Raymond, her father-in-law.) 'Here is some water, a trickle, brown, I am afraid.' And I stumble down an ankle-snapping slope of springs and rocks and clumped grass to meet Alistair and the two ponies.

He has led them four miles up the glen beside a stream. He hands me the tethers and bounds up the hill; there are two stag to recover. The roan and the small grey pony crunch on grass. Soft tangled manes, soft eyes, soft muzzles. Peace wells up and rolls through the glen. Now the roan yanks up her head; her teeth ooze yellow foam and drip with green saliva; her eyes are transfixed on the hills, huge, tender eyes, sorrowful and apprehensive. Her nostrils quiver; these ponies detect the smell of death. We lead them to the stag. 'Hold tight the horses' heads!' I cower under the roan's neck, holding her reins tight. She is loaded and in a halo of midges we set off down the glen, an age-old outline against the dying sun, Victorian, an evocative reminder of the water colourist T M Richardson (junior) and *The Stalkers' Return*.

September 24 The Big House Ardgour Argyll

Virginia creeper flames the front façade and twists through rotting windows. Gutters, stuffed with the first fall of autumn leaves, drip plaintively; slate roofs, outhouses and barns and cracked chimney-stacks are saturated in the driving rain. Sodden sheep are bundled in sodden grass, and the scullery door sticks fast, then it opens, and we all fall into a sopping kitchen floor. An Aga emits heat, made almost ineffectual by the entrenched damp and relays of rain.

We walk down dead, dark passages to a dingy room. Pyres of household relics harking back to Victorian days are stacked to the sagging ceiling: a child's sled, three estate-made children's school chairs, and five saddlebags for picnicking on the loch, a blurred brown photograph of five girls smiling on ponies by Rannoch Moor, wood curtain rings looped up with twine and metal shoe-warmers, bedpans, and a porcelain nursery stove, a ransacked dolls' house and a black bin bag, labelled 'Interesting Christmas Cards 1919–1968'. Such a confused medley of nostalgia cannot be recommended.

Through into the main body of the house where a stuffed bison's head from Burma hints at derring–do. In the gun room there are antlers piled high like coat-hangers and threadbare stalking hats, and panamas, toasted from many suns, dangle stiffly from the walls. Come, look at this. The green kilt of the last laird lies askew on the arm of a chair, lovingly darned in several places, with creases intact from the well-fed noble abdomen; has it been lying there for sixty years? And here: the colossal tin trunk, painted rich brown in the manner of tortoiseshell, is boxed in wood and marked 'From Southampton to Calcutta'. Did the laird shoot tigers too? The tantalising relics of another dawn.

In the front hall a clock ticks and a brass barometer snug in its glass case charts an ink line and registers 55°F. Time and weather, the reassuring fundaments of life. Up the wide stairs to landings, past portraits of lairds and placid châtelaines, arms folded on laps, and dogs and babies. Where now? They ask, their mild eyes delicately deflected from the direct gaze. Another cold wet winter? We shuffle by apologetically, through rooms of unloved chairs and sofas, faded tables, empty cabinets, and wall glasses with little to reflect. Peeling paper, pale Regency stripes, and sprigged roses are smirched and sooted with damp. 'This room is haunted.' A distant cry from the east bedroom wing. We enter gingerly and a cavernous Edwardian hanging cupboard knocks and rattles as we pass. Loose ends, memories, twilight days, and high noon days; lives run and spent and spirited away, their shackles left in sorry heaps, the debris of discarded props.

September 28 St James's Church Piccadilly

The altar burns rich, red and gold with candles and autumn flowers, a retreat from the wind and rain, puddles, smeared pavements, and swirling Piccadilly traffic. A congregation of two hundred; the elderly, wan and spare and grey, some dressed in black and some in brighter shades; few hats. Pity! Freya was mad about hats. She wrote to a friend in 1946, while staying in Paris at the British Embassy, of her wish to buy 'a hat like a small pillbox with a veil. It is just heaven to be able to think of a Paris hat again.' And she adored gloves, once comparing a new pair made from softest antelope to whipped cream. But no gloves today. Women today prefer to huddle in shawls. (How drab and ignominious.)

This gathering of Freya's friends is outwardly understated with an inner core of distinguished minds and high rank and artful passion, a duke to represent her friend, the Queen Mother, with peers and patrons, ambassadors, fellow travellers, and writers, and publishers, and a throng of godchildren. A good all-supporting cast for Freya's broad passage through one hundred years. And as many as bless her in death today have crossed swords with her in life.

The first reading by John Julius Norwich is taken from Freya's books. It includes a comforting description of her grandmother, a soft, loving, unhurried landmark, with voluminous skirts and arms held wide to envelop. Colin Thubron, the travel writer, steps up. An excellent address, anecdotal and amusing with a deft delivery to include that occasion when Freya ordered a ball dress to be made in non-crush satin; it had to travel to Teheran in her saddlebag. And how her 'dearest Chief' (Field-Marshal Lord Wavell) was prevailed upon to break an important journey to inspect her latest cache of hats. Oh! Freya loved important men, clever men of position and command. It was all in the mind of course. She knew the soft spots to rub, how to cajole, to tease, and to squeeze an advance.

Freya's gallant publisher John Grey Murray ('dearest Jock') died a few weeks ago. Colin Thubron now concludes that Freya had called him up to edit her new-found material culled beyond the horizon. For Freya, the horizon was always an event about to happen.

October 15 The Whitechapel Art Gallery London E1

Anny Vaes is an inveterate culture queen. She is now la Baronne, a small fillip in exchange for those seven embassy years when she presided as the Belgian Ambassador's wife over the magnificent rooms in Belgrave Square and that Italian chef par excellence. The Belgian Embassy was famed for its parties. She and Robert, His Excellency, le Baron, now live in a bijou cottage, where superb meals still flow, unabated, under Anny's sole charge.

On this crisp sunny morning, we head east to the Whitechapel Gallery. Anny insists all four car windows are lowered; the stale stench of dogs revolts her. (The rutting season in Richmond Park is always an especial hazard with dogs rolling in the odorous excesses.) We skim through the City roads, sun in eyes and hair flying.

The artist Lucian Freud is our man of the day, grandson of Sigmund himself. A sexual open sesame cavorts across the walls, no holds barred and no taboos. We edge around the bleak, white rooms, absorbed and dumb. Here is nudity and sex à la carte; buttocks, breasts, and bulging testicles swirl and confront in competent strokes of the brush. Much flinging of heavily-endowed bodies over white sheets and floorboards, discarded in post-coital fatigue; slumped and sagging. A dour palate of mud colours to suggest phlegm, pallor, body waste, and even blood from the odd bright burst of a red rug. So much flesh, rosy-raw from rubbing, can pall. But it is strong work, and acutely delineated. The portraits of Jacob Rothschild, Lord Goodman et al are remarkable, they tap every nerve in a man. And never has bare flesh in all its conundrums been so authoritatively drawn or been less welcome on a drawing-room wall.

We tumble out into the sun and dust of Whitechapel High Street and dive into the first eaterie, a kosher restaurant. Filthy walls, floor, table tops, food and wine, and our waiter sports a dirty white crumpled jacket, awry at the collar. He looks dejected; an old Jew with more worries than we would ever guess. I am overwhelmed with a tender remorse and make no complaints.

October 22 London

The Lady Zinnia, proud, blonde, beautiful and defying her years, throws a party in the Chelsea Garden Centre. Her current paramour – that equestrian eventer – appears stolidly in her thrall. He pours champagne, standing squarely on two legs well apart to suggest a phantom horse between. Zinnia's guests are clustered and clogged on a centre stage, edged with flower pots and sacks of bonemeal, wood benches, urns and ornamental pineapples, all in danger of rolling and toppling. Leaning back on some solid trunk, I find it moves and is Reresby Sitwell. He demands a kiss, but makes off smartly when I half-stifle a sneeze.

The following night we drink at the Guards Museum, where Captain David Horn presides proudly over recent acquisitions, to include the glass and gilded replicas of the Queen's Coronation jewels. Atalanta Clifford (his romantic partner and assistant) is equally obsessed with the museum. After her three marriages, she has reverted to her distinguished maiden name. She whisks me past the glass showcases and their immaculate displays of handsome heroes; every century is depicted with appropriate chain-mail, boots, leather drinking cups, emblazoned jackets, plumed helmets, peaked hats, kilts and breeches, and khaki. The whole array dazzles with medals and silver and brass, gleaming gun stocks, hilts and swords. Atalanta, a perennial romantic at sixty, has long identified herself with each glowing effigy behind the glass.

'They are so brave. Take young Captain Thistlethwaite here; he never wrote to his mother of his pain – and half his knee shot away.' Atalanta has just completed a military-style novel.[6] What is it all about? 'Fucking and fighting in fancy dress', she answers proudly.

December 23 Victoria Square London

We shelter from the drizzle on Dame Guinevere's porch; it takes her time to reach the door. Her hair is upswept in its imperious chignon. She wears lilac tweed, elegant and fastidious always, diminished now and frail in her walk and talk. Through the long hall to the kitchen with the faded rose chintz curtains and the polished pine table. Sir John is in his chair in tweed and tie and burnished leather knee-pads. His pinched head and aquiline nose have a translucence and that transparency of approaching death. He could be alabaster sitting there. He pushes away his Lucozade and pleads with Guinevere to give him a dash of whisky which he sips with a straw.

The talk finally converges on Margaret Thatcher. 'Johnny saw her when she was eighteen years old. Tell them, Johnny, your first impression.'

Johnny breathes sharply: 'My sister was Mayoress of Grantham. She was told that Alfred Roberts, the grocer, had a clever daughter and she invited her to tea. Margaret came round and, after tea, she and I walked in the garden by my sister's chicken runs. She talked about her future plans for Oxford. But I was more struck by the white down on her face and her puppy fat.' How vividly are such vignettes stamped on a young mind's eye.

---

[6] *An Officer of Dragoons* by Atalanta Clifford, published 1994.

January 2 Hardwicke House

This diary has run for twenty-four years. Last spring the publishers, John Murray, asked to see it (on the recommendation of Selina Hastings). The senior editor wrote appreciatively and concluded 'your writing is a pleasure to read and it is a marvellous social document that you are at work on'. She (Caroline Knox) conceded that there is a wealth of material to publish but, with current market conditions, any publisher would be daunted by its volume. She also felt that the political background would gain more interest in time. I plan to wrap it up by December 1999 – a span of thirty years – Deo volente.

It has been my friend and counsel; a rambling structure with many windows lit one by one. An exercise in observation rather than a personal outpouring, a record of how it all seemed to me – a privileged record – a way to net the moment, to cherish life itself.

In today's *Sunday Times*, the second volume of the Journals of Elizabeth Smart[1] is reviewed. Nobody who has read her towering love lament, *By Grand Central Station I Sat Down and Wept*, could fail to be fascinated by her fate and frailties and pluck. She is quoted in the review saying, 'Such a strange non-thing, writing . . . writers have to construct an importance, a sacred vocation not to feel fiddling . . . even if you don't achieve it, the pursuit must have dignity.'

February 26 Lepe House The Solent Hampshire

Dense cloud. Opaque sea and light, the Solent deserted, the Isle of Wight a blur. A full tide swirls and sloshes against the breakwaters. The dogs plunge in, panting, pouncing, teeth clenched on seaweed, driftwood, a plastic canister. The far line of firs bend on the wind, creaking and lamenting a haunted smugglers' trail, running inland from the shore.

The black-shuttered Watch House, painted white, sturdy, marooned and mauled by waves. Sealed tight for winter, it is waiting now for

---

[1] Canadian writer and poet. Died 1986. Lover of George Barker and mother of his four children, Georgina, Christopher, Sebastian and Rose. Her journals, *Necessary Secrets*, published 1991, were edited by Alice van Wart, a writer and professor of literature at the University of Alberta.

spring sunsets, boats and rainbows to throw pictures through each window.

Lepe House looms gaunt on the stone sea bank, a weathered land-mark of brick and beam and many windows, frail and rambling to the eye, yet stocked to the gunwales with guests and good-living.

The dogs clear the bank and race through the grass rides that skirt the shore. Across the wide garden they tear and roll and shake out the sea. I bundle them away with an army blanket in my long-suffering mother-in-law's bedroom. She has friends to lunch, every wing at Lepe House has friends to lunch. In the evening there is a general re-shuffle over drinks and dinner, each guest from each wing is assidu-ously well-aired, well-watered, and well-fed (extremely so) and thoroughly digested.

We meet Moran Caplat, the legendary helmsman of Glyndebourne opera. With five years' Royal Navy Service in the war and his previous theatrical training at RADA, he was an obvious catch for the Glynde-bourne Group, the General Administrator for nearly forty years. 'I ran it like a ship – a leaky old frigate it was. Now it has become a state-of-the-arts battle cruiser – with mediocre management.' The new opera house has four hundred more seats. This will effectively reduce the pressure on members' tickets and retain its traditional audi-ence. (But, with standing room available for £10, the jeans and sweat-shirts will infiltrate; city suits, stale and crumpled, will merge with the dinner jackets. Will they become a stale and crumpled anachronism?)

The new Glyndebourne opera building has had unanimously good reviews. How does Caplat find it? 'The bricks are a shock; far too red.' They will tone down? Weather in the sea winds? 'They will weather . . . they are specially-made loading bricks to carry the weight of the fly tower . . . of course, with all the extra staff incurred, no more money will be made.' I forgot to ask him about the fly-on bat, a feature of every performance after the dinner interval, that frissons through the audience . . . will it swoop to the heroine's wig? Out to the audience? Tangle in the violins? As suddenly as it appears it is off into the night.

After too much lunch (a poussin each) and claret and cigars and port, Sir Dudley Forwood[2] removes himself to the terrace. The tide is out. The air is stiff with salt and mud and algae. Dudley looks superb in his eighty-third year with those rugged good looks hinting at arrogance and that excellent deportment, inured from his youth, as equerry to the Duke of Windsor. (He so enraged the Duke with his

---

[2] Equerry to HRH the Duke of Windsor 1937–39 and Chairman of Crufts 1973–89. He died in 2001.

first bow that he was rebuked, 'You look like a randy duck, now do it properly.') Poor Dudley, he still loves ducks and boys of course. Tom was on the receiving end of a hearty hug and kiss before lunch.

Dudley juts his chin forward out to sea. Tom joins him. They breathe in deeply. Dudley turns to Tom and makes some short, decisive statement. Later in the purring dark womb of the car I ask Tom what he and Dudley talked about on the terrace. 'About how happy his marriage has been and he said quite categorically – his actual words were "Prince Charles of Wales is one of us; but he will make a very good king".'

April 15 Hardwicke House

The day of the feast. The crowning glory of the hair? The attempt of a local hairdresser to sweep up my strands in a semblance of chic was disastrous. I emerged from her salon with Vesuvius erupting through my head.

At twelve noon I abandon a turmoil of organised chaos. From now on it is wholesale delegation. I park in Berkeley Street in good time for my Mayfair hair-do. In an Italian café in Lansdowne Row, cradling a cappuccino and a chocolate bun, I am amazed. What am I doing here? In between gulps and bites and snatches of the *Evening Standard*, reality hits hard. It is tonight – the dance, the ball, the feasting of four hundred. In just six hours' time I will be in my yellow dress and gold hair combs. Now in the hair salon the senior lady in the white overall clucks over my nails. And Josef whips up the hair and gingerly slides the combs in. In the car again I funk Hyde Park Corner (what if I should prang?). At home I scurry round with last-minute little things – fires to light and candles, dogs safely ensconced in the nursery with the retired Colonel.

Each crystallised detail in place – to please, to delight, to astonish, perfection set on its pedestal in that fleeting moment in time at the start of a party. Stand still, hostess, stand back and gaze a minute before you are swept away in a flood of friends. It is Tom's sixtieth birthday ball.

I admire the pretty black waitress; her long hair is elaborately coiled. Has Celia Ward[3] captured her? Sister Joy and Mother Judith from the Convent next door step in for a glass of champagne. Now a swirl of silk and voices and the party is upon us. Sixty for dinner and every

---

[3] Daughter of John Ward, the acclaimed water colourist and portrait painter, Celia Ward has herself exhibited widely. At the start of the century, she spent four years with her husband and children, painting in Romania. Her work was shown at the Romanian Embassy in London. *The yellow dress* was the title of Celia Ward's colourful oil painting of the ball.

flowered corner filling. The two long tables draped in cream linen with a gilded Rothschild dinner service. Tom's stoic double magnums of Lynch-Bages 1978 steal the show. (They were decanted and then re-filled.) On my right, Sir Edward Ford, the redoubtable octogenarian, whose mind-boggling career from tutor to King Farouk, assistant Private Secretary to King George VI, and subsequently to the Queen, has kept him remarkably agile and gallant. 'I can never refuse a party. And you look matchless tonight and Tom a mere stripling.' We eat hot wild mushroom soufflés, glazed duck and a sensational hot fruit salad and caramelised bananas and berries and strawberries and cherries served in strips on a silver tray. Sebastian on my left takes my message to Tom on the other table: 'Love you' written on my place card. Tom's speech is brief. He notes that we have twenty-two foreign friends present, from Belgium, Spain, Germany, Austria, Russia, Iran, Turkey, Argentina, and Malaysia. He then proposes the Queen's toast. Next Lord Colnbrook (Humphrey agreed to this by my pre-invitation) proposes Tom's birthday toast. Unexpectedly Juan Eduardo Fleming, the ex-Argentine chargé in London during the Falklands War, responds on behalf of the Foreigners. Port and cigars in the house dining-room and a brief respite for the ladies. The band is now well away and a swell of jubilant faces crowd into the marquee. At 12.30 wafts of breakfast. Never has breakfast been more applauded – the creamy excellence of the scrambled eggs, the kedgeree, the honeycomb, again and again, the honeycomb, the strawberries, the marshmallows in hot chocolate sauce. And we danced until 4 am.

Perhaps Robin Warrender eclipsed the hundreds of letters when he wrote to Tom: 'When everything is as faultless as your party on Friday evening it always means that the man has put in a huge amount of effort . . . the marquee was more a stately pleasure dome or pavilion. I think in fact we used to sing a hymn at school which had a line in it: Pavilioned in splendour and girded with praise.'

April 21 North Norfolk

Brancaster Sands stretch out in the receding tide. An opalescent sheen of pale sun drifts over sand and sea, and matchless shells – mottled, dappled, ribbed, and lustred pearl – and tufted dunes and sailing boats, five white sails and one blood-red. Blurred horizons of green and blue. Gilded havens untroubled by a troubled world?

'I think I should re-marry my second wife. She is sad. I am really very fond of her. I feel so guilty.' Henry Coke strides along the sand. His elderly half-sister, Hersey, looks on despairingly, for a piece of driftwood – to hit him with? 'Don't look back, Henry,' she murmurs. We trudge on through wind and sand and Henry's outburst is over-shadowed by the Caithness enquiries. (In January Lady Caithness shot herself dead in her Gloucestershire bedroom. Her husband the Earl of Caithness and their daughter Lady Iona were purportedly playing cards at the time, in the sitting-room below.)

'There are discrepancies,' Henry explains. 'Malcolm Caithness dis-closed the murder around 6 pm. But there was a shot heard by neigh-bours around 4 pm. The doctor reported the state of blood and body was in advance of Caithness's reported timing of the incident.'

Henry is the younger half-brother of Major Richard Coke, the father of Diana Caithness.

'Was Diana wonderful?' Henry demurs. 'Never much of a welcome home for Malcolm, you understand.' But he was in the arms of another? How we never do know the whole story! And half-brother Richard? He must be devastated.

'He lost his mother, you know. Killed herself. Irish blood. Then his sister and now his daughter, all suicides.' Henry's own mother boasted strains of good French blood and a more sanguine provenance. I turn to Henry again, our eyes hidden under deer-stalkers.

'You consider those two hours between Diana shooting herself and the delayed report to the police so significant?'

'Extremely so. Head wounds were found. The family are justified in holding an enquiry.'

I interject nervously, 'But Iona should know the whole story, she was there.'

'Iona has nothing to say about it.' Says great aunt Hersey. 'She has not even cried. No emotion whatsoever. We are all so worried for her.'

'I knew her headmistress at Tudor Hall. Has she been helpful?' I ventured.

'Wonderfully supportive.' (Parents killing themselves are no doubt par for the course in a top headmistress's training.)

My final suggestion that the questionable two hours were taken up telephoning for advice caused a pause on the sand but was then tossed aside.

But the House of Lords' 'line' is to back Caithness. His son and daughter show him affection and the press is rumoured to be gunning for his story.

May 22 The Manor House Chipperfield Kings Langley Herts

A fine brick front cushioned with high walls and box hedges, toy lawns and roses. The butler swings open the door. The house is silent. Are we early? Late? 'Her ladyship is receiving in the pool room. Please follow me.' Out into the pouring rain again; the portly butler and I bump hips under his magnum umbrella. 'Take care, madam, over these stones, very slippy.' The yorkstone terrace is smeared with lichen. We slip in turn and battle through rain and up a sodden slope of grass to the loggia. A cluster of white-knuckled guests clutch on champagne glasses. An old man stands still as wax, a brown homburg rammed down over his distinguished face. 'To keep the heat in,' explains his wife through purple lipstick. Complains the ex-Belgian Ambassador, 'Can't think why they ask Nicki Embiricos.' Lord Dudley, tall and handsome, props up a stone corner. 'Oh, for bougainvillaea country – what rain! And what is wrong with having our drinks in the drawing-room?' Our hostess, Gwen, is Gerald Dartmouth's second wife. French, vivacious, pretty, she points proudly at the rustic trompe l'oeils – a field mouse runs up the wall, *et voilà*, two spaniels flattened on the wainscot beside a dangling lead. Everybody is agreed the artist Graham Rust has done well by the loggia.

In the dark panelled dining-room, frozen hands are rubbed frantic-ally under the long oak table. I am seated on Gerald Dartmouth's right. The butler and maids hand us artfully-contrived dishes in the French style: sole fillets, coiled and creamy, embraced in lobster claws, a ragout in pastry cases with neatly-bundled baby asparagus, a dessert to defy all previous attempts at originality. The strawberry sorbet is piled high in an iced mould of bright incarcerated flowers, seized this morning from the sopping garden. The claret, Prieuré-Lichine 1985, is soft and full and fruity. On my right, Brian Sweeny, a veteran teetotaller, raves over the bouquet.

A loose thread of conversation loops the length of the table – Jackie Onassis's swift death from cancer. And why did she marry Onassis? To sever links with the Kennedy clan; to be independent on the arm of an incomparably richer man; to steer her two children into a European milieu, to protect them from kidnap, or worse. 'She certainly knew on which side her bread was buttered,' concluded Gerald Dartmouth. 'Did you say "bed", Gerald?' I ask. He laughs, 'You've got it in one!'

Nicki Embiricos sits motionless, through the badinage, grey and drained, a monument to ultimate social survival.

June 1 Horse Guards St James's Park

A dry, warm night; we watch the Beating the Retreat. The spectacle is preceded by a reception at Wellington Barracks. Ugly little low rooms reached by narrow stairs. Such deficiencies redressed by an imposing show of Guards officers and commanders, standing tall with proper haircuts, a flow of good manners, and champagne. Field Marshal Lord Bramall, resplendent in gold braid and scarlet and black wool greatcoat, admires my cool, pink dress. I assure him he looks splendid trussed up in gold loops and tassels. 'So hot,' he moans, 'and impossible to sit in this outfit.'

Our host Major-General Robert Corbett sweeps up his 'dead chicken' feather helmet. His niche as Commander of the Household Division and London District ends in a month. He is fifty-four, fit, handsome, and too able to retire. Offered the tenure of the Tower of London, he has opted instead for the toss and tumble of civilian life.

Night falls. The Life Guards trot down the mall, massing on the parade ground. The jingle of silver harness, the red and white and gold and glint of it all. The trumpets peeling and the drummers stolidly astride their mounts, those sturdy greys unperturbed by the din and drama, the swivelled swoop of searchlights, the clang of church bells and shrill command. An hour of marching and music of the Queen's Household Division – the horses, the bearskins, the dress helmets of red and white horsehair switches, the spurs and the buckles and belts – shimmering at the trot as they retreat into the night.

Our transient Major-General stands before the stark stone grandeur of Whitehall. He doffs his high ceremonial feathered hat. For him, it is a touch of 'Goodbye to all that'.

June 12 Swinbrook Burford Gloucestershire

Propped sumptuously on a pile of linen pillows, lace cushions, and with a breakfast tray, every prospect pleases. The view is astonishing and tugs me to the lead panes and the incomparable green peace of an English summer landscape. The folds and swells and wooded summits of beech and chestnut slope to willow and valley streams, each tree a three-dimensional mass of sharp light and shade. A pair of peacocks mince past from the wings of the lawn and skirt the ha-ha. The terrace below my window is tumbled with pale roses and clematis; flat, blue dials flung wide to the sun and a walled garden of weeping pears and pastel iris and grass closet salons beyond.

Nancy Mitford hated this house her father built in 1927. By 1935 the family had sold up. In a letter to her young brother, on July 17, 1927, she wails: 'Really this house is too hideous for words . . . like a barn badly converted.' Set high on its bluff, Swinbrook braced itself against the four winds as the Mitford sisters were cooped up for warmth in the linen cupboard, the nest that seeded their pursuits of love and political fantasies: Fascism for Diana, Nazism for Unity, Communism for Jessica, but, more especially, Nancy's own formidable literary output. Did their comparatively exclusive and solitary world stir these sisters to that passionate overflow reminiscent of the Brontë girls at Haworth?

July 14 Hardwicke House

Sister Jane I remember well. She is brisk and fun. 'All in a day's work.' Of course I could see the room; the present lady had just vacated. (Died? Gone fishing? Day-dreaming in the blue drawing-room?) Sister Jane is friendly, but clearly she has no memory of me, or indeed of my mother. We reach the small end room; and the bathroom where the regale lilies were stored at night because they smelt so strong. I walk to the French windows and the little terrace. Just one tall tree and the old brick wall with a little blue above. I sit on the bed, her bed. I see nothing as I have since remembered, no green line of trees or skies of beckoning blue.

Sister Jane plumps up the pillows and smoothes and pats each crease. 'Meet your troubles head on and kiss them goodbye.' 'She never came back to me,' I hear myself say to Sister Jane. 'My mother, she was always so spiritual, I was expecting something, some sign.' Sister Jane purses her lips and tweaks hair out of a prickly brush. She shrugs and straightens the blanket and opens wide her beautiful eyes. 'Perhaps there is nothing there,' she says cheerfully and then, by way of consolation, 'or perhaps she was just tired.'

It is daughter Lydia who finally puts me wise. 'But Janna did come back, to Luke, when he was having his bottle. His eyes followed her round the room and he looked up at her, on the ceiling, and smiled.' And Luke I remembered, too, when aged around three months I was giving him his bottle, looked up above our two heads, smiled at the ceiling, and then back at me in some significant recognition. I know my mother was there, watching. I dared not look up. Babies retain some visible link with the spiritual unknown. And we more hardened mortals? We still know when we know that we know.

July 19 Carcassonne France

We escape from the dust and tourist clangour to the cool of the medieval walls and devour yesterday's papers. In the *Daily Mail*, former Detective Chief Superintendent Roy Ranson rabbits on over the Lucan débâcle. Twenty years on, the thwarted detective is still floundering over Newhaven for clues to the Earl's body. And is he dead or alive? Has he ever searched for a hired killer? Such a man would have a lot to answer for – the wrong dead lady and then the Lord thrown in to cover the traces? Ranson has just published his book *Looking for Lucan*. According to his wife, the unsolved crime rankles in his mind night and day. He carries the Earl's photograph in his breast pocket.

Meanwhile, Lucan's son George Bingham has succeeded to the title. He works with a leading merchant bank. His two sisters, Lady Frances and Lady Camilla, gained top degrees at Cambridge. Good news is no news.

July 25 Nice

Today we forgo the beach and lapping sea, that milk-blue opalescence that draws you again and again to its primeval womb, and we drive from Nice up through the Alpes-Maritimes. Shafts of angry pink rock: purple slate and loose shale are wired back from the road like slabs of salmon caught in nets. The narrow road is sound; it loops and winds and concentrates the mind, though the paltry barrier wall gapes in places. Best not dwell on what tumbled when. We hug the nearside up and up where dense wooded foothills peak and convolute into blurred blue distance. The air is cool, clean, keen. We edge the car through a medieval village, an arch of gold, crumbling stone, a market square, a church. Major General Robert Corbett[4] and wife, Susie, live higher still, at Pierrefeu. And now we see tall terraced homes clinging to the steep rock edge and a frail bell-tower, the whole clasped by the wavering village wall.

Robert leads us up shallow steps and a cobbled lane. Children eddy in his wake around corners; he knows their names. The local restaurateur, her voluptuous bosom wedged high on her window-sill, calls out pleasantries. We pass the 1914–1918 War Memorial and Robert pauses. A fresh bouquet of red, white and blue rests at the foot of the pedestal. 'I laid that,' he says reverently. 'The village asked me.' After a distinguished career of high ceremonial, our retired hero was

---

[4] *Berlin and the British Army* by Major General R. J. S. Corbett, CB. Published 1991.

undeniably moved to have performed this small parochial service. Susie runs down the steps of their house, smiling, striking, rosy, Susie. 'The last house in the village, the end of the road, the top of the mountain!' Their tiled arched veranda is suspended high above green impenetrable gullies and a flight of mountains. 'Rather a different view from our home in Dorset,' muses Robert. 'Yet we are only four hours from London.'

We lunch on salmon trout and glistening sweet red peppers and tomatoes, excellent local wines, accompanied by a charming couple from Paris. Is Robert deflated in retirement? 'No, never. Dealing with the excessive army cuts was distressing, very wearing.' Later we touch on the emotive subject of Northern Ireland. 'I feel the only radical solution lies in re-educating the young; educate the new green shoots.' As we talk clouds bundle black over the mountains. 'You have about five minutes,' warns Robert as we hurry down the stone alley to our car. Lightning forks in menacing silence down the winding road. And now a bulldozer cavorts like a wounded animal in our path, frantically manoeuvring its steel caterpillar band on to scattered rubber tyres for insulation. The heavens open. A long haul to Nice if you run out of lemons.

August 18 The Hebridean Princess Oban

A forlorn quayside, with Oban's Edwardian front swept with wind and drizzle. The *Hebridean Princess* (two thousand tons, 235 feet – built 1964) vibrates like an oven, vast, white, red, and gleaming. We are piped on board and, through a jumble of crew and corridors, pursers and passengers, locate our cabins.

To be a transient mother to eleven-year-old Mischa[5] is no idle undertaking. He is admirably hyper-active, abseiling down narrow stairs, swinging in a wide arc from every rail, knob, cleat, or banister and hurling imaginary cricket balls. I warn him of old ladies lurking and lurching round every corner, to mind his step, to walk! Walk! Walk! The severe disappointment incurred when I ask the cabin steward to lock up his prestigious cocktail cabinet is soon redressed by the video extension to his television.

---

[5] Mischa, son of Alexandra (née Galitzine), a brave and beautiful captive of multiple sclerosis, and grandson of Prince Yuri Galitzine. His father, the Polish architect Leszek Nowicki, renovated Hardwicke House.

August 19 Rhum Sound of Mull

The Sounds are grey and swollen under a troubled sky. We pass Eigg
to starboard, too rough to land. Foaming crests flounce to the rock
shores. These great khaki island hulks, Rhum, Eigg, Muck, Soya, and
Canna; like so many monsters, hunched on prey; dribbling with rocks
and slashed with waterfalls. Steaming and white, they swing, like
tablecloths. A clutch of modest white stone lodges with pitched slate
roofs cleave to the more sheltered dips.

If it is Rhum to our port, it is Kinloch Castle; built of pink Arran
pitchstone rather than the glowering bloodstone of Rhum. A fat,
breathless custodian shows us the rooms. We have caught him
unawares; Friday is usually the *Hebridean Princess*'s Eigg day. Meanwhile
the portentous sporting home of the Edwardian Lancashire industrialist
Sir George Bullough enthrals. The gold satin-swathed ballroom, the
Lady Monica's delicately faded boudoir, and her exuberant multi-
control jet sprays are finally eclipsed by a thunderous rendition of
'Washington Post'. It reverberates through the huge cluttered rooms
and corridors and galleries masked with stuffed stags, from a mechanical
organ, reportedly built for Queen Victoria.

Back on board. It is too rough to land on Canna. We drink cocktails
with Captain David Campbell in the Tiree Lounge. He is semi-retired,
with his ruddy good looks and white beard, he could make a full-time
Father Christmas. He tells me *The Princess* was built thirty years ago
for the Secretary of State for Scotland as a potential escape and nuclear
fall-out shelter for the Royal Family. 'She may yet come into royal
service if they scrap the *Britannia*. But our *Princess* is now an old lady
herself having spent her years-in-waiting, ferrying mail and up to five
hundred passengers between the isles, in the Sound of Mull.'

August 20 Kallin Harbour Grimsay

'The sea here is all islands and the land is all lakes,' writes the geologist
James McCulloch. The fast-changing tides add to the confusion, adding phantom peninsulas and straits to the labyrinth of mouths and
inlets. On the indisputable dry land of this pocket harbour a man with
a red beard hoses out a shed of lobster tanks; a bubbling flow of sea
water keeps the catch clean and cold for export (it is Madrid on
Mondays). Claws are secured with bands. 'They did'na mind and it
saves them a killing of each other,' mutters the man through his red
beard.

An afternoon landing on South Uist, from Loch Skiport. A dire scenario to compare with *Cold Comfort Farm*. One broken-up skeletal bus, a derelict lodge in a stranglehold of wild yellow iris, matted sheep wool swings in the wind from mangled fences, lobster creels, heaped haphazardly with twine and rusted chains, line the quayside.

Freshwater lochs puddle the flat marsh and stubble to the far Atlantic shore. Sheep and rabbits shuffle through the scene along with a proliferation of greylag geese and a stretch of wind-wound corn-stooks, said to house corncrakes, one endangered species harbouring another. And now Mischa hurtles across the white coral sands to salvage pearly shells and 'obsidian' black stones; three-horned masks of rams are lugged back for home transport. The petite French lady is *enchantée*. But, horns or no horns, *The Princess* will not accommodate this savoury bounty.

It was to these gentle glens strewn with knapweed and clover that Bonnie Prince Charlie came, where the cry of sea birds and the wide arc of ever-changing skies spelt dull tranquillity. Traumatised from his deadening defeat at Culloden he could have found no better skulking ground, no better counselling. After three weeks he was disguised as Flora Macdonald's maid, whereupon that resourceful lady sailed with him from the peninsula of Rossinish across the Minch to Skye.

August 21 Eriskay

Bonnie Prince Charlie landed here in July 1745 before that ill-fated battle at Culloden. Here he enlisted troops with the help of Macdonald of Boisdale. The white coral bay that faces the Atlantic was his embarkation point. It still bears his name. A grass cemetery slopes to the sands with white marble and black granite headstones and crosses – Macdonald, MacGregor, Mackinnon, MacLellan – each family a testimony to longevity from living out their span on home ground, where skies, hills, wheeling birds, and the Atlantic are timeless, where sticky blocks of peat are stacked to dry each successive winter, and where on a high bluff, cushioned with knapweed and daisies, the Victorian Catholic church keeps the candles burning.

Mischa, untroubled by the historic freaks of humanity, religious extremes, and territorial rights, sprints over the sand towards me. Pink-faced and panting:

'I found a seal! It was dead – crisped. I buried it.'

'Where did you bury it?'

'In the sand of course.'

'What with?'

'My bare hands.'

Through these days of the closest proximity with Mischa I am astonished not yet to have noticed his hands or indeed his fingernails. Back on board at dinner he makes a desultory pass at his raspberry soufflé. 'This doesn't taste of anything.' He slumps in his chair. I urge him to look pleasant even if he does not feel it; life might be likened to a party where we should be good guests. Sometimes it seems a lousy party, but, whether a good or medium or bad party, we should honour our position. And I feel a cad; only yesterday he gave me an enchanting brooch, a tortoise with a diamond shell, studded with sapphires and rubies. 'Oh, Mischa! You shouldn't.' 'I paid cash,' he assured me (all of £5.50, I discovered). And this morning he polished my binoculars and zipped up my cumbersome life jacket . . .

Dinner is finally saved by our waiter 'Big Pete'. He bends his 6½-feet frame to Mischa's ear. 'I have a mackerel on the line, come and look.' Puffed with pride on his return to the dining-room, Mischa declares, 'I have friends in high places!'

August 22 Muck The Sound of Mull

Mischa's fishing with Big Pete from the top deck for squid and mackerel is now a regular entertainment together with gratuitous spins in the speedboat when Allan lets rip with flying leaps and wide skimming arcs. Jackie, the deputy receptionist, a rosy brunette, proffers him such titbits as brass-polishing and window-cleaning. And dashing Douglas, the young bartender in the Tiree lounge, is fast initiating him in the art of twirling a tray of drinks from the shoulder. Mischa's faculties are fully stretched with this flamboyant fraternisation with the crew. (A bicycle ride on Barra Head with Jackie? Another daunting tryst in the offing.)

Now it is Muck, where two milking cows and Lawrence MacEwan, with his tractor, welcome us ashore. We look back across the Sound to Skye and to the jagged Black Cuillins. A stink of silage and cowpats denotes serious cultivation. 'Where is your farm?' enquires the perennially-enchanted French lady. 'The whole island is my farm,' muses our host and indicates a lift on his tractor where bales of hay are scattered as further inducement. His own thick hair resembles a cornstook. 'Where have you come from?' He peers through yellow eyelashes. 'From Eriskay? Ah! Eriskay! Nice place. I was there in 1957.' We lurch over the hill where cows hug each headland and curlews haunt. A population of thirty includes five children; they now attend the island's new primary school. No cars allowed. A second tractor hurtles into view with a woman at the wheel. Who is the lady? Mrs

MacEwan, no less, and whisking the doctor from the mainland off to an islander in the last stages of childbirth, one more for the primary school pot.

August 22 Tobermory Mull

This afternoon Tobermory heaves in view. The bay densely screened with oak, larch and elm. The multi-painted harbour front glistens in rain. Tall, narrow houses, yellow, pink, grey, and blue, have modest lozenge windows. It is tiring to shuffle through shops on a wet day. We buy a tartan wool rug (Maclean) for £19.95 and mooch through the Mull Museum, an admirable ensemble of warriors' arms and dress from the fifteenth century to World War II. The affable bun-haired lady sells me a postcard. 'Mull Weather'.

Mull Weather by a Summer Visitor:

> It rained and rained and rained and rained
>   The average was well maintained
> And when our fields were single bogs
>   It started raining cats and dogs
> After a drought of half an hour
>   There came a most refreshing shower
> And the queerest thing of all
>   A gentle rain began to fall.
> Next day 'twas pretty fairly dry
>   Save for a deluge from the sky
> This wetted people to the skin
>   But after that the rain set in
> We wondered what's the next we'd get
>   As sure as fate we got more wet
> But soon we'll have a change again
>   And we shall have
>   A drop of rain
>   (By courtesy of the *Oban Times*,
>   author unknown)

'Have I given you the correct change?' The bun lady is clutching a fistful of Scottish £1 notes. (This floundering over what is the correct change is a national failing.)

August 23 Iona

We pass Fingal's Cave at 8 am. A black hole, immortalised in Mendels-sohn's Overture, *The Hebrides*, it is like a missing tooth in Staffa's black basalt jaw. The whole islet a collapsed cathedral with reeded columns toppled like blocks of peat. Iona is faintly discernible on the horizon with the black rocks of Mull to port. Iona, wide open to the Atlantic and to the rape of the Vikings – the lamb to the slaughter in the quest for Christianity. A banner of undulating emerald, the soft swards stroked by sun as rugged Mull frowns across the Sound. From the ship's bridge I scan the cathedral, squat and foursquare in its bloodstone and basalt, with the dark rock hills behind. It is as elusive to the eye as it is solid.

We leave the quay and its buoys and boats and lobster creels and skirt the rosy ruins of the nunnery. A walled vegetable garden runs alongside with meticulous rows of stalks and sprays, leeks, onions, carrots, parsnips. A bearded hero, his hair caught in a tail, shuffles in sandals as he weeds and waters. A young man in search of his soul? His sex? And new socks?

To the ordered sun and shade of the cloisters we go and to the marble altarpiece, a delicately-inscribed block of nougatine marble, veined with green serpentine and pink.

'My favourite island is Iona!' concludes Mischa.

September 3 Simpson's-in-the-Strand

Simpson's-in-the-Strand, another bastion of British excellence for the chop? Rocco Forte and his ex-ice-cream-vendor Padre, Lord Forte, are set to bag the entire Savoy camp. The Connaught, the Berkeley – Claridges? For twenty years, Lord Forte has stalked these prizes. No longer can their bottom line equate with prestige and privilege. No longer can exclusivity rule economy.

(John Major's preferred 'classless society' has bred a grey mediocrity; the dead hand of his authority homogenises across the board. We even read of the eleven-year-old ballet protégée who is told, 'Ballet is elitist and middle class'; her grant application is refused.)

But this cucumber-green and white order of Simpson's is one ulti-mate refuge.

'Where did we meet? In the East?' asks my lunch host, Sir Edward Ford.

'No, darling,' I tease, 'That was Betty Smart – you pottered around the Pyramids together.' A former girlfriend, the writer, Elizabeth

Smart. Wrote Edward: 'There were a lot of beautiful girls around in London in 1936 – but she was the intelligent one – lots of fair hair . . .'

'Poor old Betty! We should be eating beef of course . . .' It is a reassuring scene; men in dark suits, eating proper meals; the doomed silver chariots swivelled between tables where black-tied waiters skim knives through glistening roasts. I persuade Edward to join me in fish-cakes of the day. Conversation skirts around the Asprey débâcle.

(A later press reference to John Asprey in Peterborough's diary – 'that dry-throated goldsmith, Asprey' – on September 9 might have been timed to stick in the gullets of his shareholders; on Saturday, September 10, the *Guardian* announced a dismal interim report for Asprey – 'barely trading at a profit' – 'no sparkle at Asprey'.)

For a decade Asprey has depended on two golden eggs: the Sultan of Brunei and the Sultan of Oman. But these eggs hatched long ago; bored with buying, they hail new horizons. Asprey has built up no contingency revenue; no credible house style in jewellery or design. For too long the rooms have reflected the glut and outrageous glitz of mega-rich Eastern patronage.

Edward subsequently wrote me, 'I would not take the *Guardian* report as proof positive of skulduggery – yet!')

I drive Edward home, threading through heavy traffic up Shaftesbury Avenue.

'I can smell dogs . . .' I apologise. I had cleaned the car especially. 'I don't mind – it is not a bad smell – identifiable, that's all.'

Turning into Cambridge Circus, I launch into my Prince of Wales incentive.

'Do you know Sir Dudley Forwood? The last equerry to Edward VIII?'

'We met briefly of course. He left his post as I took over mine. What became of him?'

'Happily married for forty years – to a divorced lady of title. He is as queer as a coot . . .' I gabble on . . .

'And now down the Tottenham Court Road . . .' directs Edward.

'Dudley,' I press on – 'Dudley stated categorically at lunch recently – he said – Prince Charles of Wales is one of us – but he will make a good king.' Edward is silenced; the traffic stalls. 'He thinks he will make a good king – in spite of – or even because? Well, well, I don't think we can call the Camillagate tapes a reflection on this . . .'

'What people also say . . .'

'Yes, yes?' The traffic is now fairly bowling along Camden Town.

'They say that the Queen's sons are all wimps and that Princess Anne is the man; that she is the real backbone to the next generation.'

Edward – smell of dog or no dog – is now totally committed to this confidential auto-dialectic.

'Princess Anne is certainly proficient in her duties. I see her only on few occasions. She impresses us all and writes her own speeches.'

We are now in Blomfield Road, Edward's road. We kiss on both cheeks.

September 30 St Etheldreda's London EC1

Shocked and saddened, some three hundred converged on St Etheldreda's.

Colin Haycraft dead! The witty classicist, the publisher, the athlete, the husband, the family man, and the indisputable all-round achiever. Of a stroke! I look back with pleasurable guilt on that bottle of house-red we shared in his library in June.

A Catholic service unadorned. His widow Anna (alias the writer Alice Thomas Ellis), veiled and cloaked in black, her bare toes in sandals, peeking, pink and cold, from her hem. Latin plainchant – Mass and Homily and Sanctus – asphyxiating storms of incense clouded the coffin. Colin was no Catholic. He would not mind; this is Anna's pigeon.

The Address, given by Richard Gregory, a scientist from the Royal Society; a quiet eulogy with a graphic portrayal of Colin curled up with his Latin and Greek in a big chair by the fire; the matchless Welsh landscape of meadows, streams, and spinneys passing him by. A dark-haired granddaughter sat on her mother's knee beside Grand-mother Anna. She ran her ivory fingers and wrists through her mother's long hair, entwining, stroking and loving things still hers and left behind.

In the crypt, we drank warm white wine. Anna looked immediately happier, her pale lips parted in drinking and smiling. She will take on the Mantle of Duckworth. Certainly she will have tales in hand of numbing widowhood. And who is this? This plump, less grey replica of the Prime Minister? Terry Major-Ball. John Major's elder brother, and I were rammed up against a pillar. 'You look younger than your brother!' I blurted. 'John is some ten years younger than me. He was an after-thought, you know.' Our Prime Minister an after-thought? 'Yes, my mother was pretty sure she had a baby in there, but my pa was away fighting the war, he had no idea that John was on the way.' We sip companionably in disbelief at such an ignominious start. Terry Major-Ball continues. 'This is the second funeral I have seen this week. I hurt my back at the first, fell on my face stepping out of the train. This morning I had trouble shaving, awkward angle over the basin. I got this twinge and called my wife Shirley to come. She took the razor from my hand, so that I could ease the pain.' How was his book selling? (*Major Major*, Duckworth). 'I have no idea. The publishers have no idea. They want me to write another – a type of Do-It-Yourself-Disasters – in the home.'

October 20 Hardwicke House

Sir Edward Ford is lunching with me. After the weekend's provocative press coverage of the Prince of Wales's latest biography by Jonathan Dimbleby, I am all set to keep mute on matters Royal.

Down the back passage I tinker with the catchy waltz from *Eugene Onegin*, all ears on the door bell. There it rings! Edward on the dot at 12.45 pm. 'Well done,' he cries. Perhaps he feared I might have forgotten? Looked a mess? The dogs snort behind the dining-room door.

'Do you mind the Labradors?' They are promptly released.

'Well, Prince Charles has shot himself in the foot this time. What have his advisors been up to?' The ex-courtier shakes his head.

I settle Edward on the sofa with a glass of dry sherry. A dog lodges his snout up one trouser leg. 'Prince Charles is not a man. Perhaps these confessions are his coming out. Some good must come of it all. At least the Queen will now never abdicate in his favour. She will prefer to delegate to Princess Anne, lean on her daughter, time will tell.' I babble on.

'You believe in Anne, I know. But you can't bypass the heir to the Monarchy.'

'But, Edward, just imagine. When the Queen snuffs it, in say 2020, Charles will be breeding sheep in the Hebrides. Prince William will step in, with Princess Anne's support, and that husband of hers.' (I was going to refer to him as 'that Chocolate Commander'.)

We eat Coquilles St Jacques. Edward prefers Heineken lager to wine and scoops up his sauce with pieces of bread; a gratifying guest.

'Prince Charles,' I explain, reviving the theme – 'What a whinger he is – the bullying at school and endless complaints over Diana and not enough love from his parents.'

'The Queen is not a hugger, you know,' confides Edward. 'I doubt if she would do her job so superbly if she was too emotional. We will not see her shed a tear when her mother dies.'

The autumn sun fades and the dining-room darkens. I light up the glass cabinet. 'What an enviable house you have, so many lovely things. Tell me about these chairs. Eighteenth-century satinwood, you say? And these glasses? Are they very old? 200 years? Described as

'drawn trumpets'? With a tear in the stem?' But Edward's glass had
got no tear. I show him mine. He is delightfully inquisitive.

We sip strong coffee. There is something intimate in sipping coffee;
such a moment can invite confessions, indiscretions even. I am off
again.

'I worry about Princess Diana, that she might take her life, set herself
up as an icon of martyrdom. She has been treated monstrously by the
men she loved, sending her up with their sordid kiss and tell stories.'

Edward considers this morbid hypothesis. 'You envisage a Mayerling
scenario? Or Eva Peron? I have had similar fears. But the Princess of
Wales has her two sons and I feel we need not worry unduly. She is
a most dedicated mother.'

He straightens himself in his chair and levels his gaze at me; a strong,
good-looking man of eighty-four.

'Am I much changed since we first met, twenty years ago?'

'Edward, you are as slim and handsome as always you were.'

November 12 Saffron Beach Lyford Cay Nassau Bahamas

The palms and casuarinas thrashing in the high winds; fronds and
branches a frenzied scribble against the cloud and the sea boils just one
hundred yards from the French windows, half a mile offshore the
barrier reef creams furiously. Heavy rain dive-bombs steaming grass,
frogs, lizards and deserted verandas. It tumbles in sheets from ageing
eaves. We pad cautiously over stone terraces and slippery tiled floors.
Weather calls come hourly. Hurricane Gordon from the Gulf of
Mexico. Heading for Haiti? Due Nassau tonight, expect winds up to
100 mph.

Says Maria, balloon-busted and black, erect and pristine in white
starch and smoothed hair: 'This is no hurricane, Ma'am; hurricane is
when houses fly past the kitchen window.' Head thrown back, she
sways tall and majestic down the sodden path to cut yellow hibiscus
for the lunch table, and fastens one in her hair.

There is no let-up by teatime. This cascade of water devastates. The
pool overflows, crusted with leaves and baby frogs. The air is curiously
warm, a foretaste of the Mexican blast to come? Still Maria insists this
is no hurricane: 'Just a breeze, Ma'am.' And the rain does a sudden
horizontal dive through the main veranda. We stow cushions in a
frenzy and upturn tables and chairs. Palm branches litter the garden,
flapping like birds with broken wings. We finally go to our beds with
candles, closed windows, and a prayer, the only contingency plan to
beat a retreat to the garage.

November 13

A washed-up dawn with distant thunder and a flushed sky. Cheery black men sweep up debris and unclog gutters. The precious judas-tree has had a free fall over the tennis court. Banks of seaweed are hurled along the coral beach; the sea tepid, brackish and thick with shredded flotsam.

Tropical Storm Gordon makes big copy. Lives, homes, and trees have been ripped apart in a two-hundred-mile rampage across Southern Florida. The tornadoes have left six dead, having first flattened Haiti with a death toll of four hundred.

November 14

Faxed from London; news of Asprey in potential default of a £20 million loan from the Bank of Scotland, 'and may face receivership'. This suggestion is quashed as absurd by John Asprey. He is photographed in the *Mail on Sunday* (13.11.94) alongside the New Bond Street showrooms.

'The Queen's Gift Shop' up for grabs? *The Financial Times* takes up the trail (14.11.94). Share prices punctuate speculation. In early September they tumbled from 310p to 200p. In October they were knocked down to 135p in a swill of rumours, on Friday (11.11.94) they closed at 157p.

November 17 La Richelieu Hotel French Quarter New Orleans

'Gumbo' is a key word in New Orleans, a mix, mêlée of heterogeneous cuisine and culture. In the 1700s the French and Spanish merged to produce their Creole progeny. The Acadian French, on their expulsion by the English from Nova Scotia, infiltrated the Louisiana swamps around 1785. From these marsh parvenus, rich in fish and game and the all-pervasive okra plant, the Cajuns established their own distinctive cuisine. Today, a homogenised N'Awlins stews companionably in a gumbo of heat, humidity, and jazz round the clock. The spanking pull of these narrow downtrod old streets is tangible; each jazz bar, a den of smoke, blacks and whites swinging and yelling with their banjos, trombones, and drums blasting out Dixieland, Blues, and Gospel. Funeral jazz is also popular: 'Glad to see you go, Joe – you rascal you.'

The mules stand by with their fiacres, blinkered and impervious to the din.

November 18 New Orleans

A cool, clouded morning. We stroll through this old 'red light' French quarter, reputedly the safest district to find yourself (378 deaths in New Orleans this year; purportedly drug-related, between blacks), where plain-clothes police are rife and incognito, sauntering through the crowd, lurking on motorcycles and bar stools. 'I bet you one hundred dollars I can tell you where you got them shoes.' 'On our feet.' We shout back, ready briefed. Advised friends, 'Always carry one hundred dollars' hand-out trouble money; wear no jewellery, skulk in jeans and t-shirts.'

This innocent contrast of pretty architecture, pistachio pink, lemon and hot sienna façades. Each house embroidered with intricate iron balconies, valanced eaves, and shaded inner courtyards. Royal Street, Dauphine, Burgundy, and Chartres Streets, with incomparable, crazy Bourbon Street, are all preserved in this eighteenth-century *vieux-carré*; this quintessential elegance of Franco-Spanish alfresco living.

A small white group sets up a good noise in the centre of Royal Street, their samoyed dog slumped in a heap beside their instrument. Down the street by a 'topless and bottomless' bar, a black boy drums on cardboard over his knee and a pair of shapely nude legs swing electrically from a further bar window. But it is the annual February Mardi Gras carnival, a month long rave-up to end them all that draws two million to the city. The new street rule of 'four articles minimum of clothing to be worn' is interpreted by some as two socks and two gloves and letting it all hang out.

On Chartres Street we climb steps up to Beauregard-Keyes House, a typical Graeco-revival manse with four Doric column supports to the front portico. The old impoverished General Beauregard would be gratified to see the current care of his old home. The novelist Frances Parkinson Keyes, a woman of phenomenal energy, lavished all into restoring Beauregard House in 1945.

The eight-panelled white double doors are hauled open by a lady in a pink crinoline. In reverent sotto voce she leads us through the 75-foot long hall to adjoining study, drawing-room, dining-room, and bedrooms. Beeswax and rectitude engulf the house. Massive mahogany four-poster beds, where any detached ball or claw or decorative swag from their heavy encrustations could knock a body senseless. Our lady in pink explains that Frances Parkinson Keyes preferred to live in the slave quarters across the stone patio. It was there she wrote and entertained and had her privacy.

What a powerhouse of achievement. Her fifty-one books of historical fiction acclaimed world-wide; an issue of three sons and ten grandsons, and the facility to renovate and embellish properties. At the height of her output, Frances Parkinson Keyes was running three homes along the Mississippi, a mansion in New Hampshire, one in Vermont, one in Virginia, and a convent in France. Several running books would lie open, waiting completion, on desks whole continents apart. 'Mind you, I was never a beautiful woman,' she would muse. Her percipient author friend, Pendleton Hogan, observed: 'Not being beautiful herself, she must reveal beauty to others.' Her restoration of houses and gardens became her own surrogate beauty.

'Here she died. Of course she was a large lady and a special bed was brought in.' The lady in pink stands aside, her neat head bowed. We are all silent in the smooth tiled room. The French windows open to the patio where her little iron fountain trickles, in her words: 'a gentle, audible clocking of time.' The pink lady needs to sell us a book. The study walls are stocked with second-hand editions. I seize on *The Chess Player*, on the life of Paul Morphy, chess prodigy and champion born in New Orleans in 1837. It was written in 1960. Says the pink lady, 'One of her best. And if you can't play chess you soon will.' Sounds deadly. I snatch up *Lunch with Mrs Keyes* by Pendleton Hogan, a short biography, as a palliative.

The formidable Frances Parkinson Keyes, a stout matriarchal figure, as resolved as Boadicea on her intent, gazes down implacably from a battery of framed photographs. Back at the hotel, a fax from London.

'The *Financial Times* report that a stock exchange enquiry is mooted on Asprey share deal.'

November 19 New Orleans

'If you don't have a good time in New Orleans, check your pulse!' Our pretty, pert guide of the day bristles with info: 'New Orleans 95% surrounded by water; 60 inches annual rainfall; a low flat city built on marsh and brick piers. The Mississippi River one-half mile wide; water from thirty-one states drains through to an overflow network of underground canals. The Pontchartrain Lake laps the South Shore with brackish water and with a twenty-four-mile bridge to cross it. And see that Maginot Concrete wall? It keeps the show afloat. A hurricane could sink this city up to forty foot flat.'

At Memory Cemetery (built on a former race track), four acres of manicured green and monolithic tombs, we stretch our legs and scan the rich mix of names:

Famille Bougère
Family tomb Benachi
Pizzorato
Pecoraro
Bois-Doré

Next stop to grand Colonial St Charles Avenue, the American garden district where clapboard mansions and painted stucco villas are hung with West Indies-style balconies and belvederes. Our guide pipes up, 'See the bevelled glass in those doors and the chandeliers sparkling through like diamonds. And the gardens to die for. You have your elephant leaves, ginger plants, banana, and angel trumpets. The city park runs to 5,000 acres and these wide avenues are tree-lined with water oak, red oak, magnolia. What you folks fancy for dinner?' Our irrepressible lady trills, 'Cajun-Creole cookin' fried or broiled. Go Felix's in the French quarter for oysters, or The Hog's Breath Saloon for great music, or to Poppy's where your burgers are grilled under a hubcap, and to Antoine's, Arnaud's or Brennan's, for swanking it.'

We walk back through the old quarter. Dark falls early and the gas carriage lamps flare from each house. The bronze horse-head tethering posts gleam along the sidewalks; some have lost the rings in their noses; others have had their heads yanked off anyway. A collision of sound; jazz pounds from both sides of the long narrow streets. Frenzied tap dancers and skate boards, the isolated prim trot of the mules and the trundle of their fiacres running behind.

Dinner is at Antoine's. We dress chic and take a taxi. Established since 1840 by the Guste family, it is now fatigued by fame and the faceless drift of tourists. The plastered high cream walls, banded with mirror, reflect on art deco mahogany, soaring potted plants, blacks in black tie, and an astonishing swell of ballooning outsized middle-aged women. This tidal wave of fat is the American disease.

Tom sinks teeth into the famed oysters Rockefeller, served hot and smothered in a splotch of khaki cream, hinting at sage. Reported the film star, Buddy Ebsen, 'A body hasn't lived until they've blistered their tongue on an oyster Rockefeller at Antoine's.'

November 20 Nottoway Plantation Baton Rouge Louisiana

A three-hour drive to this grand plantation home through a dead land of swamp and woods festooned with Spanish moss fungi and sad, brown canals curling off from the Mississippi. We see whole families fishing for mullet, bass, and catfish. Messing about in mud is a Louisiana pastime.

'Six of the Randolph daughters were gotten married in this room.' The dead-pan Southern drawl rumbles round the 65-foot-wide ball-room, now empty, save for a chandelier, the prized hand-painted Dresden door-knobs and haunting echoes down a hundred years. Nottoway, the sugar plantation home built in 1850. The swamp shores of the Mississippi still boast a trail of these Greek Revival Italianate piles with their deep, cool verandas, classical columns, fifteen-foot sash-windows, and lawns spread to the river. 'The Randolphs entertained . . .'

I lean against the marble mantel and curse my toothache, the humid air, and that languid drawl again. 'And the windows opened up high on to the veranda. You danced out of one, kissed and dallied, and swung back through the next. The four Randolph sons had their own living quarters, the garconnière extension.' What sultry scenes of romance and sexual escapade are conjured here. The fluid pen of Frances Parkinson Keyes wrapped it up with her *Blue Camellia* and her *Victorine*.

December 18 Hardwicke House

Yesterday I saw Philip de Laszlo; he stood in the Lower Richmond Road clutching his roasting tin; it was glazed and streaked with the roasts of many Sundays. Dearest Philip, who kept scrupulous accounts of every penny and then got slayed at Lloyd's.

'I have just been across to the butcher to ask him what size of turkey we can fit . . .'

I looked at the tin more closely, 'I would guess a 15 pound bird.' Philip beamed; it was just what the butcher said.

December 23 Vienna Austria

Each car has a duvet after last night's heavy snow; bronze warriors with snow-tufted helmets sit astride haughty horses, every mane and tail bristled white. We have come for Christmas, Tom's sister Amanda, Sebastian, and self. After twenty-two consecutive years of Christmas lunches *chez nous*, the ghosts have mown a swathe across our dining table with friends and family dead or divided. But next year – Inshallah – grandson Luke will be the catalyst of a renewed spirit.

Here we bask in the mirrored bois-clair magnificence of the Imperial Hotel. Explosive chandeliers and the great marble staircase glimmer still, legacies of the mighty Hapsburg Empire coasting to its end. No parade of tiaras or ball-gowns today, but a hefty flow of fur coats sweeps the lobby. Amanda and I swan around in our racoons; grey, brown and bushy-tailed we flounce in the snow beside Tom like wolf hounds.

'Do you think Vinci could be alive?'

'He would be eighty-plus. I will look him up in the town directory.'

Tom emerges from the marquetry telephone booth. 'He is in the book? And what of Martha?' Prince Windischgraetz was Christie's representative in Vienna. Twenty years ago he piloted us round Vienna. His wife, Martha, was a handsome Hungarian and an artist. I remember well her white satin mackintosh, her platinum hair, libidinous, glossy red lips and that lurking laughter in her blue eyes.

'The Viennese are dull beside us Hungarians.' Vinci is a survivor, her third husband and married fifty years.

Vinci is on the telephone. His voice firm and mellifluous. He will lunch Monday. And was Martha . . . ? Would Martha . . . ? 'I will ask her.' Muffled murmurs off . . . 'Martha has one arm broken. She will not embrace you as always before, but she accepts with pleasure.' Again a fleeting vision of Martha liberally sifting her apple fritters with icing sugar some twenty years ago in some *gemütlich* retreat in the Vienna woods.

Vienna under snow this afternoon is handsome, still, stark and reserved. Mozart, Schubert, Strauss *père et fils* brood in bronze, each colossus an island in the snow where the seagulls stand by mute and hungry. The town and parks seem strangely empty, and the wide avenues of soaring nineteenth-century solid Baroque façades of grey, cream and white stone, barnacled with balconies and floral pediments, bring to mind a glorified extention of Selfridges. A skyline of cupolas and green copper domes pleases. Little dogs are linked osmotically to their old mistresses, thatched in mink and racoon. Across the Danube (at 2,500 km, the second largest river in Europe to the Volga), the Vienna woods swell above the far banks, pale in snow. Now the seventeenth-century splendour of Schönbrunn shimmers across a vast court of frosted cobbles, a majestic curve of gold with a glittering sixty-foot Christmas tree and a huddle of booths selling handmade Christmas decorations, candles, roasted chestnuts and apple fritters.

In this muffled glow of sweet sounds and smells it is macabre to think on that final nadir of the Hapsburgs: the Empress Elisabeth's frantic screams in giving birth behind these golden walls to Rudolfo, the yearned-for heir, in her delirium she even saw the fall of the Empire with red flags waving through Vienna. Years on, her protracted grief for the suicide of her adored cousin Ludwig II of Bavaria and the cancerous death of her amitié amoureux, Count Andrássy, prime minister of Hungary. Above all one shivers for that moment on Wednesday, January 30, 1889 at noon when Elisabeth was told of her son's death at the Mayerling hunting lodge. She was interrupted in her Greek lesson by her devoted old courtier, Baron Nopsca; sobbing unrestrainedly, she went to her room. On hearing the Emperor's footsteps she straightened up to break the tragic news: 'Let him in and may God help me now.'

December 24 Vienna

Christmas Eve in Stefansplatz; the cathedral locked and silent. We had thought to see whole families thronging there with phalanxes of burning candles, music, singing, furs and faces, the old and the young, pale, flushed, ecstatic, sad, belonging somewhere. We stroll down narrow streets and across wide squares. Swags of yew and scarlet ribbon stream with showers of gold and silver glister to hang around the frozen night. Shops are lit and locked and every restaurant barred. A stage set with no players.

December 25 The Hofburg Chapel

From our loggia we look down directly on the altar which groans with rich trappings. Ten tall silver candlesticks, two Christmas trees dripping with tinsel and poinsettias, scarlet bursts between a blaze of white linen and lace, the whole topped by a porcelain stove which on closer look is a marble shrine with funeral ormolu urns set round its roof. The candles are now lit with ceremony and caution. A vast chandelier hangs close by, which turns and turns again; its gold-washed branches entwined with heavy pendants sparkling crimson, blue and orange. In the gallery a small string orchestra collects; the renowned Vienna Boys Choir file in alongside. Dressed in sailor suits with pretty necks and proper hair cuts, they settle down, chatting and grinning. It is the orchestra that streaks ahead with waves of glorious sound flowing like silk through water, to the boys' hosannas and '*stille nachts*'.

We edge down the crowded stairs and landings of the palace into the courtyard. Another cold and cloudy morning. Sebastian agitates for a fiacre and a pair of steeds. We pick the first from the solemn line-up by the main archway. Have they stood just there through the centuries? Our handsome coachman, buttoned up in black and a peaked hat, hands up plaid rugs to tuck round knees.

December 25 Evening

To the State Opera to see *Figaro*. Despite the gilded swagger, the mirrored grandeur, the sweep of marble stairs and the blaze of chandeliers, there is a lacklustre in this Viennese éclat; the lighting effects are as flattering as a station waiting-room. That déclassé veneer, inherent from ninety years of Republican rule or as once described by Vincent Windisch-Graetz 'pinstripe suit socialism', eats into the heart of things. Humour and spontaneity are lost on the streets and stages of Vienna. The opera sets are tedious with all light and colour flown. But there are no beggars or vandals, no graffiti to mar the scene. One envies such urban order and fastidiousness.

The Crickhowells in the interval are an unexpected light relief. They lead us to a bar cellar after the performance. A zealous accordion greets us with 'The Third Man' and 'Edelweiss' accompanied by a loud lady singer. Her voice ricochets through the vaults. Anne Crickhowell writhes and tears at her napkin stuffing her ears with paper pellets; I offer her little balls of bread. She rummages in her bag and finds earplugs, a strange precaution to carry around when off to a Mozart opera.

Nicholas Crickhowell[6], the longest-serving Cabinet member during Mrs Thatcher's tenure, despairs of the Conservative Party today; he concedes that John Major is a clever man, 'but he is hopeless at appointing the proper man for the job'.

[6] Lord Crickhowell, Secretary of State for Wales 1979–87, Life Peer 1987, publications to include *Westminster, Wales and Water* 1999.

1995

Every ten years Tom is lured by some persistent friend to take up his gun. This entails borrowing son-in-law Rupert's gun, booking in for two or three lessons at the West London shooting grounds, sustaining blisters as a result of these preliminaries, and on this occasion a touch of gout in his right toe. But he always succumbs.

'Men who shoot are deaf, pissed, or boring,' this valediction from Susie Bulmer as she waves us off from her Hereford folly. 'And the wind is whipping up, we have a tree down. You won't shoot tomorrow if it's like this.' We swoop down from her wooded summit and climb again to 900 feet to Burwarton, the 12,000-acre estate of the Lord Lieutenant of Shropshire.

Our host, tall, blue-eyed and handsome, greets us in jeans. His black labradors ravage my skirt (so recently vacated by our own). His wife, Rosemary, again tall and willowy, smiles through her delicate face; 'Since falling on my head with so much eventing, I don't remember so much.' But she makes it apparent that we are expected.

The house is High Victorian with plaster ceilings coagulated with bold white icing. Blazing wood fires and a round-the-clock newly-fitted gas boiler keeps the temperature to a uniform 68°F. We meet in the library before dinner; dress – black tie. I have put on my Pucci long wool, thinking to save my scarlet décolleté velvet (now in its twelfth year) for tomorrow night. The other ladies, although not in décolletés, are shimmering in taffeta and silver thread. Our hostess's wool stole is dripping with black ostrich feathers. However, all is not undone; my own dress (also in its twelfth year) came from the Faubourg Saint-Honoré after all.

We have an excellent dinner; the roast grouse understandably tough. In the glow of many candles, the Zoffanys and the Frans Hals and the embossed velvet curtains, faded from rich pre-war crimson to worn brown, induce a cosiness. The conversation is general with shooting hardly mentioned; but with much talk of respectively-owned labradors. They are all sworn to perfect performance in the killing fields and are sleeping the night out in Land Rovers. (The Lord Lieutenant's black labrador is called Peter. Why? Some Russian family connection? 'No, No,' explains his lordship, and he lowers his voice. 'Personally I don't much care for the name; but, when Rosemary threatened to call

our son and heir Peter, I quickly pre-empted the name with every
successive dog.' Our host glances through the gleaming tangle of
candelabra from his end of the table and is surprised to see Tom and
Jamie Illingworth sitting beside each other.

'We should have asked along Biddy Cash,' he remarked. 'Bill is
away, but she doesn't like to drive herself home at night.' I suggest
that Tom and Jamie would have been only too happy . . . And then
the Lord Lieutenant's eyes momentarily light up. 'The most beautiful
girl in Shropshire will join us for lunch tomorrow.' (If one was really
beautiful would Shropshire be a prestigious enough platform?)

Tom and I retire to the day nursery with a comfortable mattress.
The all-prevailing 1930s round-point electric plugs necessitate a bit of
jiggery-pokery; the hot blanket plug fits the bedside light-socket which
shares the wall plug with the two-bar fire. The bathroom, down a
passage and past a rocking horse, has an intriguing door off. Tom
opens it on our second night in search of shampoo; he is confronted
with a line-up of old nursery cures in brown bottles, syrup of figs, cod
liver oil, milk of magnesia, dettol, and a scattering of wooden spatulas
to hold down little ailing tongues. Another cupboard is gloriously
crammed with a fire-hose reel, a badly-singed lampshade, crumpled
tennis shoes, and paperbacks wedged in every cranny.

January 11

The horizon is streaked stormy red. The morning still dark at 8 o'clock.
The wind has dropped with no rain. We collect for breakfast in muted
tweeds and wool – sage, beige, brown. One lady appears in bright
emerald with a pink shirt. Later she is swamped in khaki like everybody
else. The view from the dining-room windows confirms that we are
a good 150 miles from London. Spinneys, copses, magnificent oak and
beech; the far blue-blur of the Malvern hills and the moon still brilliant
in a fast-emerging cloudless sky. We set off in Land Rovers, parked by
barns, and spill out over a field of winter wheat. Tom's swollen toe is
comfortably packed in his wellington boot. The black labradors, after
last night's vaunting, are marginally out of control. Exasperated calling
to heel and the yelping and cavorting are reduced to squirming in the
mud at their masters' feet.

Wood after field after copse with five drives before lunch, then back
to the house. Tom puts up a good show, breaking his duck on the
first drive with a high shot. A hum of approval from the hedgerows
and then a yell from a fellow Grenadier: 'Don't shoot that one, Tom!'
It's a buzzard sweeping the skies. 'Go on, shoot!' shouts the next man.

Another Grenadier friend, Jamie Illingworth (a superb shot), complains of a swollen knee. 'It will be a football by lunchtime.' Birds are dropping all around us in ditches, streams and spinneys. The two men, incapacitated with their gout, rely on me to retrieve their loot. Another contender asks me to hold his gun while he unravels the pink twine fastening the gate. 'I am too old to climb over.' But Jamie is the flavour of the month. Good shots are in particular demand at the end of the season – to finish off the birds. 'I had to turn down the Queen this weekend at Sandringham. Breakfast is quite an experience; every conceivable newspaper is laid on, all full of the latest muck on the monarchy. The Royal Family flicks through them, quite unconcerned, and makes no comment.'

It is the last drive, and dusk and cold mount on the hills. The Lord Lieutenant blasts on his Austrian horn; the beaters crash through the woods and holler through their teeth – Brrrrh! Brrrrh! Louder and louder. Now the fly-past of the put-up birds and it is the killing fields. A brief silence and a blast on the whistle to end it all; the drive is completed. The Lord Lieutenant's lady has been leading the beaters in a handsome feathered hat. She supervises a search of the more inaccessible birds. 'How many cocks did you have, Jamie? Did you mark them?' She looks lithe with colour in her cheeks. 'My father brought me up as a boy. We would shoot together and walk the land.'

Later, I come down to dinner resplendent in the décolleté red velvet dress to find my hostess in warm slacks. However the Lord Lieutenant has redressed this sartorial imbalance with his smoking jacket. 'You are good to bother to dress,' he says disarmingly. I kick myself for not wearing it the previous night. But the vagaries of evening dress in mid-week shooting parties are hard to anticipate.

'Where's Peter? Who saw him last?' Nobody is interested in Peter. It is time for bed. Halfway up the stairs we hear growls and reprimands. Peter, with a pheasant stolen from the game larder hanging from his jowl, stands on the front-door step. He is unrepentant and wags his tail. Another well-trained dog.

March 10 Laughing Waters St James Barbados

Silence as Mervyn the butler and maids Isabel and Eglantine hand down each breakfast order – two fried eggs please, Isabel, and no tomato . . . just crispy bacon for me, Isabel . . .'

The Countess glances over yesterday's *Daily Mail*. She stops short at Dempster's Scottish Diary. 'Ah! Daughter Georgina! But the photograph is at least five years old. Look, darling! She met that travel man, Clive Anderson, when he passed through Calcutta.' (The Lady Georgina Murray once hailed as the most beautiful girl in Britain. They say she is tattooed and has since trailed a blaze to Mother Teresa.) The Earl scrutinises the picture of his gorgeous Georgina, décolletée across the page in a swirling dress; 'very nice too,' he says. And is it not her birthday today? The Countess blushes. 'What do you think, darling? Do you really believe it is Georgina's birthday?' The Earl ladles more guava jelly over his bacon. 'Pretty sure. We can look her up in Debrett's after breakfast.'

Our host's family trustee has lost a pair of Y-fronts. He is a stocky man; no other male guest could have appropriated them. The house laundry is excellent with starched shirts and pants winged back in hours. The trustee is poised to leave on Concorde at 12 noon. 'A double breakfast day,' he beams, 'and home for supper.' Our hostess assures him his pants will follow.

A skein of sybaritic days where each dawn parts the curtain on a gilded stage; on the idle dance of sun and waves and monkeys shaking shade from the mahogany tree. Now the purple cloud swells up behind our white-hot coral ramparts. It bursts all over, drenching tropicalia and setting off tree-frogs in a rhapsody.

Books dozed over, barely read, languid bathes in a painted sea, light meals and easy conversation, fond teasings and provocations, in-house jokes and speculation on those beyond. A propensity for nicknames runs through the more established residents of Barbados. We are already familiar with the Swiss chocolate General and his wife – La Contessa – whose tangled East European pedigree leaves you reeling. 'The Body'. 'Nimble Knickers'. 'The Fragrant One'. 'Fat Annie'. 'The Moor' (that charming Italian Count whose suntan has exceeded all credibility), and the latest arriviste on the scene, a young Frenchman, who is unanimously dubbed 'S&M'; his shaved head and macho physique spark this ripple of satanic fantasy. Sipping champagne by the moonlit pool, he and I talk of books, but his shorn head suggests to me a vulnerability, convalescence from cancer perhaps?

Barbados, where the crescent moon hangs on its back, a silver hammock in the stars. Halcyon days for some. That last party on the terrace, black with night and the tall French windows lit behind. Our hostess a streak of silken tanned limbs in a twist of black (her gold lamé bikini is renowned). The last party when the monkeys, tired from a day's scampering in the garden, are curled up high in the geranium trees, the flame-red petals fluttering down on the back of the night breeze. The last party; drinks, the clink and the hum and the laughing. The serving minions with their bottles and trays and matchless canapés, water chestnuts, crab tarts, cheese tarts, and caviar. For the last party the Ionic coral columns stand serene by wide verandas, stone terraces descend to the sea and a creek of satin sand. Renovated and extended by Oliver Messel thirty years ago (he lived here with his companion 'The Great Dane'), this captivating villa is now sold again. It is the last party of all.

April 23 Buchowina – Oswiecim Krakow Poland

Kasimir waves from his sun-baked wood veranda. We take a last look at his mountain lodge. The Tatra mountains shimmer white behind and tumble water to the trout streams, the foothills, and fields below. A medieval landscape. Poland still uses five million horses to work the strips of winter wheat and plough. We swing to the left through the roly-poly plains of the Carpathian mountains strung along the Slovakian border, past spaces of saffron flower open deep-blue to the sun, and orchards in white blossom. Apple and plum and lime-trees and willows shiver in crinkled new green. Wood houses with steep, pitched roofs loom above barns, hens and horses, dogs and logs, and Hovis haystacks. This part of Poland (1772–1918) was part of the Austro-Hungarian Empire – and the river, the Skava, has the purest water used in the making of the famous local beer. Jan, our guide, unravels in a steady monotone. 'We Poles are a naïve people, we do not like the Jews. They work in banks. They have exploited us for moneys. They used us poor people for their gains.' (I am reminded of the observations of a Hungarian: 'If the Germans had not exterminated the Jews at Auschwitz, the Poles would have done.')

We near Oswiecim (Auschwitz); parched, flat land with crops of barley, rye, and wheat, puddled with carp ponds. Poplars line the road and spinneys of silver birch, a single track rail and a level crossing bar. We wait as a train passes by slowly, slowly nearing its terminus, as so many trains have passed slowly by, just here.

Make your mind a blank. We are at Auschwitz on a glorious day. Birds sing and spring waves an artless wand over this place of exceptional horror.

'*Arbeit macht frei*'. The worn lettering is arched over the entrance to the death camp. Says Jan, 'Here, under this arch, you lost your name and became a number.' Beside us, a lush wide space of grass suggesting a playground or cricket pitch informs. 'A gravel pit where prisoners of war working on this place were maltreated and murdered.' The warm rose-brick façades of the Auschwitz barracks belie their guilt – the azure sky, the soft breeze, the orderly military architecture of things. But these gutters were choked with smashed skulls and bones and blood; screams day and night pulled the air apart, each shrill of terror sudden, unexpected, unheeded. Shots rang out in spates by the death wall, where, in an intimate courtyard, two victims at a time would be executed, naked – untried, innocent – still asking why. And from the dungeons and dark stone torture cells rose moans and stench – the suffocating cells, the starvation cells, the standing only cells – and that final beating-up in the undressing rooms.

Emblazoned above the main entrance to the Auschwitz Museum of Martyrology are George Santayana's words: 'The one who does not remember history is bound to live it again.' It is salutary to see streams of schoolchildren guided through this history of holocaust – Dutch, Swedish, Polish, and German. Finally released from the evil corridors of death, they stretch languorously in the hot sun and sink teeth into oozing red pizzas. Auschwitz is young history; a warning to the young.

We lunch in the cafeteria. 'They say the ashes from the crematoria still dance in the sunbeams.' Jan relishes such details. And I remember reading of Roosevelt swallowing ash with his cornflakes, of Churchill mixing them with his burnt umber and putting them on his canvasses. Our baked beans arrive and black specks swim in the sauce. I can't eat. Jan switches to another savoury morsel of information. 'The ashes were scattered in the Vistula river below the town, where gold was found. The rich Jewesses swallowed their rings and small effects when trapped in the undressing rooms.' And I remember a drawing, hurriedly pencilled by a prisoner, of voluptuous Jewish mothers, hair thick and black on white skin, being chivvied to the gas chambers, their little children, frantic, terrified, screaming, encircling their arms around those mothers' ample thighs.

We drive the two miles to the vast, dread plain of Birkenau, the death factory in which as many as 24,000 persons were gassed and cremated daily. Jan hovers beside me with a *sotto* spiel of horror. 'Actually I would like to be alone now, to keep quiet and think about things on my own,' I say and trudge along the wood sleepers, the half-mile track that runs from the gate of death to the gas chambers and crematorium, the last lap of life for two and a half million Jews; Poles, Soviets, and Dutch, 1942–5. I feel blank, unmoved, unshocked, and shocked that I am not shocked. This is Auschwitz-Birkenau, where the Nazis' mindless machine of death rolled night and day, where bodies were shoved from gas to flame, heads shorn, gold teeth extracted, luggage sifted, and sardines and figs and silk underwear and jewels siphoned off to mates and the wives of SS commandos. And I remember the old Polish lady framed up close on the TV screen. 'There was no love lost between the Jews and the Poles; the Jewesses would sit in front parlours opening eyes on our men, while we worked hard in old clothes. Yes, we saw the trains pass through Auschwitz town on their way to the death camp. But what was to be done? And so you threw another rabbit in the stew pot, hung out the washing, and flicked the ash from your linen cupboard.'

The blue sky arches with innocence and sun and air. I look right and left and see, suddenly, in shock, the greenness of the billowing grass, juicy, thick and brilliant grass, in mounds and ditches and in between. Grass, vibrant with the dead, profane in its contrast to the bald, khaki, grazed surrounding plains and hills. Now I am shocked. To my right are the ruins of the sheds and barracks, blackened and burnt. The waspish look-out towers are perched high above the old electrified wire fence demarcations. Imagine the spill of a fresh load, on a freezing black night, of children, mothers, old men, old women, all curtly headed into the undressing rooms, to the gas chambers, where those who could not be squeezed in were shot outside. At the end of the line, I turn to see that mocking low red barrack with its central tower, that evil pivot, where each load of victims stumbled from the trains to be assigned to death or near-death.

Ahead there is a dell, lush green with treacherous troughs and little holes and ditches; it would be too ignominious to break an ankle at Auschwitz. Death throws up its own fertile cover. How green are death's valleys? I stand by a pond throttled with lilies with Jan beside me. 'Here are bone particles.' He pours white chips into my hand; they are indecipherable from the Cyclon B gassing pellets. 'You have seen the crematoria, the gas chambers? The storage rooms? The dynamited remains? The Nazis tried to cover their tracks in 1945.' The bombed display before us gapes in guilt at today's new world; it remains a tangible warning of crimes too evil for comprehension. Why? you cry. It is a warning. This explicit eyeful of horror must remain. And on the bronze plaques positioned alongside is written in every language:

> Forever let this place be
> A cry of despair
> And a warning to Humanity
> Where the Nazis murdered
> About one and a half million
> Men, women and children,
> Mainly Jews,
> From various countries of Europe.
> Auschwitz–Birkenau
> 1940–1945

We drive through evening sun to Krakow. They say you are contaminated by Auschwitz for a week. You can't share Auschwitz. It scrapes the barrel of all emotion, your sob strangled, your inner eye smothered by all those other eyes – uncomprehending, beseeching, and asking why. Auschwitz is a fundamental part of every European's culture. To be cautioned and humbled, to be newly alerted to a man's inhumanity to man, is essential. But the perplexing conundrum of Auschwitz remains. Who was guilty? It was a collective job as only the Germans could effect the ferocity of a few führers over the passive majority of driven 'caddies'.

Sebastian and I have tickets for *La Traviata*. The opera house is Baroque and bulky, a hulk of gold stone. We fall into our seats and feel soothed by the red plush and the swirling gilt and cream architectural extravagance. A packed house, an excellent performance to loud applause. We stroll through the old quarter of this medieval city, cobbled corners and arched alleys, past clock towers and Renaissance façades, through marble colonnades. The fifteenth-century Wawel Castle straddles the hill above the largest, the most beautiful, and untouched square in Europe. In Krakow, you find Florence, Vienna, Paris, Amsterdam, and in its untroubled consistency, a peace and solidity.

Secreted in a side-street we seize on a McDonalds and sink our teeth into the first red meat for days.

April 25 Warsaw

A *gratin* of gentry still dusts the drawing-rooms of Warsaw. Princess Maria Sapieha heads operations from her pretty rooms. Friends and family are winched in to pilot us around, to drive us, to dine us, to definitively educate us.

'Tomek must take you to the film of Warsaw's total devastation by the Germans' and 'Piotr to a dinner – herrings and sour cream – in an old vodka cellar, and Maryjka to the far bank of the Vistula where you see the Warsaw sky line.' And then the Wilanow Palace and the Lazieñki Palace, the lake and the peacocks, and the baroque ceilings. (Possibly the only ceilings not to be dynamited by the Germans.) The Sapieha Palace, a pale strawberry edifice encrusted with cartouches, urns, and pediments, is now a home for the deaf and dumb. I climb on to a ledged railing to take a picture. A few children dot the wide terrace. An old retainer sweeps leaves behind me. 'This was a park of beautiful trees.' But the whole of Warsaw was then full of beautiful trees and grass and parks and elegant ladies promenading with parasols and plumes. This old Warsaw fortunately was painted by Bellotto, an entire room in the Royal Castle is dedicated to his elegant eighteenth-century views. His accurate work was instrumental in reconstructing the city after the war and his period details and colour tones were closely imitated.

Sebastian and I have a final tea party with Maria. She confides to me that her two years as a prisoner-of-war in Berlin were the happiest and the most romantic. 'Of course they put bromide in our food. To dull the sexual urges.' Maria has a talent for enigmatic allusion. 'I have shoes,' she continues in a conspiratorial undertone, 'bought in Sloane Street six months ago. Most unfortunately they are the wrong size. Could you, dear Penelope, change them for me?' The shoes are produced. 'I will buy them off you, Maria.' The price is startling but infinitely preferable to any abortive negotiation in Sloane Street. 'Is there anything I can do, Maria?' She answers gaily – 'Just ring Father Napier of the Brompton Oratory to say I am well and expecting him back here soon for tea.'

May 19 Barnsley Cirencester

Barnsley is a conglomerate of gold in a sea of green with the sheep running and everywhere the honey breath and froth of cow parsley. Inside, the hall and library are silent in the scent of lilies. It is the *Marie-Celeste*. But there is a fire in the library and now a light step across the stone hall, 'I am Sarah's aunt, Lady Margaret Colville.' Charley arrives by train for dinner in his city suit, 'I am still vibrating.' He leaves the library in search of a drink and loose clothes.

The weekend revolves around the Queen Mother's entourage, Lady Margaret, her long-distance lady-in-waiting, Sir Hardy Amies, her long-distance dress designer, and Lord Charteris, the Queen's longest-serving assistant private secretary.

Tucked away in the Cotswold village of Langford, we admire Sir Hardy and his boxed parterres. Bent double on his sticks, listing to the grave, he totters around his roses and his bowers of clotted clematis. Actinidia, a leaf that variegates from green to white to pink, screens a wall, like the patterned silks of several dresses. 'I am busy with the Japanese just now; working with them on a collection for 2001.'

Tom takes tea with Lady Margaret in the library. I retreat to that rest in the four-poster bed; only to be savoured in a house not your own. Tom later reports that Lady Margaret has trouble keeping up with the Queen Mother. She exhausts her household with her schedule and will not let them retire. She keeps going and they must keep going. Her aged retinue are all on 'No Doz'[1] pills. But we have all noticed Lady Margaret dropping off at the table and Sarah worries about her aunt's driving. 'But what the Royal Family is really worried about is the new book on Prince Philip, already published in the States and over here in a month. Desperate scandal.'

May 21

Lord Charteris comes to lunch along with his wife and other distinguished neighbours. The high-flown achievements of his life have not knocked his modesty, but his unsteady hand sends the plum tart flying. 'I am the dirtiest eater west of Suez!' Earlier in the meal he had a coughing fit. He assured Sarah, and Sarah assured us, that we should take no notice; all offers of pats on the back were vigorously declined. 'Time and prayer, time and prayer,' he assured us with the authority of a former Provost of Eton.

After lunch Charley orchestrates a gentle constitutional through the Nash conservatory. Lord Charteris seizes on a huge lemon, the size of a melon; the thick yellow skin is moist and puckered. Now an adept sculptor, his lordship sees its possibilities and twirls it on its stalk. 'Came off in my hand, dear boy.' And the man who has everything, has seen everything, has done everything, needs that lemon to perfect a day.

June 9 Royal Opera House Covent Garden

Verdi's *Stiffelio* is not familiar. First produced in 1850, it was deemed unfortunate and rechristened *Aroldo*, a resounding success. But this morning we are back with *Stiffelio* and our great Verdi conductor, Sir Edward Downes. The music is immediately captivating, the scenes are evocative and severe, the priestly, parochial overtones are masterfully at variance with the tripwires of adulterous passion that prompts the tale. Edward Downes, in short sleeves, manipulates the orchestra with busy, strong arms. He calls to mind an osteopath. Sir Edward Ford is my guest in the orchestra stalls. Is he happy? Is it too loud? Can he see? Would he like to move in the interval? 'I like to see the works,' he assures me and hands to me his opera glasses. His daughter-in-law descends on us in the interval. She is extremely pretty. Edward is nicely wedged by the bar in the coffee queue. He introduces us. She

---

[1] *No Doz* – an American product, containing caffeine, to revive one from fatigue.

gives me an old-fashioned look. 'Edward,' she talks proprietorially, 'you are coming next weekend to help with the fête? To move furniture, lots of jobs I have for you.' 'I think I would prefer to arrive on Saturday,' says Edward, fumbling with his diary. 'I think I am busy on Friday. Yes, the Prince of Wales, some function.' And another lady comes up and kisses him and looks at me askance. Edward puffs a little as we take the narrow side-stairs and rests his hand on my shoulder.

'You are rugged-up today.' I have wrapped my Kashmir ring shawl round my silk dress. He looks approving and we walk down to the Strand for lunch at Simpsons. We wait on the kerb when to my blank horror I see Edward step out in front of a bus. He indicates I follow, but with hands wound up in a rug I cannot pull him back. He recovers himself in time. 'Must not send you back to Tom half-maimed; silly of me; it was that car waiting to turn right muddled me.' At eighty-four Edward is wonderfully in control. More stairs at Simpsons, asparagus and fish cakes, his with lager and mine a glass of house red.

'We met an admirer of yours, Lady Margaret Colville. She told me she found you so intelligent.' Edward laughs. 'She was married to a very intelligent man herself. Jock's diaries were extremely entertaining. But I don't know if his stories of Churchill were always accurate.'

'Lady Margaret takes "No Doz" pills,' I volunteer. 'Yes. She drove me from her home in Hampshire to Dorset last weekend. She had taken her pills; no dropping off at the wheel. Do you know? I sat next to Edward Heath at a Goldsmiths' dinner recently; he slept through two courses! I tried him on every subject. He told me that he much preferred parties where he knew nobody.'

'Did you see in your paper today that Prince Charles is holding Camilla's dog at Highgrove while she is away? Perhaps they should marry and set up in Florence and get on with their watercolours? But you know how I feel, Edward, that Princess Anne is the man and then it's up to William. Let's hope he does well at Eton.' Edward grunts at these loose conjectures.

'I am afraid Princes Anne is becoming very scraggy. She doesn't eat.' 'Oh – not another one.' 'No, nothing medically untoward, but she will pack so much into her day, and then have a sandwich instead of lunch. Of course she likes to keep her weight well down for the riding she does. Tell me, with your crystal ball, how long do you give the Queen Mother?' 'Two or three years I would say, Edward. And have you any travel plans?' 'A week here and there; I never go far for long. Virginia could need me at any time. Yes, she is comfortable in the nursing home, lost a lot of weight. But I would like to go to Prague.'

June 12 *A private drawing-room London W2*

Lady Howe is unprepossessing; in fact her gender is hardly discernable under a cropped helmet of hair; is she wearing a wig? She challenges the versatile journalist, Geoffrey Wheatcroft, in the pretty drawing-room of a friend; her right foot jabs the carpet emphatically. I edge up and on two glasses of wine feel free to join the fray: 'The fact is, Lady Howe, this government is in the kindergarten.' I interject. Her short neck bulges – 'The kindergarten?' Her voice assumes Lady Bracknell dimensions. 'Explain what you mean.' Geoffrey Wheatcroft sidles off and I move in closer. 'This government is a shambles.' I get into my stride – 'No direction – no leadership. It has become an anachronism, Lady Howe. In the 1980s Mrs Thatcher showed us how to make money. To stand on our own two feet – use our initiative. Today many of us have a fax in the back room, are in touch with the Pacific Rim and run our affairs *irrespective* of Government guidance. And, if the dustmen fail, the individual entrepreneur will deliver. I repeat, Lady Howe – in my opinion – this government is an anachronism.' Her husband, Sir Geoffrey, shuffles up. 'I want to go home, Elspeth.' 'Now, Geoffrey. It is too early and I am in the middle of a dispute. Go and find a corner – I will pick you up later . . .' (Sir Geoffrey – who as Mrs Thatcher's trusted Chancellor finally turned traitor, prompted by his wife some say – and thus provoked that lady's untimely downfall.)

Lady Howe scours me with disdain. 'I suppose you want a dictatorship!' 'No, Lady Howe, just leadership – real leadership.'

July 6 *Hardwicke House*

John Major has pulled off his leadership gamble; re-fastened his grey grip on the Conservative party. The fractious Right and Eurosceptics are angry; will they pester him soon again? We now race towards a Euro Buro straitjacket; the party is tilted left. John Major's *pis-aller* cabinet reshuffle, with Europhile Michael Heseltine as his 'Deputy Prime Minister' and Euro Malcolm Rifkind as his Foreign Secretary, has caused fresh alarms. Far from allaying hostilities within his cabinet John Major has roughed it up with sawn-off edges. One observation: 'The worst day since Mrs Thatcher was forced out in November 1990.'

September 5 Itteringham Norfolk

Says the young man in the corner shop through a mop of black curls. 'Oh! You mean Elsbeth. Through those trees, along the track. You can't miss it.' Bintry House beckons through woodland, an old brick sprawl lapped with long grass and nettles and the mangled miscellanea of things not put away. A clutch of picturesque barns thrust into a paddock beyond. I skirt around to the front door. It looks abandoned and is barred by a battered croquet set. The bell is defunct; the knocker sounds as a rebuke. 'Who is it?' A tall woman with her head in a towelled makeshift turban introduces herself as Elsbeth Barker.[2] 'Washing my hair. Do come in.' She will lunch with us at the Walpole Arms? In an hour's time? 'A liquid lunch for me. What a delightful idea.'

At 1.15, Bass and I are well into a coke and a pernod. The lady is late. The telephone rings: the barman advances. 'A call for you.' Elsbeth, my new friend, is she ratting? 'I am running late, the vet hasn't come.' 'What will she drink?' 'Red wine, French red wine.' (And is the vet to tend herself or an animal? It is not uncommon in the shires to eschew the GP for the vet.)

Elsbeth finally arrives in a flounce of waterproof and thick black hair. She seizes her carafe of house red with delight and apologises for her lateness. It was Portia, her Vietnamese pig; her toenails curled up like Moroccan slippers, could hardly walk; the vet clipped with horrendous difficulty and Portia dancing in a mad fear.

'Is it awful being widowed?' 'You never get used to it, it is four years now. You are on your own and you love him still.' Does she write herself? 'I am on my second novel. The first *O Caledonia* is selling well, about my Scottish childhood.' (It won a literary award.) 'Our daughter Raffaella writes. Her first novel *Come and Tell Me Some Lies* has been well received. All about the family of course, thinly disguised. Elizabeth [Smart] is Eliza. Of course I need the work and the money. I do book reviews for the *Independent*, the *Guardian*, *Harpers & Queen*.' And Elizabeth? What of Elizabeth? (Elizabeth Smart who bore George Barker four children and hit the literary jugular with her exposé of their celebrated love.)

Two hours on and we still talk at Bintry at the long polished kitchen table. The Aga is out, an economy. Bass is vilified and caressed in turn by a menagerie of five cats. The bottle of Gateway Red Côte de Gascogne tastes good (at £2.95).

---

[2] Second wife of George Barker, Elsbeth is a writer and journalist and the commended author of *O Caledonia*, 1991.

'Elizabeth? She and I were good friends. She would sit where you sit now. George headed the table between us in this big chair.' I look at the fire-engine-red wood carver beside us. Hard and angular, it gapes for its hero.

'Elizabeth would come up from Suffolk, on her moped, and stay a night or two. We would talk of George, tease him, laugh together, and he would hare off in a rage. Elizabeth liked to drink. And George had his own drinking room next door. He could be violent; knocked us all up. Always throwing plates around the table. It was best to sit close to him – out of firing range.'

And what of Elizabeth's *BGCS*? 'You know she wrote half of it before she ever met George. And then almost manipulated events. They had periods of living together but could not sustain it.'

Elsbeth looks out from her kitchen and her memories; her grey-green eyes, high bones and white skin denote her beauty, a bold beauty and a capable woman, a mother of five children, now alone, pausing on her laurels, coasting cannily to more literary acclaim. Tomorrow she is off to London to a party in Hampstead. Literary? Left-wing? She wrote the review for Salman Rushdie's *The Moor's Last Sigh* in last Sunday's *Independent*.

'My London suit.' She smiles at the flimsy black two-piece swinging on the garden washing line. It is time to leave. I will read her book, her daughter's book, and her favourite Nabokov *Speak Memory*. And perhaps I will introduce her to Elizabeth's biographer, Alice Van Wart? 'We tried to meet but always missed each other.'

September 6 Holkham North Norfolk

We pile into Bryan Basset's new Range Rover and swing down his narrow drive. The beautiful Lady Carey waves us off; thankful perhaps to be left alone. She cooked a great lunch. (Sebastian showed her how to turn out the ice cream from its mould – by a nifty dip in hot water.) She rewarded him with a flat stone from Holkham beach – painted over with a red pig and signed by his distinguished hostess.

To our left – a field like a burst duvet – where white geese flap for space. 'Not popular with the management,' mutters Bryan. 'Feathers make mess.'

We approach Holkham through the South Gate Arch. A herd of caramel bullocks with rounded rumps and retroussé snouts cavort in the sun and flies. 'Proud of my bullocks. This lot came down from the Massif Central. Now I must introduce you to my chicken-handler. He was torpedoed twice in the war.' We are whirled around some bushes into an enclosure of hens and cockerels and more geese and flattened feathers and the old man.

'Afternoon! You all well? That hen has a bad leg – you'd better kill it and have it for your dinner. Lot of flies around here – and they all seem to be landing on you. You'd better take a bath!' The wily old boy gives his landlord a savvy look. Mr Basset is known for his blunt turn of phrase. (The hairdresser at White's is said to refer to 'Mr Basset's mood swings'.)

'Next, the eel trap I must show you. We will drive to the lake.'

After the week's rain the water is crystal-clean with polished stones. The dogs leap in. Joss dives under and Toby yanks out a log, dripping with viscous black weed. Bryan is delighted to see them jostling in the water. 'But the new cream carpet in your boot will be ruined!' I wail. But Bryan Basset is not to be deterred and we round on Holkham, lurching at random over the parkland. We stop on a rise by its stern south façade.

'You can't call it beautiful; personally I prefer brick. The glazing bars have been painted white; an improvement on the old brown . . .' A four-square, compact, Palladian monument in local gold stone; it took forty years to build. Beautiful? Handsome, more; fine; a superb package with its Capability Brown setting; the woods, the slopes, the lake, the wide radial avenues, obelisks, temples.

'Like to see round inside?' We decline; he is very kind; we were there ten years ago; another time perhaps. Interrupting this exceptional peripheral tour is not a consideration. How is the châtelaine? Eddy Leicester's second wife? (Wife number one had jibbed at the running of Holkham and is now moored nearby in Burnham Market.)

'You mean Eddy's wife, Sarah? She does a good job about the place; works very hard – a little wren type . . .' We turn into the 200-year-old ilex avenue.

'In the days of the Grand Tour, the Italians would pack the marble statuary and busts in ilex branches for transport to Britain. And some clever man this end stuck the acorns in the ground.'

We near the South Gate again and its attendant obelisk. 'I bashed into this – one foggy morning.' 'Is there a mark?' I ask ingenuously. The Range Rover mounts the grass dome and we circle the plinth. 'There! There!' Bryan points to a shrapnel-like dent and narrowly avoids a second attempt.

September 16 Hardwicke House

Celia Ward came at ten o'clock to put finishing touches to 'The Yellow Dress'. We propped her easel in the upstairs sitting-room to catch the morning light. Rupert stood for forty minutes; his head needed attention. And Reresby Sitwell's hair had lighlights added. Finally the Lynch–Bages double magnums were labelled. We now have a sensational record of Tom's 60th birthday ball, 'The Yellow Dress' by Celia Ward, April 16, 1994 will be a work to be reckoned with.

'Did Elsbeth tell you that we met?'

'Oh yes! She thought you were the vet.'

September 28 The Turkish Embassy (Residence) 69 Portland Place

The newly-appointed Turkish ambassador – Özdem Sanberk – is locked in talk; the delicate issue of exporting crude oil from Baku, Azerbaijan, has antagonised Russia and Turkey for months. A diplomatic compromise is almost breached; the edgy neighbours will have an oil pipe each; one to run through Russian Georgia to the Black Sea, the second to the west, skirting Armenia, through Turkey, to the port of Ceyhan on the Mediterranean. To have such a prestigious exit point must be the stuff of dreams for a Turk.

'The men still talk,' explains His Excellency's diminutive wife; a sleek black tube capped with sleek black hair. She looks uneasy in the bright-lit rooms; the residence has been re-glazed cream and gilt; crimson swags, glittering chandeliers, silk rugs and brocaded carved sofas do little to induce intimacy. We sit gingerly and admire the nineteenth-century fine marquetry floors laid through the enfilade of rooms. The rugs and the polished floors prove a treacherous match; one young footman does a near perilous fandango with his loaded tray.

And now! The double doors thrown wide. Our old friend from Istanbul Professor Emré Gönensay and His Excellency enter, beaming; their oil pipe secured on paper at least. Emré, plump and serene in his success. Position has aged him; his moustache is grey. (I recall Tom's comment, 'I have always distrusted facial hair. How do you cope with scrambled eggs?')

It was in March 1994 that Emré lunched with us at Hardwicke House and branded his Prime Minister, Tansu Çiller, as an adventuress and worse. And now? He has become her trusted right-hand man! He leaves the dinner table, his plate of baklava swimming in syrup untouched, as he is called to the telephone. On resuming his seat he whispers some delightful confidence to Tom. (He has had an ecstatic call from Tansu Çiller. He lights a cigar, unbuttons his double-breasted jacket; 'What a woman!'

October 5 Le Shuttle Dover – Calais

'Attention please! Attention please! An incident has been detected in the next carriage. As a precaution passengers will be joining your carriage while the Shuttle continues its journey. Please remain calm; there is no danger to this carriage.'

'Attention s'il vous plaît! Il se produit un incident dans le wagon voisin – veuillez rester calme . . .'

We are halfway through the channel tunnel at eighty miles an hour; each carriage compartment of four vehicles is contained by bomb-proof glass fire-doors. We bounce and sway a bit. Again and again the tannoy belts out its staccato drill. We have seventy feet of deep blue sea above us and a blazing sky. But no sign of sea or white cliffs or Dover Castle as you set off on this computerised rail track through the skeletal props of the station; a journey devoid of contours.

The grey painted high-sided containers – prison-like with peep-hole windows – even suggest holocaust deportation vans. The interior reflects intensive care; shining white, shining steel; red fire extinguishers, red emergency fire buttons; green for passenger alarm. A family of Sephardic Jews swarm the front car, their large, clever heads are shaven except for their plaited little bell-pulls that swing from each temple. Their children scurry like mice in search of a lavatory. A nervous female official with a mobile explains that the tannoy has never come on before and nobody knows how it turns off. But what is the trouble? A bomb? A gunman? A car on fire? It is the bus, she explains; a little boy playing with a smoke-detector.

We reach Calais – to the triumphant strains of 'Land of Hope and Glory' played full tilt in the car behind. A posse of armed police and *pompiers* in silver helmets dance around the bus as it is ostracised to the corner of the arrival esplanade.

'The Shuttle continues its journey' is a pragmatic warning with sinister innuendo to those caught in an 'incident' carriage.

October 17 Hardwicke House

As read in *The Times* diary today:

'Sir James Goldsmith, the billionaire Euro MP, has already recruited 180 would-be MPs to join his anti-Europe party at the next general election. He may also have picked up a first-class economist to advise them. Yesterday he was spotted lunching with Alan Walters, the economist so admired by Baroness Thatcher.'

Good on them! And to Bill Cash, John Redwood and any other accountable leaders to go for the jugular of bureaucratic bungling and bullying – go for it!

October 24 3 Impasse du Château Roquebrune

Long shots are necessarily streaked with fantasy and daydreams soar beyond sense and scaffolding. But how else to meet my heroine? How else but to arrive at her door? At Garavan; the village sloping up from the French Corniche, within a breath of Italy.

I have brought Russian tea as a lure; little packets of 'Georgian' tea, 'Russian Breakfast' tea and 'Stravinsky' tea procured in a Russian Tea House in the Fulham High. And a pamphlet on bygone Richmond; its old mansions and its evocative riverside, where she had once lived and walked her dog along the tow path.

My friends' heart-warming testimonials and suggestions that she meet me – 'but Penelope adores your books; has travelled through Russia and Turkey; speaks Turkish . . .' – have met with an incontrovertible 'so what?'

Lesley Blanch is honed to a deadline, her rooms are a minefield of papers piled on stools and sofas and nests of tables. Says my hostess on this matchless gold morning – 'We will have a picnic in the Arrière Pays. We can drop off your tea on the way. Alice might be there to let us in.' And how is this Alice? 'She has an expressive bottom,' sighs my octogenarian host, 'and red-gold hair – dyed,' adds my hostess. Alice is a Scot, is our heroine's factotum and something of a phenomenon. 'She's got a lover; a widowed Frenchman; he gives her clothes; he comes to stay.' An intriguing ménage. Does he help with the cooking? Perhaps a sighting of Alice would be even more edifying than her mistress . . .

We chug through Cap Martin-Menton; neat, high-rise encrustations slotted between the towering backdrop of wooded cliffs and the sea. Up a small road in Garavan we confront a steel gate with a steep flight of steps to a pert, pink villa above. With the daring of an errant

schoolgirl my hostess buzzes the bell. A pause and then – a voice; a
voice of arctic and unalloyed dismissal:

'Who is there?
What do you want?
Is it a big parcel?
Alice is out shopping . . .'

'We will leave our parcel inside the gate.' My hostess is remarkably
sanguine. My trophies caught in the little white bag from the Stravinsky Tea House are dropped tenderly through the security system,
landing unceremoniously on their side.

I saw her once; I saw her twice; how often do we meet people in
our ignorance of their achievements? Thirty years ago I saw her;
reclining on a window seat, in a nest of colourful shawls and a cloud
of rosy hair; at Zoffany House on Strand-on-the-Green where our
hostess, Enid Box, would paint her dinner guests with a lion sat in
between. And then again, in 1977, she was in Teheran, writing her
biography: *Farah Shahbanou of Iran*. It was not such a good book; not
to be compared with those stirring profiles of wilder shores. She
inscribed a copy for our mutual friends:

For Marianne & Lanham
(à Roquebrune)
In remembrance of a Persian path they smoothed for me and over
and over again.
With love and gratitude
Lesley B

August 1978

And in 1965 she has written in the flyleaf of '*The 9-Tiger Man*' – a
romantic tale:

Something frivolous to lighten the sadder moments of the last
summer among the roses at
Kuche Tarakol 23 (Tehran)
With love from Lesley.

October 25 Roquebrune

Today we fitted in Monte Carlo, the Empress Elisabeth of Austria and Gustave Eiffel's glass rotunda in the Hermitage all before lunch – the last item served as an *amuse-gueule* if you like, as we collapsed underneath it with a drink. Especially evocative is Elisabeth's monument. A white marble obelisk with the words:

'Nous avons élevé cet humble obélisque à Reine Elisabeth, car vous aimiez le soir à venir respirer la senteur lentisque, et parmi les rochers près d'ici vous asseoir.' The thrush and robin sing and the two imperious eagle heads are locked in bronze and proud memento. A single parasol-pine fans out in obeisance against that profoundly blue sea.

November 5 Hardwicke House

I have had a card from my heroine Lesley Blanch.

'How very kind of you to shower me with Russian tea and a review of Gore V's book. He is an old & cherished friend so the Amis review grates. Gore is too clever, witty, generous and kind and good-looking and so arouses jealousy everywhere. I find the book enchanting.[3] Marian tells me we met in Persia. I do not recall this. Forgive such vagueness. I am deep in work, late on my deadline which must be my excuse for not inviting you to visit me here.

All good wishes
Lesley Blanch
Madame Lesley Blanch
9 Chemin Vallaya
06500 Garavan-Menton

November 14 Christie's St James's

John Partridge of Partridge (Fine Arts) Ltd is rosy from champagne and the hunting season. 'The Great Rooms' reverberate to a Private View of Important English Furniture. What does John Partridge think of the Asprey take-over? 'I would adore to be taken over by the Sultan of Brunei!' he exclaims. 'Simply longing to be taken over!' And you can see him purring in his shop – a Cheshire cat grin – with every gilded table-leg set wide apart – and *not* thinking of England.

---

[3] (Martin Amis concluded his review of Gore Vidal's autobiography – in so many words – 'only once did he touch on the *Wilder Shores of Love* and *Shipwreck*)'.

November 16 Hardwicke House

Despite our arid night life, there have been day encounters – notably one sun-bright morning this week: as I launched the labradors through the front gates, Harrods' van halted before us. I was handed a slim package. What could this be to merit a delivery? 'One pair of gold-plated nail scissors, Madam, with blades replaced.' It will have to be seen if the new owners of Asprey – the Sultan of Brunei's family – will match such Edwardian service.

And how about the Asprey family? Two hundred years of a family inheritance and tradition tossed to the winds of change. At an excessively good price, of course; the £200 million mark; a mere drop in the Pacific Rim for the Sultan who is billed as the world's richest man with over £20 billion.

Having lunched on Wednesday at Boodles ladies annexe with Esmond and Susie Bulmer (a particularly good Graves 1983) I walked up St James's Street to Asprey. I had hoped Susie would come too; John Asprey adores redheads. However, Esmond's Mercedes was revving over for Herefordshire; for their rotunda on the hill.

Clutching a necklace of Persian glass beads for re-stringing, I braved the front portals to face a pretty girl (the assistants at Asprey have recently been ascribed 'porcelain vowels' by the tabloid press).

'I would like to see John Asprey – I am first going up to the jewellery department.' And from there a man ushered me in to John. He was exceedingly friendly and admired my Black Cross mink jacket. He looked well and handsome – quite untouched by the pangs and procrastinations of his lost family empire. 'We fixed it up over a glass of Champagne – a wonderful deal. You must realise that the Sultan could go *phut*[4] in two or three years' time and then I would have lost my best client; Asprey would be finished. We are retaining a 10% family interest.' His sons? 'They are happy; they are all uninterested in the business . . .' I congratulate John on being the Sultan's chosen one and inwardly marvel at his total lack of clan sentimentality. A more circumspect man in his shoes would be on his third nervous breakdown.

---

[4] 'Phut' in the *Oxford Dictionary* – 'The sound of a bladder collapsing'.

November 22 Hardwicke House

The Princess of Wales put up a remarkably sanguine performance for her television interview on Monday's *Panorama*. One hour's in-depth interrogation on her life and loves and fears was handled with a circumspect grace. She was articulate, expressive and devastatingly honest – shedding skin after skin with equanimity; some would argue an equanimity to belie all sincerity. Her performance was compelling; according to the national grid, her audience was captive throughout the country. Her long legs were crossed in blue tights; her blonde head tilted to attention and her oceanic eyes intent on her male interrogator (suitably plain and monotone).

She talked of the Palace's 'whispering campaign' – 'the enemy within'. The Princess is sensible to speak out. Eddy, Duke of Clarence's 'clearance' from the Royal Family can draw chilling parallels with her own voiced fears. (The diaries of Inspector Abberline, the head of Scotland Yard 1892–96, make pertinent reading one hundred years on.)

November 25 Burwarton Bridgnorth Shropshire

Rosemary Boyne feeds bread into the toaster. Breakfast smells spiral up stairs and winding passages; coffee, bacon and egg and sausage are cushioned with that musky aroma of mushrooms. 'Did you sleep well? Enough blankets? We aired the sheets for two days . . .' Never do you feel more cosseted than on that first morning after the first night; the guest on honeymoon. And you forget that juggle with those Edwardian electrics in that rush to change for dinner; the rumpled sausage of carpet on the landing (fitted and laid by the Lord Lieutenant for Shropshire himself). If you aren't sent flying as you negotiate the nursery bathroom in the dark, beware the rocking horse.

From the wide-plate Victorian windows we see the sun steal up this bowl of green with tawny trees. A rare pocket of country, this midland East England, untrammelled by road or industrial development. Now the housekeeper darts through the dining-room door. A fox in the rose bed! A fox! A fox! Eating two of your bantams, Lady Boyne!' Rosemury hurls herself at the window. 'A fox in the rose bed! My bantams, my precious, best bantams! Michael! Michael. Get your gun on the rose bed!' On the first floor the Lord Lieutenant hoists his 20-bore through a bedroom window but he holds his powder over the wrong roses. Silence ensues. For a good five minutes he skins his eyes. 'Michael – where are you?' From the dining-room we watch in awe as the fox crunches luxuriantly on the wodge of flesh and creamy feathers. Suddenly, he starts and drags his loot clumsily across the lawn to a rhododendron bush. Michael appears on the lawn; tall, patrician, handsome and splendid in tuxedo and red shooting garters. He circles the bush and steps inside its hollowed bower. And the fox is off! A streak along the terrace; a shot, two shots.

A day of fresh air and sun and shooting all the way. Our two labradors acquitted themselves well enough. Their first day on the killing fields, when they preferred to charge around with sticks and logs in their jaws instead of dead birds. The keeper butted their big heads with blood and feathers but could not induce any working enthusiasm.

The dinner table groans with grouse and silver. A beautiful woman – 'the most beautiful woman in Shropshire' according to our host and hostess – joins the party. The grouse is rare and *tiède*. I ladle a heap of redcurrant jelly on to my plate. A pink pool expands as I struggle with the breast. Now Michael's bird shoots off his plate on to the floor between us. 'Have mine!' I lift my nearly-new aberration on to his plate and a dog is called in to lap up the grease.

Light banter in the Library after dinner. Much comment and speculation on the Princess of Wales's television interview; on her claim that the Palace wants to 'eliminate' her, that Prince Charles is not necessarily the ideal candidate for the throne, that she should be a globe-roving ambassador, that she should be 'Queen of people's hearts'. And I tell them how, the morning after the interview, I had heard Princess Margaret trill from her cubicle at the hairdresser's – David and Josef – 'It is the Prince that matters'.

Michael, with his KCVO fresh on his shoulders from the week's Royal Investiture, masks himself with *The Times* and silence.

December 16 Hardwicke House

Bobby Nicolle telephoned this morning. In the course of conversation – 'Did you know Michael Boyne?' – 'We were shooting with him at Burwarton just three weeks ago.'

'Hold tight – some bad news coming – Michael dropped dead yesterday – massive heart attack at a board meeting.'

We read today in *The Times'* Deaths – 'Boyne – Gustavus Michael George – 10th Viscount, KCVO. On December 14th aged 64 very suddenly in London . . .'[5]

[5] 'Dear Penelope, Found in the Library. Who were you paying?' Love Michael. (My Peter Jones account card, which I had mislaid.)

1996

January 10

Dinner at the Garrick Club with our host, Anthony Gray. A small party in the main Zoffany dining-room. An elderly member shot out of the sacrosanct recess under the stairs.

'Margaret!' he gasped, ramming up his nose an inch from mine. 'Not Margaret – Penelope!' I corrected him as he scanned my face accusingly and slunk back to his cupboard.

January 13 Hardwicke House

Dr Christian Carritt and her son Luke come to lunch. Christian brings home-made fudge in pretty green bags. 'I have to find Christmas presents for 150 patients and I make them fudge.' Christian – a septuagenarian, adored, depended on, stunning and self-deprived.

Luke disappears from the lunch table ... does he know the way ... ? He returns and moans through fingers on his face that he has been sick in the kitchen sink. Later we blame the dogs for swiping the left-over sausages. Christian telephones the next morning. How is Luke? He had confessed to her that he had binged on the sausages – 'And last week,' she continues distractedly, 'I found a hoard of mashed potato in his anorak pocket.'

January 30 La Poissonnerie Restaurant Sloane Avenue SW3

Selina Hastings lunches with me. Dover sole for two. She drinks nothing; I have one glass of house white. The bill soars to £75.

It took Selina a year to persuade the Mitford family to allow her to write a biography of Nancy. She urges me not to be disheartened if Lesley Blanch refuses to authorise me to write her biography. 'These distinguished old ladies take a lot of wooing.'

February 6 Colindale North London

'That Dare Devil Mood'. I spend an absorbing day wrestling with the heavy volumes of the *Sunday Times* and *Spectator* and the *Times Literary Supplement*, shuffling through the frail, yellowed paper for reviews of Lesley Blanch's books. The above caption refers to her first book *The Wilder Shores of Love* published in 1954. It was translated into eleven languages.

Operating the Museum's food and drink vending machines exacerbates all frustrations.

February 12 Royal Society of Literature Hyde Park Gardens W2

Chill, high-ceilinged rooms; the handsome premises tenanted by the RSL. A lone girl in charge photocopies for me letters from Lesley Blanch to the Society secretary. This didactic lady seems permanently to be in need of subscription money. Lesley Blanch is understandably hard-pressed to attend to such exigent requests for three guineas . . . 'I am just back from Afghanistan' . . . 'a few days before leaving for Central Asia' . . . 'upon my return from Upper Egypt'. Her far-flung travels spur on the secretary to ever more disciplinary demands.

February 13 Hardwicke House

One incontrovertible refusal from Lesley Blanch to authorise my writing her biography. She is writing her own; anything that I might consider doing on an unauthorised stand would be condemned as 'mal vu'. She urges me to refrain from '. . . continuing to approach any more of my friends or accquaintices [sic]* to obtain unauthorised information . . .' and ends, 'Let me wish you well writing on some other, more accessible subject.'

Yours sincerely
Lesley Blanch
A copy of this letter has gone to my agent, Mrs Pat Kavanagh.

*spelt incorrectly in her scorn and fury.

February 14 The Tate Gallery

The Cézanne Exhibition

At his best he is unassailable – *The Card Players* – it is to die for. But what a restricted diet: apples and more apples; Mont St Victoire and those gangling grey nudes, feigning pious arches with their bony arms. No charm or smiles or hint of sex; his wife, pale and patient and pushed into a chair to pose; again and again. Our hero, saturnine, bold, or glowering from under his slouch hats. Cézanne was no party man but he could have afforded a variety in models. *The Lady in Blue with a Hat* (from The Hermitage in St Petersburg) is stunning; not least because of its solo diversity. And his towering mentor – Mont St Victoire – in the right, bright light with the paint on clear is an enduring triumph.

February 20 The Arts Club Dover Street W1

The dining-room is deadening and brown; an aberration of style after the Georgian elegance of the marble entrance hall. Selina Hastings introduces me to John Saumarez Smith of Heywood Hill, the book-sellers: that literary nest in Curzon Street where Evelyn Waugh would gossip with the wartime châtelaine, Nancy Mitford.

Selina and John know that I have been clipped and muzzled by Lesley Blanch; that she is writing her autobiography; another? John warns me that she draws a fine line between fact and fiction. He will write, he says, and try and oil my passage.

February 23 Hardwicke House

Aylın Gönensay telephones. She is staying with Sir Bernard and Lady Burrows in Fulham. I thank her for sending me the back copies of *Cornucopia* – the Turkey-orientated magazine, published in Istanbul (and edited by John Scott, second son of the Duke of Buccleuch). The article on Pierre Loti by Ömer Koç I had especially enjoyed; Lesley Blanch had written Loti's biography in 1983. 'Ah . . . ! Lesley Blanch!' shrilled Aylın down the mouthpiece. 'At this moment I hold a cushion stitched by her . . . for "Bernard and Inez".' I mention my contretemps with the lady . . . 'I tell Inez to write to her about you – immediately.' I do not demur.

February 29 Hardwicke House

Spring birds and daffodils and a sharp white sun. Edward Ford lunches. ('What about taking a leap and plumping for 29th February?')

A scrunch of gravel and I wave from the balcony. Coquilles again and 'you are a delicious hostess and provided me a delicious luncheon – the coquilles were delicious as was the wine with which we washed it down'.

The Princess of Wales he had termed as 'aggressive'. 'She needs corralling. An older man to guide her.' We strolled in the sun. It was that sort of day. 'Where is Ham House?' asked Edward. 'I'll get in your car and show you.' We weaved slowly down Ham Street past the patched up 300-year-old brick walls and halted at the main iron gates. The leaded windows and the lugubrious north front frowned in shade. 'Charles II stayed here often,' I ventured . . . 'Did he *really*?'

March 2 Coast Guard Cottage Lepe Hampshire

Lydia, nursing a forty-eight-hour hangover, stood by the kitchen window cajoling spaghetti into boiling water. At her grandmother's funeral the previous day, followed oddly by a night's dancing, champagne had flowed, unceasing.

'Where is Sunny?' demanded great-grandson Luke. He stomped through the familiar cottage rooms. 'Where is she hiding?' Said Lydia, 'Sunny's gone shopping.' Sunny was certainly not down on the beach because her red wellingtons were standing in place in the porch. Ten minutes later Luke hoisted himself up beside Lydia at the kitchen window . . . 'Mummeeeee . . . Sunny is sitting in the garden.'

March 12 Hardwicke House

Georgie Vassiltchikov telephones to cancel our tête à tête tomorrow with acute back pain and a paralysis induced by a poisonous oyster – he can't think or move or see. Last week he was his bright voluble self – 'Romain Gary was my good friend. In the late 1950s we worked together in the United Nations. He often asked me back to supper. Lesley Blanch was an excellent cook. She would wait for us, lolling on the sofa like a Turkish odalisque.'

March 18 Bruges

Dung and damp hang on the night air. A crowd of campaniles set off their clanging as the fiacres race through the dark cobbled streets. Floodlit, ethereal, each Gothic tower and Dutch gable etched in night's black void. Lead-paned windows flank the streets in ordered Renaissance. Vitrines of intricate lacework underline the parochial mores of a well-ordered country.

March 19

To the Memling museum and *Sibylla* (1480), the girl with gold rings on her fingers, the corner of her brown eye veiled by a wimple. But in the Begijnhof – the square – for the Nuns, the modest white houses need a coat of paint. On the centre green with the tall trees, the white doves coo. Here sat Winston Churchill and painted a day out of his life.

March 21 The Vermeer Exhibition 1632–1675 The Mauritshuis The Hague

The girl with the red hat, c. 1665: an androgynous face peers out from the froth of red feathers. She could be a boy. 'The girl is painted over a portrait of a man.' That explains it.

Girl with a pearl earring (recently restored). Exquisite with luminous use of paint. An open gaze to equivocate an innocence and invitation. Vermeer's 'light' accents are clearly visible with pinpricks of white in the corners of the mouth.

In *The Milkmaid* we are transfixed on detail. The shadow on the white wall from the driven nail; the light pouring in through a broken window pane. Tom thinks this painting needs cleaning.

The young woman fastening a strand of pearls round her neck certainly needs cleaning. Her yellow satin ermine-trimmed jacket is dulled with dirt. The following year – 1665 – a woman writing a letter wears the same jacket – conspicuously more yellow and cleaned.

From our own National Gallery *A lady seated at the virginals* in or before 1675 was painted in the last year of Vermeer's life. The hands hovering over the keys are clumsily depicted, more like pigs' trotters. Memling's Sibylla – painted 200 years before – puts such hands to shame.

The exhibition is crowded, a six-deep foray before each picture. You have to be still and intent to eke out the peace and light.

March 23 Hardwicke House

A letter from Selina Hastings:

'John Saumarez Smith had a call from Lesley who is very distressed at the thought of anyone writing about her . . . She is planning some kind of autobiographical work herself . . . This is all in the day's work in my view and part of the biographer's lot.'

March 28 Hardwicke House

John Jolliffe[1] telephones (currently at work on his commissioned tome on Glyndebourne). 'Shamyl's descendants will be in London on April 18. You must meet them. I told them you are working on Lesley Blanch's biography.' Shamyl, the Imam of Daghestan, the hero of Blanch's *The Sabres of Paradise.* Of course I will meet them: Aydın and Kim Erkan. Their elderly relation, Habibe Erkan, from Istanbul, gave to me, fifteen years ago, the enamelled paper knife by my bedside today.

April 18 10 Alma Terrace London W8

Lady Monson is an accomplished hostess. She edges me towards Aydın and Kim Erkan from Istanbul. They inherited the deceased Habibe's flat in Besiktas. The Caucasus they still view with caution; they had plans to visit but the Chechnya war intervened. Kim remembers Lesley Blanch well and has a fund of stories; for another time. Tom, John Jolliffe and I dine in an Italian restaurant – Il gallo d'oro – in High Street, Kensington. The men exchange Glyndebourne stories. I promise to send John comments by Moran Caplat on the new building.

June 12 Hardwicke House Ham Common

Luke had his three-year assessment last week at the National Health baby clinic. He warned off the lady in charge when she checked his testicles, complaining that she was tickling him. She next proffered him a picture board of animals to identify. 'Don't know – don't know – dunno.' Disappointed, she offered him fish. Luke pointed enthusiastically at the lobster in the middle. 'That is a lobster . . . at my home, we *eat* lobster.'

[1] Grandson of Raymond Asquith and author of books on Virginia Woolf and Glyndebourne.

July 12–19 Lourdes South-West France

36° celsius in Lourdes. The mountain river Gave sweeps green and
cold through the congested town.

Sebastian and I help push the sick in hooded Victorian perambu-
lators – to the Rosary Basilica, the Grotto, the Baths. A ceaseless
procession of international pilgrims, singing and praying and moving
on through heat and exhaustion. Sebastian has attached himself to an
Anglo-Irish-Indian girl with red flowers in her black hair and a tend-
ency to squeal and gurgle in the darker recesses of prayer.

Our Benedictine monks line up on their platform like a choice of
ice cream in such sartorial variety. My fellow pilgrims surprise me with
their need to confess so frequently, such incontinent consciences. And
I never did discover why the senior Father had a washing line of
rosaries and clanging crosses dangling across his bottom.

One day I surprised Father Jock in a unisex lavatory. 'I do love
these communal loos,' he said as I turned to wash my hands. There
was a silence from his allotted space. 'Shall I whistle for you?' Later he
shared with me a peeled orange. I told him he looked handsome
without his sunhat and he squashed it on to my head. Celibacy at
thirty-eight? What a prospect. It took him one whole year to say
goodbye to his girlfriends; they came to Rome one by one.

The Penitential Service at the Chapel of St Joseph – the Procession
of the Blessed Sacrament – Mass in the Basilica of St Bernadette – The
Torch Mass; the human chain, stronger in its weakness, hope and
conjunction. At The Grotto I stand beside the little plaque commemorating the spot where St Bernadette first saw the Virgin Mary in the
rocks above; poised in white; smiling; as young as the little village girl
herself she had seemed, with her long blue sash and yellow roses on
her toes.

And how did everybody fare in the baths? Stripped and swathed in
an ice-cold shroud you are dipped in a trough of mountain water –
like sheep. Pretty Victoria swears she trembled uncontrollably; all the
evil coming out, we console her. Having skinned my knees in a free
fall between pews at St Joseph's chapel, I do not bathe. 'Are you going
to have a bath, Penelope?' 'No – I have an infected leg . . .' 'Oh!
But that doesn't matter. People go in the baths with every kind of
infection.'

July 24 44 Ladbroke Grove London W11

Lunched with Laurence Kelly (author of *Tragedy in the Caucasus*), his
wife Linda, and son, Nicky, who is studying to be a solicitor. Nicky
knocked a glass of water over the dining table; nobody turned a hair
and I deftly saved Laurence's white wine as he waved aside a point.
Linda left promptly to see her publisher and Nicky had a poem waiting
upstairs.

Laurence walked me up to his study-cum-library. Cairns of books
and manuscripts lay in ambush on the floor. 'Sorry about the mess –
I am in the middle of a book – Alexander Griboyedov[2] – husband of
Nina Chavchavadze. Have a look at the Caucasus section – W. E. D.
Allen – John Baddeley. Now that Fitzroy[3] has gone, we Caucasians
must stick together. You should get Moshe Gammer on *Muslim Resist-
ance to the Tsar, Shamil and the Conquest of Chechnia and Daghestan*.' I
scribbled down titles; I must not tire him, or irritate. It was pouring
with rain. 'It is pouring with rain! Have you an umbrella? A car?
Forgive me if I don't come downstairs with you . . .' I shut fast the
heavy front door and waited comfortably in the porch for the storm
to pass.

July 31 Reykjavik Iceland

An eight-hour bus tour encircling the geographical marvels of south
Iceland. We are a polyglot party of Americans, Japanese, Germans; no
British except for Sebastian and me. We see Gullfloss (Golden Waterfall) described as 'the most beautiful in Iceland'. It thunders in tiers to
a twisting orgy a hundred feet below – stand alongside and you are
stunned with sound and spray.

This vast, volcanic plain is probed with lakes and falls and gorges.
Geysers bubble and steam in their sulphurous red-earth holes. The
renowned Strokkur geyser ejects seventy feet of boiling spume every
six minutes; a most gratifying performance for tourist enterprises.
'Stand back,' urges our guide as the sodden sulphur swells furiously
before each burst. 'People get caught with boil burns every day.'

A lone white Lutheran church on a green hill – Skalholt Cathedral
– is positioned on the ancient seat of Iceland's first bishopric (ninth
century). It recalls the church and spire staged at Covent Garden for

[2] Czar Nicholas's ambassador to the Shah of Persia. He was assassinated in Teheran.
[3] Sir Fitzroy Maclean, the acclaimed writer on the Caucasus, author of *Eastern Approaches*
1982.

Verdi's *Stiffelio*. Inside we shelter from driving rain as a visiting orchestra rehearse their Bach.

August 2 Vik South Iceland

Our bus takes a clear straight road through emerald grazing slopes; ponies, cows and sheep; a glowering mountain backdrop and the undulating volcanic steppes. Lumped and hollowed tracts of lava paved over with moss, and threaded through with purple thyme, white clover, pink wood-cranebill and dazzling daisies. Yellow lichen clots the rocks like powdered egg. The Ölfusa mountain river – Iceland's most voluminous – swirls through volcanic scrub, milky with accumulated glacial silt and rubble. There are 130 rivers in Iceland. Dairy farms cluster the green lowland space with outbuildings of quake-resistant steel, concrete, stucco, brightly painted red, blue, and ochre. Hay is stored in livid white vacuum packs. Wool is the main export; sheep spot the foothills black and white. A corral of snow-capped mountains with the massive volcanic Mount Hekla, the roaring Skogafoss waterfall where rainbows glance, the hollowed cliffs and gorges combine in a forbidding ring around these lush valleys bent on husbandry. Tourism is a prime national concern. Expense is everywhere. Import tax and national tax fan the prices. (Three American dollars for a cup of coffee in a Nissen hut – twenty dollars for a lamb burger.)

What is this dichotomous land of fire and ice, green sanctuaries and sea? The Sound of Mull comes to mind with Rum and Eigg and Muck, Cumbria's Scafell Pike and Ireland's emerald sweeps. Just south of the Arctic Circle, an island in the middle of the Atlantic ocean, it still sustains vast icé–floes barracked by hundred-feet-high glacial walls. It is a chameleon land.

Pierre Loti, the nineteenth-century sailor, fisherman and writer, describes Icelandic effects of cloud and sea and light in his novel *Pêcheur d'Islande* (1886). They have not changed today. As the bus lurches up a winding cinder path we pant with fear. The summit! The cliff edge! We are rewarded by a sheer satanic rock face stuffed with a nesting puffin colony. 'Most of us live on some sort of volcano. Dangers are everywhere,' murmurs our guide laconically. The black dust beaches on this south-east coast bear out his words. Pierre Loti's lines on clouds reflect the sudden storm now massing from the west: 'Accumulation of grey wads, forming, as it were, soft walls round the sea . . . The great shag of clouds . . . a suspended shag trailed over the distance like an immense curtain of mourning.' He describes the light: '. . . a few yellow openings by which the sun sent down its rays in sheaves.'

August 3 Reykjavik Iceland

A minor gale. Barracudas of grey cloud bolstering the horizon. We embark off Keflavik in a small motorboat to whale-watch. Warns Olaf from the tiller; 'This is a cold-tempered oceanic climate. There is no understanding of the Icelandic weather.' Helga points out puffins and guillemots. Gulls wheel and scream above. Forty minutes out to sea and things look bad. A choppy sea, much swelling and frothing. We head back to shore, gulping at spray and wind.

Iceland is a treacherous indent of rocks and fjords on its north and east coasts. The British, French, Dutch and Spanish have wrecked their fishing boats on these shores through centuries. The crews were rescued and sheltered in isolated farmsteads, pending their return to foreign climes. Offspring evolved inevitably. The population in the north can boast dark skin and eyes to this day. And many an Icelander will tell you he feels more Celt than Scandinavian.

August 16–17 The Manor House Cholderton Wiltshire

An early eighteenth-century red-brick gem; some bricks blackened with a vitrified glaze. The date 1732 is clearly incised on the lead drainpipe heads. A sweeping lawn, a lily pond stuffed with iris and carp and golden orfe – and timbered barns; older than the house itself the owner, David Brooke, told me. His distinguished ancestors hung in the intimate Georgian rooms; a handsome line-up by Lely, Van Dyck, Gainsborough and Romney. On the brick terrace we drank champagne from the palest blue crizzled glasses. The dinner dance to celebrate my brother Stephen's fiftieth birthday was a thirty-minute drive through rolling country paled by the August sun. In a village school hall, as remote as a Norfolk church in fields, a marquee, a band, champagne, candles, flowers had converged from another world. John Jolliffe, graced the scene in a bottle-green smoking jacket on the hottest night of the year. Barbara Goalen's daughter, Sarah, chic, rich and widowed, was assiduously whirled round the floor by that rogue charmer, David Cotton.

1997

From Denpasar, the capital (Pasar equals Market), we drove through a ribbon Hindu-Buddhist toyland. The black volcanic terrain repeats in black rock, granite, shore lines, cement and dust. A sombre scene in rain. Stores and shacks bulge under their red-tiled and tin roofs with canework, coconuts, fanciful wood-carving and exotic fruits that often look better than they taste. The Hindu temples glowing in imported red brick are barnacled with stone gods and gargoyles and reptilian grotesques. Small Buddhist temples, private garden temples and grand public temples clearly ensure that folks are kept busy, appeasing the evil spirits and invoking the great and the good before yet another party celebration. The blood from a cockfight is the favoured cleanser for the courtyard or patio. Everywhere their wicker cages are seen, placed in the shade to rest before the next contest.

Up to the central mountains through swaying green fans of coconut, with banana, lychee and orange groves. We see far below us women in bright sarongs slap and scrub and stretch out their washing on river boulders. We skirt the wedged emerald rice terraces where streaks of water reflect sapphire from the blazing sky. Coolies with wide hats and shoulder poles ferry weed and hay in pails to feed their oxen.

A blue mist hangs over Lake Batur. The gaping mountain crater soars above. After two devastating eruptions in 1911 and 1926, when thousands were killed and 2,000 temples wiped out, the present village is still embraced by a serpentine torrent of petrified black lava. We stroll through eleventh-century garden temples and centuries-old stone villages (the Balinese are vague on dates) – where dogs sleep as if dead and roosters crow all day; and the black family pig is fattened for slaughter and women fry flat cakes for the next party. In the street, peddlers tout preposterously-carved elephants ('made of bad wood', we are warned), florid bolts of batik, incense gongs and every conceivable offering to the beneficence of the Hindu gods. Vishnu, the preserver and giver of rain (often depicted on his charging Nandi bull destroying and then re-cycling the spirit), Dewi-Sri – the goddess of rice, Ganesh – the remover of obstacles; always a popular god to have around if you are giving a party. We marvel at every Buddhist altar where saucers and bowls are piled with flower heads, their stalks stuck in between, like so many half-eaten salads discarded on the sideboard. The more important confections are awarded a joss-stick. The wisps of smoke suggest a more self-indulgent plea to the gods – or a more exceptional thanks.

March 18

On the east coast we luxuriate at Amankila – 'Peaceful Hill' – a stylish complex of marble terraces and thatched wind temples tiered down to the sea, with the island, Nusa Panida, a blue bluff on the horizon. Wayan, a frangipani blossom behind each ear, massages me with coco-nut oil, sandalwood and steel fingers.

At sunset we join a small group of Australians and Japanese on the sea shore. We sit in a modest circle sipping the beach boy's lemonade and wait for the start of the renowned 'Kecak' – the monkey dance. A ferocious band of half-naked male dancers brandishing flared torches race into the bay. They leap exultantly while their Chieftain Rama (the legendary hunting prince and romantic avenger) exhorts his troops to a frenzied nonsensical chant – Chak – Chak – Chak – to resemble chattering monkeys. Our muscle-bound hero and his team next avenge evil and greed with a frantic twirling of their flaming torches which are finally flung to the sand. Hundreds of arms and fingers thrust up, black against the sky, encircle our hero, Rama. He leaps up a tier of bent naked backs, tossing his tails of black hair against the red night sky and in a tortuous fandango of wrestling with evil he plunges to the sand. It is to be hoped that he did not land on a chip of coral.

Back in our cliff-top haven we are again entreated to dine. On no appetite. The graceful persuasion of the Balinese once more lands us in spicy squid salad, chop-grilled chicken and beancurd, wok-fried egg noodles, green mango salad, lemon grass-lime-chilli sauce – such culinary assault in 100°F heat and 75% humidity is best soothed by rice and sago in a pool of palm-sugar-sweetened coconut milk.

March 19

At Amlapura, the original seat of the Balinese Karangasem Royal family, we step into a palace open to the public. Puri Kanginan is a dishevelled complex of late nineteenth-century ceremonial temples grouped around a lily lake. Beautifully carved and gilded doors open on to empty dilapidated rooms. A makeshift show of old photographs of the Royal family are propped on the veranda. To the left an imposing temple which acted as 'the place for teeth-filing ceremonies' (at puberty the pointed canine teeth are filed even). A Temple for Praying and a Temple for Dancing compete with another, 'the place where bodies were laid before cremation'. A resourceful family pleasure dome all told.

We stop briefly at the ruins of a Royal water palace, at nearby Ujung. The last King of Karangasem was a water freak. A terraced cascade of ornamental lakes and swim pools and fountains framed in a folly of pavilions and balustrades, completed in 1921, is now become an agreeable enough shambles; the lakes clogged by cress and wild lilies and the province of plump white geese.

May 4 Quito Ecuador South America

Quito – 'the place of the sun' – lies 9,000 feet above sea level. Its cluttered poverty sprawls across the valley floor. The sixteenth-/seventeenth-century red-tiled squares, the spires and the companias draw rich and poor alike. Dim, grand interiors, stiff with gold, make gemütlich retreats for all; gargantuan Baroque does not intimidate. Peasants and gypsies set up stalls on cobbled terraces alongside and bleat their wares. Traveller, chest your money. Thieving thrives.

Jagged mountains frayed in cloud rise steeply round, their slopes parcelled up in maize, corn, potatoes. Pine and eucalyptus splash the valleys green. We are driven through the more prosperous villages – Tijus, St Raphael, and Catalina. Cattle, corn and horse-breeding. Next, to the hallowed precincts of the National Park and the 19,000-foot Cotopaxi volcano. Our guide promises puma, deer, boar – and bear besides? We jolt and judder across this vast plate of ash and lava, with rock and stones flung wide; the unclaimed debris of eruption 1904. We scan this arid plain of couch grass and dykes for the rare white-tailed deer? The dwarf deer? We detect distant pigs – black – and horses – wild – and mushrooms. Cotopaxi's sharp cone is fluffed in cloud when – 'The Andean teal!' squeals our guide (black and white). 'A humming bird' (phallic blue beak).

Lava ash is a rich sponge for wild flowers, lichens, mosses. We admire this scattered rash of yellow, purple, scarlet. And everywhere the national flower, the chuquiragua, its thistle calyx flares an orange flame. It is used as a diuretic and purported to soothe coughs.

'Let's turn around right here. No bears, no pumas. I don't mean to be autocratic but ... enough is enough.' We silently applaud our outspoken travelling companion and head back for lunch at a 300-year-old hacienda.

A white colonial pilastered façade approached by an avenue of giant eucalyptus. A Mississippi old plantation comes to mind. We are elegantly served in the beamed and boarded family dining-room. A hot cream potato soup with wedges of avocado, sea bass, and a pineapple compote.

Returning along rough country roads to Quito it is a challenge to place the physiognomy of these mingling mountain folk. Indian, verging on the Tibetan, Mongolian? Thick, black straight hair; black, slanted eyes in round brown faces; full lips, Gauguinesque, handsome, bold. It has been mooted that the Latin Americans who pioneered the Mexican, Peruvian and Chilean cultures were of Asian stock. Crossing the Bering Strait in the seventh century AD at the time of an existing land bridge, they poured into Alaska from Russia, Mongolia and Tibet, to stamp their cast and civilisation on more southern climes.

An evening stroll in the old stone Plaza by the sixteenth-century monastery, San Francisco. Despite extensive restoration from earthquake damage it stands untouched by time. Nearby shops display a palpable poverty. Rugs, leather goods, panama hats. Mothers begging, children scampering. I see one boy of three or four crawling along a pavement; exhausted, he wedges his little begging cap in the corner of a doorstep and lays down his head.

May 6 Baltra Island Galapagos Islands Ecuador

'A separate centre of creation,' proclaimed Charles Darwin. He came to the Galapagos archipelago – 600 nautical miles from the Ecuador shore – in 1835. He was twenty-six years old and roundly condemned the black marine iguanas in his diary as 'large – 2–3 feet – most disgusting, clumsy lizards'.

The sea-lions sprawl and squirm in the afternoon haze – in pairs or in groups. Such spoony, moony posturing as to knock any courting couple into the kindergarten. Black volcanic rock, red lava rock and Sir Reresby Sitwell flat on the white sand snapping an iguana close up. Our guide – a pocket Ecuadorian in bio-degradable sandals – indicates a blue-footed booby with his full white chest and brown wings. It is spectacular – our first sighting of Galapagos bird life. Who has ever seen cerulean webbed feet before? Next a male frigate bird curiously hampered by a scarlet balloon billowing out from under the beak. How come? 'He is courting. That is his inflated red pouch for all the ladies to see.'

Our guide, now bent on some more inaccessible trophy, lures us through a mangrove swamp of rock pools, slippery boulders and a swarm of mosquitoes. I follow close behind Reresby. His collapsible stick jams in the red mud as he sways, perilously launching his stalwart frame in advance of certain disaster. I throw my bottom sideways into a mud pool – a better option than being flattened by even the best of friends. The spoils of this hazardous trail amount to one tattered silvery skin of a long-departed snake.

May 7 (morning) Española Island Gardner Bay

Our rubber panga boat noses the red and black basaltic cliffs. The rock face is grizzled and pocked – the scars of primeval boiling lava exploding in the deep. Sea-lions skew beside us; sensual and agile in water and cavorting like labradors in the surf. Along the white arc of Gardner Bay they flop and wallop, arch their wet torsos, squawking and barking. Blue-footed boobies dive-bomb for fish and red luscious crabs dart lightly over black boulders where iguanas take up their pose.

We bathe in a clear sea – some snorkle. Tom spies a negroid monster with yellow lips. Reresby resembles a tropical fish himself, bathing in a vivid cape dropping to well below his knees.

May 7 (afternoon)

On the cliff tops of Punta Suarez we saunter through yellow flowering cordia bushes – a popular shelter for the albatross. With their long curved yellow beaks, gentle, dark eyes, white bibs and a wing span of seven feet, they are the aristocrats of the Galapagos. The largest marine birds in the East Pacific and magnificent flying machines. They can spend long periods at sea without landing.

Our guide enlarges on the virtues of the albatross; one mate for life and just one chick tended between them. We watch a pair bill-clicking – a courting preliminary, and pass broody females sitting on ostrich-sized eggs. Who is watching whom? We pass within inches of these birds and mammals. Their remarkable lack of fear and suspicion is the responsibility of all.

The black rocks far below are streaked white with foam from the incoming tide; the rocks above stream white again, with excrement. We watch a sea-lion guarding his fiefdom. Alarmingly prehistoric in girth with a neck size of four to five feet, he threshes the boisterous waves with fierce, raw screams.

May 8 Punta Cormorant Floreana Island

The human population on the Archipelago has risen to 16,000. Tourism mounts steadily and a ninety-day visit restriction is now enforced. Darwin himself only spent five weeks in the Galapagos and only nineteen days ashore. On board HMS *Beagle*, as a naturalist companion to the autocratic geologist Captain Robert Fitzroy, the young Darwin professed to prefer the more tangible charms of Tahiti – their next port of call.

Punta Cormorant is a sublime cove of butterscotch sand. Shade is at a premium. Penelope Sitwell and I wedge ourselves against a screen of mangrove bushes only to be plagued by insects. We are soon distracted by the perching yellow warblers, finches and juicy grasshoppers; yellow, green and orange to compare with a Fabergé brooch.

Behind us laps a fresh-water green lagoon dabbed with pink flamingoes. Over a stoney scrub-wood cliff we reach a coral bay – a turtle nesting stronghold. Five to six thousand turtles emerge from the sea to lay eggs on Galapagos in three nestings annually. Eighty eggs per turtle are buried under the sand to incubate in the rainy season, March, April, May. The candelabra cactus-trees form an erect guard on the cliffs above – like Giacometti statues, says Tom. We are urged to tread a careful narrow passage to avoid any incubating eggs. What are they like anyway? Our guide circles his arms and fingers and wide eyes – 'They are like golf balls – but with a soft shell.'

May 9 Santa Cruz

The main town of the Galapagos where the corrals of the renowned giant tortoises (translated in Spanish as Galapagos) are sited at the Charles Darwin Research Station (founded 1964). Fascinated, we watch these endangered carapaces with their elephantine legs creep round their fiefdom of mud pools, caves and edible greenery. The scraggy reptilian necks stretch long and questing from their black cumbersome crusts; eyes blank with acceptance, mouths trapped in a genetic curve. They could each live for 150 years, wallowing in mud and laying eggs the size of tennis balls.

Darwin notes that it is impossible for two grown men to roll these heavy creatures on to their backs, the captive position. I find them disgustingly ugly, an image of despair.

At the Darwin station a pretty American talks compellingly on endangered ecology. Feral dogs, cats and rats threaten the fabric and goats (introduced by fishermen in the 1960s as an alternative food source) savage the vegetation, depriving all land species of their staple sustenance. Seventy thousand goats have been shot already, we are told. Her ardent appeal for help in this wholesale demolition incites us to round up all restless adolescents back home to come out and finish the job.

We drive up a red ash road to the highlands. Dense green. Banana-trees clumped with green fruit, coconut palms, woods canopied with the endemic Scalesia tree and wild, waving grasses. Cows champ, up to their udders in this rampant tropicalia where the datura trumpets and yellow hibiscus fold for the night.

May 10 Genovesta

Past a colony of red-footed boobies nesting in the mangroves, I find a baby black marine iguana. He slithers and sways provocatively over the white sand – too slim to adopt the more customary waddle. He lures me to the shore rocks, pausing to cock his ear to gauge the lie of the sea. I want to put a rhinestone collar round his rubbery neck and make him mine.

May 11 Isabela

The crew wake us at 5 am. We near Isabela, the largest of these volcanic islands and still erupting. We scan the grey dawn sea for whales and dolphins. A spectacular sunrise silhouettes great haunches of green scrub cliffs. In the panga we circumvent the sheer lava cliffs, striated black, grey and pink; pendulous, bulbous, these arcane fulmi-nations are veritable sculpted gargoyles. But the diesel fumes and blue smoke from our outboard motor aggravate us. And are the scarlet crabs we annotate, the pelican and portly penguins, aggravated too? Such a medley of species – basking, fishing, swimming in commendable har-mony; like a compound of disparate diplomats evolving a code of respect and tolerance. Returning to our boat, *Isabela 2*, we see a fin and the flick of a tail. A shark is diagnosed. Or perhaps a shark is eating a sting-ray? We eddy round this perplexing upheaval. The botanist with the shapely brown legs and auburn beard (to recall D H Lawrence) proclaims a sting-ray and no shark. Perhaps it is both? I suggest they might be copulating rather than fighting or eating each other and secretly long to be back on board the safe haven of *Isabela 2*. I have already envisaged our entire dinghy-load overboard with all this excited rushing to one side, binoculars burning.

It later transpires as we drink companionably on the top deck that my heroic botanist does in fact hale from Nottingham. 'I was born two miles from D H Lawrence's home.'

May 11 Fernandina

The top west point of the Archipelago where the petrified black lava fields swirl inland on a vast three-million-year crust – a raging combative flow since cracked with formidable crevasses. (Some years ago a woman paused on such lava, to re-tie her shoelace. 'Go on ahead,' she urged her companion – her body was discovered six months later, fallen through a crevasse.) The surrounding mangrove swamps are live with warblers and flightless cormorants and retching sea-lions; fat black iguanas sprawl and spray salt from their nostrils; the desalination glands in their heads process this unique ejection. 'Clever of this ropey black lava to take on the camouflage of the iguanas,' remarks Reresby. Lord Byron [the poet's cousin] records his own visit to Fernandina in March 1825, sharing the general revulsion towards iguanas:

> . . . The ugliest creatures we ever beheld. They are like the alligator but with a more hideous head and of a dirty sooty black colour, and sat on the black lava rocks like so many imps of darkness. As far as the eye could reach we saw nothing but rough fields of lava that seemed to have hardened, while the force of the wind had been rippling its liquid surface.

Our guide calls out – 'Stay right behind me. These depressions in the sand are the incubating nests of iguana eggs – and here you see where two lava flows converged.' A massive wrestling into bedlam chunks of shunting, crashing lava as it cooled. A desolate black rockscape under an orange sun.

I ask the wise Ecuadorian doctor: 'Which is the cleverest of all? Which species is the King of the islands?' He replies: 'Each species is wise in his own way.'

May 15 Peru

In a doughty camper van through a switchback of Andean hills and valleys we drive from Cuzco to the ancient market village of Pisac. Rough, narrow roads hedged with wild pampas and eucalyptus, where the Urubamba river, a tributary of the Amazon, curls wide and green through this spectacular valley. Terraced cultivation of barley, maize and lupins for fodder marks the green slopes mounting sheer to snow-peaks. Adobe villages where black pigs, llamas, alpacas, cows and donkeys are herded in a congenial mix by peasant women. Sturdy and bright in their vivid wool shawls and wide skirts, with broad-brimmed hats of felt or panama to crown those black plaits and black eyes.

At Ollantaytambo (tamba. place of rest), you are confronted by vertiginous terraces effectively guarding this massive Inca fortress. In 1536 the Conqueror Spanish General Pizarro and his men and horses were blasted off these terraces by the boulders and arrows hurled down by the Inca. Still a daunting climb today; Penelope Sitwell and I rest in the field below where ancient farm hovels of rough stone and reeded thatch suggest a ravaged Petit Trianon.

Our next jewel in this sacred trail is Machu Picchu, the world's most enthralling Inca settlement. A three-hour train passage through the forested mountain gorge alongside the Urubamba river reveals a feast of flora. If we are short-changed on deer, fox and pandas munching on bamboo cane, the sheer rock face is flushed with scarlet eritrena and sprayed with yellow broom. Fierce silver cacti stab the grass banks with prickly pear and its round red fruit. We reach Machu Picchu through the hushed, dark gloom of fir groves.

A dream ruin of Inca stone works set in emerald and an unfathomable provenance, Machu Picchu − 'Old Peak' − is suspended between mountains 6,000 feet above the river valley. The Incas had no written language; their origins date plausibly from the twelfth century with the sixteenth-century Chronicles alluding to sun worship and sacrifice. Human? Such a suggestion is waved aside and llamas are mooted as a substitute. But to press the point at least eleven human sacrifices have been exposed atop Andean mountains over the last fifty years.

We wander through these ordered precincts. Each stone of each wall of each house is restored to the original. Some are roofed in reed, high-pitched for the heavy rains. The whole site first evokes a Roman settlement with ceremonial baths, agricultural terraces, residential sector, industrial sector, central plaza, more ceremonial baths beside 'the prison group' − but then a predominance of temples and tombs indicates the Inca ethos: the Principal Temple, the Temple of the three windows, the Temple of the sun, the sacred plaza, the Royal tomb, the funerary rock. These strange, spectacular slabs of stone are wedged awkwardly in caves or open to the stars. Eight centuries on and the flagitious emanations of sacrifice rites still pervade these walls and grass plateaus, temples and terraces.

Swarthy gardeners scythe the terraced grass ledges. Our guide picks a feathery aniseed leaf and crumbles the white daisy flower in his fingers. 'Come again to our ruins,' he urges in a low voice. 'Come a wet early morning. You are alone, the mountain cloud around you.'

In 1911, July 24, the American historian Professor Hiram Bingham happened upon Machu Picchu. A serendipitous find as he was in fact looking for the lost city of Vilcabamba. The broken walls, entangled with centuries of forest growth took intermittent teams of men some twenty years to clear. But why did this apparently sophisticated, well-endowed and regulated community abandon ship? With the Spanish Conquest of the Inca capital, Cuzco, in 1533, that city's support life-line to Machu Picchu snapped. It would seem the prudent mountain villagers upsticked in the teeth of any such disastrous non-communication.

May 18 Sacsayhuaman

Another steep terraced fortress which staged a definitive siege in the Conquest of the Incas. But the subsequent death of Pizarro, by a stone hurled at his head, was an ironic twist of fate.

The name Sacsayhuaman means 'satisfied falcon', from the swoop of vultures and Andean condors that devoured the dead abandoned on this fierce battle plain. Certainly eight condors feature in the Cuzco City coat of arms (1540). Today you can see chill corridors of chiselled stones with each one prised and placed in a perfect balance. But these tumbled homes around the temples, sacred plazas, sacrificial caves are devastated, dead. Lean against a wall and catch the frenzied neigh of ruined horses, the whistle of slingshots and spears and the hoarse cheers and groans of ravaged men.

A strange uncontrollable shivering steals over me. Tom buys me a thick llama jacket. At lunch I down two glasses of red wine and opt out of a tantalising afternoon; a stroll through the sixteenth-century plazas with their intricate deep wooden balconies, the Baroque churches and the colourful crafts markets.

I slide into bed, shivers, aches, hints of nausea, a devastating lassitude. The head touches the pillow and sinks thirty feet. It is a curse to lift it for a glass of water. No hope of drifting off to glowing sleep on red wine. A pounding headache and the doctor is called. Charming with his white coat, his round brown head and smiling voice, he jabs me in each buttock to a chant of 'no pain, no pain lady, no pain, no lady pain'. In 'Facts for the visitor – Health' I read a section on Altitude Sickness: Breathlessness, a dry irritative cough, severe headache, loss of appetite, nausea ... lack of co-ordination and balance are real danger signs.

'No butters,' insists my affable doctor and, 'No wines – just boiled chicken and sleep and . . . potatoes,' he beams, as though conferring treat upon treat.

May 20 Lima

Lima was established as the Peruvian capital by Francisco Pizarro in 1535. With the Spaniards a marine race rather than mountaineers, he had eschewed the stronghold of Cuzco. Lima developed fast as a trading post for Polynesia and India but in 1746 disaster struck; an earthquake flattened the city. Subsequently scarred by a population explosion, Lima has become an ugly agglutination of villas intermixed with tower blocks. Half-dead cannas – red and yellow – and palm-trees divide the avenues of incessant traffic. A sense of fear stalks private walls where armed bodyguards glower through steel spikes and grilles.

'Show us the Japanese ambassador's residence,' we urge. The seventy-one hostages plus one gallant volunteer Jesuit priest have finally been rescued by Army Commandos. Their ordeal lasted 126 days as negotiations for the release of hundreds of Tupac Amaru prisoners in Peruvian jails foundered. Our driver halts in a spacious street where white villas dance in the white-hot sun. A colonial-style façade with pediment and pillars denotes the Japanese residence. Down an adjacent side-street two modest villas are indicated. They were rented by the Peruvian guerrillas for observation and tunnelling purposes.

Later we dine with Don Juan Antonio Azula and his Donna Camilla. Their hacienda is a dream oasis encompassed by the shabby streets; the courtyard is a cascade of flowers and fountains where we drink champagne and flirt with foie gras. There is talk of the siege. It ended finally on April 22. Donna Camilla recalls a frenetic day of telephone calls, traffic jams, lunch dates abandoned, appointments missed and then, in the early afternoon, the explosive reports that rocked the city. 'The Commandos timed the raid when they knew the guerrillas would be playing their daily football. They made their balls from newspaper, socks and rubber bands. Twelve young men they were and two eighteen-year-old girls. All guerrillas. All shot.'

Our host Don Antonio is a prodigious authority on French and English history. Tall with strong, commanding looks, he has been likened by Reresby Sitwell to a conquistador. We are elegantly served at the gleaming Azula table with a seafood pâté, the rarest fillet beef and a sensuous chocolate mousse. The congenial Don Antonio dusts his anecdotes the while. Penelope Sitwell later remarks that it is Antonio's irrepressible laughter that endears him all the more.

May 22 Easter Island Chile

Through 75 mph winds, our night plane from Santiago sways and leapfrogs alarmingly, as on some desperate quest for an earth-shattering orgasm. This most remote island in the world is marooned in the south Pacific Ocean. The size of our Isle of Wight, it was accidentally discovered on Easter Sunday 1722 by the Dutch admiral, Jakob Roggeveen, who named it so. Today it boasts a five-mile landing strip laid in anticipation of any space shuttle grounding in an emergency. Easter Island, Rapa Nui, in the Maori tongue, translates as 'the Big Scream'. An apt reflection on this wild rough night as palm-trees flatten obsequiously as we pass along the hotel veranda. Beyond the headland the sea races white before the wind and a full moon boxes with the clouds.

May 23

A blood-streaked dawn and a blue-denim sea. Red hot pokers blister the sky; the rustle of guava, hibiscus, banana, fig. Our breakfast is single-handled by yesterday's barman. Any agitation from his captive patients and you are banished to the end of the queue.

Pierre Loti, nearing Rapa Nui in the French frigate *Flore* in 1871, noted in his journal:

> Slowly the strange island approaches and becomes clearer; under a sombre clouded sky it reveals reddish craters and desolate rocks. A high wind blows and the sea is covered in white spray. Rapa Nui is the natives' name for Easter Island, and merely in the consonants of this word there seems to be the sadness, the savageness of night . . .

We stroll down the central red baked street of Hanga Roa, the solitary town on the island, population 3,000. Sturdy ponies with extra-large Rapa Nui men, slumped bareback, can suddenly gallop past. Feral horses and cattle roam and graze the island, its hills and craters and vast sweeps of downland sloping to the ubiquitous sea. Catholic missionaries have marked with three white crosses a high green hill at Puna Pau. A rounded, mysterious summit under a clear dome of sky. A simple zig-zag track leads up the grass side to this popular, though arduous, rendezvous. Celebrations for weddings, memorials and Christmas are not daunted by the haul.

This strange scape of swooping downland, smooth grass mountains, frothing sea and no rivers, black lava walls and no roofs, gigantic heads of rain-roughened rock and no bodies, that back the sea and not the land with stern and sightless eyes. It is a conundrum.

Lobster for dinner and Tom's vahiné has flown in from Tahiti in a flurry of hair and frangipani.

May 24 Easter Island

The billowing grass slopes of Rano Raraku are strewn with stone heads, the renowned Moais of Rapa Nui. Some toppled, some upright still, with sun and shadow playing on their profiles; their deep-gouged eyes and spare stern lips seem more honed to wind and battle than smiles and kissing. We are shown a deep cave scooped out of the rock hillside; the original workshop where the black basalt was mined and cut to make the Moais. The softer red basalt 'topknot' assumed to be a cylindrical hat or hairpiece or even crown was finally plugged through the head. But whence these leaders of millennia ago? A Polynesian provenance? Or Asiatic? A racial mix through bloody conflict? We do know that the race of the long-eared, more patrician physiognomy from Asia was soundly ousted in the seventeenth century by the short-eared and comparatively runtish Polynesian. Originally cast as serried coastguards there are roughly some 245 long-eared heads restored and in place today. In my opinion they are endemically Asian; the long straight noses and high cheek bones denote the Russias more than the Marquesas. Accounts wobble over their arrival date, anything goes from 400 AD. But those topknots spell astrakhan titfers to me.

Our observant travelling companion Robin Halwas notices in the distance a fifteen strong-contingent – to include topknots – facing inland, their backs to the pounding sea. 'They present a threatening macho guard to any islander thinking of escape,' he comments darkly. Our vahiné shudders. She is cold. Where are the flowers and suns and spices of her own blue silken seas?

May 25 Anakena Easter Island

A chill wind. In a sheltered bay of shoe-engulfing sand we picnic under palms. Our military friend Michael TelferSmollett, enters the water with the dash and spirit of his calling, our leader to the end; our *sommelier* from the start. We admire him and applaud.

September 8 Hardwicke House

Letter to a friend on the death of Diana, Princess of Wales:

Your 'little' Diana. You remember we spoke of her briefly? You were indignant of her falling for an Egyptian, when I was glad she had found a man to shower her with love and money; to shield her from her persecuted life. And now, days later, she is dead.

August 31, 1997 – the *Sunday Times:* 'Dodi is killed, Diana badly injured in Paris car crash.'

The *Sunday Telegraph:* 'Princess Diana and Dodi are killed in Paris car crash.'

Headlines to numb the nation and then, suddenly, in a wave of compassion for this child, our Princess Diana, we are kick-started into vindicating the message of her brief life. Compassion was her essence.

Let us put aside recriminations, the dark side of things, the salacious scoops, and think instead on her vulnerability, her humanity, her . . . compassion. She is described by Prime Minister Tony Blair: 'The people's princess'. Possibly the only apt statement he will ever make . . .

Perhaps one of the murmured blessings of an ultimate tragedy is that it can never be anticipated. And would she have behaved so freely and been so roughly served if her father had been alive? He was such an English gent. He died in 1992 when so much tradition took a downhill coaster – Lloyd's – the Church – the Law – the black tie – 'bread and butter' letters. And so our classless society has now 'progressed' to 'people power'. We live in interesting times, In her words: they are 'daunting'.

But good must evolve. Prince Harry is now to be accepted into Eton to be with his big brother. A significant bonus for them both.

Princess Diana's death is a tragedy to overwhelm us all. But the view clears a little when trees are felled. I cannot contemplate your own prognosis over this glut of . . . mischance!

October 4 Tangier Morocco

Touch down at Tangier; sky, sea and mountains merged in mist. Dusk rolls in; palm-trees silhouetted like sabres, fastened to the fading light. To a world of tasselled fez and fretted screen; to Islamic mosaic, to mosque and mule and souk. The yearning call of the muezzin troubles our sleep.

October 5

Narrow streets curl up the hill from the shore to the souks and the Kasbah. Battered pavements and stinking gutters of squelched garbage; rotting fruit and fish-heads and 'potage garbure' – to translate as vegetable soup, from the mutton stock steaming in the inner courtyards – adds to this whole malodorous gunge.

I buy a chocolate-brown yashmak from a crone cross-legged on her mound of cotton sundries. I pay 100 dirhams (£7). Far too much. She will feed her grandchildren for a week. This Muslim custom of covered heads and noses holds fast in Tangier, women, shamelessly swollen under their gender-obfuscating jellabas, splash the dusty scene – magenta, mustard, flame and indigo.

An Arab country without oil, Morocco has no significant export. Tangier, referred to as Sodom-on-sea – the arse-hole of Europe – was once the entrée to cheap drugs, drinks and little boys. Through the 1930s, '40s and '50s, such literary sophisticates as Paul Bowles, William Burroughs, Gore Vidal and Tennessee Williams straddled the scene. The French mandate imported a degree of civic order on to this whole rakish conglomerate between 1912 and 1956. Today Tangier totters in shambolic structures, regrettable restaurants and a filthy shoreline, where no tourist dares.

And is Paul Bowles still alive? 'He is sixty-six years with Tangier. Now with his Moroccan friend, he is fed with spoon and tended in a dark room. He is ninety-seven years. No more visitors please.' And Barbara Hutton is now dead? 'There go Barbara Hutton's palace.' Our guide indicates a blazing white multi-terraced confection adorning the flaking ramparts of the spiralling Kasbah.

'When she came, it was party time. Many people, pretty lights and music. Her three black Rolls came through the gate of the Kasbah. Some streets she made wider. We watched her parties on the terraces.' The fact that she was sometimes too tired or sad or too drunk to attend the parties herself was overlooked by her admiring neighbours.

It is clean and quiet in the Kasbah, an enclave of family living and prayer. We wander through dazzling courtyards and deserted courtyards where marble pillars soar to a blazing canopy of sky. We are pie-eyed with pattern and the prismatic play of light and shade on stone and stucco tracery.

October 7 Fès

A front of hard rain. On the North Atlantic coast road. I see a dead donkey; sodden, depleted, by the roadside. Juniper-groves, fir and oak and now a boy clasping a huge fish swept in by the heavy seas. Through Lixus, where the sands are blown thick across the road; to Larache and Asilah where camels plough the rich red soil and a girl canters side-saddle on a mule, her veil and skirt billowing like a spinnaker. More mules and donkeys with loaded panniers waver across the moorland, criss-crossed with brimming dykes; crops of ripening yellow-skinned melons are heaped by the road. Who will buy? And why are none offered at our hotel? The bleached bald plain gives way to green waves of sugarbeet. The road narrows and twists up wooded peaks. Caught in cloud, a white sun splashed hurriedly on hills and the distant blue sweep of the Atlas mountain range.

'Fès!' shouts Achmed the driver. A blur of mist and mountain hangs above the city, stretched below like a cobalt blindfold. From a high ridge in the city wall we look down on the medina; glazed emerald roofs, gold stone made more gold in the evening sun; the slim, fretted minarets, simple and dominant. Giant palm-trees gush green through the tight-packed roofs. Fès, a bowl of rosy terraces and marble courts with water playing in mosaic pools and the shade and peace of orange-groves and olive. Suspended from the tail of the Rif mountain and the start of the formidable Atlas range, the medina guards its medieval supremacy. No cars, no machinery must invade the mystique, the silence, the arcane toil of hand-crafts.

Shouts of 'Balek! Balek!' – 'watch out – out of the way!' Old men wave arms and clear a passage for the mules – the only permissible transport through these dark and narrow lanes. Their panniers are crammed to bursting with rotting refuse, tinware, fruits, dead poultry, carpets, and brass. Tom is pinned against a wall with one such bulging onslaught. He is almost asphyxiated and fears for his ribcage. We find camel skin moccasins for the grandchildren and a cedar walking-stick in screwed sections; of passionate interest to subsequent security checks who were all hell-bent on discovering drugs stowed inside.

Edmondo de Amicis, a diplomat, gave an account of Fès in the 1880s:

. . . blind alleys, recesses, dens full of bones, dead animals and heaps of putrid matter . . . the dust so thick, the smell so horrible, the flies so numerous . . . we can scarcely breathe in the press and heat and move slowly on, stopping every moment to give passage to a Moor on horseback or a veiled lady on a camel or an ass with a load of bleeding sheep's heads.

Today these same labyrinths and tunnels and inner courts are swept
four times a day.

Fès can possess you. You listen to its silences and feel through its
sounds. The muezzin at dawn is compelling. The live voice, insistent,
clear and strong; not intrusive, hypnotic rather; winding, spiralling,
repeating in the dead of dawn. You sense the medina is on tenterhooks,
taut with attention, transfixed. After thirty-five minutes, a brief chorus
and silence. A cock crows on cue and another; the whole caboodle.
To be a Muslim! Tom slept through the entire indelible performance

October 12 La Mamounia Hotel Marrakech

A continual flow of water from the Atlas mountains from November to
June ensures this perennial oasis. From our balcony, an ocean of
swaying green palm-groves, olives, oranges, figs and mimosa, jacaranda
trees – a burst of blue in the spring – shade the long avenues to the
Ville Nouvelle.

In his latter years, Winston Churchill would stay in this renowned
old hotel in the winter months. Sitting on his terrace with canvas and
brushes he would scan the distant Atlas range, the rose wattle walks of
the medina below and the bewitching glades and brilliant flowered
parterres.

'Plus de cent ans,' said the boy pointing to the towering olives as
he edged past me with donkey and cartload of pruned red hibiscus.

October 14 Marrakech

Our 6' 4" guide, Hatim, is resplendent in cream cotton jellaba and
black skull cap. His black wavy hair tumbles round his shoulders.

'Black and white are my favourite colours. I feel crazy with more
than two colours on me. Foods? I like chicken and vegetables – no
fats or sweets.'

'What? No desserts? No puddings?'

'Sometime I can fall for a stupidity . . .'

We drive through the Ourika Valley to the foot of the Atlas mountains. Red rock, earth, adobe villages, donkeys laden for the souk, boys
riding side-saddle, the river L'ourika (eternal springtime) below cheats
its role; reduced to a parched trickle gurgling like a death rattle. We
encourage Hatim to talk on.

He describes his country as happy, peaceable and family-orientated.
Algeria and Spain are jealous neighbours. 'But why? They have oil!

We have to import oil from Russia. We stay politically calm with our neighbours.' And their King Hassan? His sons? His wife?

'We have no Queen – it is a morganatic marriage. She is the mother of the King's sons.' The two sons (same mother?) will marry when the King says. They are in their early thirties. 'I could not keep a wife – in her dresses, her meals and her entertainments. We would live with my mother of course. I try to be a good Muslim. We are all Muslim or Christian – but we have to be good ones. If a Muslim is a bad Muslim he is a nothing to do.' With his polished English, his education in America and France and his informed conversation we wonder if Hatim is a disarming reporter.

1998

March Vietnam

The perception that a country is judged by its traffic is exemplified in Vietnam. With private cars taxed at 200% it is an army of cyclists that swarms the roads in Saigon. With each saddle rammed into the vertical above the pedals and at a measured speed of 15 mph, this sedate parade of straight backs and skinned eyes forge an unstoppable course through red lights, pedestrian crossings . . . and pedestrians. Girls in bright pyjama suits and flowered boaters further indicate a chic road mode for the millennium with their anti-pollution yashmaks and gloves to the elbow. Family Hondas, to include the baby and the rooster in a tight-packed kebab, intersperse this tidal flow, together with cycle rickshaws (the cycle-pousse of the French old days).

This dogged mix of discipline, pragmatism and eyes on the ball has propelled Vietnam – 'People from the South' – through ten centuries of siege and wars. Invading landlocked neighbours, Laos and Cambodia, the colossal conglomerates of China and Russia and more recently France and America, have all been shown the door. 'Vietnam is a country not a war,' propounds this proud English-speaking people, finally at peace. Halcyon days? Any such strategic coastline must be cut out for contest. In a voluptuous 'S' bend, Vietnam skirts the Gulf of Tonkin and the South China Sea, with her north and south extremities splayed wide in deltaic rivers and fertile rice-beds. Reserves of gas and oil are purported to be in her territorial waters. Today's rumbling shenanigans over the Spratly Islands again sharpen Vietnam's profile. '*Plus ça change, plus c'est la même guerre.*' And succeeding generations, fuelled with a genetic vengeance, will rise to expel the enemy.

In an 80% agricultural country farmers now own their land and pay taxes. With three bumper harvests per year, rice is the main hard currency export. But the new youth (and 75% of the 75 million population are under twenty-five) rigorously spurn this knee-deep squelching in mud under a blazing sun. More and more they head for the cities where work in cafés, on building sites or street stalls is an alternative. Vietnam's recently-increased factories for hulling and processing cashew nuts are another source of employment. Her phenomenal cashew export is second only to India. Ironically, in order to keep on 70,000 workers during the no-crops season (November–

February) Vietnam is compelled to import more cheap unhulled cashews from Africa.

On the rough road north to the coral sea haven of Nha Trang you see a rustic narrative unfurl. Sleek cows sprawl in banana groves, tossed hay is stacked in stupas around a central pole, white egrets perch on emerald paddy fields and on the banks of muddy klongs, reeds and palm fronds are bleached for plaiting the roofs on bungalows and shacks. Logs and planks are neatly piled, breeze-blocks and bricks. On cane screens, rounds of pasted rice dry out into paper to wrap round the spring fried rolls. Ducks, dogs, pigs, buffalo, bikes and babies make each mud alley a picture hanging there. Women in slacks and tunics swing along in a light trot with their shoulder poles and baskets. Men play cards, cross-legged in the dust, hammocks swing alongside the family wash and families eat in shade on stools. A tableau vivant of incessant activity – ploughing, planting, building, ferrying and every-where the bobbing and bending of those conical straw hats.

A panoply of eucalyptus-trees, tamarind and teak, coconut-palms and rubber-groves fringe these straggled villages and rivers. Crops of maize, tobacco, stooked corn, coffee and cashew open wide to the blurred blue mass of the distant Truong Son Mountains. This formid-able range, reaching a height of 9,000 feet, stretches the length of Vietnam's borders with Laos and Cambodia. A captivating landscape, of untrammelled green and sky. Village sidewalks jostle and spill over with gaudy stalls and awnings. Vast wicker panniers are heaped with pyramids of papaya, persimmon, pineapple, milk apple, and the furry rose mangosteen. Clumps of ripe green tiny bananas, limes, and avo-cado and that whole gamut of gold and scarlet nuts and spices and sprigs of fresh green betel palm. A glut of pots and pans, glazed earthenware, trophies of carved teak and sandalwood and buffalo bone are joined by piglets in cages, ducks in a row, and puppy dogs. (Cats and snakes are also valued culinary delicacies but random killing has made them scarce).

Vietnam's religious mores have proved a well-seasoned mélange through ten centuries. Buddhism from across the Thai, Tibetan and Chinese borders artfully linked Royal patronage with the village masses through the tenth to the thirteenth century. Pink brick pagodas and stupas were erected through the realm. Next the Confucian scholars pressed their suit, and promulgated the virtues of education. The subsequent inclusion of Hindu deities and Taoist spirit forces adds a final flush to the archetypal marinade that exists today. Having ogled the glories of Isfahan, the Taj Mahal and the stupendous mosques of the Golden Horn, I still stick resolutely to Chartres. But nothing prepares you for the half-ravaged temples and palaces of the Imperial

City of Hue, traditionally the centre of Vietnam's culture and religious studies. That poignant piecing together of history as you pass through the pillared stone courts and swooping eaves of the Forbidden Purple City. Those nineteenth-century emperors' sleeping quarters where only eunuchs and concubines feared to tread, the long-burnt library, the lost theatre. A massive room with its high-pitched ceiling, beamed in jackfruit wood, displays glass cases of porcelain, silver and jewels. A sumptuously-gilded throne stands back in lame apology and, in the ruined Royal enclosures, vegetables now grow.

'Mon marriage eut lieu le 20 mars 1934 . . . très belle, elle entrait dans la grande salle où je l'attendais sur mon trône. Elle venait devant moi, se prosternait trois fois et s'asseyait à mon droit. La Cérémonie ne dura pas longtemps. Maintenant, je l'eus à mon côté. Tous nous deux, l'un près de l'autre, nous marchions dans la joyeuse musique. Nous traversions la cité pourpre interdite pour entrer après au palais de Kiên Trung, l'endroit où nous dormions et travaillions.'[1] As recounted by the last Emperor Bao Dai in his book *Le dragon d'Annam*. The Emperor finally conceded the Nguyen Dynasty (1802–1945) to the Revolutionary Communist Forces of Ho Chi Minh (when the Imperial library was burnt to the ground and treasured papers were snatched up by the market for wrapping fish).

Look back on Hue from the Perfume River, with its broad sloping banks, ruffed in reed. The tiered rose-brick towers and temples and massive stone tombs, with honorary guards of elephants, horses and deities, are ranged in formal silhouette. Two centuries of mist and rain have smudged their façades black with damp. Beside the Imperial lotus pools, faded wood verandas reflect their wavering balustrades, where once was music and all dalliance with concubines. The tomb of Emperor Tu Duc (ruled 1848–1883) is set in the peace and grandeur of courtyards, lakes and pavilions. Faded if not jaded, these tombs of the Nguyen dynasty are an agreeable antidote to the outré exuberance of some of today's restorations. Rest a space by these eighteenth-century grand, blue Chinese bowls, bronze urns with serpent handles, splayed palms in vast marble jars and the rocking scents of the frangipani-trees, jasmine and gardenia. Hue – 'Peace' or 'Harmony' – can haunt you. The prevailing sea cloud mist from the nearby Truong Son mountains hangs softly here where death is still the best-kept secret.

---

[1] 'My marriage took place (the 20th March 1934 . . . very beautiful, she entered the grand Salon where I awaited her on my throne. She came before me, prostrating herself three times, and sat on my right. The ceremony did not last long. Now I had her beside me. We both, close to each other, walked in the joyous music. We crossed through the Forbidden City and entered the Palace Kien Trung, the home where we would sleep and work.'

The black sandstone breast sculpture at Danang's Cham museum strikes a cheerful contrast. The voluptuous posturing of these Hindu and Thai nude dancing girls harks back to the second century. The Chams' culture of breast-worship was channelled well into the fifteenth century by their Hindu-orientated neighbours. Meanwhile, at the main Cham sea port of Hoi An, trading reached its zenith in the seventeenth century. Today the web of narrow streets are a teeming treasure trove of local wares, elaborate handicrafts and food markets. Look up at the nineteenth-century fretted wood house shutters and balconies and the old 'Yin and Yang' roof tiles, snug in their convex/concave fit and tufted in moss. Hoi An's eighteenth-century temples and family houses are relics of the Japanese and Chinese traders. Tan Ky house, set on the Cai River and home to the same family for seven generations, consists of dark, panelled rooms with a bright, balconied central courtyard where you come up for air. The diminutive family, who speak fluent French and English, entertained us on high-backed, ebony-carved settees, with trays of green tea balanced on sandalwood tables. A collection of rare Chinese and Japanese porcelain, ranged on deep shelves, indicates the former elegant life of these rich old traders.

Back at our immaculate Chinese-style hotel another diversion is in store.

'The Hotel Regulations:
Do not leave key in key hole.
Guests are requested not to cook or launder in the hotel rooms.
Bicycles, motor bikes, pets, fire arms, explosives, inflammables, stinking things and even prostitutes are not allowed in the hotel.'

Finally up north to Hanoi (the city in the bend of the river). With its expansive parks and jade lakes and tamarind tree-lined boulevards Hanoi is often compared with Paris. Under French rule for one hundred years the Vietnamese regained independence in 1954. But the Ho Chi Minh mausoleum set high on concrete columns still emits a frisson, a cautionary cuff from the old Comintern guard. The entrenched ideological differences between North and South Vietnam – Hanoi and Saigon – are tolerated. In the interests of a viable Sino/Vietnamese economy, a merger compromise has evolved; to the Western observer, this enlightened system suggests a coup-de-grâce of capitalism, Communism and corruption.

Today, tourism is Vietnam's fast lane industry. Hotels throughout the country have been well-renovated or newly-built. The luxurious Ana Mandara beach hotel at Nha Trang is incomparable in its exquisite solo setting on a transparent, turquoise sea. A tiger balm beach massage round the clock must be a further inducement. Vietnam's national cuisine and natural *soins* combine well with French traditions, especially when taken with the Chardonnay imported from Australia. The staple diet of chicken broth and noodles keeps the Vietnamese slim with good bones and teeth – obesity is unknown. But, with the huge variety of raw materials to include the largest fresh lobsters, crabs and prawns and the legacy of croissants and patisserie, visitors to Vietnam can eat like . . . Emperors.

Hardwicke House July 26, 1998

The first birthday of our granddaughter Jemima. We gave her a Folio edition of *Alice in Wonderland*. Seven years on she would be filmed by Devlin Crow, an independent film-maker. A table for tea was set up in the garden of Hardwicke House. With her long fair hair and her imperturbable poise, Jemima presided over the party, to include a garrulous Mad Hatter and the White Rabbit.

November St Petersburg

It was at Prince Yusupov's palace in St Petersburg that I sensed a vestige of that old *nyet* network. The sumptuous colonnaded yellow façade overlooking the frozen Moika Canal had lavished on us a stream of elegant rooms to include the rococo family theatre. But it was the drama of Rasputin that we had also in mind. Could we see the room in which he had dined with Prince Felix Yusupov?

'*Nyet*' said the babushka in her ticket office. 'Rasputin not possible.' But we had come from London . . . Our formidable mentor turned to others in the queue. My hackles stirred with memories of Leningrad in 1963 and those phalanxes of sturdy women, topped with tightly-coiled hair and bound with belts of keys. '*Nyet*' was still clearly an on-line option. Again I troubled our lady. 'Is it possible to see the room where Rasputin was poisoned?' She crumpled. 'Rasputin is in the lower rooms; the cellars. He is not now possible until 5.15 pm.' Two hours to wait . . . and then that magical volte-face which is one of the mysteries of the *nyet* network . . . 'You go now,' and a girl guide stood beside me.

Rasputin was surely dismayed, the evening of December 17, 1916, to have been led to his host, Felix Yusupov, through such a labyrinth of dingy passages. And then we turned down narrow curling stairs to the cellars. The small vaulted rooms were thronged with Russian students, crowded around wax figures seated at a table; the young Grand Duke Dimitry, who listened by the door as they waited tensely on events, an army officer, a doctor and the fervent czarist, Vladimir Purishkevich. In a nearby room where we surged in a body, Rasputin himself sat at a table, his thick hair tumbling to the shoulder, his right hand clasped to his white shirt-front. 'Arsenic poisoning,' hissed my guide. 'Just two glasses of wine and two cakes.' Rasputin, disappointed that the Princess was not at dinner, was next persuaded by Felix Yusupov to turn and admire an icon on the wall. He was shot in the back and fell to the floor. Seconds later he lurched up the narrow stairs. Yusupov's party, horrified at his brute survival, found him in the courtyard. They shot and beat him dead with sticks. Not to be further outwitted they bound him and pushed him under the frozen Neva. Three days later Rasputin's body was found, holding on to a bridge support with water in his lungs.

The occasional spurt of exceptionally soft brown bath water evoked another fond memory of Leningrad forty years ago. And those ubiquitous cream ruched window blinds still encompass palaces and shops; bus seats and gilded chairs are still tied with dust-covers to suggest a children's party. The first-class hotels of Leningrad in 1963 boasted flamboyant entrance halls of pillared marble floors, mirrored walls and handsome iron banisters. A faint smell of cloakrooms was prone to waft through the assembled opulence. The beds were hard with thin mattresses and duvets. It was difficult to book a single room; three or four guests could be put together irrespective of sex or relationship. The dining-rooms were a drab conglomerate. The old high-ceilinged rooms would be filled with small standard chairs of the time; a hard seat of scarlet or purple cord with a curved back resting on black peg legs. The functional glare of harsh neon striplights and chandeliers gave no concession to lighting effects.

Light and colour are now a prime prerogative of St Petersburg and no landmark can be more glorious than the gilded dome of St Isaac's Cathedral. At dusk the massive red granite columns and bronze pediments are bathed in a silvery light. Next the gilded lantern, set like an upturned pendant in the dome, blazes gold through vaults and porticoes below. Light splashes on the night snow from the luxury hotels – the Astoria and the Grand Hotel Europe. With their renovated glowing marble interiors, their glut of chandeliers and their sweeping staircases they can conjure an illusion of former days. That revolution leads to restoration is no paradox in Russia's today.

Caviar bars, handsome Cossack dancers, erotic exotica, beautiful girls, casinos, opera at the elegant Mariinsky Theatre, ballet at the

Mussorgsky – St Petersburg now pulsates with nightlife and sound.

In 1963, it was a challenge to go off piste at night. Tourist initiative was not approved. But the odd disconsolate band would play in a modest bar. It was the time of the 'Twist' which was categorically not allowed. But tourists were tourists and the Russians joined in. The few restaurants were drab and the waiters listless. Our ignorance of the cyrillic script added to the frustration of what to order. Any circumvention of the menu invariably ended in chicken Kiev or boeuf Stroganov. Lunch and dinner for group travellers would start with caviar or sturgeon; one of the few perks, pre-Intourist. Today in St Petersburg there is a riotous worldwide choice of restaurants. A Caucasian meal of beef and lamb shashlyk in the Kavkaz bar, near the Fontanka river, is a popular choice. The red and white Georgian wines are excellent, and chewing gum is handed out on your departure, to combat the pungent pickling and spices of the meat. At the Adamant fish restaurant on the Moika Canal you are overwhelmed with a choice of sturgeon, swordfish, trout and succulent scallops, crayfish and tiger prawns. But it is in the Log Cabin at Tsarkoe-Selo, the Tsar's village, south of St Petersburg, that you will eat superbly. It is the borsch soup that will revive you after shuffling through Pavlosk Palace and Maria Fyodorovna's Amber room, the Lapis-Lazuli room with the scagliola inlays, the bois-clair doors and the marquetry floors. 'Wood is everywhere in Russia,' explained our Russian guide with her Zsa Zsa Gabor bones and eyes. (She had been brought up on Shakespeare and Chaucer.) 'It has no commercial value. These door surrounds are of lime; a soft wood and easy to carve.' We admired the intricate moulding of the birds and flowers on the architraves. 'On the floors you have maple, beech and fir.'

But in the Log Cabin we found Cossacks with concertinas and hunting songs, and wolf and bear skins leering from the beams. And, when you are seduced by a troika and whisked through the park in two feet of snow, have a thought for Tsar Nicholas II, who, under house arrest in 1917, shovelled snow to pass the days. And it will not be two bears you see ahead, on a collision course with the horses, but a pair of Russians submerged in fur. Every restaurant and museum lobby overflows with fur; the hooks heaving with sable, mink and polar fox.

Religious freedom is now encouraged throughout Russia, with many old monasteries and long-neglected churches revived. Church attendance has been restored. Forty years ago it was a sad and different tale. The eleventh-century cathedral of St Sophia in Novgorod, shouldering its gold and grey domes, stood silent in the market square. Beside it soared the Yaroslav bell tower, its five belfries empty and open to the wind. At Zagorsk, an original seat of the Greek Orthodox Church, a curious medley of little churches, smacking of intermingled Gothic, Moorish and Byzantine, were grouped on the top of the hill. The old square, overshadowed by the mosaic brick columns of a fifteenth-century chapel, was crowded with strutting pigeons and black-clad peasant women. Some sat talking on the benches, while one or two were stretched out on the church steps, in complete abandon and sleeping heavily. Others thronged the two churches, in which services were still held. We followed them in.

Their lips worked in a slow, tremulous chant as they filed past a priest: a young man with shoulder-length hair, resplendent in a mitre-type hat and brocade gown. He held a glistening sceptre to their ardent lips. They prostrated themselves throughout the church, feverishly kissing statues and paintings of the saints. Their devotions continued unabated in the square as they caressed the frescoes in the walled arches, prostrating themselves devoutly. The last shreds of the people's past religion died with these old women.

The Russian Orthodox Church now holds a daily Divine Liturgy. At St Isaac's Cathedral we converged on a side chapel, where chanting led by a priest in bass tones wafted through the incense. Young acolytes in yellow silk chasubles tossed their silver bells and fragrant caskets. The massive malachite columns, the mosaics, the icons and gilded sculpture were lit by magnificent chandeliers and the 300-feet dome.

As an antidote to this tour-de-force of palatial treasures our guide led us off the Nevsky Prospect to the Kuznechnyy food and flower market. Engulfed by waves of tomato, cheese and sturgeon, we were promised Dostoyevsky to follow. He had died in the corner house up the street in 1881, having completed *The Brothers Karamazov* in 1880. (Although, in her own literary prowess, she told us that Dostoyevsky had been working on a trilogy and that *The Brothers* was merely the first tranche.) 'And there was no market here in 1963. No money. No food.' I had a fleeting memory of those meagre fruit stands in the streets; the discoloured grapes, the small, bruised, pitted apples. The stone and marble precincts of the Kuznechnyy covered market were as vast as an ice palace. The vegetables from Georgia – with tomatoes the size of cantaloupes – had to be seen; the catchment area stretched to Azerbaijan. Lime and maple honey, pickled cucumbers, soft dried figs and apricots and seductive slabs of sturgeon and swordfish swept us along a path of plenty. We had no energy for Dostoyevsky. The next day it was Pushkin and his apartment over the Moika Canal.

It is hard to believe that these solemn rooms once thronged with

Pushkin's wife, Natalya, their four children and two aunts. His impressive library of leather-bound books, in several European and Oriental
languages, mount a silent guard round his deep wooden sofa. It was
there on the worn leather cushions that Pushkin bled to death; writhing
in agony after his duel with Natalya's admirer, D'Anthes. Pushkin's
study has been left untouched since his death. His desk is pleasantly
cluttered with scattered sheets of faded writings, his cherished inkstand
with the Ethiopian boy, his pen and ivory paper knife and a small
bronze bell. Opposite his desk, a Turkish sabre, presented to him in
the Caucasus, is hung on the wall. Pushkin spent some of his happiest
years in the Caucasus, where he had begun his celebrated novel in
verse – *Eugene Onegin*. Lesley Blanch in a haunting recollection of
Pushkin's study from her own visit in *Journey into the Mind's Eye* found
it 'very quiet in the little house, yet it seemed to vibrate with the
agonised cries that were wrung from the poet during his thirty-six
hours of dying. The afternoon was overcast and the room felt very
cold.' She left in tears.

Postscript

February 2001 Masai Mara

> So have I heard on Afric's burning shore
> A hungry lion give a grievous roar;
> The grievous roar echo'd along the shore.

That drama buff, William Barnes Rhodes, let slip these lines in his *Bombastes Furioso*. Two hundred years on, in Kenya, on safari, we were deluded; no lion, no roar. It was the fleeting glimpse that thrilled. Across waves of green, gold savannah we saw them; two lionesses, slicing through long grass, intent on gazelle or jackal or warthog. Hacking and galloping across the Loita plains, our polo ponies deftly dodged hyena holes, stumps spiked with thistles, rhino skulls, elephant bones half-scrunched and scattered, bogs and dykes and strange mud castellations to resemble the Nabatean tombs at Petra or our own Tower of London; the earth-works of termite ants, in which a fat white slug lurked in the bowels of each confection.

'Let's have a canter through that herd of wildebeest . . .' (or zebra or impala or hyena). 'Look out for rocks in the grass – and lion of course.' Our safari leader Tristan Voorspuy (ex-officer in the Blues) was a dynamic man. Whatever the obstruction or destruction, the dire danger or unpalatable potential, we his followers knew that the situation would be resolved. Two articulated lorries, sunk deep in the main earth track across the plains, had been unceremoniously yanked out by the nose. And we had continued in our Land Rover, lurching and jumping like a sick rhino through gutters running with mud. Runaway horses had on the whole been recaptured – whole – and electric storms had held off until we had breached evening camp. Any proximity to elephant was Tristan's cue for ultimate nonchalance.

When our Land Rover had halted in swampy ground some fifteen feet from a mammoth specimen with virgin white tusks linked in a skipping rope beneath flapping bellows, my heart stood still. What did it take to swallow one's tongue? Tristan (now upgraded to 'Titan', after his Herculean mud battle) gave a laconic résumé on the superb mammal placed so advantageously before us. My relief at moving on was cut short as we halted before yet another hefty monster. But when a rhinoceros a half-mile away set up a voluptuous bucking and kicking and bundled towards us, Tristan drove off rapidly. With the recent rains, a lush glut of green had swept the rich, red earth of the Masai steppe. Scarlet, white and yellow butterflies flitted between the horses' hooves, and flowers, bright blue and gold and heliotrope, threaded the grass. In the burning noon sun the cicadas shrilled incessantly. Our riding party of nine included two junoesque girl grooms, scooped from the home hunting shires, and a lithe black boy who brought up the rear; his prime brief was to retrieve fallen damsels, stirrups, hats, whips, stethoscopes and binoculars . . . It was reassuring not to be the last in the field. My doughty mare, under the chronic conviction a hyena was poised to leap on her back, would set off at a break-neck gallop, gathering speed as the geldings passed her with their overbearing stride. 'Might I suggest . . . ?' The sportif Wykehamist had closed in beside me after a particular pasting – 'Might I suggest that you shorten your stirrups?' His timely advice was spot on. Having been confined to thirty years of collected canters in Richmond Park, the long stirrup was painfully hors de combat on the Masai plains.

As we squelched through marsh and mounds, Tristan would point out indistinct herds of game lined along far hills and horizons; water buffalo, zebra, wildebeest. We passed several orderly Masai cattle and goat herds, with their tinkling hand-made bells. Each herdsman stood straight and slim and silent, with a red tartan 'shuka' slung across one shoulder. His bamboo stick and bow and poisoned arrows were his only protection. By sunset he would steer his herd to a 'boma': the ubiquitous thorny enclosure, securing the livestock from any night marauders.

One day, the Siria escarpment beckoned us; elusive, teasing, it receded from each successive horizon. A low elephantine sweep to stretch forty-five miles, lapped in mist and blue distance; it appeared a Hebridean illusion. Antelope, impala and baboon leapt ecstatically in the wild green sea of grass. And there were eagles; the great white fish eagle with its seven-foot wing span, the white headed vulture, the hooded vulture, the secretary bird and a quirky range of whi-dah birds. They were identified as the red-collared and the yellow-rumped variety. These small weaver birds, now popularly named widow birds, had marked out their nesting patch across the plains. A central tuft of grass is marked by a bald earth surround, where the mother hen has hopped and hopped to bare her fief. But it was the 'boo-boo' bird that urged us from dawn to dusk to 'work harder – work harder' or even 'push harder – push harder' – to depend on your fancy.

We covered forty miles that day, galloping up to each horizon, staked out by some lone flame-tree. Furtively and silent we passed through a rock gorge where leopards lurked. We found none. Instead

Tristan indicated a gardenia-tree with its glossy leaf and white waxen petals. We picnicked in a glade of acacia. Some of our party – to include the intrepid Viscountess – frolicked in a deep mud pool where elephants had drunk and defecated. It occurred to me that, after the rains, crocodiles might also have availed themselves of this pleasurable waterhole. I preferred to sip red Chilean wine in the shade and watch our unsaddled horses roll and kick in the grass.

Enjoying a post-prandial ride through the setting sun, the Lord[1] and I were suddenly split apart by a vicious kick from my mare on his left tibia; the impact was savagely etched on his suede chaps. Naughty 'Tharala'. Was he hurt? No – just numbed. When we reached camp I would naturally share with him my tiger balm; an asphyxiating camphoric ointment for 'migraine, ague and any ponderous muscles'.

The heavens opened on our return at dusk. An exhilarating sword dance of rain and lightning, as we juggled with the leather gourds of hot water in our shower tents, open to the clouds. The camp fire was soon blazing through rich, nutty wafts of acacia wood. Within an hour of the storm, Tristan had the dining-table set up under the stars. 'In Africa you have to get on with life,' he reminded us. His bearers, immaculate in white gloves and mess-jackets, served us roast zebra.

That night we were pitched by the Mara river. My tent, with its same cosy bed, rug and table, magically resurrected at each successive site, was positioned right on the bank. A mud path, denoting regular riparian exit and entry, appeared to lead directly to my zipped-up front flap. Later, as I lay in a paroxysm of fear, ears cocked for trouble, the grunting and gurgling and wallowing in the river beside me was clearly set to run. Whenever a faint pause interrupted this gross gurgitation, I imagined a surge of hippopotami converging on my privacy. Their short legs and gigantic low-slung bellies would knock my paraffin lamp, my tent pole, would lunge on to my bed, scrunching me in their scrofulous snouts . . . I needed a day off; a rest day, a day at leisure; rather in the way that altitude sickness is cured by immediate descent. A day in the hammock with Elspeth Huxley. A little light reading, with no hyena holes, no lion, no elephant . . . But to be left behind with a bevy of virile stable lads? The entire team of willing tent hands? The cooks and bearers? Tristan ran a formidable retinue. No – and mindful of Hilaire Belloc's cautionary lines: 'And always keep a hold of Nurse, For fear of finding something worse' – I tried again to sleep. In the early darkest dawn I badly needed a slash. With the hippos at large any tentative sortie into the great green outside was

[1] Lord Patrick Beresford, with his services to the SAS and his world-wide riding on an Olympian scale, kept the show on the road.

not an option. Any opened tent flap can be tantamount to trouble. It was my Henry Maxwell riding boot that stepped into the breach; the obvious and only receptacle. Had I known that, just hours later, it was, in turn, to be submerged by the Mara river, any shame would have been mollified. Early wake-up call from Dominic, with sweet milky tea and warm washing water; the usual breakfast banquet under the trees; scrambled eggs or poached? Sausages, crispy bacon, porridge, toast to die for from the camp bakery, marmalade and marmite.

Announced Tristan: 'Hippos in the Mara this morning – they are used to the horses. We will cross over straight after breakfast.' Saddled up and mounted, we eyed them from the bank. Some fifty yards away, a cordon of twenty monsters glugged and spewed with gusto in the choppy brown water. We crossed the bouldered river-bed without incident. Thirty minutes later, the Mara – always a challenge, with its flow from Lake Victoria right up north to the Nile – by some serpentine feat had reappeared. It was deeper now with a visible current and waves flecked with spume. Seven towering giraffe appeared from nowhere and gazed down on us with mild disinterest. 'First let's see if they cross and then we can gauge the depth.' The giraffe were not tempted. Continued Tristan: 'We are well within our depth. Keep the horses' necks turned left into the wind – or you will be carried downstream. The river-bed has big boulders with gaps between. The horses might suddenly drop a foot or two. Right, off we go . . .' I tucked 'Tharala' right behind our infallible leader; no dithering on the mud shore. We plunged in and after five yards my boots and bottom and saddlebag took in a rush of water. And 'Tharala,' her head to the wind, was comfortably swimming. So diverted by the novel sensation, I lost a stirrup; caught just in time before she did the splits on landing on the opposite bank.

'When I was in Patagonia,' recalled the Lord, as we were all later ranged round a quarry of rose quartz, drying out and drinking. 'When I was in Patagonia, we crossed a swollen river. A girl's horse flipped over. Righting himself in the water, he plunged in his fore legs on either side of her head. She never knew how close she had been to death. She was facing the other way at the time . . .' But our Dorsetshire lady, an elegant and accomplished rider, had sustained an agitating crossing. Her gelding had snapped his martingale and had flung up his head at her eye. Furthermore her cherished binoculars had been drowned. However after a gallop and a blow in the wind she could now report that they had recovered their sight. The tethered horses whinnied and became suddenly restless. 'We are sitting in a lion haunt,' warned Tristan. And the baffled girl grooms confirmed that, only last week, a lioness had lolled throughout lunch, in the middle of the tree to our left. Too bad.

After an arresting six days in the saddle our safari was ended. Twelve horses were stalled, nose to tail in their travel box, with a nosebag each for the three-hour journey. Destination 'Deloraine', near Lake Naivasha, in the Rift Valley; the home of Tristan and his wife, Lucinda. Built in 1920 by Lord Francis Scott, younger son of the 8th Duke of Buccleuch, the house stands today, perhaps more finely than ever, with its screen of mature trees, its brilliant flowering shrubs and terraces. Lucinda schools around sixty thoroughbred ponies on the estate, for polo, hunting and safaris. She took us on an evening ride up the side of a mountain, through fig and yellow fever-trees, gum and acacia. We came to a clearing on the peak and she pointed out to us the distant Aberdare range to the north of Nairobi; a vast chain, blurred and amethyst in the fading light. We reached the stables at dusk, where grinning stable boys poured out like bathwater to seize our ponies.

The gleaming old cedar verandah at Deloraine, the spacious landings and wide stairs denote the colonial style. But the charm and elegance of Lucinda's house-style calls the tune; the smiling maids in their blue kerchiefs and dresses, poised by bedroom doors with water jugs or pressed laundry, could even suggest the household vignettes of Frith or Vermeer. The handsome dining-room hung with the portraits of Lord Francis – reputed to have been the best bridge player in Kenya – and his Lady Eileen, daughter of the Earl of Minto, Viceroy of India, is a haven of indulgence. Whether it be calamari stuffed with nuts and onions or roasted impala, the food and wine are superb.

Finally, we lunched at the Muthaiga Club, before catching our London flight. The 1930-style rooms, cool and sparse with comfortable wicker chairs, overlooked the garden. The caccia-tree, clustered with its yellow globes, the pink-flowered chestnut and the candelabra tree shaded the lawns.

Mingle shades of Joy and woe, Hope and fear, and peace and strife, in the thread of human life.

Sir Walter Scott

Index

NOTE: Titles of rank are generally those applying at the time of mention